# THE HISTORY OF
# WISCONSIN

# THE HISTORY OF
# WISCONSIN

## VOLUME III

*Urbanization and Industrialization,*
*1873–1893*

## ROBERT C. NESBIT

WILLIAM FLETCHER THOMPSON
*General Editor*

1985
STATE HISTORICAL SOCIETY OF WISCONSIN
MADISON

Manufactured in the United States of America by
Worzalla Publishing Company, Stevens Point, Wisconsin

*Library of Congress Cataloging in Publication Data*
(Revised for Volume III of the History of Wisconsin)
THE HISTORY OF WISCONSIN
Includes bibliography and index.
CONTENTS: v. 1. From exploration to statehood,
by Alice E. Smith. v. 2. The Civil War era, 1848–1873,
by Richard N. Current. v. 3. Urbanization and
industrialization, 1873–1893, by Robert C. Nesbit.
1. Wisconsin—History. I. Thompson, William Fletcher
F581.H68          977.5          72-12941
ISBN 0-87020-122-0 (v. 1)

# PREFACE

AT FIRST GLANCE, the prospective reader might be tempted to ask whether an account of the years 1873 to 1893 is apt to provide anything essential to his understanding of Wisconsin's history. (Indeed, when he was first invited to write this book, the author was heard to remark: "Pretty thin gruel.") After all, the period seemingly lacks the large-scale and dramatic events around which other volumes in this series have been built: the grand sweep of history from exploration to the attainment of statehood; the supreme test of the Union in the Civil War era; the origins of the Progressive movement and its second flowering in the years between the wars; and so on. By way of contrast, the period 1873–1893 begins and ends with years in which there occurred severe national financial panics which ushered in depression, business failures, and widespread industrial unemployment.

In fact, however, as we shall see, the two decades between 1873 and 1893 also witnessed sweeping changes in Wisconsin's economy and in the ways in which people lived, worked, associated, and responded to the society around them. Probably no other twenty-year period in the state's history—not even the years of the Great Depression and the Second World War—encompassed such a major transformation of the state's economy. What had been in 1873 an extractive frontier economy producing primarily grain and lumber had by 1893 emerged as a mainly urban-centered economy operating on the leading edge of contemporary industrial technology. During the same period, Wisconsin's farmers largely abandoned wheat as a cash crop and undertook the long but successful transition to dairying and other forms of intensive agriculture. By 1893, urban and rural settlements dotted those parts of northern and western Wisconsin which had been only temporarily occupied twenty years earlier, and a complex railroad network crisscrossed the state.

These changes in the economy inevitably wrought far-reaching adjustments of Wisconsin's social and political structures. This period was one of great population mobility, as people moved from farm to village and city and from south to north, while others entered the state for the first time or left it for new opportunities in the West. With one of the highest foreign-born populations in the nation, it became necessary for Wisconsin to accommodate immigrants within her social and political systems. The often painful transition from a craft to an industrial system of production led to extensive unrest among Wisconsin's working people and to frequent and sometimes dramatic confrontations between capital and labor. Women entered the paid labor force in increasingly larger numbers. Local and state governments began to respond to the basic requirements of an emerging urban and industrial society by providing what has in our time come to be known as the infrastructure. At the same time, organized society also wrestled with the problems of the needy, in the course of which the state began to assert the type of leadership which usually is associated with the subsequent Progressive period.

\* \* \*

One of the advantages of writing about a period as brief as twenty years is the opportunity to examine the society in some detail. Both in the text and in the photographic essays which accompany it, we have attempted to provide a portrait of the circumstances and quality of life as enjoyed and endured by both the ordinary and the extraordinary.

This six-volume *History of Wisconsin* represents an effort to gather in narrative rather than topical form an unusually large body of historical research based upon manuscripts, state and local government archives, newspapers and other contemporary publications, and published and unpublished scholarship, most of which is housed in the State Historical Society of Wisconsin and the University of Wisconsin's Memorial Library sitting opposite one another on the Madison campus. Pulling this material together represents the work of many hands and minds beyond the infinitely greater number of those who created the original manuscripts and gathered basic data, others who preserved and collated it in usable form, and those who drew upon it for general or specialized studies. For this particular volume the author recognizes special debts. James Cavanaugh was research assistant for this volume for three years—longer ago than I like to admit—and was fortunately self-directing in a highly intelligent and productive way while I was completing my one-volume survey of Wisconsin history and serving as assistant chairman of the history department during what may fairly be characterized as interesting times on the Madison campus. Almost ten years later the National Endowment for the Humanities furnished me with a year of support and with another two years of part-time assistance; Charles Bulger was loath to leave any stone unturned.

A very considerable debt is owed to William F. Thompson, general editor of the series, who directed a corps of research assistants for the series and occupied the office next to mine during the latter years of this marathon while he was writing Volume VI among other distractions. Three members of that research team deserve special mention: George H. Roeder, Jr., Dale E. Treleven, and John O. Holzhueter, the latter our walking Wisconsin general encyclopedia. The University's Student Work-Study program provided Robert Munson, who ran through much of the available Milwaukee German-language press material, making notes and translations on selected topics.

The completed manuscript was too long, and it can only have profited from the necessary pruning and meticulous editorial scrutiny. If some parts remain obscure, or just plain wrong, the credit lies with the author.

ROBERT C. NESBIT

*Madison, Wisconsin*

# CONTRIBUTORS

The State Historical Society of Wisconsin

The University of Wisconsin

Western Publishing Company, Inc.

First Wisconsin Foundation, Inc.

The Journal Company

The Northwestern Mutual Life Insurance Company

Pabst Breweries Foundation

Schlitz Foundation, Inc.

Appleton Coated Foundation, Inc.

Appleton Wire Works Corp.

Banta Company Foundation, Inc.

Bergstrom Foundation

The Falk Corporation

Fox River Paper Co.

Kimberly-Clark Foundation, Inc.

The Marine Foundation, Inc.

Marshall & Ilsley Bank Foundation, Inc.

Thilmany Pulp and Paper Company

Wisconsin Electric Power Company

The Johnson's Wax Fund, Inc.

Miller High Life Foundation, Inc.

Nekoosa-Edwards Foundation Incorporated

Wisconsin Michigan Power Company

Wisconsin Natural Gas Company

Wisconsin Public Service Corporation

Charles W. Wright Foundation of Badger Meter, Inc.

ix

# CONTENTS

## Part III: Politics and Government

## ILLUSTRATIONS

Following pages 128, 352, and 432 are selections of photographs from the last quarter of the nineteenth century. Unless otherwise noted, the illustrations are from the Iconographic Collections of the State Historical Society of Wisconsin. The editors would especially like to thank the Milwaukee County Historical Society and the H. H. Bennett Studio of Wisconsin Dells for their generous assistance.

# MAPS

*Designed by*
CURTIS J. MUSSELMAN

*Prepared by*
The University of Wisconsin Cartographic Laboratory

# PART I

# The Economy

". . . [C]an more be wanting to manifest the design of Heaven, to which from long aforetime the forces of nature have labored, that here shall be for a duration beyond all prescience of man an intelligent, prosperous, happy State?"

WILLIAM F. VILAS
United States Senator, 1891–1897
In *Harper's Magazine* (April, 1891)

NOTE ON CITATIONS

| | |
|---|---|
| *DWB* | *Dictionary of Wisconsin Biography.* Madison, 1960. |
| *SHSW Proceedings* | *Proceedings* of the State Historical Society of Wisconsin, 1874–. |
| SHSW | State Historical Society of Wisconsin. |
| *Wis. Hist. Colls.* | *Collections of the State Historical Society of Wisconsin.* 21 vols., Madison, 1855–1915. |
| *WMH* | *Wisconsin Magazine of History.* |
| WSA | Wisconsin State Archives. |

Unless otherwise indicated, all manuscripts, broadsides, and pamphlets cited are in the collections of the State Historical Society of Wisconsin.

# 1

# Agriculture

## THE FARM IN TRANSITION

IN 1873, two out of three Wisconsinites lived on a farm, or in a farm-oriented hamlet of two hundred or fewer inhabitants. Just under 20 per cent of the population lived in an urban setting (2,500 or more), and the remainder inhabited farm-related villages or lumber camps and other rural settings not directly associated with farming. Twenty years later, the rural (mostly farm) population had increased by about one-third, but the urban population had nearly trebled. Nonetheless, agriculture remained a dynamic part of the economy in 1893, and not simply because it added something less than half again the number of acres in farms as well as farmsteads, thereby increasing the percentage of improved land. More importantly, it had become more highly commercialized, capitalized, and mechanized while developing new specializations which were better adapted to the land, as well as more sophisticated marketing techniques which required higher levels of co-operation.[1]

It is difficult to characterize the agricultural enterprise of the times. There was a vast difference between a prosperous farm in

[1] Walter H. Ebling et al., *A Century of Wisconsin Agriculture, 1848–1948*, Wisconsin Department of Agriculture, Wisconsin Crop and Livestock Reporting Service, *Bulletin No. 290* (1948), 4, 13, 16. The state's population figures were:

|      | Urban   | Rural     |
|------|---------|-----------|
| 1870 | 207,900 | 847,571   |
| 1880 | 317,204 | 998,293   |
| 1890 | 562,286 | 1,131,044 |

The percentage of total state land in farms, the number of farms, their acreage, and the

Dane County in the 1870's, well located with respect to available
rail lines and markets, compared with subsistence operations in
areas of nearly equal potential, say in Marathon or Pierce counties. The Dane County farm would have been under cultivation
for a generation and valued at probably fifteen to thirty times the
initial government price ($1.25 per acre) as raw land. The Mar-
athon and Pierce county farms would be relatively new to the
plow, or still covered with a variety of timber or stumps, not so different from the Dane County farm of the 1850's. The differences
in farmland, relative newness, location, and marketing opportunities were as varied as the people involved and the experience
which they brought to the agricultural enterprise.

Averages of farm values, income, and so forth are only general
indicators. Traversing the rich farm counties of southern Wisconsin, one can readily see that democratic equality of opportunity
does not extend to the land itself. A generalized map of soil provinces fails to show the inequalities created by glacial action and
other forces. Even the best areas harbor islands of inferior soils,
rocky hills thinly covered, drowned lands, and prospective farms
cut by ravines and meandering streams subject to flooding. The
familiar rectangular survey system adopted under the Northwest

percentages of improved and unimproved land were:

|  | Land in Farms | No. Farms | Acres | Improved | Unimproved |
|---|---|---|---|---|---|
| 1870 | 33.6% | 102,904 | 11,714,321 | 50% | 50% |
| 1880 | 43.8% | 134,309 | 15,343,118 | 60% | 40% |
| 1890 | 48.0% | 146,409 | 16,787,988 | 58% | 42% |

The 1880–1890 variation in the ratio of improved to unimproved land occurred because
some former pinelands were converted to agricultural use, while some improved farmland
was withdrawn from the agricultural base in urbanizing areas. The ratio of improved to
unimproved farmland was greater in Wisconsin in 1880 than at any other time before
Ebling and his colleagues compiled their statistics. Although certainly subject to serious
reservations, particularly with regard to agricultural labor that was seasonal and casual (and
much of which did not receive wages), an indicative summary is as follows:

|  | 1870 | 1880 | 1890 |
|---|---|---|---|
| Total Labor Force | 292,808 | 417,455 | 576,290 |
| Agriculture | 175,712 (60%) | 223,992 (53.7%) | 257,516 (44.7%) |
| Manufacturing | 53,013 (18.1%) | 88,871 (21.3%) | 140,326 (24.3%) |

See Harvey S. Perloff et al., *Regions, Resources and Economic Growth* (Baltimore, 1960;
reprinted, Lincoln, 1967), 613–614, 622, 624.

Ordinance of 1785, which applied to almost all Wisconsin land, treated these discrepancies with democratic indifference. But it was the nature of the settlement process that even land with very poor prospects was soon settled when it was located adjacent to better lands which enjoyed the necessary amenities—"infrastructure" is the current term—of roads, schools, hamlets, trade cen-

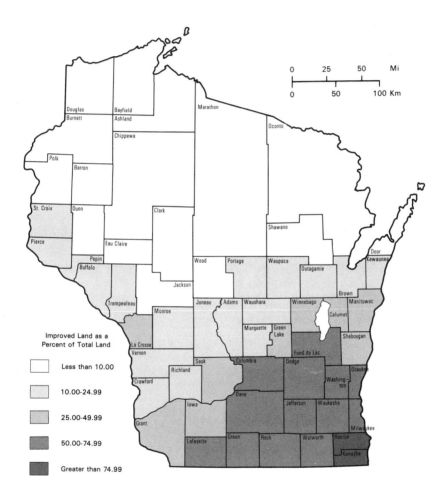

FARM DENSITY, 1870

ters, and railroads. One may observe this phenomenon immediately west of Madison, where the abrupt hills and narrow coulees of the driftless area vividly differentiate between the westernmost two tiers of townships in Dane County from the leveler land to the east. These hills and valleys lie in a north-south direction. The pioneer railroads that connected Milwaukee with Prairie du Chien and La Crosse ran within easy reach. Despite its limited possibilities, this land harbored generations of hard-working farm families who struggled, not always successfully, to achieve more than a subsistence level of existence. Such places lie adjacent to other rich farmlands in southern Wisconsin, or in similar coulee country between the lower Wisconsin and St. Croix rivers.

The presence of this poorer land and—by the 1870's—the opening of good prairie land in western Iowa, Minnesota, and the Dakotas at government or railroad prices retarded northern agricultural settlement in Wisconsin. This was particularly true of real Wisconsin cutover, which roughly describes most of the land lying north of a line from Marinette to Grantsburg in Burnett County. This area experienced very little agricultural settlement before the late 1890's. But pioneer farming was still to be found in the years after the Civil War on less attractive land well behind the skirmish lines of northern settlement.[2]

If no typical Wisconsin farmer appears in this chapter, it is partly for want of a prototype. Farmers were more numerous by far than any other occupational group, and more various in origins, age, education, prospects, expectations, preparation, and relative success. They will be met along the way as the many

---

[2] Joseph Schafer's *Wisconsin Domesday Book: Town Studies* (Madison, 1924), 149–151, compares several townships for the census years 1850 through 1880, demonstrating growth in valuation. See also the *Eleventh Census of the United States, 1890: Agriculture, Volume V*, 234–235, which demonstrates that farmland values rose three to five times between 1850 and 1890 in the counties represented in Schafer's *Town Studies*. Schafer gives an 1870 average value of $37 per acre for the farmland in Pleasant Springs, a town southeast of Madison, and $19 per acre for Primrose to the southwest and not as well favored. The 1870 value-per-acre range for the twenty-three towns in southern Wisconsin included in Schafer's *Town Studies* is from $12 for the Town of Castle Rock in northern Grant County to $67 for Brookfield in Waukesha County.

aspects of the economic, social, and political profile of Wisconsin
society in the period 1873–1893 unfold. There are so many portraits available as to be overwhelming. They appear in autobiographies, biographies, fiction, scholarly exposition, government
reports, the publications of agricultural and historical societies, the
popular county subscription histories of the time—nor does this

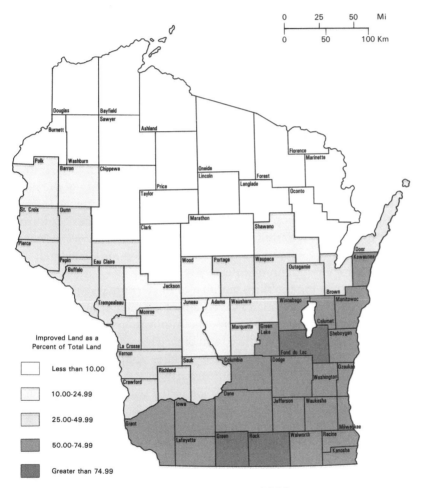

FARM DENSITY, 1890

exhaust the list—and from these a variety of portraits will appear. But the immediate emphasis is upon that portion of the revolution in Wisconsin farming which belongs in the period of this volume, ultimately resulting in the phrase that we have come to accept as commonplace: "America's Dairyland." Farming as a way of life, popular and personal views of rural life, and farming as a vocation will appear in due course.

There are differences to note between a society that was more than half directly involved in farming and the overwhelmingly urban society of the present. For one thing, most urbanites in the 1870's, 1880's, and 1890's came from a farm background. Another difference was the very real limitations upon opportunities for other careers. Much was heard in that period about the perils for an agrarian society that was losing its young people to the cities. Scant concern was expressed for the misfits who lacked talent for farming and might have flourished in some other occupation. It is little wonder that there was much indifferent farming and hence that many families led stunted lives. The city of the late nineteenth century had no monopoly on poverty, overwork, meager returns, and people caught in a bootless existence. Onward and upward is the familiar theme in general discussions of Wisconsin farming. The misfits are usually ignored, or considered as an uncharacteristic minor category.

The astonishing mobility of much of the farm population in the period under discussion, the creation of ethnic enclaves and the gradual erosion of most of them, the implications of ethnicity for distinctive types of agriculture, and other characteristics related to time and place will be dealt with in later chapters. It is worth mentioning here that the Populist party of the late eighties and early nineties, which is correctly identified with agrarian discontent on the Middle Border, was largely an urban phenomenon in Wisconsin. This suggests either that Wisconsin farmers were too diverse in interests and origins to mount a significant political movement, or that they were relatively less discontented. Scholarship suggests the latter, for the reason that many Wisconsin farmers had moved beyond the risks of wheat farming to mixed farming, largely based on dairying, livestock, and feeding. The failure of Populism to catch fire might also suggest that the major parties, and the state government, were sufficiently responsive to agrarian interests. Or even that the railroads, the credit system, farm machinery manufacturers, and farm marketing instrumentalities were identified by farmers as largely local and somewhat competitive—or realistically apprehensive about effective regulation—rather than simply as dark forces controlled from afar. The result does suggest a degree of maturity for Wisconsin agriculture not yet achieved immediately to the west.[3]

It usually comes as a surprise to Wisconsinites in the late twentieth century to discover that the state was once a leading wheat producer—third in production and second in commercial surplus in 1859—not simply because of the well-known identification with dairying but also because today's agricultural landscape seems to belie our notion of what wheatlands should look like. Wheat was, however, the standard cash crop of pioneer commercial agriculture. It kept well, was comparatively high in value and portability, almost always found a market, and was well adapted to extensive and relatively careless cultivation. That its supremacy as the singular cash crop was passing by the 1870's is a truism in Wisconsin agricultural histories. Wheat growing did not vanish dramatically from the agricultural scene, but rather it moved in a generally northwesterly direction and ceased to be the standard commercial crop which it had been on the limited prime soils of southern Wisconsin. There wheat had literally worn out its welcome, while factors unrelated to the waning fertility of the abused soils were raising taxes and land values.[4]

---

[3] See J. Martin Klotsche, "The 'United Front' Populists," in the *Wisconsin Magazine of History*, 20 (June, 1937), 375–389.

[4] Joseph Schafer, *A History of Agriculture in Wisconsin* (Madison, 1922), chap. 5; John G. Thompson, *The Rise and Decline of the Wheat Growing Industry in Wisconsin* (Madison, 1909), 63–64, 68–69, 73–74, 78, 82–83, 91–92; Eric E. Lampard, *The Rise of the Dairy Industry in Wisconsin: A Study in Agricultural Change, 1820-1920* (Madison, 1963), 25–56; Wilbur H. Glover, *Farm and College: The College of Agriculture of the University of Wisconsin, A History* (Madison, 1952), 161–166; Ebling et al., *Century of Wisconsin Agriculture*, 27–28. The *Wisconsin Farmer*, new series, 1 (November 20, 1869), 369, observed of the 1869 wheat crop that yields were little better than the averages of ten to fifteen previous years. Yields of twenty bushels per acre could be found on recently opened land, "but throughout the greater portion of the State, it has been from 12 to 15 bushels, and we have reports of some localities where it was only 9 or 10." It was time to consider whether it paid to continue with wheat, which took so much from the soil for the prevailing returns.

Contemporaries were not aware of the dilemma they faced in southern Wisconsin:[5]

> Wheat was the staple product of the town [Town of Dane in Dane County] for the first twenty years, covering a period of time from 1850 to 1870. During this time there were but few failures of the crop, and all that was required of the husbandman was to break up the virgin soil, sow the seed, and a bountiful harvest was insured. For seven or eight years [before 1877] this crop has been less cultivated, and it is doubtful if the wheat crop of the town for three years back has paid expenses.

This brought a period of adjustment which was well in hand. Nearly all of the Town of Dane farmers had turned to mixed farming with an emphasis upon general livestock and dairying. Feed grains, grasses, and hay did particularly well, and livestock was helping restore the soil. A cheese factory, built about 1874, was handling the milk from some 250 cows and another was just started.

One contemporary witness of the agricultural scene was William W. Daniells, professor of chemistry and agriculture at the University of Wisconsin. Although he had a Michigan farm background, Daniells was uncomfortable in the agricultural portion of his professorship and had difficulty conveying the practical value of his work to farmer audiences who were generally prejudiced against "book farmers." Appropriately, Daniells took the long view when asked to write a sketch on agriculture for a Wisconsin atlas published in 1878. Wisconsin's pioneer wheat farming he characterized as "mere land-skimming. . . . It was always taking out of the purse, and never putting in." Because the farmer had "every obstacle to contend with except cheap and very fertile land, . . . *poor* farming was the only profitable farming," but it left the inevitable legacy of exhausted acres and "the habit of loose and slovenly farming acquired by pioneers." Change was coming, however, "to a rational method that will preserve the soil's fertility and pay for the labor it demands." The changes could not

---

[5] Robert Steele and Mansfield Arries, "Dane," in William J. Park and Co., *Madison, Dane County and Surrounding Towns* . . . (Madison, 1877), 465.

be expected from those pioneer farmers addicted to land-skimming, but would come "with the replacement of the pioneer farmers by immigrants accustomed to better methods of culture. In such cases the pioneers usually 'go west' again, to begin anew their frontier farming upon virgin soil, as their peculiar method of cultivation fails to give them a livelihood."[6]

Professor Daniells had been exposed to his share of hostile grangers who preferred to look for the roots of their distress elsewhere than in their own land-skimming techniques and their devotion to wheat. These they found in plenty: exorbitant railroad and elevator costs subject to monopoly practices; a "fixed" marketing structure; a government insensitive to the hardships for agriculture caused by a deflationary monetary policy; inadequate credit available only at ruinous interest rates; the high costs of rapidly changing technology in grain farming; taxes rising with land values that could be capitalized only by selling or assuming new debts and new practices; and "book farmers" brimming with unwelcome advice.

Another contemporary critic of Yankee farmers was John Wesley Hoyt, publisher of the *Wisconsin Farmer and Northwest Cultivator* (1857–1867) and, from 1859 to 1872, secretary of the Wisconsin State Agricultural Society. In the society's *Transactions* for 1871, Hoyt administered a typical scolding to the "wheat maniacs" and lambasted the typical farmer for the impractical nature of his periodic forays into agricultural fads. Such farmers spent too much time watching their neighbors and taking up whatever was the fashion, and soon made it the next local disaster. "No class of people on earth," Hoyt fumed, "manifest so little independence or so blindly and implicitly follow the prevailing custom. . . ." Farmers in the shadow of a city might raise wheat, while those in a remote location would raise potatoes and turnips despite the lack of a market or transport. Hoyt was an angry man when he contemplated the Wisconsin agricultural scene, which he departed in

---

[6] Merle Curti and Vernon Carstensen, *The University of Wisconsin: A History, 1848–1925* (2 vols., Madison, 1949), 1:456; William W. Daniells, "Agriculture" in Snyder, Van Vechten and Co., *Historical Atlas of Wisconsin . . .* (Milwaukee, 1878), 160.

1878 to become governor of Wyoming Territory, where not much farming was going on at the time.[7]

The outcome of this clash between pioneer farming practices (and prejudices) and men like Professor Daniells who sought rational solutions is now well known. The answer lay not in the popular experimental temper of the 1860's, stimulated by war-induced shortages and inflated prices, but rather in the accept-ance of proven alternatives. These were to be an emphasis upon feed crops, livestock, small grains, and dairying. However, there was no reason to infer that dairying would inevitably emerge by the 1890's as Wisconsin agriculture's most viable alternative. Its success was to require considerable proselytizing, much experi-mentation, many scientific and technological advances—and some taxpayers' money. The fact that more satisfactory wheatlands, still selling at a fraction of the prices for farmland in southern Wiscon-sin, lay immediately westward helped the dairying equation. What is more, Wisconsin's recently consolidated railroad lines were more interested in carving out their "rightful domains" west of the Mississippi than in expanding Wisconsin's network in the face of popular and official hostility epitomized by the Potter Law, passed in early 1874. Finally, only the southernmost tier of Wis-consin counties shared in the growing promise of the midwestern corn belt, given the limitations of nineteenth-century corn varieties.[8]

While the total Wisconsin acreage devoted to wheat did not hit its peak until 1878, then declined rapidly after 1881, the early 1870's saw a leveling off which amounted to a relative decline, because between 1840 and 1880 a near-average of 3,500,000 acres and 30,000 new Wisconsin farms per decade were being added. The rate of farm expansion dropped sharply in the decade 1880–1889 when Great Plains agriculture was all the rage. Even before the marked decline after 1881, wheat acreage in the state drifted

---

[7] Wisconsin State Agricultural Society, *Transactions*, 1871, pp. 18–19; *DWB*.

[8] Lampard, *Rise of the Dairy Industry*, chap. 2, draws much upon Frederick Merk, *Eco-nomic History of Wisconsin During the Civil War Decade* (Madison, 1916; reprinted, 1971), chap. 1. The Potter Law, a rigid rate schedule which proved both controversial and impractical, is discussed in more detail in Chapter 3.

in a generally northwesterly direction. Wisconsin, about equal in total land area to either Illinois or Iowa, has only about half as much potential farmland as either neighbor, and much less than that of prime land. As an example of the shift in wheat culture northwestward in Wisconsin, Dane County, centered in southern Wisconsin, had the largest wheat acreage of any county in the state in 1870 with 239,232. This dropped to one-tenth of that total, 24,990 acres, by 1890—fairly typical of southern Wisconsin agriculture.[9]

The railroads had much to do with the shift of wheat to the counties northwest of La Crosse. It was not all the work of chinch bugs, smut, rust, and depleted fertility in southern Wisconsin. The railroads brought these counties higher land values and higher taxes as they opened the way to major markets. Beginning in the 1870's, they also created formidable rivals (as milling centers and grain markets) of the Twin Cities and Duluth, while opening new grain lands westward into the Dakotas. The lure of cheaper, more open land west of the Mississippi was more compelling than the recently cleared timberland of northwestern Wisconsin. But the ten-county area north and west of La Crosse to St. Croix County, with its advantageous location in relation to markets and railroad lines, accounted for 25 per cent of the farm acreage added in the state between 1870 and 1890.[10]

While the railroads clearly enhanced the attractiveness of northwestern Wisconsin for wheat culture, they worked the opposite effect in the south-central counties. Although southern Wisconsin was amply served by the railroads, the competition was muted there and did not benefit from the alternative markets at the

[9] George Wehrwein, "Agriculture (Land Use)," in Wisconsin State Regional Planning Committee, *A Study of Wisconsin: Its Resources, Its Physical, Social and Economic Background* (*First Annual Report*, Wisconsin Regional Planning Committee, and *Bulletin No. 2*, Wisconsin Regional Planning Commission, 1934), 206; Ebling et al., *Century of Wisconsin Agriculture*, figure 41, p. 39, table 8, p. 90, figure 38, p. 38; Allan G. Bogue, *From Prairie to Corn Belt: Farming on the Illinois and Iowa Prairies in the Nineteenth Century* (Chicago, 1963), 12.

[10] Ebling et al., *Century of Wisconsin Agriculture*, 87; Henrietta M. Larson, *The Wheat Market and the Farmer in Minnesota, 1858–1900* (New York, 1926), chaps. 3 and 4. The ten counties northwest of La Crosse were Buffalo, Dunn, Eau Claire, Jackson, La Crosse, Monroe, Pepin, Pierce, St. Croix, and Trempealeau.

Twin Cities or Duluth. Despite this disadvantage, and the damage to the soils after a generation of wheat cropping, the average value per acre of land and buildings in 1870 was about three times that in northwestern Wisconsin, while the average yield per acre from wheat was sharply down.[11]

The rapid decline in total Wisconsin wheat acreage after 1881, even as it was increasing in newer agricultural counties, is illustrated by the total drop from 1,940,130 acres in wheat in the 1870 federal census to 744,080 acres twenty years later. Corn acreage rose in the same period from 462,115 to 1,120,341 acres, tame hay from one to two and a quarter million acres, and oats from 565,000 to 1,635,000 acres. Hog raising had an irregular expansion, reflecting markets and the relative ease of moving in and out of this activity as compared to beef or dairy cattle. Raising beef cattle was a relatively highly capitalized activity. Successful stockmen were the agricultural elite. Dairy cattle, by contrast, provided a more immediate return, and the number of them increased steadily, from 308,377 to 792,620 in the twenty years.[12]

Somehow virtue has come to reside in those Wisconsin farmers who remained behind to make the difficult transition to mixed farming with an emphasis upon dairying. There is more than a hint that Daniells' scornful references to "land skimmers" and good riddance were widely shared. But the truth is, wheat farming was more than a way to farm sitting down, interspersed with ample leisure while nature took its course. Wheat commanded prices, well into the 1870's, that were comparatively high. "We were all worshippers of wheat in those days," wrote Hamlin Garland. "The men thought and talked of little else between seeding and harvest, and you will not wonder at this if you have known and bowed down before such abundance as we then enjoyed. Deep as the breast of a man, wide as the sea, heavy-headed, supple-stocked, many-voiced, full of multitudinous, secret, whispered colloquies,—a meeting place of winds and sunlight,—our fields

---

[11] Thomas J. Pressly and William H. Scofield, eds., *Farm Real Estate Values in the United States by Counties, 1850–1959* (Seattle, 1965), 32.

[12] Robert C. Nesbit, *Wisconsin: A History* (Madison, 1973), 283; Ebling et al., *Century of Wisconsin Agriculture*, 98, 106.

ran to the world's end." Grain farming had become highly mechanized, particularly after the Civil War, greatly increasing the
operator's efficiency and permitting him to handle much larger
acreages. But this increased efficiency was expensive. The Achilles
heel of wheat farming was the harvesting, which was limited by
the weather and the susceptibility of ripe wheat to shattering from
the head in heat, wind, and hail, or flattening to the ground in a
rain shower. Hence the early emphasis upon horse-drawn reapers
and binders to replace the scythe, and hand tying to ready the bundles of wheat for stacking or storing in the barn to await the visit
of the neighborhood thresher and his crew. It was therefore reasonable for the well-equipped wheat farmer to capitalize on his
Wisconsin acreage and move his investment in horses and
machinery west to broader and cheaper acres. Even the marginal
grain farmer had the incentive of capital gains and a speculative
repetition of the gain farther west.[13]

One is left with two questions about those who moved west primarily to follow wheat raising. Were they, as William D. Hoard
suggested, simply following "the easy go-to-town-every-other-day
sort of a life they have in raising grain" and therefore unwilling to
submit to the "close, steady confinement which *success* demands of
the dairy farmer"? And if there was a grain-raising "type," was
he most typically a Yankee who readily sold out the family farm,
confident of success on a new frontier?[14]

---

[13] Fred A. Shannon, *The Farmer's Last Frontier: Agriculture, 1860–1897* (New York, 1945;
reprinted, 1968), 142–145, claims that one hour of labor in the best-equipped wheat fields
in 1896 was worth eighteen and a half hours with the equipment of the 1830's. Bogue, *From
Prairie to Corn Belt*, 165–167, cites studies which indicate that grain farming enjoyed a much
greater increase in labor productivity in the general period than did agriculture generally.
The attitudes of the wheat farmer are described in numerous sources, but nowhere more
eloquently than by Wisconsin's Hamlin Garland in *A Son of the Middle Border* (New York,
1917), 144–160.

[14] Wisconsin Dairymen's Association, *Report*, 1877, p. 32, as quoted in Glover, *Farm and
College*, 164; Joseph Schafer, "The Yankee and the Teuton in Wisconsin," in *WMH*, 6
(December, 1922), 6:143. Schafer often repeated this point of view in his voluminous writ-
ings. Fifteen years later he was less sure of what the inconclusive federal census records
implied about this, but repeated: "Native Americans were more mobile than foreigners."
See Joseph Schafer, "Editorial Comment: Peopling the Middle West," in *WMH*, 21 (September, 1937), 98. Schafer was correct. See Chapter 6 below.

Contemporary evidence confirms that the generation concerned thought that it was mainly the Yankee farmers who chased wheat and cheap prairie land westward. The historian Frederick Jackson Turner, for instance, remarked in a letter to his colleague and mentor at the University that he had noticed, on a fishing trip in northern Wisconsin, recent German arrivals "dispossessing whole townships of Americans and introducing the customs and farming methods of the fatherland." The published census does not tell us about such moves, only that the children of the foreign-born were less likely to move than were the children of American-born parents.[15]

Joseph Schafer, one of Turner's students and himself a historian, devoted twenty years of scholarship to the question of who settled where and the results. His published works exhaustively record the displacement of Yankee farmers by immigrant farmers—and particularly Germans since they were, by a wide margin, the largest group among Wisconsin's foreign-born. Schafer conceded the Yankees a talent for pioneering, but he certainly qualified the concession. They were overconfident that public improvements would be made to put them in easy contact with markets; they also hated to pay a speculator's price for land, and this drove them ever westward. In addition, they had forgotten their own traditions of scientific farming, were easily bored with their present situation, and lacked the German's doggedness and attachment to the land.[16]

The wheat farmers have found their defenders. There were progressive and successful farmers on the Wisconsin scene who

[15] Turner to William F. Allen, July 11, 1888, as quoted in Ray Allen Billington, *Frederick Jackson Turner: Historian, Scholar, Teacher* (New York, 1973), 47–48. The eleventh United States census for 1890 was the first to account for the distribution of native-born according to parentage.

[16] Louise Phelps Kellogg, "Joseph Schafer, the Historian," in *Joseph Schafer: Student of Agriculture*, foreword by Edward P. Alexander (Madison, 1942), 1. Schafer's observations about the pioneering qualifications of Yankees and their demerits as farmers are summarized in his long article, "The Yankee and the Teuton in Wisconsin," which ran in the *Wisconsin Magazine of History* between December, 1922, and December, 1923. His larger works on the subject were the five volumes in his *Wisconsin Domesday Book* (one volume of *Town Studies* and four of *General Studies*) published between 1922 and 1937.

kept well abreast of the rapid changes in machinery, methods of cultivation, and experiments with new wheat varieties. A comparison of wheat prices with those of other commodities, including dairy products, does not give dairying an incontrovertible advantage. Efficiency of production rather than favorable prices kept both dairying and wheat farming viable during the general downtrend of agricultural prices from the 1870's into the 1890's. The advantage of dairying, in the context of Wisconsin's available land, was that increased productivity included more intensive use of the land. Wheat farming, by contrast, increased its productivity by the application of improved machinery to extensive land use. As Wisconsin wheat growing trended northwestward, it found comparatively cheaper land, but land that was hilly in the driftless area and much that had been heavily forested. Both of these conditions worked against the efficient use of machinery. Also, the new roller-milling processes put a premium on the formerly less desirable hard spring wheat varieties. Wisconsin's climate had not been favorable to the softer winter varieties, so this change first appeared as an advantage. But spring wheat fell victim to wheat stem rust, a hazard not conquered in time to halt the rapid decline of the crop.[17]

The rise of Wisconsin dairying is a story rich in detail and apt quotations, in part because it was actively promoted by a crew of New York Yankees who loved an audience. They wrote, and they sought public platforms. One served as governor and others held public office by election and appointment. They wrangled among themselves, usually cheerfully but with occasional asperity, and eagerly took on all comers who doubted that dairying represented the way of salvation. Their rhetorical range is hinted at by W. C. White's dictum, "Speak to a cow as you would to a lady," and by Governor William Dempster Hoard's exasperated comment: "One reason why there is so much truth in the oft-reiterated remark,—'Farming don't pay'—is that there is not another busi-

[17] Glover, *Farm and College*, 161–164; Schafer, *Agriculture in Wisconsin*, 93–96; John D. Bowman and Richard H. Keehn, "Agricultural Terms of Trade in Four Midwestern States, 1870–1900," in the *Journal of Economic History*, 34 (September, 1974), 592–605.

ness on the face of the earth that, in proportion to the numbers engaged in it, supports so many incompetents."[18]

The rhetoric, chafing, and wrangling all had their purpose and served a vital function in the shift to dairying. The market, the marketing instruments, the mechanical technology, and a basic understanding of the demands of the crop were all there for the Wisconsin wheat farmers, but not for the dairymen. Oddly, this proved to be advantageous for the pioneer dairymen. The wheat farmers had little reason for co-operation in the production of their crops. The dairymen, by contrast, had to be drawn together to solve the kinds of problems that were handled by others for the grain farmer. Where was the market? In what form would the products most advantageously reach the market? How were the special requirements for transportation, handling, and marketing to be met? How could the products be standardized to ensure market confidence? How could the products be produced in sufficient quantities to command the market? How was the market to be reached? How could the dairy year be extended into the winter months? All of these questions suggest a co-operative effort well beyond the inclinations or resources of a pioneering agricultural community. The success of the endeavor, within a single generation, possibly accounts for the argument, begun by William Daniells back in the 1870's and carried on since by historians, as to who were the "land skimmers" who went west with the wheat, and who stayed on to milk the cows.

The Civil War decade was a period of experimentation with alternatives to wheat culture and cattle raising. Experimentation was encouraged by wartime shortages, especially for substitutes for cotton, sugar cane sweeteners, tobacco, and other possible alternatives to uncertain wheat crops on expensive but tired soils. Most were short-lived or, like tobacco farming, limited in application. Dairying emerged as one of the better alternatives which fit a broad range of available soils, topography, and climate conditions. But it was an alternative that seemed open only to well-financed farmers able to operate on a fairly large scale. The Dane County farmer who manufactured choice butter from his superior

[18] Lampard, *Rise of the Dairy Industry*, 159, 424.

herd for shipment directly to a Philadelphia buyer was illuminating an opportunity although not exactly setting an example for the ordinary farmer who possessed a half-dozen grade cows supplying a modest surplus during the flush season. There was a long way to go and many hurdles to overcome.[19]

Picture the husbandman of the 1870's as, lantern in hand, he rouses his manure–matted cows from their beds of warm dung. With grimy fingers he coaxes their milk into an open pail as kittens frisk in the hay at his feet. From the fragrant product, the busy farmwife skims the cream, setting it aside to ripen in a crock near the stove where her husband's socks and boots are drying. Nearby, the family dog pursues the nimble flea with tooth and nail. The butter resulting from such casual dairying was known as "Western grease." It was sold in Chicago by the hundredweight as the base for wagon lubricants—in short, as axle grease.[20]

The task was to upgrade existing dairy operations and products, establish markets, and find methods for reaching them. The instrument was the Wisconsin Dairymen's Association, organized in 1872 to establish a central market for butter and cheese. The nine founders had Yankee backgrounds. A majority was from New York, and all but two of them were private dairy farmers. The best known among them, William Dempster Hoard of Fort Atkinson, was a country newspaperman who later founded the nation's outstanding dairy publication, *Hoard's Dairyman*. With the formation of this organization, Wisconsin's dairy revolution was fairly launched.[21]

Except for those fortunate to have an established private mar-

[19] Merk, *Economic History*, chap. 1; Park and Co., *Madison, Dane County and Surroundings*, 447; Charles L. Hill, "John V. Robbins, Pioneer Agriculturalist," in *WMH*, 34 (Summer, 1951), 230–232; Richard N. Current, *The History of Wisconsin. Volume II: The Civil War Era, 1848–1873* (Madison, 1976), 374–379, 452–464.

[20] Adapted from Earl Hayter, *The Troubled Farmer, 1850–1890: Rural Adjustment to Industrialism* (DeKalb, 1968), 68–69.

[21] The organization of the Wisconsin Dairymen's Association had been preceded, in 1869, by a regional organization centered in Rockford, Illinois, and by the first county organization in Fond du Lac County in 1870. See Lampard, *Rise of the Dairy Industry*, 124–125. The same source (p. 340) nicely captures the spirit of these Yankee prophets of dairying: "With fervor born of religiosity and language lifted bodily from Old Testament prophecy and popular Darwinism, the Wisconsin leaders denounced the errors of wheat growing and proclaimed the glad tidings of redemption through dairying."

ket, most Wisconsin dairy products before 1872 were traded at
country stores for credit, to be bought by the lot by traveling buyers, or else were shipped through out-of-state dealers, primarily in
Chicago. Both systems resulted in minimum prices which
afforded little recognition of great variations in quality. In 1872
the Wisconsin Dairymen's Association established a dairy board
of trade at Watertown, modeled on the one at Little Falls, New
York, to bring buyer and seller together in an auction setting. The
Watertown market was followed a year later by one at Sheboygan
Falls. Hoard recognized the implications for dairymen of the
refrigerator car developed by the Chicago meat-packer Gustavus
Swift for transporting chilled carcasses to eastern markets. The
cars were supplied by fast freight services, such as Star Union of
Chicago, which guaranteed six-day delivery to New York. In 1874
Hoard negotiated with this company a favorable rate which
enhanced Wisconsin dairymen's advantages of cheaper land, feed,
and labor costs in comparison to the highly developed dairy
industry of New York. Other Wisconsin Dairymen's Association
members simultaneously explored the growing British market for
American cheese.[22]

Having established new marketing mechanisms and special
transportation for the product, the enterprising dairymen next
faced the not unpleasant prospect of supplying an expanding
urban market at home and abroad with reasonably uniform products. No longer did they have to worry about frequent gluts of the
limited western market. This is where the "fervor born of religiosity" came into play. Beyond associating the saved in a better
marketing system, they needed a growing body of converts to
supply the demand and maintain the service. Borrowing again
from New York precedents, the country cheese factory supplied
the answer.

Cheese was a more complicated product than butter, and it
required skills which were beyond the reach of most households.
But good cheese had characteristics which recommended it for a
dairy economy distant from its markets and normally lacking

[22] Ibid., 125–130.

refrigeration except in transit. Cheese shipped and kept better than butter under such circumstances, and it used the whole milk. The answer was to multiply the relatively scarce skills of the competent cheese maker by establishing cheese factories in dairy districts within hauling distance of neighboring herds.

Given the state of nineteenth-century Wisconsin roads and horse-drawn transport, the accepted maximum radius for a country cheese factory was between two and three miles; but the minimum supply for economical operation was the milk from at least 200 cows. This is where the necessity for converts came into play. In order to enjoy the enhanced income promised by an emphasis on dairying, farmers already in the cause had to recruit fellow enthusiasts.

That the proselytizing worked there can be no doubt. Wisconsin had 308,377 milk cows in 1870 and produced 1,696,783 pounds of factory cheese. Iowa had 369,811 cows but produced only 256,906 pounds of factory cheese. In 1890 Wisconsin had 792,620 cows to Iowa's 1,498,418, but produced 53,708,595 pounds of factory cheese to Iowa's 4,705,576 pounds—more than eleven times Iowa's production with about half as many milk cows on the farm. The point is that Wisconsin was primarily committed to cheese production, being second only to New York in 1890, with close to half New York's production of factory cheese. Twenty years earlier, Wisconsin had produced only one forty-sixth as much as New York: an impressive single-minded pursuit.[23]

The leaders of the revolution had winning arguments, principal among these that acceptance of the discipline and advancing technology of dairying assured predictable profits, on an increasingly regular basis, while restoring the fertility of the soil. These were difficult arguments to ignore, even when stubborn neighbors occasionally hit extraordinary yields or prices for their wheat. But

---

[23] See *Ninth Census of the United States, 1870: Wealth and Industry, Volume III*, 147–148, 280–281, 594; *Eleventh Census of the United States, 1890: Manufacturing, Volume VI, Part 1*, pp. 694–695; *ibid., Agriculture, Volume V*, 285, 314. It should be noted that these statistics all apply to factory-made cheese, as distinguished in the census tables from cheese produced on the farm. In 1870, Wisconsin produced 1,591,798 pounds of cheese on the farm; Iowa, 1,087,741 pounds. Lampard, *Rise of the Dairy Industry*, 392–393.

the dairy arguments needed constant reinforcement because starting a dairy herd was relatively expensive, mainly for a barn, even
if the farmer started with a dozen cheap cows at $20 to $25 apiece.
It was little wonder that diversified farming appealed to many. If
some variation of livestock feeding was the logical course, sheep
or hogs required much less outlay and emphasis could be varied
from season to season more readily. If cattle raising promised better returns, it was tempting to listen to those who spoke in favor
of the dual-purpose cow that provided both milk and beef.[24]

These alternatives challenged the dairy enthusiasts in the agricultural press and at meetings. The Wisconsin Dairymen's Association adopted a variety of techniques for involving a wider
audience. The emergence of a specialized press devoted to dairying was one. *Hoard's Dairyman* was launched in 1885, a logical
outgrowth of Hoard's *Jefferson County Union*, started in 1870, in
which he had carried a dairy column since 1872. Hoard's timing
was correct, for dairy journalism had just begun to find sufficient
subscribers and interested advertisers for survival. By 1889,
Hoard's journal was the leader in the field with 6,000
subscribers.[25]

The "experience meeting" developed by the Wisconsin Dairymen's Association drew appreciative audiences and became the
model adopted by county and other local associations. The state
convention of the Wisconsin Dairymen's Association became
something of a traveling show which played to interested audiences in the small towns where the dairymen met with the purpose of taking their message to farm communities. Governor
Hoard had much to do with this. As a young man he had worked
as a song leader and was also a Methodist lay preacher. He knew
country audiences. After twenty years with the Wisconsin Dairymen's Association as secretary, member of the board, and president, Hoard confessed that "to retain the confidence of my co-
workers in this field, has been an ambition with me more than
money, and my wife says often more than herself." The dialogues

[24] Lampard, *Rise of the Dairy Industry*, 105–109.
[25] John T. Schlebecker and Andrew W. Hopkins, *A History of Dairy Journalism in the
United States, 1810–1950* (Madison, 1957), chaps. 3 and 4.

of these conventions and experience meetings, with their spirited give-and-take between speakers and audience, became the basic element of the farmers' institutes, begun in 1885, which the College of Agriculture of the University of Wisconsin pioneered.[26]

The purpose of this persuasiveness, pitched to the widest possible audience, was the acceptance of a discipline which characterized industrialization—a subordination of individualism to the demands of an industrial process. This was particularly necessary in the organization of a community cheese factory which depended upon regular deliveries of fresh milk that met an empirical standard. The final product was the result of an imperfectly understood chemical process which careless practices in feeding, milking, handling, or delivery on the part of one patron could taint or ruin for his neighbors. Dairying, and especially the factory cheese making that became so characteristic of Wisconsin dairying, demanded an uncommon devotion to co-operation and the discipline imposed by the demands of the process.[27]

The esprit of the Wisconsin Dairymen's Association was such that it shortly became the dominant agricultural organization in the state. This had important implications for the adjustment of Wisconsin agriculture to the point that by 1890 dairying was the state's principal speciality, and nearly 90.5 per cent of her farms reported dairy cattle in 1900. Dairying had moved, with much the same pattern as wheat raising, from pioneer centers along Lake Michigan and in south-central Wisconsin, in a westerly and northerly direction. Unlike wheat culture, this was not a temporary adaptation enforced by pioneering conditions. The older dairy regions already had gone through the experimental phases, and these did not therefore have to be recapitulated in the newer areas.[28]

A crucial factor in the rapid rise of the Wisconsin Dairymen's

---

[26] *DWB*; Wisconsin Dairymen's Association, *Report*, 1892, p. 108, as quoted in Glover, *Farm and College*, 69. Hoard was a good show, always armed with a supply of apt stories that made him a favorite of audiences.

[27] This aspect of Wisconsin dairying is particularly emphasized by Lampard, *Rise of the Dairy Industry*, 91–94, 108–109, 146–147.

[28] *Ibid.*, 192, 266–274.

Association was that it came just at a time when the new agricultural program of the University needed a sense of direction and organized support animated by strength of purpose. The Wisconsin Dairymen's Association provided them. In 1863 the legislature had accepted the terms of the Morrill Act, which offered generous federal land subsidies to states for creating agricultural and mechanical colleges. Not until 1868 did the University of Wisconsin get around to hiring a professor of agriculture and chemistry. The appointee, William W. Daniells, was unable to implement either an educational or experimental program which satisfied any constituency. The logical directing organization was the Wisconsin State Agricultural Society, which had been in existence since 1851. The society, chartered to organize the state fair and assist local fairs, had become the province of gentlemen farmers—City of Milwaukee farmers, as a matter of fact—interested in maintaining Milwaukee as the permanent site for the state fair. The society's publications often lent substance to the traditional "dirt farmer's" scorn for both "book farmers" and "gentlemen farmers" who were believed to have little practical knowledge or experience.[29]

Not surprisingly, the Wisconsin State Agricultural Society failed to provide a sense of direction to the future college of agriculture. The smaller Wisconsin State Horticultural Society broke off from the agricultural society in 1865 to answer the needs of this more specialized farming. Fruit growers had assumed that most

[29] Gerald L. Prescott, "Yeomen, Entrepreneurs and Gentry: A Comparative Study of Three Wisconsin Agricultural Organizations, 1873-1893" (doctoral dissertation, University of Wisconsin, 1968), chap. 7. John Mitchell, son of Alexander Mitchell, the Milwaukee banking and railroad tycoon, regularly listed his occupation as "farmer." John was a horse breeder, a popular specialty of the time. Such gentlemen farmers were normally more interested in thoroughbreds and harness horses than draft animals. Harness racing was the most popular entertainment at agricultural fairs. Mitchell once professed that he avoided any interest in cost accounting on his farm for fear of learning how much his hobby really cost. See John L. Mitchell, "Fine Horses and Horse-Breeding Facilities," in W. J. Anderson and Julius Bleyer, eds., *Milwaukee's Great Industries: A Compilation of Facts Concerning Milwaukee's Commercial and Manufacturing Enterprises, Its Trade and Commerce, and the Advantages It Offers to Manufacturers Seeking Desirable Locations for New or Established Industries* (Milwaukee, 1892), 117-121.

varieties from New England would thrive here, but Wisconsin's climate made fruit culture an uncertain enterprise, whatever the seeming resemblances of weather and other growing conditions to New England and upstate New York. Trial and error was an expensive process for orchardists. Indicative of the dilemma, by 1890 Wisconsin had fewer than 1.4 million apple trees producing less than 2 million bushels; Michigan had 8.5 million trees and a harvest of over 13 million bushels. In soft fruits the disparity was just as great.[30]

A more realistic contender as spokesman for Wisconsin agriculture at this time was the Patrons of Husbandry, universally known as the Grange. It first took successful root in early 1871, then grew rapidly after the fall of 1872 when Colonel John Cochrane of Dodge County became grand master. Two years later there were 300 local granges and upwards of 20,000 members. The problem with the Grange was that it went up like a rocket and came down like a stick. Conceived by its founders as a social organization, modeled after the Freemasons, for the purpose of overcoming rural isolation, it was seized upon as an instrument of militant protest in the hard times following the 1873 panic. The Grange became identified as the farmers' spokesman for railroad rate regulation, currency inflation, and general antimonopoly sentiment. Flush with membership dues, the national organization encouraged a plunge into co-operative purchasing and even machinery manufacturing which ended as discordantly in Wisconsin as it did elsewhere. The membership of 18,650 reported in 1875 slid to 8,592 by 1878 as the Grange began a long readjustment to its original role.[31]

The Grange often played a spoiler's role in the field of formal agricultural education. Governor Jeremiah M. Rusk recognized that Grange membership represented only the tip of the iceberg

---

[30] Glover, *Farm and College*, 37; *Eleventh Census of the United States, 1890: Agriculture, Volume V*, 82–83. The Wisconsin State Horticulture Society was a revival of the Wisconsin Fruit Growers Association, which existed between 1853 and 1859.

[31] LaVerne H. Marquart, *Wisconsin's Agricultural Heritage: The Grange, 1871-1971* (Lake Mills, 1972), 1-21, 28. "Grange" is a medieval term for farm. See also D. Sven Nordin, *Rich Harvest: A History of the Grange, 1867-1900* (Jackson, Mississippi, 1974).

among those who considered themselves "practical farmers" as
opposed to the gentlemen farmers, educators, and urban types
who took part in the annual winter meetings of the state agricultural society. To browse through the society's *Transactions* (published and distributed by a generous state subsidy) is to recognize
the social, economic, and intellectual barriers that set its members
apart from the vast majority of farmers. Indeed, most of the
spokesmen who appeared at those meetings were there because
they could afford the trip, were accustomed to staying in a hotel as
well as to performing before an educated audience. Therefore
many were gentlemen farmers, and urban gadflies looking for a
likely forum, and men who were prominent for reasons other than
their farming skills. One thing most of them had in common was
a childhood spent on a farm, and most could aver that this experience had been enhanced by a wider education. So what about
those who did not belong to an agricultural society or otherwise
expose themselves to what was available in farm journals or other
media that dealt with their craft and its problems? Undoubtedly
many such were among those who invited the exasperation of their
betters for their failure to adopt progressive agricultural practices
and preferred to spend their winter idle hours around the stove in
the hamlet general store cussing the monopolists and their political allies.[32]

Happily there *was* a flourishing institution of the times that successfully reached much of this silent majority: the county fair. In
1884 there were fifty-four fairs, usually one per county, but nine
of which had two fairs at different locations to reach a wider audience. Burnett, Barron, and Taylor counties were the northernmost of them. Nearly forty of these local fairs were listed eleven
years earlier. By the mid-eighties the county fair was taking on
more of a carnival atmosphere with harness racing and even beer
tents raising complaints just as they did at the larger state fair,
which was controlled by the state agricultural society. While the

---

[32] Henry Casson, *"Uncle Jerry": Life of General Jeremiah M. Rusk, Stage Driver, Farmer,
Soldier, Legislator, Governor, Cabinet Officer* (Madison, 1895), 158–160; Wisconsin State Agricultural Society, *Transactions*, 1885, pp. 376–380. Pages 8–13 list life members of the society with post office addresses.

state fair, which did not finally settle down in Milwaukee until 1886, was a much greater attraction, the local fairs must have reached a larger farm audience.[33]

In the early years, local fairs emphasized their educational functions with exhibits, livestock judging, field trials, machinery displays, and competitions of various kinds. These fairs afforded an opportunity for the self-proclaimed practical farmer to examine what farm equipment manufacturers were offering, talk to exhibitors, and compare notes with a wider sampling of successful fellow farmers than his local neighbors offered, even if he was not inclined to seek opportunities to attend lectures or read up on his craft.[34]

Another agency which aimed to take practical agricultural knowledge to the local level in a more serious setting than a county fair claims a unique Wisconsin origin: the farmers' institutes. Hiram Smith, the pioneer Sheboygan County dairy farmer who enjoyed visible material success as a "scientific farmer," gave an address at a fair in neighboring Manitowoc which fired the enthusiasm of a local lawyer who shortly won a seat in the state assembly. Collaborating with Smith, the new assemblyman, Charles A. Estabrook, introduced a bill calling for a substantial state subsidy to fund farmers' institutes. The measure passed and is claimed to be the first such in the United States. Given Smith's active role in the Wisconsin Dairymen's Association and the fact that the law placed the direction of the institutes in the hands of the University regents, the programs of the institutes were strongly biased towards dairy farming. Institutes were held from November to April when farm work was slack. Hudson claims the first of thirty institutes held that first season (1885–1886). So popular was the program that the appropriation for the third year of operation was raised from $5,000 to $12,000, eighty-one institutes were held throughout the state, and a total attendance of 50,000 was

---

[33] Wisconsin State Agricultural Society, *Transactions*, 1873–1874, pp. 42–43; *ibid.*, 1885, pp. 112–115, 118, 124–126. In 1885 the executive board of the society voted 12–1 to exclude intoxicating liquors, including beer, from the state fair.

[34] Bogue, *From Prairie to Cornbelt*, 204–206; Einar O. Hammer, "One Hundred Years of Wisconsin State Fairs," in *WMH*, 34 (Autumn, 1950), 12–13.

26             THE HISTORY OF WISCONSIN

claimed. An average of seventy annually were held through 1893.

After a speech on "Agricultural Institutes" by Hiram Smith at the 1886 meeting of the state agricultural society, one enthusiast remarked: "I endorse what has been said . . . that we should have a wider dissemination of the proceedings of these farmers' institutes. I have attended some of those institutes and one thing has pleased me more than any other. We come up here [to Madison] and we see a great many gray heads, but the young men and young women, where are they? These farmers' institutes meet that want. I attended one in Rock county where I think one-half of the entire audience, and the audience was very large, were young men and young women, the very parties that the institute ought to reach. . . . The young people gather in our towns and larger villages at these institutes when they will not come here." The farmers' institutes doubtless eased the long and rocky path followed in defining the structure, aims, and location of the state's college of agriculture by developing a farmer constituency for it.[35]

Dissatisfaction with the agricultural program at the University did not succeed in dislodging the program from the school. In 1878 the farm organizations persuaded the governor to appoint a farmer to the Board of Regents. He complied by nominating Hiram Smith. Thereafter, dairymen would have a central role in shaping what was to become the College of Agriculture of the University of Wisconsin. Regent Hiram Smith was not long in making his influence felt. He persuaded the board in 1880 to create a professorship solely in agriculture, to replace Daniells (who moved wholly into chemistry, which was more congenial to him).

---

[35] E. L. Luther, "Farmers' Institutes in Wisconsin, 1885-1933," in *WMH*, 30 (September, 1946), 59-68; Robin Hood, "The Progress of Our Farmers' Institutes," in *Wisconsin Country Magazine*, 10 (April, 1916), 332-333; *DWB*. Wisconsin State Agricultural Society, *Transactions*, 1886, pp. 107-128, contains the paper by Hiram Smith on "Agricultural Institutes," followed by one of many on the then–burning question, "A Separate Agricultural College," and subsequent discussion of both papers. Bogue, *From Prairie to Corn Belt*, 205-207; Lampard, *Rise of the Dairy Industry*, 158-159, 169. Glover, *Farm and College*, 28-31, 94, 106-109, 149-156, shows the relationship between the 1885 law creating the institutes in Wisconsin and the ongoing debate over the form, purposes, and role of the agricultural college in Wisconsin.

The new man brought in was William A. Henry, who had just graduated from the agricultural course at Cornell University.

Henry, with enthusiastic support from his constituency, built up the physical plant and the budget of the college as well as its faculty. Seemingly shy when he first appeared on the Wisconsin scene, within four years he felt no hesitancy in appearing at the office of an important ally, Governor Jeremiah M. Rusk, without a prior appointment, and going off with him on the spur of the moment to do battle with the Regents over the college budget. ("Come on, Henry, we will straighten this out," Rusk promised.) Henry learned to get what he wanted and became a masterful performer before legislative committees or in impromptu barnyard demonstrations. He turned the adjoining University farm (now part of the campus) from a communal picnic ground and woodlot into a vital facility in American agricultural experimentation.[36]

William A. Henry was to become one of the country's best-known deans of agriculture, and by the early nineties had refused flattering offers from Iowa, Stanford, and the New York department of agriculture. He came to Wisconsin with an open mind in search of a constituency for whom to build a program. He began his search by courting the Grange, but by 1890 he was elected president of the Wisconsin Dairymen's Association. His election was an indication of the influence of Regent Hiram Smith and of the state's dairymen as a powerful group, open to experimentation and the application of science to agriculture. After a few false starts, including another attempt (which Henry abetted) to separate the Morrill Act program from the University, the relationship settled into a mutual admiration society that helped to mold the College of Agriculture into the nation's leading dairy sciences school. William Henry, near retirement in 1906, stated simply: "The Wisconsin State Dairymen's Association is the true parent of the Wisconsin College of Agriculture of today."[37]

Like Wisconsin agricultural history generally, the College of Agriculture of the University of Wisconsin has been written about

[36] Glover, *Farm and College*, 89–102, 133–148.
[37] *Ibid.*, chap. 5.

a good deal. The farmers' institutes and short courses became models for reaching farmers and for giving practical scientific instruction in dairy manufacturing to those with a common school education. While it was a committee of the Regents that forced Dean Henry and the faculty to accept students without high school or other college preparation, it was Henry himself and the agricultural school faculty who finally made the program a success. Henry was a good judge of men as well as an administrator who offered direction and support. The best known of his appointees must be Stephen M. Babcock, whose name is perpetuated in the Babcock butterfat test, which supplied a much-needed quality test for fluid milk. Babcock and a younger colleague who later replaced Henry as dean, Harry L. Russell, pioneered studies of cheese making which led to cold curing and control of sportive bacteria in the process. Russell, who had studied with the physician and bacteriologist Robert Koch in Berlin, did pathbreaking work on tuberculosis in dairy cattle. Other members of Henry's faculty did important work which led to competitive offers for their services. Henry's own scientific study was summarized in his handbook, *Feeds and Feeding* (Madison, 1898), that continued, with revisions, as a standard for many years. By his continuing scientific and practical work on ensilage, Henry helped to extend the dairy season into the winter months. He did much in the years to come to make the silo a ubiquitous feature of the Wisconsin landscape.[38]

The idea was widely held that a cow was more productive during the brief milking season, beginning in the spring when she had her calf, if she had a long rest during the months when fresh feed was not available. This was a rationalization to justify the fact that abundant feed to fuel milk production was difficult to supply after October. As a result, cheese factories and creameries normally

[38] Glover, *Farm and College*; Curti and Carstensen, *University of Wisconsin*; and Lampard, *Rise of the Dairy Industry*, all have extensive treatments of the College of Agriculture in the years 1873-1893. See also Edward H. Beardsley, "The Making of a Scientist: Harry L. Russell in Europe," in *WMH*, 49 (Autumn, 1965), 3-15, and "An Industry Revitalized: Harry Russell, Stephen Babcock, and the Cold Curing of Cheese," in *WMH*, 49 (Winter, 1965-1966), 122-137.

operated only four or five months on the average, during what was known as the "flush season." This gave little incentive to the many small farmers who supplied the cheese factories and creameries to extend their milking season.

In 1877 a Frenchman, Auguste Goffart, published the results of twenty-five years of experimentation with silage—green feed fermented in a tightly enclosed space. Dr. H. S. Weeks of Oconomowoc, using Goffart's book as a guide, began experiments within three years of its publication. But farmers were traditionalists and there was much resistance to feed so radically altered as to be offensive from downwind. Dean Henry seized upon Dr. Weeks's experiments, and in 1881 he was successful with a request for a special legislative appropriation of $4,000 to build an experimental silo on the University farm. Refinements of the process produced a product that was acceptable to the University herd, and had none of the dire consequences predicted by doubters. Hiram Smith, the Sheboygan dairy pioneer, kept careful records of his own experiments with the process which showed that he could winter three cows on the green corn silage from one acre, while it required the hay from two acres for a single cow. This ability to provide more generous nutriment in the fall and winter extended the milking season. Like other aspects of the dairy revolution, acceptance of the silo required strenuous preaching to the obdurate on the part of Henry and his faculty, editor Hoard, and other early converts and experimenters. Even so, as late as 1904, a statewide census reported only 716 silos in Wisconsin.[39]

Dairying benefited as well from significant mechanical inventions. The centrifugal cream separator perfected in Sweden by Dr. Carl De Laval was available by 1885 in simple, hand-cranked models for the individual farm. This replaced the unsatisfactory method of allowing cream to rise to the top of shallow pans of whole milk for skimming. As one can imagine, this required many pans, much space and intermittent labor, and less than complete separation. Also, it was difficult to keep the milk cool enough to ensure that the cream did not turn. The separator permitted the

[39] Nesbit, *Wisconsin*, 290-291; Lampard, *Rise of the Dairy Industry*, 155-162.

dairy farmer to deliver his cream to the butter manufacturer—the creamery—in much fresher condition, while he kept the skim to feed his pigs and other livestock.[40]

Success in spreading the dairy gospel soon raised the specter of overproduction. Traditional dairy markets for Wisconsin farmers were the nearby, growing urban markets. But, as Hoard commented in 1879, during those early years the Wisconsin dairyman's Chicago market could be glutted for a week with the shipment of three carloads of cheese. The product simply did not carry over very successfully, given the storage facilities of the times; and storage was no solution anyway, because storage and a large inventory had to be financed. Accumulated product was, therefore, simply a glut that threatened current production and any realistic price structure. Inevitably, these periodic gluts were mostly the problem of the men who operated the cheese factories, whether as individual owners or as managers. This is why these men were those most interested in organization and sometimes found themselves at odds with the milk producers. But the factory and creamery men were those who solved the problems of finding wider markets, including overseas, by developing boards of trade and an auction system to regularize prices, and by securing special rates and handling, including the use of refrigerator cars, negotiated with the railroads.[41]

All is not gold that glitters, nor does the course of true love always run smoothly. So it was with Wisconsin agriculture. Having developed a growing export market, particularly in Great Britain, American dairymen unfortunately discovered that they could market their butterfat separately and replace it with lard or other fats in skim milk cheeses. This seems to have worked sometimes with domestic consumption, but the adulterated cheese was particularly offensive to British palates. The "filled cheese" contagion is alleged to have spread from New York, and Wisconsin dairymen had caught it by the mid-eighties. Filled cheese ruined

---

[40] Lampard, *Rise of the Dairy Industry*, 204–210.

[41] Wisconsin Dairymen's Association, *Report*, 1879, p. 129; Lampard, *Rise of the Dairy Industry*, 102–141.

the export market, dealing a severe blow to Wisconsin with its emphasis on cheese manufacture and its dependence on export markets. It is reasonably contended that the need to establish standards for dairy products and to regulate products such as filled cheeses, oleomargarine, and butterine developed a progressive bias among Wisconsin dairymen—a bias later to be exploited by Robert M. La Follette.[42]

Farmers assumed that their interests were general rather than special, and politicians usually responded ungrudgingly. It was certainly common for Wisconsin's governors to provide the legislature with some recommendations specifically addressed to agricultural problems. The recommendations of two governors in particular during the 1880's are worthy of notice. Governor Jeremiah Rusk, Dean Henry's staunch ally, was to become Secretary of Agriculture in President Benjamin Harrison's cabinet in 1889, a few weeks after the post was raised to cabinet rank. He set an impressive record as an administrator and spokesman for the country's agricultural interests. As governor he successfully sought appropriations for Henry's experiment station, for a state veterinarian to inspect dairy products and livestock exports, and for financial support for the new program of farmers' institutes. Rusk, who proved to be both effective and popular, was governor for seven years from January, 1882, to January, 1889—three terms plus a year added by a change to the even-numbered years for gubernatorial elections. His unusually long tenure—he refused to accept a fourth term which he doubtless would have won—gave his vigorous advocacy of agricultural, particularly dairying interests, an important impact.[43]

The Wisconsin Dairymen's Association generally had abjured involvement in the popular concerns usually identified with midwestern agrarian revolt: railroad regulation, currency reform, and

---

[42] Lampard, *Rise of the Dairy Industry*, 244–257, 333–351.

[43] Leonard D. White, *The Republican Era: A Study in Administrative History, 1869–1901* (New York, 1958; reprinted, 1965), chap. 11; *Messages and Executive Communications to the Legislatures of Wisconsin, and Public Proclamations of Governor Jeremiah M. Rusk, 1882–1889* (Madison, 1888), pp. 13–14 [1882]; pp. 9–10, 24 [1883]; pp. 16–18 [1885]; pp. 15–16 [1887]. See Chapter 11 below.

antimonopoly agitation. The Wisconsin Dairymen's Association
pursued more immediate goals in dealing with railroads, their
markets, and production problems. The dairymen did not neglect
politics. Their alliance with Governor Rusk helped to mold the
College of Agriculture to their particular needs and they enlisted
his aid in the beginnings of state regulation of dairy production
and marketing. As governor, Rusk's final service to the dairymen
was to declare for an open Republican convention to choose his
successor. William D. Hoard thereupon became the nominee of
an unfettered convention.[44]

Governor Hoard, probably Wisconsin's best-known dairy
leader, naturally favored the state's agricultural interests. He
congratulated the legislature for expenditures in behalf of agriculture, particularly the experiment station and the farmers' institutes, and asked the continuance of a $2,000 appropriation made
directly to the Wisconsin Dairymen's Association at the instance
of Governor Rusk. As a means of expanding the state's commitment, he recommended, successfully, the creation of a dairy and
food commission "with the power to enforce the laws against all
adulteration of foods and drinks. . . ." Wisconsin was not a
pioneer in this field. Hoard noted that neighboring Iowa and
Minnesota had such commissions "with the necessary powers and
means conferred by law for the suppression of the fraudulent
manufacture and sale of imitation butter and cheese as well as the
sale of adulterated, impure or diluted milk."[45]

Hoard came a cropper, after a single term, because of his
enthusiastic support of a law (known as the Bennett Law) requiring all schools, including parochial, to teach a common body of
subjects in the English language. He was replaced by Democrat
George W. Peck, a city man with a national reputation as a
raconteur and humorist who drew upon his rural and small-town
boyhood. Governor Peck was appalled by the spendthrift ways of
the state. He pointed particularly at the expenses of the office of

---

[44] Jeremiah M. Rusk, "To the Editor," August 6, 1888, in the Rusk Papers.

[45] *Wisconsin Public Documents*, 1889, Governor's Messages and Documents, vol. 1, pp.
13–16.

the state veterinarian and the dairy and food commission as among the more dubious recent examples of such "special pleading and selfish interests." While Peck's recommendations did not prevail, he slowed the expansion of the state's commitment to subsidizing and regulating in the interest of agriculture.[46]

By the 1870's, railroad building was going forward in northern Wisconsin as a result of generous federal land subsidies granted earlier to link up Lake Superior ports and the terminus of the Northern Pacific with the developed railroad network to the south. The new lines, as a matter of course, assumed an agricultural future for their own and neighboring lands. The Wisconsin Central in particular carried on a very active campaign to attract northern European immigrants, beginning in the mid-seventies. Wisconsin's board of immigration appointed the Wisconsin Central's agent, headquartered in Switzerland, as a state agent. Publications of the state board, freely transcribed into German, Norwegian, and other languages, commonly advised immigrants not to waste time looking for land in southern Wisconsin, but to head north where land was available for homesteading or was privately owned but for sale at favorable prices and terms.[47]

The Wisconsin Central reported in 1890 that it had disposed of 250,000 acres of its 838,628-acre grant. This, however, tells little or nothing about the railroad's settlement activities, because the reports do not segregate agricultural land sales from timberlands. The latter may be assumed to have been the major share by far of these sales. The railroad men's hope in the 1880's was that the sale of railroad lands would revive because "the best government lands have been already taken up." The other northern railroads were similarly involved with their grants, but, like the Wisconsin Central, they accepted the evidence of sawmill towns as settlement.[48]

[46] *Ibid.*, 1891, Governor's Messages and Documents, vol. 1, pp. 1–6.

[47] Wisconsin Board of Immigration, *Wisconsin: What It Offers to the Immigrant* (seventh edition, Milwaukee, 1881), *passim*; also the Board of Immigration's *Publications*, a volume consisting of bound pamphlets issued mainly in the 1880's. Chapters 3 and 11 below discuss these railroad grants at more length. See also Current, *Civil War Era*, 42–48.

[48] Wisconsin Central Railroad Company, *Annual Report*, 1878, p. 13; *ibid.*, 1880, p. 9, and subsequent reports through 1890; Arlan Helgeson, *Farms in the Cutover: Agricultural Settlement in Northern Wisconsin* (Madison, 1962), 4–5.

Private owners and promoters of settlement who were active before 1895 operated mostly in the counties south of the true Cutover. Pine lumbering operations, which hit their peak in northern Wisconsin in the 1880's, naturally attracted a limited agricultural population. The mill towns and camps created a ready market for food and feed crops for men and beasts engaged in lumbering, and logging provided off-season employment for farmers and their teams. But many of the lumber companies were of two minds about selling their cutover lands to settlers, or to speculators who would attract settlers. Farmers meant more voters and demands for outlandish services—such as schools, and roads that did not end at a log dump on a stream bank. It was much cozier to control the county by voting the company's payroll and suppliers while holding down taxes on company lands. Further, the Cutover contained many merchantable hardwoods and stands of immature evergreens, neither of which a lumberman is likely to have ignored. Only the most sanguine could conceive of farms in an area so recently a wilderness.[49]

A soils map of Wisconsin will show an irregular patch popularly known as the Sand Counties, where much of the soil is excessively sandy, while extensive areas are swampy. Much drowned land also lay immediately eastward between the Sand Counties and Lake Winnebago. This forbidding combination inhibited settlement there, and immediately north, until lumbering and railroad construction began, in the 1870's, to draw agricultural population into the lands lying immediately south of the true Cutover and north of the Sand Counties. People who enthused over the agricultural possibilities of "northern Wisconsin" referred usually to pioneering in counties like Barron, Chippewa, and Marathon, leading agricultural counties before 1900, rather than the true Cutover. Clearing and breaking logged-over land or

[49] Helgeson, *Farms in the Cutover*, 6–7; Alice E. Smith, "Caleb Cushing's Investments in the St. Croix Valley," in *WMH*, 28 (September, 1944), 7–19; Lucile Kane, "Settling the Wisconsin Cutovers," in *WMH*, 40 (Winter, 1956–1957), 91–98; Ray Stannard Baker, *Native American: The Book of My Youth* (New York, 1941), 16–19.

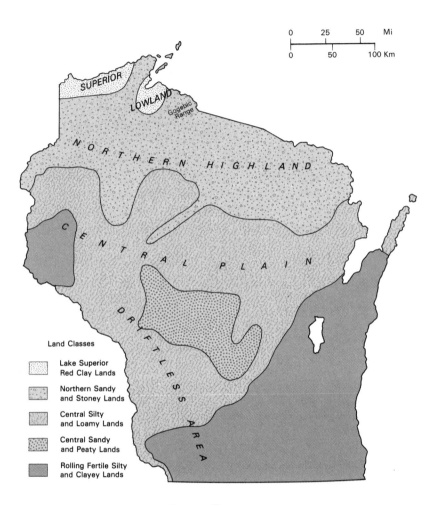

LAND CLASSES

hardwood stands was a formidable task on poor as well as good soil.[50]

It may be possible that historians overemphasize dairying in their histories of Wisconsin agriculture between the 1870's and 1890's. But dairying truly became the dominating interest both in transforming the older settled sections and in offering an alternative to cash crops for the more limited soils and climate conditions in northern Wisconsin. Dairying is of interest because of the production and marketing problems to which solutions were found in intensive co-operation and co-ordination among producers and manufacturers, and in the energetic use of the state and its university to serve the industry. There is a contrast between the granger's vision of the state as regulator of monopolies and the dairyman's use of the state as regulator of the product and the purveyor of the benefits of science to his industry. (One thinks of Andrew Carnegie's observation that he was the only American ironmaker to employ a chemist in the early 1870's.) Wisconsin's dairymen were turning towards the light of science as well as searching for pragmatic solutions, and contempt for "book farmers" was on the wane.[51]

Returns from cash crops fell to less than 50 per cent of Wisconsin agricultural income by 1880, primarily owing to the steady rise of the livestock industry. The state's swine population increased by 162 per cent between 1870 and 1890, but this was modest when compared with Iowa's 511 per cent increase. The figures for what may be interpreted as beef cattle (the breeds were not differentiated very clearly in the census) are comparable. Small grains and hay crops were becoming the mainstays in Wisconsin, along with some other specialities. In 1890 the state ranked first, second, and third nationally in the production of rye, barley, and oats grown

[50] See William A. Henry, *Northern Wisconsin: A Handbook for the Homeseeker* (Madison, 1896), 148–160. Henry's book, with its many illustrations of bumper crops, invites comparison to the New Deal resettlement project in the Matanuska Valley of Alaska—which, ironically, attracted refugees from the Wisconsin Cutover who no longer had been able to eke out a living. One sees the same gigantic cabbages on proud display in the most disheartening surroundings.

[51] Andrew Carnegie, *The Autobiography of Andrew Carnegie* (Boston, 1920), 181–183.

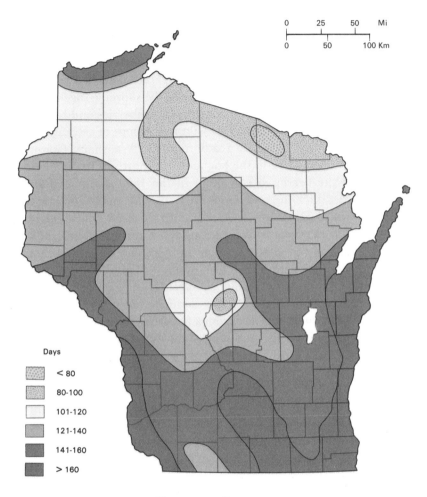

GROWING SEASONS

as cereals. This is impressive when Wisconsin's acreage available for farming is compared with that of other leading agricultural states. It also defines the difference in her agriculture from that of more favored neighbors like Illinois and Iowa.[52]

[52] *Eleventh Census of the United States, 1890: Compendium, Part III*, 620, 632–639.

Potato production, concentrated in the central counties of Portage, Waupaca, and Waushara, was also becoming a Wisconsin speciality in the sense that acreages and yields were on a par with those of Illinois and Iowa. Hay, small grains, roots, and vegetables, in strains suitable to a north temperate climate, were the state's best adaptations; but dairying was the supreme speciality.[53]

Among the state's unique specialities, cranberries and tobacco come to mind. Cranberries grew wild in the bogs of central Wisconsin and early found a ready market. Waushara County pioneered the industry in the boglands just north of Berlin. Cultivation of the berries began there in the 1860's with planting experiments, ditching, and damming to provide quick flooding to forestall frost damage—a constant hazard. It was a typical boom-and-bust business requiring large outlays. Bogs had to be graded and ditched, and the water brought in by canals; and, as in most horticulture, the operator had to wait a few seasons for a satisfactory return. But profits could be spectacular. Another hazard, oddly enough, was fire. In a dry summer the bogs, which are based on peat, could take fire from a forest fire or careless burning of slashings and would continue to smolder even when flooded. Official interest in fire control did not exist until some measures were taken late in the century.

Cranberry culture spread westward into the bogs of the Sand Counties, generally promoted by horticulturists from the Berlin area. The usual technique was to buy a wild marsh for the extensive improvements required. Like hops, which boomed in the 1860's, cranberries were a labor-intensive crop at harvest. The technique of flooding the bogs and raking the berries from the vine was a late development. Large growers traditionally provided a dance hall and even musicians to attract pickers, many of them Indians.

The culture and marketing of cranberries tended, like dairying, to bring growers together in co-operation. Cranberry culture was an exotic among agricultural pursuits. Growers had to be con-

[53] *Ibid.*, 654–658; Ebling et al., *Century of Wisconsin Agriculture*, 40–41, 97.

cerned with riparian law which, in Wisconsin, usually reflected the special needs of lumbering. The market was highly seasonal and no one outside the industry was particularly concerned with hazards to a crop that could grow wild in a bog. The cranberry growers organized their own association in 1887 and financed experiment stations on members' properties. Wisconsin subsequently became one of the leading producers among the few states, stretching from Maine to Washington, where the cranberry is an important crop.[54]

Tobacco is another Wisconsin crop which attracts notice because it requires rather special conditions and unique handling. It early became highly specialized geographically as well. Many farmers grew a few plants for their own use to chew or smoke in a pipe, though apparently the Wisconsin product of the time was not particularly well suited for either use. In addition, tobacco is a temperamental crop, subject to various diseases and insect infestations. It must be transplanted as seedlings and carefully cultivated; much labor is involved in harvesting and preparing it for the buyer.

Some years passed after the introduction of tobacco as a cash crop in southern Wisconsin before it could find a regular market widely sought by speciality buyers. Tobacco acreage rose sharply in the late 1870's, and passed 10,000 acres in 1880. This coincided with the growth of warehousing and processing facilities in Edgerton and Stoughton, where this crop became centered, and the development of cigar manufacturing in Milwaukee, owing much to its German population. The product became standardized, as much in response to soil and climate as to experiments with seed types. It was known as Wisconsin binder tobacco and was used primarily in cigars. For those puzzled by this specialization, one successful grower summed it up: "It has one virtue which no other state's tobacco possesses in so high a degree, viz.: It burns well—and without this quality no tobacco, however fine

---

[54] Neil E. Stevens and Jean Nash, "The Development of Cranberry Growing in Wisconsin," in *WMH*, 27 (March, 1944), 276-294; Wisconsin State Cranberry Growers' Association, *Proceedings*, 1889-1902.

its flavor, is marketable." In 1885 the crop hit a peak of 27,000 acres which it did not attain again until the late nineties, presumably because production was running well ahead of the growth of consumption.[55]

The use of tobacco had its detractors within the late-nineteenth-century generation accustomed to firm moral judgments. After an optimistic presentation of tobacco culture prospects by a couple of growers before the state agricultural society meeting in 1885, interested queries soon were silenced by a member who remonstrated: "I have lived here forty years. I thought when I carried wheat from here [Madison] to Milwaukee that I was laboring to an end in raising a family and trying to inculcate in them principles of industry and integrity, and how can any sane man entertain this audience with a subject [i.e. tobacco] that has not a moral thread in it from beginning to end?" This led several of the like-minded in full cry.

One of the accused growers thereupon responded by quoting an old tobacco grower: "Gentlemen, if you will grow tobacco, grow the best and ask God to forgive you." Another bluntly asked: "If that gentleman who was shooting off his mouth had any objections why did he not say so?" A bemused member of less certain convictions commented facetiously: "I thought that when we excluded beer from the fair grounds and censured the executive committee for using so much of it, that we would soon have this question upon us. I think the executive committee ought to be prohibited from using tobacco, cigars, or anything of that kind." The president of the agricultural society, not surprised by this turn of affairs, opined: "The chair would modestly suggest that he has known a good many individuals that claim they do not have any habits. If a man don't have any habits, I feel sorry for him.[56]

[55] Ebling et al., *Century of Wisconsin Agriculture*, 42–43, 91; F. W. Coon, "The Ins and Outs of Tobacco Culture," in Wisconsin State Agricultural Society, *Transactions*, 1885, p. 308.

[56] This exchange over the "morality" of tobacco culture appears in the Wisconsin State Agricultural Society, *Transactions*, 1886, pp. 301–316. A century ago, tobacco was considered immoral as well as unhealthy by many; hence the comment about "not a moral thread," which may baffle a generation more attuned to the health hazards. That audience in 1885 was probably aware of the resonance of the presiding officer's comment about a man without any habits: it was a direct steal from one of Mark Twain's set pieces.

Oddly, Wisconsin Norwegians have long been identified with tobacco growing in Wisconsin. They were, of course, already settled in areas coinciding with the developing Wisconsin tobacco regions in Dane and Rock counties, later extended into Vernon and Crawford counties to the west. But Norwegians would have been somewhat impervious to some Yankee moral imperatives, besides which they had large, disciplined families well suited to undertake the drudgery of tobacco culture. (This also suggests something about the adaptation of ethnic groups to successful forms of agriculture and crops suitable to local conditions, whether or not they had any previous familiarity with them. So much for Norwegian and German "affinity" for dairy cows!)[57]

The change from cash crops, with a concentration on wheat, to feed crops, better adapted to the soils and climate, characterized the period 1873–1893 in Wisconsin agriculture. The specialization in cheese making, in what became essentially a dairy economy, called for a degree of co-operation and self-imposed discipline which makes the shift remarkable at the very least. The long-term benefits were the creation of a relatively stable agriculture as evidenced, even by the 1890's, in an unusually high proportion of owner-operators living on solid, well-kept family farmsteads. Dairying, for obvious reasons, also contributed to the growth and stability of small towns and villages, a notable feature of much of the Wisconsin countryside.[58]

The upward trend in land values that characterized the latter half of the nineteenth century for Wisconsin's proven farmlands was accompanied, after 1873, by disturbing counter trends. Taxes and rising expectations of what local and county government

---

[57] Ebling et al., *Century of Wisconsin Agriculture*, 29, 42–43; The Tobacco Institute, *Wisconsin and Tobacco* (Washington, 1960), 1–12; *Wisconsin Then and Now*, 22 (September, 1975), 4–6; Wisconsin State Agricultural Society, *Transactions*, 1885, pp. 301–316. Schafer, *Agriculture in Wisconsin*, 51, says of these Norwegian immigrants: "Almost all of these people were farmers, some being farm laborers and some of the women household servants. In the older settlements they frequently took up left-over lands. . . . But they were not deterred from taking open prairie where it was available and openings—the favorite lands—were scarce." Schafer also says in *Town Studies*, 141, that "those leftover lands in the heart of a settled and prosperous community appeared to them more desirable than wild lands lying at the actual frontier."

[58] Lampard, *Rise of the Dairy Industry*, chap. 10.

should provide; the downward secular trend of farm prices; the inherent difficulties presented by fragmentary understanding of profitable alternatives to wheat, the traditional money crop; the increasing commercialization of agriculture bringing new marketing uncertainties; and the capital demands of more varied land uses for equipment and stock: all added to the uncertainties. Of course the rise in farm values also presented a variety of opportunities. An obvious choice was to find a buyer, capitalize the rise in values, and move westward to cheaper land of equal or greater promise. This was the choice of many confirmed grain farmers with an investment in equipment and stock. Another alternative was to rent and move to the village for a second career in business. Still another choice was to make use of the increased value by way of a mortgage to stock and equip for more intensive or varied types of farming. The 1880's saw a growing interest on the part of eastern investors in western farm mortgages while Wisconsin's growing economy was creating a similar class of prospective creditors.[59]

Comparing Wisconsin with the four states whose borders adjoin hers, in 1890 she had a lower percentage of tenant farmers, ranking forty-second in this respect among the forty-eight states and territories. (Minnesota was thirty-ninth, Michigan thirty-sixth, Iowa twentieth, and Illinois fourteenth.) Illinois had 36.72 per cent of her farms operated by tenants, Wisconsin only 13.1 per cent. Wisconsin similarly had a lower percentage of owner-occupied farms with mortgages, with the exception of Illinois. (Iowa had 53.29 per cent; Michigan, 49.35; Minnesota, 46.39; Wisconsin 42.85; and Illinois, 36.71) These states were all in the upper reaches nationally, the average for the United States being 28.22 per cent. The reasons for Wisconsin's relatively favorable show-

[59] Merle Curti, *The Making of an American Community: A Case Study of Democracy in a Frontier Community* (Stanford, 1959), 269–285; Ebling et al., *Century of Wisconsin Agriculture*, 25, 75; Bogue, *From Prairie to Corn Belt*, 173–175; Allan G. Bogue, "Farming in the Prairie Peninsula, 1830–1890," in Allan G. Bogue, Thomas D. Phillips, and James E. Wright, eds., *The West of the American People* (Itasca, Illinois, 1970), 434–436. Shannon, *Farmer's Last Frontier*, 183–190, has a discussion of the credit problems of prairie farmers, much of it applicable to Wisconsin farmers between 1873 and 1893.

ing with respect to farm tenantry and mortgage debt doubtless owed much to the character of her farm population. A higher proportion of that population was made up of the foreign-born and their children from German and Scandinavian backgrounds; and the largest group, those of German background, characteristically did not view its farms as marketable property. Germans generally avoided debt and were inclined to buy up neighboring farms to keep their adult children nearby. It was those of Yankee background—using the term loosely—who were much more apt to follow wheat culture and cheaper acres westward, and very likely those Yankees who remained were culturally more likely to assume mortgages than were their neighbors of German and Scandinavian background. Also, it is fair to generalize that they had the earliest pick of the land to be sold or mortgaged at a higher figure than its cost. The Norwegians, by far the largest Scandinavian group in Wisconsin, followed a different pattern, generally arriving with fewer financial resources than the earlier German settlers and being more readily movable. They therefore often took poorer land that was left in fairly settled communities where they could work for neighbors and farm their own land on a subsistence basis. The result was that they were less attractive prospects for someone with money to lend, and less likely to seek a loan from a Yankee villager.[60]

The state's bureau of labor and industrial statistics, begun in 1883, took a concentrated look at agriculture in its report for the 1895–1896 biennium. The bureau often had used questionnaires previously with industrial workmen and the building trades to elicit information, opinions, and attitudes on job-related as well as public policy issues. There was little that was scientific about

---

[60] *Eleventh Census of the United States, 1890: Report on Farms and Homes, Proprietorship and Indebtedness in the United States, Volume XIII*, Diagram 3 following p. 24, Diagram 4 following p. 26, and pp. 34–40; Joseph Schafer, *The Winnebago–Horicon Basin: A Type Study in Western History* (Madison, 1937), 239–242; Joseph Schafer, *The Wisconsin Lead Region* (Madison, 1932), 220–229; Bogue, "Farming in the Prairie Peninsula," in Bogue, Phillips, and Wright, eds., *The West of the American People*, 433–437. Chapter 6 below discusses the relatively heavier migration westward of Yankee farmers and the characteristics of Wisconsin's foreign–born and their children.

either the sampling techniques or the questions, and the farmers'
rate of response was barely 10 per cent. But those 549 who took
the trouble to fill out and return the questionnaire provided valuable insights into farming and the agrarian mind in the waning
years of the nineteenth century.[61]

The bureau's 1895 farm questionnaire posed forty-three questions, ranging from those requiring only a number or a word in
response to such ramblers as: "Is female help scarce; if so, what is
the reason?" "What in your opinion are the chief causes that lead
to a farmer's failure?" "Is the general tendency of unmarried
farm laborers to acquire and own a farm or is there a desire to go
and live in the city?" Those responding were in general agreement to this leading question that young people preferred to go to
the city. And no one could be harder on the foibles of his neighbors who were not making it than a successful farmer. The printed
returns are not identified by location or name, but only by country or state of birth. The foreign-born are considerably underre-
presented; however, many doubtless were American-born of
immigrant parents. The responses left no doubt that those farmers who favored the bureau with a completed questionnaire considered themselves successful.[62]

The questionnaire did not ask directly about farmers' incomes,
but rather asked whether they had accumulated savings over the
past year, or over the preceding five years. While only half the
respondents had come out ahead over the past year (51.8 per
cent), five out of six (83.2 per cent) has accumulated savings over
the five years preceding. The number of respondents who said that
they had run into debt during the past year (16.1 per cent) coincided with the number who had not made savings over the past
five years. The questionnaire did not ask whether the respondent
might be a tenant, but in 1890 four out of five Wisconsin farms
(81.9 per cent) were owner-occupied, and doubtless a higher pro-

[61] Wisconsin Bureau of Labor, Census and Industrial Statistics, *Biennial Report*, 1895–
1896, pt. 2, "Farmers' Returns" section, pp. 1–135.

[62] *Ibid.*, 2–24, 96, 110; *Eleventh Census of the United States, 1890: Population, Volume II*,
624–625.

portion of these respondents owned their own farms. Of the 48 per cent of respondents who had not accumulated savings over the past year, apparently only one in three had gone into debt as a result. Thus, while the year 1895 certainly represented a low point in agricultural prices over the preceding twenty years, most of these Wisconsin farmers had not suffered unduly.[63]

Only nineteen of the 549 respondents belonged to "any grange or labor organization." If they had one characteristic in common, it was their scorn for any neighbors who failed at farming. Governor Hoard knew his audience when he remarked that farming supported more incompetents than any comparable line of endeavor. He would have found agreement among those who responded to the bureau's query as to why some farmers failed: "Sitting on boxes at the corner grocery squirting tobacco juice and telling fish stories." "A little more brain, even at the expense of some brawn, would prevent many failures." "Laziness, ignorance, carelessness, the credit system, forgetting to mend their fences and to change their crops from year to year. Not using manures. Too large a mortgage and a hole in their pockets large enough for everything to run through."[64]

All in all, the bureau's sampling of articulate Wisconsin farmers, as they found themselves in that year of depression, did not turn up many who disagreed with Commissioner Halford Erickson's comment that "during the last three years the farmers have not suffered more disappointments than those engaged in other occupations." They did have some appreciation for how the other half was living. As one respondent put it: "I have been a farmer all of my life and have no fault to find; farming is satisfactory to me as a life calling. Of course some years the crops do not turn out very well. I have even had almost a total failure in everything I tried to raise for more than one year in succession. But on the whole it averaged up pretty well. There are not near as many failures among farmers as in other businesses."[65]

[63] Wisconsin Bureau of Labor, Census and Industrial Statistics, *Biennial Report*, 1895–1896, pt. 2, pp. 99, 109.

[64] *Ibid.*, 110, 112–123.

[65] *Ibid.*, 137, 122.

# 2

# Lumbering

## ORGANIZING BEYOND WOODS AND MILLS

WHAT were commonly known as Wisconsin's pinelands covered roughly the northern three-fifths of the state. The southern limits of these pinelands were very irregular, with a lobe stretching far to the south, almost to Sheboygan, along the Lake Michigan shore. Other southern lobes followed the Wolf, Wisconsin, La Crosse, and Black rivers; then the pinelands turned northwesterly, avoiding the western uplands, towards the St. Croix watershed. The upper reaches of the Chippewa River and its tributaries were said to contain one-sixth of the white pine lying west of the Adirondacks, a portion of the forest which stretched across much of Michigan, northern Wisconsin, and Minnesota, into Canada. The term "pinelands" was more a commercial designation than an accurate description of the forests, for while there were large areas in central and northern Wisconsin dominated by pine, much of it was largely in hardwoods. Any extensive tract near a driving stream containing one or two mature pines per acre was designated by government surveyors and lumbermen as pinelands.[1]

The reasons for this generous application of the term pinelands are apparent. White pine was the standard of the early lumber

[1] Robert C. Nesbit, *Wisconsin: A History* (Madison, 1973), 9, 296–297; Robert F. Fries, *Empire in Pine: The Story of Lumbering in Wisconsin, 1830–1900* (Madison, 1951), 5–7; Frederick Merk, *Economic History of Wisconsin During the Civil War Decade* (Madison, 1916; reprinted, 1971), 65.

industry, although other conifers were available in the same area, to be exploited as the preferred white pine became scarce. White pine is a light softwood, easily worked and straight-grained. It holds its dimensions well when milled, and, being resinous, resists rot. The standard method for getting timber to the mill was by floating it on a driving stream. The white pine floated very nicely, but the non-buoyant hardwoods, like the inaccessible conifers, had to await the railroads, or later trucks. Also, hardwoods were plentiful in southern Wisconsin where most of their industrial users were located. But the opening prairie lands immediately west of Wisconsin lacked pine. This conjunction was viewed by many as a deliberate gift of divine Providence.[2]

The statistics of the lumber era are overwhelming. It is estimated that the Michigan, Minnesota, and Wisconsin sawmills cut 165 billion board feet of pine lumber in the years 1873–1898. Wisconsin's share of this was 60 billion board feet, or 36 per cent. Reducing these numbers to more manageable terms, Wisconsin mills cut an estimated 1,240,000,000 board feet in 1873. This amount had doubled in 1882, and more than trebled by 1892, the peak year, when 4,010,000,000 board feet of lumber were cut. Added to Wisconsin's total for the period were another estimated 6 billion board feet cut for shingles and lath.[3]

These increases in production came more from an expansion in capacity of the larger mills than from a simple addition of mills, although new mills were a factor as the railroads opened new areas to exploitation. The average mill of 1860 produced about 50,000 board feet of lumber in a twelve-hour day. If we extrapolate a 170-day average cutting season—May to November—we get an annual production of 8,500,000 board feet. Ingram, Kennedy and

---

[2] Fries, *Empire in Pine*, 5–6; James I. Clark, *The Wisconsin Pineries: Logging on the Chippewa* (Madison, 1956), 3–6. There are other descriptions of Wisconsin's pineries. See John T. Curtis, *The Vegetation of Wisconsin: An Ordination of Plant Communities* (Madison, 1959), 171–176; Filibert Roth, *Forestry Conditions and Interests of Wisconsin*, U.S. Department of Agriculture, Division of Forestry, Bulletin no. 16 (1898), 22; *Tenth Census of the United States, 1880: Part 9, Report on the Forests of North America (Exclusive of Mexico)*, opposite 554.

[3] Roth, *Forestry Conditions of Wisconsin*, 44–45. A board foot is 12 by 12 inches, one inch thick. George W. Hotchkiss, *History of the Lumber and Forest Industry of the Northwest* (Chicago, 1898), 745.

Company of Eau Claire was the sixth largest mill operation on the upper Mississippi in 1875–1879, with an annual average production of 23,800,000 board feet, equal to 140,000 daily by the same extrapolation. The same mill in 1888 produced 22,900,000 board feet and had fallen to forty-fourth place.[4]

By 1888, when Wisconsin's pine logging hit its peak, a big mill could process 200,000 board feet per day. This required 1,000 logs, averaging 200 board feet. A mature white pine averaged four to four and a half logs running from 140 to over 200 board feet each, meaning that it required somewhere between five and seven logs to make 1,000 board feet. By 1897, it took an average ten logs to make that measure of the preferred white pine. Not that the trees had shrunk, but there was more clear cutting by 1897. A yield of 25,000 board feet per acre was considered very good, the average running less than half of that. Assume an average of 12,000 board feet per acre and the 200,000 board-feet-per-day mill required the timber from sixteen and two-thirds acres per day, or about 2,832 acres per season. Figure 333,333 acres (about 520 square miles) to provide the 4 billion board feet cut in 1892. This does not allow for timber left in the woods and lost while driving the logs to the mill, or for standing timber destroyed by fire, disease, and decay. In 1898 Filibert Roth estimated that the twenty-seven northern Wisconsin counties surveyed had contained, in the original stand of pine, 129,400,000,000 board feet of which only 17,400,000,000 remained. Most of the logged-over land was not left in condition to encourage renewal. The outcome was predictable.[5]

The temper of the times was certainly acquiescent to a generous use of Wisconsin's timber resources. Federal legislation set the

---

[4] Fries, *Empire in Pine*, 64–65. Fred W. Kohlmeyer, *Timber Roots: The Laird, Norton Story, 1855–1905* (Winona, 1972), 162–163, reproduces a useful chart of the fifty largest mill companies on the upper Mississippi for 1875–1879, 1888, and 1898, which he compiled from the *Mississippi Valley Lumberman and Manufacturer*.

[5] Fries, *Empire in Pine*, 245–246, estimates that "perhaps more good pine timber was burned than ever reached the sawmills," and discusses wasteful practices by all concerned. Roth estimates "26 billion feet as probably wasted, chiefly destroyed by fire." This was 20 per cent of the original stand of pine in the twenty-seven northern counties. Roth, *Forestry Conditions of Wisconsin*, 29–32, 45.

tone. The assumption of such legislation was that the end use of all public lands was agricultural development. The rule was: Hasten the lands into private hands, either directly or as subsidies for desirable public improvements conditioned on quick sale. The pull and haul of farm settlement versus speculation or exploitation on a large scale was solved by increasing generosity to both interests. The State of Wisconsin was not inclined to develop more conservative land policies in competition with the U.S. General Land Office. In any case, the state lacked both the will and the bureaucratic competence to handle the business differently. The contemporary notion that lumbermen were performing a service by turning "the encumbering forest into . . . an incalculable source of wealth to the nation" was not wide of the mark.[6]

Local land offices first opened in the pineries in 1848, but the 1857 business panic effectively halted the rush until after 1862, when Morrill Act scrip (assignable claims to a share of the public domain to support agricultural and mechanical arts colleges) came on the market. Other scrip, which had been granted to veterans for service prior to the Civil War, was also on the market. The Homestead Act of 1862 made land scrip bonuses redundant for Civil War veterans, but opened possibilities for homestead applications in timberland. For land entry purposes, Wisconsin timberland was treated no differently than open prairie until after 1892, when less than 200,000 acres of federal public land remained in Wisconsin.[7]

Unauthorized lumbering activities went forward on public

---

[6] J. Willard Hurst, *Law and Economic Growth: The Legal History of the Lumber Industry in Wisconsin, 1836–1915* (Cambridge, 1964), 52–61; Hotchkiss, *Lumber and Forest Industry*, v. Roth, writing in 1898, roughly classified the pinelands: "About 20 per cent of the area is good farm land, about 40 per cent medium, while nearly 40 per cent is either not fit at all or only doubtfully suited to farming. . . ." He was arguing, of course, for forest reserves. Roth, *Forestry Conditions of Wisconsin*, 24. Arlan Helgeson, *Farms in the Cutover: Agricultural Settlement in Northern Wisconsin* (Madison, 1962), 112, observes that by 1920, if one subtracts the six southernmost counties around the rim of the Cutover (Shawano through Polk)—which had 60 per cent of their lands in farms, half of that cultivated—the remaining counties lying to the north had not more than 7 per cent of their lands in farms.

[7] Jerry A. O'Callaghan, "The War Veteran and the Public Lands," and Thomas LeDuc, "State Disposal of the Agricultural College Land Scrip," both in Vernon Carstensen, ed., *The Public Lands: Studies in the History of the Public Domain* (Madison, 1963), 109–119, 395–410; Fries, *Empire in Pine*, 162.

lands before they came on the market. Federal efforts to control cutting on federal lands received small financial support from Congress and were met with hostile indifference locally. Until Interior Secretary Carl Schurz tried to change the system in 1877, federal agents were encouraged to compromise with timber thieves by collecting a nominal amount for stolen stumpage based upon the standard $1.25 per acre plus legal expenses. Although lumbermen complained of these costs, the arrangement was so standardized that Land Office clerks often gave prior consent to trespass.[8]

Men and companies owned princely tracts of timber, numbering in tens of thousands of acres, generally acquiring them in units known as "quarters"—really quarters of quarter sections, that is forty-acre tracts. Acquisition was a selective and cumulative process; an owner's units were not ordinarily in a solid block. These were not estates, but raw materials to be stored, traded, sold, or contracted for stumpage on the appraisal of a timber cruiser, who might well be the only party to the transaction who actually visited the tract before the loggers arrived. Fortunes were accumulated, but because of theft and fires they were certainly much at hazard until a man retired from the game.[9]

The state followed a similar course in exercising its claims on federal land, finding timber theft endemic and widely tolerated locally. But as timber adjacent to driving streams came to be perceived as a finite commodity rapidly passing into private hands, there was a change in popular attitudes. By the early 1880's more substantial lumbermen were forced to buy timber to protect future supplies and therefore could no longer abide casual trespass on their lands. The old days were passing when a lawyer would advise a timber owner, whose lands had been stripped, that "you can't get a jury in all that country that will bring you in a verdict of

[8] Fries, *Empire in Pine*, 184–196; Lucile Kane, "Federal Protection of Public Timber in the Upper Great Lakes States," in Carstensen, ed., *Public Lands*, 439–447.

[9] Arthur R. Reynolds, *The Daniel Shaw Lumber Company: A Case Study of the Wisconsin Lumbering Frontier* (New York, 1957), 155–157; Gilson G. Glasier, ed., *Autobiography of Roujet D. Marshall, Justice of the Supreme Court of the State of Wisconsin, 1895–1918* (2 vols., Madison, 1923 and 1931), 1:349–357.

guilty, no matter how great and strong your evidence may be.''[10]

Natural hazards and socially acceptable timber theft certainly discouraged early speculation in remote timber. This probably served a democratic function, not implemented by the laws and their administration, in that it discouraged efforts to monopolize timber. The possibility of monopoly held a fascination for those earliest on the scene. Moses Strong of Mineral Point envisioned ''a complete monopoly of the whole lumber business on the [Wisconsin] river.'' Cyrus Woodman and his partner, C. C. Washburn, entertained even more ambitious plans to monopolize the Wisconsin-Minnesota pineries. Most such undertakings came up against the hard fact that men with money would not take the chances involved, or could not see the speculative value of timber which they doubted would reach the market within the foreseeable future. By the time the equation was right, the rush was on, and a rough democracy of opportunity prevailed even if long purses, rigged sales, dishonest clerks and registrars, and public and official indifference all combined with organized hustle to make possible some princely timber domains. Ezra Cornell accumulated 499,000 acres of Wisconsin timber with which he endowed the university which bears his name. A Detroit capitalist, Francis Palms, acquired 112,567 acres to become the greatest individual owner. Knapp, Stout & Company of Menomonie entered 120,000 acres. Of fifteen owners of 25,000 or more acres, eight were not Wisconsin residents or lumber companies.[11]

One of the last public auctions of pinelands in the Chippewa Valley took place in 1869, evidence of how rapidly it had been engrossed. Initial bidding drove prices to three or four times the minimum $1.25 per acre. In a not unusual community of inter-

[10] Fries, *Empire in Pine*, 195–200; George Henry Warren, *The Pioneer Woodsman as He Is Related to Lumbering in the Northwest* (Minneapolis, 1914), 58.

[11] Kenneth W. Duckett, *Frontiersman of Fortune: Moses M. Strong of Mineral Point* (Madison, 1955), 149–150; Larry Gara, *Westernized Yankee: The Story of Cyrus Woodman* (Madison, 1956), 116–118, 142–143, 164–166; Paul W. Gates, *The Wisconsin Pine Lands of Cornell University: A Study in Land Policy and Absentee Ownership* (Ithaca, 1943; reprinted, Madison, 1965), 34–35, 56–57, 70–120; Hurst, *Law and Economic Growth*, 9–142; Fries, *Empire in Pine*, 122–128, 161–203; Richard N. Current, *Pine Logs and Politics: A Life of Philetus Sawyer, 1816–1900* (Madison, 1950), 103–145.

est, the main bidders formed a "ring" to end the competitive bidding and then split the melon and took most of the 250,000 acres
at the minimum price. It was a procedure that Land Office officials had come to expect and did not question. They readily served
outside speculators as locators and influence peddlers, and they
even juggled the books occasionally. Outlying timber of average
quality was generally bought by private sale from both the federal
and state governments. The choice forties having prompted an
auction, the remainder could be picked over with the reasonable
assumption that the price of pine stumpage would rise enough to
make a modest pine cover valuable within the near future. Less
desirable timberland was also subject to homestead entry, almost
always fraudulently, because those who filed had no intention of
residing on and improving their claims. The Commissioner of the
U.S. General Land Office commented in 1875 that vast areas of
the pineries were thus entered, yet "scarcely a vestige of agriculture appears."[12]

One must not assume that timberland speculators served no
purpose other than to enrich themselves. The usual speculator was
not a magnate, but had accumulated scattered holdings through
purchase at the land office. Timber in large blocks usually came
by purchase from a railroad grant or similar holdings. Magnates
such as Frederick Weyerhaeuser, Philetus Sawyer, and Isaac Stephenson, as well as many other large corporate owners, acquired
blocks of timber in this manner and handled it differently. Smaller
holders could not set the price on local timber, assumed considerable risk in holding timber, and performed a service by providing stumpage on credit. Selling on credit, they made the timber
more accessible to logging contractors and small mill operators.
Conceding an economic function for the speculator rests upon the
recognition that federal and state governments offered no better
solutions.[13]

---

[12] Gates, *Wisconsin Pine Lands of Cornell University*, 110–113; Current, *Pine Logs and Politics*, 121–123; Hurst, *Law and Economic Growth*, chap. 2; Fries, *Empire in Pine*, 179–184.

[13] Fries, *Empire in Pine*, 172–177; Gates, *Wisconsin Pine Lands of Cornell University*, 208–
243.

There can be little doubt that Frederick Weyerhaeuser, Isaac Stephenson, Philetus Sawyer, and other successful lumbermen would have become men of substance had northern Wisconsin been covered only with hazel brush in their time. The lumber era furnished them with a spectacular opportunity. Students of the industry have viewed them differently over the years. To a contemporary (1898) they were:[14]

> . . . [E]nterprising operators who within the past sixty years have added more than four billion dollars to the national wealth, principally in the employ[ment] of labor in the forest and mill, in turning the encumbering forest into a means of adding an incalculable source of wealth to the nation in the development of a region which but for the availability of a cheap building material must have lain dormant for centuries to come.

A half-century later, a leading scholar of the history of the public lands observed of the lumber industry in Wisconsin:[15]

> Its rise was swift, its heyday short, its effects devastating, and its decline precipitate. From it were derived numerous family fortunes, the present owners of which live elsewhere and take no interest in the counties that were the source of their wealth. A few lumbermen gave libraries, parks, and colleges to the pine-land communities in which they made their money, but for the most part the wealth made in lumbering was not put back into the area from which it had been drawn. . . . These self-made men, real individualists, were contemptuous of the rights of labor and they paid little heed to federal and state laws which forbade certain practices in which they were engaged. Their struggle for wealth changed the rich pineries, the product of centuries of growth, into a shambles within a generation.

What is missing in these characterizations is a statement about the uncertainty of conspicuous success. The most successful entrepreneurs were those who combined strong and diverse capital in a number of mills and locations, and even in non-lumbering ventures. A near monopoly of a particularly choice body of timber, as in the case of Knapp, Stout & Company, could also reap

---

[14] Hotchkiss, *Lumber and Forest Industry*, v.
[15] Gates, *Wisconsin Pine Lands of Cornell University*, 121.

generous rewards, but this company too spread its risks in a number of mills and allied enterprises. The depression years from 1873 to 1879 shook out many of the weaklings. The common pattern of the 1880's was a combination of outside capital, particularly from the great wholesale lumber center of Chicago, with a Wisconsin lumberman who had proved his mettle on the site. One set of figures confirms this pattern. In 1897, there were 101 incorporated Wisconsin lumber firms and sixty-six which operated as partnerships. These 167 firms involved only 632 stockholders and 105 partners. It was not a business of wide ownership, and there was considerable overlap of individuals with multiple holdings.[16]

The single-mill enterprise of the 1870's was overcommitted financially, within a range of choices which could and often did turn sour in response to a multitude of natural and market forces over which the entrepreneur could exercise little or no control. The wonder is that there emerged a number of millionaires in the face of all the potential varieties of disaster. The continued vigor of the market, the cheapness of the raw material, and ingenuity in loading operating costs onto the labor force, contractors, suppliers, timber owners, and the general public—in taxes evaded or valuable franchises won—all kept the often financially desperate industry afloat. Successes and failures came at great social cost.

If a man had real capital behind him and a measure of business sophistication, he probably sensed that he could do better dealing in timber than by building a sawmill in the wilderness. There is justification in Matthew Norton's aggrieved statement that, when Chippewa pinelands were going at the federal land office for $1.25 an acre, "the poverty of the lumbermen was good reason why they were not found at these sales in great numbers as purchasers." Since Norton was referring to Frederick Weyerhaeuser, among

[16] Fries, *Empire in Pine*, 102–103; Hotchkiss, *Lumber and Forest Industry*, 489–492; Hurst, *Law and Economic Growth*, 414; Wisconsin Bureau of Labor, Census and Industrial Statistics, *Biennial Report*, 1895–1896, pp. 450–451, and *Biennial Report*, 1897–1898, pp. 560–561. Goodspeed Publishing Company, *Industrial Chicago: The Manufacturing Interests* (6 vols., Chicago, 1891–1896), 3:123, claims that in 1884 Chicago millmen and lumber dealers handled 34.2 per cent of the lumber cut in Wisconsin lying east of the Wisconsin River, and 31.4 per cent of that cut west of the Wisconsin River, including eastern Minnesota.

others, his remark draws attention to the economics of sawmilling. A sawmill was both omnivorous and omnifarious in its appe-
tites for capital and talent. Timber speculation called for initial
judgment as an insider with respect to the mechanics of acquisition, as well as vigilance, luck, patience, and capital. Sawmill men
usually lacked the last-named attributes: patience and capital.
They added, however, a considerable confidence in their abilities
to manage other men and the processes amenable to human decision and enterprise. They were not patient men. This was no virtue in dealing with a finite resource in a market which offered no
incentive, or even practical methods, for conserving that resource.
Most of them knew, early on, that they were not building enduring monuments to their enterprise.[17]

Wisconsin's lumber entrepreneurs came from a greater variety
of backgrounds than did the state's brewers or tanners, for
instance, but then they were a larger business group. The overall
impression from the biographical literature is that Yankee types
from Maine, New Brunswick, and neighboring states and provinces dominated the northern pineries, while the smaller, hard-
wood mills to the south had a heavy leaven of continental
European types. There were important exceptions to this general
pattern. Wisconsin's greatest lumber tycoon, who came into control of much of America's richest white pine stand, was born on a
farm-vineyard in the Rhine Valley which he did not leave until he
was seventeen. Although never a resident of Wisconsin, Frederick
Weyerhaeuser called the tune on log production in the pineries of
the Chippewa River Valley. The biographical literature also indicates that lumbermen were generally self–made men; this certainly was true of the few for whom we have more complete
information because of their relative success. The Yankee lum-

---

[17] Matthew G. Norton, *The Mississippi River Logging Company: An Historical Sketch* ([Chip-
pewa Falls?], 1912), 92. Orrin Ingram was a fair representative of the sawmill men. In 1857
he started what became the Empire Lumber Company, when he was twenty-six. The main
mill in Eau Claire, his monument, ceased operations in 1898. Ingram lived another twenty
years, watching his money grow but with considerable dissatisfaction over his passive role.
See Charles E. Twining, *Downriver: Orrin H. Ingram and the Empire Lumber Company* (Madison, 1975), 265–290.

bermen were usually country boys with ambition, prospects, and little capital. The phrase, "a modest education in the district school of the times," is standard. Many served an apprenticeship working for others in lumbering and rose to managerial rank.[18]

The lack of both investment and working capital, and the want of institutional facilities to provide these necessities, were compensated for in a variety of ways. The basic resource itself, timber, was the common substitute. Both federal and state governments put it into private hands for the basic $1.25 per acre, with minor variations as to price and terms. Timber, because of its relatively dependable rise in value after it was mostly in private hands, was usable in lieu of long-term investment capital. From stump to mill to market, timber served as a substitute for working capital in a skein of credit relationships which called for special legislative recognition.[19]

Aside from the relatively free and legal use of land and timber in lieu of investment and working capital, the great alternate source was the plowing back of cash into the enterprise. One could not represent this plowback as profits, for it was a business that lived on a heavy liquidation of assets, assuming the ownership of timber. A great flow of cash was generated for the operator who had large timber holdings or options on stumpage at favorable prices.

Working capital was a constant concern that called for much improvising in the absence of a well-developed banking system. This accounts for the tenacity with which lumbermen clung to the

[18] Among the biographies of lumbermen important to the Wisconsin pineries are: Twining, *Downriver* (Orrin H. Ingram); Current, *Pine Logs and Politics* (Philetus Sawyer); and Ralph W. Hidy, Frank Ernest Hill, and Allan Nevins, *Timber and Men: The Weyerhaeuser Story* (New York, 1963). Also see Isaac Stephenson, *Recollections of a Long Life, 1829–1915* (Chicago, 1915). Any sampling, such as the fifty-five men identified in the *DWB* as active in the period 1873–1893 primarily as lumbermen, is skewed, in this instance because they were often included in the volume for reasons other than business success.

[19] Investment banking was a late arrival on the American financial scene and its services were strained to supply capital to the rapidly growing railroad network. See Vincent P. Carosso, *Investment Banking in America: A History* (Cambridge, 1970), 29–50; William G. Rector, *Log Transportation in the Lake States Lumber Industry, 1840–1918* (Glendale, California, 1953), 59, 139–140, 235–237; Hurst, *Law and Economic Growth*, 309–321.

right to delay payment to their labor and then to pay with evidence of indebtedness rather than cash, as well as exacting a penalty for the failure of workers to complete the season. Another aspect of this was the ubiquitous credit system: providing food, lodging, and a company store with enforced credit, in the mill town as well as in the woods. It was the need for working capital that directed the lumbermen to the wholesale and retail end of the business. A captive lumberyard could be forced to disgorge its cash without the heavy obligations imposed by a middleman advancing cash.[20]

Banks there were, particularly by the expansive 1880's. But there were not many banks capable of advancing a line of credit that might run from the first snows of November until the first cash from the lumber rafts, which probably meant late summer or early fall, to cover payrolls for several hundred men. Most bankers of the 1880's operated on the maxim that the first requirement of a worthy creditor was to prove that he didn't really need the money, and lumbermen were geographically remote from more enlightened metropolitan bankers.

Sawmills serving the Chicago market, such as those in established lumber centers like Oshkosh, certainly had less acute cash flow and credit problems than those serving the Mississippi River trade. It is doubtful that many lumbermen consciously separated credit and cash needs for operations from capital investment, which compounded their credit needs. Expedients were various. Daniel Shaw of Eau Claire had a wealthy brother living in Maine to whom he was able to turn. After Daniel's death, his son and successor, Eugene, had to post collateral with his uncle until he could terminate the arrangement. For Orrin Ingram, also of Eau Claire, the chronic lack of operating funds was a way of life which he came to feel was an advantage for keeping his operations lean, with all cash and credit hard at work. His driving spirit was essentially optimistic, based on a firm belief in an expanding market which, despite inevitable gluts and hard times, justified his faith.

---

[20] Fries, *Empire in Pine*, 100–103, 206–212; Twining, *Downriver*, 72–104; Kohlmeyer, *Laird, Norton Story*, 205–209.

Ingram was surrounded, however, by nervous partners who learned to defer to his decisions. Philetus Sawyer of Oshkosh, representing a generation of lumbermen who had found financial success somewhat earlier (largely as a result of location), was already by the 1870's seeking profitable investment for surplus funds.[21]

Another boon to the lumberman was the public acceptance of the corporation as an instrument of private enterprise. It was particularly useful for organizing, financing, and controlling co-operative ventures among lumbermen, such as joint log-driving facilities and booming companies, and for developing state franchises for dams and stream improvements. Such franchises themselves, whose value went beyond simple conveniences for log driving or rafting, were in effect capital subsidies. Then there was the law itself, as interpreted by the courts or created by legislatures, which was consistently favorable to the active role played by the lumber entrepreneur in converting trees into economic goods and in providing employment. The effect of this benign attitude, free of regulatory or conservationist initiative, encouraged rapid capital formation for further exploitation.[22]

The beauty of this scheme of things was that Wisconsin lumbermen were not compelled to subvert the legislative process or do violence to popular attitudes. This is not to say that there were not occasions when they did so, particularly when lumbermen found themselves at odds with one another, with their labor force, or with the local community over taxing and spending. But the generally favorable climate encouraged these naturally self-confident men to test the outer limits of public acceptance with the considerable economic and political power at their disposal. The results were surprising, less for what they got than for what they failed to acquire by these means.[23]

If the easy acquisition of timber, stream alteration franchises,

[21] Reynolds, *Daniel Shaw Lumber Company*, 133–134; Twining, *Downriver*, 52, 252–253; Current, *Pine Logs and Politics*, 103–145.

[22] The general ideas in this paragraph are among the themes developed in Hurst, *Law and Economic Growth*.

[23] *Ibid.*, 142, 256, 261.

generous corporate charters, and the consistently favorable bias of the legal system were positive forces in promoting the lumber industry, there were other broad areas of decision that determined success or failure over the long pull. Whatever a man's particular managerial strengths, he had to cope with a diversity of problems that went beyond those in most industries of the time. If the railroads developed the first coherent managerial bureaucracies necessary to huge enterprises, the lumbermen were forerunners to the conglomerate of the 1960's. A lumberman had to understand and balance priorities as diverse as the efficiency of his sawmill operation, the timely acquisition and management of his timber holdings, his woods operations, participation in stream improvements and in co-operative log driving, sorting and booming, whether to ship his products by raft or rail, and how to participate in or influence the wholesale and retail end of his business. Because their operations were geographically extensive and often remote, it was normal for lumbermen to operate steamboats, railroads, dams and waterways, build roads, direct extensive construction of mills, operate farms to feed men and animals, buy and sell draft animals, maintain retail stores, operate food-processing plants, sell fuel and power, furnish housing as well as board and room, and provide fire protection for a community. Some maintained their own employment bureaus in Milwaukee or Chicago and handled contracts for licensing patents. It is little wonder that those who succeeded in such diverse roles tended to be dictatorial and firmly paternalistic. When challenged, they did not shrink from a contest of wills, nor were they given to doubts.[24]

The seeming epitome of malign monopoly, large mill owners dominated whole communities and even counties, controlling practically all available employment, wage rates, retailing, law enforcement, and services. At the same time, the record is full of mill and timber owners who insisted, with some justice, that they were the victims of ill-conceived new counties, authorized by a complacent legislature and controlled by settlers and townsmen for

---

[24] Fries, *Empire in Pine*, 124–128; Twining, *Downriver, passim*. Isaac Stephenson's *Recollections* celebrate his diverse talents.

the express purpose of loading taxes upon timber and mill properties for unneeded services and for subsidies to promote railroads. While a great milling company might justifiably appear as
an absolute monopoly on the local scene, the lumber business
remained fragmented and generally unable to adopt any effective
restraints upon its own truly destructive competitive spirit. "Cut
and run" remained the rule. While commanding fortunes did
emerge—based more upon rising timber values than milling
enterprises—many mill owners simply traded dollars in marginal
operations. They destroyed a great resource while providing seasonal employment at poor and uncertain wages, with wretched
living accommodations and highly hazardous jobs.[25]

Logging in the woods was necessarily a relatively small enterprise carried on from a base camp with its perimeter limited by
how far the crews and animals could travel economically to and
from their labor. The distance to the driving stream, to which the
logs had to be hauled, was also a limiting factor. Large operations
simply multiplied the number of camps. Elsewhere, logging railroads would change these conditions radically, but they were not
widely used in Wisconsin, which had only eleven such railroads
by 1887, six built within the preceding two years. Since most of
the large lumber mills were built on waterways to facilitate log
driving, booming, and lumber rafting, one may assume that some
of the logging railroads—which averaged only seven and a half
miles in length—were a later development related to the exploitation of hardwoods that would not float.[26]

The lumber camp of the 1870's was usually isolated and
received its supplies by way of the river—by boat or sled on the
ice—or by the tote road, which was rudimentary but could be
negotiated by teams hauling sleds. In Wisconsin, logging was
necessarily a winter activity, as snow and ice provided the means
by which animal power moved the logs to the loading area and the

[25] Hurst, *Law and Economic Growth*, 503–533; Bernhardt J. Kleven, "Wisconsin Lumber
Industry" (doctoral dissertation, University of Minnesota, 1941), 273; Fries, *Empire in Pine*,
222–224.

[26] Rector, *Log Transportation in Lake States Lumber Industry*, 215–237; Reynolds, *Daniel
Shaw Lumber Company*, 58–63.

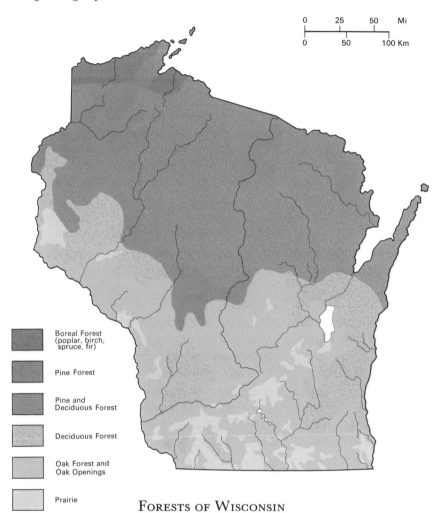

0    25    50    Mi

0         50    100 Km

Boreal Forest
(poplar, birch,
spruce, fir)

Pine Forest

Pine and
Deciduous Forest

Deciduous Forest

Oak Forest and
Oak Openings

Prairie

FORESTS OF WISCONSIN

surface on which the heavily loaded sleds reached riverbanks
where the logs were stacked to await the spring freshet. Northern
Wisconsin was richly supplied with driving streams, but these
usually had to be improved by a system of dams to retain and control the runoff.

Logging camps might be operated by an integrated lumber
company cutting from its own or contracted lands. Independent

logging contractors commonly cut for a mill, for a timber owner, or speculatively on shares with a timber owner without a definite buyer in hand. Getting into business as a logging contractor required a minimum of capital, some knowledge of the business, and a source of credit. Mill companies ordinarily owned an inventory of tools, harnesses, sleds, and even draft animals. The work in the woods was all done with muscle power, fired by beans and hay. Everyone involved both furnished and existed on credit. The worker, who was paid at the end of the season when the logs were delivered, furnished his labor on credit. The mill company provided bed and board, usually with borrowed money. Often the oxen and horses belonged to northern farmers who contracted as teamsters. It was a long chain of credit that made the mare go.[27]

Having struck his deal, the logging contractor headed for the woods before winter with a skeleton crew. There they threw up a rough camp, cut roads, built dams, and did necessary clearing. The main crew was brought in with the beginning of winter. The camps offered primitive living conditions and seldom served more than a single season. The northern winters and outdoor work were widely believed to contribute to the general health of the men in what were essentially unhealthy, close quarters. The romance of the logging camp makes light of vermin-infested clothes, unwashed bodies, animal and human waste as part of the immediate landscape, and crowded living with nowhere else to go. It could not have been all jolly jacks yarning and singing about the cheery stove. One suspects that the food may have been monotonous as well, despite tradition. Much of it came out of a barrel, either dried or in brine.[28]

All of this is by way of suggesting that much of lumbering was

[27] Reynolds, *Daniel Shaw Lumber Company*, 11, 63; Fries, *Empire in Pine*, 207–210; Twining, *Downriver*, 249–250.

[28] Hurst, *Law and Economic Growth*, 490; John Emmett Nelligan, as told to Charles M. Sheridan, *The Life of a Lumberman* (n.p., 1929), 117–132; Vernon H. Jensen, *Lumber and Labor* (*Labor in the Twentieth Century* series, ed., Henry David et al., New York, 1945), 51–58. The Wisconsin State Board of Health paid little attention to logging camps in its annual reports.

a prosaic enterprise. Wisconsin's pines were cut down one at a time by ordinary mortals and hauled away by oxen or horses of normal proportions. When the logs were floated to the mills the operation, while hazardous, involved keeping the timber in water deep enough to float it more often than it did riding a log through the rapids or fighting a jam there. None of this required a special breed of men. That is a delusion of memorialists who have been told they led exciting lives in a setting which is forever gone, or of romantics, regional authors, and eager folklorists. It is the province today of advertising agencies pushing fabricated pancake mix and imitation maple syrup. They should be condemned to a season in a logging camp of the 1870's.

Photographers of the lumbering scene were not often drawn to the "sacking," which consisted of poling the logs out of the shallows, nor did they often show the work-a-day life within the mills. There are plenty of pictures of mills in panorama, with the busy pond and belching stacks, but few of boys and girls cutting laths, bundling shingles, or clearing trash from the whirling trimmer saws.[29]

The railroads and opening of farmlands in or near the pineries brought relative refinements: window glass, some cut lumber, fresh meat, and root vegetables. But the temporary character of the accommodations and the employment discouraged any passion for comfort. The lumber industry generally was indifferent to its record as one of the poorest-paying and most hazardous of America's major industries. It clung fiercely to the right to pay at the end of the season and to dock substantially any worker who left before. The industry accepted with equanimity its dependence upon an itinerant labor force and seems to have counted on isolation in a winter landscape, combined with fierce supervision, to keep the men at their drudgery. Retaining a cook who at least did not suffer by comparison with the standard in other camps was the

[29] The author recalls working in a small lumber mill in the Cascades of the Pacific Northwest in 1934. A year later, as a college student, he met on the train from Seattle another teenager who was still at the mill and was returning from treatment for a severed right hand.

principal concession to making working and living conditions
tolerable.[30]

Lumbering was a young man's game. A family man was less
inclined to spend five months in the woods. Working and living
conditions were worse than Spartan, and demanded physical
stamina. There probably is something to the notion that work in
the woods, or on the rivers, attracted a mesomorphic breed. But
the times, open immigration, and economic conditions also produced many ordinary men who never established themselves with
a trade, a farm, a family, or steady work, whatever their youthful
intentions. The nation's and Wisconsin's discovery of the "tramp
menace" in the late 1870's is indicative. Reason would suggest
that logging, driving, and rafting depended upon a more youthful
and footloose work force than did the sawmills.[31]

Farm boys found work in the woods a change from the drudgery of fall plowing and other chores. It fitted in with the seasonal
farm work where they had some experience working with tools and
handling horses or oxen. The mills normally shut down before
winter set in, having exhausted the log supply. Some of the mill
crew men took to work in the woods in winter, but certainly not
all of them. Logging was quite a different activity. Many who
considered themselves lumberjacks disdained working in the mill.
Accurate employment figures are impossible to find. The 1890
federal census gives a variety of numbers to consider. By one
account, there were 7,211 Wisconsin lumbermen and raftsmen,
599 woodchoppers, and 13,325 working in the mills. A special
report, also part of the 1890 census, gives the number 32,755 as

[30] George B. Engberg, "Lumber and Labor in the Lake States," in *Minnesota History*,
36 (March, 1959), 153–166; Hurst, *Law and Economic Growth*, 480–485; Jensen, *Lumber and
Labor*, 51–58.

[31] George B. Engberg, "Labor in the Lake States Lumber Industry, 1830–1930" (doctoral dissertation, University of Minnesota, 1949), 19–104; Jensen, *Lumber and Labor*, 50–
51; Ruth Stoveken, "The Pine Lumberjacks in Wisconsin," in *WMH*, 30 (March, 1947),
322–334; Thomas J. Vaughan, "Life of the Wisconsin Lumberjack, 1850–1890" (master's thesis, University of Wisconsin, 1951); Paul T. Ringenbach, *Tramps and Reformers,
1873–1916: The Discovery of Unemployment in New York* (Westport, Connecticut, 1973).

the average number of employees in Wisconsin's lumber mills and related woodworking.[32]

The pioneers of the Wisconsin lumber industry, both owners and workers, were from the Atlantic seaboard lumber states and provinces, in general from Pennsylvania northward. By the beginning of the 1870's, however, there was a heavy foreign-born component in the industry's work force, almost one-to-one with native-born. In 1869, Scandinavians, Germans, and Canadians—a majority of the latter of British extraction—made up 77 per cent of the foreign-born workers in lumbering; by 1889, 87 per cent. In the latter year the foreign-born constituted nearly 60 per cent of the total work force. For many immigrants, lumbering was an employer of last resort, and the industry took full advantage of that fact.[33]

Meaningful averages are hard to come by in assessing the work of woods crews. It was generally conceded that getting the logs cut and hauled to the driving stream was the largest single manufacturing cost in lumbering. An average cost of about $3.50 per 1,000 board feet would be close. Any advances in techniques or equipment were pretty well offset by smaller timber and longer distances hauled. An average camp of sixty men would get out 4,500,000 to 6,000,000 board feet in a season. A big mill cutting 30 million board feet annually required at least five such camps. Time was money in lumbering. The woods boss for the Empire Lumber Company of Eau Claire summed up his expectations in commenting on an argument with a teamster: "He thinks it is fat horses, not logs that are wanted and says it will kill the team to do

[32] Fries, *Empire in Pine*, 204–206; Jensen, *Lumber and Labor*, 49–51; Engberg, "Lumber and Labor in the Lake States," *Minnesota History*, 36:153–166; *Eleventh Census of the United States, 1890: Volume XXXI, Special Report on Occupations*, 52–57, and *Eleventh Census of the United States, 1890: Manufacturing, Volume VI, Part 3*, p. 611. The lower figure (21,135) is the sum of what people reported as their occupations to the census taker; the higher (32,755) is that reported by the employers. The figures doubtless fail to jibe because most workers could fall into different categories at various times of the year. The census would have been finished by June, when there were fewer loggers in the woods.

[33] Engberg, "Labor in Lake States Lumber Industry," 55; Jensen, *Lumber and Labor*, 50–51; Fries, *Empire in Pine*, 204–205.

any more. If that be so I think they had better try it [and] if it does kill them it would be better so, than to have them a[n] expense to the company. . . .[34]

There were a few jobs in the woods that demanded some basic skills: cook, blacksmith, scaler, faller, bucker, loader, and teamster. The scaler in the woods tallied the day's work and might mark logs to be taken from a fallen tree. The fallers downed the tree where it would do the least damage to itself and its neighbors. The crosscut saw, generally in use by the 1870's, had about doubled the average output of a falling and bucking crew over what could be accomplished with axes alone. There were not many other successful technological refinements at this point in the process. The tree was limbed, scaled, and marked, then cut up by a bucking crew. The teamster's job was to haul the logs to the loading area, where they were loaded on sleds, using poles as an inclined plane and a crude boom and tackle, operated by a team, to top off the load. The ultimate in hazardous jobs was that of the top decker who guided these logs into place. Another teamster then hauled the sled load to the landing where the logs were off-loaded and stacked by the driving stream.[35]

The log drive came with the spring thaw. This is usually represented as the most exotic employment offered in lumbering. French-Canadians are alleged to have excelled at riding a log through rapids. Germans were competent loggers, but they seldom took part in the spring drive. Since the drive required only about half the number of the woods crew, the others took off for

[34] Reynolds, *Daniel Shaw Lumber Company*, 162; Twining, *Downriver*, 223. See *Tenth Census of the United States, 1880: Part 9, Report on the Forests of North America (Exclusive of Mexico)*, p. 557, which estimates production per man per season at 80,000 board feet, and at over 100,000 board feet in the richer Chippewa River pineries. H. C. Putnam, "The Forests of Wisconsin," in Wisconsin Horticultural Society, *Annual Report*, 1892, pp. 184–185, gives the following average costs: "It will cost on an average $3 to $3.50 per 1,000 feet to cut and haul this to the driving streams or to the mills near the timber, also an average cost of $1 per 1,000 feet to drive or float the same to mills farther down the stream to be sawed, and some $2.50 per 1,000 feet sawing and added expense at the mills before the lumber is ready for market."

[35] Engberg, "Labor in Lake States Lumber Industry," 111–119; Jensen, *Lumber and Labor*, 56; Fries, *Empire in Pine*, 29–33.

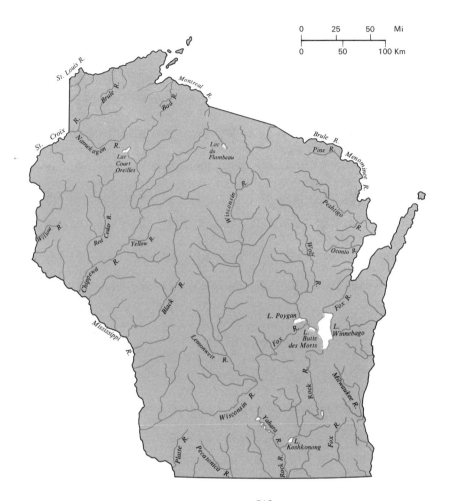

HYDROGRAPHY OF WISCONSIN

town to celebrate or returned to mill, farm, or family. The log
drive was uncomfortable as well as potentially hazardous—the
hazards depending upon the character of the river as well as the
volume of water required for the drive. Early spring could be cold,
as was the water. The men were wet much of the time, had to

camp out, and hot meals were few and far between, even with cooks and floating wanigans accompanying the drive.[36]

Drives on the Chippewa River were remarkable for a number of reasons. For one, it is estimated that its drainage basin contained fully 40 per cent of the merchantable white pine in Wisconsin. It fell nearly 1,000 feet in about 200 miles, maintaining a strong flow from below Chippewa Falls to its mouth at the Mississippi, and offered little in the way of natural slack water for booming and sorting logs. It also became the principal source of logs for the great mills downriver on the Mississippi at Wabasha, Winona, Dubuque, Clinton, Davenport, Burlington, Rock Island, Keokuk, and Hannibal. A long struggle took place between the big mills at Eau Claire and those located at and above Chippewa Falls over the right of the Eau Claire interests to dam the river and create slack water at its lower dells. The mills above opposed this project as a hazard to their rafts of cut lumber which were floated down to the Mississippi to market. Eau Claire finally won in 1876 after repeated legislative efforts tainted with fraud and chicanery.[37]

A greater threat came from the Mississippi mills under the organizing genius of Frederick Weyerhaeuser. A natural sorting works existed at Beef Slough, a long backwater paralleling the Chippewa for several miles where it met the Mississippi. The Eau Claire lumbermen thought they had immobilized Beef Slough by getting a legislative charter in 1866, reserving privileges there for themselves to forestall any real development. They were beaten at their own game by a legislative ruse, and the Mississippi lumbermen developed the slough. The so-called Beef Slough Wars began in 1868, with Chippewa lumbermen trying to block improvements and, failing that, holding all logs upriver. The Mississippi men countered by releasing water from their dams at various headwaters and driving great masses of logs into the sorting

[36] Engberg, "Labor in Lake States Lumber Industry," 47–59; Nils P. Haugen, *Pioneer and Political Reminiscences* (Evansville, 1929).

[37] Twining, *Downriver*, 172–182; Hurst, *Law and Economic Growth*, 253, 259; Fries, *Empire in Pine*, 21.

booms, with their driving crews instructed to break the booms if need be. The upriver men had the local law and numbers to defeat such methods, but they could not counter a disastrous flood in 1880 that inexorably swept booms, logs, cut lumber, and several mills down the river. Weyerhaeuser and his allies ended up with possession of most of the season's log cut. Legend has it that he was magnanimous in victory, and in 1881 he rationalized the exploitation of the Chippewa timber by means of the "Chippewa Pool," a group of companies representing all interests to control timber buying, damming, driving, sorting, and the division of logs among the mills on both the Chippewa and the Mississippi. Weyerhaeuser may have been magnanimous, but he was an authentic autocrat who left little room for decisions by lesser autocrats. Donald Kennedy, Orrin Ingram's original partner in what became the Empire Lumber Company, pretty well summed it up eight years before, in an unrelated matter: "I may be mistaken but I don't think that there will ever be much pleasure in lumbering on the Chippewa."[38]

As the Beef Slough story illustrates, the drive was one of the many hazardous operations of lumbering, not only for the crew but for the timber owners and mill operators as well. Too little water and the drive might be aborted. Two years in the stack allowed rot and insects to destroy several inches of the outer wood in the log. Too much water and logs ended up far from the stream in sloughs, bracken, and farmers' pastures. An uncontrolled freshet, as in 1880, could carry all before it—logs, dams, booms, mills, and towns. Nothing was so useless to a mill owner as a log several miles downstream. Log brands and marks were developed along with an equitable system of credit for strays, assuming that they were recovered by responsible persons. Another hazard was the log jam. A famous jam on the Chippewa in 1869 contained 150 million board feet of logs extending fifteen miles and piled thirty

---

[38] Twining, *Downriver*, 106–113, 140, 182–192, 204–207, 215; Fries, *Empire in Pine*, 141–160; Kohlmeyer, *Laird, Norton Story*, 82–116; Norton, *Mississippi River Logging Company*, *passim*; Hurst, *Law and Economic Growth*, 266–270; Glasier, ed., *Autobiography of Roujet D. Marshall*, 1:272–295.

feet high in places. Wisconsin's rivers tended to be modest streams most of the year, which made a large jam a long-term affair.[39]

These hazards account for the co-operative instincts of Wisconsin lumbermen. Most major driving streams were co-ordinated by a damming, log drive, and booming company, organized as a corporation owned by the interested timber and mill owners. Isaac Stephenson wrote of his role in organizing and directing such a company on the Menominee. These companies usually were treated as service organizations rather than what today would be called profit centers, but many returned substantial dividends and retained valuable water powers into the electrical age.[40]

Much merchantable timber lay along small waterways that were seemingly quite intractable, or was so distant from any stream as to make water transportation of the logs impossible. But Philetus Sawyer, the Oshkosh lumber tycoon, opened a tract of timber on the upper Wolf River by undertaking major improvements on the available streams, a project his competitors thought impossible. The success of the venture led to a comfortable fortune, much of which he invested in Chippewa Valley timber, in part by becoming a major stockholder in one of the land-grant railroads there. Sawyer and others then combined this and other lines into what was known popularly as the "Omaha," which in turn was combined with still others into the "Wisconsin Lumber Line." Sawyer's milling interests were in Oshkosh and Marinette in eastern Wisconsin, so he functioned as a timber speculator in western Wisconsin's Chippewa Valley, allying himself early with the Weyerhaeuser interests. Sawyer's business career was not atypical of Wisconsin lumbermen. He invested heavily in timber and in land-grant railroads with vast acreages in the pineries. Most of his fortune thus came from shrewd timber speculations, rather than from his considerable lumber manufacturing interests, or his links with the Chicago lumber trade.[41]

[39] Fries, *Empire in Pine*, 45–48.

[40] Stephenson, *Recollections*, 161–163; Rector, *Log Transportation in Lake States Lumber Industry*, 135–146; Current, *Pine Logs and Politics*, 112; Hurst, *Law and Economic Growth*, 194–197.

[41] Current, *Pine Logs and Politics*, 103–145.

Railroads had a greater impact upon the marketing of cut lumber than they did upon the traditional means of transporting logs to the mill. Despite the great physical and logistical problems posed by the log drive, water transportation was much cheaper. This remained true even though lumbermen estimated an average loss of 10 per cent of the logs in river drives. In years of poor water conditions, losses were much higher; and logs delayed deteriorated rapidly. Early experiments with crude tramways led to the development of highly flexible railway equipment. This could follow the loggers from location to location on temporary tracks laid almost as cheaply as roads could be improved to handle heavy loads. They had the great advantage of extending the logging season, doing away with dependence on snow and ice to facilitate sledding great loads. But this light, often narrow-gauge equipment was not widely used in Wisconsin during this period.[42]

The regular railroad network in Wisconsin trebled from 1,975 miles in 1872 to 5,925 by 1893. The greatest increase came in northern Wisconsin, where log and lumber hauling became a large part of its business. The Wisconsin Central, as it built northward beyond Stevens Point, was overwhelmed by the business generated by the lumber industry. Both to secure this traffic and to enhance the value of its land grant, "whenever there appeared a chance to push a spur or branch into the deep woods, the Central's exchequer seldom failed to produce the means to finance the project."[43]

It became the common pattern, as pine adjacent to driving streams was swiftly depleted, for railroads to carry logs to the mills or to nearby waterways. The prevalent notion that water transportation in the lumber industry had almost ceased by the eighties is accurate for cut lumber, not sawlogs. The peak year for log driving on the Chippewa was in fact 1892, when 632,350,670 board feet in logs—probably something like 3.5 million logs—

[42] Rector, *Log Transportation in Lake States Lumber Industry*, 185–186, 215–231; Fries, *Empire in Pine*, 53–54.

[43] Roy L. Martin, *History of the Wisconsin Central* (Railway and Locomotive Historical Society, *Bulletin* no. 54, Boston, 1941), 26–27, 79; *Commercial and Financial Chronicle*, 44 (June 25, 1887), 807; *Wisconsin Blue Book, 1895*, p. 455.

were floated to the mills. (Those 3.5 million logs represented perhaps 800,000 pine trees.) The Mississippi River mills normally took 65 per cent of the total, made up in log rafts at Beef Slough or across the river in Minnesota at Reads Landing to be pushed downstream by a stern-wheeler, with a smaller vessel secured at right angles on the raft's bow to steer. Rafts covering the equivalent of ten city blocks each were not uncommon.[44]

Lumbering employed the largest work force of any industry in the state. In 1889 it accounted for over 25 per cent of all industrial employment and over 21 per cent in 1893, when the second-largest labor force—in the railroad car shops—was just 6 per cent of the state's industrial work force. Because of the seasonal nature of the work and the high proportion of unskilled labor, lumbering continually ranked near the bottom among major industries in average annual wages. In 1887–1888, for instance, lumbering ranked twenty-fourth among the state's twenty-five leading industries in this category, with an average annual wage of $255.17 compared to $416.75 in brickmaking, $476.33 in tanning, $495.63 in meat-packing, $501.06 in foundries and machine shops, and $538.16 in brewing. These are telling comparisons, since brickmaking, tanning, and much meat-packing were also seasonal in character.[45]

A report by the Peshtigo Lumber Company for 1893 of wages paid for all phases except lumber rafting may be taken as illustrative of the range and proportion of skilled to semiskilled and common labor. Of 356 men employed in the woods, only the camp foremen and cooks received monthly wages above $26. Foremen were paid $50, cooks $35 to $40. Teamsters, the largest group, received $26, and the sawyers $24. Together with eight scalers, who also earned $26, the teamsters and sawyers accounted for over three-fourths of all the men in the company's camps. Of the remaining one-quarter, wages ranged from $16 to $22 per month.

[44] Twining, *Downriver*, 291; Rector, *Log Transportation in Lake States Lumber Industry*, 155–162; Norton, *Mississippi River Logging Company*, 31.

[45] Wisconsin Bureau of Labor and Industrial Statistics, *Biennial Report*, 1887–1888, xv–xviii; Fries, *Empire in Pine*, 206–207; Jensen, *Lumber and Labor*, 56–58.

The log drive required less than half this force, 149 men, who were paid $2.70 per day, suggesting that the drive was both hazardous and even more rugged than work in the woods. Sorting logs in the boom paid $1.50 per day for forty-five men. Twenty-seven skilled workers, out of the 231 men employed in the mills (the firm operated a steam mill and an older water-powered mill), were paid $2 or more per day. The saw filers were the highest paid at $3.50 to $5, and head sawyers were next at $3.13 to $3.50, but these together accounted for only eight men. Other jobs ranged from 75 cents per day for nine boys to $2 for men running the edgers. The number of low-paying jobs so overbalanced the few really skilled ones that the average wage in the steam mill was $1.58 and $1.51 in the water mill.[46]

Lumbermen were complacent about their labor supply, accepting a high turnover as characteristic of the trade. Winter was the season of high transient employment, when the woods crews were at work. This remained so even after the railroads made it practical to log in other seasons. In part, this was a response to tradition, but also to the availability of labor and conditions in the woods. Standing water, flies, mosquitoes, and lack of sanitary measures were less troublesome in winter. Transient labor was more easily available in winter because much of it came from the agricultural sector, from the city where jobs were scarce, and from railroad construction, which usually shut down in winter. Mill wages were usually advanced a fraction during wheat harvest. Payment of wages was often made in time checks or due bills, promising payment at a later date, usually following the spring drive or after logs had been cut into lumber and sold on the wholesale market, thus temporarily replenishing the employer's supply of working capital. These time checks or due bills were so standard in the industry that banks and merchants dealt in them at substantial discounts. Even lumber companies would discount their own time checks for payment in cash. The industry also got exception in legislation to preserve the substantial reduction in

---

[46] Wisconsin Bureau of Labor, Census and Industrial Statistics, *Biennial Report*, 1893–1894, pp. 84–87; Fries, *Empire in Pine*, 62–63.

wages for not finishing out the season, arguing that the difference really represented a premium to those who stayed the course.[47]

Lumbering was insulated, to a considerable degree, from the pressures that labor organizations could bring to bear in cities with their more varied industrial mix and leadership available from a body of skilled workers who had some traditions of trade unionism to draw upon. Eau Claire, for example, although a city of 10,118 in 1880 and growing very rapidly, was virtually a single-industry center where employment was highly seasonal. Aside from such cities as Eau Claire and Marinette where there was a concentration of lumber mills, the more characteristic pattern was of smaller communities dominated by one or two mills. Eau Claire exhibits the difficulties of organized action by labor, these difficulties being magnified in more isolated lumber towns with only one or two large employers. Most every mill had its "regular" employees, identified with the community because they were usually the foremen and skilled workers and likely to be family men. Having more of a stake, they were the least likely to lead or join a strike action. The majority of mill workers had no particular skill and were itinerant, single men. The seasonal nature of employment in both the mills and the woods depended upon men who were not particularly identified with their jobs, including farmers who were seldom inclined to unionism.[48]

The "Sawdust War" in Eau Claire in 1881 was a case in point. Several hundred men employed by the Eau Claire lumber companies went on strike in July apparently with little preliminary negotiation because, characteristically, they found their leader-

[47] Engberg, "Lumber and Labor in the Lake States," *Minnesota History*, 36:153–166; Lumber Industry Engberg, "Labor in Lake States Lumber Industry," 260–262; Vaughan, "Wisconsin Lumberjack," 48–50; Kleven, "Wisconsin Lumber Industry," 442–444; Fries, *Empire in Pine*, 204–206; Jensen, *Lumber and Labor*, 49–50; Hurst, *Law and Economic Growth*, 391–394, 407, 481–486.

[48] *Wisconsin Blue Book, 1887*, p. 346; J. Rogers Hollingsworth and Ellen Jane Hollingsworth, *Dimensions in Urban History: Historical and Social Science Perspectives on Middle-Size American Cities* (Madison, 1979), 61, 66, say that, while no unemployment data are available for the 1880's, "the newspapers suggest that in any season of the year there were large numbers of unemployed men in Eau Claire." See also Jensen, *Lumber and Labor*, 58–59; and Fries, *Empire in Pine*, 210–212.

ship only after going out. Their grievance was the twelve-hour day, which they wanted reduced to a ten-hour day. The Eau Claire *News* recognized the justice of their cause and acknowledged their "clear right to refuse to work if they wish to. But it by no means follows that they have a right to prevent others who wish to labor from doing so." Governor William Smith was persuaded to visit the scene later in the week, when some 1,500 men were out, many of them unwillingly so because of forcible action by the strikers. The governor responded with what the Madison *Daily Democrat* sarcastically characterized as "nearly the whole of the state militia," though the force consisted of only some 375 men. This was more than enough to discourage the strikers. The mills were able to start up again the following Monday, although shorthanded, "the strikers having largely left the place to seek employment elsewhere." Although there was evidently more talk than overt action, there was a marked about-face on the part of the press, because the threat of violence to keep the mills closed had existed before the militia arrived. Everyone seemed relieved to announce that the brief threat was the action of footloose Norwegians and "bummers" who had no stake in the community.[49]

The Knights of Labor were rising rapidly nationally in the mid-eighties and had an energetic organizer on the Wisconsin scene in the person of Robert Schilling. In the summer of 1885 the lumber workers on the Menominee River organized their own union, which shortly affiliated with the Knights. Marinette lumber workers found the basis for a grievance when, in June, 1885, the Michigan legislature imposed a ten-hour day on the state's major industries, including sawmills just across from Marinette. There remained a way to circumvent the legislation by individual contracts with the Michigan workers. The attempt to do so solidified

[49] Eau Claire *News*, July 23, 30, 1881; Eau Claire *Daily Free Press*, July 29, 1881; Madison *Daily Democrat*, July 24, 26, 30, 1881; Wisconsin Bureau of Labor Statistics, *First Biennial Report*, 1883–1884, pp. 151–153; Fries, *Empire in Pine*, 212–214; George B. Engberg, "Collective Bargaining in the Lumber Industry of the Upper Great Lakes States," in *Agricultural History*, 24 (October, 1950), 205–211; Jerry M. Cooper, "The Wisconsin Militia, 1832–1900" (master's thesis, University of Wisconsin, 1968), 250–253; Twining, *Downriver*, 237.

union sentiment on both sides of the river. A minor concession on hours failed to mollify the militant workers. Fortunately for the workers, the mills were vulnerable to selective strikes since successfully shutting down one or two mills would embarrass the operations of the common boom company that held and distributed the logs to all of the mills. Both parties agreed to accept the good offices of Robert Schilling, as neither owners nor labor were spoiling for a test of wills at that point. After some maneuvering, an agreement on a ten-hour day was accepted late in the milling season. As the chief cynic among the mill operators predicted, the union soon fell apart, the leaders left town, and there was a return to business as usual on the Wisconsin side of the river.[50]

Other local assemblies of the Knights of Labor flourished briefly during 1885–1886 in important lumber centers: Eau Claire, Oshkosh, Peshtigo, and Wausau. But it was rare for a labor organization to exist as a directing agency for a strike prior to the action. Even in those yeasty months when the Knights were at their brief peak, the Wisconsin Bureau of Labor Statistics reported only nine isolated strikes in the lumber industry. Aside from Marinette, the others were in small mill towns. One, in Pineville, northeast of Clear Lake in Polk County, was over the issue of conditions in the company boardinghouse; the others were over wages or for a shorter work day. The longest strike lasted two weeks, the shortest fifteen minutes. There were a number of strikes that should have been characterized as lockouts by the employers, although these normally grew from some threatened action on the part of workers. The Wisconsin Bureau of Labor Statistics counted ninety sawmills that conceded the ten-hour day, but another 120 continued at eleven hours.[51]

[50] Carl Krog, "Marinette: Biography of a Nineteenth Century Lumbering Town, 1850–1910" (doctoral dissertation, University of Wisconsin, 1971), 204–210; Milton M. Small, "The Biography of Robert Schilling" (master's thesis, University of Wisconsin, 1953), 191–195; Jensen, *Lumber and Labor*, 59–63.

[51] Small, "Robert Schilling," 191–195; Engberg, "Collective Bargaining in Lumber Industry," *Agricultural History*, 23:205–206; Jensen, *Lumber and Labor*, 58–59; Fries, *Empire in Pine*, 210–218; Wisconsin Bureau of Labor and Industrial Statistics, *Biennial Report*, 1885–1886, pp. 238–247, 309–310. Both the Wisconsin Bureau of Labor and Industrial Statistics and the U.S. Commissioner of Labor collected data on strikes, but there are dis-

There was a minor resurgence of strikes in 1892. Robert Schilling, who figured in these as well, had turned his attention to the national Populist party campaign. The action started in the Wisconsin River mills this time, over the usual grievances of hours, wages, and terms of payment. It began at Merrill and Eagle River late in July and soon spread from there. City officials at Merrill promptly called for the militia, but Democratic Governor George Peck did not oblige. Instead, they got Robert Schilling, between campaign speeches. He negotiated with the mayor and mill owners and won a concession of the ten-hour day and arbitration on wages. This apparently encouraged other strike actions, following the usual pattern of spontaneity with little prior notice or organization. The strike wave hit Eau Claire near the middle of September. The mills shut down, as it was late in the season and they were short of logs. Predictably, at Rhinelander someone pointed out that the strike was in the hands of men who did not work in the local mills; three strike leaders named Rafelle, Pecor, and Beaulieu were arrested. At Stevens Point, the strike was blamed on the Poles.[52]

Sawmill workers over the years wrung small concessions in their wages and hours of labor, but mill owners enjoyed a steady increase in their productivity. Labor remained cheap while greatly improved machinery increased capacity—at increased cost, of course. Technological advances were more dramatic in the sawmills than in the woods. Millwrights were inventive men, surrounded by mechanical contrivances under one roof, where

---

crepancies between the two sources with respect to the number of strikes, where they occurred, their causes or goals, and their duration. For the federal data for 1885 and 1886, see U.S. Commissioner of Labor, *Annual Report*, 1887, pp. 9–10, 604–607, 612–615. See Chapter 8 below for an extended discussion of the rise of the Knights of Labor in Wisconsin.

[52] U.S. Commissioner of Labor, *Annual Report*, 1894, vol. 1, pp. 1242–1243, lists strikes in 1892 at La Crosse, Merrill, Eagle River, Superior, Stevens Point, Wausau, Schofield, Eau Claire, Woodboro, Rhinelander, and Marinette. See also "Correspondence Concerning Strikes and Riots, 1858–1909," Records on Social Unrest, Disasters and Relief, and Investigations, Series 88, Executive Department, WSA; Milwaukee *Sentinel*, July 30, 31, August 2, 3, 4, 6, 22, 23, 25, 31, and September 1, 2, 6, 13, 1892; and Small, "Robert Schilling," 275–276. Strikes in the woods were more obscure, and there simply does not seem to be much of anything in the literature about them.

unsatisfactory performance by one machine could halt the production line and idle many men. An advantage of size was that a big mill multiplied the number of production lines from head saw to trimmer, which ensured a flow despite the failure of one machine. Lumbermen could not do much about the vagaries of the weather or other elements that controlled logging, driving, rafting, fires, infestations, or market conditions; all the more reason to concentrate on the controllable processes. Work at the mill comprised something on the order of one-third of the labor costs for getting lumber from the stump to the product in the stack. As part of a lumberman's capital investment, the sawmill in 1890 represented an average one-sixth. A very rough calculation, taken from census reports, gives an average Wisconsin lumber company capitalization of $15,900 in 1870; $28,200 in 1880; and $99,000 in 1890. Even if the one-sixth invested in the mill is assumed as a constant, the average investment in the mill increased sixfold from $2,624 in 1870, to $4,653 in 1880, and to $16,335 in 1890. During those twenty years, the average number of employees per mill had only doubled (from 17.3 to 38.4). As a mass-production process, the productivity of mill labor was subject to great improvement with better machines and more efficient working conditions.[53]

Steam had released the sawmill from the limitations of waterpower years before, but the steam mill really came into its own in the 1870's with the development of much more reliable, heavy, low-pressure, constant-speed engines. It was a perfect marriage, for it tied the increasing power demands of the new technology to a plant that produced an embarrassment of fuel in sawdust, slab,

[53] H. C. Putnam, in the Wisconsin Horticultural Society's annual report for 1892, pp. 184–185, estimated a cost of $3.00 to $3.50 per 1,000 board feet to cut and stack, $1.00 for driving, booming, and sorting, and $2.50 from log to manufactured lumber at the mill. See also Fries, *Empire in Pine*, 60–65, 103–104, and *Eleventh Census of the United States, 1890: Report on Manufacturing Industries in the United States, Volume VI, Part 3*, pp. 597, 611–613. In 1870, Wisconsin sawmills were using 16,119 horsepower produced by steam and 11,668 produced by water. In 1890, steam produced 50,878 horsepower, water 11,852. See *Ninth Census of the United States, 1870: Volume III, Statistics of the Wealth and Industry of the United States*, 453; *Eleventh Census of the United States, 1890: Report on Manufacturing Industries in the United States, Volume VI, Part 1*, pp. 902–903.

and other waste. The band saw, which came into general use in the latter 1880's, was no faster than the rotary saw, but it wasted less lumber in sawdust at high speeds and required less maintenance by the saw filer. Lumbermen also concentrated on lumber-finishing equipment—planers, edgers, shapers, and drying kilns—as railroad delivery began to replace rafting of lumber, thus making it possible to finish the lumber at the mill. Continuous technological improvement was encouraged not alone by a competitive market and cost consciousness, but also by the regularity with which an appalling number of sawmills burned down each year. Almost invariably they arose phoenix-like from the ashes—bigger and more modern than ever. Few were not replaced unless the available timber was near exhaustion.[54]

By 1873 the older lumber towns, Oshkosh and Fond du Lac in particular, which drew upon depleting pineries, were already well along in converting their remaining lumber to higher uses in sash and door plants, furniture factories, and carriage and wagon manufactories. They had the necessary ingredients: capital, a settled labor force, nearness to markets, and railroad connections.[55]

Change was as marked in lumber marketing as in other aspects of the business. Most cut lumber moved by water in the early seventies. The mills between Green Bay and Marinette logically shipped on the Great Lakes, mainly to the great Chicago wholesale market, but increasingly eastward to ports such as Cleveland, Buffalo, and Oswego, as Lower Michigan's pine resources were exhausted. Lumber rafts were navigational hazards on the Great Lakes. By the seventies, lumber was barged under tow or carried by the lumber fleet, generally made up of older sailing vessels. A leaky hull did not make much difference to a cargo of lumber.

---

[54] Walter F. Peterson, *An Industrial Heritage: Allis-Chalmers Corporation* (Milwaukee, 1978), 20–27, 42–44. A common phrase referring to fires destroying small mills in hard times or when timber resources ran low was "sold to the insurance company." Insurance was a problem; lumber mills accounted for about half the industrial fire losses in the state between 1885 and 1891. See Kleven, "Wisconsin Lumber Industry," 240–242, 253–256; Fries, *Empire in Pine*, 61–62, 105–106.

[55] Current, *Pine Logs and Politics*, 112–121; Joseph Schafer, *The Winnebago-Horicon Basin: A Type Study in Western History* (Madison, 1937), 265–279, 290–294.

Vessels were often dismasted and converted to barges for ease in loading. Railroads, which had taken most of this business by the latter 1880's, offered greater convenience, efficiency, and were competitive in rates by then.[56]

The Wisconsin River basin furnishes still another example of change. In the early years, practically all of its lumber production went to market by raft down the Wisconsin and Mississippi. By 1880, the new railroads built there had taken over much of the log hauling as well as most lumber carriage to market. The Wisconsin, badly shoaled in its lower reaches, had never been very satisfactory for transporting either logs or lumber. The railroads gave a welcome link with the local markets of southeastern and central Wisconsin, while Chicago was an assured cash market for any surplus.[57]

The other river basins emptying into the Mississippi found their markets mostly at the river landings on the west shore from Wabasha, Minnesota, southward to St. Louis. Each mill had a rafting works which assembled cut lumber into cribs, generally sixteen feet square and one to two feet in depth, held together by heavy stringers bound by tough roots. A deck load of lath, shingles, or lumber was common, but the raft was made of green lumber which meant it did not have much freeboard or carrying capacity. Cribs were secured in strings, depending on the nature of the river. A Wisconsin River lumber raft, for instance, was usually three cribs wide and seven long. It was the tricky navigation of these rafts, carried by the current with steering provided by improvised sweeps at bow and stern, that made upriver millmen nervous about rapids, booms, and dams franchised to competitors below them on the river. Dam franchises specified the width of spillways and required log chutes to skid the rafts to the river below. Rapids required special care, usually taking the raft through by pieces and reassembling them below. Some men made a good living piloting through particularly hair-raising rapids. The Wisconsin River alone claimed forty lives in the rafting season of

[56] Fries, *Empire in Pine*, 70–71, 74, 80; Merk, *Economic History*, 80–81; Stephenson, *Recollections*, 168–169.

[57] Hotchkiss, *Lumber and Forest Industry*, 517–518; Fries, *Empire in Pine*, 91–92.

1872. The railroads were a welcome alternative above the fall lines of the rivers, for lost men usually meant lost lumber as well. The hazards of running the upper tributaries of the Mississippi contributed to the romance of the industry. Involving unusual skills and responsibilities, raft piloting was comparatively well paid and considered a profession. Experienced steersmen, too, were always in demand, but most rafting crews contained a fair number of greenhorns who saw the work as partly adventure.[58]

Reaching the main river, the lumber rafts were bound together into huge Mississippi rafts sometimes covering literally acres. Rafts no longer depended upon the current, but were pushed by towboats in the same manner as the log rafts. Lumber rafting was an expensive method of marketing the product, but not many mills in northwestern Wisconsin had an alternative in the early seventies. The cost of rafting depended much upon water conditions and luck. A general estimate for the Wisconsin River was that it cost about $5 per 1,000 board feet to raft lumber from the upper reaches to St. Louis. This included construction of the rafts, wages of the crew, and the cost of the towboat on the Mississippi. The towboat might be delayed by low water, fog, adverse winds, and the necessity to solicit business along the way or to unload lumber. The great expense, of course, was the condition of the lumber delivered by raft. It arrived sodden, muddy, and much of it damaged. In low water, the rafted lumber became even more waterlogged and the bottom courses in the rafts suffered from contact with rocks or scouring by sand. Rafted lumber was unfinished, and wholesale yards in the Mississippi River towns had to clean it, dry it, saw it to dimension, and finish it.[59]

---

[58] Wilbur H. Glover, "Lumber Rafting on the Wisconsin River," in *WMH*, 25 (December, 1941–March, 1942), 155–177, 308–324; Fries, *Empire in Pine*, 66–75; Walter A. Blair, *A Raft Pilot's Log: A History of the Great Rafting Industry on the Upper Mississippi, 1840–1915* (Cleveland, 1930), 34–36, 204; Merk, *Economic History*, 81–84.

[59] Supposedly the largest Mississippi raft was run in 1901. It was 270 feet wide by 1,450 feet long and contained 9 million board feet of lumber; see Blair, *A Raft Pilot's Log*, 203; Glover, "Lumber Rafting on the Wisconsin River," *WMH*, 25:317–318; Twining, *Downriver*, 132–134. Fries, *Empire in Pine*, 75–76, notes that the cost of rafting took nearly 50 per cent of the returns on a lumber raft in the 1860's. In 1878, the cost of a towboat for a thirteen-day trip came to $1,027.09—but was an improvement over drifting and trying to make market stops.

Sending a raft of several million feet of lumber down the river, into what was often a buyers' market, with only a salesman up ahead or the raft's pilot authorized to make a deal, could be a stomach-churning exercise of many days' duration for the mill owner. Of course there was the telegraph, but it might tell the lumberman only that he had a choice between recovering part of his costs or telling the raft to continue on. St. Louis was the market of last resort and therefore usually of the lowest price. One could not call up and down the river for customers—only down.

Most successful lumbermen learned the lessons to be had from this style of marketing. They saw that it was the retailer and the wholesaler who first claimed the consumers' dollars, which gave the wholesaler, in particular, the advantage in dealing with cash-starved lumbermen. The wholesaler provided the credit at both ends: to the mill and to the small retailer. There were a number of options open to the lumberman who could get beyond a hand-to-mouth existence. He could establish his own wholesale yards at strategic locations. A more attractive option was a corporate tie with one or more established wholesalers. While wholesalers saw the cash earlier, much of their credit was based upon accounts receivable and lumber in the yard. The lumberman with a mill and standing timber had a broader credit base and could ensure the wholesaler's supplies.[60]

Railroads offered another marketing strategy. Lumber companies maintained retail yards along the lines and became concerned about their "legitimate territories" in relation to rivals. Railroads presented a peculiar marketing problem for lumbermen in northwestern Wisconsin. The Mississippi was bridged at La Crosse in 1876, followed by other railroad bridges at points above as rival railroads vied for the growing traffic originating at Minneapolis-St. Paul and the rapidly opening agricultural areas south and west of there. This expanding railroad network became a lively factor in marketing Wisconsin lumber westward, especially what became popularly known as the Wisconsin Lumber

---

[60] Twining, *Downriver*, 115–167; Reynolds, *Daniel Shaw Lumber Company*, 105–128; Kohlmeyer, *Laird, Norton Story*, 204–231.

Line, allied with a combination called the Chicago, St. Paul, Minneapolis and Omaha, commonly called the ''Omaha.'' This offered favorable lumber rates to carry the traffic westward, directing lumber from as far east as the Green Bay district. Many lumbermen, who had been rafting their lumber, made the necessary changes to take advantage of rail delivery of finished lumber. This involved planing, finishing, kiln drying, and seasoning, which tied up more capital in machinery, facilities, and inventory.[61]

Chicago railroads and lumber wholesalers watched these developments with concern. The Lumber Line reached into their supply area in the upper Wisconsin River valley. In 1883, the Omaha became part of the Chicago and North Western system, disrupting the Lumber Line. Chicago railroads and lumbermen could then exert more leverage. They re-established Chicago's rate advantages and, by placing Eau Claire at a disadvantage vis-à-vis La Crosse and other Mississippi River points, briefly restored lumber rafting on the Chippewa. Eau Claire carried on a long campaign to have the new Interstate Commerce Commission, created in 1887, set aside the differential. Although a ruling favorable to Eau Claire came in 1892, the railroads ignored it with impunity for some years. White pine was becoming scarce enough by then to warrant paying railroad rates to much more distant markets, and Chicago lost her primacy as wholesaler of the commodity.[62]

Price, of course, was an important consideration in lumber marketing. Pine lumber experienced less price volatility between 1873 and 1893 than one might have expected from the record of the previous twenty years. Despite a near trebling of average annual output from Wisconsin mills, the increased demand resulting from agricultural, industrial, urban, and transportation expansion, plus the greater marketing reach by rail, absorbed the

[61] Kohlmeyer, *Laird, Norton Story*, 211–215; Current, *Pine Logs and Politics*, 131–133; Fries, *Empire in Pine*, 84–89.

[62] Reynolds, *Daniel Shaw Lumber Company*, 100–103; Current, *Pine Logs and Politics*, 142–143; Fries, *Empire in Pine*, 89–99.

increase. Average annual prices for Laird, Norton Company at
Winona were $16.84 per 1,000 board feet in 1873 and $14.22 in
1893. The lowest average was $12.49 in 1879; $18.18 in 1882 was
the high. Despite a fairly steady rise in the value of stumpage,
lumber prices fluctuated rather narrowly. Profits depended upon
the price paid for stumpage, an advantageous location with respect
to timber and markets, or more efficient milling operations.[63]

Advantages of scale in the individual mill were limited. The
more successful operators exercised a variety of options at all
points in the process, but particularly by investing in a number of
locations for both manufacturing and marketing. Lumbering was
a business that dealt in variables far beyond national or local business cycles: the price of wheat, the snow pack, winter tempera-
tures, river levels, railroad rates, fires in the woods or at the mill
or in Chicago or inflammable Oshkosh—the list could go on—and
of course a very seasonal and disorderly market. Survivors, and
those who prospered spectacularly, needed shrewdness—and not
a little luck.

At some point in every successful lumberman's career there
came the time when the desperate pursuit of cash and credit to
meet expenses and to expand was replaced by the problem of what
to do with a growing cash surplus. A mill visibly exhausting its
available timber resources was not an attractive investment. The
first thought of many was to start over in a new timber bonanza.
This decision was easy for Philetus Sawyer of Oshkosh, who was
a wealthy man before 1870 and a very wealthy man by 1880, made
so by his timber speculation in the Chippewa Valley. Making
money continued as a consuming interest for Sawyer, but a political career which led to the United States Senate and recognition
as "boss" of Republican party politics in Wisconsin furnished
diversion that occupied his considerable talents after 1875.[64]

[63] Glover, "Lumber Rafting on the Wisconsin River," *WMH*, 25:314–315; Fries, *Empire in Pine*, 107–113; Kohlmeyer, *Laird, Norton Story*, 216. Chicago and the Mississippi River markets provide most of the figures because there is little information on domestic con-sumption in Wisconsin.

[64] Current, *Pine Logs and Politics, passim.*

Isaac Stephenson of Marinette, who was even wealthier than Sawyer, had a less satisfactory political career, which he apparently considered more in the nature of a recognition of his financial and managerial success than an opportunity to run things. Following a common pattern, he invested heavily in southern yellow pine, which preceded Pacific Northwest fir and California redwood in the Chicago market as a competitor of white pine and hemlock.[65]

Orrin Ingram of Eau Claire invested in timber in Washington State, but, full of years, he never seriously considered moving westward—as did many others of Weyerhaeuser's associates—after he closed down his Eau Claire mill in 1898. But as a hobby, Ingram retained his mill at Rice Lake. He served as president of two Eau Claire banks and was vice-president of the Dells Paper & Pulp Company, in which his interest was strictly financial. He also had financial interests in Eau Claire utilities, serving as titular head of several. On the side, and quite unplanned, Ingram had investments in Florida orange groves, a Texas rice plantation, and an Arizona copper mine.[66]

Wausau lumbermen set an example not generally followed. Provided leadership by a hired manager, David Clark Everest, who was brought in to direct their paper mill which later became the Marathon Corporation, the so-called Wausau Group developed hydroelectric power and utilities. Masonite Corporation and Employers Mutual of Wausau, long after 1893, were further interests. Most of the mill towns and cities of northern Wisconsin, unless they were on a power site or at a location particularly adaptable to the growing pulp and paper industry, had a difficult time finding other industrial pursuits. Moreover, they could seldom count on the talents or capital of the lumber barons to offer much help. Fairly typical was the Peshtigo Harbor Mill which, having run night and day for many years, closed down in 1895. It

---

[65] Hotchkiss, *Lumber and Forest Industry*, 302.
[66] Twining, *Downriver*, 265–290.

was characteristic of the industry to abandon a community when the local timber resources were exhausted.[67]

The legacy of the lumber era is familiar. The social cost of nearly abandoned communities which have persisted continues in underemployment and poverty. Hardwood lumbering, exploitation of less desirable species for dimension lumber, and the paper and pulp industry—all had their beginnings before 1893, but they did not fill the void left by the pine. In the end, nearly three-fifths of the timber was wasted, and not over 40 per cent reached the mills. In 1928, of the 11 million acres in Wisconsin's seventeen northernmost counties, 82 per cent remained in stumps and brush. The effort to turn it into agricultural land had failed. It is interesting to reflect that Congress passed the Timber Culture Act in 1873 to subsidize and encourage the farmers of the Great Plains to plant cottonwood groves—and then waited nearly twenty years before concerning itself seriously with the vanishing conifers.[68]

[67] Steven B. Karges, "David Clark Everest and Marathon Paper Mills Company: A Study of a Wisconsin Enterprise, 1909–1931" (doctoral dissertation, University of Wisconsin, 1968), chap. 3; Howard R. Klueter and James J. Lorence, *Woodlot and Ballot Box: Marathon County in the Twentieth Century* (Stevens Point, 1977), 47–49, 92–115; Fries, *Empire in Pine*, 242–245. "Philetus Sawyer, Jesse Spalding, the Witbecks, the Hamilton and the Merryman brothers all gained large fortunes from their mills in Marinette, but left the community little except cut-over tax-delinquent lands, sawdust where mills once stood, and memories. . . . The sons of these Marinette lumbering families moved to . . . new unexploited regions. Most of the lumbering families of Marinette spent only one generation in Marinette." Carl E. Krog, "Markets and Mills: The Growth and Development of the Marinette Lumber Industry After 1860" (unpublished manuscript, courtesy of the author), 31–32.

[68] Helgeson, *Farms in the Cutover*, 113. The commissioner of the General Land Office observed in 1876: "It is an anomalous fact that the Government is giving away the rich alluvial soil of Iowa, Nebraska, Kansas, and Minnesota to any citizen who will plant a few acres of cottonwood or other inferior timber, while under the provisions of the pre-emption and homestead law it is granting a license to destroy millions of acres of pine forests of almost incalculable value, which should be preserved as a national heritage." Quoted in Hurst, *Law and Economic Growth*, 439–440.

# 3

# Transportation

## THE AGE OF STEAM AND HAY

"PEOPLE can make more money in farms and other industries than in rrs. . . . And it is only the Eastern capitalist, who
cannot use his money to advantage at home who is willing to risk
it in western railroads," complained the president of the Chicago,
Burlington & Quincy to an Iowa railroad commissioner in 1885.
The comment sounds both paradoxical and self-serving, coming
as it did from one of the accused monopolists of the Granger Era.
There was in fact much that was paradoxical and self-serving
about the western railroads. They were grinding monopolies and,
at the same time, helpless pawns caught in fierce and often ruinous competition. They were shamelessly courted where they did
not exist and cordially hated where they did. They acknowledged
their role as public highways when it suited their purposes, but
assumed the rights of an individual ordering his private property
for most other occasions. They corrupted politics and then
claimed, sometimes correctly, that this was necessary to protect
them from corrupt politicians. They played upon local sympa-
thies while nursing regional or even transcontinental ambitions.
They were too vital to hobble and too intransigent to be given free
rein.[1]

The railroads were the great instruments of the vast expansion
of opportunity enjoyed by industrial entrepreneurs, businessmen,
and farmers in the post-Civil War years. The wonder is that the

[1] Charles E. Perkins to J. McDill, January 26, 1885, as quoted in Thomas C. Cochran,
*Railroad Leaders, 1845-1890: The Business Mind in Action* (Cambridge, 1953), 98.

railroads themselves, and midwestern lines in particular, continued to attract the huge amounts of capital necessary for their insatiable expansion. It is true that some—the Chicago, Milwaukee and St. Paul (CM&StP) and the Chicago and North Western (C&NW) among them—had moved from speculations to investment status by the 1870's, but it was a status under constant threat of insolvency both from the hazards of business cycles and the actions of their own promoters and managers.[2]

The railroads serving Chicago and Milwaukee to the westward were greatly overbuilt by 1873, given the stage of development of the territory served. But there was no pause for settlement and the growth of traffic to catch up with the facilities. Costs and profits had to be taken from the available captive traffic while meeting competition at points where most of their business was generated. The rule that rates were based upon "all the traffic will bear" was tempered by special terms for favored shippers or commodities to encourage volume, for railroad men recognized the urgency of fixed costs. Railroad rates inevitably became political issues. Government regulation seemed the only feasible means of control over giant enterprises that responded so erratically to the accepted rules of the marketplace. But after the political fires died down, the hazards of unbridled competition continued. "Contractors and too enterprising Railroad projectors and raiders . . . are worse than the Grangers," wrote a despairing Boston financier in 1880, "in fact we may again welcome Granger legislation as a check to over production of Roads."[3]

There was no doubt about the part the railroads had to play in the economy. By the 1870's, the dream of cheap, competitive, interior waterways for Wisconsin was fading. The federal government took over the best hope, the Fox–Wisconsin waterway, in 1872, but it was becoming evident that the Wisconsin River defied

[2] Alfred D. Chandler, Jr., comp. and ed., *The Railroads: The Nation's First Big Business* (New York, 1965), 9–12; Dorothy R. Adler, *British Investment in American Railways, 1834–1898*, ed. Muriel E. Hidy (Charlottesville, Virginia, 1970), 205–211; Edward C. Kirkland, *Industry Comes of Age: Business, Labor, and Public Policy, 1860–1897* (New York, 1961), 52–74.

[3] S. F. Van Oss, *American Railroads as Investments: A Handbook for Investors in American Railroad Securities* (New York, 1893), 452–454; John Murray Forbes to Frederick L. Ames, September 8, 1880, as quoted in Cochran, *Railroad Leaders*, 339.

conquest of its shifting shallows. Nor was the Upper Mississippi reliable; there were years when boats could not pass the rapids at Rock Island. The Mississippi's tributaries in Wisconsin brought logs and lumber rafts to the big river, but offered very limited opportunities for navigation into the interior. Public roads were no alternative. Animal power could not compete with steam and an iron wheel on a rail, even on the best of roads, and Wisconsin's roads were beyond hope.[4]

Railroading in Wisconsin had entered a new phase in its development prior to 1873. The pioneer railroads had been civic promotions to penetrate a city's hinterland. Every Lake Michigan port had its quota of paper railroads; interior towns were similarly blessed; so was every aspiring village. Thirty-three new railroads were incorporated in Wisconsin between 1861 and 1868, although only 130 miles of new line were built. There were many more paper railroads that never achieved the formality of a charter.[5]

The railroads that had actually put down some rail were a different problem. They existed in the real world and had taken on a life of their own. Their birth pangs had been prolonged, difficult, and uncertain in most cases. Establishing ownership and control after bankruptcy—in the 1857 panic every Wisconsin railroad had gone broke—was equally prolonged, difficult, and uncertain. One thing assured was that much of the original promotional capital and subsidies—the notorious farm mortgages and municipal bond issues which eager farmers and municipal corporations had exchanged for railroad stock—was mostly lost.[6]

[4] Richard N. Current, *The History of Wisconsin. Volume II: The Civil War Era, 1848-1873* (Madison, 1976), 445–450; Richard N. Current, *Pine Logs and Politics: A Life of Philetus Sawyer, 1816-1900* (Madison, 1950), 93–94, 216–217; Samuel Mermin, *The Fox-Wisconsin Improvement: An Historical Study in Legal Institutions and Political Economy* (Madison, 1968), 145–151; John B. Sanborn, "The Story of the Fox-Wisconsin Rivers Improvement," in the *Proceedings of the State Historical Society of Wisconsin* (74 vols., Madison, 1875–1958), 1899, pp. 186–194 (hereinafter cited as *SHSW Proceedings*); Paul W. Brown, "The Collapse of the Steamboat Traffic upon the Mississippi: An Inquiry into Causes," in *Proceedings of the Mississippi Valley Historical Association,* vol. 9, pt. 3 (1917–1918), 426.

[5] Frederick Merk, *Economic History of Wisconsin During the Civil War Decade* (Madison, 1916; reprinted, 1971), 277.

[6] *Ibid.,* 238–270; Current, *Civil War Era,* 35–41, 243–250; John W. Cary, *The Organization and History of the Chicago, Milwaukee & St. Paul Railway Company* ([Milwaukee, 1893]), 17–18; George H. Miller, *Railroads and the Granger Laws* (Madison, 1971), 142–143.

The next logical step was the consolidation of the pioneer railroads into larger systems. In the 1860's, the Chicago, Milwaukee and St. Paul combined the two lines out of Milwaukee that had reached the Mississippi River at Prairie du Chien in 1857 and La Crosse in 1858. Racine was the only competing Wisconsin port city that before 1870 had a railroad connection with the Mississippi. The CM&StP gathered this line in as well, giving it another river port at Savannah, Illinois.

The Chicago and North Western started with a line to the Mississippi due west of Chicago to Fulton, Illinois. A spur branched at Belvidere, Illinois, and entered Wisconsin by way of the Rock River valley. Before the end of the 1860's, this line carried a branch from Beloit to Madison, and a longer one from Janesville to Fond du Lac had reached Oshkosh and beyond Green Bay. A line along the shore of Lake Michigan connecting Chicago with Milwaukee was absorbed by the C&NW, along with Kenosha's railroad to the Mississippi, which had gotten as far as Rockport, Illinois. The CM&StP countered with a parallel line, completed in 1874, along the lakefront to Chicago; and in adding Chicago's name to its title it recognized that city's dominant position in the growing railroad network of the Midwest.[7]

In simplest terms, the Milwaukee-based CM&StP controlled both lines reaching the Mississippi from the city, plus Racine's westward line. This reflected Milwaukee's interest in the grain trade. The CM&StP helped carry the expansion of wheat culture into the Dakotas by driving westward from points across the river from Prairie du Chien at McGregor, Iowa, and at La Crescent, Minnesota, opposite La Crosse, even before throwing bridges across in the mid-seventies. The C&NW's main thrust in Wisconsin was northward, cutting across the other's lines, to the lumber centers on Lake Winnebago and Green Bay and then to the Michigan iron mines beyond. By 1870, the CM&StP and the

---

[7] Richard L. Canuteson, "The Railway Development of Northern Wisconsin" (master's thesis, University of Wisconsin, 1930), 137-143; Alice E. Smith, *George Smith's Money: A Scottish Investor in America* (Madison, 1966), 144; William F. Raney, "The Building of Wisconsin Railroads," in *WMH*, 19 (June, 1936), 394-395.

C&NW controlled all but a very few miles of Wisconsin's railroad lines.[8]

The consolidation of the railroads was not viewed with equanimity by their customers. Railroad rates rose rapidly during the Civil War, along with grain prices. Antimonopoly sentiment had reached a peak of activity in Wisconsin by the end of the Civil War as grain carriage rates doubled what they had been in 1860. Railroad regulation bills continued as a feature of postwar legislative sessions, but nothing important was passed until the Potter Law of 1874. The railroads and their friends usually had the votes and demonstrated the political and economic power inherent in combination.[9]

Much of the political agitation was directed against the consolidation of the lesser lines into the C&NW or the CM&StP, for the idea died hard that competition was invariably a force on the side of right and justice, even with respect to railroads. But it was difficult to argue with the fact that two strong companies, able to afford necessary improvements and efficient in operation, were preferable to a disjointed collection of small, inefficiently run, mostly bankrupt lines. Moreover, the CM&StP made political capital from its local identification. Ownership actually was in Europe and New York, where a majority of the board of directors lived, but management was visibly local. Alexander Mitchell became president in 1865 and the general manager was Sherburn S. Merrill, who had been associated with companies in the consolidation since 1850.[10]

As the owner of the city's oldest and most powerful bank and of Wisconsin's largest personal fortune, Mitchell was a sometimes controversial figure. He had come to Milwaukee from his native Scotland in 1839 to manage the bank owned by his countryman,

[8] Merk, *Economic History*, 80, 271–278, 289–300; Current, *Civil War Era*, 33–34, 381–382, 437–444.

[9] Merk, *Economic History*, 243–299; Miller, *Railroads and the Granger Laws,* 143–151; Frank N. Elliott, "The Causes and the Growth of Railroad Regulation in Wisconsin, 1848–1876" (doctoral dissertation, University of Wisconsin, 1956), 266–274.

[10] Merk, *Economic History,* 299–304; Wisconsin Railroad Commissioners, *Annual Report,* 1875, Official Papers section, 35–60; *DWB.*

George Smith, a Chicago investor with broad banking and real estate interests in the Midwest and Georgia. Mitchell bought out Smith's interest in the Milwaukee bank in 1854. Smith, enormously wealthy, retired to London after the 1857 financial panic, largely unscathed by it. He had vast interests in midwestern railroads and was Mitchell's mainstay in his fight for control of the CM&StP. (The Smith estate still had about $20 million in securities of the CM&StP when World War I was in the offing, as well as a large position in the Burlington.) Mitchell, with Peter Geddes, agent for Smith's investments in America, had financial leverage well beyond his own resources. Polite but determined, he was a force to be reckoned with in economic and political affairs.[11]

The agitation for railroad regulation and control was rather easily contained for a time. A glance at maps showing railroad mileage in 1860 and 1870 in Wisconsin suggests some reasons why. Not a mile was added between 1864 and 1867. There remained simply too much settled area not yet served by a railroad, which meant people more eager for promotion and construction than for regulation. The railroads argued, on the basis of the hiatus in new construction, that the hostile political climate generated by agitation for regulation was frightening capital away from the task at hand. The arguments were effective. Iowa and Minnesota were simply more hospitable, had even larger federal grants, had not accumulated as many railroad problems, and their agriculture was expanding even more rapidly. The arguments of the railroads were therefore self-fulfilling. The CM&StP was financially able to enlarge its mileage and was doing so . . . west of the Mississippi.[12]

---

[11] Smith, *George Smith's Money,* 135–140, 146–156.

[12] Wisconsin Regional Planning Committee, *A Study of Wisconsin: Its Resources, Its Physical, Social and Economic Background,* Bulletin, no. 2 (Madison, 1934), maps on pp. 371–373; *House Executive Documents,* 44 Cong., 2 sess., no. 47, pt. 2 (serial 1761), appendix, 239; *Wisconsin Blue Book, 1905,* p. 1004; Merk, *Economic History,* 277, 279–280; Robert S. Hunt, *Law and Locomotives: The Impact of the Railroad on Wisconsin Law in the Nineteenth Century* (Madison, 1958), 126; *Commercial and Financial Chronicle,* August 15, 1874; Miller, *Railroads and the Granger Laws,* 143; William H. Stennett, comp., *Yesterday and Today: A History of the Chicago and North Western Railway System* (Chicago, 3rd edition, 1910), 89–91; Russell Sage to Joseph T. Dodge, August 28, 1873, March 27 and June 18, 1874, in the Joseph T. Dodge Papers, SHSW (microfilm edition).

With its terminals at Prairie du Chien and La Crosse, the CM&StP depended on the Mississippi to gather the traffic west of the river. Bridges at these two points were not in use until 1874 and 1876 respectively. But already in the mid-sixties, the CM&StP was building and buying lines beyond the river. In 1867 it bought the Minnesota Central which made a connection from St. Paul to McGregor, Iowa, opposite Prairie du Chien. A second line on the Minnesota side was opened in 1871, and reached St. Paul from La Crescent, opposite La Crosse. These reduced the railroad's dependence on the river. Before 1870, the C&NW was reaching in the same direction. It bought a couple of short lines in the vicinity of La Crosse in 1867 and in 1870 commenced a line from Madison on the franchise of the Baraboo Airline Railroad to Winona, Minnesota, crossing the Mississippi just north of La Crosse.[13]

The CM&StP and the C&NW had their choice of the usual strategies as they began to parallel one another with routes into the growing St. Paul market: competitive war to the knife or some form of accommodation. Briefly, there was a nervous harmony between the two. In 1868 they exchanged members of their boards of directors, and Alexander Mitchell for a few months in 1869–1870 was president of both roads. But diverging interests and public hostility made this arrangement impractical. The two roads, of course, had their eyes not only upon one another, for other competitors were certain to follow. By 1870, one competitor was already in operation, carrying the growing wheat traffic of the northern plains off to Lake Superior. St. Paul capital, aided by Jay Cooke who was promoting the Northern Pacific, had completed a rail link with Duluth at the head of Lake Superior. Duluth took some time to establish itself as a major competitor of Chicago and

[13] Temporary bridges on the ice preceded the permanent installations. See *House Executive Documents,* 50 Cong., 1 sess., no. 6, pt. 2 (serial 2552), 19–20, and H. J. Hirshheimer, "Bridging the Mississippi at La Crosse & Winona," in La Crosse County Historical Society, *La Crosse County Historical Sketches,* series 6 (La Crosse, 1942), 33–40, for the story of the two bridges. Cary, *Chicago, Milwaukee & St. Paul Railway Company,* chaps. 7, 9, 12, 13, and 15; Julius Grodinsky, *Transcontinental Railway Strategy, 1869–1893: A Study of Businessmen* (Philadelphia, 1962), 126–131; Stennett, comp., *Yesterday and Today,* 73.

Milwaukee as a grain shipping port, but the potential was clearly there with a rail haul about one-third as long.[14]

Between 1871 and 1874, the CM&StP and C&NW joined in a common effort to force the St. Paul to Duluth line (Lake Superior and Mississippi Railway) to the wall financially. They had the longer haul, but also the longer purses and other territory from which to recover their losses. In the spring of 1873, they strengthened this alliance with a tentative agreement to pool their earnings. Governor Cadwallader Washburn sought an opinion on the pooling agreement and was advised that the state could probably move legally against the railroads by *quo warranto* proceedings. The companies backed away from their agreement—maybe in response to Washburn's threat, and possibly because the C&NW elected a new president, Albert Keep, who was less inclined to ally with Mitchell. The matter became less urgent within a few weeks. The Northern Pacific took over the Lake Superior and Mississippi in September of 1873, about the time that Jay Cooke and Company went bankrupt. The Duluth line gave up the rate war in the confusion. The CN&StP and C&NW celebrated by raising the rates on wheat more than two cents a bushel all along the line beyond St. Paul. This rate increase came in the fall of 1873, shortly before the gubernatorial and legislative elections. The railroads' political dams would be washed out in the freshet of protest that followed.[15]

[14] Grodinsky, *Transcontinental Railway Strategy,* 33; Merk, *Economic History,* 298–300; Miller, *Railroads and the Granger Laws,* 133. Jay Cooke, a Philadelphia financier, was the principal promoter of the Northern Pacific. The failure of his banking house in the autumn of 1873 precipitated the financial panic of that year.

[15] Alpheus B. Stickney, *The Railway Problem; With Many Illustrative Diagrams* (St. Paul, 1891), 40–44; Herman J. Deutsch, "Disintegrating Forces in Wisconsin Politics of the Early Seventies," in *WMH,* 15 (March, 1932), 288–289, 293; Miller, *Railroads and the Granger Laws,* 132–133, 154, 159; Dale E. Treleven, "Railroads, Elevators, and Grain Dealers: The Genesis of Antimonopolism in Milwaukee," in *WMH,* 52 (Spring, 1969), 213; *Commercial and Financial Chronicle,* May 17, June 5, 7, 21, 1873; Stennett, comp., *Yesterday and Today,* 76.

Railroad rates were wildly erratic. Elliott, "Railroad Regulation in Wisconsin," 288, says the general rate raise on wheat was approximately 3 cents a bushel. Treleven, 213, says 2 cents, citing two Milwaukee newspapers. Individual freight agents had wide discretion not only in setting commodity rates but also special rates for individual shippers. Within the bounds of current managerial policy, rates might vary almost daily depending upon the

The CM&StP's hold on the grain traffic to and through the port of Milwaukee was illustrative. The railroad owned nearly every grain elevator in the city. These structures permitted handling the grain in bulk, rather than in sacks, effecting great economies. They also were effective instruments for control of the business. In this instance, as in many others, it was difficult to distinguish among the interests of Alexander Mitchell, the Wisconsin Marine and Fire Insurance Company bank, and the CM&StP. The bank controlled over 35 per cent of Milwaukee's total bank assets, giving Mitchell considerable leverage over the grain market by the simple device of casting an eye over credit to grain dealers. These middlemen in the movement of grain operated on narrow margins and had high capital requirements. Mitchell had every advantage. He liked to deal in sure things.[16]

Able to call the tune so effectively over the city's most important commercial activity, Mitchell was not without allies in maintaining the grip of the railroad and his bank. A circle of other business leaders found it prudent and profitable to support his point of view. Mitchell spoke with authority in meetings of the Milwaukee Chamber of Commerce, of which the grain exchange was the nucleus, and wherever the city's commercial destiny was discussed. What Mitchell claimed, with general success, was that the fortunes of the city were bound up with those of the railroad. It was difficult, given the circumstances, for a Milwaukee businessman in open meeting to suggest that the emperor had no clothes.[17]

---

immediate competitive situation, the season, the availability of cars, the size of the crop, the amount of business originated by the shipper, and prevailing prices for grain, lumber, or other commodities. In other words, whatever the traffic would bear. Miller, *Railroads and the Granger Laws,* 16–23; Wisconsin Railroad Commissioner, *Annual Report,* 1878, p. 342; Elliott, "Railroad Regulation in Wisconsin," 251–263; *House Executive Documents,* 44 Cong., 2 sess., no. 46, pt. 2 (serial 1761), 59–66.

[16] Elliott, "Railroad Regulation in Wisconsin," 288; Treleven, "Genesis of Antimonopolism in Milwaukee," *WMH,* 52:206–208; Deutsch, "Disintegrating Forces in Wisconsin Politics," *WMH,* 15:293.

[17] Treleven, "Genesis of Antimonopolism in Milwaukee," *WMH,* 52:208–209, 212–213. Mitchell often looked upon his own works and found them good. See E. E. Barton, *Industrial History of Milwaukee: The Commercial, Manufacturing and Railway Metropolis of the Northwest . . .* (Milwaukee, 1886), 31.

The state election of 1873 upset the normal Republican majority which had been in control since the 1850's. Agitation for railroad regulation was the central issue in the election. All parties
favored it, a large number of Republicans probably more strongly
than either the Democrats or the self-styled reformers. It was an
issue whose time had come. This near-unanimity was a response
to rising farmer discontent. The year 1873 was a bad one for Wisconsin grain farmers. The wheat crop of 1873 was comparatively
good, but the September rise in freight rates agreed upon by the
two dominant Wisconsin railroads and a decline in market prices
threatened to cancel the benefits of the good harvest. High Wisconsin intrastate rates helped to make up for the competitive rates
prevailing in the St. Paul market and the slim pickings from the
sparse settlements on many of the western extensions across the
Mississippi. The CM&StP took two-thirds of its earnings from its
Wisconsin mileage in 1873, although this mileage represented
only half the total in its system.[18]

Farmers were aware of this arithmetic. Resentment centered
upon discriminations in rate structure which penalized some
localities over others fortunate enough to have competitive carriers. Farmers did not ordinarily encounter the more galling discriminations between individual shippers. They did see as
discriminatory the prevailing higher rates from Wisconsin points
to Milwaukee or Chicago than were paid from St. Paul to those
cities. The reasons for such a seeming inequity might be clear to
a railroad manager, but the rate advantage in the Milwaukee
market for farmers located farther west on cheaper, more productive acres was difficult to explain to a Wisconsin granger. Despite

[18] William L. Burton, "Wisconsin's First Railroad Commission: A Case Study in
Apostasy," in *WMH*, 45 (Spring, 1962), 190–192; Wisconsin Railroad Commissioner,
*Annual Report*, 1878, p. 342; *ibid.*, *Annual Report*, 1874, p. 27; Graham A. Cosmas, "The
Democracy in Search of Issues: The Wisconsin Reform Party, 1873–1877," in *WMH*, 46
(Winter, 1962–1963), 97–99. The politics which led to the passage of Wisconsin's Potter
Law are discussed at more length in a later chapter. See also D. Sven Nordin, *Rich Harvest:
A History of the Grange, 1867–1900* (Jackson, Mississippi, 1974), 173–175; Miller, *Railroads
and the Granger Laws*, 10–11; Herbert W. Rice, "Early History of the Chicago, Milwaukee
and St. Paul Railway Company" (doctoral dissertation, State University of Iowa, 1938),
243–244; and Treleven, "Genesis of Antimonopolism in Milwaukee," *WMH*, 52:206, 209.

the impractical nature of the remedy, the grangers favored a flat rate based upon mileage—the pro-rata formula that was supposed to settle the long-haul/short-haul controversy. They did not generally favor a railroad commission with any discretionary powers. Events had taught them to distrust politicians dealing with railroads.[19]

Alexander Mitchell had a commanding voice in the Democratic party in Wisconsin and served in Congress from 1871 to 1875. Given Mitchell's role, it was hardly surprising that the CM&StP provided favors and assistance to the state's Democrats. It was also common knowledge, on the other hand, that the C&NW had its political affairs looked after in Wisconsin by the "Madison Regency," a term borrowed from New York politics to designate the leadership of Wisconsin's Republicans. A conspicuous figure in the Regency was Elisha W. Keyes, Madison's postmaster and the state chairman of the party. Keyes administered federal patronage. Aside from these levies on the salaries and services of federal employees, the C&NW provided further staples in the form of cash and free passes for the Keyes war chest.[20]

Republican awareness of the agrarian temper was acute in 1873, for the party had a broader rural following than did the minority Democrats. Keyes's predecessor as state chairman, Horace Rublee, had been rewarded by the Grant administration

[19] See Nordin, *Rich Harvest, passim.* Also see Solon J. Buck, *The Granger Movement: A Study of Agricultural Organization and Its Political, Economic and Social Manifestations, 1870–1880* (Cambridge, 1913); Miller, *Railroads and the Granger Laws;* Deutsch, "Disintegrating Forces in Wisconsin Politics," *WMH,* 15:289; Cosmas, "Democracy in Search of Issues," *WMH,* 46:94. Wisconsin Railroad Commissioners, *Annual Report,* 1874, pp. 24–27, 117, notes that the CM&StP had less than half of its mileage within Wisconsin, but that half brought in two-thirds of the road's income in 1873. While not spelled out, it suggest the differential outlined above. Van Oss, *American Railroads as Investments,* 88, sums up the dilemma nicely: "Rates, strange to say, are fixed somewhat arbitrarily, and by men who know little about them." He was referring to railroad traffic managers, not unfriendly railroad commissions.

[20] Richard W. Hantke, "The Life of Elisha Williams Keyes" (doctoral dissertation, University of Wisconsin, 1942); Richard W. Hantke, "Elisha W. Keyes and the Radical Republicans," in *WMH,* 35 (Spring, 1952), 203–208; Richard W. Hantke, "Elisha W. Keyes, the Bismarck of Western Politics," in *WMH,* 31 (September, 1947), 29–41; Miller, *Railroads and the Granger Laws,* 150–151; E. Bruce Thompson, *Matthew Hale Carpenter: Webster of the West* (Madison, 1954), 112.

with the ministerial post in Switzerland. He kept a cynical eye on party affairs at home. In a playful letter to Keyes, Rublee expressed his confidence that the members of the Madison Regency would be well drilled so that none could be "more hard-fisted, horny-handed, and agricultural looking than they, and that they will leave a trail of hay-seed behind them wherever they go."[21]

The grangers were equally cynical towards the Regency, although it was difficult for Yankee or Scandinavian farmers to break their traditional allegiance to the Republican party. The incumbent Republican governor, Cadwallader C. Washburn, who was seeking his second term in 1873, was a leader of the anti-railroad, anti-Regency wing of the party. He had been talking railroad regulation for years and was the probable author of an 1866 rate bill that had gotten nowhere. Washburn, a wealthy man with varied interests, also used his messages to the legislature to argue for nationalizing the telegraph. On railroads, he observed that they had grown to represent vast concentrations of capital "without any general system and with little responsibility to the people of the state, and the opinion among railway managers seems generally to prevail, that their will is the supreme law. This is an error which ought to be corrected."[22]

The Republicans had a number of crosses to bear both nation-ally and locally—the price of long-continued power. President Ulysses Grant was a divisive figure in the party. The Liberal Republican bolt from Grant in 1872 had ended in fiasco. Grant, easily re-elected, placed the Liberal Republicans in outer dark-ness. Many non-Catholic Germans, who considered themselves Republicans, were still sulking over the treatment meted out to Carl Schurz, a critic of the administration in the Senate and a leader of the Liberal Republican revolt. Keyes and his corps of

[21] Keyes and Rublee are in *DWB;* see Rublee to Keyes, August 19, 1873, in the Elisha W. Keyes Papers.

[22] Deutsch, "Disintegrating Forces in Wisconsin Politics," *WMH,* 15:282–296; Miller, *Railroads and the Granger Laws,* 147, 152; Current, *Civil War Era,* 591–592; Nordin, *Rich Harvest,* 223–224. The quote is from *Wisconsin Public Documents,* 1870–1871, Governor's Message, vol. 1, p. 22.

federal officeholders in Wisconsin were identified with Grant. The Germans were further alienated by the Graham Law, a stringent liquor control measure passed in 1872 with Washburn's enthusiastic support. They looked upon this as a revival of nativism in the Wisconsin Republican party.[23]

The loosening of party ties in the majority party invited a third-party bridge between the liberal dissidents from the Republican ranks and the minority Democrats. Reformers organized a Milwaukee convention which cemented an alliance with the compliant Democrats. What finally emerged was a fusion party without a name officially. It is usually called the Reform party, although it sometimes got lost behind the Democratic label as the Democrats had the organization, the votes, and the money. The fusion was an unlikely mixture. The Democratic party was dominated by the Milwaukee organization, funded and influenced by Alexander Mitchell. The "out-state" Democrats, a term in common use to identify party units outside Milwaukee, sought alliance with Liberal Republicans, unhappy agrarians, and anyone else who might help to pry loose the party control from Mitchell and his conservative Bourbon allies and ethnic ward bosses. But Mitchell, who worked both sides of the political street, was also intent upon the defeat of Governor Washburn, a resident of La Crosse, who had recently vetoed a heavily lobbied bill to permit the CM&StP to bridge the Mississippi just north of La Crosse. Another part of the alliance was an anti-Graham Law organization of Germans calling itself the American Constitutional Union, which the Republican Milwaukee *Sentinel* sarcastically characterized as "The mighty host of brewers, liquor dealers, turners, sharp-shooters, Catholic association leaders, free thinkers, free singers, free drinkers and free lovers of lager. . . ."[24]

---

[23] Cosmas, "Democracy in Search of Issues," *WMH*, 46:93–108; Current, *Civil War Era*, 586–589; Deutsch, "Disintegrating Forces in Wisconsin Politics," *WMH*, 15:170–172; Herman J. Deutsch, "Yankee-Teuton Rivalry in Wisconsin Politics of the Seventies," in *WMH*, 14 (March–June, 1931), 263.

[24] Cosmas, "Democracy in Search of Issues," *WMH*, 46:93–101. Alexander Mitchell was a Johnson Democrat, having left the Republican party with President Johnson and Wisconsin Senator James Doolittle. See *DWB*; Horace S. Merrill, *William Freeman Vilas: Doctrinaire Democrat* (Madison, 1954), 32–33; Western Historical Company, *History of La*

The fusionists hoped to shake a few grangers loose from their traditional Republican loyalties. Accordingly they nominated a prominent state Grange leader, William R. Taylor of Madison, for governor, and cautiously endorsed railroad reform—Mitchell was supplying the cash for reform—and repeal of the Graham Law. The Republicans made railroad regulation their central issue in the campaign. This was good politics, given their normal rural strength and Governor Washburn's record, but their legislative record suggested railroad domination. Taylor, with his Grange background, offset this new Republican enthusiasm. Curiously, Taylor was also a member of the Good Templars, a temperance organization, but the Reform-Democratic coalition was pledged to repeal of the Graham Law, which the Republicans would not repudiate.[25]

The "reform" coalition swept the field in the election of 1873, leaving the Republicans in control of only the senate, and that by a narrow margin of only one vote. Because attention upon this political upset subsequently centered upon the Potter Law, it became the received truth that 1873 was a great granger triumph. But what happened was that the rural Republican vote, presumably Grange members or sympathizers, stayed home rather than vote against their traditional party. Closer examination of returns shows that the rural vote was down nearly 41,000 from the returns of the 1872 election, and that the urban vote was down by fewer than 3,000—considerably less proportionately, given a rural-urban population ratio of four to one. It was not a presidential election year as 1872 had been, but it was plain that the urban vote had turned out, more exercised by liquor regulation than by animus against the railroads.[26]

---

Crosse County, Wisconsin (Chicago, 1881), 590–597. For background, see Herman J. Deutsch, "Political Forces in Wisconsin, 1871–1881" (doctoral dissertation, University of Wisconsin, 1926). This valuable dissertation is abstracted in a series of articles in Volumes 14 and 15 of the Wisconsin Magazine of History. The quote is from the Milwaukee Sentinel of August 7, 1873.

[25] Cosmas, "Democracy in Search of Issues," WMH, 46:99–100; Current, Civil War Era, 593–594.

[26] Deutsch, "Yankee-Teuton Rivalry in Wisconsin Politics," WMH, 14:277–278; Burton, "Wisconsin's First Railroad Commission," WMH, 45:192; Cosmas, "Democracy in

The Potter Law had almost as anomalous an origin as did the election victory for reform. The really continuous leadership for railroad regulation was from the Milwaukee business community, particularly some of the grain dealers. In 1871, Francis West, a commission merchant who had been leading the antimonopoly business forces, was elected president of the Milwaukee Chamber of Commerce. Dissatisfied with the timidity of legislators easily frightened by Mitchell, West ran successfully for the state assembly on the Reform ticket.

West's problem as a politician was that he lacked sound political moorings. He had joined the Liberal Republicans in 1872, but they had little organizational strength in the Reform-Democratic coalition. The Democrats, who furnished the basic party structure for the coalition, were claiming victory and the rewards. West, who should have been a legislative leader within the coalition on the basis of his record, went his own way with his own bills for the regulation of elevator and railroad charges, disgusted with others' trimming to Mitchell's pressure.[27]

The regular Republicans, better organized even in defeat, were in a position to embarrass the Reform coalition. They were determined to redeem their pledges for railroad regulation and to reclaim their errant rural vote. While Governor Taylor and his supporters had responded affirmatively to the election issue of railroad regulation, the Bourbon Democrats and particularly Alexander Mitchell were a restraining influence within the Reform coalition. The Republicans were well aware of the opposition's dilemma. The majority Republicans in the senate fixed upon the Potter Bill, introduced by one of their members, Robert L. D. Potter of Waushara County. It proposed a schedule of maximum rates below those rates which the railroads had posted the

---

Search of Issues," *WMH,* 46:101. Governor Washburn, somberly assessing his chances in a letter to Cyrus Woodman, bitterly concluded that the "combined powers of darkness, Whiskey, Beer, R. Roads & a sprinkling of Grangers, have been on my trail and are confident of my defeat." See Washburn to Woodman, November 4, 1873, in the Cyrus Woodman Papers. Also see Deutsch, "Disintegrating Forces in Wisconsin Politics," *WMH,* 15:294–295.

[27] Treleven, "Genesis of Antimonopolism in Milwaukee," *WMH,* 52:209–219; Cosmas, "Democracy in Search of Issues," *WMH,* 46:102.

previous September. A three-man commission was to gather and publish information on the railroads and have the power to lower but not to raise rates beyond those proposed.[28]

Potter's bill was only one among a jostling crowd from all quarters on the railroad question, but it had the advantage of support from an organized minority in the assembly and from the Republican majority in the senate. A conference committee had worked out a bill based upon the Illinois law of 1873. This was really a conservative approach which provided for a railroad commission with the power to set fair and equitable rates. After extensive maneuvering the Republican senate majority substituted the Potter Bill for the conference committee bill, pasted it over under the same number, and sent it to the assembly for concurrence. The coalition forces in the assembly had frittered away their chances to write a bill more to their liking, and because they had made a great campaign issue of economy, they feared the political effects of extending the session to get their own railroad bill. Thus it had come down to adopting the Republicans' Potter Bill or nothing on the railroad issue, and they could not fault the Potter Bill as too mild a measure. They concurred on the bill, and in March, 1874, Governor Taylor signed it.[29]

The Potter Law was not a satisfactory solution to the problem and deserved much of the criticism it subsequently received. The railroads were correct in claiming that rate making was a highly complicated business which could not be settled equitably for the railroads or the shippers on a simple pro-rata formula of a maximum allowable charge per mile for each class of freight. The Potter Law attempted to meet those objections partially by setting up

[28] Burton, "Wisconsin's First Railroad Commission," *WMH,* 45:193–194; Cosmas, "Democracy in Search of Issues," *WMH,* 46:103–104; Miller, *Railroads and the Granger Laws,* 157–159. As Cosmas points out (p. 103), the port cities enjoyed an advantage in railroad rates over interior points because of the competition of water transportation. The Bourbon strength of the Reform coalition was concentrated along the lakefront where Democratic (Reform coalition) strength was motivated more by opposition to the liquor control law (Graham Law) than by railroad rates. See the *Wisconsin Blue Book, 1875,* p. 240, which compares the gubernatorial votes of 1871 and 1873.

[29] Miller, *Railroads and the Granger Laws,* 156–159; Cosmas, "Democracy in Search of Issues," *WMH,* 46:103–104; Robert T. Daland, "Enactment of the Potter Law," in *WMH,* 33 (September, 1949), 45–54; Graham A. Cosmas, "The Reform Party of Wisconsin, 1873–1877" (master's thesis, University of Wisconsin, 1962), 99–100.

a higher schedule of rates for the minor railroads. As the chairman of the legislative joint select committee on railroad matters later wrote, none of the members had practical knowledge on the subject and the railroad lobbyists were careful not to offer any.[30]

The history of the Potter Law, which was repealed within two years, gave rise to the view that it was a misfired scheme between the railroad lobbyists and some sympathetic Republicans to press legislation so harsh that a majority would fearfully reject it and fail to agree upon a substitute. But there was a wide range of alternative bills available, several of which might have been approved. It seems more likely, on the basis of the evidence, that it was a bad year for railroad lobbyists. The Republicans had redeemed their pledge and could blame their opponents if the enforcement proved faulty. It was legislation whose time had come.[31]

As it turned out, the enforcement was faulty, the legislation was faulty, and the response of the railroads proved faulty. Armed with an advisory opinion from distinguished counsel that the Potter Law was clearly unconstitutional and would surely be struck down by the federal courts should the state courts fail to do so, Alexander Mitchell politely informed Governor Taylor that the CM&StP would not abide by the law. His main argument was that the mandatory rates would cut the railroad's earnings by 25 per cent, that this amount was well over the projected net income, and that to acquiesce in the mandated rates would destroy the company's credit. "I regret the necessity that compels the company to take this course," he explained to the governor, "but it is the only one left to preserve the property, and properly test the question raised by the act." The president of the C&NW similarly refused to comply. His letter was less assertive than Mitchell's, but both took the same course of action: defiance of the law.[32]

The railroads may have expected Governor Taylor to tempor-

---

[30] Frederick W. von Cotzhausen, *Historic Reminiscences and Reflections* (5 pts., [Milwaukee], 1906-1918), pt. 2, pp. 32-33; Hunt, *Law and Locomotives*, 101-103, 127-129.

[31] Hunt, *Law and Locomotives*, 53-54; Burton, "Wisconsin's First Railroad Commission," *WMH*, 45:194. Cotzhausen, *Reminiscences*, pt. 2, p. 33, writes: "Who was the real author of this bill, has always remained a profound secret." He goes on to suggest that Senator Potter, a lawyer, clearly had advice from someone familiar with the railroads.

[32] Wisconsin Railroad Commissioners, *Annual Report*, 1874, Executive and Legal Documents section, 1-6.

ize, or to find some formula for a quick test of the constitutionality
of the law without making a public issue of the refusal to comply.
There certainly was evidence in the governor's private and public
remarks that he was not enthusiastic about the Potter Law. To his
credit, Taylor responded to the issue of direct defiance of the law
rather than to the arguments supporting defiance. He maintained
stoutly that the railroads must obey the law and issued a call for
individual citizens to enforce the law vigorously by haling railroad
employees before a justice or circuit court to recover damages.
The real contest should have been between organizations of shippers and the railroads, but the issue there was seldom as clear-cut
as the complaint of a passenger put off a train. Freight rates came
in a great variety of classifications and circumstances. Also, the
urgency of either shipper or receiver usually dictated that the
freight be paid and the remedy pursued afterward. This could be
a touchy business if one needed service in the future. The Milwaukee commercial community shrank from a head-on confrontation with the major railroads. It was not a propitious time to
push the matter, because Milwaukee was losing more and more of
its grain trade to Chicago and the Twin Cities.[33]

There was no provision in the Potter Law for state executive
action to sue a railroad company directly for violation of the statutory rates, only for suit against the agent involved by the individual passenger or shipper. This was awkward, to say the least.
The railroads implemented their defiance in a calculated manner,
publishing a new set of rates which conceded something but still
were above the Potter Law rates. There followed a cat-and-mouse
game in which railroad employees exercised wide latitude. Passengers who insisted upon tendering the legal fare might carry the
day, or they might be put off the train short of their destinations.

[33] Deutsch, "Disintegrating Forces in Wisconsin Politics," *WMH*, 15:392–396; Treleven, "Genesis of Antimonopolism in Milwaukee," *WMH*, 52:220–221; Cosmas,
"Democracy in Search of Issues," *WMH*, 46:104; Hunt, *Law and Locomotives*, 102–103.
Wisconsin Railroad Commissioners, *Annual Report*, 1874, p. 94, remarks that wheat receipts
at Milwaukee for August 20 to November 10 shipping dates in 1873 and 1874 had dropped
from about 12 million to 6 million bushels.

Challenges to illegal freight rates were naturally less newsworthy. The railroads had the better of this game in the short run. The average difference between posted and Potter Law rates for passengers was nominal. It took more determination than most travelers possessed to take a railroad conductor into a local court for a contest with the railroad's legal staff. The satisfaction of winning such a contest could only be purchased at a cost which bore little relation to the award. And winning proved little except that justice presumably had been done in the single instance.[34]

The whole controversy took a new turn when it occurred to the state attorney general to enter *quo warranto* proceedings against the railroads, asking that their charters and privileges be revoked for defiance of the law. This was a line suggested earlier by Governor Washburn's administration. The railroads already had failed in attempts to get the federal courts to test the constitutionality of the Potter Law. The effect of the attorney general's action was to put the matter before the state supreme court, which circumvented the awkward remedies of the Potter Law. This was much more satisfactory to the public, who could not understand a procedure in which the state and the railroad commission helplessly stood by as spectators.[35]

The denouement is a familiar chapter in Wisconsin's legal history. The chief justice, Luther S. Dixon, resigned at this point for personal reasons, giving Governor Taylor the opportunity to appoint a successor. Taylor made sure of his man on the railroad question and appointed the brilliant but irascible Edward G. Ryan of Milwaukee. Ryan, who had long hoped for a judgeship, did not fail him. His opinion in *Attorney General v. the Railroad Companies*, pronounced in September, 1874, presently became a landmark decision upholding the right of the state to regulate railroads. The railroads did not contest further, but sought relief where Ryan had pointed them: in the legislature. Meanwhile, the roads continued

[34] Hunt, *Law and Locomotives*, 101–108; Burton, "Wisconsin's First Railroad Commission," *WMH*, 45:195–196; *Commercial and Financial Chronicle*, June 6, 1874.

[35] Hunt, *Law and Locomotives*, 107–108.

to make the law a burden on the public by curtailing services.[36]

The railroad commissioners appointed by Governor Taylor were active critics of the Potter Law. One of the three, George H. Paul, was editor of the Milwaukee *News,* a Democratic paper controlled by Alexander Mitchell. Paul also functioned as a principal advisor and wrote state papers for Taylor. John Wesley Hoyt, a Republican who had been secretary and manager of the Wisconsin State Agricultural Society, was about as close to being an expert on railroad matters as anyone, aside from railroad employees. The third commissioner was Joseph H. Osborn, former purchasing agent for the state Grange.[37]

Interest in enforcement of the Potter Law had faded rapidly by 1875. It had not solved much beyond the assertion of the state's authority to regulate the railroads should it choose to do so. This served the purposes of those who wished to abandon the experiment. Milwaukee feared the impact of the law upon the city's commerce and, indeed, its grain commerce was in decline. Grange membership, which had boomed in 1873–1874, went into a rapid decline in 1875. Alexander Mitchell won renewed local popularity in the summer of 1875 when he and his allies forced the Wall Street speculator, Russell Sage, from the vice-presidency and board of directors of the CM&StP, and then reconstituted the board so as to include four Wisconsin members. Finally, the railroads, aided by the financial stringency following the 1873 business panic, were winning converts to the belief that Wisconsin could not expect to attract investment in new lines in the face of the publicity given the Potter Law.[38]

---

[36] *John B. Winslow, The Story of a Great Court: Being a Sketch History of the Supreme Court of Wisconsin, Its Judges and Their Times from the Admission of the State to the Death of Chief Justice Ryan* (Chicago, 1912), 339–345; Alfons J. Beitzinger, *Edward G. Ryan: Lion of the Law* (Madison, 1960), 113–122; Hunt, *Law and Locomotives,* 108–126; Miller, *Railroads and the Granger Laws,* 114–115, 129, 134–138, 140–142, 156, 170, 175, 180.

[37] Wisconsin Railroad Commissioners, *Annual Report,* 1874, p. 93, comments: "Still, it cannot be denied that the law [Potter Law] is really obnoxious to just criticism, even if the objects aimed at are allowed to be in themselves desirable." See also Burton, "Wisconsin's First Railroad Commission," *WMH,* 45:194–195; Deutsch, "Disintegrating Forces in Wisconsin Politics," *WMH,* 15:392.

[38] Nordin, *Rich Harvest,* 29–40; Buck, *Granger Movement,* 192–193; Treleven, "Genesis

In 1875, Governor Taylor was defeated by the amiable Harrison Ludington, who as Republican mayor of Milwaukee had ignored enforcement of the locally unpopular Graham Law to control the liquor trade. Taylor lost narrowly while other state officers on the Democratic-Reform ticket won re-election. Not too openly, Mitchell supported Ludington. Ludington's victory was matched by a return to Republican control in the legislature. The Potter Law was soon replaced by the Vance Law of 1876, which reduced the railroad commission to a single commissioner who had only advisory powers and whose reports contained only whatever publicity and information value he could give them. Governors' messages and railroad commission reports subsequently reflect a benign complacency for some years. The railroads had been shown the strong arm of the state and remembered the lesson—for a term. Marvin Hughitt, who later rose to the presidency of the C&NW, wrote to Elisha Keyes in 1878: "We are on our good behaviour . . . and we hope that the good people of Wisconsin will recognize our good conduct and let us severely alone."[39]

The repeal of the Potter Law was not due solely to the success of the railroads in changing public opinion, or to the decline of the Grange and of organized militance. In justification of repeal, Governor Ludington emphasized the impact of the Potter Law upon the fiscal reputation of the state and its municipalities among prospective creditors, as well as curtailed railroad construction.

---

of Antimonopolism in Milwaukee," *WMH*, 52:220–221; *Commercial and Financial Chronicle*, June 19, 1875. Other sources on the panic years and on Wisconsin and Upper Midwest railroads are Van Oss, *American Railroads as Investments*, 39–41; Grodinsky, *Transcontinental Railway Strategy*, 122–147; *House Executive Documents*, 44 Cong., 2 sess., no. 46, pt. 2 (serial 1761), 180–182; Paul Sarnoff, *Russell Sage: The Money King* (New York, 1965), 271, 368. Sage was a large stockholder in the CM&StP because of his earlier control of the La Crosse and Milwaukee, absorbed by the former. The appearance of local directors on Mitchell's successful slate "was regarded by the general public as a concession to their views." Wisconsin Railroad Commissioner, *Annual Report*, 1878, pp. 345–347.

[39] Fred L. Holmes, ed., *Wisconsin: Stability, Progress, Beauty* (5 vols., Chicago, 1946), 1:157; Deutsch, "Disintegrating Forces in Wisconsin Politics," *WMH*, 15:409–411; Deutsch, "Yankee-Teuton Rivalry in Wisconsin Politics," *WMH*, 14:271–272; Cosmas, "Democracy in Search of Issues," *WMH*, 46:106.

The proof of this he found in the sharp decline in new railroad mileage. This was true enough, but equally true elsewhere because of the long depression beginning in 1873.[40]

The CM&StP survived the hardships of the Potter Law and the depression. It proved that it could bring one-third of gross earnings down to net and that less than two-thirds of net were required to service the funded debt. The C&NW was similarly strong. Both continued as investment-grade railroads.[41]

Wisconsin's other railroads did not ride through the storms of Potter Law and depression so buoyantly. D. M. Kelly, general manager of the Green Bay and Minnesota Rail Road Company, indulged in a philosophical exchange with Commissioner Hoyt on the impact of the Potter Law upon the newer, independent lines. Kelly emerges as one deserving of sympathy, but he also illustrates the misguided promoters of the time, a tribe infinitely more numerous than the Alexander Mitchells. With single-minded energy, Kelly and others linked Green Bay with the Mississippi. The city responded with its customary caution. The best indication that Green Bay was never a threat to Milwaukee was that the CM&StP ignored the GB&M as a competitor. The latter remained weak, often reorganized, but independent into the 1970's.[42]

Railroad building in northern Wisconsin came to a halt shortly

[40] *Wisconsin Public Documents,* 1874–1875, Governor's Message, vol. 1, pp. 9–12. Charles Francis Adams, Jr., chairman of the Massachusetts board of railroad commissioners, helped to make Wisconsin's Potter Law infamous among conservatives by branding it "the most ignorant, arbitrary, and wholly unjustifiable law to be found in the history of railroad legislation." See "The Granger Movement," in the *North American Review,* 120 (April, 1875), 416.

[41] Chicago, Milwaukee and St. Paul Railway Company, *Annual Report,* 1875, p. 8; Wisconsin Railroad Commissioners, *Annual Report,* 1874, pp. 22–32; *ibid., Annual Report,* 1875, pp. 20–24.

[42] Wisconsin Railroad Commissioners, *Annual Report,* 1875, Official Papers section, 293–300. The *Laws of Wisconsin,* 1874, pp. 599–601 (Potter Law), put the Green Bay and Minnesota, Wisconsin Central, and West Wisconsin railroads in Class B, allowing them only a slightly higher passenger rate but not on freight. Lee F. Pendergrass, "Businessmen and Politicians in the Urban Development of Green Bay, Wisconsin, 1866–1882" (master's thesis, University of Wisconsin, 1968), 4–6, 15–31, discusses the want of a unified community spirit of interest. Also see Ray Specht and Ellen Specht, *The Green Bay Route, Including the Green Bay and Western, Kewaunee, Green Bay and Western, La Crosse Branch, Stevens Point, Green Bay and Northern, Waupaca, Green Bay and Western, Iola and Northern, Ahnapee and Western*

after the 1873 financial panic, which was a useful coincidence for enemies of the Potter Law. But lumbering was expanding there. For the year ending in June, 1875, the Wisconsin Valley Railroad reported three-fourths of its total freight business was hauling lumber; the Wisconsin Central reported one-half. The railroads drew farming population as well as lumbermen and promoters of nascent cities and villages into what the historian Joseph Schafer designated the "New North," which, he felt, was limited in its development after 1870 by the rival attraction of fertile prairie land farther west.[43]

Railroad construction revived in the latter seventies as the depression eased. The importance of the business cycles is readily reflected in mileage built. The basic commodity in new construction was eastern and European capital. When investment and speculative interest revived in New York and Boston, capital looked for opportunities in western railroads which combined high interest rates, expansion possibilities, and federal land grants.

As the long depression lifted, the CM&StP, which had been looked upon by the market as a conservative, relatively small road whose securities were largely held by European capitalists, embarked upon an aggressive campaign of expansion. The president of the C&NW complained that the CM&StP seemed "to be building, buying and negotiating for almost every Road in the market." Soon the C&NW, the Chicago and Rock Island, and the Chicago and Burlington were locked in combat with the CM&StP and with one another. The world of finance, expressing dismay over this disorderly world, nevertheless ran the stock of the CM&StP up from 34 in 1879 to 128 in 1882. The stocks of her rivals also reflected their shifting fortunes in the game.[44]

---

(Railway and Locomotive Historical Society, *Bulletin,* no. 115, Boston, 1966), 10–26; Canuteson, "Railway Development of Northern Wisconsin," 204–207; Milwaukee *Journal,* December 11, 1977, in the Sunday "Business News Section."

[43] Wisconsin Railroad Commissioners, *Annual Report,* 1875, p. 10, and Official Papers section, 141, 151; Joseph Schafer, *A History of Agriculture in Wisconsin* (Madison, 1922), 137–139. County lines do not follow the physical boundaries between the agricultural area of the "New North" and what is generally know as "The Cutover."

[44] Adler, *British Investment in American Railways,* 136, 184–185; Albert Keep to M. L. Sykes, May 6, 1879, as quoted in Grodinsky, *Transcontinental Railway Strategy,* 128. Stock prices and rivalries are discussed in *ibid.,* 203, and Van Oss, *American Railroads as Investments,* 463–477.

The reasons for the burst of expansion were various. One was simply geography. As settlement moved westward, the railroads did not merely follow; they hurried on ahead. "We could better afford to take the risk of having some property on our hands which would not pay very much *directly,* than to take the chance of having the country occupied by our enemies," wrote the president of the Burlington in 1886. The territorial imperative was a highly developed reflex, but one difficult to define. "Each must have a line to every place where any competitor has a line." Minneapolis–St. Paul was one of these new competitive points. It had been the preserve of the CM&StP briefly. By the latter eighties, this rapidly growing center had become a great grain collection point which was served by six railroads connecting with Chicago. The CM&StP replied to these incursions by pressing southwest to Council Bluffs, Iowa, which lay opposite Omaha, the domain of its Chicago-based rivals. (Earlier sovereigns of the plains had been confined on reservations for making such sudden raids and warfare a way of life!)[45]

Railroad warfare was dependent upon a long supply line to the rear—where money was raised. Speculative capital ran to the weaker transcontinentals and the myriad local roads favorably located for inclusion in larger systems. The difference between speculation and investment was a fine distinction. The market's valuation of the CM&StP put it in an enviable position for buying up smaller lines or borrowing at favorable terms. The stock market also provided opportunities for tests of strength between powerful rivals. Railroading was not entirely concerned with laying tracks and running trains.[46]

In 1873, not more than one-fifth of the 3,750,000 acres in Wisconsin designated for railroad subsidies had been earned by accepted construction. The bulk of the St. Croix grant, to subsidize connections in northwestern Wisconsin with Lake Superior

[45] Charles E. Perkins to T. J. Potter, January 5, 1886, as quoted in Grodinsky, *Transcontinental Railway Strategy,* 272; *Railroad Gazette,* October 2, 1885, as quoted in *ibid.,* 278. See *ibid.,* 122–147, and *Senate Reports,* 49 Cong., 1 sess., no. 46 (serial 2356), 48–50, 375 (Cullom Report), for railroad rivalry in the early 1880's.

[46] Grodinsky, *Transcontinental Railway Strategy,* 122–147.

ports, continued to attract suitors. This reflects the accepted view that unearned grants did not revert for failure to meet the time limits imposed—the initial grant was made in 1856—but continued within the gift of the legislature in the absence of contrary congressional action. Congress seemed to confirm this in 1864 by enlarging the St. Croix and northeastern Wisconsin grants and by adding another which was eventually earned, in part, by the Wisconsin Central.[47]

The general assumption seems to have been that railroads would encourage settlement, and since such railroads would have to precede settlement, they required generous inducements to attract capital. Hence the 1864 increase in the grants to 6,400 acres per mile—ten sections chosen from each twenty-mile strip. The Northern Pacific grant, with its eastern terminus at the head of Lake Superior, was the westward linkage for these subsidies.[48]

Congressional assumptions did not deal with the one overwhelming attraction that drew capital to northern Wisconsin: the pineries. Agricultural settlement was to be minor in the granted areas for years to come. Meanwhile, not until 1872 was the portion of the St. Croix grant between Tomah and Hudson earned. It was 1883 and 1884 before the connection from Hudson to Bayfield and then Superior was made. The twenty-eight-year interval since the original grant saw a scramble for ownership of timberlands as stumpage rose in value.[49]

While pineland owners and lumbermen had reason to welcome railroads when they opened inaccessible timber to exploitation,

[47] Current, *Civil War Era*, 430–433; Merk, *Economic History*, 279–286; John B. Sanborn, *Congressional Grants of Land in Aid of Railroads* (University of Wisconsin, Bulletin no. 30, *Economics, Political Science and History Series*, vol. 2, no. 3, Madison, 1899), 85–92, 98–102; Paul W. Gates, *The Wisconsin Pine Lands of Cornell University: A Study in Land Policy and Absentee Ownership* (Ithaca, 1943; reprinted, Madison, 1965), 178–179; Canuteson, "Railway Development of Northern Wisconsin," 108–136.

[48] Sanborn, *Grants of Land in Aid of Railroads*, 14–18; Gates, *Wisconsin Pine Lands of Cornell University*, 179.

[49] Sanborn, *Grants of Land in Aid of Railroads*, 100–101; Gates, *Wisconsin Pine Lands of Cornell University*, 106, 242; James P. Kaysen, comp., *The Railroads of Wisconsin, 1827–1937* (Boston, 1937), 33; Current, *Pine Logs and Politics*, 104–106, 114–115, 121–125, 131–133.

provided improved marketing opportunities, or replaced lengthy tote roads and costly supply transport, their welcome was not unalloyed. Much valuable timberland lay near the driving streams that served as their transportation medium to the mill. Railroads carried with their charters the right of eminent domain through this timber, and they greatly increased the danger of fires. But the sorest point of all: leading lives of noisy financial desperation, the railroads mendaciously promoted local subsidies inimical to the lumber interests.

Timber owners found themselves sitting ducks in the game of railroad subsidies as played in northern Wisconsin. With little agricultural settlement, it was the timber owners and sawmill men whose real and tangible property was pledged to pay off the subsidies, which generally were in the form of municipal and county bond issues. Given a sparse population, much of it highly mobile in lumbering and railroad construction, the absentee timber owners were usually no match for the railroad promoters and their local supporters in turning out the vote. Prospective cities and villages, and most of the sawmill centers, courted railroad connections. In the event that a county subsidy did not receive a favorable vote, the action moved to Madison, where railroad lobbyists found friendly help. Not infrequently, a new county would be carved from the body of a recalcitrant one, followed by a favorable vote on a subsidy. This is part of the northern Wisconsin legacy of underpopulated counties.[50]

The St. Croix grant continued its amazingly tangled history. Closely allied with the West Wisconsin was the North Wisconsin, which succeeded to the portion of the St. Croix grant from Hudson to Lake Superior after a legislative battle with the CM&StP. The latter won the grant in the 1873 session, but the West Wis-

---

[50] Gates, *Wisconsin Pine Lands of Cornell University,* chaps. 8 and 9; J. Willard Hurst, *Law and Economic Growth: The Legal History of the Lumber Industry in Wisconsin, 1836-1915* (Cambridge, 1964), 270-281; James R. Donoghue, "The Local Government System of Wisconsin," in the *Wisconsin Blue Book, 1968,* pp. 90-96. Wisconsin had sixty-three counties in 1880, of which twenty-nine had populations under 16,000, eight under 5,000, and four less than 1,000. Those with populations under 5,000 were all located north of an east-west line between Marinette and New Richmond. See the *Wisconsin Blue Book, 1883,* pp. 366-367.

consin's friends in the legislature so loaded it with conditions that Mitchell spurned the prize and the West Wisconsin got it. Unfortunately for their immediate plans, this was the panic year of 1873 and the halcyon days for railroad construction were over for a term.[51]

The extended depression of the seventies was too much for the fragile West Wisconsin and North Wisconsin lines, which had little real money or railroad talent behind them. When the depression eased, the CM&StP emerged as the terror of its competitors. Most outraged by this development in northwestern Wisconsin was the C&NW, no longer closely allied with the Milwaukee-based company. William Vanderbilt, infinitely more cautious than his father, had recently become a controlling voice in the C&NW, and he did little to counter the CM&StP. This irritated a former C&NW director, Henry H. Porter, a Chicago steel magnate, who enlisted Wisconsin's Philetus Sawyer and others in the creation of the Chicago, St. Paul, Minneapolis and Omaha from the West Wisconsin, North Wisconsin, and two other derelict railroads. The Omaha, as it was known, attracted Sawyer because of the pinelands claimed from the St. Croix grant. As intended by Porter, the Omaha frightened the C&NW both by its ability to deliver lumber westward in competition with Chicago's dominant wholesalers and by the threat that it might complete its abortive line into Chicago. There was also danger of an alliance of the Omaha with either the CM&StP or the revived Northern Pacific, which was also looking for entry into Chicago. In 1882, the C&NW bought the Omaha. (Senator Sawyer, who was a director of Mitchell's bank, could get along with anyone who gave him what he wanted.)[52]

The CM&StP ventured into northern Wisconsin more cautiously than on its westward drive beyond the Mississippi. In 1880

---

[51] Gates, *Wisconsin Pine Lands of Cornell University,* 184–187; Merk, *Economic History,* 282–283; Canuteson, "Railway Development of Northern Wisconsin," 108–136. Speaking of the northern Wisconsin land grants, Frederick Merk observed (p. 280) that "the tardiness with which most of the beneficiaries of such subsidies fulfilled the obligations imposed upon them defeated the object for which they were given."

[52] Current, *Pine Logs and Politics,* 131–143; Grodinsky, *Transcontinental Railway Strategy,* 126–134.

it bought the so-called River Roads, running northward from Clinton, Iowa, to Minnesota, from the Burlington, after scandals involved with their construction split the Burlington management. These purchases reinforced the CM&StP's competitive position in the Chicago-to-Twin Cities scramble. It therefore could look with some equanimity upon the acquisition of the Omaha by the C&NW. The CM&StP tapped the Chippewa lumber region by acquiring the Chippewa Valley and Superior Railway, which by 1883 ran from Chippewa Falls to Wabasha, Minnesota. The Wisconsin Valley Railroad, which met the CM&StP's main line at Tomah, was started in 1873 to build northward along the Wisconsin River. Promoted by James F. Joy, a Detroit railroad figure intimately involved in the Burlington, the Valley line was bought by the CM&StP in 1880 and extended as far as Minocqua by 1892.[53]

The CM&StP shared in the ownership and promotion of the townsites at present-day Merrill and Tomahawk. As a sample of this type of opportunity, Tomahawk, in 1886–1887, was advertised as an ideal manufacturing site with great waterpower potential. Lots were vigorously promoted at auctions held in Milwaukee. Railroad insiders rewarded their own acumen by taking personal ownership in the boom company at Merrill which held the valuable waterpower privileges at Grandfather Falls. Such opportunities were, of course, limited in southern Wisconsin.[54]

[53] Richard C. Overton, *Burlington Route: A History of the Burlington Lines* (New York, 1965), 128–148; Cary, *Chicago, Milwaukee & St. Paul Railway Company,* 233–245. When Alexander Mitchell died in 1887, the CM&StP system operated 5,669 miles of railroad, of which about 1,500 were within Wisconsin. The company had meanwhile organized, absorbed, or leased some thirty-seven separate companies in Wisconsin which were involved in the completion of this mileage. See Raney, "Building of Wisconsin Railroads," *WMH,* 19:393–394; Kaysen, comp., *Railroads of Wisconsin,* 20–32.

[54] Cary, *Chicago, Milwaukee & St. Paul Railway Company,* 283; George O. Jones et al., comps., *History of Lincoln, Oneida and Vilas Counties, Wisconsin* (Minneapolis, 1924), 38; Letitia H. McQuillan, "The Industrial and Social Development of Merrill, Wisconsin" (bachelor's thesis, University of Wisconsin, 1914), 7–9. The annual reports of the CM&StP between 1886 and 1896 were examined for any mention of the Tomahawk and Merrill boom companies as "paying investment[s] to the stockholders," in Cary's language. The ordinary stockholder certainly had no way of knowing that he shared in this investment, although he could discover the cost of a crossing gate in any village along the right-of-way.

The Wisconsin Central was another railroad brought into existence to acquire a generous federal land grant. The local promoters looked to Boston for the necessary capital and found it with Gardner Colby, who had made a fortune in textiles during the late war. Colby sent his son, Charles, and Elijah B. Phillips, supposedly a practical railroad man, to manage the interests of the easterners putting up the money. It was not long before the Wisconsin promoters were frozen out.

The transition from a local promotion to control by outsiders was a common pattern. The local promoters had successfully solicited the usual generous municipal bond issues in exchange for stock in the railroad—$553,000 according to the first annual report of Wisconsin's railroad commissioners. Subsidies, donations of rights-of-way, and having grading done preparatory to laying rails were common practices of the time, hoping for outside money to provide the expensive railroad iron and equipment. Colby and Phillips arrived on the scene in 1871 and proved a bit too peremptory for the neighbors who had put the promotion together. The locals, at first embarrassed, soon found themselves without any effective voice in the railroad's affairs.[55]

The Colbys created the Phillips and Colby Construction Company, with an initial capital of $200,000. The controlling officers of the construction company also controlled the railroad. It was the familiar device of the "inside" construction company, with the officers of the railroad making contracts with themselves as the construction company. Following the usual pattern, the construction company subcontracted the actual work. They made an arrangement whereby the construction company should provide the entire line for $35,000 in stock and $25,000 in bonds of the railroad for each mile constructed. The railroad commissioners reported that in 1873 the average real cost of the state's railroads was $34,221 per mile. This figure included the first-class lines, while the Wisconsin Central was a slapdash affair over much of its mileage. The bonds and preferred stock were marketed, mostly in

[55] Roy L. Martin, *History of the Wisconsin Central* (Railway and Locomotive Historical Society, *Bulletin,* no. 54, Boston, 1941), 1–13; Wisconsin Railroad Commissioners, *Annual Report,* 1874, p. 36; Merk, *Economic History,* 244.

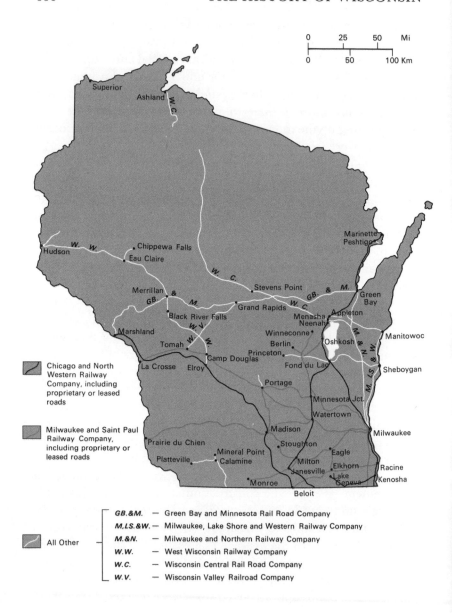

RAILROADS IN WISCONSIN, 1873

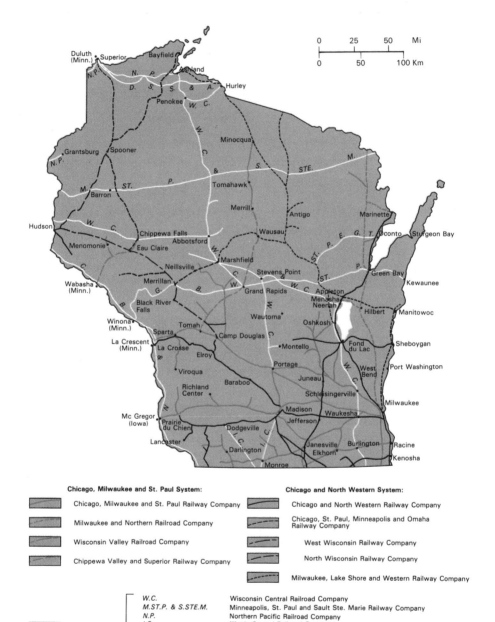

Chicago, Milwaukee and St. Paul System:

Chicago, Milwaukee and St. Paul Railway Company

Milwaukee and Northern Railroad Company

Wisconsin Valley Railroad Company

Chippewa Valley and Superior Railway Company

Chicago and North Western System:

Chicago and North Western Railway Company

Chicago, St. Paul, Minneapolis and Omaha Railway Company

West Wisconsin Railway Company

North Wisconsin Railway Company

Milwaukee, Lake Shore and Western Railway Company

| | |
|---|---|
| W.C. | Wisconsin Central Railroad Company |
| M.ST.P. & S.STE.M. | Minneapolis, St. Paul and Sault Ste. Marie Railway Company |
| N.P. | Northern Pacific Railroad Company |
| I.C. | Illinois Central Railroad Company |
| C.B. & N. | Chicago, Burlington and Northern Railroad Company |
| G.B.W. & ST.P. | Green Bay, Winona and St. Paul Railroad Company |
| D.S.S. & A. | Duluth, South Shore and Atlantic Railway Company |
| ST.P.E.G.T. | St. Paul Eastern Grand Trunk Railway Company |

**All Other**

RAILROADS IN WISCONSIN, 1893

Boston. The floor under these securities was not the railroad and
its prospects, but the federal land grant estimated to be worth $8
million.[56]

Very few things worked out well for the Wisconsin Central. The
land grant kept shrinking. It had been estimated originally at
2,387,000 acres. In 1870 Colby requested an examination by the
General Land Office of the acreage remaining in the reservation
and was given the figure 1,357,000 acres; but this too proved to
be optimistic. The railroad's agents found only 800,000 acres
reserved on the local land office books for the grant. The secretary
of the interior cut this further by a ruling in 1877 to about 600,000
acres.[57]

The credit of the Wisconsin Central suffered a similar decline.
Elijah Phillips apparently was not a competent manager of large
affairs, and Charles Colby had no compensating talent. The first
sixty-three miles, from Menasha to Stevens Point, were built with
dispatch and opened to traffic in November, 1871. One can imagine the problems of maintaining an army of 2,000 men, 600
horses, and 200 oxen engaged in clearing and grading. Bridges,
culverts, and trestles also had to be built before the railroad iron
could go down. But the real challenge lay in the 187 miles of wild
country that stretched between Stevens Point and Ashland on
Lake Superior.

Railroad construction was a contest with the weather, the
financial market, the terrain, the logistics of supply and of maintaining a labor force, and a thousand other distractions. Much
money had been spend attacking the wilderness from both Stevens Point and Ashland, and the managers of the Wisconsin Central had behaved somewhat like the military commander who
splits his forces in the face of a superior foe. Even before the collapse of the financial market in 1873, the line was in trouble.

Ashland had a population of five when the railroad surveyors

[56] Martin, *Wisconsin Central,* 1–17, 32, 34; Wisconsin Railroad Commissioners, *Annual
Report,* 1874, pp. 51–61, and Official Papers section, 72; Canuteson, "Railway Development of Northern Wisconsin," 158–160.

[57] Wisconsin Central Railroad Company, *Annual Report,* 1878, pp. 6, 12; Wisconsin
Railroad Commissioner, *Annual Report,* 1878, pp. 383–384.

arrived. It was transformed into a boom town by the sudden influx of lumbermen, laborers, and the footloose. Over 200 buildings were built between March and November of 1872, in addition to the bustle of 1,000 to 1,300 men working on the railroad grade running south. These first thirty miles of road reached Penokee Gap through the Penokee Range, where iron mines were later developed. This bobtail line was served by way of the lakes from Ashland, requiring new docks and other facilities. The Colbys also reared a sprawling, 400-room wooden hotel, the Chequamegon, planned as one of a chain of tourist attractions along the railroad.

The boom was brief at Ashland. Work on the railroad was abruptly shut down in December, 1872, while rumors flew and everyone hoped that it was only the usual winter layoff. The pause stretched into 1873, when the financial panic assured a longer hiatus. Construction did continue on the line running north out of Stevens Point. Another fifty miles were added there during 1873, to make a total of 101 miles, but a gap of about fifty-six miles remained which had to cross some of the worst terrain in the northern highlands. Early in 1874 the subcontractors, unhappy with Phillips and Colby, left the job which Phillips failed in his efforts to complete. The gap was not closed for three and a half years. It was 1876 before enough money could be found to resume the work, which was completed the following year.[58]

It was a curious sort of depression for the unfinished railroad. Despite the fifty-six-mile gap in the northern wilderness and the unsettled character of the country, the road had more business than its limited equipment and frail line could handle. Sawmills sprang up like mushrooms beside the tracks, and a passenger train which ran each day to the end of the line from the south was alleged to be insufficient to carry the traffic. Nor did Ashland lie down and die. The lumber business grew on the pigtail line to Penokee Gap and there was activity in the iron deposits of the Penokee. To the south, the Wisconsin Central operated into Milwaukee over the line of the Milwaukee & Northern and by way of

[58] Martin, *Wisconsin Central*, 14–28, 30–31, 40–41.

the CM&StP, into the city. Business was encouraging, but it was necessarily local in character.[59]

An uncompleted railroad is the proverbial bear by the tail: once release your hold and all is lost. In the case of the Wisconsin Central, to leave the line incomplete jeopardized the federal land grant. To adopt a common expedient—confessing judgement (bankruptcy) and reorganization under nominally new ownership—would risk the loss of the tax-free status of the granted lands as provided in the grant and subsequent extensions. The eastern financial angels were forced to hang on willy-nilly. Somehow they found the funds, and despite the hard times the gap was closed in 1876–1877. After years of financial travail, they had a railroad running from Menasha to Ashland. But if they wanted something more than an overcapitalized logging and lumber railroad, they had to connect to more important points than those defined in the land grant. They were unable to maintain their lease on the Milwaukee and Northern, which was absorbed in 1890 by the CM&StP. The CM&StP, however, accommodated Wisconsin Central trains into Milwaukee and attached its cars to CM&StP trains to Chicago.[60]

One option was to head westward towards St. Paul–Minneapolis, encouraged by friendly overtures from the Northern Pacific which was looking for a route southward independent of stronger competitors. The Wisconsin Central incorporated a new subsidiary, the Wisconsin and Minnesota, which built westward from present Abbotsford, which lies in Clark County due west of Wausau, to Chippewa Falls. It completed the line in November, 1880, when it connected with the Chippewa Falls and Western. This gave the Wisconsin Central connections for marketing lumber from its territory to the western plains. It also aroused unfriendly sentiments on the part of the CM&StP and C&NW, not only for

[59] *Ibid.*, 26–29, 37–38; Snyder, Van Vechten and Co., *Historical Atlas of Wisconsin* . . . (Milwaukee, 1878), 189.

[60] Martin, *Wisconsin Central*, 37–38, 43–44, 47–48, 54; Wisconsin Railroad Commissioner, *Annual Report*, 1878, pp. 379–384; Cary, *Chicago, Milwaukee & St. Paul Railway Company*, 270–279; Arthur Borak, "The Financial History of the Chicago, Milwaukee & St. Paul Railway Company" (doctoral dissertation, University of Minnesota, 1929), 63.

entering territory served by them, but for a possible alliance of the Wisconsin Central and the Northern Pacific, which was indeed formalized in 1886. The CM&StP refused to handle traffic originating at competitive points over the entry which it afforded to the Wisconsin Central into Milwaukee, threatening to cut off that access. Evidently the Wisconsin Central sought a separate entry into Milwaukee and Chicago; the right-of-way was secured in 1881 from Neenah to present Slinger (formerly Schleisingerville) for this purpose. Frustrated by litigation over its contract with the CM&StP and that company's grip on Milwaukee terminal facilities, the Central set off for Chicago through Waukesha and Burlington, Wisconsin, to Antioch, Illinois, where it joined the line building from Chicago. This was done in a surprisingly short time during 1885 and early 1886, but arrangements for reaching its terminus took some months longer. This new construction, the need to improve the hastily built early mileage up north, and financing the entry into Chicago left the Central badly in need of a new infusion of capital.[61]

It was remarkable that the Colby group retained its hold upon the management of the Wisconsin Central through all these years of towering expenditures. This was a tribute to their fortunes, their determination, and probably to their financial skills, rather than to their talents as railroad men. They did find a competent manager to replace Elijah Phillips in Frederick Norton Finney. The various properties were reorganized as the Wisconsin Central Company in 1887, with Charles Colby, Edwin H. Abbot, and Colgate Hoyt holding all of the stock as trustees for the allied investors.

An influential outside connection came shortly after the reorganization, through the agency of Henry Villard of New York, who was a close friend of the Colbys. Villard, a bold financier of a most optimistic temper, returned to the board of the Northern Pacific in 1887, where he was joined by Colby, Abbot, and Hoyt of the Wisconsin Central. The Northern Pacific, with terminals at

---

[61] Martin, *Wisconsin Central*, 49–50, 52–53, 55–56, 58–68; Grodinsky, *Transcontinental Railway Strategy*, 286, 316; Kaysen, comp., *Railroads of Wisconsin*, 64–68.

Duluth, Superior, and Ashland, intended the Wisconsin Central, which it later leased in 1890, as its entry to Chicago. The generous contract to pay for the Central's terminal facilities there was often cited as one of Villard's ill-advised arrangements that in 1893 forced the Northern Pacific again into bankruptcy. The Wisconsin Central Company toppled with it, to become part of the "Soo Line" sixteen years later.[62]

The Minneapolis, St. Paul and Sault Ste. Marie Railway (Soo) was built across northern Wisconsin in the mid-eighties. It was a Minneapolis promotion using existing lines and new construction to create a direct west-to-east line from the northern wheat plains, paralleling the water route out of Duluth. Given the winter closure of the water route for five months of the year, the advantages in distance of this line over railroads running through Chicago, or to water at Milwaukee, are clear. A further advantage was that it operated in conjunction with Canadian railroads to reach Atlantic ports. This confounded regulation of rates by the Interstate Commerce Commission. The Soo came under the financial control of the Canadian Pacific in 1888, the year after the adoption of the federal interstate commerce law creating the commission.[63]

The Milwaukee, Lake Shore and Western, begun under other corporate names in the seventies, ran from Milwaukee northward through Sheboygan and Manitowoc, reaching Wausau in 1880. The principal promoter was F.W. Rhinelander of New York, whose name is memorialized by the only city in Oneida County. The road, always closely allied with the C&NW, developed feeders running into the northeastern part of Wisconsin. In 1893 it became part of the C&NW. The Milwaukee and Northern had a similar history. Promoted by Milwaukee men in 1870, it reached Menasha and Green Bay by 1873 and was operated until 1880 by the Wisconsin Central. The management of the Milwaukee and

[62] Martin, *Wisconsin Central*, 49, 63–66, 71, 80–82, 117; Canuteson, "Railway Development of Northern Wisconsin," 180–196; Grodinsky, *Transcontinental Railway Strategy*, 376–377, 403–410; Stuart Daggett, *Railway Reorganization* (Cambridge, 1908; reprinted, New York, 1967), 270–291.

[63] Albro Martin, *James J. Hill and the Opening of the Northwest* (New York, 1976), 246–247, 285–289, 384, 475; Grodinsky, *Transcontinental Railway Strategy*, 398.

Northern was allied with the CM&StP, which absorbed the local line in 1893.[64]

The Burlington and Northern was built in the middle eighties to give the Chicago, Burlington and Quincy (CB&Q) an efficient entry to the heavy Twin Cities traffic between there and Chicago. It paralleled the Mississippi River on the Wisconsin shore. The line carried little traffic originating in Wisconsin. Its rate reports served to point up the continuing Wisconsin grievance: the regional railroads connected points west of Wisconsin to Chicago and Milwaukee at rates substantially below charges from interior Wisconsin points. This was what the long-short haul controversy was all about.[65]

Wisconsin's additions of railroad mileage, as elsewhere, followed a pattern of feast or famine which corresponded to the optimism or pessimism of financial centers with regard to western railroads. Mileage nearly doubled between 1870 and 1873, picked up again in the years 1879 to 1884, and increased over 1,500 miles between 1885 and 1893, after a brief hiatus caused by the 1882–1883 recession.[66]

It is difficult to find information on the recruiting of labor for what was surely one of the major sources of employment in the period. The Wisconsin Immigration Commission, for instance, which widely distributed its booklets in several languages, generally made little or no mention of railroad construction work. The emphasis was upon farming, farm work, and urban job opportunities. The lumber industry was often noted as a source of winter employment for agricultural settlers in northern Wisconsin. Chicago was the center of labor recruiting for railroad construction. The retention of a cadre of men who understood the logistics and techniques was more vital than the problem of gathering sufficient

[64] Kaysen, comp., *Railroads of Wisconsin,* 16–17, 29–31; Cary, *Chicago, Milwaukee & St. Paul Railway Company,* 270–271; Stennett, *Yesterday and Today,* 104–108; Norma M. Huber, "History of Rhinelander" (bachelor's thesis, University of Wisconsin, 1920), 2.

[65] Martin, *Hill and the Northwest,* 324; Grodinsky, *Transcontinental Railway Strategy,* 320–349; William Z. Ripley, *Railroads: Rates and Regulations* (New York, 1912; reprinted, 1973), 452–453, 474–484.

[66] *Wisconsin Blue Book, 1905,* p. 1004.

hands. The C&NW solved this by maintaining a construction department. A more common solution was to depend upon railroad contractors who had their own organizations of key men. Just as today, these contracting firms were highly mobile outfits that not uncommonly came from hundreds of miles away. If the key men were at hand, a sufficient work force could be assembled through employment agencies and from the pinery, where employment normally slumped after the spring drive.[67]

Railroad men were a mobile labor force. It was common for those in managerial positions to move around the country from one line to another, as they made their way up through a recognized series of ranks. The organization within each company was almost military in its ordering and in the deference paid those at the top of the operations hierarchy. Being a train conductor or a locomotive engineer was considered a glamorous occupation, although the glamor was not always apparent between stations. Railroading remained a hazardous occupation, and neither commissioners nor courts exhibited much imagination in alleviating working conditions or discovering remedies for the dangers and hardships involved.[68]

Technologically, railroading changed rapidly between the 1870's and 1890's. There was room for individuality still in the 1870's, and it was common for an engine to bear a name as well as a number. Engines were usually assigned to a particular locomotive engineer and his crew who frequently added personal touches such as the engineer's own whistle and cord. The Wisconsin Central, through the seventies, was ordering wood burners with diamond stacks, weighing thirty-five tons. By the early

[67] See the annual and biennial reports of the commissioner (and later the board) of immigration for Wisconsin, 1871 to 1900, and the booklets in English and other languages bound with them in the library holdings of the SHSW. See also Martin, *Wisconsin Central,* 14–15, 23–24, 30; and the Joseph T. Dodge Papers. Dodge was chief of construction on a number of western railroads in Wisconsin, Iowa, and Minnesota during the years of this study.

[68] Martin's *Wisconsin Central* is an excellent railroad biography that contains much of interest about the physical facts of railroading in the period. Also see Hunt, *Law and Locomotives,* 151–157; and J. L. Ringwalt, *Development of Transportation Systems in the United States* (Philadelphia, 1888; reprinted, New York, 1966), 361–376.

eighties, locomotives had greatly increased in weight, power, and efficiency and were fired with coal. Locomotives built in the 1890's were still doing mainline duty in the 1920's. Except on a logging spur, a locomotive from the era of the 1870's was soon an antique. Fifteen miles per hour was the limit for freight trains on many lines in the seventies, twenty-five for passenger runs. Speeds of forty to fifty miles per hour were a commonplace by the mid-eighties. The difference was in a new generation of heavier engines, carrying higher steam pressures, usually built for more specialized service, and running over lines that had been converted from fifty-six-pound iron rails to steel rails ranging from seventy-two to eighty-five pounds per foot. Roadbeds and bridges had been reworked to carry the heavier trains at higher speeds. These changes remind us that increasing rail mileage was only one measure of the railroads' growing capacity to move freight and passengers.[69]

By the 1880's agitation for a return to more stringent rate regulation was muted. In 1886 Milwaukee traders did argue that Milwaukee deserved a lower rate than Chicago on northwestern grain on the basis of lesser mileage. The railroad managers bent a little, but not much, and included a lesson in rate making. They pointed out that Milwaukee enjoyed equality of rates with Chicago on grain going east. To alter the balance from the west would raise the issue with Chicago of equitable rates eastward: "They stated to your committee that establishing rates of freight to and from the different sections of the country was a very difficult and complicated problem to solve, but that in all cases they had endeavored by all means in their power to deal justly with the different localities along the various lines of their roads, and to avoid discriminating against such localities. . . . That they had fully considered the capital invested and the business interests of all these localities when making rates. . . . That they had found it an

[69] Martin, *Wisconsin Central,* 150–168; Kent T. Healy, "Development of a National Transportation System," in Harold F. Williamson, ed., *The Growth of the American Economy* (New York, 1951), 367–370; Wisconsin Railroad Commissioners, *Annual Report,* 1874, Railroad Statistics section, 76–77; *ibid.,* 1887–1888, xxxiv–xxxv; Ringwalt, *Development of Transportation Systems,* 295–299, 316–336; Kirkland, *Industry Comes of Age,* 47–51.

impossibility for them to establish a system of rates based on a scale of distances."[70]

What the railroad managers were telling the Milwaukee businessmen was that rates had been adjusted to the competitive pressures of all concerned, as well as to the growth of the territory concerned. They reminded Milwaukeeans that their city enjoyed the advantage of very low rates westward on coal and thereby had a "very large and prosperous coal trade . . . which when its immense capital and its employment of labor is considered, stands unrivaled in the West." In other words, it had devolved upon the railroad managers to determine by their rate structures what economic activities should receive positive encouragement. With its supremely advantageous geographic position and consequent greater economic power, Chicago could exert more pressure than could Milwaukee in making these determinations. Milwaukee had to exploit to the fullest her position on the lakes to maintain her commerce. She was caught between Chicago and the Lake Superior ports when competing for the grain trade, and between Chicago and the Twin Cities when competing for wholesale trade westward. The railroads determined where she could compete advantageously.[71]

The railroads were able to tamper with geography. The pressures from Chicago lumber wholesalers, carrier competition, and the search for bulk commodities to ship westward to balance the heavy eastward flow of grain had the effect of erasing the advantage of such lumber-producing points as La Crosse and Eau Claire, which were closer to many western markets. Differential rates favoring Chicago lumber were a source of irritation to western Wisconsin lumbermen. These differentials grew, and in 1884 they were formalized in a railroad pool agreement among the

[70] Vol. 12, Minutes of Board of Directors Meetings, 1877–1887, January 11, 1886, in the Milwaukee Grain Exchange Collection.

[71] W. J. Anderson and Julius Bleyer, eds., *Milwaukee's Great Industries: A Compilation of Facts Concerning Milwaukee's Commercial and Manufacturing Enterprises, Its Trade and Commerce, and the Advantages It Offers to Manufacturers Seeking Desirable Locations for New or Established Industries* (Milwaukee, 1892), 130. Milwaukee's coal receipts grew from less than 100,000 tons in 1870 to an 1890 total in excess of 1,000,000 tons.

major roads. Such inequities soon became the cake of custom, and efforts to overturn them excited successful reactions from Chicago in particular.[72]

The creation of the federal Interstate Commerce Commission in 1887 eased further agitation for state legislative action. Wisconsin's railroad commissioner estimated in 1888 that fully 80 to 90 per cent of railroad freight traffic carried in Wisconsin was interstate in origin or destination and therefore not subject to state regulation. Of the remainder, an undetermined amount was carried at terminal or commodity rates, indicating competition. Rates on in-state carriage that were noncompetitive showed a general decrease between 1872 and 1887 of only 10 per cent, however, compared to an average 60 per cent reduction of through (interstate) rates. Wisconsin intrastate rates were alleged to be an average 27.5 per cent above comparable Illinois rates.[73]

There is little evidence that Milwaukee manufacturers complained about their rates in comparison with rates out of Chicago. Most complaints on this score originated with intermediate points in Wisconsin that found themselves paying higher rates than terminal points such as Minneapolis–St. Paul on articles shipped from the east, or from Chicago or Milwaukee. This dissatisfaction was not unique to Wisconsin cities. The effects of water competition and terminal rates placed much of interior Wisconsin at a competitive disadvantage and accelerated the concentration of population and industry at the favored locations. The tendency of the ICC was to confirm these inequities as justified.[74]

There is a sense of disappointment that Wisconsin had learned so little about applying the lessons of 1851–1867, when the pioneer

[72] Robert F. Fries, *Empire in Pine: The Story of Lumbering in Wisconsin, 1830–1900* (Madison, 1951), 93–99.

[73] Wisconsin Railroad Commissioner, *Biennial Report,* 1888, xxxviii; E. P. Bacon, comp., "Comparative Rates on Freight between Milwaukee and Points in Wisconsin, as per Tariff of CM&StP RW, June 15, 1872 and February, 1887," a printed document, undated, found attached to the back of vol. 12, Minutes of the Board of Directors Meetings, August, 1877, to August, 1887, in the Milwaukee Grain Exchange Collection. One must remember that advances in railroad technology and the general deflation following 1873 were active ingredients in the decline of rates.

[74] Wisconsin Railroad Commissioner, *Biennial Report,* 1886, ix–xiii.

railroads were built, went bankrupt, and were reorganized by financiers like Alexander Mitchell. They repeated the whole experience in northern Wisconsin a generation later. One wonders, at least, what the consequences would have been had northern Wisconsin waited for the CM&StP and the C&NW, or other strong regional companies, to seize the opportunities that were there. The results might have been a little more systematic, only a bit later, and undoubtedly much cheaper. It remains a puzzle that so little Milwaukee money was involved in the development of Superior, Ashland, and Bayfield. They were potential rivals, of course, but they also represented opportunities; their subsequent histories, however, might be taken as evidence of excellent judgment on the part of Milwaukee financiers. No matter who directed the building of the northern Wisconsin railroads, the problems that flowed from the creation of the cutover and the misplaced population there would not have been avoided. The railroads were a legacy of the exuberant meeting of available technologies and opportunities which Americans have always accepted as inevitable, necessary, and good.

* * *

The post-Civil War generation in Wisconsin, although certainly enamored of railroads, retained a keen appreciation of water transportation and its possibilities. A great many Wisconsinites had come earlier by way of the Great Lakes, most often from Buffalo, and had generally reached there by river and canal. Parallel rail transportation had been possible since the mid-fifties, but conveniently only since the war. A loyal Milwaukeean would readily point out to visitors that the great advantage of his city over its arch-rival, Chicago, was its superior harbor and a position some eighty-five miles closer by water to the ports of Lake Erie.

It was just as well to look on the cheerful side. Water carriage was cheaper, but it had its drawbacks. There was the long sweep around the lower peninsula of Michigan that made the journey considerably longer than by land. Shallows in the passage between

View of Fountain City (Buffalo County), c. 1885.

Municipal officials in front of the fire house, Fountain City, c. 1888.

Sauk Road and Pheasant Branch crossing, Middleton (Dane County), c. 1873.

Chicago, Milwaukee & St. Paul depot, Kilbourn City, c. 1880.

Ogema (Price County), c. 1890.

Bonnie Mine boardinghouse, Hurley (Iron County), c. 1890.

Main Street, De Forest (Dane County), c. 1875.

Near Sherry (Wood County), 1895.

A pair of Dane County farms, photographed about 1875.

Drugstore, Main Street, Oshkosh, 1894.

The fruits of gardening in the Cutover, near Marinette, 1895.

Elementary school, Kilbourn City (Columbia County), c. 1880.

Business district, Merrimac (Sauk County), c. 1890.

Loggers retrieving stranded logs from a sandbar at Alma
(Buffalo County), c. 1890.

Making silage near Waupaca, 1895.

Electric streetcar, Eau Claire, c. 1890.

lakes Huron and Erie limited the draught of vessels using the route. Violent weather, navigational hazards, and narrow or shallow seas were a constant danger to both sailing ships and underpowered steamers. Then winter closed navigation on the lakes for a third or more of the year, although Lake Michigan was an exception to this, at least on the Wisconsin side, because the prevailing winds piled most of the ice on the Michigan side. But it was the mid-nineties before Milwaukee solved the competitive advantage offered by winter navigation across Lake Michigan with car ferries. Prior to the development of the car ferries, vessels had to be loaded and unloaded from and into railroad cars.[75]

By 1873 the shift in the grain trade was already being felt, particularly in terms of the rise of Duluth–Superior as an alternative milling and shipping point. Milwaukee did a lot of bragging during the latter 1860's about her unassailable position as the primary wheat market, but by 1870–1874 Chicago was ahead again. By the early 1890's Milwaukee's shipments were only about one-seventh those of twenty years earlier. Chicago had shipments averaging about twice those of the early 1870's. Wheat and flour shipments through both cities reflected the rise of Minneapolis as the country's primary wheat market and milling center.[76]

The emphasis upon the grain trade tended to obscure the more vital role of the lakes in giving Wisconsin's port cities a rough equality of industrial opportunity with respect to other cities located closer to the basic resources. More and more, Lake Superior iron ore was carried to the coal fields, which meant the Lake Erie ports. But the economics of carriage on the lakes was such that eastbound freight was always well in excess of westbound, hence favorable rates on coal, pig iron, and steel from Lake Erie to Lake Michigan ports. It was this that made possible the growing pattern of Wisconsin industry with its emphasis on heavy

---

[75] *House Documents,* 55 Cong., 2 sess., no. 277 (serial 3679), 42; U.S. Commissioner of Corporations, *Transportation by Water in the United States* (4 vols., Washington, 1909–1913), 1:25–27; 2:163, 165, 168.

[76] *Ibid.,* 2:162–174; Milwaukee Chamber of Commerce, *Annual Reports of the Trade and Commerce of Milwaukee,* fifteenth through thirty-sixth, 1872–1893; Bayrd Still, *Milwaukee: The History of a City* (Madison, 1948; reprinted, 1965), 325–329.

machinery and metalworking. By the mid-nineties, coal was delivered from Lake Erie ports to Duluth–Superior for as little as twenty cents per ton and only slightly more to Milwaukee. Coal made up three-fourths or more of westward freight by then.[77]

Lake Michigan was also vital to the growth of Wisconsin's lumber industry. As the railroads penetrated the pineries in western Wisconsin, the cheap water carriage from Marinette and other milling centers on Lake Michigan and Green Bay had much to do with setting rail rates. Chicago was the unchallenged lumber wholesaling market for Michigan and Wisconsin lumber. But the St. Croix, the Chippewa, and other driving and rafting rivers in northwestern Wisconsin carried logs and lumber to the Mississippi, which was their highway to market. If Chicago hoped to command any of this lumber, the railroads had to meet the competition. In the 1870's and 1880's, Chicago got 85 per cent or more of its pine lumber by way of the lake. By 1893, as the lakeshore timber neared exhaustion and the city drew supplies from farther afield, and as the railroads become more competitive, Chicago's lumber market was served by waterborne and rail carriage at a ratio of about three to two.[78]

As the Twin Cities emerged as a primary wheat-handling and flour-milling center, the battle for the carriage of this trade was between Lake Superior and Lake Michigan as well as between rival railroad connections. In the early 1870's, Duluth–Superior simply lacked competitive handling facilities. These followed upon the completion in 1881 of larger locks at Sault Ste. Marie. The subsequent exploitation of the Vermilion and Mesabi iron ranges in Minnesota assured further development at Duluth–Superior. The completion of the Soo railroad in 1887 created an alternate rail route many miles shorter than going around the lower end of Lake Michigan. As noted earlier, shipments of wheat from Mil-

---

[77] *House Documents,* 55 Cong., 2 sess., no. 277 (serial 3679), 80–93; Kirkland, *Industry Comes of Age,* 200; also see Chapter 4 below. Rates were not fixed for water carriage, and fluctuated competitively.

[78] *House Documents,* 55 Cong., 2 sess., no. 277 (serial 3679), 94–101; U.S. Commissioner of Corporations, *Transportation by Water,* 2:180–187; Fries, *Empire in Pine,* 77, 82, 90, 93–99.

waukee fell drastically again. It was almost with a sense of relief that the president of the Milwaukee Chamber of Commerce confirmed the city's rapid decline as a wheat handler: ". . .[T]here is some satisfaction to know that this large decrease in our wheat trade has been almost wholly beyond our power to remedy in the past, because it is due to the inevitable changes in the tides and channels of business: to changes in agriculture, the rapid development of a new and fertile country North & West, and to the establishment of other important commercial centers and markets."[79]

It is difficult to compare lakes rates with railroad rates, for both fluctuated throughout the season and the services were different. Any comparisons cited always represent some unrealistic average, or highs or lows. Rail rates were somewhat more stable, influenced by longer-term competitive situations, but rising when winter closed the lakes. Lake rates were quoted practically daily, starting from schedules posted at the beginning of the shipping season. The lakes shippers had better luck maintaining a competitive position in grain shipment, for the technology of bulk handling of grain was developed fairly early and favored the larger capacity of a vessel over railroad cars. Although the lakes carriers and ports lagged in the overall competition, during a period of particularly fierce rail competition roughly between 1875–1885, improvements begun in dockside elevators, development of larger freighters adapted to this equipment, and general acceptance of grain trading by established grades rather than by sample—all worked to the advantage of the lakes.[80]

In flour shipping, the rails were highly competitive. Flour was not truly a bulk cargo that could be handled like grain, ore, or

[79] Frank Andrews, "Grain Movement in the Great Lakes Region," U.S. Department of Agriculture, Bureau of Statistics, *Bulletin 81,* pp. 19–37; U.S. Commissioner of Corporations, *Transportation by Water,* 2:172, 205; vol. 9, Minutes of General Meetings, 1886–1902, April 11, 1887, in the Milwaukee Grain Exchange Collection.

[80] *House Documents,* 55 Cong., 2 sess., no. 277 (serial 3679), 2–48. The Soo railroad opened in 1886 as direct competition to the Great Lakes water route eastward, which spurred the improvement of better dockside handling facilities, just as improvements in the Sault Ste. Marie locks, the passage between lakes Huron and Erie, and larger, more powerful vessels put waterborne carriers back in competition.

coal; it was more perishable than wheat, and more valuable. In general, the railroads had superior terminal and warehousing facilities for flour. Unlike wheat and other grains, flour was difficult to hold over to await the opening of the lakes shipping season. Rail shipment took nearly two-thirds of the flour from Milwaukee in the aggressive competition that followed the 1873 panic, but by the mid-eighties, these shipments were more evenly divided.[81]

The lumber trade got the rag, tag, and bobtail of the Great Lakes fleet—even derelicts. Many of the mills around Green Bay were on a shallow shore and had to float or lighter their cargoes to the vessels. Lumber rafting was not satisfactory on Lake Michigan because of too much open water. Isaac Stephenson modestly took credit for the innovation of barging lumber from his Marinette mill on special barges built for the purpose. The usual technique was to use a steam tug to tow two or more. Towing by tug became common for other carriers as well, including dismasted sailing vessels retired to the lumber trade. Steam-powered barges were the next refinement.[82]

Great Lakes shipping underwent a great technological revolution between 1873 and 1893. At the beginning of this period, sail outnumbered steam vessels on the lakes by two to one. Steam vessels averaged about half again as large as sail in tonnage, but these were not impressive figures: 156 tons for sail, 223 tons for steam. Wooden construction was the standard for both. By the mid-eighties, steel and iron hulls became practical in cost, and steam vessels began to grow in average tonnage with the increase of the newer vessels. By 1888, there were 1,342 steam vessels registered on the lakes compared to 1,277 sail. (Like commerce figures, these figures are suspect, for anything which had rigging, even though

[81] U.S. Commissioner of Corporations, *Transportation by Water,* 2:168–171; *House Documents,* 55 Cong., 2 sess., no. 277 (serial 3679), 34. Grain and flour that crossed Lake Michigan as interrupted rail traffic was counted as rail traffic, which was about one-third of the total flour shipped between 1875 and 1894.

[82] U.S. Commissioner of Corporations, *Transportation by Water,* 2:149, 180–187; Isaac Stephenson, *Recollections of a Long Life, 1829–1915* (Chicago, 1915), 168; James D. Rae, "Great Lakes Commodity Trade, 1850 to 1900" (doctoral dissertation, Purdue University, 1967), 57–60.

it was always towed, rated as a sailing vessel. Many once proud sailing ships were moved under tow, although their shortened masts were occasionally used in a favorable following wind.)[83]

The fortunes of lake carriage in competition with the railroads, particularly for carrying grains and flour, related rather directly to technological developments both in vessels and shoreside cargo handling equipment. Into the early 1880's, steam and sail competed somewhat equally for commodity freight business. The principal advantage of steam was that the vessel could maintain a schedule, and therefore the small wooden steamers of the time were used in packet service to carry passengers and package freight, which was more profitable than commodity carriage. They were fired with wood, and frequent fueling stops were necessary. Nonetheless, they were able to move an estimated two-and-a-quarter times as much as a sailing vessel of equal tonnage.[84]

The technological changes appear dramatically in tonnage comparisons after the mid-eighties. Steel or iron hulls combined with coal-fired boilers to extend the size and speed of steam vessels. (In a hull, steel is about 45 per cent more buoyant than oak, and the strength and flexibility of steel permitted designs better adapted to commodity loading equipment.) The elimination of the old side-wheeler, the most popular design for wooden steamers, made more efficient use of canal locks, cargo space, and dockside loading devices. The transition to the typical Great Lakes design, with the engine aft, took some time. It was the carriage of iron ore from the western lakes that most encouraged the evolution of this design. Large steam vessels were expensive, and the trend towards fleet ownership was already established by the eighties, with the railroads as owners. The great proprietary fleets, many belonging

[83] Richard J. Wright, *Freshwater Whales: A History of the American Ship Building Company and Its Predecessors* (Kent, Ohio, 1970), 4–5; George A. Cuthbertson, *Freshwater: A History and a Narrative of the Great Lakes* (New York, 1931), 237–256; *House Documents,* 55 Cong., 2 sess., no. 277 (serial 3679), 4–5, 8–9, 12–16, 26–27.

[84] Ralph G. Plumb, *History of the Navigation of the Great Lakes* (Washington, 1911), 6, 26–29, 35, 75; Ralph G. Plumb, *Lake Michigan* (Manitowoc, 1941), chaps. 3 and 4; *House Documents,* 55 Cong., 2 sess., no. 277 (serial 3679), 4, 12–15, 26.

to steel and ore companies, began to appear around the turn of the century.[85]

For a variety of reasons, much of the shipping built, owned, and operated from ports on Wisconsin's Lake Michigan shore represented a technological backwater. The construction of iron and steel vessels logically became a speciality of the Lake Erie ports. Wisconsin shipbuilders continued to work with the traditional oak, and on smaller vessels; the Lake Michigan ports furnished more business for local coasters. Another factor at work was the conservatism of the Scandinavian sailors, who had taken enthusiastically to this trade. But oak and Norsemen were no match for the new technology. Milwaukee had maintained two important shipbuilding yards in the 1870's and 1880's, which by 1891 had merged and were engaged mainly in repair work. This change marked the passing of oaken vessels, and the attraction of the harbor with its ample anchorage space and docks made it a winter haven for a large number of ships. However, the fleet vessels that served the port in season were not Milwaukee-based, nor were the predecessors of the car ferries that linked her with the Michigan railroad terminals.[86]

Another technological advancement that greatly aided Wisconsin ports on Lake Michigan was the introduction of car ferries on the runs that crossed the lake throughout the year, a technique apparently introduced in 1888 on the narrower waters at the Straits of Mackinac. The cross-lake ferries came to Lake Michigan in 1892, the first on the crossing between Kewaunee and Frankfort, Michigan. As noted, this cross-lake traffic to railheads on the western Michigan shore had been an effective part of Mil-

[85] U.S. Commissioner of Corporations, *Transportation by Water*, 1:131–132, 158–161; *House Documents*, 55 Cong., 2 sess., no. 277 (serial 3679), 8–9, 15–16; Cuthbertson, *Freshwater*, 252.

[86] Edward J. Dowling, "The Ships That Made Milwaukee Famous," in *Inland Seas*, 4 (Summer, 1948), 83–95; Knut Gjerset, *Norwegian Sailors on the Great Lakes: A Study in the History of American Inland Transportation* (Northfield, Minnesota, 1928), 84–86, 96–101; John R. Wolf, "Milwaukee's Lake Commerce," and Louis Bleyer, "The Ship Building Industry," both in Anderson and Bleyer, eds., *Milwaukee's Great Industries*, 132–133, 135–138; Wright, *Freshwater Whales*, 59–73.

waukee's fight for equal rates eastward with Chicago. The car ferries, which took loaded freight cars aboard on rails where they
were secured by special equipment, did away with the necessity for
breaking cargo at each end of the voyage. This was a realistic
enough alternative to all rail traffic eastward to maintain the
prized equality of rates. It was a rugged and hazardous business
during the winter months to maintain this scheduled service. An
advantage was that the railroads, in effect, had 100 miles over
which they did not have to maintain a right-of-way, and government agencies improved the harbors.[87]

Interesting, though they turned out to be a technological blind
alley, were the whaleback steamers built for the Great Lakes by
the American Steel Barge Company at Superior. The driving
force behind the company was a Scot, Alexander McDougall, who
had conceived the design. As the name whaleback suggests, it was
a distinctive vessel shaped like a cigar above the waterline and flat-
bottomed below it to reduce roll and accommodate the shallow
waters of Great Lakes harbors and waterways. The whaleback was
a success as a navigator on the lakes; she was fuel-efficient and stable when she encountered heavy wind and rough water. But the
design was not well adapted to the new loading and unloading
systems developed for handling ore and grains. There were forty-
one whalebacks on the Great Lakes by 1897, most of them built
between 1890 and 1896 at McDougall's West Superior yard. They
were a familiar sight on the lakes for many years. The best-known
whaleback was the *Christopher Columbus,* which had been adapted
for passengers with a superstructure and was an attraction of the
Chicago World's Fair in 1893.[88]

The federal government was a partner in maintaining the competitive position of the Great Lakes with relation to the railroads.
The most obvious assistance was in the installation of navigational aids and the improvement of channels between the lakes,

[87] George W. Hilton, *The Great Lakes Car Ferries* (Berkeley, 1962), 57, 69–76, 169; Plumb, *Navigation of the Great Lakes,* 28.

[88] Wright, *Freshwater Whales,* 41–57; Edward J. Dowling, "The Story of the Whaleback Vessels and of Their Inventor, Alexander McDougall," in *Inland Seas,* 13 (Fall, 1957), 172–183.

especially the passage between lakes Huron and Erie. The general government also supplied subsidies for canal projects such as the Sturgeon Bay Ship Canal and the locks at Sault Ste. Marie. The latter were maintained on the American side by the state of Michigan until 1881, when the federal government took over. The larger facilities, the Weitzel Locks, were opened that year. The Sturgeon Bay Canal, which bypassed the hazardous passage around the tip of the Door Peninsula, completed in 1882, was built by private capital, specifically lumber money. In 1892, the federal government took it over.[89]

The year 1866 had been critical in federal relations with Great Lakes improvements. The ingrained Jacksonian prejudice against federal expenditures which benefited particular localities was overcome by the eagerness of the Radical Republicans to bind the midwestern populations to their cause in that election year. Wisconsin was fortunate that Philetus Sawyer of Oshkosh had arrived in Congress for the 1865 session. Sawyer and Governor Lucius Fairchild made harbor improvements and the Fox-Wisconsin waterway their specialty. When Congress started filling the pork barrels from the generous revenues provided by the tariff, Sawyer was in a position to report to Fairchild in 1872: "I am as usual getting up the River & Harbor bill, and that dont damage our prospects any." The federal government spent an average $51,850 on Milwaukee annually during the 1880's to the city's average $20,000. Lesser ports were treated with comparable generosity. Both the federal and Wisconsin governments enjoyed revenue surpluses in the 1880's, which must have encouraged municipal expansiveness.[90]

[89] Ralph G. Plumb, "Early Harbor History of Wisconsin," in the *Proceedings of the Mississippi Valley Historical Association,* 4 (1910–1911), 189–198; U.S. Commissioner of Corporations, *Transportation by Water,* 1:50, and 3:chap. 3 *passim;* Plumb, *Lake Michigan,* 77–79.

[90] Current, *Civil War Era,* 580–584; Sawyer to Fairchild, February 15, 1872, in the Lucius Fairchild Papers; *Wisconsin Blue Book, 1895,* pp. 191–192; Laurence M. Larson, *A Financial and Administrative History of Milwaukee* (University of Wisconsin, Bulletin no. 242, *Economics and Political Science Series,* vol. IV, no. 2, Madison, 1908), 117; *Senate Reports,* 43 Cong., 1 sess., no. 307 (serial 1588), 222–228; *House Executive Documents,* 51 Cong., 1 sess., no. 1, pt. 2 (serial 2718), appendix II, pp. 2067–2075.

The Wisconsin River ultimately defied efforts to make it a part of a useful waterway. But the Fox-Wisconsin project made for good politics. By 1872, Congressman Sawyer and Senator Timothy Howe (a resident of Green Bay) had arranged for the federal government to purchase the Fox-Wisconsin navigation improvements from the Green Bay and Mississippi Canal Company, a somewhat tangled affair. It was an interesting arrangement whereby the federal government declined to buy out waterpower rights and structures, which proved to be immensely valuable over subsequent years. The extensive land grant had gone into private hands.[91]

The federal engineers remained baffled by the problem of what to do with the project. One recommendation was to build a canal paralleling the Wisconsin River rather than trying to tame the intractable river. They settled upon a system of wing dams to direct the current and scour a channel through the shifting sandbars. Meanwhile they argued about the function of the waterway, should they ever succeed in creating a useful one, even as commerce was dying on the Upper Mississippi. With Sawyer directing the flow, federal money poured into the project. The treasury had spent $2,745,875 by 1889, which should be measured against something. The following Congress was the first to manage a billion-dollar budget for a biennium. A sum of two and three-quarters millions was an expenditure worth noting.

The wing dams were not a success. The Army Engineers, showing more independent judgment, had by 1884 lost their optimism and recommended abandonment of work on the Wisconsin River. The Lower Fox, where work continued, required seventeen locks to accommodate the 170-foot drop from Lake Winnebago to Green Bay. The growing industries along the Lower Fox with waterpower rights or contracts occasionally jeopardized the

[91] Current, *Civil War Era,* 580–584; Current, *Pine Logs and Politics,* 64–71; Ray F. Whitbeck, *The Geography of the Fox-Winnebago Valley* (Wisconsin Geological and Natural History Survey, *Bulletin,* no. 42, Madison, 1915), 32–40; Mermin, *Fox-Wisconsin Improvement,* 113–133; Robert W. McCluggage, "The Fox-Waterway, 1836–1872: Land Speculation and Regional Rivalries, Politics and Private Enterprise" (doctoral dissertation, University of Wisconsin, 1954), 336–354.

use of the canals. Traffic on the Lower Fox became quite local in character. There was still considerable traffic on Lake Winnebago and the river systems feeding into Lake Poygan, particularly the Wolf, an important lumbering stream. The dream of the Green Bay to Mississippi canal died in the 1880's.[92]

Wisconsin's other rivers were never very important for carrying a general commerce by steamboat. This was partly a fault of the streams themselves, partly competition from the railroads, and partly because logs, lumber rafts, and steamboats did not mix very well. Lumbermen shied away from supporting improvements that would encourage boat traffic. The lumber interests were strong enough to have their way politically, but navigation rights have always had federal support. Except for some traffic on the lower reaches of the Chippewa and on the St. Croix, most of the steamboat traffic was confined to the Mississippi. Lumber rafting was giving way to railroads by the 1880's, but it remained an alternative when railroad rates were deemed to be too high.[93]

Steamboating on the Upper Mississippi was on the decline from the mid-seventies, when the railroads bridged the river at Prairie du Chien, La Crosse, and other points. The business had an aura of continuing health for some years simply because the adjacent country was growing in population and economic activity was burgeoning so rapidly that the river continued to get a share. The grain trade on the river declined precipitously, but there was an increase in the passenger trade and general freight to the river towns. Log raft tows remained a part of the river scene, supplying the Weyerhaeuser syndicate downriver. "Commodore" William F. Davidson and the Northwestern Union Packet Company generally monopolized the river above La Crosse from the mid-sixties

[92] Milwaukee *Sentinel,* May 5, 1882; General John Newton to General H. G. Wright, Chief of Engineers, January 5, 1884, in the Breese Stevens Papers; Mermin, *Fox-Wisconsin Improvement,* 104–107, 144–151; Joseph Schafer, *The Winnebago-Horicon Basin: A Type Study in Western History* (Madison, 1937), 127–131; *House Executive Documents,* 51 Cong., 1 sess., pt. 2 (serial 2718), appendix II (as in JJ), pp. 2085–2094; Breese J. Stevens to General John Newton, President, U.S. Army Board of Engineers, December 19, 1883, also in the Stevens Papers; Whitbeck, *Geography of the Fox-Winnebago Valley,* 34–36.

[93] Fries, *Empire in Pine,* 56–58, 89, 91, 95; Hurst, *Law and Economic Growth,* 145, 261–263, 281; Robert C. Nesbit, *Wisconsin: A History* (Madison, 1973), 196–197.

until his death in 1887. He and his family's operations were big business in La Crosse, but were dogged by hard luck and declining revenues. In the three years 1882–1884, they lost $125,000 in sinkings and fires alone. The days when a boat could pay for itself in one or two seasons were long gone. Rivermen kept building new boats—larger and more expensive ones—but the traffic to sustain them kept dwindling.[94]

* * *

Wisconsin roads of the time were a scandal. In 1906 the Wisconsin Geological and Natural History Survey published a helpful manual for township road supervisors entitled *Rural Highways of Wisconsin*. The author, exhibiting an appreciation for the time and the subject, added to his preface an extended quote from Thomas Babington Macaulay's *History of England* on the condition of English roads in 1685: "One chief cause of the badness of the roads seems to have been the defective state of the law. Every parish was bound to repair the highway which passed through it. The peasantry were forced to give their gratuitous labor six days in the year. . . . A change was at length effected, but not without much difficulty. For unjust and absurd taxation to which men are accustomed is often borne more willingly than the most reasonable impost that is new." The portion quoted here conveyed a picture of turn-of-the-century Wisconsin.[95]

Influenced by the debacles in neighboring states over investment of public funds in railroads and canals, which ended disastrously in the 1837 panic, Wisconsin's constitution provided that the state should never "be a party in carrying on such works." This was construed to include highways. It excluded only the

[94] Brown, "Collapse of Steamboat Traffic," *Proceedings of the Mississippi Valley Historical Association*, 9:422–428; Lester B. Shippee, "Steamboating on the Upper Mississippi After the Civil War: A Mississippi Magnate," in the *Mississippi Valley Historical Review*, 6 (March, 1920), 470–502; Mildred L. Hartsough, *From Canoe to Steel Barge on the Upper Mississippi* (Minneapolis, 1934), 168–211; H. J. Hirshheimer, "La Crosse River History and the Davidsons," in *WMH*, 28 (March, 1945), 263–276.

[95] William O. Hotchkiss, *Rural Highways of Wisconsin* (Wisconsin Geological and Natural History Survey, *Bulletin*, no. 18, Madison, 1906), [viii].

administration of federal grants for transportation improvements. The effect of the prohibition was to make the state essentially a noncontributing partner in the construction and maintenance of public highways.[96]

The legislature followed territorial precedent by designating state roads from point to point, often via a certain route or intervening points, and appointing a commission for each such road to supervise its creation. "Creation" is the proper term, for the commissions administered no funds. The prohibition against spending or assuming debts for public improvements, however, did not extend to counties, towns, cities, or villages. But the enthusiasm of local governments for subsidizing railroads had led in 1874 to a constitutional amendment, limiting such indebtedness to 5 per cent of assessed valuation.[97]

An indication of the relative importance attached to railroads, as opposed to roads, may be gleaned from the division of municipal bonded indebtedness in aid of railroads as opposed to bridges and roads at the end of 1875: $5,707,700 for railroads, $119,960 for roads and bridges, or a ratio of 48:1. One cannot assume too much from such figures, however. Roads did not usually involve much cash outlay, since rural taxpayers normally paid their road taxes in labor. It is therefore fair to assume that most of the bonded indebtedness charged to roads and bridges was for bridges. The urban centers had the lion's share of these bonded improvements.[98]

More indicative of the casual attention given to Wisconsin's roads is a comparison of the number authorized by legislative action with the number completed within a reasonable time. Leg-

[96] Wisconsin Constitution, Article VIII, Section 10.

[97] Edwin D. Karn, "Roadmaking in Wisconsin Territory" (master's thesis, University of Wisconsin, 1959), 77, 96–98; Wisconsin Constitution, Article XI, Section 3 as amended November 3, 1874; Wisconsin State Highway Commission and United States Public Roads Administration, *A History of Wisconsin Highway Development, 1835–1945* (Madison, 1947), xxvii. See also Gates, *Wisconsin Pine Lands,* 179–180; Hunt, *Law and Locomotives,* 147–149.

[98] Hotchkiss, *Rural Highways of Wisconsin,* 123–127; *Wisconsin Blue Book, 1877,* pp. 334–336; *ibid., 1887,* pp. 283–286, which shows that the City of Milwaukee owed $153,000 of the total $416,865 debt of 1885 for roads and bridges.

islatures were generous with authorizations that involved no appropriations. There were 560 separate authorizations made between 1849 and 1891, all but fifty-two of them prior to 1871. Of the 508 roads authorized through 1870, only 127 had been declared open before 1874. Eighteen of the fifty-two authorized in 1871 or after were open by 1891. The longest of these was 58.8 miles; the shortest, 4.5 miles. The average was 22.4 miles.[99]

As the record shows, it was much easier to authorize a state road than it was to have it built and opened for use. The legislature in 1849 placed the responsibility for construction of all roads upon the town governments. In turn, the towns passed the responsibility on to road districts within the town, commonly six or more to a town. Voters within each road district elected one of their fellows to be the overseer of highways. It was his responsibility to collect the road taxes and oversee their expenditure, whether they were collected in labor or in money. The overseer rendered a financial report to the town clerk.[100]

As a common jape had it, this system mixed local politics with large rocks to assure poor roads. The single virtue of the system was that it was strictly local in character, so that a man's labor or taxes were applied to roads in his immediate neighborhood. The town supervisors were the road commissioners, but they depended upon the road district overseers almost entirely.

The defects of the system were legion. In the majority of districts, where road taxes were as a rule paid in labor, the job of highway overseer, or pathmaster, was not eagerly sought. Someone might be elected by his fellows as a practical joke, or the job was passed around, or someone was elected for being a good fellow who could be depended upon to render an acceptable report to the town clerk. In the few districts where some part of the taxes were paid in money by anxious absentees or gentlemen farmers, the job was more desirable, for the pathmaster was allowed to pay himself at a daily rate and could keep 5 per cent of all taxes he collected. If he needed help, he had some jobs in his patronage (and

[99] State Highway Commission, *Wisconsin Highway Development*, 15, 231–241.
[100] *Ibid.*, 14–16; *Wisconsin Annotations*, 1914, p. 396.

could be depended upon to make his labors and the cash come out even).

There was general agreement that the condition of the roads fared better where the least work was done because most of the roads were poorly laid out and lacked any foundation, drainage, or gravel. It did not improve them to have the sod removed and the loose dirt roughly graded to the center, as was frequently done. One observer wrote in 1885: "As a consequence of the reign of the district pathmaster and his experiments in subsoiling the road, in order to raise his annual crop of weeds, we have at the end of his 40 year reign, a highway the only solid parts of which are the places where he and his assistants have rested, as they lay under the trees and worked the roads at $3.50 per day, with 'Old Sledge' and similar utensils."[101]

It is strange that comment about this system of road building and maintenance was so subdued, but the public discussion that began only in the latter eighties supplies many of the answers. The railroad era in Wisconsin killed off interest in roads between urban centers. Energy was concentrated upon getting a railroad connection rather than a turnpike. When the railroads appeared, toll roads—which generally meant plank roads in Wisconsin—lost support. The system of long-distance stage lines that existed in the 1850's was pretty much a thing of the past by the 1870's. What remained were short feeder lines that shifted as the rail network expanded.[102]

Except in northern Wisconsin, where there were some long and uncertain routes following federal post and military routes—which were generally cleared trails rather than roads in many places— the remaining local stage lines could reach most post offices with a trip of less than thirty miles. These stage lines became the property of local liverymen, hotelkeepers, or postmasters. It is difficult to discover how these lines coped with adverse weather and road

[101] Hotchkiss, *Rural Highways of Wisconsin*, 94; J. C. Ford, "Our Country Roads," in Wisconsin State Agricultural Society, *Transactions*, 1885, p. 213.

[102] Current, *Civil War Era*, 448–450, describes the process of change in the 1860's and early 1870's. The *Wisconsin State Gazetteer and Business Directory*, 1876–1877, p. 610, lists only three local stage lines, two with addresses in Waupun and one in Lancaster.

conditions, but there must have been many times when they simply did not try. The stage lines that earlier had operated out of the larger cities either disappeared or else made the transition to local omnibus lines.[103]

With the passing of the intercity stage lines, the system of state roads became something less than an urgent matter for urban folk. With the railroad ready to haul a ton of freight from Madison to Milwaukee at a fraction of the former cost by team, no one considered long-distance freighting by road. Roads were a means to get to town or to the nearest railroad station, which probably meant ten miles or less for the majority of commercial farmers in southern Wisconsin. It is little wonder that Wisconsin's state road commissions experienced difficulty implementing their instructions. All they could do was tell the county boards, who told the town supervisors, who told the road district overseers, who did as they pleased.[104]

There was no pretense that state roads were all-weather roads. Farmers were accustomed to stay at home, or severely restrict their traveling, during about six months of the year. To be sure, there were areas where the character of the land favored adequate drainage and firmer road surfaces, as well as localities where road money and labor had been well spent. But, as was frequently pointed out, a road with only one bad stretch—a mudhole, a steep grade, a swamp, or rocky footing—determined both the use and the load capacity of the entire road.

One might expect that the shift to dairy farming, with its need for regular transportation, would have increased the agitation for improvement of farm-to-market roads. Oddly, the annual reports of the Wisconsin Dairymen's Association indicate no great interest in the problem. The speeches and papers listed in the series through 1894 make no reference to roads in their titles. There were only three papers on the subject in the *Transactions* of the

---

[103] Harry E. Cole, *Stagecoach and Tavern Days in the Baraboo Region* (Baraboo, 1923), 34–36; Barton, *Industrial History of Milwaukee,* 200–201.

[104] Of course, the state roads actually declared open required only a survey of existing township roads and some nominal linking together.

Wisconsin State Agricultural Society between 1873 and 1893, the
first one in 1885. The University's Farmers' Institutes began to
agitate the issue at about the same time in their first *Bulletin*
(1887).[105]

Once the issue arose, agreement on the problem was almost
universal. The roads were terrible and the system of township and
road district supervision, with road taxes paid in labor, did not
work. The comments of those farm leaders who sought legislative
action indicated, however, that this system was something of a
sacred cow. A farm leader who tried some lobbying complained:
". . . [T]o a man, every one of the members [of the legislature]
were in favor of some remedial of our road system, and yet not one
of them seemed to dare to introduce a bill. . . ." This was a frequent theme in discussions. What it boiled down to was that
farmers were loath to give up the privilege of paying their road
taxes in labor and feared that any real change would result in
heavier taxation without that option. They liked the particularism
of the district system. They apprehended that a road system,
administered even at the county level, would concentrate upon
roads between cities and villages. Any comment that reflected
upon the reluctance of the voters in villages and cities to support
rural roads drew enthusiastic agreement from farm audiences. As
for administering roads at the state level, this was considered even
more hazardous: "When we get about two city men to one farmer
in the legislature I don't know how you are going to bring them
to time. They are pretty shrewd, these city men."[106]

There were new forces at work which gradually overcame both
rural and urban inertia. Some farm leaders were prepared even to
entertain the idea of state control over all roads. This was considered extreme by the majority, but at least it got farmers to thinking about the possibility of the town or county taking the
responsibility away from the very inefficient road districts. Aside

[105] John Dawson, "Good Country Roads Will Pay," in Wisconsin State Agricultural
Society, *Transactions*, 1892, pp. 226–229; John M. Olin, "Better Roads—A Plan for
Improving County Highways in Wisconsin," *ibid.*, 1893, pp. 283–319; Robert Fargo,
"Our Country Roads," in Wisconsin Farmers' Institutes, *Bulletin*, no. 1 (1887), 209–215.
[106] Wisconsin State Agricultural Society, *Transactions*, 1885, p. 218; *ibid.*, 1892, p. 238.

from the growing recognition of their need for adequate roads for their own business and social requirements, farmers had their attention called to a new use for rural roads: free delivery of mail to rural addresses. It was not a new idea; but in 1891 John Wanamaker, the Philadelphia department store magnate who was President Benjamin Harrison's postmaster general, proposed delivering the mail to everyone, rather than just to the one in four Americans who lived in cities with more than 10,000 population. He appealed to the national farmers' organizations for support, and they in turn generated a flood of affirmative mail to Congress. Wanamaker was ahead of his time, but his proposal aroused farmers' interest in their roads. "Imagine Uncle Sam wading through this sea of mire," said one rural legislator, "making his proposed free deliveries of mail in the rural districts next spring." Rural free delivery did not appear in the spring of 1893, but one prerequisite of such service surely was all-weather roads.[107]

Road reform was attracting a coalition of city people, village merchants, farm leaders, people in the mail-order business, and others. A new group that helped to revive interest in intercity highways was the cyclists. "Safety" bicycles with uniform wheels, chain drive, and pneumatic tires came on the market in the mid-eighties and caught on with a rush. By the early 1890's, there was a veritable bicycle craze and, for a few years, cycling was a favorite American sport. Cycling clubs were organized by those interested in touring or sponsoring cross-country races. Particularly popular were "century races" that involved point-to-point runs of 100 miles. The popularity of cycling and cycle races was an incentive to agitate for road improvements long before the automobile became a significant factor.[108]

The first real break with the old system of road building came in the 1893 legislative session. Chapter 284 did away at one stroke with the road district and the elected pathmaster. The reform was

---

[107] Wayne E. Fuller, *RFD: The Changing Face of Rural America* (Bloomington, 1964), 18–26; Dawson, "Country Roads Will Pay," in Wisconsin State Agricultural Society, *Transactions,* 1892, p. 227.

[108] Ballard Campbell, "The Good Roads Movement in Wisconsin, 1890–1911," in *WMH,* 49 (Summer, 1966), 273–283.

kept within modest bounds, however. The town board, not the county, was given full supervision over roads. The town supervisors now appointed a single supervisor for a term of three years. Road taxes were to be paid in money, unless a majority of voters in the town voted to continue the old system of paying in labor. But the hired supervisor and the town board could determine where and when labor should be applied, which reduced its attraction. The board was empowered to buy machinery and gravel and to hire labor. Road reform grew from this measure. And, by the fall of 1896, the U.S. Post Office was also experimenting with rural free delivery, a further incentive to break with the past.[109]

Urban transportation changes in Wisconsin between 1873 and 1893 were not particularly unique, save for the pioneering application of hydroelectric power to the trolley car in Appleton. In the main, cities of the size to sustain a public transportation system on tracks started with horsecars sometime before the practicality of the trolley was established in the late 1880's. As early as 1860, Milwaukee had horsecars running on franchise routes. The trolley greatly expanded the possibilities. These will be considered in more detail later in descriptions of urban life.[110]

Societies adapt readily to revolutionary changes. The initial excitement of the coming of the railroad—the wonder of it all— soon gave place to casual groups of loafers attracted to the depot to see who was coming and going. Railroads concentrated transportation activity which has since been fragmented among trucks, intercity buses, automobiles, and airplanes. After 1893 additional Wisconsin railroad mileage was largely a matter of filling in the network. The passing of this convenient, economical transportation is occasionally regretted by any oldster who has passed an

[109] *Laws of Wisconsin*, 1893, pp. 383–385; Fuller, *RFD*, 34–35.

[110] Louise P. Kellogg, "The Electric Light System at Appleton," in *WMH*, 6 (December, 1922–1923), 189–194; G. W. Van Derzee, "Pioneering the Electrical Age," in *WMH*, 41 (Spring, 1958), 210–214; Clay McShane, *Technology and Reform: Street Railways and the Growth of Milwaukee, 1887–1900* (Madison, 1974), 1–17; Still, *Milwaukee*, 248–249, 368–369.

uncertain time sitting in an airport or searching for public parking in a major city.

The railroads made possible the change from the extensive, rather careless agriculture of grain farming to the more intensive requirements of dairying and livestock by providing the means to reach distant markets with a perishable product. (This change, incidentally, brought farmers generally into closer contact with urban centers and provided them with more assured and regular incomes as participants in the developing consumer society.) The railroads also opened the possibility for industries to develop in cities and villages of the interior. One thinks of Madison, Beloit, Beaver Dam, Stoughton, and others without frontage on the Great Lakes or canal connections to Lake Winnebago. By the time La Crosse looked to an industrial future that extended beyond lumbering and boat yards, it was not its river frontage but rather the railroad bridges across the Mississippi that assured its markets. Even before the evolution of the Great Lakes commodity carriers of the latter decades of the century, and the concomitant development of harbors, adequate locks, channel improvements, and navigation aids, the mixed fleet of smaller sail and steam vessels assured Wisconsin's lake ports of a flow of raw materials and coal at a cost that made possible the commitment to heavy industry. The railroads extended this possibility into the interior cities and villages. What had been an urban, commercial economy, based upon grain, lumber, and the requirements of the westward push of railroads and northern plains agriculture, was transformed in twenty years into a much more varied, urban-centered economy with a growing urban labor force and intensive capitalization of factory and farm.

# 4

# Industry

## HEYDAY OF THE ENTREPRENEUR

A HISTORIAN of American industrialization remarked in 1928 that "between 1873 and 1893 the United States was rapidly attaining maturity as an industrial nation." While there is not universal agreement about these dates, they do neatly bracket an era in Wisconsin's industrial history. Edward P. Allis made his bold bid to build Milwaukee's ambitious new water system in 1872. A decade earlier the Reliance Works, with which Allis began his industrial empire, had gone broke. In 1873, the Kohlers established their foundry business in Sheboygan. Merrill and Houston, organized in 1871 from a foundry and machine shop dating back to 1855, would evolve into the Beloit Corporation, world leader in the manufacture of papermaking machinery. The Philip Best Brewing Company was incorporated in 1873 with a capital of $300,000. In 1892 the company, renamed for Captain Frederick Pabst, was capitalized at $10 million.[1]

The secretary of the Milwaukee Chamber of Commerce observed in 1892 that many an obscure job shop of past years was now an imposing edifice "filled with the latest machinery and giving employment to hundreds of busy workers. The old-time pro-

[1] Victor S. Clark, *History of Manufactures in the United States, 1860–1914* (Washington, 1928), 154; Robert T. Hilton, "Men of Metal: A History of the Foundry Industry in Wisconsin" (master's thesis, University of Wisconsin, 1965), 35–39, 42, 44–45; Beloit Daily News Publishing Company, *The Book of Beloit, 1836–1936* ([Beloit], 1936), 211–213; "Wisconsin's Industries," in the *Wisconsin Blue Book, 1958,* p. 119; Thomas C. Cochran, *The Pabst Brewing Company: The History of an American Business* (New York, 1948), 66–67, 84.

prietor is now president of a corporation that pays its stockholders
good dividends and makes money enough besides to enlarge the
plant every year or two." The changes implied had been enthusiastically promoted but were not seen as inevitable from the perspective of 1873. In March of that year, the Milwaukeeans who
shared in the invention of the first practical typewriter contracted
to have their machines built by E. Remington & Sons of Ilion,
New York. Efforts to fabricate the machines locally had forced
them to the conclusion that Milwaukee had no shops that could
produce the necessary standardized parts. This would have
seemed an incongruous assumption within a few years, given the
city's identification with the metals trades, but it was accurate at
the time.[2]

The Old Northwest was the most important manufacturing
growth area to emerge in the period following the Civil War. The
five Great Lakes states, from Ohio through Wisconsin, in 1869
contributed 18.07 per cent of the total American manufacturing
value of product. This increased by 1889 to 24.35 per cent, despite
substantial growth in the traditional industrial regions of New
England and the Middle Atlantic States. Wisconsin, in its turn,
more than held its own. In 1869 she contributed 10.07 per cent of
the regional manufactured value of product; in 1889, 10.55 per
cent. Illinois enjoyed phenomenal growth in the same period,
from 24.57 per cent to 37.86 per cent. Wisconsin's share was the
only one of the remaining Great Lakes states that did not shrink
relative to the great growth of Illinois.[3]

Wisconsin's comparatively spectacular industrial growth
between 1870 and 1890 was partly a matter of where she ranked
industrially at the beginning of the period. Figuratively, she was

[2] Milwaukee Chamber of Commerce, *Annual Report,* 1891–1892, p. 40; Richard N.
Current, *The Typewriter and the Men Who Made It* (Urbana, 1954), 53–55, 62–65. The appel-
lation "Milwaukee Chamber of Commerce" is in fact a library bindery title applied to the
annual reports of the association commonly known as the Milwaukee Grain Exchange.

[3] Harvey S. Perloff et al., *Regions, Resources, and Economic Growth* (Lincoln, 1960), 153–
159; Simon Kuznets, Ann R. Miller, and Richard A. Easterlin, *Analysis of Economic Change,*
vol. 2 of Simon Kuznets and Dorothy S. Thomas, eds., *Population Redistribution and Economic Growth: United States, 1870–1950* (3 vols., Philadelphia, 1957–1964), 2:125.

on the threshold of a boom fueled by heavy railroad construction
building westward as well as filling the intervening spaces; the
mechanization of grain farming, which was also expanding rapidly westward; the demands of farm and city building; the accompanying explosive growth of the lumber industry, which like the
grain-milling industry was undergoing great technological
changes; the expansion of mining as a high-tonnage undertaking
for iron and copper ores; and the growth of urban utilities.

Geography played an important role as well. Wisconsin's Lake
Michigan ports had the advantage of cheap access to some of the
industrial requirements that were lacking here: principally coal
but also steel, pig iron, other metals and alloys, petroleum products, and so on. (Remember the problems of the railroads and
Lakes vessels in finding westward-moving traffic to balance the
heavy eastward flow of grain, lumber, ores, and other bulk commodities.) Wisconsin's lake ports benefited from that, as did the
interior cities from the equal eagerness of the railroads to develop
westward traffic. Carrying at less than cost was better than traveling empty, and encouraging manufacturing centers resulted in
highly profitable carriage. A windmill or a piece of farm machinery from Beaver Dam more than paid its way to Dakota.

Michigan and Chicago men in the lumber business had venture capital a decade or two before most Wisconsin lumbermen
began looking for investment opportunities other than more
standing timber or a large improved sawmill. A general use of
extended partnerships, and then of the corporate form with
broader stock ownership and limited liability, eased manufacturing financing problems somewhat. As a general proposition, however, manufacturing enterprises had less in the way of tangible
assets to attract capital than did competing enterprises such as
railroads, canals, lumber companies, mining companies, and others with large holdings of real estate, ore bodies, or standing timber, or urban utilities with prospectively valuable franchises. But
the potential market was there—less protected from better-estab-
lished eastern competitors because of greatly improved transportation and communication, but more protected by the increasing
specialization of the customers' needs. This trend towards spe-

cialized equipment gave the Wisconsin manufacturers certain advantages because they were closer to local conditions affecting their customers. This applies especially to foundries, machine shops, and equipment manufacturers, of course, rather than brewers or pork packers; but Wisconsin's foundry and machine industries outstripped even the brewers in growth during the last twenty years of the century. It was a combination of being lean and hungry, more direct contact with the working millwrights—the practical inventors of the day—the presence of vocationally and university-trained craftsmen and engineers from Europe in a day when such formal training was difficult to obtain in the United States, and the adaptability of local entrepreneurs who lacked an established clientele for standardized machinery and equipment. What follows is intended to illustrate these generalizations.

"If God had designed Wisconsin to be chiefly a manufacturing state, instead of agricultural, which she claims to be, and is, it is difficult to see more than one particular in which He could have endowed her more richly for that purpose." Quoted in the late 1870's, this bit of folk wisdom expressed the standard assumptions of the post-Civil War generation. But it flew in the face of some salient facts, foremost of which was Wisconsin's lack of many basic mineral resources. She had no coal, and would prove to have no petroleum or natural gas, despite popular opinion to the contrary at the time. High-grade Bessemer iron ore deposits in the Gogebic-Penokee Range, reached by the Wisconsin Central in 1873, were exploited early on the Wisconsin side, but when other steel-making processes competed successfully with the Bessemer converter, they were soon eclipsed by the more cheaply mined ores of the Mesabi in Minnesota. By the 1880's, charcoal iron was becoming a technological anachronism, for reasons over and beyond the growing scarcity of hardwoods convenient to the ores or to waterside shipping points. The economics of iron and steel reduction increasingly favored carrying the ore to the metallurgical coal, which was closer to the major markets commanded by the Lake Erie ports and Chicago. The wishful belief persisted that "the probabilities are great that coal will yet be found in Ashland Country, [for] wherever iron ore is found, coal is invariably

at hand. This coincidence has held true the world over. . . ." But
Providence let Wisconsin down. The scientists of Wisconsin's
state geological survey, instituted in 1873, frequently had to dissuade hopeful diggers from their search for coal in terrain that
superficially resembled areas with producing mines elsewhere.[4]

Yet another resource that held infinite promise for the future in
the eyes of the pioneer generation of Yankee settlers was Wisconsin's waterpower. It proved illusory, however, save in a few
favored locations. Perpetually optimistic, the hydraulic Yankees
promoted townsites across southern Wisconsin wherever a modest stream ambled through the landscape. There are and were, of
course, important waterpowers in the state, but Wisconsin's terrain is limited in providing dependable stream flows, except at
important fall lines in the north as on the lower Fox River, or by
means of expensive hydroelectric developments as on the lower
Wisconsin River. But the age of hydroelectric power was just
dawning by the 1890's, which meant that earlier development was
necessarily confined to the site. The state's developed waterpower
had a modest gain from 33,714 horsepower in 1870 to 56,811 in
1890. Steam power, in the same period, increased from 30,509
horsepower to 121,149.[5]

One can sense the shift in attitudes towards waterpowers in the
official literature. The federal census of 1880 included an enthusiastic endorsement of their continuing potential for development
in southern Wisconsin. Twenty years later that enthusiasm had
waned. The land behind dams was expensive to flood, and quiet
ponds were of little use without a strong stream flow. Local his-

---

[4] The comment about God's design is from H. H. Giles, "Commerce and Manufactures," in Western Historical Company, *The History of Fond du Lac County, Wisconsin. . .*
(Chicago, 1880), 209. See also Clark, *History of Manufactures,* 64–67, 74, 208–209, 258–
260, 552–554; George J. Kuehnl, *The Wisconsin Business Corporation* (Madison, 1959), 154–
155; Roy L. Martin, *History of the Wisconsin Central* (Railway and Locomotive Historical
Society, *Bulletin,* no. 54, Boston, 1941), 26, 119; Lawrence Martin, *The Physical Geography
of Wisconsin* (Madison, 1935), 375–382. On the presumed presence of coal, see a publication typical of the time: Art Gravure and Etching Co., *Ashland, Wis., Illustrated* (Milwaukee, 1891), 6. See also Thomas C. Chamberlin, *Geology of Wisconsin: Survey of 1873–1879*
(4 vols., Madison, 1877–1883), 2:13.

[5] *Twelfth Census of the United States, 1900: Manufactures, Volume VII, Part 1,* pp. cccxviii–
cccxx.

tories and gazetteers document the deterioration of hopes as waterpower concessions passed from one use to another in rapid succession. Most of the industries located on lesser waterpowers that succeeded had been quick to supplement it with steam. Consequently, Milwaukee and neighboring ports became important points for receiving and shipping coal which came mostly by water from Lake Erie ports.[6]

Lumber and flour milling in the years 1873–1893 were Wisconsin growth industries despite their dim long-term prospects. Both were transformed by steam power, produced by the reliable, variable-load, constant-speed-governed heavy engines that became a Milwaukee speciality. Flour milling was a notoriously migratory industry, as was wheat growing. Just as Milwaukee and some interior Wisconsin cities had developed export mills that short-circuited the flow of Wisconsin wheat to Buffalo and Rochester, the rapid growth of Minneapolis as a milling center was to put Wisconsin mills in the shadows. Ironically, the entrepreneur who did the most to put Minneapolis in the forefront by exploiting a period of great technological change in flour milling was Cadwallader C. Washburn of La Crosse, a one-term governor of Wisconsin (1872–1874). Washburn had come into control of a large share of the waterpower at the Falls of St. Anthony in Minneapolis. Although Wisconsin flour-milling production doubled in the years from 1870 to 1890, Minnesota production, which was a bit less than half that of Wisconsin in 1870, was over three times as great twenty years later.[7]

The greater power demands of "high milling," a technique

[6] James L. Greenleaf, "Report on the Water–power of the Northwest," in the *Tenth Census of the United States, 1880: Reports on the Water-power of the United States, Volume XVII, Part 2,* pp. 5–13; Leonard S. Smith, *The Water Powers of Wisconsin* (Wisconsin Geological and Natural History Survey, *Bulletin,* no. 20, Madison, 1908), 263–265; Clark, *History of Manufactures,* 533–535; *House Documents,* 55 Cong., 2 sess., no. 277 (serial 3679), 80, 81, 90, 93; Milwaukee Chamber of Commerce, *Annual Report,* 1890, pp. 35–36.

[7] J. H. H. Alexander, "A Short Industrial History of Wisconsin," in the *Wisconsin Blue Book, 1929,* pp. 34–39; Clark, *History of Manufactures,* 359–360, 533–534, 686–687; Frederick Merk, *Economic History of Wisconsin During the Civil War Decade* (Madison, 1916; reprinted, 1971), 129–240; Charles N. Glaab and Lawrence H. Larsen, *Factories in the Valley: Neenah-Menasha, 1870–1915* (Madison, 1969), 67–77; Bayrd Still, *Milwaukee: The History of a City* (Madison, 1948; reprinted, 1965), 328–329; Edward C. Kirkland, *Industry Comes of Age: Business, Labor, and Public Policy, 1860–1897* (New York, 1961), 175.

using a series of stones rather than a single set to crush the hard spring wheat, which in turn was replaced by roller mills of greater capacity, meant that few locations in Wisconsin other than the lower Fox Valley could continue to compete as waterpower mills. This was certainly true of Milwaukee. Janesville and La Crosse also were export mill centers that came to depend more on steam power. Lumber milling also saw great changes in technology and scale of operations. Indeed, lumber mills turned even more readily than flour mills to steam, for fuel was no problem.

As these changes occurred, Wisconsin cities, and particularly Milwaukee, became increasingly important for their foundries and machinery manufactories, which served the mills' needs for power application, as well as for other specialized machinery which was developed in a symbiotic relationship with local machine makers. These were technologies to which Wisconsin's struggling shops brought ingenuity, adaptability, and a generous leavening of often superior European training, education, and experience. It was a time when much basic technological information was communicated quite casually in the varied experience of these men and their Yankee counterparts.[8]

A vital element in achieving industrial diversity (aside from the conjunction of the opportunity and the individual entrepreneur with the requisite talents) was finding the necessary capital to develop a modest shop to the point where it had the potential to become an industrial enterprise. Many felt called, but few were chosen. It is worth noting—and was so noted at the time—that in the 1870's a prospective Wisconsin industrialist suffered disadvantages in a search for capital. Frontiers were traditionally short of capital. The conventional wisdom assumed that the proper role of banks was to move the harvest and to cover ordinary commercial transactions.[9]

---

[8] Glaab and Larsen, *Factories in the Valley,* 53–77; Still, *Milwaukee,* 337; Gerd Korman, *Industrialization, Immigrants and Americanizers: The View from Milwaukee, 1866–1921* (Madison, 1967), 16.

[9] James Seville, one of the founders of the Reliance Works which was sold in bankruptcy proceedings in 1861, spoke of the experience to the Old Settlers' Club of Milwaukee County thirty-six years later: ". . . [A]ll new enterprises were supposed to have their own capital, for if they had not the chances were small for accommodation at the banks. . . . The com-

Until the 1890's at least, incorporation was not an avenue to easier financing, even for relatively large and expanding enterprises. While the corporate form was widely adopted in the 1880's, the advantages were mostly legal rather than providing for broader financial participation. In lumbering, as noted earlier, of 100 corporations reported in 1896, there were only 541 stockholders involved, many with multiple holdings. Wisconsin's industrial entrepreneurs suffered with their counterparts elsewhere from the lack of a market for industrial securities on the American scene and a want of investment bankers.[10]

Milwaukee industry, on the average, bore a relatively heavy capitalization. This was certainly characteristic of the large breweries, flour-milling operations, tanneries, and the growing foundry and machine firms. The federal census of 1890 illustrated this with figures showing the average capital investment required to generate $100 of value of product:

|             | 1880    | 1890    |
|-------------|---------|---------|
| Milwaukee   | $43.17  | $70.92  |
| Cleveland   | 39.98   | 61.58   |
| Detroit     | 51.67   | 58.23   |
| Chicago     | 27.64   | 54.13   |
| Minneapolis | 30.04   | 51.43   |

It was a matter of local pride by 1892 that Milwaukee's banking capital "is almost wholly owned by Milwaukee people, and her merchants and manufacturers have so much capital of their own that they have no occasion to lean upon extraneous aid to a large extent." This was the opinion of the leading spokesman for Milwaukee bankers, Alexander Mitchell's nephew, John Johnston.

---

mercial interests were the paramount objects in view by the banks then in existence, and anyone having sufficient 'nerve' to go into manufacturing must do it on his own resources or 'bust.' " John G. Gregory, *History of Milwaukee, Wisconsin* (4 vols., Chicago, 1931), 1:544–548.

[10] It is difficult to find even fragmentary data on the financing of Wisconsin industries in the years under discussion, but see J. Willard Hurst, *Law and Economic Growth: The Legal History of the Lumber Industry in Wisconsin, 1836–1915* (Cambridge, 1964), 414; and Kuehn, *Wisconsin Business Corporation,* 138–139, 156–157. See also Thomas R. Navin and Marian V. Sears, "The Rise of a Market for Industrial Securities, 1887–1902," in the *Business History Review,* 29 (June, 1955), 105–138; and Vincent P. Carosso, *Investment Banking in America* (Cambridge, 1970), 42–44.

Such were not the sentiments some years earlier of those who struggled to expand their industrial enterprises.[11]

Industrialization was increasingly an urban phenomenon, even though the dominant lumber industry was widely dispersed. The availability of cheaper and more reliable steam power, advantages of location with relation to transportation facilities, the presence of an adequate labor pool, availability of suppliers, subcontractors, jobbers, and many other ancillary services tended to concentrate industry. In 1870, when Milwaukee had 6.77 per cent of the state's population, it had 19.2 per cent of Wisconsin's industrial and mechanical workers. The comparable figures for 1880 were 8.79 per cent and 36.6 per cent; for 1890, 12.08 per cent and 32.4 per cent.[12]

In 1870, Milwaukee's industries reflected close ties with the agricultural hinterland. Flour milling was of prime importance. Pork packing provided some early fortunes, particularly during the Civil War. Although of minor consequence compared to Chicago, by 1871 Milwaukee was fourth in the nation as a packing center. By 1880 meat-packing was the leading industry in the city in total value of product, although it ranked only sixth in amount of capital investment and ninth in aggregate wages. The hog dominated the packing industry in Milwaukee, and Milwaukee dominated the industry in the state.[13]

The pioneers of pork packing were John Plankinton and Frederick Layton. The two came to Milwaukee in the 1840's, Layton as a boy of sixteen from Cambridgeshire, England, and Plankin-

[11] *Eleventh Census of the United States, 1890: Manufacturing Industries, Volume VI, Part 2*, p. xiv; John Johnston, "Banks and Banking Facilities in Milwaukee," in W. J. Anderson and Julius Bleyer, eds., *Milwaukee's Great Industries: A Compilation of Facts Concerning Milwaukee's Commercial and Manufacturing Enterprises, Its Trade and Commerce, and the Advantages It Offers to Manufacturers Seeking Desirable Locations for New or Established Industries* (Milwaukee, 1892), 72.

[12] *Eleventh Census of the United States, 1890: Manufacturing, Volume VI, Part 1*, pp. 628–629; Still, *Milwaukee*, 570–571; Alexander, "Industrial History of Wisconsin," in the *Wisconsin Blue Book, 1929*, pp. 34–37. Alexander's 1890 figure for industrial employment is 132,031, but should be 120,015 as he included office workers and owners and officers in his count.

[13] Still, *Milwaukee*, 333–334; Ray H. Whitbeck, *The Geography and Economic Development of Southeastern Wisconsin*, Wisconsin Geological and Natural History Survey, *Bulletin*, no. 58 (Madison, 1921), 103–105; *Tenth Census of the United States, 1880: Manufactures, Volume II*, 411–412.

ton as a young man from Delaware. They joined forces in 1852 as Layton and Plankinton, with a loan of $3,000 from Marshall and Ilsley, private bankers. They dealt more in a commodity than in industrial facilities. The partners went their separate ways in 1861. Two years later, Plankinton formed a partnership with Philip D. Armour, and the firm branched out to other cities. Twelve years later, Armour moved on to Chicago while Plankinton retained the Milwaukee plant, taking Patrick Cudahy as partner. Cudahy, an Irish immigrant, began working at age fourteen and rose to be superintendent of the Plankinton plant and then a partner. In 1888, he took over the business with his brother when Plankinton retired. The Cudahys soon moved to a location south of Milwaukee named Cudahy, after the metropolis grew restive about the packing industry as an expanding neighbor in the Menomonee Valley; the tanneries were noisome enough. The Plankinton name was again attached to the old Milwaukee plant when it was taken over by Plankinton's son William after the Cudahys moved.[14]

The Plankintons made other industrial investments. William was closely identified with the Milwaukee Cement Company, the Johnson Electric Service Company, and the Fuller-Warren Company, the last a New York stove-manufacturing firm that located a large branch factory in Milwaukee in 1890. The Plankinton name was also readily identified with fast action in the commodities market and with politics, philanthropy, the Plankinton Bank, street railways, and real estate ventures.[15]

[14] *DWB;* Whitbeck, *Economic Development of Southeastern Wisconsin,* 104–105; Merk, *Economic History,* 150–151; Still, *Milwaukee,* 64, 186–187, 196, 333–334, 411–412; Milwaukee *Sentinel,* January 1, 1892. Layton continued until 1900 as head of his own firm and made his mark in Milwaukee as a philanthropist and patron of the arts. The Layton Art Gallery, founded in 1888, added greatly to the city's cultural institutions.

[15] Ellis B. Usher, *Wisconsin: Its Story and Biography, 1848–1913* (8 vols., Chicago, 1914), 5:1098–1107; Still, *Milwaukee,* 249, 327, 342; Milwaukee *News,* April 29, 1905; Milwaukee *Journal,* August 16, 1919, and February 19, 1924; Howard Greene and William T. Berthelet, "The Milwaukee Cement Company," in *WMH,* 33 (September, 1949), 28–39; E. E. Barton, *Industrial History of Milwaukee: The Commercial, Manufacturing and Railway Metropolis of the North-west. . .* (Milwaukee, 1886), 60, 64, 84, 86; Peter McGill, "Pork Packing Business of Milwaukee," in Anderson and Bleyer, eds., *Milwaukee's Great Industries,* 184–191. See also *ibid.,* 233–234, 236, and Theodore A. Andersen, *A Century of Banking in Wisconsin* (Madison, 1954), 68–84.

Another aspect of Milwaukee's industrial development was the prominence of Germans in the leading growth industries. It is almost as if the Yankees sought the most obvious opportunities: waterpowers, real estate, townsite promotions, timber, finance, transportation, the grain trade, and general commerce, which often led them out of the future metropolis. Their German counterparts put down their kits, began building, and soon took possession of some of the most profitable sectors of the city's industrial economy. So much so, indeed, that the Yankees soon learned to take them on as partners and fellow directors, appoint them as officers in banks, insurance companies, and industrial and commercial enterprises, and seek their participation in business community promotions. By the 1870's they were an integral part of the general business community, despite the lag in their social integration.[16]

Germans controlled most of the flour milling in Milwaukee. There were seven large mills by 1892, the largest owned by Bavarian-born John B. A. Kern. He made a comfortable stake as a tobacconist in Philadelphia, lost it in a printing venture there, came to Milwaukee and in 1859 started in the milling business. Thirty years later he was reputed to control the largest flour-milling business in the country under one man's ownership and management. (Kern illustrates the hazards of ethnic generalizations about Germans settling in one place and doggedly building upon a trade, a piece of land, or an opportunity.) Other large flour mills in Milwaukee were operated by C. Manegold and Son; Faist, Kraus and Company; F. H. Magdeburg and Company; and B. Stern and Son. But these mills were not necessarily identifiable as German-owned. Kern's mill, for example, used the brand name "Eagle"; other brand indentifications were "Reliance," "Duluth," "Gem," and "Jupiter."[17]

[16] The terms "Yankee" and "German" are used in the broadest sense, more or less as the contemporaries perceived one another. See Richard N. Current, *The History of Wisconsin. Volume II: The Civil War Era, 1848–1873* (Madison, 1976), 550–556, for a discussion of ethnicity as the 1870's began. The documentation for the above generalizations is scattered through every volume of Milwaukee history cited in this chapter and in comparable volumes of local history. See Still, *Milwaukee,* 112, 188–189, 264–267.

[17] Howard L. Conrad, ed., *History of Milwaukee County from Its First Settlement to the Year 1895* (3 vols., Chicago, 1895), 3:169–170; L. R. Hurd, "Milwaukee's Flouring Industries," in Anderson and Bleyer, eds., *Milwaukee's Great Industries,* 149–151.

There was no mistaking the German grip on brewing, malting, leather tanning and currying, and a number of less important industries. Germans had a vital role in building large firms in the general field of foundries and machinery manufacturing. German-Jewish firms dominated men's clothing manufacturing and tobacco manufacturing.[18]

Brewing was the most spectacular growth industry on the Milwaukee scene. The value of product in 1890 was over fifteen times that of 1870. By 1890, it was the city's leading industry in both value of product and capital invested. Milwaukee's emphasis on brewing was not necessarily the result of local factors. It was not that she was the most German of major American cities, nor more favorably located with relation to good water or to fields of choice midwestern barley. It was, rather, her location with respect to other large urban markets, particularly Chicago. The brewers of Chicago, New York, Baltimore, St. Louis, and Cincinnati were comfortably located in the midst of much larger markets of thirsty German-Americans and other urbanites learning to appreciate lager beer. American industry frowned upon hard liquor or wine, but employers were learning to tolerate beer on or near the premises in these major cities. Milwaukee brewers, lacking a local market as large as other brewing centers, were tempted by those larger markets and moved in on them. Milwaukee brewers also filled the void created by the destruction of Chicago's breweries in the great fire of 1871.

This effort involved solving the formidable problems of delivering the temperamental brew, in barrels or bottles, to distant cities. The process was immensely expensive. It was not simply a matter of technology at the point of production; it also involved the control of financing, distribution, wholesaling, advertising, and retailing in very lucrative and therefore highly competitive markets. This led to heavy real estate investments in those markets where Pabst and other Milwaukee brewers took over choice locations, even building hotels or restaurants for advertising pur-

[18] Margaret Walsh, "Industrial Opportunity on the Urban Frontier: 'Rags to Riches' and Milwaukee Clothing Manufacturers, 1840–1880," in *WMH,* 57 (Spring, 1947), 175–194; "Men's and Women's Clothing," in Anderson and Bleyer, eds., *Milwaukee's Great Industries,* 154–155.

poses, as they did in Milwaukee, Chicago, Minneapolis, New York, and San Francisco. An expanding brewery business was financially a bottomless pit.[19]

Along with their tremendous capital needs, the brewers had extremely heavy operating expenses, offset by immense flows of cash. They were quick to eliminate middlemen and replace them with their own wholesalers or branch managers. It is not remarkable that the brewers got into the banking business early. The Second Ward Bank, started in 1856, was identified with the German business community. It was dominated by the brewers; the leading stockholders and officers were Frederick Pabst, Valentine Blatz, Philip Best, Joseph Schlitz, and August Krug's nephews, the Uihleins. Pabst started his own bank, the Wisconsin National, in 1892. The West Side Bank was controlled by the brewer Adam Gettelman and others.[20]

A talent for advertising and promotional work was a necessary attribute for a successful brewer. Frederick Pabst was the archetype, but others shared in local philanthropies, took prominent roles in the chamber of commerce, and promoted Milwaukee industrial expositions. They also provided the local equivalent of a public parks system, probably as much for public relations as for profit. Brewing money was certainly respectable in the business community. As investors, the brewers inclined towards banks, real estate, and street railroads. A large number of sons followed their fathers in brewing, but other opportunities were open to them. In the second generation, Otto and Herman Falk were identified with the Falk Manufacturing Company, and Otto became president of Allis-Chalmers. Frederick Gettelman was an inventor of some importance, making contributions in the fields of road and farm machinery as well as brewing equipment.[21]

[19] Cochran, *Pabst Brewing Company*, 70–159, 196–199, 210–213; William O. Baldwin, "Historical Geography of the Brewing Industry: Focus on Wisconsin" (doctoral dissertation, University of Illinois, 1966), chap. 4.

[20] Cochran, *Pabst Brewing Company*, 85, 260; Milwaukee *Sentinel*, February 26, 1898; *DWB*; Milwaukee *Telegram*, February 15, 1925.

[21] Cochran, *Pabst Brewing Company*, 67–68, 213–225, 255–270. Cochran comments (p. 67): "For business reasons, if for no other, it was important for a brewer to be a well-known figure."

Another industry in which Milwaukee gained a wide reputation was the leather industry. At its peak it was dominated by Germans. Tanning migrated westward in company with the meatpacking industry. At the time, it also depended upon a primitive chemistry based on the natural tannin in the bark of hemlock and oak trees, which were plentiful in Wisconsin. Bark was the heaviest component in manufacturing leather, after water; it took about a ton of bark to tan 200 pounds of green hides. This equation gave Milwaukee an advantage over Chicago, the packing center, as Milwaukee was closer to the sources of bark and had cheaper handling facilities at her extensive riverside locations. In 1879, Wisconsin accounted for only 3.9 per cent of the nation's consumption of hides and skins. By 1890 Milwaukee was first in the world in plain leather production.

Wisconsin tanners concentrated on processing cow and calf hides used mostly in shoes, harness, saddles, and industrial belting. Cowhide leather manufacturing required a large capitalization for plant and inventory. By 1890 the pioneer firm of Pfister and Vogel was the dominant one in Milwaukee and the state. This local giant employed more than 600 men in three tanneries in the city. The remaining tanneries, controlled by seven firms, were all German-owned, mostly by former employees of Pfister and Vogel. Both Guido Pfister and Fred Vogel, who moved their leather and tanning operations from Buffalo to Milwaukee in the 1840's, were integrated into the financial community by the 1870's; Pfister was a trustee of Northwestern Mutual Life Insurance Company and his name remains on Milwaukee's leading hotel. His son Charles became a leader of the Republican stalwarts in their struggles with Robert La Follette.[22]

Wisconsin's leather industry fell on hard times immediately after 1892. Depression and chronic oversupply problems were complicated by the introduction from abroad of important

[22] Henry Eskuche, "Leather and the Tanning Industry," in Anderson and Bleyer, eds., *Milwaukee's Great Industries,* 157–158; *DWB;* Charles E. Schefft, "The Tanning Industry in Wisconsin: A History of Its Frontier Origins and Its Development" (master's thesis, University of Wisconsin, 1938), 1–73; Edgar M. Hoover, Jr., *Location Theory and the Shoe and Leather Industries* (Cambridge, 1937; reprinted, New York, 1968), 136; Still, *Milwaukee,* 334–335.

advances in the chemistry of the industry which freed it from bark supplies. With these changes, the great packinghouses invaded the industry. The established tanneries countered with further consolidations and trust arrangements. Leather in the 1890's ceased to be the growth industry for Milwaukee that it had been through the 1880's.[23]

An industry tied to the growth of the leather industry was the manufacture of boots and shoes. One of the early fortunes in Milwaukee was that of Charles T. Bradley, who had come from Massachusetts in 1843 and was in this business for the next fifty years. The Bradley and Metcalf Shoe Company had made the transition during the 1860's from a cottage industry to partially mechanized factory operation. Western shoe manufacturers were generally limited to supplying the western market with work shoes. Most of Milwaukee's leather for shoes found its market in the New England towns that traditionally had dominated the industry. While significant for Milwaukee—by 1890 shoe manufacturing employed 1,140 people—it provided less than 2 per cent of the gross value of product for the city.[24]

Iron ore concentrations in small amounts are common almost everywhere throughout the United States, and before the 1870's charcoal was the standard fuel for iron reduction. Wisconsin had convenient and ample supplies of both ore and charcoal, and the industry enjoyed considerable expansion in the early 1870's. But charcoal-iron production soon declined because of the rapid development of iron and steel technology and the greater use of coal in place of charcoal. As new ore bodies were discovered, particularly in Minnesota, and processes were adapted for their use, the industry concentrated in western Pennsylvania, Ohio, and Illinois, close to the metallurgical coal and to the major markets.[25]

[23] Clark, *History of Manufactures,* 467, 762; Schefft, "Tanning Industry in Wisconsin," 54–71; Hoover, *Shoe and Leather Industries,* 137–155.

[24] Merk, *Economic History,* 170–171; Hoover, *Shoe and Leather Industries,* 224–226, 269–271; Clark, *History of Manufactures,* 131; *DWB.*

[25] Kirkland, *Industry Comes of Age,* 165–166, 200–201; Peter Temin, *Iron and Steel in Nineteenth-Century America: An Economic Inquiry* (Cambridge, 1964), 199–206; Kenneth Warren, *The American Steel Industry, 1850–1970: A Geographical Interpretation* (Oxford, England, 1973), 41–80.

Milwaukee's iron-using industries profited temporarily from the uncertainties accompanying this technological and organizational transition. An ore body of considerable size at Iron Ridge in Dodge County had been exploited for some years before 1865 by furnaces near the ore and in Milwaukee. Iron mines were opened in the early 1890's near the Wisconsin border in the Menominee Range of Michigan. But limited supplies of Michigan ore evidently were available earlier as there were charcoal iron furnaces built between 1869 and 1872 along the lower Fox River. These early furnaces were based upon nearby supplies of hardwoods, owned as acreage by furnace operators or made available as land was cleared for agriculture or cut for tanning bark. The largest of the four companies in the lower Fox River had an annual production capacity of 13,500 net tons, which was probably sufficient to meet local needs in Appleton. Until the depression of the 1870's, local iron commanded good prices, protected as it was by tariffs and the distance from more economical producers.[26]

Iron supplies for Milwaukee industry were further assured by the Milwaukee Iron Company, whose rolling mills and furnaces at Bay View, just south of the city, were in operation by 1870–1871. This was the creation of Eber Brock Ward of Detroit, a pioneer midwestern industrialist. Steel technology in the United States owes much to Ward and his experiments at a jerry-built plant near Detroit. Ward was determined to follow the market westward, which meant that railroads were his primary customers. He enlisted the interest of Alexander Mitchell, who controlled a growing railroad empire as well as the Bay View site. Ward kept control of the enterprise. Bay View began as a furnace and rolling mill for reworking iron rails. Simultaneously, Ward promoted what was to be the North Chicago Steel Company, where he built blast furnaces and converters to produce Bessemer steel. The Milwaukee Iron Company apparently was well financed, and with Ward's leadership and energies behind it the

[26] Whitbeck, *Economic Development of Southeastern Wisconsin,* 111–114; Usher, *Wisconsin,* 1:139–149; Ray H. Whitbeck, *The Geography of the Fox–Winnebago Valley* (Madison, 1915), 68–69; Ellis B. Usher, "Nelson Powell Hulst, 'The Greatest American Authority on Iron,'" in *WMH,* 7 (June, 1924), 392–393; Clark, *History of Manufactures,* 67.

plant was expanded to include two large furnaces for reducing Lake Superior and Iron Ridge ores, with anthracite and coke brought from Lake Erie ports. The furnaces were followed shortly by the Minerva Iron Company furnace, a smaller coke-using reduction furnace at Bay View. (These three furnaces, like the scattered charcoal operations, were iron producers, not equipped for large-scale steelmaking.)[27]

Ward died early in 1875 and, lacking his driving spirit, the Bay View plant would have been in trouble even without the further complications of the long depression. Railroads were the main customers of the industry, and new railroad construction had slacked off dramatically. Also, steel rails were coming into wider use. The failure to equip Bay View for steel production cast a shadow over its future. The plant had reached an average payroll of 800 to 1,000 men just before the depression. By 1876, it was closed down and in receivership.[28]

The iron and steel business revived after 1878, although prices continued at a lower level than in the early 1870's. Naturally, it was the large integrated operations that survived and enjoyed the technological changes that were coming so rapidly. Bay View and the Minerva furnace were taken over in a reorganization of the parent firm, the North Chicago Rolling Mills. Bay View built again to a payroll of nearly 1,500 men by the mid-eighties. It is indicative of the changes in the industry, and of Wisconsin's marginal firms, that in 1880 the state ranked sixth nationally in iron and steel production, and by 1890 had fallen to tenth, although the investment in plants had reportedly more than doubled. More reorganizations were ahead for Bay View, which (with the exception of a nail mill) was still not converted to steel production. Wisconsin became more of a factor in the ore trade, with the exploitation of its deep mines tributary to Ashland which were

[27] Usher, *Wisconsin*, 1:144–145; Whitbeck, *Economic Development of Southeastern Wisconsin*, 113; Clark, *History of Manufactures*, 67, 208–209, 236–238, 329; Usher, "Nelson Powell Hulst," in *WMH*, 7: 385–405; Bernhard C. Korn, "Eber Brock Ward: Pathfinder of American Industry" (doctoral dissertation, Marquette University, 1942), 116–198.

[28] Whitbeck, *Economic Development of Southeastern Wisconsin*, 113–114; John Gurda, *Bay View, Wis.* (Milwaukee, 1979), 18–19.

particularly adaptable to the Bessemer process for steelmaking. With newer processes, the more easily worked Minnesota iron ores began to replace the more expensive Wisconsin ores by the 1890's. But not before Milwaukee had a brief fling as the center of a boom in iron mine stocks in the mid-eighties, with its own feverish exchange.[29]

The foundry and machine industries, which are so characteristic of Wisconsin's metropolis and a number of secondary cities, marked a sort of industrial coming-of-age. There had been pioneers in the metals trades in Milwaukee, but practically none survived the 1857 panic. Opportunities were certainly present in the postwar years to supply the equipment for the growing resource-processing industries: flour milling, lumber, iron mining, brewing, tanning, and agricultural machinery; also railroad rolling stock, and carriage and wagon making. All of these industries were experiencing great growth and successive technological changes which involved more sophisticated steam engines and machines as well as metal fabricated parts to replace hardwoods in farm machines, wagons, and carriages. It was therefore logical for Milwaukee and other Wisconsin cities to develop these industries to provide power and power transmission equipment, metal parts, and subassemblies to other industries.

But there were several catches. Capital demands were heavy whenever a machine shop aspired to move beyond the status of a job shop—that is, making and repairing items to order—to produce engines or machines of their own design for a general or specialized market. Then, too, the industries to be served, such as sawmills or farm machinery makers, had heavy credit demands of their own because their capital was tied up in inventory and credit sales, which in turn resulted in their expectations of long-term credit for their purchases. And for many engines or machines, it

[29] Whitbeck, *Economic Development of Southeastern Wisconsin*, 113-114; I. M. Bean, "Our Iron and Steel Industries," in Anderson and Bleyer, eds., *Milwaukee's Great Industries*, 77-82; Barton, *Industrial History of Milwaukee*, 58; Gregory, *History of Milwaukee*, 1:555-556; *Eleventh Census of the United States, 1890: Manufacturing Industries, Volume VI, Part 3*, pp. 386-388; Milwaukee *Sentinel*, July 24, 1892; Temin, *Iron and Steel in Nineteenth-Century America*, 194-199; Clark, *History of Manufactures*, 208-209; Ferdinand Schlesinger obituaries, Milwaukee *Sentinel*, January 4, 1921, and Milwaukee *Journal*, January 3, 1921.

could be a long time between getting the order and placing the
equipment in working order on the buyer's premises. Vagaries of
weather affected their customers, farming and lumbering in particular. The fact was, many customers were marginal operators in
marginal locations, and the boom-and-slump nature of nearly
everyone's business was magnified by the near-frontier conditions. As Wisconsin industries were being drawn ever closer to the
growing national market, this also made it easier for established
eastern machinery producers to reach the western markets.
Despite technological advancements, many machines and power
plants were still sold as generic items—"one each, ten horsepower
engine"—and such sales were commonly handled through wholesale merchants or commission agents rather than directly through
the manufacturers. This meant that the former intervened
between the latter and their customers with added leverage,
because they often provided the credit for the transaction.
Increasing the uncertainty, markets were not yet well defined in
many cases. All of these factors made this type of manufacturing
a difficult field for marginally financed newcomers to enter.[30]

As the national economy began to move out of the shadow of the
1873 panic and the long depression that followed, there were signs
that Wisconsin enterprises in the machine and foundry fields were
moving to more solid financial ground and finding their markets
more assured. One of the examples of this was provided by the
Laird, Norton Company, a lumbering concern of Winona, Minnesota, which operated several large sawmills. When the company remodeled one of its mills in 1878, most of the new
equipment was manufactured in Wisconsin. It replaced equipment put in place in 1868–1869, which had come from Philadelphia, Erie, Buffalo, and Boston manufacturers.[31]

The story of E. P. Allis and Company best illustrates the early

[30] Margaret Walsh, "Business Success and Capital Availability in the New West: Milwaukee Ironmasters in the Middle Nineteenth Century," in *The Old Northwest,* 1 (June,
1975), 159–179; Glenn Porter and Harold C. Livesay, *Merchants and Manufacturers: Studies
in the Changing Structure of Nineteenth-Century Marketing* (Baltimore, 1971), 180–184; Walter
F. Peterson, *An Industrial Heritage: Allis-Chalmers Corporation* (Milwaukee, 1978), 19–99.
[31] Fred W. Kohlmeyer, *Timber Roots: The Laird, Norton Story, 1855–1905* (Winona, 1972),
185–189.

history of the machine and foundry industries. Edward P. Allis arrived in Milwaukee in 1846 from Cazenovia, New York, and entered the retail leather business. Allis was a graduate of Union College in Schenectady, which provided the usual classical course of the time. Having family credit connections from home, he joined the Allen family, also of Cazenovia, in establishing a large tannery in 1850 at Two Rivers, where Allis got valuable experience managing the plant. Of an entrepreneurial temper, Allis was either prescient or very lucky, for he sold out his interest at a good price in 1856, just before the 1857 panic, and kept his capital liquid for several years in real estate brokerage, grain trading, and other investments. His partners in the Reliance Works, which they purchased at a sheriff's sale in 1861, sold out to Allis a year later because they were not willing to invest additional funds in the property. Allis, however, had ambitious plans for his new iron-making enterprise.[32]

Allis was without background or expert knowledge in the business upon which he embarked. His phenomenal success was based upon a simple formula: Find a promising market, then find men who could envision the highest state of the art, and provide them with the best of equipment, sufficient financing, and a free hand. Allis was laconic, as good a judge of men as of a business situation, fair, honest and generous in his dealings with employees even as he moved with the financially successful of the community. Margaret Watson Allis, his wife, was likewise energetic and had an excellent business head. She shared a life of public good works, cultural interests, and business success with her husband. Early deafness was a handicap which Allis accommodated. He often rode his horse to the works, where he was a familiar figure to his workers, carrying his ear trumpet, considerate, decisive, interested in everything.

The principal business of the Reliance Works before Allis acquired the property had been in making flour-milling equipment and dressing millstones, but it was equipped for casting about four tons of iron per day, with machinery for milling and

---

[32] Peterson, *Industrial Heritage*, 4; *Columbian Biographical Dictionary and Portrait Galley of the Representative Men of the United States: Wisconsin Volume* (Chicago, 1895), 388–391.

shaping it. After the 1857 failure, it had fallen to the status of a job shop, but wartime prosperity in wheat produced a steady business for the mill machinery and French buhrstones then used for producing flour. The work force grew, and Allis was included as forty-seventh in the list of forty-eight Milwaukee men whose annual incomes were $10,000 and up. The problem was to break out of this mold of the job shop into fields with more promise. He began by expanding his works, moving the old Reliance shops and equipment from a cramped site on the Milwaukee River to a twenty-acre tract, which he had owned since 1856, located at Florida and Clinton in the Menomonee Valley. With his enlarged facilities, particularly for iron founding and casting, Allis began making simple, basic steam engines. He soon bought out his largest local rival, the Bay State Iron Manufacturing Company.[33]

At the beginning of the 1870's, the enlarged foundry led Allis into another field, which proved to be an ill-timed move. The makeshift water system of Milwaukee was being replaced with unified pumping systems taking from Lake Michigan. Allis won the contract to provide cast-iron pipe for the Milwaukee system as well as pumping equipment, but he had neither pipe-casting equipment nor men experienced in this work. He hired two experts who proved able to deliver the desired results, but not without considerable confusion and unforeseen expense. This experience also drew him into building steam engines and pumping equipment of unusual size. He soon had machinery and skilled workmen in a variety of plants, some recently acquired, scattered in several locations around town. He had expanded from a work force of about seventy-five in 1866 to 400 in 1875, and some of his plants were working two shifts. It was the cast-iron pipe venture and heavy purchases of iron from the Milwaukee Iron Works that brought Allis to the brink of financial disaster.[34]

The 1873 panic and succeeding depression caught Allis over-extended. He was sole owner of his enterprises and heavily in debt. Unfortunately, a large part of the debt was owed to the Milwaukee Iron Company, which went into receivership in 1876. But

[33] Peterson, *Industrial Heritage,* 8–9; Hilton, "Men of Metal," 36–38.
[34] Peterson, *Industrial Heritage,* 9–15.

Allis had been a familiar and successful businessman in the Milwaukee financial community for more than twenty years, and he had not neglected the public relations aspects of his rapid rise as a manufacturer. He now had one of the largest payrolls in the city of skilled men, homeowners who took an active part in church, community, and lodge affairs. (Machinists and foundrymen were among the elite of the local labor force, mostly German, British, and American in background.) Local pride was involved. His creditors and their creditors saw to it that Allis had an opportunity to settle his debts at a considerable discount, and to retain control of his company.[35]

This brush with ruin did not alter Allis' optimistic and expansive temperament. It did have the salutary effect of concentrating his energies upon three of the most promising fields: grain milling, lumber milling, and power equipment. George Hinkley was a millwright-inventor who in 1870 had started his own sawmill machinery shop in Milwaukee, but with indifferent success. In 1873 he accepted an invitation from Allis to head an expanding sawmill machinery division of the Reliance Works. It was a wise choice. Allis financed patents in Hinkley's name, revolutionizing the lumber industry in conjunction with the more powerful constant-speed, reliable steam engines of Allis manufacture. In 1889 the company sold the first successful bandsaw mill. Hinkley's inventions harnessed steam to do much of the heavy work in the mills that formerly had been done by human muscle. The Allis Company catalog of sawmill equipment grew to seventy pages. By the 1880's, the company was the acknowledged giant in its field.

William D. Gray came to the Reliance Works in 1876 as head of the flour-milling machinery department. Like Hinkley, he was both an inventor and a competent manager. It was Gray who coordinated with experiments, financed in part by C. C. Washburn at his Minneapolis mills, to produce the machinery for the first large-scale use of the roller process in this country. Allis-built machinery became the new standard in this field.

As flour and lumber mills increased in size and capacity, there

---

[35] *Ibid.*, 15–16; Korman, *Industrialization, Immigrants and Americanizers,* 16.

was a need for ever larger and more reliable engines. Allis knew
that he must win, and hold, a leading place in engine manufacturing to continue his expansive ways. He also recognized his own
limitations as a manager of a conglomerate of industries producing machines dependent upon rapidly changing and increasingly
sophisticated technologies. He advertised in the *American Machinist*
for a nonpareil to fill his requirements, and found him. Edwin
Reynolds earned the handsome salary of $5,000 as general super-
intendent of the Corliss Steam Engine Company of Providence,
Rhode Island. Corliss was then the country's leading engine
maker. Reynolds had overseen the manufacture of the giant Corliss engine which was the central jewel of Machinery Hall at the
Centennial Exposition in Philadelphia in 1876. Allis offered Reynolds a free hand, $3,500, the shop to build his designs, and the
opportunity to develop his improvements on the Corliss engine,
for which the basic patent had run out. Reynolds came in 1877
and took charge of designing as well as overall management. He
carried on as manager of the firm after Allis' death in 1889,
although Allis never shared ownership with him.

Reynolds, like Allis, was confident and venturesome. He did
not hesitate to sell monster engines, incorporating new and sometimes untried features from his designing board, with bold guar-
antees. He offered on occasion to accept the savings in fuel costs
in lieu of the price of his new engines. He found his work force less
skilled and the equipment inferior to that at his command in
Providence, but he was correct in his assessment that Allis would
find the money to make good the deficiencies. By 1882, steam
engines and pumping equipment were about two-thirds of company sales. Reynolds' designs dominated the growing municipal
pumping applications and similar engine needs to the 1920's,
when electricity took over large pumping applications. About half
the lumber mills in the South and West, as the industry migrated
from the Midwest, used Milwaukee engines and mill equipment.
The firm continued its pre-eminence in flour-milling equipment,
sawmill equipment, mine power equipment, blower engines for
steel mills and for ventilating the deep mines of northern Wisconsin and Michigan, and high-capacity pumps for keeping down the

water level. Allis' company later entered the field of electrical generating equipment.

Edward P. Allis died in 1889, the sole owner of a company which, characteristically, was still scattered in various locations around Milwaukee, sometimes still in ramshackle buildings but housing the best in equipment. The company did not move to the West Allis location until some years later. The company Allis left behind had a payroll approaching 1,500 and was important in national and international markets. The physical assets were valued at approximately a million dollars, plus working capital of $500,000. He owed $415,000, of which $243,000 was borrowed from the Northwestern Mutual Life Insurance Company, on whose board of directors he had served for years. He owed an unsecured debt of $160,000 to a wealthy sister.[36]

By 1880, the well-publicized success of the E. P. Allis Company seemed not only secure but capable of conquering new and growing markets. This success helped to improve the fortunes of the machine and foundry industries in Milwaukee and in Wisconsin generally. Characteristically, specialty manufacturing tended to cluster in proximity to firms that played a leadership role. More important, these specialty firms became more interesting to capital investors, the main factor that separated the successes from the also-rans. Milwaukee had the usual booming, breast-beating organizations to attract new industries and outside capital and to enlist local capital in industrial opportunities, though the results are difficult to measure. As banking became more sophisticated and commanded greater resources, Milwaukee machine industries found financing more available through channels not so readily available earlier. But to keep a shop and skilled employees together through the frequent and sharp business fluctuations of the times required owners with skills in improvisation.[37]

[36] The principal source for E. P. Allis' career is Peterson, *Industrial Heritage,* 1-72, 84. See also Hilton, "Men of Metal," 35-39; Still, *Milwaukee,* 337-339, 380; Current, *Civil War Era,* 483; Gregory, *History of Milwaukee,* 1:550-553, 3:12-21; James I. Clark, *Edward P. Allis: Pioneer Industrialist* (Madison, 1958); and Korman, *Industrialization, Immigrants and Americanizers,* 37-38.

[37] Still, *Milwaukee,* 348-353. Ralph L. Andreano, ed., *New Views on American Economic Development: A Selective Anthology of Recent Work* (Cambridge, 1965), counts five distinct peaks

At a time when technological knowledge and craftsmanship were not yet institutionalized, much of it was transmitted casually, by word of mouth and by example. Milwaukee had about the richest possible mixture of men who had practical acquaintance with new technological developments in Europe as well as those in the northeastern states where the American machine tool industry centered. This available knowledge and talent, the insecurity which characterized the industry, and the needs of manufacturers and other customers to handle and process materials ever more rapidly and efficiently required innovative tool and equipment makers, situated in close communication with the industries served.[38]

The problems of finance for specialty manufacturers were partially relieved by support from the industrialists served. It was logical, for instance, that Delos L. Filer, a wealthy Michigan lumberman, should see a financial opportunity in bankrolling John M. Stowell, a self-taught machinist, in what became another leading Milwaukee firm in the sawmill machinery manufacturing field, Filer, Stowell and Co. Other machine and foundry shops that served the growing technological requirements of the brewing industry found the brewers' ready cash flow a boon. Captain Fred Pabst, who liked to have his money and credit work full time, subsidized Henry Harnischfeger in slack times by giving him brewery equipment orders. Harnischfeger met the Saturday night payroll with cash fresh from the brewery, ensuring a mixture of gratitude and bargain prices for Pabst.[39]

The career of Henry Harnischfeger, whose name at this writing still graces a major American industrial enterprise, well illustrates the international character of the machine and foundry

and troughs between 1873 and 1894 in American business activity; see pp. 258–259. Henry Harnischfeger, in his *Autobiography,* remembered vividly the numerous times when insolvency threatened his early years as a manufacturer of machinery.

[38] The best illustration of the above generalizations is given in Harnischfeger's brief *Autobiography;* Hilton, "Men of Metal," 55–65, is also useful. For the ways in which various crafts and technologies were learned, see [Frank A. Flower], *History of Milwaukee, Wisconsin. . .* (Chicago, 1881), 1283–1317.

[39] Walsh, "Business Success and Capital Availability," in *The Old Northwest,* 1:164–166; H. R. Page and Company, *History of Mason County, Michigan, with Illustrations and Biographical Sketches of Some of Its Prominent Men and Pioneers* (Chicago, 1882), 26; [Flower], *Milwaukee,* 2:1290; Harnischfeger, *Autobiography,* 9, 18, 22–23.

industries in Wisconsin. Born in Hesse-Nassau in 1855, he came to New York in 1872 and through acquaintances got a job with the Singer Sewing Machine Company. Trained in the locksmithing trade, Harnischfeger followed every opportunity to expand his technical education. He worked for Singer, the Rhode Island Locomotive Works, Brown and Sharpe, the leading machine toolmakers in the country, and took engineering classes sponsored by a Turnverein he joined in Elizabeth, New Jersey. In 1881 he followed friends from the Turnverein class to Milwaukee and a job with the Whitehill Sewing Machine Company. Robert Whitehill was an inventor who got backing from New York and Milwaukee capital. The Whitehill plant appeared full-blown in impressive quarters on Milwaukee's south side. It was less than a decade since the Milwaukee developers of the first typewriter had decided that Milwaukee lacked machine and foundry facilities and skilled labor to fabricate interchangeable parts.[40]

Whitehill proved to be a better inventor than manager and soon broke the firm with a continuous flow of design changes. Alonzo Pawling, a patternmaker put at liberty by Whitehill's failure, started a machine shop with Maurice Weiss, with whom Harnischfeger had roomed in New York. In 1884 Harnischfeger took over Weiss's interest to form Pawling and Harnischfeger, the forerunner of what was to become, after the older Pawling's retirement, the Harnischfeger Corporation.[41]

The machine and foundry industries, encouraged by the favorable business climate of the early eighties and surrounded by successful competitors and prosperously expanding client industries, began to grow expansively in Wisconsin. A man with a new idea or an invention was tempted to build a business of his own, and venture capital was becoming more readily available. Harnischfeger's account of his own early years gives a sense of this optimism. One meets a stream of engineers and inventors, several brought to Milwaukee by that active recruiter, E. P.

---

[40] Harnischfeger, *Autobiography*, 1–4; Still, *Milwaukee*, 353; Barton, *Industrial History of Milwaukee*, 129–130; Current, *Typewriter and Men Who Made It*, 62. G. C. Trumpff, president of the South Side Savings Bank, appears as secretary of the Whitehill firm, indicating some Milwaukee money in the venture. See [Flower], *Milwaukee*, 2:1087.

[41] Harnischfeger, *Autobiography*, 4–6.

Allis, who soon ventured forth on their own. Some, like Bruno Nordberg, a graduate of the Polytechnic Institute of Helsingfors (Helsinki), had the advantage of European engineering academic training; most others picked up technological backgrounds less formally. Nordberg had invented a poppet valve governor for achieving a constant speed, under varying loads, with heavy steam engines. Pawling and Harnischfeger manufactured the valves to Nordberg's designs. Nordberg left Allis and rented loft space above the modest shop of Pawling and Harnischfeger. Another who came for custom work to the shop was Christopher W. LeValley, who later started what became Rex Chain Belt.

There was much trading of talent and ideas, without apparent regard for the ethnic divisions still evident in where one lived or mixed socially. Bruno Nordberg's early financial backers were Alonzo Straw, Fredrick L. Horneffer, F. A. Wilde, and Jacob E. Friend. Straw was a Vermont Yankee, partner in the Straw and Ellsworth Manufacturing Company, a profitable firm that manufactured hats, caps, and gloves for the western market. Horneffer was secretary-treasurer of that firm. Wilde was a successful Neenah druggist. Jacob Friend, a Milwaukee lawyer, was the son of a German-Jewish clothing manufacturer. Friend Brothers was the largest of several Milwaukee clothing manufacturing firms. Jacob Friend later became president of the Nordberg Manufacturing Company in 1895. Nordberg also attracted financial support from Fred Pabst and Emil Schandein, owners of Best Brewing Company. Nordberg was an early licensee of Rudolf Diesel's engine patents in the United States, and the firm specialized in marine applications of the diesel engine. Later, Nordberg and Rex Chain Belt were combined in the Rexnord Corporation.[42]

Henry Harnischfeger's firm was similarly built from work of a

[42] *Ibid.*, 7 ff.; Anderson and Bleyer, eds., *Milwaukee's Great Industries,* 223; Usher, *Wisconsin,* 7:1926-1928; Robert E. Schultz, "Nordberg: Men and Machines," in *Creative Wisconsin,* 4 (Winter, 1957), 42–46; Walsh, "Milwaukee Clothing Manufacturers," *WMH,* 57:175–194; *DWB;* [Flower], *Milwaukee,* 2:1262; Military Order of the Loyal Legion, Wisconsin Commandery, "In Memoriam: Companion Ferdinand August Wilde," published as *Circular No. 4,* series 1920, whole no. 608 (Milwaukee, 1920).

bewildering variety. His memoir does not mention his own financial backers, if any; possibly a want of them caused him to recall so vividly those who backed Nordberg. Like so many Milwaukee firms, Pawling and Harnischfeger depended upon internal growth and taking long chances wherever business led them. Some ventures involved large outlays for machines, foundry capacity, or other equipment and space. He remembered that his own initial contribution to the firm was his life savings, $2,500, which he invested in machine tools. The next thirty years brought variations on the same theme: spend to meet new opportunities and new technologies.[43]

Industrial booming was endemic to American cities in the post-Civil War years, but Milwaukee did present an unusual opportunity, as well as some good reasons for urgency. By the mid-seventies, it was becoming clear to many that the Milwaukee wheat trade was fading, and within a few more years it would be equally evident that Chicago and the rising Twin Cities of Minnesota were seriously restricting the scope of Milwaukee's hinterland for wholesaling and jobbing opportunities. Industrial promotion did take on a bit more sophistication, although it was derivative. At least Milwaukee had moved beyond the idea of economic self-sufficiency so characteristic of frontier communities, deploring every item of eastern manufacture as if it were an expensive import from a foreign land. The Merchants' Association, the Chamber of Commerce, and the city council joined in 1879 to organize an industrial fair patterned after the successful Philadelphia Centennial Exposition. They built at a cost of about $200,000 an odd structure of "modified Queen Anne . . . architecture, in which Norman and Gothic elements" were evident. Chicago and other western cities already had similar structures for the same purpose.[44]

---

[43] Harnischfeger, *Autobiography, passim.*

[44] Current, *Civil War Era,* 454; Still, *Milwaukee,* 346–350; Gregory, *History of Milwaukee,* 1:495–506; William E. Derby, "A History of the Port of Milwaukee, 1835–1910" (doctoral dissertation, University of Wisconsin, 1963), 291–294, 334–337. See Barton, *Industrial Milwaukee,* 69–70, on the Exposition Building.

Expansion followed the business cycles rather than the decennial census, and the large growth years of industry were from about 1879 to 1883, reviving again in the late 1880's until 1893. As midwestern railroads achieved investment status and found a national and international market for their securities, railroad promotions required less local capital. Street railroads, other urban services, and real estate improvements soaked up much of this. Milwaukee capital no longer concentrated on the seasonal movement of grain, and more and more it found its way into manufacturing and trade in other processed goods. With capital

GROWTH OF MILWAUKEE INDUSTRIES, 1870–1890

| Year and Industry | Establishments | Average Number Employees | Average Capitalization |
|---|---|---|---|
| Machine and Foundries | | | |
| 1870 | 31 | 18.5 | $   15,123 |
| 1880 | 30 | 48.9 | 42.882 |
| 1890 | 44 | 74.2 | 125,413 |
| Breweries | | | |
| 1870 | 16 | 14.6 | 43,000 |
| 1880 | 13 | 80 | 364,000 |
| 1890 | 9 | 243.1 | 1,448,300 |
| Men's Clothing | | | |
| 1870 | 56 | 17.1 | 12,414 |
| 1880 | 52 | 82.7 | 36,445 |
| 1890 | 20 | 124.4 | 143,426 |
| Flour Mills | | | |
| 1870 | 14 | 13 | 35,786 |
| 1880 | 11 | 24.1 | 96,909 |
| 1890 | 10 | 37 | 175,174 |
| Hats and Caps | | | |
| 1870 | 4 | 4 | 10,900 |
| 1880 | 3 | 7.3 | 8,667 |
| 1890 | 9 | 38.2 | 26,696 |
| Trunks and Valises | | | |
| 1870 | 3 | 19.3 | 7,633 |
| 1880 | 4 | 65.8 | 45,750 |
| 1890 | 5 | 99 | 170,309 |

SOURCES: *Ninth Census of the United States, 1870: Statistics of Wealth and Industry, Volume II,* p. 744; *Tenth Census of the United States, 1880: Manufactures, Volume II,* pp. 411–412; *Eleventh Census of the United States, 1890: Manufacturing Industries, Volume VI, Part 2,* pp. 334–345. The 1870 figures are for Milwaukee County; 1880 and 1890, for the city.

needs for operations more readily available as loans, or on commercial paper, manufacturers could separate investment capital from operations, a luxury denied them in the earlier years.[45]

As many Milwaukee shops turned into factories, the census averages reflected the obvious. If the number of establishments in an industry did not actually decline, which was normal in many lines, the average number of employees and the capital invested illustrate the tendency to concentrate. (Bear in mind that these years were a deflationary period.) The table exhibits the trends in selected Milwaukee industries.

Milwaukee industry rapidly broadened beyond those concerned with the processing of basic commodities. One is surprised, for instance, to find the city ranked third nationally in 1890 in the production of trunks and valises, even if the logic of combining leather, wood, and metal is apparent. The late 1880's saw uncommon expansion in knitting mills, inspired by technological improvements in machinery using worsted, a combination of cotton and wool. A special market existed for these goods in the Upper Midwest lumber industry and in other outdoor occupations sharing the rigorous climate. In 1890, Milwaukee was fourth in the production of hosiery and knits. There was perhaps a connection between the growth of these types of industries and the toolmakers brought to Milwaukee earlier by the unsuccessful Whitehill Sewing Machine Company; Henry Harnischfeger and others were familiar with the technology.[46]

Diversified industry was, naturally, more of an urban phenomenon than were those industries devoted to the conversion of natural resources or agricultural products. Lumber, however, was a widely dispersed resource industry which helped create some important Wisconsin cities and smaller communities. Northern Wisconsin was dotted with villages—soon to be cities—advantageously placed with regard to water, rails, and timber, which were

[45] *The Commercial and Financial Chronicle,* August 6, October 15, November 5, 1887; John Johnston, "Banks and Banking Facilities in Milwaukee," in Anderson and Bleyer, eds., *Milwaukee's Great Industries,* 69–75.

[46] Clark, *History of Manufactures,* 443–445, 775; "Men's and Women's Clothing," in Anderson and Bleyer, eds., *Milwaukee's Great Industries,* 154–155; Walsh, "Milwaukee Clothing Manufacturers," *WMH,* 57:175–194; Harnischfeger, *Autobiography,* 4–7.

joint promotions by the railroads and lumber interests. Merrill, Tomahawk, and Rhinelander are examples. Other lumber towns preceded the period when railroads became vital to the business. Wausau and Eau Claire, for example, continued as cities after the timber was exhausted because they discovered other uses for their waterpowers, local capital, and labor, and continued to exploit their strategic locations.[47]

The dairy manufacturing industry was also widely dispersed from the beginning. It did not find ranking among the first three dozen industries in the state in 1870, measured even by value of product. It ranked sixteenth by 1880, and seventh by 1890, reflecting the rapid rise of factory processing of milk to serve distant markets. It gave employment in 1870 to only 177, but by 1890 to 1,817. Dairy manufacturing helped to keep many villages and hamlets in existence as it brought farmers with money in their pockets to town regularly to shop and socialize.[48]

Industrial diversity could flourish where location encouraged competitive transportation costs for bringing together varied resources and for reaching markets. Racine and Kenosha were early competitors of Chicago and Milwaukee as primary grain forwarders and entrepots on Lake Michigan. But despite valiant efforts, they could not compete with Chicago's superior location nor with Milwaukee's superior port. Attempted port improvements brought indifferent results at Kenosha, and Racine's artificial channel kept filling with sand. Both incurred staggering debts in the unsuccessful efforts to command the agricultural hinterlands behind them, only to find themselves on railroads controlled in Chicago and Milwaukee. Racine established a fairly independent industrial destiny for itself, while Kenosha was more

[47] James B. Smith, "The Movements for Diversified Industry in Eau Claire, Wisconsin, 1879-1907: Boosterism and Urban Development Strategy in a Declining Lumber Town" (master's thesis, University of Wisconsin, 1967), 26-115; Steven B. Karges, "David Clark Everest and Marathon Paper Mills Company: A Study of a Wisconsin Entrepreneur, 1909-1931" (doctoral dissertation, University of Wisconsin, 1968); *Wisconsin Blue Book, 1897,* pp. 417-418.

[48] *Ninth Census of the United States, 1870: Wealth and Industries, Volume III,* 583-584; Alexander, "Industrial History of Wisconsin," in *Wisconsin Blue Book, 1929,* pp. 34, 36; C. J. Galpin, *The Social Anatomy of an Agricultural Community,* University of Wisconsin Agricultural Experiment Station, *Research Bulletin,* no. 34 (Madison, 1915), 1-11.

of a satellite of Chicago. Individual entrepreneurs had a decided impact upon both cities, particularly J. I. Case in Racine and Zalmon G. Simmons in Kenosha's early years. Kenosha's industrial growth came in a rush, mostly after 1893.[49]

Racine, which spent heavily and received generous congressional aid for improvement of her rather unpromising harbor, was an attractive location for bringing together lumber, coal, iron, hides, and tanbark to fuel her growing industries: farm machinery, tanning, and foundries and machine shops. Jerome I. Case came west from New York state as a young man with a few crude threshing machines known generically as groundhogs. He had already decided that southeastern Wisconsin was a good location to manufacture and market such machines. He had started at Rochester in western Racine County, then quickly decided upon Racine as a better location. Case was an innovator rather than an inventor. He readily paid for patent rights and ideas in his determination to build and stand behind the best possible machines. In the late 1870's Case pioneered the use of steam power on the farm. Rapidly expanding markets and the adoption of mass production methods enabled the company to grow with internally generated funds. Unlike E. P. Allis, Case did not make a point of individual ownership and control, but took in partners during the Civil War and incorporated in 1880, a relatively early date. By the 1870's, the J. I. Case Company was one of the largest manufacturers of threshing machines in the world.[50]

Case's success drew other manufacturers to Racine and made it

[49] Carrie Cropley, "When the Railroads Came to Kenosha," in *WMH,* 33 (December, 1949), 188-196; Whitbeck, *Economic Development of Southeastern Wisconsin,* 148-156, 162-168, 187-196, 201-211; John Andreas, Jr., "Zalmon G. Simmons: Business Innovator," in Nicholas C. Burckel and John A. Neuenschwander, eds., *Kenosha Retrospective: A Biographical Approach* (Kenosha, 1981), 31-60; Harry J. Herzog, "The Economic History of Racine, 1838 to the Present Date" (bachelor's thesis, University of Wisconsin, 1916), 14-22; Eugene W. Leach, *Racine: An Historical Narrative* (Racine, 1920), 25-30, 33-43; *DWB.*

[50] Reynold M. Wik, *Steam Power on the American Farm* (Philadelphia, 1953), 30, 70-81; Stewart H. Holbrook, *Machines of Plenty: Pioneering in American Agriculture* (New York, 1955), 14-112; Merk, *Economic History,* 145-146; James I. Clark, *Farm Machinery in Wisconsin* (Madison, 1956), 3-16; *DWB;* Harvey Schwartz, "The Changes in the Location of the American Agricultural Implement Industry, 1850 to 1900" (doctoral dissertation, University of Illinois, 1966), 46.

an important center for agricultural equipment. In 1880, Racine
was a minor city of about 16,000 population, but it had eleven
manufactories of agricultural equipment, plus five making carriages and wagons, and three foundry and machine shops. These
nineteen firms had over 1,800 employees, more than half of the
local industrial employment. Ranked seventh in 1890 among
American cities in the manufacture of agricultural implements
and machinery, Racine still had only a modest 21,000
population.[51]

Wagon manufacturing as a village industry was dying out in the
face of factory production models. Racine had three large wagon
firms in 1890. One of these, Mitchell and Lewis, later made the
transition to auto manufacturing. Among the unusual specialty
industries associated with Racine, the Horlick Malted Milk Company started in 1875, pioneering dried milk production. The
origins of the S. C. Johnson Company (Johnson's Wax) began in
1882, when Samuel Johnson started to sell parquet flooring;
twelve years later he bought the bankrupt Racine Hardware
Manufacturing Company. Research about floor care methods led
to the more lucrative wax-products business.[52]

The consolidation of the agricultural machinery business, as
illustrated by Racine's history, brought changes to an industry
that seemed to spring up wherever a practical inventor progressed
from tinkering to manufacturing. There existed an insatiable
market for grain-handling machines that could multiply a man's
efficiency in the critical grain-harvesting cycle. One such Yankee
tinker, who established a flourishing business on the basis of his
inventions and improvements, was George W. Esterly of Whitewater. Starting in the 1840's with a reaping machine of his own
design, he experienced frustrations because he sent to a foundry
in St. Louis for castings of some vital parts. The parts failed under

[51] Whitbeck, *Economic Development of Southeastern Wisconsin*, 161–168, 173–174; *Eleventh
Census of the United States, 1890: Manufactures, Volume VI, Part 2*, p. 649.

[52] Margaret Walsh, *The Manufacturing Frontier: Pioneer Industry in Antebellum Wisconsin,
1830–1860* (Madison, 1972), 156–157: Whitbeck, *Economic Development of Southeastern Wisconsin*, 164–168; Leach, *Racine*, 44–45, 51–52, 56–58; Chauncey Thomas, "American
Carriage and Wagon Works," in Chauncey M. Depew, ed., *1795–1895: One Hundred Years
of American Commerce* (2 vols., New York, 1895), 2:519–520.

operating conditions on machines that he had sold. Heavily in debt as a result, Esterly and his son George built their own integrated plant in Whitewater. They worked their way out of debt, achieving success with a reaper that incorporated the basic twine binder, invented by Wisconsin's John F. Appleby.[53]

Other small Wisconsin cities were also the home bases of ventures in agricultural machinery that grew with the application of useful inventions. Some survived early growing pains and the business cycles. The Van Brunts of Horicon, a village in Dodge County, took over the structures built earlier on the waterpower that had found only temporary tenants. Inventors in 1860 of a seeder or drill which frustrated the voracious passenger pigeons, the brothers made 1,000 of the machines in 1864 and by 1869 were selling 3,800. Willard Van Brunt, a successor to George and D. C., the founders, was a wealthy sportsman well known in Milwaukee circles. The firm continued under Willard's control well beyond the turn of the century when it became a plant of the John Deere Company.[54]

John S. Rowell of Beaver Dam invented a slip tooth for seeders on which the Van Brunts paid him royalties. Rowell had numerous patents used by his own J. S. Rowell Manufacturing Company, established in 1855. Rowell was still at its head in 1895. Success made him an important figure in Beaver Dam with interests in a foundry, the Beaver Dam Cotton Mills, utilities, and banking. Rowell helped to give this small, interior Wisconsin city an impetus as a manufacturing center which it retains to this day.[55]

Farm wagon manufacturing, a village craft, was an industry in which a man could get a modest start and build a substantial busi-

[53] George W. Esterly, "Autobiography," typescript in the George W. Esterly Papers; Clark, *Farm Machinery in Wisconsin*, 7–8. Appleby is claimed by both Mazomanie and Beloit; see Current, *Civil War Era*, 456–457, and *DWB*.

[54] Western Historical Company, *The History of Dodge County, Wisconsin*. . . (Chicago, 1880), 482–483; Bill Hooker, *Glimpses of an Earlier Milwaukee* (Milwaukee, 1929), 52–53; Francis F. Bowman, *Why Wisconsin* (Madison, 1948), 153; Milwaukee *Sentinel*, June 6, 1935; Fond du Lac *Commonwealth-Reporter*, June 14, 1935; Horicon *Reporter*, October 17, 1963.

[55] S. C. Judson, comp., *Beaver Dam, Wisconsin, in 1888* (Milwaukee, [1888]), 6, 10; *Columbian Biographical Dictionary and Portrait Gallery of the Representative Men of the United States: Wisconsin Volume*, 212–217.

ness on the basis of a favorable local reputation. An advantageous location with respect to hardwoods, merchant iron, and shipping facilities could lead to success in a near bucolic setting. T. G. Mandt started in Stoughton in 1865 with a capital of $100 and himself as the labor force. Fifteen years later his establishment occupied fifteen large buildings on a seven-acre site and turned out a wagon every twenty minutes, in addition to buggies, sleighs, carriages, and agriculture equipment. Mandt found a loyal regional market. Other village wagon makers who did not expand suffered the consequences of the adaptation of the factory system to their craft.[56]

A student of the growth of Wisconsin industry, John W. Alexander, asked himself why manufacturing prospered in the Rock River Valley when it had not in other similar areas. He decided that the initial thrust came from the modest waterpowers, which were more easily controlled in the narrow valley than in other wider Wisconsin river valleys with more potential power. Next was a population, both Yankee and northern European, that was inventive and quick to seize opportunities. (Both Janesville and Beloit had a surprising number of successful inventors in this period.) The valley was also early served by railroads building out of Chicago and Milwaukee which provided competitive freight rates. As local wheat milling was displaced, the power and water at Beloit was largely used for papermaking. From this conjunction, and the availability of pig iron and fuel at favorable railroad rates, came the Beloit Iron Works, which developed skills in manufacturing papermaking machinery and became the dominant firm in that field in the United States. When in 1885 Fairbanks, Morse and Company purchased the Eclipse Wind Engine Company and the plant of the Beloit Wagon Works, the business community was quick to further Morse's expansive plans with desirable acreage and cash subsidies. Inventive mechanics, local capital willing to assume risks, favorable railroad connections, skilled labor located in small cities where living costs were relatively low: all added to the formula for success.

[56] Western Historical Company, *History of Dane County, Wisconsin*. . . (Chicago, 1880), 850–851.

Despite the depressed financial conditions of 1873–1874, the Janesville business community subscribed to $120,000 of stock in the Janesville Cotton Manufacturing Company. Although "they were regarded by the rest of the inhabitants as a band of escaped lunatics," the enterprise continued and was modestly successful. Certainly it was a unique expression of local confidence, backed by local capital. Woolen mills, mostly of a marginal character, were common in the Upper Midwest at the time, but not cotton mills making sheeting.[57]

Madison was a natural transportation center which made the city a minor wholesaling point and a good location for the manufacture and distribution of agricultural machinery. Beaver Dam and Watertown, also in the upper Rock River Valley, had waterpowers that were used in the early years mainly for flour milling. The CM&StP gave in-transit rates, a point of controversy, to these and other interior milling points which made it possible for them to compete successfully with Milwaukee millers. With the relative decline of the milling business, these locations and others like them had to find alternative industries. Beaver Dam's transition has already been noted. Watertown at the 1885 state census had, aside from six flour mills, machine shops, a small cotton mill, a woodenware factory, and other industries; but its lack of significant population growth in 1870–1900 speaks of limited expansion of its industries. Fond du Lac had capital from early lumbering and an attractive site for manufacturing as a crossroads at the foot of Lake Winnebago. She lost out to Oshkosh as a basic lumber-milling town, and had a difficult time hanging on to other industries. The city lost the La Belle Wagon Works to Superior, the Wheel and Seeder Company to La Crosse, and McDonald Manufacturing to Minneapolis where it was the nucleus of a large

---

[57] John W. Alexander, *Geography of Manufacturing in the Rock River Valley,* University of Wisconsin, School of Commerce, Bureau of Business Research and Service, *Wisconsin Commerce Papers,* vol. 1, no. 2 (Madison, 1949); Western Historical Company, *The History of Rock County, Wisconsin. . .* (Chicago, 1879), 567–569; Norman L. Crockett, *The Woolen Industry of the Midwest* (Lexington, Kentucky, 1970); Beloit Daily News Publishing Company, *Book of Beloit,* 205–230; William F. Brown, ed., *Rock County, Wisconsin: A New History of Its Cities, Villages, Towns, Citizens and Varied Interests, from the Earliest Times, Up to Date* (2 vols., Chicago, 1908), 2:564–565.

agricultural machine works. Slightly larger than Oshkosh in 1870, Fond du Lac actually lost population in the following twenty years while Oshkosh nearly doubled. Fond du Lac eventually developed a mix of industries based upon wood and metalworking. The Fred Rueping Leather Company and a machine-tool maker, Giddings and Lewis, were both substantial industries before 1890.[58]

Oshkosh, located strategically where the logs from the Wolf River entered Lake Winnebago, was by 1870 a mature lumber town already directing its capital into wood-related industries: sash-and-door and furniture factories, agricultural implements, matches, planing mills, iron founding, and machinery works specializing in sawmill and woodworking machinery. The city's name entered the American language as the generic word for the provincial small city trumpeting its own greatness. Oshkosh loyalists saw nothing funny about the city's name or business success. It was also somewhat famous for its phoenix-like reincarnations, always bigger and better, from the disastrous fires which earned it its sobriquet, the Sawdust City. Oshkosh took pride in its enterprise, exemplified by its lumber millionaire, United States senator, and political boss, Philetus Sawyer.[59]

Sheboygan was relatively late in reaching out to its hinterland. The usual local promotion was begun in 1856 to carry a rail line

[58] Historical Publishing Company, *Historical Review of the State of Wisconsin, Its Industrial and Commercial Resources, Descriptive and Biographical. . .* (New York, 1887), 132; Agnes M. Larson, *John A. Johnson: An Uncommon American* (Northfield, Minnesota, 1969). Johnson was partner in an agricultural machine works in Madison and in 1889 founded the Gisholt Company, a machine-tool manufacturing plant with a world market. Whitbeck, *Geography of the Fox-Winnebago Valley,* 42–47; Schafer, *Winnebago-Horicon Basin,* 258–284; Maurice McKenna, *Fond du Lac County, Wisconsin: Past and Present* (2 vols., Chicago, 1912), 1:324–331.

[59] Whitbeck, *Geography of the Fox-Winnebago Valley,* 47–52; Joseph Schafer, *The Winnebago-Horicon Basin: A Type Study in Western History* (Madison, 1937), 285–297; Richard J. Harney, *History of Winnebago County, Wisconsin, and Early History of the Northwest* (Oshkosh, 1880), 167–173; William and Clara Dawes, *History of Oshkosh, 1938* ([Oshkosh], 1938), 19–37; Historical Publishing Company, "Oshkosh," in *Historical Review of Wisconsin,* 87–92; Clinton F. Karstaedt, ed., *Oshkosh: One Hundred Years a City, 1853–1953* (Oshkosh, 1953), 211–255. Avery O. Craven, a distinguished historian, once told the author that when he left a high school teaching job in Milwaukee in 1919 to attend graduate school at Harvard, Professor Albert Bushnell Hart (born 1854) invariably referred to Craven as "Oshkosh," though Craven had no connection whatsoever with the Phoenix City. Obviously the word had entered the language.

to Fond du Lac. It did not achieve its destination until 1869, and the first rail link to Milwaukee was made in 1872, bringing a bonded indebtedness of nearly $20 per head to Sheboygan citizens. The town was somewhat more precocious in discovering its industrial future. It did have the great advantage of location on Lake Michigan with a port. In the summer of 1882, the Milwaukee *Sentinel* reported a meeting of the Western Chair Manufacturers' Association, and stated that Sheboygan produced about one-quarter of all the chairs manufactured in the West. Evidently Sheboygan, popularly known as Chair City, had found its destiny. Its population of only 5,310 in 1870 had tripled by 1890 and Sheboygan had become Wisconsin's sixth city. Along with this growth went a generalized industrial development to supplement the several large chair-manufacturing firms as well as the Kohler Company, which had started with the manufacture of agricultural implements, general foundry work, and enamelware.[60]

Like Sheboygan, Manitowoc and neighboring Two Rivers bonded themselves heavily for the construction of railroad links that were slow in coming. Manitowoc also spent heavily to improve her harbor. She looked out upon the lake, and one finds repeated references to a want of local venture capital for industry because local citizens put their money into small, locally built sailing vessels that still carried much of the Great Lakes traffic. It was also an important commercial fishing center and a stopping place for early steam packets to take on wood. The Goodrich Lines wintered many of its vessels at Manitowoc. Out of this grew drydock and repair facilities in addition to the small boat yards. Wooden steamers and tugs were built there in some numbers until iron and steel began to replace oak. The yards had fallen on hard times by the 1890's, to be revived by the world wars of the twentieth century. The aluminum ware industry began in Two Rivers and Manitowoc in the late nineties.

[60] Joseph E. Leberman, *One Hundred Years of Sheboygan, 1846-1946* ([Sheboygan?], 1946); Phoenix Publishing Company, *Pen and Sunlight Sketches of the Principal Cities of Wisconsin* (Chicago, 1893), 136-150; Milwaukee *Sentinel*, July 19, 1882; Trudi J. Eblen, "A History of the Kohler Company of Kohler, Wisconsin, 1871-1914" (master's thesis, University of Wisconsin, 1965), 8-29; Wisconsin Commissioner of Labor and Industrial Statistics, *Biennial Report*, 1893-94, Inspection Reports section, 148a-152a.

Manitowoc and Two Rivers also evolved a distinctive hard-wood industry which started with the manufacture of wooden-ware tubs, pails, and butter firkins. Manitowoc Manufacturing Company became the largest of these firms after it turned to making school furniture. Burned out in 1892, it was rebuilt by local subscription and subsequently sold to a national combine. Two Rivers was the home of J. E. Hamilton, who built a large manufacturing plant from a one-man operation making wooden display type. It developed into a leading national firm in the office furniture and equipment field. Of a size with Sheboygan and Green Bay in 1870, Manitowoc lagged behind Green Bay in growth over the next twenty years—and Green Bay was noted for its somnolence.[61]

Wisconsin's oldest city had been disappointed in its hopes by the intractable nature of the Fox-Wisconsin waterway. Over the years, Green Bay remained sure that logic compelled the completion of the waterway, which would make the city the entrepot of a flourishing commerce between the Great Lakes and the Mississippi. With the development of regional and interregional rail lines, the hope arose that the federal government would take over the project as an alternate route to apply pressure upon railroad rates. (Not an absurd hope, to be sure, for the Corps of Engineers after 1870 sank nearly $3 million in the attempt.)[62]

Happily, Green Bay's location assured the city a reasonable industrial and commercial future as the doorway to the waterpowers on the lower Fox River, as a lumber center for the driving streams feeding into the bay, and as a port. The city developed from these opportunities an industrial profile more varied, probably, than that of any other Wisconsin city of comparable size. A typical watergate city, Green Bay moved coal up the lower Fox where the growing paper industry required heat as well as water-

[61] Ralph G. Plumb, *A History of Manitowoc County, Complete and Illustrated* ([Manitowoc], 1904), chaps. 6 and 17; Phoenix Publishing Company, *Pen and Sunlight Sketches,* 242–249; Hibberd V. B. Kline, Jr., "The Minor Cities of Lake Michigan" (doctoral dissertation, University of Wisconsin, 1941), 225–250; Louis Falge, ed., *History of Manitowoc County, Wisconsin* (2 vols., Chicago [1912]), 1:114–138, 375–378; Mark R. Byers, *J. E. Hamilton* (Two Rivers, 1932); Wisconsin Commissioner of Labor and Industrial Statistics, *Biennial Report,* 1893–94, Report of Inspection, 64a–66a.

[62] See Chapter 3 above.

power. Handy to heavy waterborne resources, she provided many of the foundry and machinery needs of the industrialized valley behind. Green Bay also became a processor, wholesaler, and supplier to a growing agricultural hinterland. She would become identified as the processing center for varied agricultural products; hence, eventually, the Green Bay Packers.[63]

A federal census report of 1880 on the waterpowers of the United States took those of New England as a standard which no location in the Great Lakes states could rival, until one considered the lower Fox River. It had excellent watershed facilities on the upper reaches of the Wolf River, an immense natural reservoir in Lake Winnebago, good underlying strata, a favorable precipitation pattern, and, within a distance of only 37.5 miles, a fall of 170 feet concentrated at several favorable locations. While waterpower costs were hard to compare because of many variables, New England's fall points averaged about $3.50 per horsepower annually. This made Appleton's average cost of $1.00 to $2.00 an enviable resource. When the federal government took over the waterway, it had refused the offer of water rights, which remained with the Green Bay and Mississippi Canal Company. The company and other lesser owners of waterpower rights could tap any water not needed for navigation, while the government maintained the storage dams which served both locks and waterpowers.[64]

Papermaking shortly transformed the economy of the lower Fox Valley. Settled by Yankees who recognized the value of the sites, the cities on the waterpowers below Lake Winnebago attracted enough capital to build a number of prosperous industries based primarily upon woodworking and flour milling. Like Milwaukee, they found their relative share of grain falling off seriously as

[63] Whitbeck, *Geography of the Fox–Winnebago Valley*, 68–75; Phoenix Publishing Company, *Pen and Sunlight Sketches*, 249–269; Werden Reynolds, comp., *Exposition of the Natural Resources, Commercial Facilities, Business Industries, Social Institutions, and Miscellaneous Attractions of the Cities of Green Bay and Fort Howard, Wisconsin* (Green Bay, 1889), 35 ff; Gazette Publishing Company, *Men Who Are Making Green Bay, with an Outline Sketch of the Green Bay of Today, and Some Portraits of the City's Representative Men* (Green Bay, 1897).

[64] Greenleaf, "Report on the Water-power of the Northwest," in *Tenth Census of the United States, 1880: Reports on the Water-power of the United States, Volume XVII, Part 2*, pp. 15, 19–20.

wheat culture moved northwestward and Minneapolis millers intervened. Papermaking provided the alternative, though the pioneer papermakers had to compete for the rags which were the basic raw material. Wood, which had to be reduced mechanically by grinding, competed with straw, rope waste, and other vegetable material as alternatives to rags. The sulphite process was introduced from Europe in 1884, but had a slow growth in the United States because of a $10 per ton royalty and for want of an established chemical industry. In 1872, John A. Kimberly, who had started as a lumberman and miller, with his partners began the shift to papermaking on a gradual basis, followed cautiously by others at Neenah-Menasha. The new industry grew rapidly, led aggressively by Kimberly, Clark and Company.

Papermaking required larger capital outlays than did flour milling, and also a larger work force. But the new industry was less seasonal and had no difficulty finding growing markets in the Midwest. Local capital met most of the need, and the rewards proved generous. Paper came to dominate the waterpowers on the Fox. Much of the subsidiary industry developed to serve the paper mills. A pioneer woolen mill at Appleton, for instance, became a specialty mill providing felts for paper machines. Foundries and machine shops similarly specialized in equipment for the mills. Papermaking became a particularly stable industry, with an almost predictable growth curve, long before economists talked in such terms. Early in the game, Wisconsin papermakers learned the value of the development of specialty papers to maintain a competitive edge. Prosperity created a socially satisfied society: generous profits for owners, stable employment with a high proportion of skilled jobs, and desirable living conditions in a setting of attractive small cities. Many small towns, particularly on the upper Wisconsin River, followed this lead with the aid of Fox Valley capital.[65]

[65] Whitbeck, *Geography of the Fox-Winnebago Valley*, 7–23, 42–83; Schafer, *Winnebago-Horicon Basin*, 130–131; James Bertram Nash, "The Development of Manufacturing at Appleton" (bachelor's thesis, University of Wisconsin, 1901); Glaab and Larsen, *Factories in the Valley*, chaps. 3, 4, and 5; Maurice Branch, "The Paper Industry in the Lake States Region, 1834–1947" (doctoral dissertation, University of Wisconsin, 1954), chaps. 2 and 3; Clark, *History of Manufactures*, 485–491, 820–821.

La Crosse grew wonderfully in the years following the Civil War. Comparable in size to Watertown in 1870, it doubled its population in the next ten years, and by 1890 almost doubled again to 25,090; for a brief time, it was Wisconsin's second-largest city. In the mid-seventies, when the CM&StP built a bridge across the Mississippi just north of town, La Crosse felt bypassed. This turned out not as disastrously as some expected. The bridge, which was one of several crossing the Mississippi or St. Croix rivers, did spell the end of the reign of steamboats on the upper Mississippi for which La Crosse had been the center. To compound the city's temporary troubles, the pineries tributary to it were about exhausted at nearly the same time. But the sawmills and boat yards had left a residue of capital, machinery, and skilled labor just at the time when steam was succeeding waterpower as the prime power source (La Crosse had no significant waterpower). Excellent rail connections provided a market, particularly to the west, and cheap rates on coal and merchant iron from the east. La Crosse became an important manufacturing point. Location offered opportunities for manufacturers of consumer items as well as agricultural equipment. In 1889 the city claimed that it exported more beer than did Milwaukee. It also manufactured and wholesaled tobacco products, food, clothing, and hardware. This was a hard row to hoe in the shadow of Chicago, Milwaukee and the Twin Cities, but La Crosse, like Oshkosh, was filled with booster spirit and organized competitive determination.[66]

Eau Claire had less in the way of locational advantages than did La Crosse for making the transition to a trade center with a varied industrial base. Primarily a one-industry town, her businessmen could see that lumber milling had a limited future. Already by the 1880's the conspicuously successful were buying timber elsewhere, preparatory to moving on. Like La Crosse, Eau Claire had an active board of trade. The general policy pursued was to offer subsidies in cash, land, waterpower, and other inducements to

[66] Albert H. Sanford and H. H. Hirschheimer, *A History of La Crosse, Wisconsin, 1841–1900* (La Crosse, 1951), 174–183, 206; Phoenix Publishing Company, *Pen and Sunlight Sketches,* 179–204; La Crosse Board of Trade, *Annual Reports,* 1882–1890.

industry. Some of these efforts paid off over the years. In particular, the Eau Claire Pulp and Paper Company was created as a
result of a package of inducements which included a money subsidy, a ten-acre site, and waterpower rights to an Indiana industrialist. This proved to be a successful business. Otherwise, the
inducements seemed to attract promoters who were long on
schemes but short on performance, or local capital seeking subsidies for minor enterprises. Eau Claire's lack of population growth
between 1890 and 1910 marks this awkward period in finding a
new economic role.[67]

The feverish air of speculation and exaggerated press agentry
accompanying the revivals of Superior and Ashland in the 1870's
and 1890's curiously parallels the fervid booming of Tacoma,
Seattle, and Everett 2,000 miles westward. One finds many of the
same cast of characters: Jay Cooke, Henry Villard, James J. Hill,
John D. Rockefeller, Colgate Hoyt, Charles L. Colby—even a
whaleback steamer. The undercurrent of big money, moving
mysteriously through agents on the scene but quick to cut its losses
or find interesting possibilities elsewhere, was a common feature.
So were the boom-and-bust cycles that were so familiar to railroad
townsite promotions in the nineteenth century.[68]

The problem with Wisconsin's Lake Superior cities was that
they had little connection with the transportation, industrial,
commercial, or financial interests of the state's metropolis. One
looks in vain for an occasional flicker of interest on the part of
Milwaukee. Unfortunately for Superior, Minneapolis and St.
Paul money maintained an active interest in rival Duluth and its

---

[67] Smith, "Movements for Diversified Industry in Eau Claire," *passim;* Charles E.
Twining, *Downriver: Orrin H. Ingram and the Empire Lumber Company* (Madison, 1975), 268–
269; Ralph W. Hidy, Frank E. Hill, and Allan Nevins, *Timber and Men: The Weyerhaeuser
Story* (New York, 1963), 145–146; William F. Bailey, ed., *History of Eau Claire County, Wis-
consin, Past and Present: Including an Account of the Cities, Towns and Villages of the County*
(Chicago, 1914), 474–488.

[68] Robert C. Nesbit, *"He Built Seattle": A Biography of Judge Thomas Burke* (Seattle, 1961),
chaps. 4, 8, 9, 11, particularly pages 269 and 288–289 describing Rockefeller's similar
investments in conjunction with Hoyt and Colby in western Washington. See also Allan
Nevins, *John D. Rockefeller: The Heroic Age of American Enterprise* (2 vols., New York, 1940),
2:269, 274–279; and Richard J. Wright, *Freshwater Whales: A History of the American Ship
Building Company and Its Predecessors* (Kent, Ohio, 1969), 48–51.

potential to influence their fortunes. This interest dated at least from the 1864 chartering of the Northern Pacific with its princely land subsidies from Congress. The charter specified the connection of the western end of Lake Superior with Puget Sound. The prospects of such a direct link to Duluth from northern Dakota Territory spelled trouble for the control which Minneapolis and St. Paul were building over the expanding grain lands to the west, and the cities' strategic location as wholesalers and suppliers of industrial goods. In conjunction with Jay Cooke, who controlled the Northern Pacific until his spectacular financial collapse in 1873, the Twin Cities managed a rail connection with Duluth before Cooke's failure. They proceeded to build up Duluth as a transportation center for their grain and flour, using the alternate Lake Superior water route to bypass Chicago and Milwaukee.[69]

The location of Superior should have been a greater asset in its rivalry with Duluth. It was on a broad and level site in contrast with Duluth's rocky headlands, which were formidable challenges to railroad engineers. But history was against Superior. A brief, abortive boom in the mid-fifties left a tangle of land claims in the hands of political and financial families stretching back to the East and into the South. The pioneer settlers drifted away and gloom settled over the site. Even the timber tributary to Superior was exploited from the south by lumbermen based in the St. Croix and Chippewa valleys and was cut and taken out by way of the Mississippi rather than Lake Superior. Interest in Superior first revived in the 1880's when Henry Villard completed the Northern Pacific to the Pacific Northwest and James J. Hill was constructing the rival Great Northern. Then, with the opening of the Mesabi iron ranges later in that decade, it had the promise of becoming a rail center as well as a potential ore-shipping point. The Northern Pacific allied with the Wisconsin Central through Superior and Ashland, and earlier in 1882 the C&NW took over the "Omaha," which owned the North Wisconsin reaching from Hudson to Superior, Bayfield, and Ashland.

[69] Albro Martin, *James J. Hill and the Opening of the Northwest* (New York, 1976), 116–119, 180–193.

The claims of the absentee owners in the original Superior townsite speculation were so tangled that new promoters developed other sites around it which were later incorporated into the original plat. West Superior was floated by General John Hammond, a midwestern promoter who had been involved in promotions at Chillicothe, Missouri, and Clinton, Iowa. Hammond had social and financial ties with Colgate Hoyt and Charles Colby, who were assisting John D. Rockefeller to invest part of his growing personal fortune while his own attention was fully occupied with the Standard Oil Company. They were the ones who got Rockefeller involved in Superior, Mesabi iron, and allied enterprises.[70]

Hammond's promotional work eventually led to a rational plan for Superior, with a terminal and beltline commonly owned by several railroads that gave all of them equal access and created valuable commercial and industrial sites with both rail and water frontage. James J. Hill's interest led to the development of a great grain shipping terminal for the Great Northern railroad. This involved shops, elevators, and ship-loading facilities. Hill cut grain rates from the west, which made serious inroads upon the grain trade of the Twin Cities as well as of Milwaukee and Chicago. Later, with the opening of the Mesabi iron range, he brought the first ore-carrying railroad into Superior and built the world's largest complex of ore-loading facilities.[71]

Rockefeller's main interest, initially, was to use Superior as a likely distribution point for petroleum products, but he was drawn in by the others as a bondholder in Alexander McDougall's shipyard and the West Superior Iron and Steel Company. The latter company was to provide plates for the whalebacks which McDougall built and for other expected industrial users. Lehigh

[70] Frank A. Flower, *The Eye of the North-west: First Annual Report of the Statistician of Superior, Wisconsin* (Milwaukee, 1890), 102–112; Nevins, *John D. Rockefeller*, 2:277–279, 292, 359–390.

[71] Richard McLeod, "The Development of Superior, Wisconsin, As a Western Transportation Center," in the *Journal of the West*, 13 (July, 1974), 17–27; Kendall A. Birr, "Social Ideas of Superior Business Men, 1880–1898" (master's thesis, University of Wisconsin, 1948), 5–28; Helen M. Wolner, "The History of Superior, Wisconsin, to 1900" (master's thesis, University of Wisconsin, 1939), 113–147; Flower, *Eye of the North-west*, 121–147.

Coal and Iron Company, for example, built a coking plant in 1881 to serve western furnaces. Superior was also developing as an important coal-shipping point. Superior's industrial future seemed bright as manufacturing plants, lured by subsidies and the city's apparently strong financial support, began to mushroom. Flour mills, sawmills, and smaller industries were attracted.[72]

But the panic of 1893 brought a chill wind to Superior. Rockefeller's partners were overextended and mostly frozen out. With a bottomless purse, Rockefeller fell heir to the steel furnaces, the shipyard, and finally to a lion's share of the Mesabi iron range and the railroad that served it. (He had taken bonds rather than stock in the ventures and thereby held the mortgages.) Rockefeller sold out the iron-ore interests to the United States Steel Company in 1901 when J. P. Morgan put that combination together. The shipyard and the local iron and steel company were reorganized a number of times, but were never again more than marginal, intermittent operations.[73]

Superior did not collapse as it had before, but its sense of destiny became subdued. Its main business remained the transfer of commodities from rail to water and the receipt of coal for the Upper Midwest. Duluth kept possession of most of the wholesale functions of the location and a brighter industrial future. Superior's adjustment, aside from the loss of some highly visible industries, was to the realization that the world's largest ore docks did not require a large labor force. This was equally true of grain elevators, flour mills, and coal docks. The city was the victim of a harsh climate that closed down its lakes commerce for five months of the year, and a business community that was too enthralled by the promotions of outsiders. Duluth enjoyed closer ties with the capitalists of St. Paul and Minneapolis, whose interest was not as fleeting as that of General Hammond's New Yorkers.[74]

Ashland's rise and decline paralleled Superior's, although on a

[72] Flower, *Eye of the North-west,* 167–188; Nevins, *Rockefeller,* 2:277–279; McKenna, *Fond du Lac County, Wisconsin,* 1:327 ff.

[73] Nevins, *Rockefeller,* 2:277–279, 359–390, 417–422; Clark, *History of Manufactures,* 580, 678–680.

[74] Wright, *Freshwater Whales,* 49–52; McLeod, "Development of Superior, Wisconsin," *Journal of the West,* 13:25–26; Birr, "Social Ideas of Superior Business Men," 12–28.

lesser scale. It had two false starts: the first in the 1850's and the second in the early 1870's, when the Wisconsin Central began the long effort to link Ashland and Stevens Point. But in the 1880's, the rich iron ore of the Gogebic and Penokee ranges made Ashland an important shipping point with large docking facilities built to accommodate the traffic. British capital built a huge charcoal iron furnace there in 1888, but it was soon superseded by the extremely low rates on eastern coal brought westward on the Great Lakes. In 1905, the charcoal furnace shut down for the last time. Another conspicuous industry that developed was the quarrying of brownstone of good quality, but unfortunately it was not a building material that remained in favor for a long time. The novelist Edith Wharton wrote the epitaph for Ashland brownstone: "This little, low-studded rectangular New York, cursed with its universal chocolate-coloured coating of the most hideous stone ever quarried, this cramped horizontal gridiron of a town without towers, porticoes, fountains or perspectives, hidebound in its deadly uniformity of mean ugliness."[75]

Lumbering flourished, but as everywhere it was a finite resource at the rate the industry used the timber. Tourism was developed by the Wisconsin Central Railroad, which made its Chequamegon Hotel a well-known landmark for a brief time, but the season was short and competition was keen for the limited tourist dollars of the times. Ashland was almost equal in size with Superior in 1890; the cities had 9,956 and 11,983 citizens respectively. Superior drew well ahead in the decade of the nineties, 31,091 to 13,074. But each city trended downward in later years. Both had depended upon the flow of outside capital which proved all too sensitive to any downturn in the general economy or to suggestions that the blush might be off the boom on Lake Superior.[76]

[75] Edith Wharton, *The Age of Innocence* (Signet Classic edition, New York, 1962), noted in the foreword by Louis Auchincloss, page v.

[76] Charles R. Van Hise and Charles K. Leith, *The Geology of the Lake Superior Region,* U.S. Geological Survey, *Monographs* (55 vols., Washington, 1890–1929), 52:40–41; Henry C. Campbell, ed., *Wisconsin in Three Centuries,* 1634–1905 (4 vols., New York, 1906), 4: chap. 9; Clark, *History of Manufactures,* 208–209; J. M. Dodd, "Ashland Then and Now," in *WMH,* 28 (December 1944), 188–196; Art Gravure and Etching Company, *Ashland, Wis., Illustrated;* Phoenix Publishing Company, *Pen and Sunlight Sketches;* Ashland *Daily Press, Annual Edition, January 15, 1892;* Flower, *Eye of the North-west.*

Wisconsin cities were not unique in fostering organizations that demanded participation by public and private agencies in promoting the welfare of the business community. Milwaukee had a merchants' association, organized in 1861, which by the seventies was trying to lure eastern capital to Milwaukee. Other organizations followed. A popular activity was organizing excursion parties of businessmen and local dignitaries to visit the hinterland and, presumably, make a winning impression. Merchants' association, board of trade, advancement association, or whatever the title, Milwaukee followed the lead of other cities to attract trade, lure industries and wholesalers, pressure the railroads for rate advantages, and boom the city's natural and contrived advantages. Lesser cities followed the promotional pattern with similar devices and ardor. Like real warfare, civic boosting led naturally to a degree of escalation that was difficult to maintain. Citizens today are bemused to learn of heated rivalries between candidates for metropolitan status that involved elements other than those of paid athletes from distant parts. How could people have had such an emotional involvement in the business pulse, industrial output, or quality of life of their community—always in contrast with their neighbors?[77]

The logical escalation from tours and expositions was to seduce payrolls from other places. Milwaukee had one conspicuous success in this game. In 1892 the Bucyrus-Erie Company was lured from Bucyrus, Ohio, by the gift of an extensive acreage in South Milwaukee in a subsidy package said to total $94,000. It was a good investment. This and lesser victories were offset by news or rumors of possible losses to other cities engaged in the same game. The man who held the patent on the three-motor electric crane could not find local capital to back him, so he accepted a subsidy offer from a Michigan city. There developed in Milwaukee a consciousness that hunting industries with subsidies was tantamount to living by the sword, and it was a difficult game from which to withdraw.[78]

[77] Gregory, *History of Milwaukee,* 1:489–498.

[78] Harold F. Williamson and Kenneth H. Myers II, *Designed for Digging: The First 75 Years of Bucyrus-Erie Company* (Evanston, 1955), 44–45; Harnischfeger, *Autobiography,* 16; Milwaukee *Sentinel,* January 1, 1892; Robert H. Odell, "History of the Association for the

Milwaukee enjoyed a vigorous growth in wholesaling and jobbing, despite the limitations imposed by geography upon her and other Wisconsin cities. Celebrations of this growth did well to ignore comparisons. Milwaukee's wholesale grocers, for instance, gave ground grudgingly, even though "confronted on the north and on the south by the most enterprising, exacting and audacious merchants in the wide mercantile world. . . ." While Milwaukee's wholesaling grew between 1873 and 1895 from an estimated $46,800,000 to $98,300,000, St. Paul, between 1877 and 1889, went from $27,800,000 to $109,000,000. Wholesale business for Minneapolis from 1876 to 1892 ballooned from $5 million to $131 million, and Chicago's broke $1 billion before 1900.[79]

Essentially, the same factors were at work that had broken Milwaukee's brief supremacy in the wheat trade: geography and railroads. The railroads easily captured the lion's share of general merchandise and manufactured goods because of better insurance, storage, scheduling, in-transit segregation, pickup and delivery service. The results favored Chicago to the extent that wholesaling and jobbing underwent a great change in the Midwest. Merchants seldom took buying trips to eastern sources, but dealt with Chicago houses either directly or through traveling salesmen. Chicago became so central to the new pattern that eastern houses found that they could neither bypass it nor give significantly lower prices.[80]

The Twin Cities became a strong echo of Chicago, enjoying terminal rates from there, diminishing any cost differential

Advancement of Milwaukee," in Anderson and Bleyer, eds., *Milwaukee's Great Industries,* xiii–xxi.

[79] Henry M. Mendel, "Groceries and the Grocery Jobbing Business," in Anderson and Bleyer, eds., *Milwaukee's Great Industries,* 124; Bill R. Moeckel, "The Development of the Wholesaler in the United States, 1860–1900" (doctoral dissertation, University of Illinois, 1953), 62, 85–91. Harold Barger, *Distribution's Place in the American Economy Since 1869* (Princeton, 1955; reprinted, New York, 1976), 198–215, lists nearly 400 titles in a bibliography of pre-1919 periodicals in retail and wholesale trade. Only one, the *Northwestern Trade Bulletin,* successor to the *Northwestern Grocer,* was published in Milwaukee between 1879 and 1884. Chicago had twenty-nine published there between 1873 and 1893; Minneapolis had four.

[80] Moeckel, "Development of the Wholesaler in the United States," 56–63.

between Milwaukee and the Twin Cities on rail shipments from the East or from Chicago. By the mid-eighties Milwaukee could not successfully compete for wholesale business across much of northern Wisconsin against wholesalers from St. Paul and Minneapolis. It was remarked by those who saw Milwaukee's destiny as primarily a producer rather than a middleman that this would be less of a disadvantage than assumed: "The tendency of the times is towards the extinction of the trader and the enlargement of the scope of the manufacturer, who is all the time getting closer to the consumer." This was surely true of many of Milwaukee's and Wisconsin's major industries that were producing capital goods and goods that went to consumer-goods manufacturers. Her advantage lay with the Great Lakes carriers and their competition for the carriage of bulk commodities that could be stockpiled, especially coal, pig iron, and iron and steel plates and bars.[81]

The circumstance of Wisconsin cities' general engagement in manufacturing rather than wholesaling doubtless contributed to the frequent self-congratulation that permeated the local literature of the period. There was a consensus that Wisconsin businessmen were more responsible and capable, growing within their own means, yet innovative. The work force was celebrated for similar virtues: skilled, productive, sober, home-owning. Much of what this society thought about itself was based upon dubious evidence, but it had its uses. The frequently invoked negative example of Chicago was common currency. Chicago businessmen took every unfair advantage; they were feverishly speculative; their affairs were always unstable. Milwaukee took pride in contrasts. "The banks of Milwaukee are like the city itself and the business men of the city," remarked banker John Johnston, "conservative, substantial and safe."[82]

[81] Walter W. Pollock, "Milwaukee's Manufacturing Industries," in Anderson and Bleyer, eds., *Milwaukee's Great Industries,* 200. The St. Paul *Pioneer Press* remarked on January 1, 1890: "Quite one half of the State of Wisconsin is the almost undisputed territory of St. Paul jobbers." Quoted in Mildred L. Hartsough, *The Development of the Twin Cities (Minneapolis and St. Paul) as a Metropolitan Market* (published doctoral dissertation, University of Minnesota, 1924), 53.

[82] Johnston's remarks (1892) appeared in Anderson and Bleyer, eds., *Milwaukee's Great Industries,* 69. The Milwaukee banks would be jolted the following year by five closures, two of them permanent, one banker in jail, and another a fugitive. It was the end of an era. For

There is much that one may infer about the economy of the twenty years after 1873 in Wisconsin and its effects upon peoples' lives that is not subject to documentary proof. An industrial economy in which the production and use of heavy engines, milling, mining, and papermaking machinery were leading industries must have required the services of a high proportion of millwrights, mechanics, engineers, and skilled installation crews, many of them more or less itinerant; more of such, relatively, than it needed of traveling salesmen for wholesalers and jobbers. Possibly one should be satisfied that from two of Wisconsin's traveling salesmen came the Christian Commercial Men's Association of America—universally known as The Gideons. That may be an essential difference. What would a couple of drummers out of Chicago in 1898 be doing in Boscobel of a September eve?[83]

---

twenty years Milwaukeeans had recalled with pride that in 1873 there were no bank failures. Twenty-seven Wisconsin banks closed permanently in 1893 and many more suffered temporary closure, including Alexander Mitchell's bank, which was saved by his heirs (who included John Johnston, president of the bank), who pledged their personal fortunes. See Andersen, *Banking in Wisconsin,* 72–84; Still, *Milwaukee,* 324.

[83] Linda Blythe, "Crowded Hotel Was Catalyst for Gideons," in *Wisconsin Then and Now,* 19 (January, 1973), 6. It should be noted, however, that the national headquarters of the Gideons is in Chicago, not Wisconsin.

# 5

# Making a Living

THAT ancient Chinese malediction, "May you live in interesting times," certainly applied to Americans of the post-Civil War decades, particularly where rapid urbanization and industrialization prevailed. David A. Wells, a leading economist of the time, wrote: ". . . [I]n the increased control which mankind has acquired over the forces of Nature, and in the increased utilization of such control is to be found a cause sufficient to account for most if not all the economic disturbance which, since the year 1873, has been certainly universal in its influence over the domain of civilization. . . ." In the early seventies, Wisconsin felt itself a part of these changing times. A Dane County chronicler, writing in the American centennial year, referred to those simpler days of early settlement, not many years past, when "the shams of modern society had no place here. . . . Degrees of wealth were not recognized as degrees in the scale of humanity." That may have been, but not for lack of striving for a few degrees of wealth.[1]

The pioneers who seized upon the future site of Milwaukee had represented themselves as true Jacksonian yeomen come to create orderly corn rows where the Gimbel brothers would, while some of these pioneers were still about, plant their department

[1] David A. Wells, *Recent Economic Changes and Their Effect on the Production and Distribution of Wealth and the Well-Being of Society* (New York, 1890), 61; H. A. Tenney, in William J. Park and Co., *Madison, Dane County and Surrounding Towns. . .* (Madison, 1877), 550.

store. Byron Kilbourn, the most enterprising of all, wrote a preamble for the Milwaukee Claims Association. Kilbourn declared that he and his fellow pioneers "had removed to and settled in that section of country for the purpose of bettering their condition by agricultural pursuits." This seemed a dubious proposition, even to contemporaries. So sure was Kilbourn that he had struck a promotional bonanza in the future townsite, at $1.25 per acre, that he had little thought about farming or neighbors as farmers.[2]

Byron Kilbourn knew what he was about, though of course his vision of Milwaukee's future was concerned mostly with commercial possibilities. He promoted a canal project and two railroads during the city's first twenty years to extend its reach westward. By the 1870's, Milwaukee's greater industrial potential was becoming plain to some of Kilbourn's successors. Indeed, between 1873 and 1893, the United States emerged as one of the leading industrial powers of the world. Wisconsin's strategic geographical position, natural and human resources, and rapidly developed transportation network meant that her metropolis and other urban centers, including those in the interior, were included in this emergent industrialization. The appearance of the huge iron reduction works at Bay View, the extension of Milwaukee's railroad beyond the Mississippi, and the new possibilities of steam in the types of industrial production for which the city had become a center: all gave a heady sense that a simpler past was slipping swiftly away.

Aside from lumbering and such large construction work as railroads and canals, there was in the early 1870's a lag evidenced in the thinking of many people about Wisconsin's manufacturing opportunities. They saw the future in small scale,

[2] Isaac Gimbel in *The National Cyclopaedia of American Biography*, 23:133–134; Robert C. Nesbit, "The Federal Government as Townsite Speculator," in *Explorations in Economic History*, 7 (Spring, 1970), 294–295; Moses M. Strong, *History of the Territory of Wisconsin, from 1836 to 1848. Preceded by an Account of Some Events During the Period in Which It Was Under the Dominion of Kings, States or Other Territories, Previous to the Year 1836* (Madison, 1885), 242; Bayrd Still, *Milwaukee: The History of a City* (Madison, 1948; reprinted, 1965), 13–19.

related tŏ the development of waterpowers, which in most of southern Wisconsin represented a real limitation. In 1878 the Milwaukee *Commercial Times*, envious of Janesville's cotton sheeting mill, noted that "the water power of our Milwaukee River could be greatly increased by the construction of reservoirs." This was a hope that certainly exceeded the probabilities and ignored the revolutionary changes already effected by the new generation of steam engines being produced right under the editor's nose.[3]

Speaking to the state agricultural society in 1873, President John Twombly of the University of Wisconsin propounded a cure for the monopoly prices charged westerners for manufactured articles: "We can make Wisconsin New England with a western expansion," because Wisconsin possessed waterpowers "to drive the machinery of an empire." But he envisioned this expansion as dispersed among farm communities to occupy their idle times. "Start an establishment for the manufacture of whips, buttons, shoes, thread, hats, spades, knives, clocks, clothing or other useful articles, and many hands are at once stretched out for something to do." Governor Cadwallader C. Washburn was turned downright surly by Twombly's "able and exhaustive address," which ran to about 7,500 well-chosen words, with numerous tables from which he doubtless read. Washburn, more expansive and a land speculator turning successful industrial entrepreneur, had a wider vision than Twombly. In his first message to the legislature, the governor asked: "With the best iron ore in the world, why should nine-tenths of all the iron consumed in the state be brought from a distant state or from Europe? Why send our wool to New England . . . ?"[4]

Oratory aside, most people in fact did think of Wisconsin's future industrial growth as a multiplication of modest work-

[3] Milwaukee *Commercial Times,* March 13, 1878; Walter F. Peterson, "E. P. Allis: A Study in Nineteenth Century Business Technique," in the *Marquette Business Review,* 6 (Fall, 1962), 44–48.

[4] Wisconsin State Agricultural Society, *Transactions,* 1873–1874, pp. 93–112. Washburn was on the platform to endure Twombly's address; the governor was mercifully brief. *Wisconsin Public Documents,* 1870–1871, Governor's Message, vol. 1, p. 26.

shops—maybe not the seasonally operated buggy whip factory envisioned by scholar Twombly, but something within the common experience. Meanwhile the railroads, Great Lakes shipping, and reliable steam power were opening new possibilities. Like the lakes carriers, the railroads were desperate for westbound traffic, and coal was a logical commodity. Small towns and villages that had strained to develop shoestring industrial enterprises on the basis of minor waterpowers now found a new generation of entrepreneurs moving in, attracted by the mill and factory buildings on the riversides where waterpower had proved inadequate for sustained, large-scale operations. Their future was with steam power.[5]

This era of change, with its renewal of opportunities deferred and horizons expanded, was an aspect of Wisconsin's location on the western edge of the rapidly growing industrial heartland, with more than half the continent just opening for exploitation to the westward. It brought an appreciation that Wisconsin's future was to supply machinery, goods, and services rather than to compete for commercial hegemony. These winds of change would be felt in the daily lives of people who retained their identification with such pioneering enterprises as opening new land and providing transportation links.

Industrial capitalism soon arrived on this intermingled frontier. John Plankinton, Jerome I. Case, and Edward P. Allis, with thousands of others similarly motivated, were changing the workaday worlds of their fellow citizens, tying them ever more firmly to an expanding market economy of increasing complexity. The years immediately following the slow recovery from the 1873 depression realized tremendous changes in how most Wisconsinites made their livings, where they lived, the level of comforts they enjoyed, and how they perceived themselves and others in the economic, social, and political scheme of things. Definitions of the good life became increasingly discordant, while the

---

[5] George G. Tunnell, "Lake Commerce," in *House Documents,* 55 Cong., 2 sess., no. 277 (serial 3679), part 4, "Coal Traffic."

power of the few to impose a definition upon the many was increased.

A student of these changes has remarked upon the uses of American industrial city architecture for gauging human relations in the same period. Wisconsin offers an interesting field for such study, for it was a center for the production of those lithographed bird's-eye views so popular in the nineteenth century. Views of Milwaukee in the mid-1850's showed a commercial city dominated by its lakefront and interior waterways. Churches, grain elevators, quayside warehouses and lofts were the largest structures. Thirty years later, the surrounding open country had disappeared over the horizon, and there appeared pretentious commercial and public buildings near the heart of the city, together with some new institutional buildings. Dominating almost every quarter of the city were belching stacks attached to workplaces ranging from the utilitarian sprawl of the Bay View iron reduction works and the Chicago, Milwaukee & St. Paul car shops, to the eclectic Germanic castles of the rapidly expanding breweries. It was these coal-fired stacks, casting their smoky pall and soot over the city, that defined the workplace and the lives of the growing industrial army. Smaller urban centers expected and got the same artistic license—larger-than-life industrial stacks spreading their evidence of prosperity.[6]

Contemporary commentary on the new society was as mixed as it is today. David A. Wells, while he early remarked the problems of technological unemployment which accompanied the rapid adoption of inventions and factory methods to production in often unsettled markets, also contrasted factory conditions,

---

[6] Alan Dawley, *Class and Community: The Industrial Revolution in Lynn* (Cambridge, 1976), 122–128; Elizabeth S. Maule, comp., *Bird's Eye Views of Wisconsin Communities: A Preliminary Checklist* (Madison, 1977); Thomas Beckman, ed., *Milwaukee Illustrated: Panoramic and Bird's-Eye Views of a Midwestern Metropolis, 1844–1908* (Milwaukee, 1978), especially catalog nos. 3 (1854), 8 (1856–1858?), 10 (probably 1858), and 41 (1886) shown as the endpapers. A profusely illustrated example of the genre is W. J. Anderson and Julius Bleyer, eds., *Milwaukee's Great Industries: A Compilation of Facts Concerning Milwaukee's Commercial and Manufacturing Enterprises, Its Trade and Commerce, and the Advantages It Offers to Manufacturers Seeking Desirable Locations for New or Established Industries* (Milwaukee, 1892).

real wages, and living standards of the new economy quite favorably with the former cottage industries and home workshops dominated by artisans rather than by business entrepreneurs. By contrast, others have seen most of the evils of society growing out of the disorienting influences of the new economic order.[7]

It is difficult to frame a coherent picture of people's lives at work and away and of their perceptions of themselves in the social system that accompanied these marketing and industrial changes. The 1870 federal census exhibits an awareness of these changes in its handling of occupational and economic data, but the conception shifted in the two succeeding censuses, placing severe limitations upon any matching of the data. The definition of what constituted industrial employment underwent great modifications. This was partly because the 1870 definitions were too loosely constructed, and partly because the occupations themselves were undergoing great changes as factory production divided former artisans' skills into separate processes, and workshops lost out to factories. Equally obscured are the people engaged in occupational specialties that were ancillary to the new economic order.[8]

In a gross way, the federal occupational census reports tell us something about the differences distinguishing Wisconsin's industrial profile from those of its immediate neighbors. Wiscon-

[7] Wells, *Recent Economic Changes*, 396–418; Robert Hunter, *Poverty: Social Conscience in the Progressive Era*, ed., Peter d'A. Jones (New York, 1904; Harper Torchbook edition, New York, 1965), 27–40, 51–56; Herbert G. Gutman, *Work, Culture, and Society in Industrializing America: Essays in American Working-Class and Social History* (New York, 1976), 3–47. See also Sidney Pollard, *The Genesis of Modern Management: A Study of the Industrial Revolution in Great Britain* (Cambridge, 1965), 162; and Melvyn Dubofsky, *Industrialism and the American Worker, 1865–1920* (New York, 1975), 5.

[8] Carmen R. Delle Donne, *Federal Census Schedules, 1850–1880: Primary Sources for Historical Research*, National Archives and Records Service, General Services Administration, Reference Information Paper, no. 67 (Washington, 1973), 12–15; *Sixteenth Census of the United States, 1940: Population, Volume XII, Comparative Occupation Statistics for the United States, 1870 to 1940*, pp. 87–89, 104–112 (listing occupational categories, 1870–1930, many of them aggregated); Harold Barger, *Distribution's Place in the American Economy Since 1869* (Princeton, 1955; reprinted, 1976), 4–5, 101–108, discussing the problem of 1870–1900 census figures on employment. See also Glenn Porter and Harold C. Livesay, *Merchants and Manufacturers: Studies in the Changing Structure of Nineteenth-Century Marketing* (Baltimore, 1971), 116–165.

sin in 1870 had a smaller proportion of her workers in trade and transportation than any of her neighboring states except for Michigan, and between 1870 and 1890 this group of states experienced the smallest increase. But in the manufacturing and mechanical industries, Wisconsin in 1870 was second only to Michigan among the adjacent states, and second only to Illinois in the 1870 to 1890 increase. Wisconsin was, in effect, becoming a workshop caught between Chicago and the Twin Cities, where trade and transportation employment loomed larger.

The industrial growth of the 1880's was broad-based but quite uneven. If one takes the top ten counties in industrial employment—setting Milwaukee County aside as *sui generis*—these ten included 41.2 per cent of the 1870 industrial jobs in the state (Milwaukee County accounted for 19.2 per cent), 34.1 per cent in 1880, and 32.6 per cent in 1890. Milwaukee's relatively greater surge came during the 1870's; in 1880 her share was 37.3 per cent of the industrial jobs compared to 34.1 per cent for the next ten counties. Only three counties appeared in all three decennial census years among the ten following Milwaukee: Winnebago, Racine, and Fond du Lac. In all, the names of twenty counties, at one time or another, were ranked between second and elev-

PROPORTION OF POPULATION REPORTING OCCUPATIONS
(expressed in percentages)

| TRADE AND TRANSPORTATION INDUSTRIES | | | | | |
|---|---|---|---|---|---|
| Year | Wisconsin | Illinois | Iowa | Michigan | Minnesota |
| 1870 | 7.4 | 10.8 | 8.2 | 7.3 | 8.0 |
| 1890 | 11.9 | 18.2 | 13.9 | 15.4 | 15.4 |
| % increase | 4.5 | 7.4 | 5.7 | 7.4 | 7.4 |

| MANUFACTURING AND MECHANICAL INDUSTRIES | | | | | |
|---|---|---|---|---|---|
| Year | Wisconsin | Illinois | Iowa | Michigan | Minnesota |
| 1870 | 18.3 | 18.0 | 13.7 | 20.4 | 14.0 |
| 1890 | 22.4 | 23.6 | 14.2 | 21.3 | 17.9 |
| % increase | 4.1 | 5.6 | 0.5 | 0.9 | 3.9 |

SOURCES: *Ninth Census of the United States, 1870: Population, Volume I,* 674–685; *Eleventh Census of the United States, 1890: Population, Volume I, Part 2,* pp. 302–303.

enth. This represents a great variation in industrial growth rates, or relative stagnation. The great expansion of the lumber industry accounts for much of this shifting about, but there were also eighteen counties that suffered a positive loss in the number of industrial jobs during the twenty years. All of the eighteen lay south of a line from Brown to Pepin counties, both of which lost jobs.[9]

What these figures meant, over the years, was that there were a good many places where industrial employment was marginal. One can trace some of this ebb and flow after 1883 in specific communities by reference to the factory inspection reports of the state's bureau of labor and industrial statistics. De Pere in Brown County, for example, had 480 jobs in eight plants inspected in 1887–1888. This was reduced to 264 jobs in five plants in 1893–1894. The village had lost a woodenware plant employing 200, two sawmills with 153 workers, and a charcoal iron furnace with a payroll of seventy. It had gained a paper mill employing about 200. According to the state censuses of 1885 and 1895, De Pere doubled in population in those years, from 2,149 to 4,292. There were 120 women employed in the new paper mill, whereas none were reported employed by industries in 1887–1888. If one subtracts the 120 jobs from the 264 remaining, male industrial employment suffered a net drop of 338 jobs out of the 482 reported there five years earlier.

Fond du Lac likewise suffered its industrial ups and downs. It was Wisconsin's second city in population in 1870, but by 1890 it had dropped to eighth, actually losing 740 over the twenty years as the population fell to 12,024. It was an important sawmilling and woodworking center, but its timber sources were much closer by rail and water to its main rival, Oshkosh. Fond du Lac's hard luck included the removal in 1876 of the Chicago

---

[9] Wisconsin Historical County–Level Data Program, Economic Series: Manufacturing, in History of Wisconsin Project files. Seven of the eighteen counties that lost industrial jobs in the period 1870–1890 had urban centers (2,500+), and eleven did not. Lumbermen, raftsmen, and woodchoppers were counted in the agricultural schedules during the period. Many of these were sawmill and planing mill workers, depending upon the season when the mills operated or were closed down.

and North Western railroad's car shops. Five years later, the promoters of Merrill—insiders of the CM&StP railroad—raided Fond du Lac's woodworking plants, claiming one of its big sash-and-door plants and many of its 400 employees with the lure of prebuilt homes and easy mortgages. In 1890, the La Belle Wagon Works, which had 150 hands in 1887–1888, moved to Superior for a subsidy; the Wheel and Seeder Company, seventy hands,

WISCONSIN COUNTIES RANKED BY NUMBER OF INDUSTRIAL WORKERS, 1870–1880–1890

| | 1870 | | | 1880 | | | 1890 | |
|---|---|---|---|---|---|---|---|---|
| COUNTY | RANK | NUMBER OF WORKERS | COUNTY | RANK | NUMBER OF WORKERS | COUNTY | RANK | NUMBER OF WORKERS |
| Milwaukee | 1 | 8,433 | Milwaukee | 1 | 21,308 | Milwaukee | 1 | 39,222 |
| Winnebago | 2 | 3,005 | Racine | 2 | 3,561 | Winnebago | 2 | 7,786 |
| Fond du Lac | 3 | 2,325 | Winnebago | 3 | 3,442 | Chippewa | 3 | 5,186 |
| Racine | 4 | 1,882 | Rock | 4 | 2,207 | Racine | 4 | 4,594 |
| Brown | 5 | 1,880 | Sheboygan | 5 | 1,705 | La Crosse | 5 | 4,116 |
| Rock | 6 | 1,707 | Fond du Lac | 6 | 1,699 | Marinette | 6 | 3,394 |
| Dodge | 7 | 1,671 | Brown | 7 | 1,599 | Marathon | 7 | 3,352 |
| Jefferson | 8 | 1,560 | Ozaukee | 8 | 1,462 | Eau Claire | 8 | 3,155 |
| Oconto | 9 | 1,526 | La Crosse | 9 | 1,337 | Lincoln | 9 | 2,624 |
| Sheboygan | 10 | 1,474 | Manitowoc | 10 | 1,311 | Outagamie | 10 | 2,581 |
| Chippewa | 11 | 1,063 | Eau Claire | 11 | 1,168 | Fond du Lac | 11 | 2,394 |
| Totals | | 26,526 | | | 40,799 | | | 78,404 |
| State Total | | 43,910 | | | 57,109 | | | 120,015 |
| Milw. % of State | | 19.2% | | | 37.3% | | | 32.7% |
| #2–#11% of State Total | | 41.2% | | | 34.1% | | | 32.6% |

SOURCES: For county data, see *Wisconsin Historical County-Level Data Program, Economic Series: Manufacturing,* in History of Wisconsin Project files. State totals are from *Ninth Census of the United States, 1870: Wealth and Industry, Volume III,* 583; *Tenth Census of the United States, 1880: Manufacturing, Volume II,* 189; *Eleventh Census of the United States, 1890: Manufacturing, Volume VI, Part 1,* pp. 634–637. *The Sixteenth Census of the United States, 1940: Population, Comparative Occupation Statistics for the United States, 1870 to 1940,* pp. 87–88, emphasizes that because of the many changes over the years of census taking in defining, collecting, and presenting data on occupations, one must be cautious in using such data for comparative purposes.

moved to La Crosse about the same time; and a smaller threshing machine works, McDonald Manufacturing Company, was
lured away to Minneapolis, which at the same time captured the
George Esterly Harvesting Machine Company of Whitewater.[10]

Chance and geography played large roles in employment
opportunities and in the prospects of entrepreneurial success.
The two were inextricably tied together in an emerging economic
order that often baffled the shrewd and calculating as well as the
majority for whom life was simply a happening. Not only was
much industrial employment highly seasonal, it was also chancy
in a multitude of other ways that were not readily recognized:
location with relation to raw materials and markets; financing;
business cycles; the influence of new methods, machinery, and
technology; and the general nature of the new Darwinian world
with its widening markets matched by wider and fiercer competition. It was an awkward age, caught between the acceptance of
scarcity as the prudent rule of life and an abundance of production looking for customers. Steam power and the factory system
were creating new abundance, while the new economic order was
organizing consumers strictly to the ends of production, marketing, and profits, but without thought to their roles as consumers.
Not only was it an awkward age, it was an insecure one.

By 1873, the way was cleared for the new economic order
and the ascendancy of the entrepreneur. Our trouble in understanding the change is that the entrepreneur so often has been
characterized as the "Robber Baron" of the "Age of Enterprise." Francis A. Walker, who developed the ninth federal
census of 1870 and tried to fit in the emerging economic facts,
was one of the first to point out the distinction between a capitalist and a true entrepreneur. The latter was the agent who directed
the efficient functioning of labor and capital. He had to have
access to capital, but he was not necessarily a capitalist. It was a

[10] Wisconsin Bureau of Labor and Industrial Statistics, *Biennial Report,* 1887–1888,
Synopsis of Reports of Inspection, 255, 258–259, and *ibid.,* 1893–1894, Synopsis of
Reports of Inspection, 25a–26a, 33a–35a. Factory inspection reports are arranged alpha-
betically by city and town. Also see Maurice McKenna, ed., *Fond du Lac County, Wiscon-
sin: Past and Present* (2 vols., Chicago, 1912), 1:327–329; and George W. Esterly,
"Autobiography," typescript in the George W. Esterly Papers.

fierce game of survival in which only a few survived. These survivors possessed a hardness necessary for success. The great majority who felt called upon to act as entrepreneurs often claimed the sympathy of the public, yet their lack of the qualifications for success constituted the greatest tax upon labor because success eluded them.[11]

Even sufficient drive and shrewdness did not ensure success. The twenty years from 1873 to 1893 were subject to two full-fledged business panics, in the beginning and terminal year, plus what we would now term two sharp recessions in the eighties. All in all, ten of these twenty years were dominated by the dislocations of panics and depressions. Business failures were a commonplace. As competent an entrepreneur as Edward P. Allis suffered the stress of near-bankruptcy as a result of the 1873 panic, coming away from the experience with a pronounced aversion for bankers and the gold standard. It was not a time entirely dominated by hard-eyed men who understood and controlled their own destinies. Entrepreneurs, like the rest of mankind, lived with uncertainties beyond their control.[12]

Harsh judgment upon the great majority of American businessmen whom success eluded is not the usual stuff of local history "mug books." The popular subscription histories of local lore with their potted biographies celebrated successes, both large and small. Gazetteers invariably found "thriving" or "flourishing" villages and cities in the hands of "energetic businessmen" who were "well posted in all branches." One must look for the variants. They do exist, in literature and biography.

Hamlin Garland wrote to his brother in 1889: "Doesn't the whole migration of the Garlands and McClintocks seem a mad-

[11] Joseph Dorfman, *The Economic Mind in American Civilization* (5 vols., New York, 1946-1959), 3:101-109; *DAB;* Edward C. Kirkland, *Industry Comes of Age: Business, Labor, and Public Policy, 1860-1897* (New York, 1961), 306-314.

[12] Edward Kirkland, *Dream and Thought in the Business Community, 1860-1900* (Ithaca, 1956; Quadrangle edition, Chicago, 1964), 6-10. Howard N. Ross, "Economic Growth and Change in the United States Under Laissez Faire: 1870-1929," in Frederic C. Cople, ed., *The Age of Industrialism in America: Essays in Social Structure and Cultural Values* (New York, 1968), 6, notes that in the years 1870-1890 the American economy was actually contracting as many months as it was expanding, but new output increased by about ten times during those years.

ness?'' Edna Ferber's father failed four times as a merchant before her mother took over the family store-keeping: "He had never got the trick of turning his money over quickly—that trick so necessary to the success of the small-town business." Zona Gale recalled her father's efforts at business. Charles Gale was a railroad engineer on the CM&StP, dissatisfied with his occupation. "He left the railroad, left the town, went into a strange city," she wrote, "with a blindness which breeders of quail or of fish do not permit to a live thing that they wish to persist. . . . Three times in three cities in a period of twelve years the man sought a way out through business. . . . Ulysses of three consecutive Odysseys, he fared forth with such initiative as America duplicates and buries, sun by sun."[13]

The failure of a manufacturing firm of any magnitude was a matter of public record. But while the manufacturing sector of the economy experienced great expansion in the years 1873–1893, there was, particularly in growing urban centers, an accompanying expansion of the wholesale and retail trades and ancillary services such as finance, insurance, and real estate. These absorbed an increasing number of small entrepreneurs and their employees. A great many of these businesses were socially costly because they were poorly financed, poorly conceived and managed, paid low wages, and frequently went to the wall. There were 522 recorded business failures in Wisconsin, as reported by the publishers of *Bradstreet's* for the years 1880–1884. Probably the majority of small businessmen then did not observe the formalities required for a notice in *Bradstreet's* when they closed their doors, any more than did a small sawmill operator or a logging contractor when they came up short at the end of the season.[14]

[13] Hamlin Garland, *A Son of the Middle Border*, ed., Henry M. Christman (Macmillan paperback edition, New York, 1962), 342; Edna Ferber, *Fanny Herself* (New York, 1917), 5; Zona Gale, *Portage, Wisconsin, and Other Essays* (New York, 1928), 53–54.

[14] Wisconsin Bureau of Labor Statistics, *Biennial Report*, 1883–1884, p. 255; Thomas C. Cochran, *Business in American Life: A History* (New York, 1972), 147. Cochran comments that the small firm with the same ownership for five years was a rarity. Also see Merle Curti, *The Making of an American Community: A Case Study of Democracy in a Frontier County* (Stanford, 1959), 227.

The federal census did not offer consistent statistics on whole-saling and retailing until 1929. An effort to project these figures backward, using fragmentary evidence, concluded that margins or value added charged to distribution by wholesaling and retail-ing were remarkably stable over the years, rising slowly from 32.7 per cent in 1869 to 37 per cent in 1929. The labor force engaged in distribution showed a steady upward trend between the Civil War and World War I, but output per man-hour in distribution increased much more slowly than in agriculture, mining, and manufacturing.[15]

Small retail stores came and went rapidly. Credit was rela-tively easy in good times, secured in part by the merchandise itself. A person owning a piece of urban real estate was a partic-ularly good credit risk. Cities and towns experienced strong growth, and specialized retailing and financial districts were emerging in the cities as the horse car, and later the trolley, tempted the well-to-do to the new suburbs.

Real estate speculation in growing urban centers was a fre-quent subject for criticism. A characteristic comment appeared in an 1892 publication of the Association for the Advancement of Milwaukee: "A leading occupation of perhaps too many . . . recently has been dealing in real estate. . . . If these talented gentlemen would devote one-half of the abundant energy they display in converting suburban farms into city lots to the build-ing up of manufactures . . . a solid foundation for great and continuing prosperity would be established." General John Hammond, the promoter of West Superior, likewise complained: "Hundreds of speculators and promoters of every kind took up my time and interfered with the business of the company. . . ."[16]

A superfluity of retail establishments was also a subject for criticism. In 1872 a Kenosha editor commented: "In passing through Main Street and counting up the grocery stores thereon,

---

[15] Barger, *Distribution's Place in the American Economy*, x–xi, 56–57, 81–84.

[16] Blake McKelvey, *The Urbanization of America, 1860–1915* (New Brunswick, 1963), 12; I. M. Bean, "Our Iron and Steel Industry," in Anderson and Bleyer, eds., *Milwau-kee's Great Industries*, 81–82; Frank A. Flower, *The Eye of the North-west: First Annual Report of the Statistician of Superior, Wisconsin* (Milwaukee, 1890), 110.

one could almost wish some of the money invested in coffee, tea, pepper and starch could be applied to manufactories.'' Apparently it was a common notion that retailing was overcrowded. Entries for 1875 in the diary of a young man who kept store depict the dissolution of a dry goods and grocery store in Manitowoc which he managed for an employer who owned other stores. In February, the two agreed that ''Manitowoc is a played out Town for Merchants, there are too many stores for the demand.'' An auctioneer was hired to dispose of the stock. The clerk took part of his back pay in goods, bartering for fancy boots and other items. He and his employer parted company with wages $265 in arrears, which must have been several months' pay. The young man—he was just twenty—took to the road selling fire insurance, which also proved a losing venture. Fortunately, he had a home to go to and tended his parents' garden for the summer, drifted about from one thing to another until 1878 when he caught on as a successful correspondent for the Chicago *Inter-Ocean*.[17]

Depression periods were hard on retailers. Village storekeepers had to contend with Grange co-operative stores in the depression years of the seventies. Wisconsin grangers were not enthusiastic co-operators, and they shopped at Grange stores only when they offered better prices, while damning the village storekeepers who had been carrying them on credit and accepting butter and eggs as payment, which naturally meant higher prices for goods. Then, as the railroad network was extended, the village and country stores faced new competition. The cities, now more easily accessible, offered more varied shops and the new department stores. Equally handy were the Montgomery Ward and Sears, Roebuck mail-order houses in Chicago. Nationally advertised brands, which the local merchant had to stock usually at lesser margins, complicated his life further.[18]

[17] Carrie Cropley, *Kenosha: From Pioneer Village to Modern City, 1835-1935* (Kenosha, 1958), 46; Charles Burmeister Papers, Green Bay Area Research Center.
[18] LaVerne H. Marquart, *Wisconsin's Agricultural Heritage: The Grange, 1871-1971* (Lake Mills, 1972), 14-21; George Cerny, ''Cooperation in the Midwest in the Granger Era, 1869-1875,'' in *Agricultural History*, 37 (October, 1963), 187-205; ''A Farmer with Lib-

Despite the new competitive atmosphere, general stores proliferated in villages and hamlets. In the *Wisconsin Gazetteer* of 1871, there were approximately 1,350 general stores listed, located in some 550 communities. Twenty years later there were nearly 2,900 at more than 1,220 post office locations. Although the general population had increased only 61 per cent, it had of course extended geographically. In general, communities of over 2,500 population had fewer general stores at the later date, with the exception of rapidly growing newer communities in northern Wisconsin. General stores tended merely to persist rather than increase in the older communities of southern Wisconsin that were in the 800 to 2,500 population range. Retail groceries almost tripled in number (788 to 2,025) during these twenty years, indicating the trend towards retailing specialization.

A rough comparison of Wisconsin gazetteer entries for 1871 and 1891 indicates a proliferation of services extending even to villages that were very stable in population numbers. The 1871 gazetteer listed 105 bankers, brokers, and banks in fifty-eight cities and villages, nineteen of which had more than one. The 1891 edition, listing banks only, had 272 separate listings in 172 communities, of which sixty-seven had more than one bank.[19]

There were, in 1871, sixty-four villages and cities with livery stables offering rigs for hire. By 1891, there were 293 post office addresses offering this service. In 1871 there were forty-two village and cities boasting a professional photographer; by 1891 there were 182. If a person in 1871 sought the services of a dentist, there were only forty-two communities with a listing. By 1891 this service could be found in ninety-one cities and villages. By contrast, in 1871 there were 183 breweries located in 110 cities and villages, which by 1891 had declined to 160 breweries in 109 communities. Industrialization and the new marketing

---

eral Views,'' undated letter to the editor in the Dodgeville *Chronicle,* March 19, 1875; Lewis Atherton, *Main Street on the Middle Border* (Bloomington, 1954), 49–57; Daniel J. Boorstin, *The Americans: The Democratic Experience* (New York, 1973), 118–129.

[19] *Wisconsin State Business Directory, 1872–73; Wisconsin State Gazetteer and Business Directory, 1891–1892.* Some of these counts are not exact, having been averaged by counting a single page where long lists appeared to be quite standard per page.

order were slowly changing the distribution of producers, while services and professions became more specialized and employed more people, even in somnolent villages.[20]

Foreign visitors often remarked the eager intensity with which urban Americans pursued success in business. This probably reflected the foreigners' preoccupation with the class of people they commonly encountered. Despite the assumed universality of this drive, those who elected employment in trade as entrée to the role of owner or entrepreneur were apt to be referred to as the "non-producing classes, of whom we have too many already." It was an ambivalent role. There seems to have been a narrow line between the self-made man in the making and the derogatory references to "multitudes of farmers' and mechanics' sons seek[ing] to be salesmen, clerks, book-keepers, drummers for trade houses, and, failing to find or retain such situations, they become 'sports,' billiard-markers, bar-tenders, confidence men, dead-beats—anything, in short, but hand-soiling working-men." Although the working hours were generally longer than in industry or wholesaling, and average daily wages below those of skilled labor, a great advantage was that clerking ordinarily offered steady employment in contrast to much industrial employment.[21]

Even in seemingly stable communities—stable in numbers at any rate—we now know there was a great turnover of families, individuals, and business houses. A detailed study of five such villages in Grant County found that 56 per cent of the people listed in the 1880 federal census did not appear on the rolls of the 1885 state census. Between 1880 and 1895, fully 78 per cent dropped from view. The author suggests that most of those who

[20] The two gazetteers used were those cited in the preceding footnote.

[21] Cochran, *Business in American Life*, 170–171; Irvin G. Wyllie, *The Self-Made Man in America: The Myth of Rags to Riches* (New Brunswick, 1954); Ruth M. Elson, *Guardians of Tradition: American Schoolbooks of the Nineteenth Century* (Lincoln, 1964), 252–254; Milwaukee *Northwest Trade Bulletin*, December 31, 1883; Kirkland, *Dream and Thought in the Business Community*, 77, quoting from U.S. Senate Committee on Education and Labor, *Report Upon the Relations Between Labor and Capital, and Testimony Taken by the Committee* (4 vols., Washington, 1885), 2:964; Wisconsin Bureau of Labor and Industrial Statistics, *Biennial Report*, 1887–1888, p. 125, and Table V, pp. 189–213.

left were "wage earners rather than petty entrepreneurs," but this is at variance with the findings of a better-known study of Trempealeau County that small businessmen were equally mobile.[22]

This movement reflected the search for greater opportunity, much of it simply hopeful, some of it calculated. Business colleges experienced a healthy growth in Wisconsin as elsewhere. Only two of these institutions were listed in the Wisconsin gazetteer for 1872–1873, one in Milwaukee and the other in Oshkosh. Twenty years later there were some twenty of them located in fourteen communities. Milwaukee supported six, Eau Claire three, and Janesville two, while the smallest community to have one offered the Stoughton Academy and Business College. This was a particularly fertile field for private enterprise, as the business college could offer concentrated courses of a few weeks or evening classes to accommodate students with other employment.[23]

Leo Wieland, one such student, came to Milwaukee about 1877 from Baden, Germany. He was sixteen at the time. His trip was financed by his sister and her husband, L. J. Miller, a hardware merchant in Milwaukee. Miller agreed to advance Leo the tuition for a three months' course at Bayer's Commercial College, a one-man operation. "He was a Jew, but he was a smart old professor," Leo recalled. Leo attended during the day and worked evenings in the hardware store, which was open six days of the week from six in the morning to nine in the evening. Wieland had a fair writing knowledge of English, acquired in the village school in Baden. Bayer conducted classes bilingually and complimented Leo on the rapidity with which he acquired a serviceable spoken English.

Wieland later was offered an office job with the John Pritzlaff Hardware Company, where he continued until his retirement

[22] Peter J. Coleman, "Restless Grant County: Americans on the Move," in *WMH*, 46 (Autumn, 1962), 16–20; Curti, *Making of an American Community*, 69–70, 443.

[23] *Wisconsin Business Directory, 1872–73*, pp. 89, 172; *Wisconsin Business Directory, 1891–2*, pp. 1127–1128, 1157–1158; Cochran, *Business in American Life*, 177; Kirkland, *Dream and Thought in the Business Community*, 77–78.

more than a half-century later. Pritzlaff Hardware was well on its way to becoming the largest hardware wholesale house in the Upper Midwest—the third largest in the nation at the time of Pritzlaff's death in 1900. Pritzlaff helped to bring significant manufacturing firms to Milwaukee. The firm did not engage directly in manufacturing but acted as a jobber for materials such as sheet iron, and was the major distributor in the area of manufactured hardware items.[24]

John Pritzlaff, born in Pomerania in 1820, immigrated to New York in 1839, arriving without a cent and owing about ten dollars, he remembered. He worked his way to Milwaukee in 1841 where he hired out as a cutter of cordwood and finally got a job as porter in a hardware store. John Nazro, the leading hardware wholesaler in Milwaukee before he was caught by the 1873 panic while expanding his operations, staked Pritzlaff in the hardware retail business. By 1884, Pritzlaff emerged as the dominant wholesaler, and by 1887 he had a payroll of 100.[25]

Leo Wieland's reminiscences, recorded in his old age, offer a vivid reconstruction of Pritzlaff's comfortable rise to wealth after his initial struggles. The whole tone is one of Gemütlichkeit and tolerance for his debtors who were engaged in the tooth-and-claw world of small-town retailing. Grown stout, John Pritzlaff sat in state in the hallway leading to the offices of his domain. "He looked at the people when they came in, you know, and he had pretty good judgment of them." Pritzlaff was known for his generous extension of credit to retailers, even to those like the one who, in Wieland's phrase, "couldn't quite concentrate himself to his position." A refrain that runs through Wieland's narrative was expressed by one of the firm's traveling men, who

[24] Transcript of Leo Wieland interviews, January 16, 22, 29, February 14, 1952, in the Matson Holbrook Interviews; John G. Gregory, *History of Milwaukee, Wisconsin* (4 vols., Chicago, 1931), 1:447–450. Wieland started with Pritzlaff at $10.50 per week, good wages for the time. "After I was there eight months then I got $12.00. I was a pretty good writer."

[25] Gregory, *History of Milwaukee*, 1:447–450, 4:729–730; Wisconsin Bureau of Labor and Industrial Statistics, *Biennial Report*, 1887–1888, p. 298; [Frank A. Flower], *History of Milwaukee, Wisconsin. . .* (2 vols., Chicago, 1881), 2:1586–1587.

said: "Gentlemen, I want to tell you right now, that if it hadn't been for the leniency of the John Pritzlaff Hardware Company, they would never have built up the business which they did."

Other Pritzlaff business practices are of interest. He expected other members of the extensive German business community to do business with him, particularly fellow members of his Lutheran church congregation. Employees were presumed to be bilingual—a normal expectation in Milwaukee. He protected his retailers by avoiding direct dealings with local contractors, including large ones. Even with large manufacturing concerns, with which the Pritzlaff firm dealt directly, there was little discussion of prices or evidence of centralized purchasing. Wieland seemed surprised by the interviewer's questions about discounts or other competitive practices. Pritzlaff's outside men dealt with "the boys," meaning shop foremen at such places as the E. P. Allis Company or the CM&StP car shops.

Despite its size during these years, the Pritzlaff firm had only minor competitors with limited lines aside from those in Chicago and Minneapolis, and it remained a highly personal business. Employees negotiated directly with their immediate superiors for raises. Three important employees, who were buyers and managers, Charles and George Davis and Fred C. Westfall, were dissuaded from starting an independent jobbing business by an offer of stock in the firm. (Pritzlaff's preference for employees of German background was certainly qualified by the Davis brothers, one of whom was the assistant manager of the office force and did the office hiring.)

Working for John Pritzlaff, particularly in his office, but also as a buyer or an outside man, surely put a man in a different category from industrial laborers or the clerks in most retail establishments. One finds an identity of views between the employer and his hired managers and clerks. They were people whom one knew and this recognition was shared right up to old John Pritzlaff, sitting in his chair in the office hallway.[26]

---

[26] Gregory, *History of Milwaukee,* 1:447–450, and 4:729–730; Wieland Transcript.

August Groth, like Leo Wieland, took the path through a business college to better things. Growing upon in Cedarburg, he was apprenticed in a willowware factory there at age fourteen, having completed seventh grade in a German-language school. At fifteen, he started as a clerk in a large general store in Cedarburg and shortly became cashier, inheriting a set of books that had not been in balance for years. He also kept time for his father's cordwood business, did the billing, ran a sewing machine agency on the side, functioned as a community banker—a service of the general store—and managed the new telephone exchange. With all of these activities going on concurrently, he received a salary of ten dollars a month from the store and room and board from his father.

Groth recognized that he had business talents as well as serious educational deficiencies. About 1891 he persuaded his father to stake him to a four-and-a-half-month course at the Spencerian Business College in Milwaukee. As the leading scholar in the college, Groth was readily placed by Spencer in the office of the Gallun Leather Company. Groth started at six dollars a week: "I thought that was very good pay." Groth later told Gallun that he did not want to be an accountant: "I wanted to find out something about the business." This seemed to please Gallun. He was put through various departments to learn the processes and hide selection, served temporarily as payroll clerk, then went on to more responsible positions with the firm and became principal buyer by age twenty-five. Groth always spoke German with Gallun: "I got on very nicely with the old gentleman, and I got more and more important work to do."[27]

Clerking was certainly not universally scorned, as some contemporary commentary might suggest. The editor of the Monroe *Sentinel* complained in 1883 that many promising young men of the community were leaving town because of a lack of business opportunities. Clerkships were being given to foreigners, making it necessary for "our Yankee lads" to go elsewhere to find work.

[27] Transcript of August Groth interview, April 8, 1952, in the Matson Holbrook Interviews; Augustus Frederick Gallun is in the *DWB*.

Monroe had been a Yankee settlement, but by 1880 Germans and German Swiss outnumbered them. By the early nineties the Germans had certainly infiltrated the business community, and a number of firm names indicate partnerships between the Yankees and their German neighbors, a recognition of the facts of life.[28]

It is hazardous to characterize the 1870's as ushering in a change of relationships between employers and employees based upon the anonymity of the swiftly growing cities and the rise of employers with work forces numbering in the hundreds. Before 1870, Milwaukee had its large packinghouses, the railway car shops, and the ironworks at Bay View. Nor were the employers of large crews, most of them either semiskilled or requiring no skills whatever, confined to the metropolis. The lumber industry, geographically dispersed and much of it in rural and village settings, employed large crews in woods and mills and depended upon casual, itinerant labor because much of the work was seasonal. Railroad construction similarly looked to casual laborers who either found the job on their own or were imported from the cities in carload lots. The charcoal iron industry flourished for a time and an occasional newspaper notice would advise that woodchoppers were needed for some location. The growing tannery business required immense tonnages of oak and hemlock bark. Although much of this was provided by farmers clearing land, some large tanneries owned forest acreage on which large crews gathered bark. Winter ice cutting and hauling also involved large numbers in season. These earlier experiences with mass labor were not the rule, but would become familiar enough within the next decade or two.

Industries outside Milwaukee had their great period of growth in the 1880's and early 1890's. As one would expect, the number of large employers increased. Between 1886 and 1894 the number of employers located outside of Milwaukee who had average

---

[28] William F. Birdsall, "The Immigrant in Monroe, Wisconsin, 1870–1900," unpublished seminar paper, in the author's files; *Wisconsin Business Directory, 1891–92,* listing for Monroe.

payrolls of 100 or more increased from 130 to 227. While isolated lumber mills accounted for many of these, 133 of the large plants in the latter years were located in cities that had from two to nineteen payrolls of over 100. In Milwaukee during the same interval, the number of employers with over 100 employees increased from sixty-five to ninety-three. Three of these had over 1,000 employees each; eight had over 500. Six years before there were only two with more than 500 employees.[29]

After 1873, the artisan shop with a few employees working under the direction of a craftsman-owner characterized a steadily diminishing segment of industrial employment. Increasingly, employment opportunities were to be found in large shops owned or directed by men whose concerns were primarily with the mobilization of capital, financing the latest in technologies, and marketing their products. As illustrated by the career of Henry Harnischfeger, an entrepreneur in the machine and foundry industries necessarily spent much of his time looking for product needs that he could fill. He did not have time to devote to hiring and firing, beyond those key employees who were essential to make the mare go. Significantly, Harnischfeger in his *Autobiography* mentions only partners, customers, and fellow entrepreneurs. While hiring skilled management and technical personnel must have been a continuing problem, this did not figure as a major concern when he looked back over the elements of his considerable success. Similarly, Edward P. Allis left this problem in the hands of his divisional managers. Milwaukee seemed to attract a flow of technically skilled men who produced a corps of managers of the rough-and-ready school demanded by the times.[30]

The employer possessed all of the advantages in dealing with labor. There was no limit, other than the relative efficiency of his operations, upon his right to hire and fire at will. With the premises and necessary equipment centralized under his control,

[29] Wisconsin Bureau of Labor and Industrial Statistics, *Biennial Report,* 1887–1888, Synopsis of Reports of Inspection, 245–337; *ibid.,* 1893–1894, pp. 3a–179a.

[30] Henry Harnischfeger, *Autobiography* (Milwaukee, 1929), *passim;* Walter F. Peterson, *An Industrial Heritage: Allis-Chalmers Corporation* (Milwaukee, 1978), chap. 2.

the employer defined all of the terms of employment: hours, wages, standards of production, work rules, conditions of the workplace, and so forth. He was free to discriminate in any way he might choose: to exclude on the basis of ethnic origin, religion, presumed attitudes, or suspected union activity; or to proscribe certain behavior ranging from conversation on the job to drinking on any occasion. This control extended beyond the limits of the plant, particularly in an isolated lumber town where the political and economic activities of the community were commonly assumed to be the principal employer's business. There he frequently owned much of the housing and the general store, and was free to pay in scrip, rent, or room and board. Proscription of "troublemakers" could extend beyond the community by means of the familiar blacklist. Even in the Milwaukee tanneries, for instance, it was accepted practice that a man needed a recommendation from his previous employer to transfer from one tannery to another.[31]

The basic conservatism of the majority of workmen led them to accept as normal the employment conditions of very large shops. The Wisconsin Bureau of Labor and Industrial Statistics began in 1887–1888 to distribute questionnaires to a large sampling of workmen. Comment was invited on home ownership, the effects of immigration, how general conditions could be improved, suggested legislation, and so forth. Despite the evident freedom of the workers' responses, one looks in vain for much about the disadvantages of large shops compared to what must have been the earlier work experience of many. Rather, many responses dealt with general issues of the day which often were remote from their specific working conditions: temperance, working women and children, convict labor, the decline of apprenticeships, hostility to unions, the mechanics of payment.

---

[31] Gerd Korman, *Industrialization, Immigrants and Americanizers: The View from Milwaukee, 1866-1921* (Madison, 1967), 3–73; Robert F. Fries, *Empire in Pine: The Story of Lumbering in Wisconsin, 1830-1900* (Madison, 1951), 206–212; transcript of William Brockman interview, February 11, 1952, in the Matson Holbrook Interviews; Daniel Nelson, *Managers and Workers: Origins of the New Factory System in the United States, 1880-1920* (Madison, 1975), 3–54, 79–100.

But there is hardly any mention of monotony in the workplace
or a lack of challenge resulting from the division of labor. About
the only comment on the size of operations was the ritual reaction to "monopolies" as remote forces that set prices artificially.
There was comment about the decline of skills from men who
had mastered a craft, but not against piecework or piecework
wages as such.[32]

Some historians have argued that, particularly in smaller
industrial towns, the community often sided with the employees
in labor disputes and exhibited prejudice particularly against
large employers. It is difficult to document such sympathy, partly
because the usual place to look for it is in the local press—not
exactly a free agent then in most communities. In one study of
such a Wisconsin community, the authors conclude that they
could not substantiate any such sentiment. They found, rather,
that community consensus favored the employers' views as being
for the good of the community.[33]

Lumbering and railroad building were obviously seasonal, but
this was equally true of industries that were clustering in the
cities. Meat-packing and brewing were seasonal prior to the use
of mechanical refrigeration, as was tanning, which was tied to
meat-packing. Other industries in turn responded to the seasonal
nature of farming, lumbering, and other resource-oriented activities. Wisconsin's climate set limits upon outdoor employment
for the building industry, construction of all kinds, and subsidiary industries like brickmaking and quarrying, as well as coal
handling, ice harvesting, iron reduction, and woodcutting. It
also made a lot of jobs miserable that were carried on in sheds,

[32] John A. Garraty, *Unemployment in History: Economic Thought and Public Policy* (New
York, 1978), 108–109; Wisconsin Bureau of Labor and Industrial Statistics, *Biennial
Report,* 1887–1888, pp. 1–115.

[33] Herbert G. Gutman, "The Workers' Search for Power," in H. Wayne Morgan,
ed., *The Gilded Age* (revised edition, Syracuse, [1970]), 31–53; Charles N. Glaab and
Lawrence H. Larsen, *Factories in the Valley: Neenah-Menasha, 1870–1915* (Madison, 1969),
222–223. For typical comment in the press on the 1881 "Sawdust War" in Eau Claire,
see: Eau Claire *News,* July 23, 30, 1881; Eau Claire *Free Press,* July 24, 31, 1881; Madison
*Daily Democrat,* July 24, 25, 30, 1881. See also *Wisconsin Public Documents,* 1885–1886,
Governor's Message, vol. 1, pp. 3–6.

foundries, tanyards, car shops, and other buildings with inadequate cover. The average worker experienced ten weeks or more of unemployment annually, whether dictated by the seasonal nature of a given industry or by business conditions which might be general or peculiar to that industry.[34]

Employment opportunities were also circumscribed by the popular ethnic stereotypes of the day. Patrick Cudahy is often cited as an example of this because of his preference for Poles and his firm notion that Mediterranean types, particularly Greeks, were "undesirables." Albert C. Vogel of Pfister and Vogel Leather Company, which had nearly 700 employees in 1893, divided them along a similar plan: "The people of Northern Europe, Germany, East Germany, and Poland and those from the Austrian and Hungarian empire, which I will refer to as Group #1, were more stocky built and slower moving than the people of Italy and Greece. . . . The latter were more of a nervous type and sought work of lighter and [one] might say of a cleaner nature. Their nervous energy caused them to work along more rapidly but also to show more fatigue after a period of time. . . . Group #1 . . . in learning any of the arts of the tanning industry . . . had a desire to learn them more thoroughly and took special pride in their production."[35]

Because most of the skilled workers in Milwaukee were of German, British, or Yankee origin, they constituted the elite of the work force and exercised their ethnic preferences according to accepted stereotypes. They were the foremen; they did most of the hiring. This was reinforced by the common practice of con-

[34] Wisconsin Bureau of Labor and Industrial Statistics, *Biennial Report,* 1898–1899, pp. 146–147; *ibid., Biennial Report,* 1887–1888, p. 226; Korman, *Industrialization, Immigrants and Americanizers,* 35–36; Margaret Walsh, "From Pork Merchant to Meat Packer: The Midwestern Meat Industry in the Mid Nineteenth Century," in *Agricultural History,* 56 (January, 1982), 135–136.

[35] Korman, *Industrialization, Immigrants and Americanizers,* 45–48, citing *Patrick Cudahy, His Life* (Milwaukee, 1912), an autobiography, and an interview with Cudahy. Albert C. Vogel responded in writing to a questionnaire from Matson Holbrook, February 21, 1952. William Brockman, who was a foreman with the Trostel Leather Company, repeated Vogel's categories; see Vogel folder and transcript of Brockman interview in the Matson Holbrook Interviews.

tracting jobs on bid to the skilled craftsmen in the machine and
foundry businesses. These men in turn hired their own crews,
often for a single job that might take less than a day to complete.
This system operated like the traditional "shape-up" in long-
shoring work, with crews picked from men who simply showed
up at the plant gate. Usually there were no set wage scales, so
that common labor could be hired at a rate reflecting the availability of such labor. A surprising number of industries operated
on this system, which relieved the employer of hiring and payroll
responsibilities.[36]

Piecework was another common method of avoiding problems
of whom to hire and what wages to pay. In Milwaukee, clothing
manufacturing, including knits, gloves, and hat and caps,
employed 6,700, a great many working at home rather than in
factories. This did not include an estimated 1,700 seamstresses
who went to their customers. Piecework was adaptable to many
industries. Work of a disagreeable nature was often left in the
hands of a minor foreman, representing one of the newer ethnic
groups, who hired workers at his home or any place frequented
by his countrymen, usually a saloon. These shops functioned in
the language of the dominant group, which jealously guarded its
prerogatives by making things miserable for any outsider who
might be hired on by higher authority.[37]

This yawning gap between the owner and his workmen was a
convenience that suited most employers. The expense of keeping
up with technology created the seeming imperative of forcing
labor to fit the rhythms and tireless energy of the machinery.
This, in turn, was limited by the vagaries of the market which
created interruptions and peaks in employment. Classical economic theory said that labor was simply another commodity to
be entered into the equation, along with rent, interest, and the

---

[36] Korman, *Industrialization, Immigrants and Americanizers,* 41–53, 61–69; Glaab and Larsen, *Factories in the Valley,* 238. The shop records of the E. P. Allis Company showed that
in 1890, with a work force averaging 1,342 men, there had actually been 11,101 separate
hirings during the year. See Peterson, *Industrial Heritage,* 78.

[37] Anderson and Bleyer, eds., *Milwaukee's Great Industries,* 154–155, 205–207; Korman,
*Industrialization, Immigrants and Americanizers,* 66–67; Nelson, *Managers and Workers,* 80–81.

cost of raw materials. How better to maintain this relationship than by divorcing ownership and management from employment? One result was that in times of labor unrest the owner was so distant from much of his labor force that he remained unaware of the source of his difficulties, and he was unable to communicate with his workers except through the foremen or skilled workers who very probably were the source of the discontent. It was easy enough to charge any such unrest to "outside agitators," another widely accepted stereotype.[38]

Another deficiency of the times was that the workplace was commonly a hazard to the health and safety of the workers. This grew out of the assumption that the surroundings of the job were simply dictated by the given conditions. Factory design was an art that arrived late on the Wisconsin scene. Makeshift sheds and adapting whatever buildings were available were the rule. Steam power was transmitted throughout the factory by means of leather belting and turning shafts which might be overhead or under the floor. Individual machines ran by belting which functioned like pulleys from the constantly turning shafts. Whether the workman's machine was engaged remotely or by physically shoving the turning belt from an idler to a fixed pulley, the power was always turning—and it did not respond to shouts or to a hand, arm, or body caught in a machine or belting or by the turning shafts. Inattention was a common denominator in such accidents, which also occurred while oiling or attempting to correct some malfunction. Sawmills and woodworking plants took the heaviest toll, but of the forty-four fatal accidents reported in 1893–1894, eight involved belting, gearing, and turning shafts in other types of plants. "Killed, wound up on shaft," was the laconic comment. Rush-hour traffic was less hazardous.[39]

Despite the liability of the employer for injuries if the worker

[38] Korman, *Industrialization, Immigrants and Americanizers,* 62–64; Nelson, *Managers and Workers,* 36–41, 47–48.

[39] Wisconsin Bureau of Labor, Census and Industrial Statistics, *Biennial Report,* 1893–1894, pp. 193a–198a; Nelson, *Managers and Workers,* 11–30; Peterson, *Industrial Heritage,* 8, 77; Korman, *Industrialization, Immigrants and Americanizers,* 17–21. Like other state agencies, the bureau changed its name from time to time over the years.

could establish that he had not been careless or was the victim of another's carelessness, sawmills were rarely equipped with elementary safeguards around saws, pulleys, and shafts. Although state factory inspectors were charged with responsibility for health and sanitary conditions as well as elementary safety under the legislation of 1883 and subsequent modifications of that law, most violations reported involved fire exits, unguarded machinery, or open elevator shafts. During 1893–1894 there were 1,075 individual inspectors' orders for changes involving worker safety, and only four orders for the installation of suction fans, presumably for the workers' comfort and health.[40]

Workplaces were not expected to have plumbing when most city homes and schools did not. If the job was excessively hot, cold, dirty, or dangerous, it was accepted as common to the nature of the work or the circumstances of the employer. Henry Harnischfeger described the first building that was constructed in 1884 to house the new firm of Pawling & Harnischfeger:[41]

> After the partnership was formed, we came to the conclusion that there was not enough room for expansion at the little shop at 292 Florida Street. We leased an empty lot at the northeast corner of Clinton and Florida Streets, 50 × 120, and erected a 26 × 50 one-story frame building on it. Since our means were limited, we put up a very cheap structure. The outside walls consisted of only one thickness of board with weatherstrip over the joints. The winter of 1884–1885 was one of the coldest that I have ever experienced. The building was finished on the ninth of December and we started to move in during a severe snow storm. The snow stayed on the ground until early spring. We suffered greatly from the cold as we had only one big stove in the center of the shop and our little 4 × 6 steam engine had to be thawed out every morning. The tools and material were so cold that our fingers stuck to them. At noon, when it warmed up a little, the tools and material started to sweat and rust. This was a condition we had to fight throughout the winter months. The roof was of the flat type and after every snowstorm someone had to go up and shovel the snow off for fear the building might collapse.

[40] Fries, *Empire in Pine,* 218–220; Wisconsin Bureau of Labor, Census and Industrial Statistics, *Biennial Report,* 1893–1894, pp. 199a–200a; Gordon M. Haferbecker, *Wisconsin Labor Laws* (Madison, 1958), 18–19, 34–38.
[41] Harnischfeger, *Autobiography,* 6.

A boilermaker working in Milwaukee remarked that "there are few boilermakers who are not more or less deaf, while their eyesight is often impaired by flying particles of steel." Another in the same trade complained that "the great majority of boilermakers are deaf, and at the age of forty-five they are pretty well played out." A machinist in the CM&StP car shops said "the smoke in the shops during winter is almost unbearable." A girl working as a knot sawyer in a Neenah shingle mill did find it "very hard work, and especially disagreeable in the spring and fall, as the weather then is cold, and the temperature of the mill, quite unfavorable. During the winter months we are out of work, and therefore the employment is not such as I should wish; but I am unable to obtain more suitable work in the town. . . ."[42]

Much of Wisconsin's growing industry in this period involved work with hot metal. Oddly, the most common complaint in this work did not concern serious burns or the extremes of temperature, but rather the cost of clothing. Men charging the furnaces at Bay View with scrap rails and molders in stove factories objected that they burned up a dozen shirts and six or eight pairs of pants each year. (These were generally of wool as it did not burn as readily as other material.) A rougher added that he went through four pairs of heavy, hobnailed shoes annually at a cost of $24. A molder said he went through three pairs. At wages averaging $2.35 per day, these added costs apparently bothered them more than did the hazards to what the shoes and shirts covered.[43]

Tanning was a disagreeable trade. It started in the tanyard with manhandling tons of bark which had to be ground and cooked to make the tanning liquor. The heavy hides had to be stirred, turned, and shifted, without mechanical aid, from one vat to another. Then there were the hides themselves. "Well, the hide house was not a very pleasant place to work . . . a storage

---

[42] Wisconsin Bureau of Labor and Industrial Statistics, *Biennial Report,* 1887–1888, pp. 79, 90, 94. The girl quoted was not complaining, for her wages had increased by one-quarter in the six years she had worked at the Neenah mill, and her workday had decreased from eleven and a half to ten hours.

[43] *Ibid.,* pp. 96, 105.

place for green, salted hides and the odor is not the very best. . . .
The hides came in bundles in carload lots and were taken into
the hide house and weighed up. . . . This odor just got into a
person's skin and clothes. At that time they did not have shower
baths and rest rooms. . . . You had to go home with those smelly
clothes.'' A proper tanner was one who took pride in meeting
these challenges. "My first recollection was that they were trying
to test me out . . . as they always do. And my first job was
sorting hides. There was a bunch of hides they had stored under-
neath the stairway there, all full of grubs. . . . I had to sort those
real smelly hides with the grubs crawling up my arms. But I
stuck it out. . . .'' And finally "[T]hey always said that a tanner
was never a tanner until he had fallen into some kind of vat in
the tannery and we all have done it.''[44]

Human labor used in loading and unloading was not necessarily cheap, but the machinery and the capital to replace humans
were sometimes slow to appear. Unloading coal, for instance,
was still handled by shovelers in the ship's hold. The clamshell
power shovel, which was self-loading, was not developed until
1892. It still left much hand shoveling to be done. Because such
work could be done only by men who were "strong and endowed
with great powers of endurance . . . the services of such men
have always been costly.'' As a consequence, coal heavers, lumber loaders, and tanbark stevedores were able to maintain strong
associations or unions and command high hourly rates. These
rates were offset by the discontinuous nature of the employment.
The Milwaukee coal heavers union, for instance, based members' pay upon a standard of sixty cents an hour shoveling in a
vessel's hold, but guaranteed that a crew of three or four would
unload 100 tons of nut or egg coal in six hours. Rates varied with
the type of coal and how far it had to be moved by hand, but not
many workers today would undertake to shovel twenty-five to
thirty tons into a bucket in the course of six hours, and keep up
the pace for ten hours or more. The rate quoted was for "horse

[44] Transcripts of George C. Laitsch interview, January 10, 1952, and A. S. Capron
interview, May 5, 1952, in the Matson Holbrook Interviews.

work," meaning that horses lifted the bucket from the hold. When steam was used, it cut the time for handling by one-third. Stevedores unloading tanbark made fifty cents an hour, compared to an average wage for common labor of $1.25–$1.50 per day for a ten- or eleven-hour day.[45]

Between 1870 and 1890, ten of the twenty-five counties of southern Wisconsin—lying mostly south of the Fox-Wisconsin waterway—lost population, or had urban centers that countered the actual loss of rural population. This phenomenon was general throughout much of the Midwest. A variety of changes brought about the loss of rural population, which was usually attributed to the lure of the cities and towns. Mechanization was certainly a contributing factor as evidenced by the relative decline in the number of farm laborers compared to the number of farms in Wisconsin. An associated phenomenon of the time was the increasing availability of farm mortgage money for investment in machinery that rapidly increased the efficiency of farm labor. Also, dairying and mixed farming required less hired labor to meet peak periods of activity than did wheat growing.[46]

One cannot discount the attraction of villages and cities for this displaced rural population, although those who took this path are difficult to trace. A common enough path was by way of education to a professional or business career. One thinks of Robert M. La Follette, Burr Jones, Roujet Marshall, Hamlin Garland, Oscar Hallam, and Joseph Schafer. An almost universal reaction of the times was a distaste for farm life expressed by those who had escaped it for something more satisfying. Finan-

---

[45] *House Documents*, 55 Cong., 2 sess., no. 277 (serial 3679), 84–85; Wisconsin Bureau of Labor and Industrial Statistics, *Biennial Report*, 1887–1888, p. 87; transcript of Christ Miller interview, April 17, 1952, in the Matson Holbrook Interviews; Milwaukee *Sentinel*, July 27, 29, 30, 31, 1872; Wisconsin Bureau of Labor and Industrial Statistics, *Biennial Report*, 1888–1889, p. 151, "Diagram of Daily Wages Paid in Wisconsin Factories."

[46] Allan G. Bogue, *Money at Interest: The Farm Mortgage on the Middle Border* (Ithaca, 1955); Jeffrey G. Williamson, "The Railroads and Midwestern Development, 1870–1890: A General Equilibrium History," in David C. Klingaman and Richard K. Vedder, eds., *Essays in Nineteenth Century Economic History: The Old Northwest* (Athens, Ohio, 1975), 307–311; Curti, *Making of a Frontier Community*, 155–156; Joseph Schafer, *A History of Agriculture in Wisconsin* (Madison, 1922), 139.

cial success often led to a return to the suburban farm as a gentleman farmer who could discharge his agricultural duties from a buggy drawn by a spanking team. Suburban farm life was less deprived in a day when many sizable towns lacked a water or sewer system, used similar heating systems but lacked a woodlot to draw upon, and townsmen were envious of a man with a fancy driving team, pasture land, and hired hands.[47]

Where did the young farm hand of less brilliant ambitions or abilities go? Oscar Hallam recalled a hired man who lit out for a railroad construction camp which offered higher wages, a shorter day, and the company of his peers. Work in the woods, or any job that drew upon skills in handling horses, acted as a magnet. Milwaukee was probably a bit fearsome for most farm youths, but the neighboring cities and villages with their expanding industrial payrolls were less of a leap into the unknown. Wisconsin's bureau of labor and industrial statistics was given to questionnaires with leading questions: "Is the general tendency of unmarried farm laborers to acquire and own a farm, or is there a tendency to go and live in the city?" (The question carried a presumption shared by both questioner and respondent.) At any rate, 75 per cent of the farmers responding affirmed that the city won out over the agricultural ladder. Governor Jeremiah Rusk endorsed this common belief in supporting a separate agricultural college "to check the dangerous rush of farmer boys to the cities and into the professions." A similar loaded question—"Do you experience any trouble in hiring first-class workmen?"—addressed to contractors and craftsmen in the building trades often led to an equally self-fulfilling answer: "They prefer to work in larger cities." The responses expressed something about what people thought was happening.[48]

[47] Schafer, *History of Agriculture,* 172–173; David V. Mollenhoff, *Madison: A History of the Formative Years* (Dubuque, 1982), 206–212, 219–227, 388–394, on the belated solutions to the problems of pure water and sewage disposal.

[48] Garraty, *Unemployment in History,* 108–109; Oscar Hallam, "Bloomfield and Number Five: The American Way of Life in a Wisconsin Rural Community in the 70s, As Seen by a Small Boy," 153, in the Hallam Reminiscences; Wisconsin Bureau of Labor, Census and Industrial Statistics, *Biennial Report,* 1895–1896, pp. 108–109; *ibid.,* 1893–

Long before 1873, the American industrial scene had not been compatible with apprenticeship training. Many long-established crafts were becoming obsolete and subdivided by the factory system. One does not have to look far for evidence that the traditional system of apprenticeship was widely disregarded or its purposes abused and the results deplored. In the large Milwaukee tanneries, for instance, apprenticeship had come to mean a young man learning to use a machine for a particular operation, such as splitting hides, rather than learning the trade as a tanner or currier. Even the traditional building trades suffered a decline of the apprenticeship system as balloon frame construction, using dimension lumber and pre-assembled sashes, doors, cupboards, scroll-saw trim, precut shingles, and so forth, made obsolete the journeyman carpenter's skills. Men who had mastered their trade through the traditional apprenticeship constantly complained that anyone could assemble a cheap set of tools and hire out as a carpenter. The confident ones wasted little time in their self-proclaimed journeyman's status and were soon representing themselves as builders and contractors. Molded bricks, poured stone, and sheet-metal cornices and caps worked a similar change in the stonemason's trade.[49]

The principal beneficiaries of change in building practices were plumbers and fitters. Rather than fabricating sinks and drains, they now worked with fittings, joints, and pipes of cast and wrought iron. They had to know some elementary physics as well as how, in practical terms, a simple plumbing system or a heating system using hot water or steam operated. Steam used for power called for considerable skill, and a gas-lighting system had to be reasonably safe and reliable.[50]

1894, pp. 12–16; *Wisconsin Public Documents,* 1893–1894, Governor's Message, vol. 1., p. 19.

[49] Robert Christie, "The Carpenters: A Case in Point," in David Brody, ed., *The American Labor Movement* (New York, 1971), 44–66; Wisconsin Bureau of Labor and Industrial Statistics, *Biennial Report,* 1887–1888, pp. 36–115; *ibid., Biennial Report,* 1888–1889, pp. 1–56, 69; Wisconsin Bureau of Labor, Census and Industrial Statistics, *Biennial Report,* 1891–1892, pp. 1–28, 40.

[50] Martin Segal, *The Rise of the United Association: National Unionism in the Pipe Trades, 1884–1924* (Cambridge, 1970), 2–16.

The insecurity of many traditional trades is indicated by the repeatedly expressed fear of displacement by unskilled, cheaper labor; the cavalier disregard for the traditional distinctions between masters, journeymen, apprentices, and the unskilled on the part of employers; a lack of rewards for hard-won skills; and the constant threat of unemployment. An 1888 questionnaire from the state's bureau of labor and industrial statistics asked skilled workmen: "What trade would you choose for a boy?" Out of approximately 540 responses, representing some eighty trades from all over the state, only about forty responded with their own trade. This bleak outlook can be partially qualified. Nearly 120 failed to respond to this particular question, and about seventy said it should be the boy's free choice. Fourteen favored "a good education," another fourteen would have steered a boy into farming, and twenty-two named a profession. Of the remaining 300 (70 per cent of those responding), almost all treated the question seriously and named a trade. By far the favorite choice was that of machinist, representing the choice of nearly ninety respondents. Of the forty who chose their own trade, eleven were machinists. (A total of forty-three machinists responded.) Aside from the few who advised the professions, farming, or a good education, there were very few who would direct a boy into an independent or entrepreneurial career: one said "merchant," one "railroad manager," and seven mentioned "banker." (This last was no doubt a facetious response, as four of the seven were upholsterers in the same Milwaukee factory.)

There is little evidence of a realistic belief that working-class boys could hope to become self-employed professionals or businessmen. Of approximately 360 workmen who commented on apprenticeship in their trades generally, some 200 expressed definitely negative reactions while only seventy had favorable comments about the situation in their trade, shop, or community. The most frequent comment was that employers took advantage of what was supposed to be an apprenticeship system to employ boys simply as cheap labor, making no effort to teach them a trade. Many blamed this on the nature of the factory system, or on piecework, but usually on simple greed.[51]

This gloomy outlook on what a majority recognized as an outmoded system makes one wonder how people chose their trades or employers in the 1880's. Except for a minority who arrived with a marketable trade—usually adult immigrants— most apparently did not do much conscious choosing. Boys whose fathers had skills that were valuable to their employers had a clear advantage, given aptitude and a desire to learn. A definite problem was the reluctance of many skilled workers to train the young, and of employers to pay for the time of the skilled work- men to do such training. For those who had no sponsor, employ- ment was rather a hit-or-miss affair depending upon the need for unskilled labor. Middle-class parents with white-collar jobs or small businesses expected to find entrée for their sons into com- parable niches in the economy. This is where the virtues of thrift, loyalty to the employer, hard work, and intelligence were expected to pay off.[52]

The same virtues could lead a working-class youth to a useful and satisfying trade and long-term employment. E. T. Stamm, who worked up through the ranks at Pritzlaff Hardware, recalled that he got a job as a boy because his brother worked there. "He was my older brother and he was here several years before I was, and he got the job for me. Those days, you know, you had to have somebody speak for you. Usually the mothers went down to the place to get the jobs." William Brockman, who went to work in 1892 at the Becker Leather Company, remembered: "My father worked there and my uncle worked there, my uncle's

[51] Wisconsin Bureau of Labor and Industrial Statistics, *Biennial Report,* 1887–1888, pp. 165–188; *ibid., Biennial Report,* 1883–1884, pp. 91–94.

[52] Albert Martin, whose father owned a tannery, offered one of the workmen $50 to teach him to operate a hide–splitting machine. The man refused. Thereupon another former splitter, who had lost his arm in the machine and made his living "selling shoe polish and shoe laces and all little trinkets of that sort" to his former workmates, taught Martin to run the machine for $25. Transcript of Albert Martin interview, January 30, 1952, in the Matson Holbrook Interviews; Cochran, *Business in American Life,* 171–173.

brother-in-law, John . . . my brother-in-law . . . one was beam house foreman, one was tanyard foreman, and the whole family [worked there] when I was a kid." This fortunate minority did not so much choose a trade as find admittance by way of a particular employer. Sixty years later, Brockman had just trained his replacement, a World War II veteran, under the G.I. Bill: "I think I've done the finest thing in the world a man can do. I figure if other people train my children, why shouldn't I train other people's children?"[53]

This sense of satisfaction in the job and a relationship of respect and friendship with the employer was common, but was hardly the rule. A great many people became part of an unstable work force that was chronically between jobs, acquired no essential skills, and contributed to the astronomical employment turnover rates of the time. A large group of workers, although they acquired skills, remained mobile and insecure in their employment. Others simply were located and remained where work of any kind was problematic.[54]

The year 1873 saw the end of a tight labor market in Wisconsin and this condition prevailed practically until World War I. Given the low scale of wages in Wisconsin, one can appreciate that this was an environment in which a surplus of labor was the norm, except in specific local cases. Evidence is lacking to show that there were many large-scale industries that ever worried seriously about the supply of labor. The largest employer by far—the lumber industry—was notoriously low-paying and exacted the harshest conditions. Apparently the formal and informal employment bureaus, newspaper advertisements, and simple word-of-mouth supplied a sufficient flow of workers. "The mobility of Europe's and America's population made the manu-

[53] Transcripts of E. T. Stamm interview, January 22, 1952, and Brockman interview in the Matson Holbrook Interviews.

[54] Korman, *Industrialization, Immigrants and Americanizers*, 37–38. See also Irwin Yellowitz, *The Position of the Worker in American Society, 1865–1896* (Englewood Cliffs, 1969), 19–20; Edward M. Lang, Jr., "The Common Man, Janesville, Wisconsin, 1870 to 1900" (master's thesis, University of Wisconsin, 1968), 50–61; and Nelson, *Managers and Workers*, 83–84.

facturing centers of England and the continent a part of the labor market for [Milwaukee's] employers,'' and to a lesser degree of the rest of the state, reaching well beyond the limits of Europe's industrial cities into the countryside. The seasonal nature of much of Wisconsin's industrial employment also worked to the advantage of employers.[55]

A recent study avers that in 1890 "the average worker in manufacturing [in the United States] was unemployed twenty days and employed 279 days. . . ." In Wisconsin, where one-

[55] Korman, *Industrialization, Immigrants and Americanizers,* 21–37; Wisconsin Bureau of Labor, Census and Industrial Statistics, *Biennial Report,* 1895–1896, p. 320; Fries, *Empire in Pine,* 205–210; Glaab and Larsen, *Factories in the Valley,* 227–229, 234–239; Wisconsin Bureau of Labor and Industrial Statistics, *Biennial Report,* 1887–1888, xviii–xxi, 142–160.

AVERAGE ANNUAL EARNINGS FOR MALES OVER 16 IN SELECTED INDUSTRIES COMMON TO 10 STATES HAVING THE LARGEST NUMBER OF INDUSTRIAL EMPLOYEES, 1890

|  | WISCONSIN AVERAGE | TEN-STATE AVERAGE* | MIDWEST† STATES AVERAGE | TEN-STATE RANGE (low–high) | |
|---|---|---|---|---|---|
| Carpentering | $539 | $643.80 | $591.80 | $518–727 | Mich.–N.Y. |
| Carriages and Wagons | 459 | 532.40 | 485.80 | 446–670 | Mich.–Conn. |
| Men's Clothing | 374 | 483.10 | 399.40 | 295–637 | Ohio–Mass. |
| Foundry and Machines | 502 | 557.80 | 536.00 | 502–598 | Wis.–N.J. |
| Masonry: brick and stone | 470 | 630.10 | 572.80 | 470–769 | Wis.–N.J. |
| Tobacco and Cigars | 455 | 484.50 | 473.00 | 377–560 | Penn.–Conn. |

*The ten states: Connecticut, Illinois, Massachusetts, Michigan, Missouri, New Jersey, New York, Ohio, Pennsylvania, and Wisconsin.

†Illinois, Michigan, Missouri, Ohio, Wisconsin.

STATE AVERAGE WAGE FOR MALES OVER 16 FOR THE SIX REPRESENTATIVE INDUSTRIES

| | | | |
|---|---|---|---|
| Massachusetts | $622.60 | Pennsylvania | $554.00 |
| Connecticut | 614.17 | Illinois | 545.33 |
| New York | 607.17 | Michigan | 498.17 |
| New Jersey | 606.00 | Ohio | 481.50 |
| Missouri | 557.50 | Wisconsin | 466.50 |

SOURCE: *Eleventh Census of the United States, 1890: Manufacturing, Volume VI, Part 1,* p. 28.

fourth of the industrial labor was then employed in the seasonal lumber industry and where the building trades and other industries faced harsh winter conditions, the average period of unemployment was considerably more than twenty days. A Wisconsin labor bureau report covering 1887 gives employers' estimates of lost time for their employees (workdays lost) which indicate tremendous variations that cannot be averaged. For instance, 152 painters in chair factories lost an average of ninety-three days, 134 finishers lost only an average of eleven days, and 161 boys doing unspecified work lost only an average of ten days. The same source, from a sample in 1885–1886, reported: "Of 653 skilled workmen, 271 report 'steady' employment, and the average time which the remainder, 382, found work in their regular trades, is 231 days. . . . The average of lost time is, therefore, 61 days per man in his chosen trade. But many of these, of course, engage in other work temporarily during the dull season and thus swell their yearly earnings. Of such earnings we have no record." Of these skilled hands, 597 reported average annual wages of $572.63 in 1887. (This average was derived entirely from round numbers, not from actual wages.) But 186 of the 653 men reporting indicated that their annual wages were $400 or less, and ninety-four of those reported $300 or less. Economic uncertainty affected the skilled ranks as well.[56]

Public attitudes in times of stress illustrate the response to the new economic order. In the summer of 1878, Beloit discovered that it had a "tramp problem." Job seekers who commonly sought harvest work, railroad construction jobs, and work in the lumber industry by riding freight trains found themselves in oversupply and meeting hostile responses wherever they congregated. The governor of Iowa had forcibly ejected some, and many gathered at Beloit where they could retreat across the Illinois state line in the event of trouble. Trouble came, in the form of armed guards hired by the C&NW to protect its "private

---

[56] Clarence D. Long, *Wages and Earnings in the United States, 1860–1890* (Princeton, 1960), 47–48; Wisconsin Bureau of Labor, Census and Industrial Statistics, *Biennial Report*, 1895–1896, pp. 294–295; *ibid., Biennial Report*, 1887–1888, xii, 118–141, 216–237.

property.'' An aroused citizenry, which just a few years before had applauded Chief Justice Ryan's decision that railroads were public highways operated by dangerous monopolies meriting regulation, now applauded the railroad's use of employees armed with revolvers and clubs to repel the unemployed. A Madison minister attracted favorable notice in the press with an address on "What Can We Do For The Tramp?'' These ''scum of the earth'' and ''robbers of the industrious,'' he said, were clearly outside the pale of civilized society. ''Now, what is our Christian duty to the tramp? *He must be treated with the utmost severity of the law.* ''⁵⁷

The legislature responded with enthusiasm to the call from Governor William E. Smith: ''The habit—I may say the crime—of vagabondage is increasing in such unprecedented ratios as to demand most serious consideration. . . . The disease . . . is too virulent and deep seated to yield to the mild remedies provided for common vagrancy.'' The definition adopted by the legislature seemed common enough and offered no litmus test to distinguish ''the honest man who in good faith travels from place to place in search of employment'' from ''modern tramps,'' a distinction which the governor easily made on the basis of whether or not the vagrant was willing to work. This test was simple: if the vagabond was willing to work, he would not be traveling about and certainly not in the company of other vagabonds.⁵⁸

The new statute provided that ''any male person sixteen years of age or over, being a vagrant''—not a resident of a community and with no visible means of support, unable to account satisfactorily for his presence—''shall be deemed a tramp. Any person

---

⁵⁷ Beloit *Free Press,* July 11, 18, August 1, 1878; Beloit *Daily Record,* July 8, 10, 11, 1878; *Wisconsin State Journal,* July 16, 1878; Whitewater *Register,* August 1, 1878.

⁵⁸ *Wisconsin Public Documents,* 1877–1878, Governor's Message, vol. 1., pp. 21–22. Twenty-four-year-old Robert M. La Follette took up the cry in a Fourth of July oration he delivered at Sun Prairie: ''Dangerous socially and politically, because reckless and vicious. Reckless and vicious because *homeless.* Needless to furnish statistics that you may grasp the awful enormity of this subject. Needless to tell you that every State in the Union has passed stringent vagrancy laws to protect the life and property of its citizens from these human parasites.'' (As reproduced in the Sun Prairie *Star-Countryman,* July 10, 1879.)

convicted of being a tramp, shall be punished by imprisonment
at hard labor in the county jail for a period not exceeding six
months, or by imprisonment in the county jail not exceeding
thirty days in solitary confinement, and to be fed on bread and
water only. . . ." Justices of the peace, police magistrates, and
county courts were empowered to enforce this. Any peace officer
was entitled to the regular constable's fee for arresting a tramp.
Offenders could be forced to work on roads and highways. Officers in charge of such details of men were to be paid $2 per day
by the town, village, or city benefited. Refusal to do such labor
could lead to two years in the state prison at Waupun. The law
even provided the right of eminent domain to erect necessary
jails and other facilities to carry out its directives.[59]

A recession in 1882 brought hard times again. When a public
soup kitchen was proposed in Milwaukee by a charitable organization, a policeman was quoted in the *Sentinel* as saying that the
last time such a kitchen was set up on his beat, open to all
comers, he had marched nineteen patrons away to the magis-
trate. Each of them was sentenced to three months for vagrancy,
and presumably the diligent patrolman collected the standard
constable's fee. A lady of charitable inclinations feared that the
institution of a soup kitchen would sap the independence and
moral fiber of those exposed to such indiscriminate charity. A
similar expression of concern came from the National Conference on Charities and Corrections, which happened to be meeting in Madison. A happier solution was a woodyard, where the
deserving could put their sincerity to the test and earn their
meals by chopping and splitting firewood.[60]

The insecure worker of the eighties is generally faceless at this
distance, although the state labor bureau's questionnaires offer

[59] *Laws of Wisconsin*, 1879, pp. 273–276. This interest in the "tramp menace" was not
confined to Wisconsin. See Paul T. Ringenbach, *Tramps and Reformers, 1873–1916: The
Discovery of Unemployment in New York* (Westport, Connecticut, 1973).

[60] Milwaukee *Sentinel*, August 12, 1882; Korman, *Industrialization, Immigrants and Americanizers*, 33. Classical economics had nothing to say about unemployment, and indeed the
word did not come into the language until 1894. See Garraty, *Unemployment in History*, 4,
104–124.

an occasional glimpse. A tailor in Milwaukee found a dull season made worse by employers who farmed out piecework to girls who did the same work for half as much—about $3 per week. A village wagon maker complained that "machine work, being sold cheap, has virtually killed the trade. . . ." A paper worker in Appleton complained that the proliferation of paper mills in the area brought prosperity to the owners but "the common labor, which constitutes 80 per cent of the work . . . is paid the same as ten years ago." And, he added, the mills "do not improve the town much." A Milwaukee worker commented that "a laborer in a brickyard is not better than an ox." Another Milwaukee laborer replied that he was a molder by trade, but "could not find work at trade; blacklisted." A Beloit laborer wrote: "On July 1, 1886, I was laid off because I would not accept a reduction from $1.50 to $1.25 per day. . . . At every application I was referred back to Beloit Iron Works where I had been working for nineteen years. . . . I am a temperate man and reliable in every respect; yet I can not get work, neither can I get out of town."[61]

The other world of the workingman was that inhabited by those in possession of an essential skill which was not displaced by the new industrial system. Or one might be relatively unskilled but have the good fortune to catch on with an employer who, from an attitude of paternalism or impressed by the practical value of maintaining a dependable work force, attempted to ensure relatively steady employment for a majority of his labor force.

The tanneries, for instance, were family affairs involving both the owners and workers. William Brockman went to work at Becker Leather in his early teens, because his father worked there. "It was hard work but as you went along, you were picked to learn a trade. They chose you from a group of other boys. . . . They called me into the office and said, 'Sign this contract,' " which involved taking $175 from the boy's wages to learn only

[61] Wisconsin Bureau of Labor and Industrial Statistics, *Biennial Report,* 1887-1888, pp. 16, 23, 98, 109, 110, 127-128, 219, 226. "Laborers," of whom 18,117 were covered in the report, were on average unemployed eighty working days and employed 230 days.

one of the steps in processing leather. (A skilled currier remarked cynically: "It takes about ten men now to make a complete tanner.")

The tannery business in Milwaukee was expanding rapidly enough throughout the 1880's to be able to mechanize and sub-divide operations regularly with little resistance from the skilled workers, who made more money at piecework with the new machines or found themselves as foremen overseeing shops devoted to a single process that engaged sometimes more men than the whole tannery had a decade before. The business was also co-operative to a degree. Many tanneries specialized in particular types of leather so they were not directly competitive, and their markets—mostly in the East—were not the same. Paternalism therefore flourished along with gentlemen's agreements not to raid one another's skilled work force and, incidentally, to present a united front in resisting unionization. When later asked whether a contract to learn leather pebbling, hand boarding, or hand shaving was what he had wanted, William Brockman replied with some astonishment: "Oh, no. You didn't want nothing. They just simply called you." The reward was that "when you was in a placement you stayed. . . . When they were slack of work they would lay you off, but not indefinitely, probably a day or two."

William Tetzlaff got a job in 1888 with Pfister and Vogel, the largest tannery operation in Milwaukee, with four locations and 590 employees. He had worked at the Plankinton packing company, but "I saw there was nothing there for me." The foreman put him on as "kind of a loafer around the place, putting the skins in sawdust and such things. . . ." By 1895 Tetzlaff was foreman in the buffing room. He did not hesitate to approach Fred Vogel, Jr., who managed the tanneries, about raises . . . and got them. Charles Jopke, another tanner who had gone to work for Pfister and Vogel in 1881, remembered that Vogel, the second-generation manager, making his daily rounds of the firm's scattered tanneries, went "all over the whole tannery and when he came, of course, then everybody had to look out. He was good to you too. . . . Fred Vogel, Sr., well, he was kind of old-fashioned in a way, you know, slow and easy going.'' Brockman, who worked at several Milwaukee tanneries over the years, had some reservations about the later generations of owner-managers who ''lost their acquaintance'' with the men, but this was after 1900. Of the three generations of the Vogels, he said: ''They are just as friendly as can be and they talk to you and they're just no more than you are.''[62]

Brewing, like tanning, was dominated by German entrepreneurs. But unlike tanning, the great expansion it was undergoing did not involve training a great many of its workers in meticulous skills. The paternalism that came to characterize the industry sprang from other sources. One was the character of the brewing process itself, with its long periods of relative idleness even though the crew was expected to be there. Another was the variety of jobs involved as the emerging giants integrated their operations to include coopers, maltsters, brewers, wagon makers, painters, bottlers, and so on. Brewing on this new scale became a natural target for industrial unionism, led by the skilled workers. As industrial unionism—the Knights of Labor—swept Milwaukee in the mid-eighties, some of the leading brewers, led by Frederick Pabst, had the wit to see that the urban working class was the backbone of their rapidly expanding market. This doubtless was the main source of their practical paternalism.[63]

Edward P. Allis was a model of Milwaukee paternalism in a big shop. He sponsored and maintained an aid society which paid sickness, accident, and death benefits to members. In April, 1886, he dealt reasonably with the Reliance Assembly of the Knights of Labor, meeting with their delegation and returning a

[62] Transcripts of William J. Tetzlaff interview, February 12, 1952, Charles Jopke interview, February 15, 1952, and William Brockman interview, all in the Matson Holbrook Interviews; Wisconsin Bureau of Labor and Industrial Statistics, *Biennial Report,* 1888-1889, pp. 70a-71a.

[63] John H. M. Laslett, *Labor and the Left: A Study of Socialist and Radical Influences in the American Labor Movement, 1821-1924* (New York, 1970), 9-53; Thomas C. Cochran, *The Pabst Brewing Company: The History of an American Business* (New York, 1948), chap. 11; Milton M. Small, ''The Biography of Robert Schilling'' (master's thesis, University of Wisconsin, 1953), 201-213; Wisconsin Bureau of Labor and Industrial Statistics, *Biennial Report,* 1887-1888, pp. 218-219.

written reply offering concessions, though qualifying that with the statement that he could not afford them given the "state of our trade" and the obvious competitive disadvantages of such concessions. His employees rebuffed attempts to close down the shop in the Eight Hour Day agitation of May, 1886. But the fact remained that Allis did not look much beyond the skilled molders and machinists whom he recognized as "old hands." A layer of supervisors, foremen, and skilled workers taking jobs on bid and hiring their own crews interposed between Allis and the unskilled workers. While a paternalistic tone might be set by the employer of hundreds, he did not usually directly control the hiring process.[64]

A so-called "jealousy table" compiled by Commissioner Flower ranked cities and villages of Wisconsin by the average per capita industrial wage. It also indicated the principal local industries. Milwaukee ranked fourteenth with an average $445.22. Baraboo, population about 4,300, headed the list with $635.23. Fifty-six per cent of its industrial jobs were in the Chicago and North Western Railway shops. Only Madison ($496.00) and Stevens Point ($449.79), among the cities of over 5,000 population with appreciable industrial bases, ranked above Milwaukee. Like Baraboo, even a larger percentage of the industrial jobs in Stevens Point were in the railroad repair shops of the West Wisconsin Railway. Railroad shops, with their relatively high wages and steady employment, also raised the average wage in such places as Green Bay, Fort Howard, Hudson, Altoona, Kaukauna, and Waukesha.[65]

[64] Peterson, *Industrial Heritage,* 76–83; Korman, *Industrialization, Immigrants and Americanizers,* 37–39, 64–65; Wisconsin Bureau of Labor and Industrial Statistics, *Biennial Report,* 1885–1886, pp. 322–323.

[65] Of Milwaukee's 25,541 industrial employees, 4,035 or 15.8 per cent were female. See Wisconsin Bureau of Labor and Industrial Statistics, *Biennial Report,* 1887–1888, xix–xxv, 238–241, 245, 249, 260, 262, 278–312, 330, 333–334. This was a much higher percentage than in most of Wisconsin's industrial cities. There were also many women in Milwaukee engaged in the needle trades who worked at home on piecework and thus were not counted. They, of course, would have pulled down wage averages. Other variations are equally difficult to assess. *Ibid.,* 278–312. The burden of the bureau's argument was that federal census figures on average wages in Wisconsin industry were much too low; but this renders the bureau's figures useless in any comparison with other states. *Ibid.,* xiv.

Madison had a variety of industries, including two modest railroad repair shops maintained by the CM&StP and the C&NW railroads. The largest single payroll, 175 men and boys, making up a quarter of the city's industrial labor force, was employed by Fuller and Johnson, an agricultural machinery manufacturing firm. The president and managing officer was John A. Johnson, a Norwegian immigrant and successful industrialist probably better known as the founder of Gisholt Machine Company, which was incorporated in early 1889. Johnson was paternalistic in the best sense. He sought to foster interests beyond the shop floor among his employees and was known as a fair and approachable employer. Johnson's firms enjoyed the advantage of a highly trained work force, although the city did not have a skilled labor pool to draw upon. This deficiency was offset by formal training offered by Johnson, something of a rarity.[66]

Recent work in American labor history emphasizes that the industrial work force of the time was recruited among people who came from backgrounds entirely at odds with what was expected of them; that is, from pre-modern or pre-industrial societies, whether abroad or in rural America. About the only demurrer for Milwaukee would be an adjustment for a certain amount of beer consumption, but this surely varied from shop to shop as a matter of cultural conditioning, particularly on the part of the employer. The evidence seems to be that the majority of workers made the necessary adjustments. It is difficult to find those who failed, except in the assertions of those who discovered the "tramp menace" or the innate "inferiority" of certain ethnic strains. One child of this pre-modern or pre-industrial society

---

[66] *Ibid., Biennial Report,* 1887–1888, xix–xxi, 270–271; *Wisconsin Blue Book, 1891,* pp. 211, 239; *DWB;* Agnes M. Larson, *John A. Johnson: An Uncommon American* (Northfield, 1969), 158–160. The "jealousy table" mentioned above placed Madison in eighth place in per capita industrial wages, and first among major cities. It was more a measure of Madison's favorable employment pattern: railroad shops, printing plants, and Fuller and Johnson offering steady employment to a largely skilled, mature male work force, and of the city's minor commitment to industry. Racine, for instance, had an industrial work force of 4,083 of whom 503 (12.3 per cent) were women compared to Madison's 679 industrial employees of whom only sixty-five (9.6 per cent) were women. Another significant difference: Madison's industrial workers comprised only 5.6 per cent of her population; Racine's, 20.8 per cent.

was Charles Jopke, who came to Milwaukee in 1881, at age thirteen, evidently from eastern Germany. His older brother, Louis, had come earlier to escape military service and found work with the Pfister and Vogel Leather Company, unloading and stacking tanbark from the schooners. Fred Vogel, Sr., found Louis a steady and willing worker, and asked if the boy had any brothers at home. The upshot was that Vogel bought tickets for the rest of the family which included Charles, two other brothers, their parents, and a sister. They repaid Vogel from their wages at the tannery. One brother, Fritz, became the Vogel family coachman and gardener. Charles later became a tannery foreman.[67]

Jopke maintained that he never had a moment's regret about leaving Germany or coming to work in the tannery. No one complained about the hours or the hard work. His brothers and fellow workers were always ready to advise anyone who expressed nostalgia for the German homeland that ships were running the other way. Other tannery men reflected similar attitudes. They enjoyed recalling how they had learned their craft and looked upon the long hours and hard, exacting, and often disagreeable features of the work as simply the given conditions of the time. The great imperative was that the work was steady and secure. Some people had a knack for certain operations—a memory of muscle and mind for highly empirical processes. But if you were a willing and reliable worker, you stayed whether or not you had a knack that made you more valuable.[68]

The greatest bargain of the time was the hired girl. E. T. Stamm remembered family life in Milwaukee in the eighties. He

[67] Gutman, *Work, Culture, and Society*, 15; Ernest L. Meyer, *Bucket Boy: A Milwaukee Legend* (New York, 1947), 1–18; Jopke Transcript.

[68] Transcripts of Frank H. Fiedler interview, February 19, 1952; Joseph Stodola interview, March 5, 1952; and Jopke, Miller, Laitsch, Brockman, Tetzlaff, and Vogel transcripts, all in the Matson Holbrook Interviews. It is true that Jopke was recalling his youth from a distance—nearly seventy years in fact—and from a position as a skilled hand and retired supervisor whose advice was still sought by the current manager, Al Vogel.

came from a family of eleven children. The hired girl, Albertina, was newly arrived from Germany: "We paid her two dollars a week. Well, she did the washing and she did the ironing and the cooking and everything else and then I had two older sisters and my mother, they used to help with the cooking."[69]

Frank Flower enjoyed embroidering his bureau reports from his own well-stocked kit of opinions: "A shop girl is tolerated in a certain grade of society below the 'upper ten thousand,' but the ordinary domestic or servant is not. A man of considerable standing may marry a milliner, a seamstress, a dry goods clerk or a book-keeper without totally paralyzing his 'high-toned' relatives; but if he should marry a kitchen girl, or a waiter, or a chamber-maid, no matter how fair her face, how graceful her deportment or how bright her mind, 'select circles' would be scandalized. . . ."[70]

The federal census for 1870 enumerated 25,555 Wisconsin women as gainfully employed. Domestic service accounted for five out of eight of these. By 1890 there were 81,061 women working for wages. The general population meanwhile had increased by less than two-thirds. Persons reporting gainful occupations doubled from 292,808 to 582,469, but this did not match the increase of 217.5 per cent in the number of women reported as wage earners. However, by 1890 domestic service accounted for only two out of five women employed. Complaints were becoming common that domestics were hard to find, despite the influx of immigrant girls and the more numerous American-born daughters of foreign-born parents, who were presumed to be of the domestic servant class. As one editor wrote: "The phenomenal scarcity of hired girls throughout the county and elsewhere this season must lead to many serious questions 'Whither are we tending?' That marriage is a failure may remain in the region of doubts, but no sane person will doubt that house-keeping is a

---

[69] Stamm Transcript.
[70] Wisconsin Bureau of Labor Statistics, *Biennial Report,* 1883–1884, pp. 112–113.

failure, where dependence is placed upon the always unstable quantity of household help."[71]

The answer to the tight market for servant girls was not necessarily the social stigma supposedly attached to domestic service. There had been a great opening of other employment opportunities for women, primarily in industry. Between 1870 and 1890, the number of female industrial workers jumped from 3,784 to 12,751. Factory-made clothing and hosiery and knitting mills, centered in Milwaukee, accounted for much of the growth, but women were also finding entrée into many other fields previously considered the preserves of men. A tinware worker complained: "When I started to learn my trade there were hardly any girls employed, but now the work is done mostly by females." His was not a lonely voice.[72]

Between 1870 and 1890, the metropolis increased its share of the industrially employed women in Wisconsin from about one-third to two-thirds. By 1890 the proportion of women workers in Milwaukee industry was nearly twice that of Cleveland, half again more than in Chicago, and a third more than in Detroit. Milwaukee's heavier proportion of women workers is mostly chargeable to the factory-made clothing industry—both men's and women's clothing—and to employment in factories making hosiery and knit goods. There were 2,904 women reported in Milwaukee's clothing factories. Hosiery and knits employed 1,449 women in Milwaukee and 210 in Cleveland (the industry was not listed in Detroit). The manufacture of boots and shoes occupied 418. In Milwaukee, 58.2 per cent of the women industrial workers were employed in clothing factories and hosiery and knits, compared to only 33 per cent in Chicago. If these figures on women industrial workers have any particular significance, it

[71] Fort Atkinson *Jefferson County Union*, June 19, 1891. Also see Wisconsin Regional Planning Committee, *A Study of Wisconsin: Its Resources, Its Physical, Social and Economic Background* (Madison, 1934), 53; and David M. Katzman, *Seven Days a Week: Women and Domestic Service in Industrializing America* (New York, 1978), 3–14.

[72] *Ninth Census of the United States, 1870: Population, Volume I*, 764; *Eleventh Census of the United States, 1890: Manufacturing, Volume VI, Part 1*, pp. 628–634; Wisconsin Bureau of Labor, Census and Industrial Statistics, *Biennial Report*, 1895–1896, p. 324.

is possible that there were more multiple-income families in Milwaukee. It may have had some bearing on the generally lower wage scale known to prevail there.[73]

For the wives and children of laboring men, one form or another of industrial wage earning was also available in smaller cities and even in bucolic settings. Wisconsin had quite a number of woolen mills located on minor waterpowers that traditionally exploited this labor source. There were even a few cotton mills. Cigar making was often a local industry using women and children to prepare the weed. Tobacco-growing areas looked to this source for sorting and stripping in local warehouses. In 1887, a laboring man in Oshkosh alleged that the city's work force was about one-fourth boys and girls under fourteen.[74]

The Janesville Cotton Manufacturing Company occupied the most imposing industrial building in town. The local projectors knew the town well. In the summer of 1880 the factory employed 250, two-thirds of them women, their median age just under nineteen. Immigrant girls and first-generation Irish and German-Americans made up 75 per cent of the women. One-third of the hands in the mill came from households headed by women, most of them widows. The remainder were mostly children of day laborers. The mill worked two shifts of eleven and a half hours, six days a week, but was never inconvenienced by a lack of available workers. Wrote a state factory inspector in 1887: "I went to these mills some time ago and found several children, whom I suspected to be under 12 years of age. The company promised to discharge them, and I have every reason to think they have done so. But there are some 300 women and children who are working $11^1/_2$ to 12 hours per day and night, the night

---

[73] *Ninth Census of the United States, 1870: Industry, Volume III,* 582; *Eleventh Census of the United States, 1890: Manufacturing, Volume VI, Part 2,* pp. 130–144, 154–165, 194–201, 334–345, and pp. 3–4 of Table 3; *Twelfth Census of the United States, 1900: Volume VIII, Part 2,* pp. 951, 994–999.

[74] Norman L. Crockett, *The Woolen Industry of the Midwest* (Lexington, Kentucky, 1970); Chicago *Knights of Labor,* March 5, 1887; Wisconsin Bureau of Labor and Industrial Statistics, *Biennial Report,* 1887–1888, pp. 90, 238–239, 264, 314–317. The factory reports of the bureau for 1887–1888 did not report city workers by age, only by sex.

being the time most of the children are employed. The work is principally piecework; but some of them work by the day. It is a hard place to work. Young persons cannot stand the strain and long hours. Even now it is almost impossible to run the mill for lack of help. Child labor is the main feature; there are many of them under 14 years of age and all have to work 11½ hours. The thermometer (I am told by one of the employees), averages in the heated season about 108°. There are plenty of openings (windows) for light and air; but if there is too much air stirring, the windows must be kept closed on account of blowing the cotton. The dressing room thermometer (I am told) runs as high as 140° and averages 110° to 120°. (Men work here 8 to 10 hours.) I am told by employees that girls who have worked since last September are quitting on account of loss of health caused by hard work and long hours; they cannot stand the intense heat at night, and cannot get sufficient sleep in the day time. They tell me they are unanimous for a '10 hour law, pure and simple—like Massachusetts.'"[75]

In 1893, Janesville had 557 women employed in industries with a total work force of 1,639, almost double the proportion of women engaged in industry in Milwaukee. Not included was the seasonal employment in tobacco warehouses in Janesville. In 1886 the season lasted four to six months, employing mostly girls and women. "The work is done in basements, or on lower floors. The girls make from $6 to $12 per week. . . . As near as could be judged some 500 females and 100 males are employed in tobacco sorting."[76]

The median age of Janesville's female cotton mill operatives was nineteen, and working women generally, with some accuracy, were described as "working girls." The Frenchman Emile

[75] Wisconsin Bureau of Labor and Industrial Statistics, *Biennial Report,* 1887–1888, p. 264. John A. Fleckner, "Poverty and Relief in Nineteenth-Century Janesville," in *WMH,* 61 (Summer, 1978), 284, states that "the mill never suffered for want of workers; the mill hands' wages, however meager, were essential to the economic survival of many poor families."

[76] Wisconsin Bureau of Labor and Industrial Statistics, *Biennial Report,* 1885–1886, p. 499; *ibid., Biennial Report,* 1893–1894, pp. 44a–47a.

Levasseur cited studies made about 1890 of the status of such workers in representative American cities. One federal study queried 17,427 working women of whom 15,387 were single, 1,038 widowed, 745 married, and 257 divorced or separated. Of the 17,427 only 2,509 lived away from home, in a boardinghouse or with a private family. Of the 14,918 single women living at home, 8,754 gave their earnings for the general support and 4,267 paid board at home. "In general the single woman makes and spends less than the single man." The implicit assumption was that a woman's wages generally supplemented a family income.[77]

The world of retailing, as well as the office and counting room of business and manufacturing, was very much a male world at the end of the decade of the Civil War. The occupational census of 1870 found just ninety-eight women in Wisconsin engaged as clerks and accountants in retail stores, two in banking, broker-age, and insurance offices, and none working as clerks or accountants in manufacturing establishments. Change did not come rapidly, but the barrier was broken initially in the retail field. By 1880, Milwaukee alone had 260 women working as clerks, sales ladies, and accountants in retailing, but only two clerks in manufacturing establishments. Then the dam broke—belatedly it would seem, since the first practical typewriter was invented in Milwaukee in the middle seventies. In 1890, 3,824 women were employed in offices and stores in Wisconsin, 781 of them as saleswomen and the remainder in offices. Stenographers and typists numbered 459; clerks and copyists in offices, 1,992. Forty-one per cent of these women employed in retailing and office work were in Milwaukee.[78]

There is other evidence of the belated, and not yet whole-hearted, acceptance of women in business offices and behind the store counter. A circular for Milwaukee's Spencerian Business

[77] Emile Levasseur, *The American Workman,* trans. Thomas S. Adams, ed. Theodore Marburg (Baltimore, 1900), 336–352, 404.

[78] *Ninth Census of the United States, 1870: Population, Volume I,* 764; *Tenth Census of the United States, 1880: Population, Volume I,* 886; *Eleventh Census of the United States, 1890: Population, Volume I, Part 2,* pp. 624, 692.

College issued in 1890 spoke defensively: "We favor business education for woman because we regard her as the equal of man, with the same natural right to self support. We believe in it because her entrance into business life carries with it a refining and healthful influence." And, with a note of hope: "Much of the prejudice which has existed among business men, against the employment of women in office and counting room has given way, and in its place has come a disposition to recognize their ability and worth. It is beginning to be understood that young women are in many cases preferable to young men, owing to their quickness of perception and motion, their uniform freedom from bad habits and consequent reliability. There is a demand, therefore, for those whose training fits them for book-keepers, correspondents, cashiers and stenographers."[79]

Teaching was one of the genteel occupations open to women, and they were an increasing proportion of the state's public school teaching force. In 1874, when almost all teaching certificates were issued annually by local school boards and city systems, women outnumbered men by two to one. By 1890 the number of female teachers had almost doubled and they outnumbered men by four to one. Numbers did not necessarily mean equity, however. Average wages for men teaching in country districts in 1874 were $47.44 per month, for women $32.13. The comparable figures for 1890 were $43.50 and $29.00.[80]

All of the county superintendents in 1873 were men. Ten years later, another barrier had been breached as three superintendents—in Eau Claire, Iowa, and St. Croix counties—were women. By 1891, ten of the seventy county superintendents were identifiable as women. But the average pay for the women superintendents, $582.50 annually, was well below the average for men in the same position, which was $823.75. Both Anna Smith of Eau Claire County and Agnes Worsley of Racine County were paid at the rate of $800, although eleven counties paid $1,000

[79] Spencerian Business College, *Circular, 1890–1891* (Milwaukee, 1890), 20–21.
[80] Wisconsin Superintendent of Public Instruction, *Annual Report,* 1874, pp. xii–xiii; *Wisconsin Blue Book, 1891,* p. 552.

and seven paid $1,200. It is not, however, possible to generalize that the more populous counties paid the higher wages. City superintendents often were paid more than county superintendents who had no jurisdiction over the city systems.[81]

In 1891, there were 175 free high schools in the state, headed by 174 male principals and by Mary J. Gillan, the principal at Plainfield in Waushara County. These jobs were very evidently plums in public education. Of course Plainfield, where Mary Gillan was principal, had a village population of only 459 so her salary was well below the average. Of the forty-three city superintendents, Ida M. Johnson of Menomonie and Belle Smith of Waupaca were the only women. Waupaca had only ten teachers and Belle Smith received $100 annually above her regular teacher's salary. Ida Johnson supervised twenty-nine teachers—Madison had only forty-seven—for an added $300 per annum. Madison's superintendent, W. H. Beach, received $2,000 and did not double in brass as high school principal, as so many other superintendents did.[82]

The Wisconsin Bureau of Labor Statistics, established in 1883, came into existence partly out of concern that the 1879 compulsory school-attendance law was not serving its purpose. A problem was that the 1879 statute exempted from its provisions children between the ages of seven and fifteen whose "time and labor are essentially necessary for the support of an indigent parent, brother or sister." However, a more general statute excluded children under twelve from work in factories or workshops. The operation of the compulsory school law was continually under question. In a characteristic aside, the superintendent of Rock County observed in his 1886 report: "The present com-

[81] *Wisconsin Blue Book, 1873*, p. 423; *ibid., 1883*, pp. 374–375; *ibid., 1891*, pp. 545, 548. *Laws of Wisconsin*, 1875, pp. 220–221, made women eligible for all elective school offices. This did not include their right to vote in those elections. That came ten years later, but was not effectively implemented until 1893. The counts are based upon the apparent custom of identifying the women by their given names, though many superintendents are identified by initials only.

[82] *Wisconsin Blue Book, 1891*, pp. 546–548; *ibid., 1903*, p. 160, for Plainfield's population of 1890.

pulsory law is a dead letter.'' This was, apparently, an irritant between school people and the commissioner of labor statistics, who in his 1888–1889 report remarked testily: ''The Wisconsin Bureau cannot furnish statistics of child labor, for the simple fact that there is no child labor in this state, in the strict sense of the word. Our inspectors have been very diligent in this matter, because of the annoyance created by irresponsible persons and newspapers, who keep harping upon the subject.''[83]

The argument was not to be won so easily. The minimum age for children in factories and workshops was raised to thirteen in 1889, but special permits, grantable by a county judge, were still available for children under fourteen. In 1899 the legislature increased the number of factory inspectors from two to seven to pursue the child labor problem more vigorously. ''We find in our state an amazing increase among our youthful employees during the last quarter of a century,'' the bureau reported a year later. ''In the older manufacturing cities of the state, conditions surrounding working children were found to exist as horrible as any which cursed the life of the factory hands of the older manufacturing states. . . .'' Inspections in 1897 reported that 9,041 workers out of 102,560 inspected were between the ages of fourteen and eighteen. Seventy-nine were under fourteen. Industries employing the largest numbers of juveniles were, in order: knitting mills, tinware, sash-and-door plants, chair factories, malleable iron, box making, candy making, and beer bottling. The average weekly wage for children sixteen and under was $2.69, ranging from $1.96 to $3.50. Of 1,226 children ''who appeared to be young or weak and whose homes were visited,'' 60 per cent came from families that owned their own home and nearly half (46 per cent) of whose fathers were regularly employed.[84]

Among the most common complaints of adult workmen was the use of child labor by employers under the guise of apprentice-

<hr />

[83] Wisconsin Bureau of Labor and Industrial Statistics, *Biennial Report*, 1883–1884, pp. 160–162; *ibid.*, 1888–1889, p. vii; Wisconsin Superintendent of Public Instruction, *Biennial Report*, 1884–1886, p. 195.

[84] Wisconsin Bureau of Labor and Industrial Statistics, *Biennial Report*, 1898–1899, pp. 124–125, 256, 283–285; *ibid.*, *Biennial Report*, 1897–1898, pp. 348–349, 540–544.

ship. Typical was an apprenticeship contract, reproduced in the state's report of labor statistics for 1885–1886, which noted "that there is not one word in the agreement providing for the instruction of the infant in some useful trade or profession. . . ." Trunk making was an industry centering in Milwaukee because of the conjunction of tanneries, metal shops, hardwoods, and abundant cheap labor. The bureau had complaints from young men in that trade who were hired as apprentices, but before they advanced to over $5 per week they were "replaced by younger boys at the foot of the ladder" or else by foreigners and their children "who come here direct from the rural districts of Europe."[85]

There are many inferences which one may draw about the family incomes and the standard of living in Wisconsin during these years. But first the reservations. The great bulk of material available on wages and income covers only industrial workers, and it is apparent that a much higher proportion of skilled workers responded to the questionnaires issued by the state's labor bureau than did the more numerous semiskilled or unskilled. And despite the emphasis upon the great increase in industrialization and urbanization, one must bear in mind that Wisconsin's population remained mostly rural. While winter, the usual slack season, brought alternate employment—logging, ice harvesting, woodcutting, and snow removal—most of these jobs took men away from home where their board and room came out of minimal, unskilled wages or piece rates. A family man working in a logging camp drew only $15 to $25 per month, beyond his board, but there seemed usually to be plenty of men available for these jobs. Winter put a lot of farm labor at liberty, shut down waterpowers, and brought most jobs in the building trades to a halt.[86]

In 1888, just over half of Wisconsin's industrial workers averaged less than $1.50 per ten-hour day. If you raise the figure to just under $2.00, this included 77.4 per cent of them. One in six made less than a dollar a day, when they had work. Three years

---

[85] *Ibid.*, *Biennial Report*, 1885–1886, pp. 268–269, 305–306, 449–450.
[86] Fries, *Empire in Pine*, 207.

later, in 1891, 70.5 per cent made under $2.00, and those mak-
ing less than $1.50 per day had fallen to 43.8 per cent. This
slightly improving trend reversed again after the panic and
depression beginning in 1893. It was standard for wage rates to
respond to business cycles. The French observer Levasseur cited
a Wisconsin study covering the years 1888 to 1895 that indicated
that only 3.2 per cent of workmen's families had incomes over
$600 annually, "while 51.6 per cent lived on less than $400."[87]

Studies indicate that the standard of living for workingmen
and their families was undergoing a qualitative improvement.
Wages did, over the long term, go up slightly. This, combined
with the long deflationary pressure on the dollar after 1873,
raised real wages by about 44 per cent. Nevertheless, a review of
Wisconsin prices in the early 1880's indicates that an average
workman traded one hour's labor for a pound of cheese or for a
pound of beef round steak, or bacon, and three to four days'
labor for a ton of soft coal. (Of course, food and fuel prices
fluctuated from year to year.) One bargain was the rather steady
decline in the price of ready-made men's clothing and shoes. To
be sure, this advance came at the expense of young women
flocking into the needle trades in Milwaukee. Nonetheless, a pair
of work pants in 1884 cost $2. Although they were about a dollar
cheaper than four years before, this was still more than an average wage for ten hours' work. A plain suit for dress cost $14—
about a week and a half in average wages.[88]

Like kerosene for lighting, ready-made clothing was a convenience that was readily adopted by the working class. Coal was
cheap and more convenient that wood for heating, but one could
not gather his own coal. The period marked a start towards
today's consumer society. Housing was doubtless cheaper and
better than formerly, with cheap dimension lumber, the balloon
frame mode of construction, and prebuilt components from sash

[87] Wisconsin Bureau of Labor and Industrial Statistics, *Biennial Report*, 1898–1899, pp.
152, 156; Levasseur, *American Workman*, 399, citing *ibid., Biennial Report*, 1895–1896.

[88] Wisconsin Bureau of Labor and Industrial Statistics, *Biennial Report*, 1898–1899, pp.
133–137; Long, *Wages and Earnings*, 61–68.

and door factories. Milwaukee was justly proud of the fact that it had one of the highest proportion of home owners of any major city in the country. Wisconsin's general average in 1890 for families owning their own homes in cities over 8,000 population was 55.2 per cent, compared to an average 47.5 per cent for the four adjoining states. It also had the lowest average mortgage debt of the five states.[89]

Upward mobility in this society was certainly not foreclosed. There are many examples of men who made it into the ranks of successful entrepreneurs without the advantages of capital, education, or special skills. But they were certainly exceptional enough always to be remarkable. More common forms of mobility were possible for those caught in the ordinary ranks of employment that was steady. "Security of employment meant a great deal to these people," commented Albert C. Vogel of the workers in his family's tannery.[90]

Yet another route towards a higher economic status was through the accumulation of property, usually a home. Leo Wieland, who worked for Pritzlaff Hardware, bought a suburban lot for $1,000 with $100 down, and sold it a year later for $100 profit "and the interest." He did this in the early 1880's, on a salary of $12 per week after he was married. ("When I got married," he commented, "then things weren't so easy," pointing up a common observation that single men had a much different life style on the prevailing wages.) The disadvantages or unlikelihood of owning a home for many workingmen was the uncertainty of employment. Indeed, the word "uncertainty" runs like a litany through the responses to a question about home ownership addressed to workers by the state's bureau of labor and industrial statistics.[91]

---

[89] *Eleventh Census of the United States, 1890: Farms and Homes, Volume XIII*, 27–32. Of the twenty-eight American cities of 100,000+ population, only Rochester, New York, with 43.98 per cent of its families owning their homes, exceeded Milwaukee's 42.13 per cent.

[90] Wisconsin Bureau of Labor and Industrial Statistics, *Biennial Report*, 1887–1888, pp. 15–36; Vogel Transcript.

[91] Wieland Transcript; Wisconsin Bureau of Labor and Industrial Statistics, *Biennial Report*, 1887–1888, pp. 15–36.

The existence of credit institutions aided home ownership for wage earners. Wisconsin had forty-nine building and loan associations in 1895, thirty-two of them having been in existence more than five years. Fifty-four per cent of the shareholders in these associations were wage earners. They made up 78 per cent of the 3,628 current borrowers, almost all of this credit invested in homes. Personal returns from 300 workers (all classified as unskilled) indicated that 118 of them owned their own homes. The highest home valuation claimed was $5,500, the lowest $66, making an average meaningless. Fifty-two of the 118 gave the value of their homes between $800 and $1,200; twenty-five were under $800. Eighty-one of the 118 carried mortgages, sixty-four of these in amounts under $800.[92]

There were a number of ways to augment or stretch family income. Janesville may be taken as typical of smaller industrial cities. It had some 2,500 acres of unplatted land and vacant lots within the city limits. Tobacco, an intensive cash crop, was grown in considerable quantities within the city, for a ready market existed for it in the tobacco warehouses. Many residents of Janesville kept pigs or chickens, and backyard root cellars, smokehouses, and kitchen gardens were common in an age predating mass-produced foodstuffs. It was not only the poor who thus reduced dependence on cash income for their food and their animals. The city assessor in 1875 reported 678 horses, 364 cattle, and 255 swine in the city. Janesville, like other cities, adopted ordinances to keep grazing animals off the streets and other people's property, but they remained a part of the local scene. Hunting and fishing were also regular sources of food. An opponent of restrictions on winter fishing estimated that 30,000 pounds of fish from a nearby lake were marketed locally in two winter months.[93]

Gardening, raising animals and poultry, keeping a cow, and

[92] Wisconsin Bureau of Labor, Census and Industrial Statistics, *Biennial Report,* 1895–1896, pp. 261–278, 506–517. These home owners, as with other questionnaire respondents reported by the bureau, were not necessarily representative. While the 300 responses came from twelve major cities, only forty-six were from Milwaukee, 116 from Sheboygan, two from Janesville, fifteen from Racine, and so on.

[93] Fleckner, "Poverty and Relief in Janesville," *WMH,* 61:281–283.

foraging the countryside were not uncommon in the metropolis, although Milwaukee got the cows and pigs off the streets a decade or more earlier than did Janesville. The old third ward, the residential area immediately south of the main business district, had gardens, hen houses, and usually a shed with a cow on many of the tiny lots of the district. This pattern prevailed until the fire of 1892 nearly wiped out the older housing in the ward.[94]

When the federal census turned its attention towards the American city for its 1880 series on the social statistics of cities, it failed to find officially sponsored public market facilities in most Wisconsin cities. Even Milwaukee managed only a "a market of small dimensions, belonging to an association of gardeners." There were, however, well-established traditional markets. There was one for firewood at Fourth and Poplar, maintained well into the 1880's when wood became more expensive than coal. There was a German market on upper East Water Street where vegetables were generally cheaper and where non-Germans learned to like rye bread and new varieties of cheese and sausage. Office workers and retail clerks, distinguishable by their plug hats, commonly carried baskets to work and shopped the German market. A German tannery worker remembered that he would accompany his father to a livestock market at Fourth and Vliet in the fall where they would buy a pig of 300 pounds and another half that size. "We tied a washline to the hind leg of [the] big pig and drove it home . . . and the whole family would get together, all the sisters and sisters-in-law. . . . One day they would make sausage here and the next day there."[95]

[94] Leora M. Howard, "Changes in Home Life in Milwaukee from 1865 to 1900" (master's thesis, University of Wisconsin, 1923), 12-13. Until the nineties, when the electric streetcar began to work its transformations, Milwaukee was a walking city with workers' homes on lots around the main industrial plants. Narrow but deep with no space used for front yards, Milwaukee lots offered room for gardens and pens at the rear. See Clay McShane, *Technology and Reform: Street Railways and the Growth of Milwaukee, 1887-1900* (Madison, 1974), 87-94; and Roger D. Simon, *The City-Building Process: Housing and Services in New Milwaukee Neighborhoods, 1880-1910* (*Transactions of the American Philosophical Society,* vol. 68, pt. 5, Philadelphia, 1978), 35.

[95] *Tenth Census of the United States, 1880: Social Statistics of Cities, Volume XIX, Part 2,* p. 672; Howard, "Home Life in Milwaukee," 27; Bill Hooker, *Glimpses of an Earlier Milwaukee* (Milwaukee, 1929), 10-11; Brockman Transcript.

Bill Hooker recalled farmers bringing produce to Milwaukee to sell in the markets or to merchants. Many brought hay and grain to provender urban horses and cows, while their wives brought dried apples on strings, berries, butter, eggs, and other items to trade at the grocers' for staples. Dried stockfish, hard as flint, was another standard item, displayed in piles like kindling. "Once in a while a farmer would fetch into some regular customer a dressed hog or a barrel of apples or a sack of potatoes and undersell the grocer. Besides, he got ready money, which was hard to get from a dealer." William Brockman's family bought potatoes in this manner, a sixty-pound bag for thirty-five or forty cents. Twenty-five bags represented a normal purchase, "and [we] put them down in the basement. . . . Of course we didn't have heat all over the house."[96]

One aspect of making a living that deserves mention was the absence of leisure time for most wage earners, except that conferred by periods of unemployment. Gardening and gathering fell largely to other members of the family. Boys learned the value of stray bits of fuel that seemed of doubtful ownership or of an occasional dime that ingenuity might produce. Fishing served more than the instinct for sport. Bill Hooker recalled catching crayfish in the Kinnickinnic marsh and selling them to German saloonkeepers, who served them to their customers. (By courtesy, they were called "crab.") The growth of the tanneries, packing plants, and coal docks in the Menominee Valley had put an end to crayfishing and similar pursuits by the eighties.[97]

Most industrial workers commonly worked a ten-hour day, six days a week. But a bookkeeper in Marinette lamented that while his employers were considerate men, they were forced to conform to the hours of competing merchants. He put in sixteen-hour days and knew others who worked a half-day on Sunday in addition. Teamsters employed as deliverymen worked a similar schedule. In many working-class households the breadwinner was a tired boarder or even just an occasional presence. A

---

[96] Hooker, *An Earlier Milwaukee*, 9–10; Brockman Transcript.
[97] Hooker, *An Earlier Milwaukee*, 13.

machinist from Wausau complained that he had not been home, except for visits, for two years. He owned a home there, but had had to look elsewhere for work at his higher-paying trade: ''I can not move my family because I do not know how long work will last.'' This speaks volumes about the quality of life for many of Wisconsin's wage earners.[98]

There are many figures available to provide a general picture of the average working-class urban family. There simply is no such measure for farm families because there was no labor market mechanism at work and the returns were so variable. And the uncertainty of employment did not impinge upon the farmer. The opportunity to turn his hand to useful labor, for his own benefit and at his own command, was of inestimable value. Privately the farmer may have envied the successful entrepreneur, banker, professional, or man of commerce, but not the marginal village tradesman waiting for a customer or the unskilled worker waiting to be hired. The wonder is that the city or the small town was assumed to act as such a lure. But farm life presented such a dull routine, and so many people in town appeared to lead interesting, well-rewarded lives.

For the ambitious who felt that they were equipped for better things, the years after 1873 opened many avenues, especially by way of some formal education beyond the district school. The complexities of an interdependent, industrialized society were opening new opportunities for many people—a minority, to be sure, but a growing minority.

[98] Wisconsin Bureau of Labor and Industrial Statistics, *Biennial Report,* 1887–1888, pp. 27, 80.

# PART II

# Communities

"It is evident that in Wisconsin, from the beginning, were mingled many and conflicting religious and social influences, and it should need no argument to determine that there would certainly be religious and social results from such contact, in modification of all of the original materials."

ELLIS B. USHER

Democratic Party State Central
    Committee Chairman, 1887–1890
In *Wisconsin: Its Story and Biography,*
    *1848–1913,* vol. 3 (1914)

# 6

# Population

## TRENDS AND COMPARISONS

THE essential character of Wisconsin's population was set early in the state's history. In 1890 Wisconsin was third among the states and territories, after North Dakota and Minnesota, in its percentage of foreign-born. These percentages were reversed in the category of American-born with foreign-born parents— Wisconsin having much the larger. This reflects the obvious: Wisconsin was settled almost a generation earlier and had an almost identical proportion of foreign-born in its 1850 population as did Minnesota twenty years later. The great difference was that a third of Wisconsin's foreign-born of 1850 were counted as Germans. The German component in Wisconsin was half of her foreign-born population by 1890, almost matched by Minnesota's Scandinavian-born in the same census. One gains some perspective by this exercise in comparisons and contrasts. What follows is an effort to place Wisconsin's population mix by looking at its adjoining neighbors to compare how people adjusted to geographic determinants, urbanization, possible migration patterns, and other factors. The comparisons are necessarily mostly statistical; the argument is that Wisconsin's population pattern showed a greater consistency than most of her adjoining neighbors' during the last half of the nineteenth century. Wisconsin also had a more general distribution of the foreign-born and their progeny with respect to urban, village, and rural environments. Thus, despite having the highest proportion of any state east of the Mississippi (and the dominance of those of German origins,

262

which was not all that unique), one can reasonably argue that the foreign-born were probably more integrated into Wisconsin's wider society. This is necessarily an assertion rather than a provable fact.[1]

In 1850, Wisconsin's population was 36.2 per cent foreign-born, compared to between 13 and 14 per cent in neighboring Illinois and Michigan. While Wisconsin's proportion of foreign-born trended slowly downward, to 34.6 per cent in 1870 and 30.8 per cent in 1890, the comparable 1890 figures were rising to 22 per cent in Illinois and 26 per cent in Michigan. Even Yankee Iowa had to adjust to an increase of foreign-born from 10.9 per cent in 1850 to 17 per cent in 1870 and 1890. By the latter date, Chicago, Detroit, and Milwaukee were very close in their proportions of foreign-born: between 35 and 40 per cent. A significant difference was that Chicago contained over half of all the foreign-born in Illinois, while Detroit and Milwaukee each had approximately 15 per cent. Although Milwaukee in 1890 had a much higher percentage (68.8) of German-born in its foreign-born population, only 21.1 per cent of Wisconsin's German-born lived in Milwaukee, while more than one-fourth of Michigan's lived in Detroit, and nearly half of Illinois' German-born lived in Chicago.[2]

In 1850, Wisconsin had 38,064 German-born in a total population of 305,391. The lasting influence of this very early pattern should be considered. As will be observed below, even though like attracted like, there were few communities that did not undergo relatively rapid change due to mobility and generational trends. Then, too, the census reported its findings by basic units

[1] *Eleventh Census of the United States, 1890: Statistical Atlas, Volume XVI,* 20, and plates 14 and 16.

[2] The federal census is an imperfect guide to ethnicity. Until late in the nineteenth century, immigrants were identified by national sovereignty rather than language and their own perceptions of who they were. An excellent discussion of the problem of identifying ethnic groups from the federal census is in Frederick C. Luebke, *Immigrants and Politics: The Germans of Nebraska, 1880–1900* (Lincoln, 1969), 8–10. Milwaukee had the highest percentage of foreign-born among major American cities, followed in order by New York, Chicago, Detroit, San Francisco, Buffalo, St. Paul, and Cleveland. See *Eleventh Census of the United States, 1890: Statistical Atlas, Volume XVI,* plates 14 and 16.

of government, and the basic unit of government in Wisconsin, the town, did not conform to ethnic settlement patterns but instead generally followed the geometric federal township survey, six miles square. People of different languages, churches, and cultures thus intermingled in the business of ordering their roads, schools, taxes, and other affairs. Another consideration is that the relatively huge German immigration of 1873–1893 and earlier was not at all monolithic in character. Germans differed more widely than did most other continental European ethnic groups in identities that mattered the most: religion, separate sovereignties (which continued to mean much even after the 1871 unification of Germany), dialects, occupations, economic circumstances, and urban or rural origins.[3]

Even so, there is no escaping the record of ethnocentrism. A study of intermarriage patterns among Wisconsin ethnic groups at the turn of the century found that six out of seven German-born who married after coming to Wisconsin did so endogamously, within their ethnic and usually within their religious affiliation. Only one in five of the American-born children of German-born parents married outside, and then often with someone of identifiable German heritage if not of the second generation. The Norwegians were even more standoffish, and they were after 1880 the second-largest Wisconsin foreign-born group. Others, particularly the Irish, British, British-American (Canadian), and those of Yankee heritage, married almost as readily outside as within their ethnic heritage, assuming no conflict of religious backgrounds. Intermarriage in 1890 was a rather final evidence of ethnic interaction.

[3] Wolfgang Kollmann and Peter Marschalck, "German Emigration to the United States," trans. Thomas C. Childers, in Donald Fleming and Bernard Bailyn, eds., *Dislocation and Emigration: The Social Background of American Immigration* (*Perspectives in American History,* vol. 7, Cambridge, 1973), 522–541; Marcus L. Hansen, "The Revolutions of 1848 and German Emigration," in the *Journal of Economic and Business History,* 2 (August, 1930), 634–635; James S. Olson, *The Ethnic Dimension in American History* (2 vols., New York, 1979), 1:99–102. Joseph Schafer's *Wisconsin Domesday Book: Town Studies* (Madison, 1924), details typical population changes, discussed below, in the Wisconsin towns.

NATIVE-BORN AND FOREIGN-BORN POPULATION

| | 1850† | | 1870 | | | 1890 | | | | 1900 | | | |
|---|---|---|---|---|---|---|---|---|---|---|---|---|---|
| | NB | FB | NB.NB | NB.FB | FB | NB.NB* | NB.FB* | FB* | Colored‡ | NB.NB* | NB.FB* | FB* | Colored‡ |
| Illinois | 736,149 | 111,892 | 1,553,856 | 470,837 | 515,198 | 1,882,693 | 1,044,804 | 840,975 | 57,879 | 2,271,765 | 1,498,473 | 964,635 | 86,677 |
| % of Total | 86.5 | 13.1 | 61.2 | 18.5 | 20.3 | 49.2 | 27.3 | 22.0 | 1.5 | 47.1 | 31.1 | 20.0 | 1.8 |
| Michigan | 341,656 | 54,703 | 695,900 | 220,149 | 268,010 | 917,693 | 613,590 | 541,601 | 21,005 | 1,026,714 | 831,653 | 540,196 | 22,419 |
| % of Total | 85.9 | 13.8 | 58.8 | 18.6 | 22.6 | 43.8 | 29.3 | 25.9 | 1.0 | 42.4 | 34.4 | 22.3 | 0.9 |
| Wisconsin | 194,099 | 110,477 | 336,838 | 353,333 | 364,499 | 435,004 | 726,835 | 518,989 | 6,407 | 585,903 | 956,303 | 515,705 | 11,131 |
| % of Total | 63.6 | 36.2 | 31.9 | 33.5 | 34.6 | 25.8 | 43.1 | 30.8 | 0.4 | 28.3 | 46.2 | 24.9 | 0.5 |
| Minnesota | 4,097 | 1,977 | 154,190 | 124,819 | 160,697 | 311,200 | 518,151 | 467,057 | 5,667 | 425,780 | 806,321 | 504,935 | 14,358 |
| % of Total | 67.4 | 32.5 | 35.1 | 28.4 | 36.5 | 23.9 | 39.8 | 35.9 | 0.4 | 24.3 | 46.0 | 28.8 | 0.8 |
| Iowa | 170,931 | 20,969 | 777,881 | 211,447 | 204,692 | 1,063,971 | 513,187 | 323,932 | 10,810 | 1,261,068 | 651,817 | 305,782 | 13,186 |
| % of Total | 88.9 | 10.9 | 65.2 | 17.7 | 17.1 | 55.7 | 26.8 | 16.9 | 0.6 | 56.5 | 29.2 | 13.7 | 0.6 |

KEY: NB = Native-born. FB = Foreign-born. NB.NB = Native-born of Native-born Parents. NB.FB = Native-born of Foreign-born Parent(s).

*White only.

†Percentages total less than 100 because place of birth was not always known.

‡In 1890, Colored includes blacks, Chinese, Japanese, and civilized Indians.
In 1900, Colored includes blacks, Chinese, Japanese, and Indians taxed and not taxed.

SOURCES: *Ninth Census of the United States, 1870: Population, Volume I, 299; Eleventh Census of the United States, 1890: Abstract, 46, 52–55; Twelfth Census of the United States, 1900: Population, Volume I, Part 1, pp. 482–483, 489.*

One mitigating point may be ventured. Because the proportions and pattern of Wisconsin's early ethnic mix did not change as much as did those of her adjacent neighbors, the largest component of her 1890 population was the American-born children of her foreign-born. They were 42.9 per cent of her total population—approximately half again that of Illinois and Michigan. Remember also Wisconsin's broader geographical distribution of her German population. The second-generation immigrants were less footloose than their Yankee neighbors, were usually comfortable in a couple of languages, understood their unlike neighbors more readily than did their parents, and could entertain a wider range of options as to occupation, participation in politics and community life, and location. This must have made a palpable difference—although not one susceptible of objective proof. This difference suggests that sheer numbers of foreign-born as a proportion of the total population had possibly less to do with processes of acculturation and adaptation than did their early appearance as a significant part of the population, their origins, distribution, mobility, the relative importance of local units of government in the political process, and most particularly the role of that mediating generation, their American-born children.[4]

Wisconsin's rate of population gain from 1870 to 1890 was closest to the national average among its immediate neighbors, although the others—with the single exception of Minnesota, which was not a contemporary in settlement—were likewise very close. The average growth rate, however, conceals a considerable variation among these states in the rates of growth during the three decennial census periods. Migration in and out was the most obvious factor at work. It was both fitful and fickle.[5]

As a rough measure of the opportunities for population expansion in the years 1873 to 1893 in Wisconsin, the net increase of 1850 to 1870 was 794,279, while the increase of the following twenty years was only 638,660. One can identify some of the

[4] Richard M. Bernard, *The Melting Pot and the Altar: Marital Assimilation in Early Twentieth-Century Wisconsin* (Minneapolis, 1980), 5-9, 44-58.

[5] United States Bureau of the Census, *Historical Statistics of the United States: Colonial Times to 1957* (Washington, 1960), Series A, 123-180.

more obvious influences that slowed growth even below that of the Civil War decade: limitations upon Wisconsin's agricultural expansion and the lure of cheap, fertile acres westward; the competing attraction of neighboring Chicago and other cities; a pronounced drop in the birth rate; the long depression of the seventies with two recessions in the eighties; and the uncertain nature of Wisconsin's industrial future as the dominant lumber industry neared its peak.[6]

Sometime before 1880 Wisconsin and Michigan were coming up against the hard fact of a limited amount of undeveloped arable land, especially when compared with Iowa and Minnesota. The expansion of acreage in Wisconsin farms as well as in

[6] The decennial increase from 1850 to 1860 of 470,490 was not surpassed until a century later in Wisconsin. See Robert C. Nesbit, *Wisconsin: A History* (Madison, 1973), 548.

DECENNIAL RATES OF POPULATION GROWTH EXPRESSED AS PERCENTAGES

|  | 1870–1880 | 1880–1890 | 1890–1900 | 1870–1890 |
|---|---|---|---|---|
| United States | 30.1 | 25.5 | 20.7 | 63.3 |
| Illinois | 21.2 | 24.3 | 26.0 | 50.7 |
| Michigan | 38.2 | 27.9 | 15.6 | 76.8 |
| Wisconsin | 24.7 | 28.7 | 22.2 | 60.6 |
| Minnesota | 77.6 | 67.8 | 33.7 | 198.0 |
| Iowa | 36.1 | 17.7 | 16.7 | 60.2 |

SOURCE: United States Bureau of the Census, *Historical Statistics of the United States: Colonial Times to 1957* (Washington, 1960), Series A 123–180.

POPULATION GROWTH, 1850–1900

|  | Illinois | Michigan | Wisconsin | Minnesota | Iowa | United States |
|---|---|---|---|---|---|---|
| 1850 | 851,470 | 397,654 | 305,391 | 6,077 | 192,214 | 23,191,876 |
| 1860 | 1,711,951 | 749,113 | 775,881 | 172,023 | 674,913 | 31,443,321 |
| 1870 | 2,539,891 | 1,184,059 | 1,054,670 | 439,706 | 1,194,020 | 38,558,371 |
| 1880 | 3,077,871 | 1,636,937 | 1,315,497 | 780,773 | 1,624,615 | 50,155,783 |
| 1890 | 3,826,352 | 2,093,890 | 1,693,330 | 1,310,283 | 1,912,297 | 62,947,714 |
| 1900 | 4,821,550 | 2,420,982 | 2,069,042 | 1,751,394 | 2,231,853 | 75,994,575 |

SOURCES: United States Bureau of the Census, *Historical Statistics of the United States: Colonial Times to 1957* (Washington, 1960), Series A 123–180; *Seventeenth Census of the United States, 1950: Population, Volume I, Part 1,* p. 3.

improved acres was, after the census of that year, certainly nominal. Indeed, the state census of 1895 claimed fewer improved
farm acres than did the 1890 federal census. Simply put, better
land that was more easily put to the plow and as readily accessible lay across the Mississippi. By 1890, one in four Wisconsin-
born lived outside the state, three out of four of them west of
Wisconsin.[7]

Neighboring Illinois and Iowa were equally generous, and by
1890 they had lost even larger contingents of their native-born
than had Wisconsin. This was evidently not only a matter of
proximity to western opportunity and the relative maturity of
their land settlement, but also a reflection of the greater readiness
of the children of American-born parents to move on. The federal census of 1890 is the first to show the distribution of each
state's native-born population according to parentage. In that
year, one of every three Wisconsin-born children of American
parents (32.9 per cent) had left the state, but only one in five
(19.4 per cent) of the children of foreign-born parents had left.
The greater mobility of those born in Illinois and Iowa must be
due, in part, to the fact that they had a much larger percentage
of native-born of American-born parents than did Wisconsin. An
estimate of the impact of migratory habits upon the populations
of the five states between 1870 and 1900 shows the continued
dependence of the Upper Midwest upon an influx of the foreign-
born to sustain a growth rate close to the national average. All
but Minnesota suffered a net loss of American-born population
in at least two decennial intervals. Wisconsin lost during all three
decades, but this was more because she failed to attract American-born from other states rather than having suffered a heavier
loss of her own native-born.[8]

Among the four states adjoining Wisconsin, Michigan lost
fewer of her home-grown citizens to other states than did Wis-

[7] Wisconsin Department of State, *Tabular Statements of the Census Enumeration and the Agricultural, Mineral, and Manufacturing Interests of the State of Wisconsin,* 1895, vol. 1, pp. 986–987, hereinafter cited as *Wisconsin State Census,* 1895; *Eleventh Census of the United States, 1890: Agriculture, Volume V,* 74–75.

[8] *Eleventh Census of the United States, 1890: Compendium, Volume III,* 22–31.

ACREAGE IN FARMS, IMPROVED ACREAGE, NUMBER OF FARMS, AND VALUE OF FARM PRODUCTS

| | 1860 | 1870 | 1880 | 1890 | 1889* |
|---|---|---|---|---|---|
| **Illinois** | *35,840,000 acres of land* | | | | |
| Acres in farms | 20,911,989 | 25,882,861 | 31,673,645 | 30,498,277 | $184,759,013 |
| Acres improved | 13,096,374 | 19,329,952 | 26,115,154 | 25,669,060 | Ave. per farm |
| No. of farms | 143,310 | 202,803 | 255,741 | 240,681 | $ 765.65 |
| **Michigan** | *36,755,200 acres of land* | | | | |
| Acres in farms | 7,030,834 | 10,019,142 | 13,807,240 | 14,785,636 | $ 83,651,390 |
| Acres improved | 3,476,296 | 5,096,939 | 8,296,862 | 9,865,350 | Ave. per farm |
| No. of farms | 62,422 | 98,786 | 154,008 | 172,344 | $ 485.38 |
| **Wisconsin** | *34,848,000 acres of land* | | | | |
| Acres in farms | 7,893,587 | 11,715,321 | 15,353,118 | 16,787,988 | $ 70,990,645 |
| Acres improved | 3,746,167 | 5,899,343 | 9,162,528 | 9,793,931 | Ave. per farm |
| No. of farms | 69,270 | 102,904 | 134,322 | 146,409 | $ 484.88 |
| **Minnesota** | *50,691,200 acres of land* | | | | |
| Acres in farms | 2,711,968 | 5,483,828 | 13,403,019 | 18,663,645 | $ 71,238,230 |
| Acres improved | 556,250 | 2,322,102 | 7,246,693 | 11,127,953 | Ave. per farm |
| No. of farms | 18,181 | 46,500 | 92,386 | 116,851 | $ 609.65 |
| **Iowa** | *35,504,000 acres of land* | | | | |
| Acres in farms | 10,069,907 | 15,541,793 | 24,752,700 | 30,491,541 | $159,347,844 |
| Acres improved | 3,792,792 | 9,396,467 | 19,866,541 | 25,428,899 | Ave. per farm |
| No. of farms | 61,163 | 116,292 | 185,351 | 201,903 | $ 789.23 |

*Value of farm products available only for 1889.

SOURCE: *Eleventh Census of the United States, 1890: Agriculture, Volume V*, 74–75, 92–93.

consin or the others. In the 1890 census, Wisconsin, Illinois, and Iowa had lost nearly one-third of their native-born of American-born parents. Michigan had lost only about half as many. The children of the foreign-born in Michigan also were less footloose: Wisconsin, Illinois, and Iowa had lost about one in five, Michigan only a bit over one in ten. Iowa, of course, had nothing to rival the attractions of the metropolitan centers in the other four states, and like Minnesota it also lay next door to the open land of Nebraska and the Dakotas.[9]

Why the anomaly offered by Michigan? Surely proximity to the current itch—the lure of the western prairie land being opened by the railroads—had much to do with it. Michigan was more remote from that action. Better situated than Wisconsin with respect to markets, her agriculture became more specialized and more productive on a nearly equal improved acreage. The influence of Lake Michigan in moderating her western shore also helped; a Wisconsin peach was a rare item indeed.[10]

A Wisconsin scholar who is of particular interest in any treatment of the population of the state during the latter decades of the nineteenth century is Joseph Schafer. He was born in 1867 at Muscoda, a village in the Town of Castle Rock in northeastern Grant County, the son of an immigrant German farmer and teacher who was a leader in his community. Schafer also taught school, and, in his early thirties, began graduate study at Madison in 1898 with Frederick Jackson Turner. He taught at the University of Oregon from 1900 to 1920, when he accepted the superintendency of the State Historical Society of Wisconsin. He came with an ambitious proposal: ". . . a Wisconsin Domesday Book . . . something quite as fundamental as the famous survey of English counties made in the reign of William the First. . . ." He envisioned this project as the groundwork for a "future great history of Wisconsin which should reach very much further down in the social life of the state than any history that has yet been

---

[9] United States Bureau of the Census, *Historical Statistics of the United States,* 44–47.

[10] *Eleventh Census of the United States, 1890: Compendium, Volume III,* 22, 28; Harvey S. Perloff et al., *Regions, Resources, and Economic Growth* (Lincoln, 1960), 622–634.

produced.'' Aside from the descriptive data, Schafer's plan included a "plat book or atlas that will give the student of Wisconsin history immediate access to the names of first settlers in each section of the state, together with an ocular account of the lands they occupied. . . .'' Frederick Jackson Turner, who had removed to Harvard some years before, gave his blessing to this "new type of historical study peculiarly suited to America. . . .''[11]

The end result of Schafer's endeavors to implement the Domesday Book, since he had Germanic work habits and considerable time for scholarship, was five volumes which appeared between 1922 and 1937. The first, *A History of Agriculture in Wisconsin*, was a survey of pioneer settlement and the development of agriculture to about the turn of the century. *Town Studies, Volume One,* represented the never-completed atlas. It contained sketches of just twenty-five widely scattered towns (townships) across southern Wisconsin. The remaining three volumes were what Schafer called "type areas"—blocks of three or four counties with some cohesive features—through which he examined settlement, economic development, population changes, acculturation, and other processes. These published works fell far short of the original Domesday Book concept, but they earned their author a national reputation. He lost no opportunity to advertise to the scholarly world his samplings designed "to penetrate deep lying strata in human affairs." Like Frederick Jackson Turner, Schafer easily slipped into oratorical flourishes while proclaiming that his technique was that of the dedicated, detached scientist. His end product, he asserted, "yields a result analogous to what the painter obtains through a study of both the spiritual and the physical lineaments of his

---

[11] Edward P. Alexander, Foreword, in *Joseph Schafer: Student of Agriculture* (Madison, 1942), v–vi; Louise Phelps Kellogg, "Joseph Schafer, The Historian," *ibid.*, 1; Clifford L. Lord and Carl Ubbelohde, *Clio's Servant: The State Historical of Wisconsin, 1846–1954* (Madison, 1967), 258–270; Joseph Schafer, "The Wisconsin Domesday Book," in *WMH*, 4 (September, 1920), 60–63. The projected atlas proved to be less readily prepared than Schafer had presumed. He expected to use county plat books, but these proved to be quite limited in their coverage.

subject.'' His Wisconsin studies were intended to establish with
''the sinking of a multitude of shafts through all the strata, social
and economic . . .'' —he liked geological and biological meta-
phors—the validity of Turner's theories about the frontier process and its results.[12]

The Wisconsin pattern that Schafer saw was the Yankee speculators moving well ahead of settlement into the interior, buying
up prospective townsites, usually associated with waterpowers,
and taking up as much adjacent good farmland as they could
command. The prospect of canals, roads, and railroads into the
interior soon drew American farmers away from the Lake Michigan shore inland across southern Wisconsin's prairies and oak
openings. The Germans, less sanguine about these improvements, wanted to remain close to the lake and to markets. They
were less inclined to exploitative agriculture—specifically wheat
farming—that used the land prodigally, and were less apt to have
access to credit sufficient for such a venture. The heavy maple
forests north and west of Milwaukee, which remained available
at government prices, were a more familiar setting, were closer
to markets, and permitted the Germans to clan together. Their
early concentration there, Schafer argued, was not due to their
lack of appreciation for the advantages of more open land. German immigrants with more financial resources readily bought
out the Americans who had settled or engrossed the best land
close to the lake. The other side of the coin was that the Americans and the Irish—the latter second in numbers to the Germans
among the foreign-born until the 1880 census—readily moved
on, taking a quick profit on their speculative ventures and
improvements.[13]

[12] Joseph Schafer, *A History of Agriculture in Wisconsin* (Madison, 1922); Joseph Schafer,
*Wisconsin Domesday Book: Town Studies* (Madison, 1924); Joseph Schafer, *Four Wisconsin
Counties: Prairie and Forest* (Madison, 1927); Joseph Schafer, *The Wisconsin Lead Region*
(Madison, 1932); Joseph Schafer, *The Winnebago-Horicon Basin: A Type Study in Western
History* (Madison, 1937). See also Joseph Schafer, ''The Wisconsin Domesday Book: A
Method of Research for Agricultural Historians,'' in *Agricultural History,* 14 (January,
1940), 23–24, 32.

[13] Joseph Schafer, ''The Yankee and the Teuton in Wisconsin,'' in *WMH,* 6–7
(December, 1922–December, 1923), 6:125–145; Schafer, ''Wisconsin Domesday Book:

By 1873, the expansion of farmland was approaching the limits imposed by the northern highlands. Physiographic and soils maps show the limits of adequate agricultural soils and help explain why. If one draws a line westward from Marinette, and then tilts about thirty degrees to the north from just below Merrill, the line will take in two lobes of agricultural soil that lie to the north of the Wisconsin Terminal Moraine. It will also include the Barron Hills and some other land of little agricultural promise. The brief Lake Superior Lowlands lie far to the north of this line. By 1880 railroads, encouraged by federal land grants and the eagerness of lumbermen to reach their markets more efficiently than by rafts and to get to standing timber less accessible for the river log drives, had penetrated well north of the line delimiting agricultural soil. But the pioneering conditions on the lobes of good soil remaining were certainly formidable, both before and after the passage of the lumbermen.[14]

The migrating farmers of the seventies and later may be forgiven if they overwhelmingly preferred to continue westward across the Mississippi rather than tackle Wisconsin's remaining frontier. Ray Stannard Baker came to St. Croix Falls in Polk County in 1875 at the age of five. Central Polk County lies just within the detached lobe of prime soil that includes Pierce, St. Croix, and Polk counties. His father was land agent there for a development company headed by Caleb Cushing of Massachusetts. The boy accompanied his father on many trips "upcountry," as the elder Baker was deaf and Ray was useful as intermediary in talking with the few Scandinavians settling on land purchased from Baker.[15]

Joseph Stannard Baker was an enthusiast. "Sometimes [wrote his son later] during our long drives my father would suddenly

A Method of Research," *Agricultural History*, 14:29–31; Kate A. Everest, "How Wisconsin came by Its Large German Element," in *Collections of the State Historical Society of Wisconsin* (21 vols., Madison, 1855–1915), 12:313, hereinafter cited as *Wis. Hist. Colls.*

[14] Robert F. Fries, *Empire in Pine: The Story of Lumbering in Wisconsin, 1830–1900* (Madison, 1951), 84–92. See also the maps in Chapter 1 above.

[15] Alice E. Smith, "Caleb Cushing's Investments in the St. Croix Valley," in *WMH*, 28 (September, 1944), 7–19; *DWB*.

break out, after a long silence, with the kind of prophecies he delighted in, as on one occasion passing through the wilderness that was then the township of Milltown [fifteen miles northeast of St. Croix Falls] in our own county":

> "Ray," he said, pointing with his whip, "I shall not live to see the time, but you will, when all of this country will be covered with beautiful farms. There will be fine painted houses and great barns and windmills and good roads and good schools and a rich and contented people."
>
> I believed it of course if father said it, but it seemed utterly impossible. On all sides were unbroken forests, great trees, jungles of brushwood, marshy brooks, miles and miles of them; even the road was all but impassable, ruts, mudholes and the remainder of huge stumps and roots. And yet, not so long ago, I drove out that very road with my brother Harry in his automobile—a fine pavement all the way. Every word my father said had come true.

But the 1880's were a long time ago, and Ray Baker's recollection of a night spent with a Danish family pioneering that wilderness, which he saw as "utterly impossible," helped to explain the lure of Iowa, Minnesota, and beyond. While father and son were made welcome and offered the rude comforts, it was certainly a heroic undertaking making a farm there.[16]

Attempting to explain why Wisconsin attracted and held a relatively smaller contingent of American-born from other states after 1870 than did neighboring states, Joseph Schafer offered the comment: "The explanation seems to lie in the state's persistent rurality. The total agricultural population was large enough by, say 1870, to occupy pretty fully the choicest farming lands lying to the south of the pine forest belt." This, Schafer felt, combined with Wisconsin's much larger foreign-born element, accounted for the state's lesser attraction to American-born from other states and a relatively larger loss of her own Yankees westward. So far, so good—except for his statement about Wisconsin's "persistent rurality" continuing after 1870.

---

[16] Ray Stannard Baker, *Native American: The Book of My Youth* (New York, 1941), 16–18, 21–25. See Chapter 1 above for a discussion of the settlement of northern Wisconsin.

The fact is that Wisconsin was urbanized between 1870 and 1900 at a rate more rapid than that of the United States generally, and comparable to that of most of her neighbors.[17]

Wisconsin's urban population in 1870 was located in twenty-seven centers ranging from Chippewa Falls with a population of just 2,507 to 71,401 in Milwaukee. Only two cities other than the growing metropolis had over 10,000: Oshkosh (12,663) and Fond du Lac (12,764). Seventeen had less than 5,000 population. Twenty years later the number of urban places had nearly doubled to forty-eight. Eleven of them had over 10,000 population, twenty-four under 5,000. In 1890 a line from Beloit to Madison to Portage and thence to Green bay, delimiting the southeastern corner of the state, enclosed twenty-eight of the state's forty-eight urban centers. A line from Marinette through Antigo and Merrill and then on due west left only four urban centers to the north of it. Three of those—Superior, Ashland, and Washburn—were on Lake Superior. The fourth was Rhinelander in Oneida County, with 2,658 population. The lumber industry created several urban centers, some fortunate enough to become commercial and industrial centers. They were, after all, located strategically in relation to watersheds and often had a significant waterpower plus rail connections as a result of their locations and lumber shipments.[18]

What properly delimited an urban place in Wisconsin between 1873 and 1893? Many—maybe most—villages and small towns harbored the ambition to become important trade centers. The

[17] Joseph Schafer, "Editorial Comment: Peopling the Middle West," in *WMH*, 21 (September, 1937), 94–101. Schafer does not identify the sources he was consulting, but on p. 95 he assigns Wisconsin a population of 1,095,000 for 1870, "almost 40 per cent" foreign-born, up from 34 per cent in 1850. According to the census figures available in 1937 and today, Wisconsin' foreign-born in 1850 comprised 36.2 per cent of the total population. In 1870, with a population of 1,054,670 and 364,448 foreign-born, the percentage was 34.6. (The scholar could nod occasionally.) See Bernard, *Melting Pot and the Altar*, 5–6. Schafer's basic argument was that Wisconsin was unique in her larger proportion of foreign-born who were rural rather than urban and were less mobile than the urban population.

[18] *Ninth Census of the United States, 1870: Population, Volume I*, 287–295; *Eleventh Census of the United States, 1890: Population, Volume II, Part 1*, pp. 357–367.

boomer spirit animated every crossroad; all things seemed possible. Just to give one instance: Alma was described in 1876 in the *Wisconsin State Gazetteer* as a "flourishing village and county seat in the west central part of Buffalo county, on the east bank of the Mississippi river. . . . Population about 500." Alma had been growing. The federal census for 1880 was a heartening 1,244, and the state census for 1885, which drew a longer bow than did even the gazetteers, gave it a population of 1,521. On the strength of this and its imperial ambitions, Alma had its charter changed from a village to a city in 1885. But the bloom was off the rose even as this was accomplished. All that the federal census of 1890 could squeeze out for Alma was 1,428 inhabitants. By 1900, it had fallen to 1,201. Many felt called, but few were chosen.[19]

Close communities of 500 to 2,499 population, whether or not they were formally incorporated as villages—or cities, as in the case of Alma—are mostly recognizable in the published federal censuses of the latter nineteenth century. It is interesting that the percentage of the total population in this category remained almost constant in the censuses of 1870, 1880, and 1890 respectively as 8.0, 8.2, and 8.33 per cent. Some figures for 1870 are questionable, but the 1880 and 1890 schedules are quite compa-

---

[19] *Wisconsin State Gazetteer and Business Directory for 1876-7* (Milwaukee, 1876), 67; *Wisconsin Blue Book, 1887,* p. 346; *ibid., 1897,* p. 375; *ibid., 1903,* p. 163; "Alma" entry in George W. Peck, ed., *Cyclopedia of Wisconsin: Comprising Sketches of Counties, Towns, Events, Institutions, and Persons Arranged in Cyclopedic Form* (Madison, 1906). The figure 2,500 to define urban centers certainly is arbitrary. One geographer, Guy-Harold Smith, attempting to find a more realistic figure to separate the farm population from those otherwise engaged, counted as urban all incorporated villages and cities having over 200 population. He argued that this division "separates more exactly the agricultural people from those who derive their livelihood from other occupations." See Guy-Harold Smith, "The Settlement and Present Distribution of Population in Wisconsin: A Geographical Interpretation" (doctoral dissertation, University of Wisconsin, 1927), 174.

Another geographer, Glenn Trewartha, argued that 150 population marked the difference between a hamlet which, before the automobile, was rural in orientation even though it might have had legal and medical services, and a village with urban pretensions. See Glenn T. Trewartha, "The Unincorporated Hamlet: One Element of the American Settlement Fabric," in the *Annals of the Association of American Geographers,* 33 (March, 1943), 32–81. *Seventeenth Census of the United States, 1950: Population, Volume I,* xv–xviii, and *Thirteenth Census of the United States, 1910: Population, Volume I,* 53–55, discuss the problems of comparing urban populations in earlier censuses.

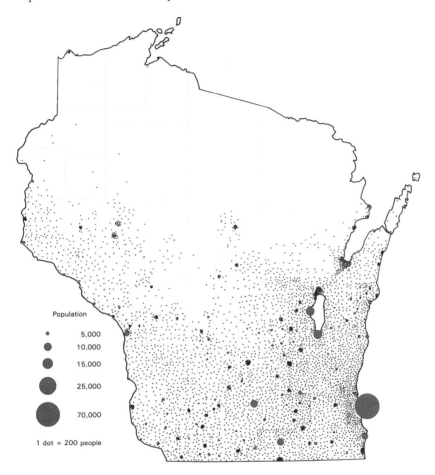

WISCONSIN POPULATION, 1870

rable. The number of such places increased from some eighty-seven to 120 between the 1880 and 1890 censuses. Meanwhile, the rural component of the census, which included communities of under 2,500 population, fell from 75.9 per cent of the total population to 66.8 per cent. This persistence of the village is part of the urbanizing process, despite a steady loss of their numbers as these communities passed the 2,500 threshold of urban status. About one in nine of Wisconsin's rural population in 1880 lived

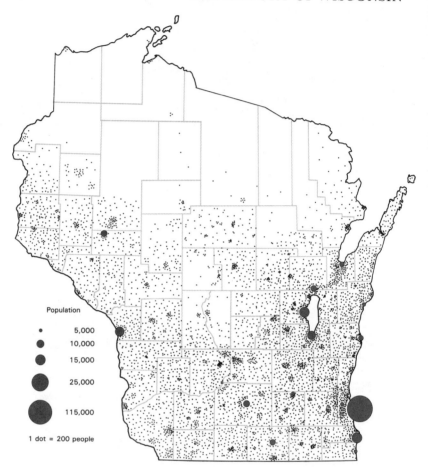

WISCONSIN POPULATION, 1880

in a village of over 500 but less than 2,500 population; one in eight by 1890.

All of this suggests a considerable movement of people. The movement into the cities was apparent already in the 1870's, even though rural Wisconsin received nearly three-fifths (57.8 per cent) of the total increase during the decade. In 1877, the *Christian Statesman,* published in Milwaukee, was urging farm boys to stay home and not come to the city. This became a

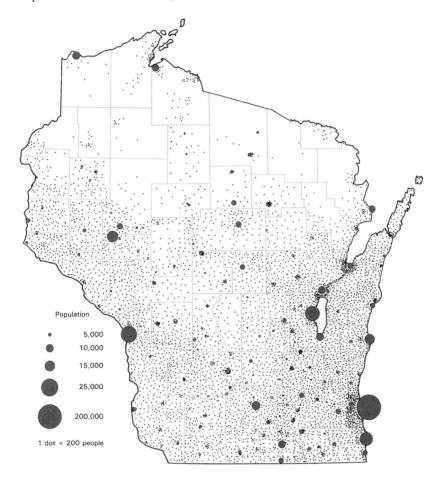

Population

●     5,000

●    10,000

●    15,000

●    25,000

●   200,000

1 dot = 200 people

WISCONSIN POPULATION, 1890

familiar theme as the expansive 1880's brought 65 per cent of the decade's population increase into urban Wisconsin. This trend, of course, continued. The presumption is that the higher birth rate in rural areas, both here and in Europe, fueled the growing movement towards urban America.[20]

---

[20] *Christian Statesman,* November 29, 1877; Charles N. Glaab and A. Theodore Brown, *A History of Urban America* (New York, 1967), 135.

We have noticed that by 1870 nearly 100,000 Wisconsin-born had moved elsewhere, and by 1890 about 300,000 still living had left, nearly 80 per cent of them to places west of the Mississippi River. There is no way in the published census to trace those born in other states or foreign countries who lived in Wisconsin, for no matter how long, and subsequently moved on. Now we get on to shaky ground. One way to check the geographic mobility of population as individuals or family units is through the federal manuscript censuses for 1850 through 1880, which have been available since 1918 in state depositories. The computer has made such projects feasible.[21]

The historian Merle Curti, in one of the pioneering studies combining this manuscript information with primitive computers, selected Trempealeau County because of a wealth of complementary records and because it had undergone an extended pioneering period in Wisconsin's western uplands. The main objective of his study was to test the theory of Frederick

[21] Carmen R. Delle Donne, *Federal Census Schedules, 1850–1880: Primary Sources for Historical Research,* National Archives and Records Service, General Services Administration, Reference Information Paper, no. 67 (Washington, 1973), 12. The manuscript census for 1890 was lost in a fire. The manuscript census identifies each household by the name of the family head and lists each member, citing age, birthplace, and sex.

URBAN POPULATION

| | 1850 | 1860 | 1870 | | 1880 | | 1890 | | 1900 | |
|---|---|---|---|---|---|---|---|---|---|---|
| | % Urban | % Urban | % Urban | Less Metro* | % Urban | Less Metro* | % Urban | Less Metro* | % Urban | Less Metro* |
| United States | 15.3 | 19.8 | 25.7 | N.A. | 28.2 | N.A. | 35.1 | N.A. | 39.7 | N.A. |
| Illinois | 7.6 | 14.3 | 23.5 | 11.7 | 30.6 | 14.2 | 44.9 | 16.2 | 54.3 | 19.0 |
| Michigan | 7.3 | 13.3 | 20.1 | 13.4 | 24.8 | 17.7 | 34.9 | 25.1 | 39.3 | 27.5 |
| Wisconsin | 9.4 | 14.4 | 19.6 | 12.9 | 24.1 | 15.3 | 33.2 | 21.1 | 38.2 | 24.4 |
| Minnesota | N.A. | 9.4 | 16.1 | N.A. | 19.1 | 7.7 | 33.8 | 11.1 | 34.1 | 10.2 |
| Iowa | 5.1 | 8.9 | 13.1 | — | 15.2 | — | 21.2 | 18.6 | 25.6 | 22.9 |

*Cities with 50,000 or more population (Milwaukee, Detroit, Grand Rapids, Chicago, Des Moines, Minneapolis-St. Paul, Duluth).

SOURCE: *Seventeenth Census of the United States, 1950: Population, Volume I, Part 1,* pp. 5, 19–20; *Part 13,* pp. 7, 9–11; *Part 15,* p. 68; *Part 22,* pp. 9, 11–12; *Part 23,* pp. 9, 11; *Part 49,* pp. 7, 9–10.

Jackson Turner that the frontier experience was central to the development of our democratic traditions. The figures developed on the geographic mobility of the Trempealeau County population indicated that an astonishing 75 per cent of business and professional people—mostly townsmen—who were present in 1870 were missing from the 1880 manuscript census. This was higher than the 67 per cent that dropped out between 1860 and 1870, presumably because of the depression of the seventies and their perception of limited opportunities. Farm operators were more persistent in the seventies than they had been earlier; however, 60 per cent of those present in 1870 were not on the 1880 census rolls. In general, non-English-speaking foreign-born farmers were more apt to leave than the others, and newcomers appearing in only one census were somewhat more mobile. This was doubtless a reflection of the large Norwegian population of the county, which was more mobile than the Germans and Poles, having generally settled on poorer land and smaller holdings.[22]

There have been other, less ambitious studies of Wisconsin geographic mobility. One, a study of five villages in Grant County, a part of the old Lead Region, showed that 56 per cent of the households reported in 1880 did not appear in the 1885 state census rolls. Seventy-eight per cent of them were missing from the 1895 state census. These persistence rates varied from village to village, but not in any direct relationship to modest growth or relative stagnation of population. In another study of

[22] Merle Curti, *The Making of an American Community: A Case Study of Democracy in a Frontier Community* (Stanford, 1959), 1–11, 65–77, Table 5, 70–71, 94–97.

| | NUMBER OF URBAN PLACES (2500+) | | | | | |
| | 1850 | 1860 | 1870 | 1880 | 1890 | 1900 |
| --- | --- | --- | --- | --- | --- | --- |
| Illinois | 9 | 23 | 47 | 69 | 79 | 114 |
| Michigan | 4 | 13 | 27 | 44 | 63 | 71 |
| Wisconsin | 3 | 15 | 27 | 34 | 48 | 61 |
| Minnesota | 0 | 3 | 11 | 14 | 23 | 37 |
| Iowa | 3 | 9 | 22 | 34 | 46 | 70 |

SOURCE: *Seventeenth Census of the United States, 1950: Population, Volume I, Part 13*, p. 7; *Part 15*, p. 6; *Part 22*, p. 9; *Part 23*, p. 9; *Part 49*, p. 7.

farm population in two Dane County towns (townships), one of prime land in the southeast (Dunkirk), and the other in the hilly southwest (Blue Mounds), the rate of persistence from 1870 to 1880 was virtually the same: 53 and 52 per cent. The American-born were more apt to move than the Norwegians, who were a large contingent in both towns. Joseph Schafer, writing of his boyhood home, the Town of Castle Rock in Grant County, says that the Bohemians and Norwegians who arrived late in the settlement process there (1860's and 1870's) took land that was left and had a bare living, many working for others who had better land. Many of the newer immigrants left when the rush to Nebraska, western Iowa, and Dakota was in full tide in the 1880's. Others among them managed to acquire better lands sold by Americans and Germans who joined the westward tide. Those Bohemians and Norwegians who remained turned to dairying and prospered. "Thus has the community been reconstructed," Schafer concludes.[23]

Population mobility studies became popular as the topics for graduate dissertations and theses after Merle Curti's pioneering Trempealeau County study. The problem with such studies is answering the question: When families disappeared from the town or county manuscript censuses, where did they go? More sophisticated computers have permitted the development of means to compare available manuscript census reports for the whole country, which ought to make it possible to pick up, by name and other identifying data, those who dropped out of a local data base between 1870 and 1880, for instance. But the results of one such search failed to find 80 per cent of the sample in other locations. The fault could lie in the data or the linkage

---

[23] Peter J. Coleman, "Restless Grant County: Americans on the Move," in *WMH*, 46 (Autumn, 1962), 16–20; James L. Jarvis, "A Study of the Composition and Mobility of the Farm Owners of Dunkirk and Blue Mounds Townships, Dane County, Wisconsin, 1860–1880" (master's thesis, University of Wisconsin, 1966), 8–9, 25. Still another study of Blooming Grove, a rural township on the edge of Madison, found a persistence rate of 60 per cent for farm operators between 1870 and 1880. See Michael P. Conzen, *Frontier Farming in an Urban Shadow: The Influence of Madison's Proximity on the Agricultural Development of Blooming Grove, Wisconsin* (Madison, 1971), 48. Also see Schafer, *Wisconsin Lead Region*, 230–231.

procedure, but the results suggest that the missing families were probably not as mobile as these local studies have suggested. An underlying problem is the imperfections inherent in the methods employed to gather census data a century ago. All of these doubts suggest that local studies of who lived where and who moved on between censuses probably exaggerate mobility somewhat. A common finding in studies limited to small villages was that families disappeared from the manuscript censuses but their names continued to appear in the county histories, often as living in the same village or town.[24]

While these indications of geographic mobility may be faulty and tend to err on the high side, there is ample evidence to assure us that resettlement—young people moving to town or the city, moving from one farm to another within the state, and the accommodation of the foreign immigrant stream—resulted in a great deal of movement. The evidence is in the brief biographies in every county history of the period, in autobiographical accounts, contemporary newspapers, and reports of government officials.

Not only did Wisconsin's population continue to expand after 1870 into areas that were only lightly settled in the Central Plains and Western Uplands and follow the railroads and the lumber industry into the pineries, but there also was a great deal of movement in southern Wisconsin, which had been well settled before the Civil War. The Yankees who pioneered the area proved most readily movable. A prominent feature of Joseph Schafer's studies was to count—in text, extended appendices,

---

[24] Richard Jensen, "History from a Deck of IBM Cards," in *Reviews in American History*, 6 (June, 1978), 229-234. See also John B. Sharpless and Ray M. Shortridge, "Biased Underenumeration in Census Manuscripts," in the *Journal of Urban History*, 1 (August, 1975), 409-439; and the comments of Francis A. Walker, superintendent of the 1870 federal census, on the imperfections of the law covering the census and the performance of many agents, in *Ninth Census of the United States, 1870: Population, Volume I*, ix-xxxiv. The author once had seminar students attempt mobility studies from the manuscript rolls covering the federal censuses of 1850-1880, using Wisconsin villages and hamlets small enough for a hand count. While not done on a computer able to match up names and related data, they did report often losing someone who, by other evidence, seemed still to be there.

and detailed studies of individual townships—the changing balance of American-born and foreign-born family heads from census to census. In the majority of cases, there was a marked increase in the number of foreign-born family heads, which usually peaked with the 1885 state census. They were the buyers. There was a frequent decline of American-born families between 1870 and 1885, before the formation of families by the American-born children of the immigrants tipped the balance again.[25]

Aside from movement to other states from Wisconsin, mostly westward, there was also a movement both of the population within the state as well as from the rural countryside towards the cities and villages. The foreign-born were presumably those most apt to migrate to a location known as a good job market—being less influenced by propinquity or local familiarity. Fond du Lac, which was in the doldrums economically and actually lost 740 of its population between 1870 and 1890, also lost 1,059 foreign-born in that twenty-year interval. Neighboring Oshkosh, which had a vigorous growth during the same years from 12,663 to 22,836, enjoyed an increase from 4,541 to 7,278 of foreign-born. This 60 per cent gain in foreign-born was less than the 80 per cent increase in the general population, but the natural trend was downward for the foreign-born, simply because, even with strong replacement, new blood was the only way to maintain such numbers.[26]

---

[25] For Schafer's findings and supporting evidence, see his "Peopling the Middle West," *WMH*, 21:85–106; "Yankee and Teuton in Wisconsin," *WMH*, 6:142–145; and *Town Studies*, 18–19. In response to a widely circulated questionnaire relative to local settlement and assimilation, a German-born resident of Wilmot, in Kenosha County, noted: "Most all the German immigrants came by and by, first they worked out then they rented farms and then they bought farms, mostly of Americans who went further west. I believe that the most farms are in immigrants hands of this Kenosha County. We find here very seldom that a German sells land he generally buys." See George Kroncke to R. G. Thwaites, March 19, 1889, in the John S. Roeseler Papers.

[26] *Ninth Census of the United States, 1870: Population, Volume I*, 287–295; *Eleventh Census of the United States, 1890: Population, Volume I, Part 1*, pp. 557–558. This is to suggest that any increase in the foreign-born over a twenty-year period required a considerable influx of newcomers. They may well have been, as urban dwellers, as mobile as any other element of the population. In ten of the twenty-five counties lying all or in part south of the Fox-Wisconsin waterway—mostly prime farmland—there occurred a net loss of pop-

The argument that "Milwaukee's early preeminence as a German city probably had more to do with drawing German immigration to this state than any other single factor" has a point. Between 1831 and 1850, over 2 million Europeans came to the United States as immigrants; 47.2 per cent of them were Irish, 28 per cent were from Germany. But as early as 1850, the German-born outnumbered the Irish by nearly three to one in Milwaukee; thirty years later, by more than eight to one. The city's second-largest foreign-born group in 1890, the Poles, were outnumbered six to one by the German-born. German-born were still seven out of ten of the foreign-born, who were two-fifths of the total city population, nearly three in ten of the total population.[27]

The German migration continued into the mid-eighties to flow heavily into the Midwest, the Irish to the Northeast and Middle Atlantic states. By 1890, Wisconsin stood third among the states, after New York and Illinois, in the total number of foreign-born of German origin. The Germans came more directly to Milwaukee than did the Irish and most other immigrants for a variety of reasons. For one thing, they could more readily afford the trip. The early German immigrants, mostly from southwestern provinces and states, were generally small farmers and townsmen who had property. Changes in the German economy, which was being industrialized, and difficulties in agriculture—particularly

---

ulation between 1870 and 1890. Five more of these counties would have shown similar losses had they not had growing urban centers that more than offset the rural losses. The ten counties were: Columbia, Dodge, Grant, Green, Fond du Lac, Iowa, Jefferson, Lafayette, Ozaukee, and Washington. The five that lost rural population that was more than offset by urban growth were Manitowoc, Racine, Sheboygan, Waukesha, and Winnebago. In Dane and Rock counties the growth of population in villages of 500 to 2,499 indicated an actual loss of the truly rural population. Glaab and Brown, *History of Urban America,* 42–44, note that this loss of rural population was common to the Midwest.

[27] Ellis B. Usher, *Wisconsin: Its Story and Biography, 1848–1913* (8 vols., Chicago, 1914), 1:52–53; Bernard, *Melting Pot and the Altar,* Tables 1.1 and 1.2, pp. 5–9; Clifford L. Lord and Elizabeth H. Lord, *Historical Atlas of the United States* (New York, 1944; revised, 1953), Appendix III, p. 207; Bayrd Still, *Milwaukee: The History of a City* (Madison, 1948; reprinted, 1965), 574–575. Poles were doubtless undercounted in the nineteenth century.

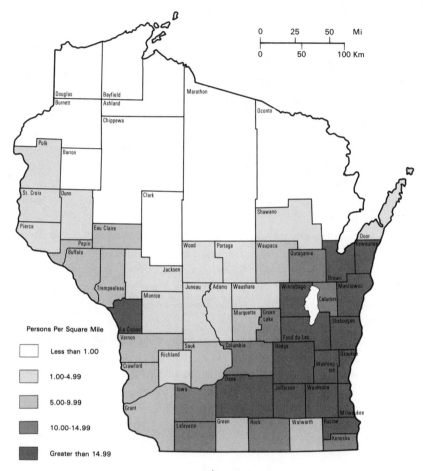

FOREIGN-BORN POPULATION, 1870

prevalent diseases of grapes and potatoes—drove them to sell out
rather than face an uncertain future. Fortunately, German farmland and other real estate commanded good prices. Also, the
Germans had a long tradition of emigration as the answer to
population pressures and economic dislocations.[28]

[28] *Eleventh Census of the United States, 1890: Statistical Atlas of the United States,* 21–22; Mack
Walker, *Germany and the Emigration, 1815–1885* (Cambridge, 1964), chaps. 2, 3, 4; Kollmann and Marschalck, "German Emigration to the United States," *Perspectives in American History,* 7:499–554; Hansen, "Revolutions of 1848 and German Emigration," *Journal
of Economic and Business History,* 2:630–658.

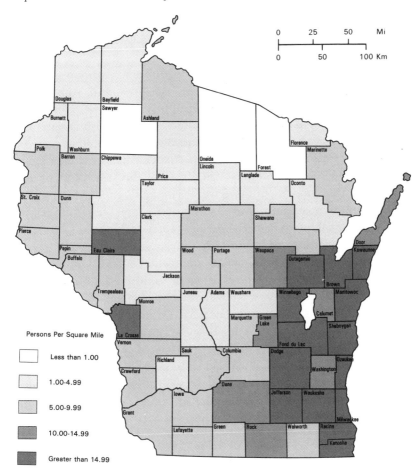

FOREIGN-BORN POPULATION, 1890

Why Wisconsin? Because Wisconsin was where the American frontier of open farmland was opening after the mid-1830's. Milwaukee and Wisconsin had a good press in Germany. Some fifty titles had been published in Germany about the United States by mid-century, in many of which Wisconsin was particularly noted. Some were travelers' accounts, but others were directed at prospective emigrants. Wisconsin offered available government land and physical features and a climate similar to much of Germany; it had a most liberal state constitution which accorded early political equality to foreign immigrants; and it had a limitation upon state debt. Also, Milwaukee was accessible by sail and steam.[29]

As early as 1844, Milwaukee acquired a German-speaking Catholic bishop, John Martin Henni of Switzerland, who in 1875 became the first Germanic archbishop in America. Henni and Father Martin Kundig attracted other clergy and financial support from Austria, Switzerland, and Bavaria, as well as a strong flow of immigrants. Most of the early German immigration to Milwaukee came from Rhenish Prussia, Bavaria, Baden, and Saxony; the majority of these were Roman Catholic.[30]

German immigration to the United States came in waves, reaching peak periods in 1845–1855, 1865–1874, and 1880–1884, and then trailing off after 1890. Germans constituted from a quarter to a third of European emigration to the United States from 1830 to 1890. Many of them continued to come from western and southwestern Germany, but by the 1870's a larger share originated from northeastern Germany: East and West Prussia, Pomerania, Posen, Brandenburg, and Mecklenburg. East Germany suffered a similar crisis of overpopulation and threatened pauperism which had prompted small holders to move abroad from western Germany a generation before. Wisconsin received a share of the landless by subsidized emigration and aid from relatives who had made the break earlier. But in general

[29] Walker, *Germany and the Emigration,* chap. 2. Everest, "How Wisconsin Came by Its Large German Element," *Wis. Hist. Colls.,* 12:312–322, notes that one German author suggested in 1849 that people would soon see Bremen steamers in Milwaukee harbor.

[30] Peter Leo Johnson, *Crosier on the Frontier: A Life of John Martin Henni, Archbishop of Milwaukee* (Madison, 1959), 77–82; *DWB;* J. H. A. Lacher, "The German Element in Wisconsin," in Milo M. Quaife, *Wisconsin: Its History and Its People, 1634–1924* (4 vols., Chicago, 1924), 2:160–162; Kathleen N. Conzen, *Immigrant Milwaukee, 1836–1860: Accommodation and Community in a Frontier City* (Cambridge, 1976), 29. Gordon Craig notes in *The Germans* (New York, 1982), 92–93, that Catholic Germans in Europe were conscious of the fact that they were a religious minority, viewed with mistrust by their Protestant countrymen. After Napoleon, it was clear that the latter intended to exclude Catholic Austria from any German union. Prussia achieved this end in 1866 at the Battle of Sadowa.

Wisconsin seems to have received relatively fewer of the pauper agrarian class or the industrial proletariat. It simply cost more to get here.[31]

Generalizations about Wisconsin's German population are all very well, but the decision to emigrate and where to go was as individual as were the families or single persons who made the break. The starting points were equally various, and one finds exceptions to any general statement very readily in the voluminous literature, the biographical sketches, and the autobiographical material available. Nonetheless, some generalizations are necessary. One is that most Germans came for economic reasons. Political refugees from the Revolution of 1848, or those who did not wish to abide the ascendancy of the Prussian Hohenzollerns in 1871, were a minor fraction of Wisconsin's Germans. Compulsory military service, particularly the Prussian variety which translated the traditional militia obligation into three years' service in the standing army, probably sent more young men and families abroad than did political convictions. But there was a natural tendency to identify with the most popular reason: to enjoy the political freedom of the United States.[32]

Economic forces, of course, worked from both directions: as reasons to leave and as reasons to head for Wisconsin. Indeed, one authority is of the opinion that economic cycles in the United States were somewhat more compelling than conditions in Germany. Emigration from Germany certainly dropped off sharply

---

[31] Richard Fapso and Richard Zeitlin, " 'My Children Will Have the Real Benefit,' " typewritten research report, November, 1975, pp. 1-17, research files, Old World Wisconsin; David Ward, *Cities and Immigrants: A Geography of Change in Nineteenth-Century America* (New York, 1971), 53; Kollmann and Marschalck, "German Emigration to the United States," *Perspectives in American History,* 7:518-535; Ira J. Kligora, "The German Element in Wisconsin, 1840-1880" (master's thesis, University of Wisconsin, 1937), 4-18; Roger D. Simon, *The City-Building Process: Housing and Services in New Milwaukee Neighborhoods, 1880-1910* (*Transactions of the American Philosophical Society,* vol. 68, pt. 5, Philadelphia, 1978), 18; Kate Everest Levi, "Geographical Origin of German Immigration to Wisconsin," in *Wis. Hist. Colls.,* 14:352 ff.

[32] Koppel S. Pinson, *Modern Germany: Its History and Civilization* (New York, 1966 ed.), 123-131; Walker, *Germany and the Emigration,* chaps. 6 and 7.

in the depression years following 1873 and 1893 and during the recessions in the 1880's. Whatever the economic push from Germany, prospective immigrants had an eye on the economy here as well. German farmers, particularly those in northern and eastern Germany, were also well aware of where the flood of cheap grain was coming from that so depressed their prices.[33]

German immigration offered a greater variety of classes and origins than most major ethnic groups that were in the state before the end of the century. They came from both urban and rural backgrounds. Nor were the Germans a homogeneous people with respect to ethnic origins and especially religious affiliations. And even rural immigration from Germany often included people who worked part of the year at other trades which took them to European cities. Joseph Schafer noted that many German farmers in the Wisconsin lead region had useful trades they could turn to—and some not so useful, such as roof tiling and thatching. Certainly many Germans appeared in Milwaukee and other Wisconsin cities with an urban skill or for the purpose of setting up in business. [34]

Apart from Milwaukee County, which had one-quarter of the state's German-born population in 1890, this ethnic group was still by all odds the largest in the remainder of the state. According to the 1895 Wisconsin state census, subtracting Milwaukee County's 69,606 German-born from the state total of 268,469 left 198,863 "out-state," a term popularly understood at the time. Scandinavians, meaning Norwegians and Swedes in this census, numbered 106,468, and only 2,437 of them lived in Milwaukee County. In other words, the second-largest foreign-born group was still outnumbered almost two to one by the

[33] Walker, *Germany and the Emigration,* chaps. 6 and 7; United States Bureau of the Census, *Historical Statistics of the United States,* Series C 88–114; Olson, *Ethnic Dimension in American History,* 1:95–97.

[34] Schafer, *Wisconsin Lead Region,* 210–213; Theodore A. Boerner to R. G. Thwaites, August 30, 1888, in the Roeseler Papers; Conzen, *Immigrant Milwaukee,* 18, 31–33; Gerd Korman, *Industrialization, Immigrants and Americanizers: The View from Milwaukee, 1866–1921* (Madison, 1967), chap. 2; Carlton C. Qualey, "Immigration, Emigration, Migration," in O. Fritiof Ander, ed., *In the Trek of the Immigrants: Essays Presented to Carl Wittke* (Rock Island, 1964), 35.

Germans outside Milwaukee County. Twenty-five years earlier, in 1870, they were outnumbered three to one. Together, in 1895, the German- and Scandinavian-born comprised over 70 per cent of the 523,877 foreign-born.[35]

But, since the Germans clustered so formidably in the metropolis, were they equally clustered in other urban settings? The answer is that they generally were not. In Dodge County, 21.3 per cent of the population was German-born in 1895; the county's five cities and four incorporated villages together were 17.6 per cent German-born; and the remaining rural population 22.9 per cent. In other counties, selected either because they were more heavily German or had rapidly growing cities to attract them, ratios usually were similar to those found in Dodge County. Sheboygan County had the greatest variation, with the city having 29.6 per cent and the remainder of the county 17.4 per cent German-born. By contrast, Sauk County, traditionally heavily German, had only 6.5 per cent German-born in the only growing urban center, Baraboo, and 17.1 per cent in the remainder of the county. The city of Eau Claire had only 7 per cent German-born while the rest of the geographically small county of the same name had 13.3 per cent. Madison, with 7.3 per cent German-born, had less than the rest of Dane County, 8.2 per cent. In predominately rural counties, the Germans did often cluster in the small communities that served the countryside, but only where they held the countryside.[36]

Germans, like other continental Europeans, tended to cluster in America according to identifiable preferences. Such preferences started with relatives, friends, neighbors—something iden-

---

[35] *Wisconsin State Census,* 1895, Part 1, pp. 60–109. See also Walter H. Ebling, "Wisconsin Territorial and State Censuses," in the *Transactions of the Wisconsin Academy of Sciences, Arts and Letters,* 55 (1966), 47–57. The 1870 figures for the state, excluding Milwaukee County, were 133,295 German-born to 47,421 Scandinavian-born who were overwhelmingly Norwegian (*Ninth Census of the United States, 1870: Population, Volume I, Social Statistics,* 376–377).

[36] *Wisconsin State Census,* 1895, Part 1, pp. 60–120. In contrast to Wisconsin, 62 per cent of the foreign-born in the United States in 1890 lived in urban places as defined by the federal census. See John Higham, "Immigration," in C. Vann Woodward, ed., *The Comparative Approach to American History* (New York, 1968), 101.

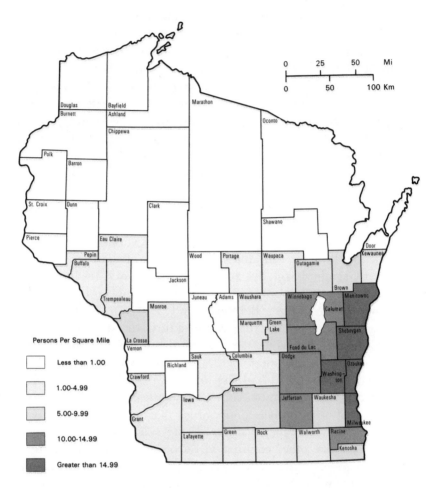

GERMAN-BORN IN WISCONSIN, 1870

tifiable as home. Or, being more venturesome, it might be just
fellow provincials who shared the dialect and the same church.
Germans did not ordinarily think of themselves as fellow nation-
als until exposed to the notion here. A Rhinelander had little use
for a Prussian for a variety of reasons, prominent among them
that the Prussian was assumed to be a Lutheran and from a

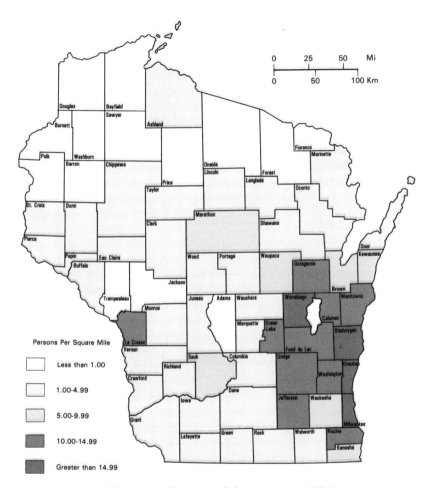

GERMAN-BORN IN WISCONSIN, 1890

militarily aggressive state. Once here, they all found themselves identified as Germans by the wider society, which helped to impress upon them a more generalized notion of who was a compatriot. The most important distinction they invariably made was whether a fellow German was a Catholic, a Lutheran, another kind of Protestant, or (most dangerous of all) an anti-cleric. We do well to remember that Americans settled in similar patterns.[37]

The adaptability of the German immigrants was noticed by Joseph Schafer, who said that they were as ready to clan as anyone. However, he used the Town of Burnett in Dodge County, a Yankee stronghold still in 1870, to illustrate how the town was gradually infiltrated by a Germanic majority. Through their children, the Germans maintained the social and political organizations that they found already in place, to the point that all concerned considered themselves part of the Yankee heritage. ("This would be farcical were it not for its historical background," concluded Schafer.) The second generation of Germans had a tendency to join the surrounding culture. Schooling, the economic realities, and the fascination of American politics had their way. The great advantage of the German-American was that he or she seldom felt like a real stranger anywhere in Wisconsin. To a lesser degree, the same applied to other groups of European origin in the state.[38]

As an interesting sidelight, it is the potential of the computer for isolating the preferences of latter-nineteenth-century voters, and their motivations, that promises recovery of much of the detail about how the German-born and others identified themselves after they became voters. Such studies go well beyond the

[37] Pinson, *Modern Germany,* chap. 9; Olson, *Ethnic Dimension in American History,* 1:93–108. George Kroncke of Kenosha County identified himself as Hanoverian and Protestant and spoke of "so called Catholic Settlements" made up of people mostly of "the south most part of German" who kept to themselves, "inter-marry very seldom and are mostly democrats." George Kroncke to R. G. Thwaites, March 19, 1889, in the Roeseler Papers. Also see Levi, "Geographical Origin of German Immigration," *Wis. Hist. Colls.,* 14:351–352; Allan G. Bogue, *From Prairie to Corn Belt: Farming on the Illinois and Iowa Prairies in the Nineteenth Century* (Chicago, 1963), 16; and Allan G. Bogue, "Social Theory and the Pioneer," in Allan G. Bogue, Thomas D. Phillips, and James E. Wright, eds., *The West of the American People* (Itasca, Illinois, 1970), 531–536.

[38] Schafer, *Winnebago-Horicon Basin,* 230–232. Germans were surprised by the readiness of the state to educate their children with the general tax. Despite their tradition of parochial education, the public schools were a constant temptation. Juliane Dittrich–Jacobi "German Immigrant Families and Schools for Their Children," typewritten research report (n.d.), 8, in History of Wisconsin Project files.

literary allusions of earlier works about who went where. The common bonds were ethnicity, defined differently than it had been in Europe, and particularly religious affiliation—ideas not always within the grasp of the generation that understands computers.[39]

One might reasonably object to lumping Norwegians, Swedes, and Danes together as Scandinavians. Discussing them separately does present less difficulty than separating Germans by thirty-nine states and provinces whose differences were meaningful to them. The saving grace for the Germans was their variety. Even after they discovered a common identity once here— brought about by unaccustomed propinquity with one another, the obtuseness of their non-German neighbors, and the creation of Germany as a nation in 1871—they remained firmly divided along religious lines which defined their politics and the degree to which they assimilated with one another. The Scandinavians had no such wide divisions as Catholic versus Lutheran and other Protestant sects; but they did have a talent for devising them, based upon intricate distinctions within the Lutheran faith. Both Germans and Scandinavians brought their own notions and prejudices based upon social class, which also underwent a sea change when transferred to America.[40]

Norwegians always had the edge among Wisconsin's Scandinavian citizens. They were five of every six in the 1870 census, and still two-thirds twenty years later. The Swedes came on strongly during the eighties, more than double the Danish immigration of that decade, and by 1890 they outnumbered the Danes by three to two. The reasons for Scandinavian emigration were

[39] See Richard J. Jensen, *The Winning of the Midwest: Social and Political Conflict, 1888–1896* (Chicago, 1971); Paul Kleppner, *The Cross of Culture: A Social Analysis of Midwestern Politics, 1850–1900* (New York, 1970); and Roger E. Wyman, "Voting Behavior in the Progressive Era: Wisconsin As a Case Study" (doctoral dissertation, University of Wisconsin, 1970), the most useful of the three.

[40] Pinson, *Modern Germany*, 3–6, 53; Olson, *Ethnic Dimension in American History*, 1:116–119; Sydney E. Ahlstrom, *A Religious History of the American People* (New Haven, 1972; Image Books edition, 2 vols., New York, 1975), 2:220–222.

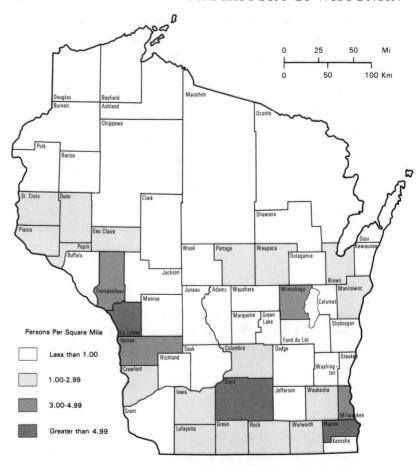

SCANDINAVIAN-BORN IN WISCONSIN, 1870

similar to those which inspired the Germans. The Norwegians
felt the pressure earliest and most acutely as they experienced a
sharp increase in their population in the early nineteenth century. They were a nation of farmers in a land of which only an
inflexible 4 per cent was arable. The landholding system was
such that there were bound to be many losers who were landless
or about to become so. There were political and religious grievances as well. But there was not a dramatic rush to America
until the end of our Civil War, although in 1860 there were
24,265 Scandinavian-born in Wisconsin. Norwegians comprised

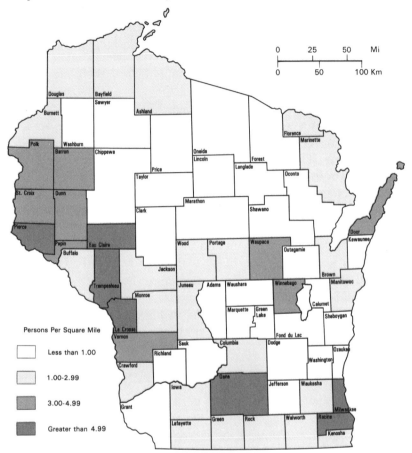

SCANDINAVIAN-BORN IN WISCONSIN, 1890

21,442 of that number—just about half of all the Norwegians in the United States.[41]

[41] Guy-Harold Smith, "Notes on the Distribution of the Foreign-Born Scandinavians in Wisconsin in 1905," in *WMH*, 14 (June, 1931), 419–436; Theodore C. Blegen, *Norwegian Migration to America, 1825–1860* (Northfield, 1931; reprinted, New York, 1969); Carlton C. Qualey, *Norwegian Settlement in the United States* (Northfield, 1938); and Ingrid Semmingsen, *Norway to America: A History of the Migration,* trans. Einar Haugen (Minneapolis, 1978), are the standard accounts. See also Philip Taylor, *The Distant Magnet: European Emigration to the U.S.A.* (New York, 1971); Joseph Dorfman, *Thorstein Veblen and His America* (New York, 1934), 3–7; and Richard J. Fapso, *Norwegians in Wisconsin* (Madison, 1977).

The Norwegian emigration began in earnest as Wisconsin's frontier was disappearing into the Western Uplands and the retreating pineries of the upper St. Croix Valley. That is where they went in numbers. Those who came before 1860 had established a first base in Illinois, where they were dissatisfied, and then followed the Rock River Valley into Wisconsin. Dane County became a base and from there colonies were settled westward into Vernon County, thence northward into the Western Uplands. The momentum carried them on to the west. Minnesota about reversed the proportions of Germans to Scandinavians found in Wisconsin; in effect, the latter leapfrogged the earlier German possession of better land. Joseph Schafer said that after the early settlements in Dane County the Norwegians were latecomers and took the inferior land that was left. This was a reflection of what they could afford. They also wanted to be near American settlements where they could find work and services.[42]

The Swedes, who began coming in large numbers later than the Norwegians and Danes, were more concentrated in or near the Cutover. Sixty-two per cent of them, by 1890, were located in twelve northern counties. The main body was in a half circle of eight northwestern counties from St. Croix County to Price County. Burnett County was 35 per cent Swedish-born.[43]

The Danes, 13,885 of them by 1890, had their largest and longest-standing colony in the city of Racine. They were more numerous than Swedes or Norwegians in Brown, Calumet, Green Lake, Kenosha, Langlade, Marquette, Oconto, Outagamie, Racine, Waukesha, Waushara, and Winnebago counties. There was also a colony in Dane County. The common pattern was that the Danes clustered more in eastern counties while the Swedes and Norwegians were found in greater numbers in central and western Wisconsin.[44]

[42] Smith, "Distribution of Foreign-Born Scandinavians in Wisconsin," *WMH*, 14:421–432; Schafer, *Wisconsin Lead Region*, 224–228.

[43] Taylor, *The Distant Magnet*, 27–32; *Eleventh Census of the United States, 1890: Population, Volume I, Part 1*, pp. 667–668.

[44] *Eleventh Census of the United States, 1890: Population, Volume I, Part 1*, pp. 667–668; Thomas P. Christensen, "Danish Settlement in Wisconsin," in *WMH*, 12 (September,

After the Germans and Scandinavians, who comprised about 70 per cent of the foreign-born of 1890, English-speaking immigrants were another 20 per cent. Three groups, roughly equal in size, made up these less noticeable foreigners: Irish, British, and Canadians. Only the latter had been increasing significantly in numbers since the Civil War. The Irish outnumbered the Norwegians in 1870, but by 1890 there were twice as many Norwegian-born. Most of the Irish-born reached Wisconsin in stages, either by way of Canada or the eastern United States. Schafer guessed that on average the Irish-born had been in America some seven years or more before making it to Milwaukee. (He was referring to those who pioneered as farmers, whom he found as ready to move as were the Yankees.) Later arrivals, attracted by industrial and construction jobs, usually came more directly, as transportation cheapened and improved. Many Irish started at the bottom for want of needed skills and funds. The 1895 state census found them very widely dispersed throughout the state. Many were farmers or farm workers, but they were found in numbers in the cities, particularly the rapidly growing ones: Ashland, Superior, Eau Claire, Madison, Appleton, and Milwaukee of course, although oddly enough less so in La Crosse and Oshkosh. The principal thing that set the Irish apart was religion, but in a population that was so heavily Catholic this was not a great disadvantage. The Irish were clustered in particular wards in the cities, more so usually than the Germans. A historian of pioneer Milwaukee remarked: "Despite the greater stability of the Irish neighborhoods, much of the sense of grass roots community action that emerges from the German experience seems absent."[45]

The other English-speaking groups from Great Britain and

---

1928), 19–40; Frederick Hale, *Danes in Wisconsin* (Madison, 1981). An old vaudeville routine had it thus: "Where was Racine ten years ago?" "In Denmark."

[45] *Eleventh Census of the United States, 1890: Population, Volume I, Part 1,* pp. 667–668; Schafer, *Winnebago-Horicon Basin,* 144–145; *Wisconsin State Census,* 1895, pp. 60–111; Conzen, *Immigrant Milwaukee,* 170–171. The Irish differed from continental European Catholics in that English was their common language and they had not widely supported parochial schools in Ireland.

British America were well-dispersed, and they readily disappeared into the general Yankee economic and social background,
which was assumed as the norm. They appeared in all walks of
life, from banker-railroad tycoon Alexander Mitchell on down
the economic scale. They were owners, managers, and foremen
in many of Milwaukee's large enterprises. French Canadians
were a minority of those from British America. By 1890, they
could readily be found in the lumber centers. There were seven
counties, aside from Milwaukee, that reported over one thousand
from Canada and Newfoundland, ranging downward from Chippewa County with 2,742, to Marinette, Ashland, Douglas, Eau
Claire, Oconto, and St. Croix counties. These were not all
French Canadians, but the numbers and their locations do suggest their presence in the lumber towns.[46]

Smaller national groups such as the Dutch, Belgians, and
Swiss were established in Wisconsin long before 1870. They
maintained or modestly increased the number of European-born
among them into the next century. The largest group, the Swiss,
numbered just over 7,000 Swiss-born in 1890, with their greatest
concentration around New Glarus in Green County. Most Wisconsin Swiss were from German-speaking cantons and were quite
generally distributed, aside from the Green County concentration. Almost half of the Hollanders were concentrated in communities around the city of Green Bay and rural townships in
Sheboygan County nearby. They were somewhat less widely
distributed than the Swiss. The Belgians centered in the adjacent
counties of Brown, Kewaunee, and Door.[47]

Two Central European peoples who came in increasing numbers after 1870 were the Poles and the Bohemians. Both are
difficult to trace in the federal and state censuses because they
lacked national sovereignty at the time. Poland lost its identity as
a nation in 1795 when it was partitioned among Russia, Prussia,

[46] Korman, *Industrialization, Immigrants and Americanizers,* 68; *Eleventh Census of the United
States, 1890: Population, Volume I, Part 1,* pp. 667–668.

[47] *Eleventh Census of the United States, 1890: Population, Volume I, Part 1,* pp. 667–668. The
volume in *The History of Wisconsin* preceding this one, Richard N. Current's *The Civil War
Era, 1848–1873* (Madison, 1976), 418–425, has maps displaying the distribution in 1870
of native-born people from eastern states, of German-born, English- and Welsh-born,
Irish-born, Swedish- and Norwegian-born, Danish-born, Dutch-born, and Swiss-born.

and Austria. Bohemia (the Czech portion of Czechoslovakia) was part of Austria until after World War I. Most of Wisconsin's Poles came from the Prussian provinces of Posen and Pomerania and were counted as part of the German immigration, as were Poles from Silesia and West Prussia. Poles on the land suffered similar attrition to that imposed on eastern Germans. In the early seventies, the Prussian chancellor, Otto von Bismarck, began a determined campaign to Germanize the Poles. This included efforts to weaken the influence of the Catholic church and to encourage the colonization of German farmers among them. Many middle-class Poles were thus bilingual and Prussianized.[48]

The Poles were a minor presence in Wisconsin until after 1880, but their earlier presence is masked by their inclusion in the Prussian and Austrian immigration. The 1890 census counted only 17,660 Poles in Wisconsin and 31,789 ten years later. A Polish authority claimed that a more reasonable figure would be 200,000 in 1900, one-fourth of them in Milwaukee, centered on the city's south side. Another long-established colony was located in Portage County around Stevens Point. Other distinctly Polish settlements were located around and in Berlin, Menasha, Manitowoc, Beaver Dam, La Crosse, and Independence, the last a village in Trempealeau County. The 1890 census, though grossly undercounting the Poles, demonstrates that they were widely distributed, despite the clusters indicated above. Although the huge colony in Milwaukee conformed to the popular notion of the so-called "New Immigration" as an industrial and urban proletariat, about a third of Wisconsin's Poles were farmers.[49]

The Bohemians arrived in numbers earlier than the Poles.

[48] Olson, *Ethnic Dimension in American History,* 2:230–249; Richard Zeitlin, "White Eagles in the North Woods: Polish Immigration to Rural Wisconsin, 1857–1900," in the *Polish Review,* 25 (no. 1, 1980), 69–92; Victor Greene, *For God and Country: The Rise of Polish and Lithuanian Ethnic Consciousness in America, 1860–1910* (Madison, 1975), chaps. 1 and 2.

[49] *Eleventh Census of the United States, 1890: Population, Volume I, Part 1,* pp. 667–668; John W. S. Tomkiewicz, "Polanders in Wisconsin," *SHSW Proceedings,* 1901, pp. 148–152. Zeitlin, "White Eagles in the North Woods," *Polish Review,* 25:71, notes that in contrast to Wisconsin nearly 90 per cent of the Poles in the United States settled in urban areas.

Similarly lacking a sovereign country, they were counted as Austrians. Before the federal census takers got around to language as a determinant, they counted 11,999 Bohemians in 1890. As with the Poles, this was evidently far short of the mark. The Bohemian settlements in Wisconsin were mostly established before 1860, coming contemporaneously with the German immigration and usually existing in proximity to German settlements. Their settlements were concentrated north from Racine along the lakefront. Racine became a center for the Bohemian presence in America through the person of Karel Jonas, a newspaperman, politician, and early spokesman for Czech-Americans. Kewaunee County also had a large Bohemian colony. Others were across the state in the coulee country of Grant, Vernon, Crawford, and La Crosse counties. Probably a good many of those in western Wisconsin came, as did the Germans, by way of New Orleans. Wisconsin was the first center of rural life for Bohemian-Americans, many of whom proved ready to move on westward.[50]

The results of Wisconsin's heavy immigrant admixture, combined with the relatively light flow of American-born coming in and more Wisconsin-born of American-born parents moving out, may be summarized briefly here. First, Wisconsin became one of the most Catholic of states in the Midwest. Close to half of the huge German group was Catholic, to which one must add most of the Irish, Poles, Bohemians, Swiss, Belgians, and French Canadians. This, of course, had profound implications for Wisconsin's political history as well as for the development of the Catholic church here. Religious affiliation was central to one's political orientation, especially prior to Robert M. La Follette and William Jennings Bryan. This made Wisconsin demography chilling enough for the Republican party—the bastion of Ameri-

[50] J. J. Vlach, "Our Bohemian Population," *SHSW Proceedings*, 1901, pp. 159–162, claimed 50,000 although the 1900 census allowed only 14,000. Very likely Tomkiewicz and Vlach were claiming all American-born descendants of Poles and Bohemians in Wisconsin. See *Eleventh Census of the United States, 1890: Abstract*, 50; Karel D. Bicha, "The Czechs in Wisconsin History," in *WMH*, 53 (Spring, 1970), 194–203; Karel D. Bicha, "Karel Jonas of Racine: 'First Czech in America,' " in *WMH*, 63 (Winter, 1979–1980), 122–140.

can Protestantism until 1896, when Bryan turned the tables. Another inescapable fact was that about 80 per cent of the foreign-born males in 1870 were over twenty-one but only 28.2 per cent of the native-born males were. (Remember that the suffrage franchise extended to any male of twenty-one or over who had filed for citizenship.) In 1880, although the foreign-born were only 30.8 per cent of the total population, foreign-born males were 55.9 per cent of those eligible to vote under Wisconsin's constitution.[51]

This discrepancy is no mystery. Even if Wisconsin attracted more foreign-born as families than as young single adults, there were always many of the latter among them, particularly after the Civil War when it was much easier and cheaper to get here and industrial jobs rather than cheap government land were the lure. As we have noted, Wisconsin was a net loser from 1870 to 1900 through the out-migration of the native-born. For these and other reasons, the foreign-born were a clear majority of the eligible voters, but certainly not of the officeholders nor possibly of those who voted. But suppose they became interested? (They did.)[52]

Negroes and Indians were two small elements of the general population who found less than ready acceptance. This attitude shows up in the federal census, where the numbers vary in an inconsistent manner from one census to the next. The 1880 census has a convenient table giving both "Colored" and "Indians" by counties for 1860, 1870, and 1880. The first thing to note is that the census counted only "Civilized Indians," mean-

---

[51] Jensen, *Winning of the Midwest,* 58–88, 269–308; Kleppner, *Cross of Culture,* 35–37; Wyman, "Voting Behavior in the Progressive Era," chaps. 5 and 7; *Ninth Census of the United States, 1870: Population, Volume II,* 579–648; *Tenth Census of the United States, 1880: Population, Volume I,* 642–643. The arithmetic is rather astonishing. There were 676,949 white males in Wisconsin counted in the 1880 census: 457,000 American-born and 219,949 foreign-born. But only 149,463 of the American-born were twenty-one or older; 189,469 of the foreign-born were in that age group.

[52] Conzen, *Frontier Farming in an Urban Shadow,* 39–42; Walter L. Slocum, "Ethnic Stocks as Cultural Types in Rural Wisconsin: A Study of Differential Native American, German and Norwegian Influence on Certain Aspects of Man-Land Adjustment in Rural Localities" (doctoral dissertation, University of Wisconsin, 1940).

ing those living among the general population who were generally recognized as Indians; it did not include Indians on reservations. The number of Indians counted under this rubric increased from 1,206 in 1870 to 3,161 in 1880, and to 3,835 ten years later. The number enumerated by Wisconsin's two Indian agencies of those in reservation status declined in those censuses from an estimated 10,115 in 1870 to 7,637 in 1880 to 6,095 in 1890, making a decline during the twenty-year period (counting both categories) from 11,521 to 9,930.[53]

Lest it be thought that Wisconsin's Indian population was running counter to the popular belief of the time that they were a dying race, the 1,955 increase of "civilized" Indians between 1870 and 1880 was partly a result of the Winnebago determination to remain in Wisconsin. Also, as Wisconsin's white population moved northward, bringing the amenities of civil government with them, census takers evidently discovered more formerly uncounted Indians, like the Winnebago, who were without reservation status and not subject to the bounty of the Federal Indian Bureau. For example, in 1880 Bayfield County discovered 252 Indians where only two had been counted in 1870; Burnett County, 266 where eleven had been before; and so on. Many non-reservation Indians did not seek contact with the Indian agencies nor did many citizens of settled habits, with part Indian blood, hasten to proclaim the fact, given the attitudes of the wider society.[54]

[53] United States Bureau of the Census, *Historical Statistics of the United States,* Series A 59–70; Alice E. Smith, *The History of Wisconsin. Volume I: From Exploration to Statehood* (Madison, 1973), chap. 5; Current, *Civil War Era,* 149–155; *Tenth Census of the United States, 1880: Population, Volume I,* 414–415; *Eleventh Census of the United States, 1890: Population, Volume I, Part 1,* pp. 435–436, 450; *Eleventh Census of the United States, 1890: Report on Indians Taxed and Indians Not Taxed in the United States (Except Alaska), Volume X,* 21–28. "Negro" was the common term of the time and is therefore employed here. The problem with "Native American" is the confusion with the common use of "native" to refer to American-born.

[54] Francis A. Walker, "Report for 1872," in Wilcomb E. Washburn, comp., *The American Indian and the United States: A Documentary History* (4 vols., New York, 1973), 1:176–190; Nancy O. Lurie, "The Winnebago Indians: A Study in Cultural Change" (doctoral dissertation, Northwestern University, 1952), 167–169; R. G. Thwaites, "The Wisconsin Winnebagoes," *Wis. Hist. Colls.,* 12:399–433; *Eleventh Census of the United*

Between 1870 and 1880 in Calumet and Brown counties, where the New York Indians farmed, there was a considerable drop recorded in their population, offset by a tripling of the Negro population. Negroes were not that common as immigrants into Wisconsin then; certainly not to Calumet County. The answer must be that many enumerators considered Negroes and Indians interchangeable. The numbers reversed again in 1890— more "Civilized Indians" and fewer "Colored." Wisconsin's Negro population outside these special areas was a tiny minority, fairly constant in numbers, mostly urban, and also highly mobile—being constant in numbers only. Indians and Negroes are dealt with at more length in Chapter 9 because of their status as special minorities, considered and treated as outsiders by the general society that surrounded them.[55]

---

*States, 1890: Population, Volume I, Part 1,* p. 450. The federal agencies involved in counting Indians had difficulties classifying "civilized Indians," using terms such as: outside of tribal relationships, non-reservation, self-sustaining, or Indians taxed. See the *Eleventh Census of the United States, 1890: Report on Indians Taxed and Indians Not Taxed in the United States (Except Alaska), Volume X,* 21–28.

[55] John O. Holzhueter, "Negro Admixture Among the Brotherton, Stockbridge, and Oneida Indians of Wisconsin" (1966), unpublished research paper in the SHSW, 16, notes: "Even after casual scrutiny, the census emerges as an unreliable source for studying admixture." Also see the *Eleventh Census of the United States, 1890: Population, Volume I, Part 1,* pp. 435–436.

# 7

# Communities

## GEOGRAPHIC AND CORPORATE

IN his oft-quoted book *Democracy in America,* Alexis de Tocqueville observed: "Among the laws that rule human societies there is one which seems to be more precise and clear than all others. If men are to remain civilized or to become so, the art of associating together must grow and improve in the same ratio in which the equality of conditions is increased." This equality, as legally defined in Wisconsin, included the generous franchise—one year's residence in the state and the declaration of intent to become a citizen for white, male immigrants—equal rights in every legal sense for this same group, and no limits upon ownership or economic opportunity.[1]

The art of associating together was another matter. Most voluntary associations reflected the ethnic and religious identities of members. This identification extended beyond churches, lodges, and benevolent societies to such organizations as choral societies, fire insurance companies, and savings banks. The Milwaukee Polish community, around the turn of the century, was said to support some eighty voluntary associations, most of them dedicated to religious, patriotic, or benevolent purposes. Milwaukee's Poles were relatively late arrivals in large numbers

---

[1] Alexis de Tocqueville, *Democracy in America,* trans. by Henry Reeve as revised by Francis Bowen (2 vols., Vintage Books edition, New York, 1954), 2:118; Wisconsin Constitution, Article III. See Chapter 8 for a discussion of the legal and other disabilities which were the lot of Wisconsin's Negro and Indian minorities, and of her women.

compared to the Germans and Irish, and they found less ready acceptance economically and socially, but the inward-looking nature of their community was not exceptional. Associating together across these barriers was a slow process. In part, this was true simply because the foreign-born and their children were an overwhelming two-thirds of the total Wisconsin population in 1870, and were still gaining at the 1890 census. While first- and second-generation Germans accounted for about half of this two-thirds of the population, they represented a divided society themselves as regards religion, states of origin, social class, economic status, and general sense of difference from fellow Germans as well as from immigrants of different national and linguistic stocks. One saving feature in all this was that Wisconsin's foreign-born, and particularly the Germans, were very widely distributed geographically and were not overwhelmingly either urban or rural. The foreign-born and their children were a familiar part of nearly every Wisconsin community.[2]

In its early years of statehood, Wisconsin saw continuing evidence of a want of associating together, marked by overt incidents. One can find a number of them in late-nineteenth-century editions of the *Wisconsin Blue Book* under the heading, ''An Outline History of Wisconsin.'' An entry for 1850 notes: ''Liquor riot at Milwaukee. Mob attacked and partially wrecked residence of John B. Smith, for introducing, while in the legislature, a bill called the 'blue liquor law.' Smith being absent, escaped injury.'' Another for 1851: ''Catholics of Milwaukee mobbed Mr. Leahy, a former Catholic, for delivering anti-Catholic lectures.'' The provocation was the work of civilized Yankees who were simply trying to better the ways of their German and Irish neighbors by sponsoring a ''Know Nothing'' lecture by one who was billed as ''Father'' Leahy. But even Yankees were sometimes capable of mob rule, as on the occasion in 1854 when Sherman Booth led

[2] Boleslaus E. Goral, ''The Poles in Milwaukee,'' in Jerome A. Watrous, ed., *Memoirs of Milwaukee County: From the Earliest Historical Times Down to the Present, Including a Genealogical and Biographical Record of Representative Families in Milwaukee County* (2 vols., Madison, 1909), 1:616; *Ninth Census of the United States, 1870: Population, Volume I*, p. 299; *Eleventh Census of the United States, 1890: Abstract*, 44–46, and *Population, Volume I, Part 1*, p. clv.

his followers in seizing an alleged runaway slave from a federal marshal. For this deed, the Wisconsin courts subsequently declared the federal fugitive slave law unconstitutional.[3]

Further instructing their immigrant neighbors in the art of associating together, the Yankee masters of the then dominant Democratic party attempted to "count out" the Republican winner of the 1855 gubernatorial election, Coles Bashford. After some tense confrontations and threats of armed violence, the losing incumbent, William Barstow, blinked first. This humiliation, plus gleeful Republican investigations of past Democratic carelessness with state lands and funds, was soon reversed by the revelation that the promoters of the La Crosse and Milwaukee Railroad had bribed Republican Governor Bashford and a wholesale lot of legislators to help secure a federal land grant. This is far from exhausting the list of moral lessons from the Yankee element or acts which conveyed to immigrant groups that they must conform to Yankee standards or remain forever outsiders. An equally depressing list illustrating Wisconsin society's failures in the arts of associating together can be constructed for subsequent decades.[4]

A rather quixotic figure came forward to put this behavior into context for his fellow citizens. Edward G. Ryan, later chief justice of the state supreme court, expressed his concern for the low state of political morality and the scofflaw attitudes of his fellow citizens in a rambling address before the 1860 annual meeting of the state historical society. The heart of his charge was that both Americans and European immigrants who peopled Wisconsin

---

[3] *Wisconsin Blue Book, 1887*, pp. 109–112; *ibid*; *1899*, p. 125. Richard N. Current, *The History of Wisconsin. Volume II: The Civil War Era, 1848–1873* (Madison, 1976), 140–141, 219–221, 270–271, and the book's index entries "Lynchings" and "Mobs and Riots", which clarify that this sort of thing was not strictly a Milwaukee activity and frequently had overtones of ethnic and religious strife.

[4] Current, *Civil War Era*, 226–230, 243–250. The Milwaukee *Sentinel* of March 1, 2, 11, 12, 13, 16, 22, and 23, 1892, details a gory lynching near Darlington of a neighboring hired hand who had murdered a respected farmer. Of the mob, estimated at 100, seven men were tried and acquitted on the grounds of what the Milwaukee *Sentinel* called "epidemic insanity." The *Sentinel*, May 3, 1892, also noted the tarring and feathering of an Oshkosh barber "by about a dozen of the most prominent business men of Oshkosh."

tended to leave behind the social bonds and moral standards of their homelands. Until these diverse elements were finally intermingled in the West, he thought it would be difficult to establish an acceptable common morality. Society, he said, would "probably remain less a community than a mob."[5]

Better known to Wisconsin, because of the presence in his audience of young Robert M. La Follette, was an address by Ryan thirteen years later, in 1873, before the graduating class of the university. The gist of Ryan's forebodings is familiar to many: "There is looming up a new and dark power. . . . For the first time really in our politics[,] money is taking the field as an organized power. . . . The question will arise, and arise in your day, though perhaps not fully in mine, 'Which shall rule—wealth or man; which shall lead—money or intellect; who shall fill public stations—educated and patriotic free men, or the feudal serfs of corporate capital.' "[6]

Ryan's concern was with free men and the political process, rather than with free men and their relationship to the impersonal economic and social forces that were turning a growing urban working class into insecure employees. Much of the violence of the ensuing twenty years would be concerned with the relations of employees with employers. As it had been previously, the main theater of overt ethnic and religious strife was Milwaukee, which contained the largest body of workers, mixed in origin and subject to great uncertainty of employment. In the eighties, they came as close as ever they would to a consciousness of themselves as a proletariat in the Marxian sense. Of course they were subject to many forces working against such consciousness, not the least of which were those ethnic, religious, and cultural differences which, in the 1850's, had given rise to occasional acts of violence.[7]

[5] Alfons J. Beitzinger, *Edward G. Ryan: Lion of the Law* (Madison, 1960), 52–53, paraphrases Ryan's speech.

[6] *Ibid.*, 104–105; Robert M. La Follette, *La Follette's Autobiography: A Personal Narrative of Political Experiences* (Madison, 1911; reprinted, 1960), 11–12.

[7] Gerd Korman, *Industrialization, Immigrants and Americanizers: The View from Milwaukee, 1866–1921* (Madison, 1967), 15–16, 20–22, 35–38, 42–46, 55–57.

If Ryan missed this latter aspect of the looming struggle between free men and economic power, he was correct in his shift of emphasis away from the inability of peoples of diverse origins to arrive at any sense of community. One outstanding feature of the period 1873 to 1893 was the increasing ability of these people of diverse origins to protect their cultural and religious interests in the political arena. The Yankees clung to the top rungs of the political ladder, and in the process they learned the arts of compromise and coalition with the other elements of the community. Conflict is more interesting than consensus, and there was plenty of the former; but ethnic and religious differences became the subjects of rhetorical and political skirmishes rather than physical confrontations. Some measure of community was being achieved despite the mountains of evidence to the contrary.

What is under examination here are the processes of acculturation and assimilation of diverse elements into a society which has a sense of itself and certain norms of belief and conduct to which members conform. This sounds simple enough until one tackles the problem of defining norms. If, as many contemporaries assumed, New England institutions and standards of belief and conduct were the necessary norms, then the process has never been completed. What has emerged in Wisconsin is a society whose norms vary appreciably from those of neighoring Illinois and Iowa. The survival of the Continental Sunday, associated with Wisconsin's widely dispersed population of German origin, is an obvious example. This variant was fairly established, and was defended in the political arena, during the period 1873–1893, and it survived the temporary setbacks of World War I and the national prohibition era.

It is no problem to find conflicting contemporary testimony on the question of whether acculturation and assimilation were actually happening. This conflict of opinion was natural enough in a society expressing itself politically along the fault lines of ethnic and religious divisions, with the gates to further immigration wide open and the tide rising. The Yankee minority had the advantage of addressing posterity in English, but not with one voice. "America is a vast conglomerate of valuable elements. All the nations of the earth contribute to it some peculiarity and some excellence. In every case there results after the lapse of a short time a grand transmogrification. The traditions of the parent country remain no longer more than a tendency in the blood. The immigrant has become an American." So editorialized the *Daily Commercial Times* of Milwaukee in the centennial year of 1876. The Milwaukee *Sentinel* was less sanguine as it observed the city's non-Yankees: "The mighty host of brewers, liquor dealers, turners, sharp-shooters, Catholic association leaders, free thinkers, free singers, free drinkers, and free lovers of lager assembled at the Academy of Music yesterday forenoon to consummate an American Constitutional Union." These "Knights of the Beer Seidel" particularly distressed the *Sentinel* because the unholy list included those Germans who had earlier allied with the Republican party. It was noted, with some relish, that the meeting was conducted in English to avoid charges of German know-nothingism—a step not calculated to assure their assimilation to the *Sentinel's* view of the American mainstream.[8]

One theory of the assimilation of immigrants and their children into American society distinguishes two important elements of the process. First, the outsiders must adapt to the host society: learn English, develop a fundamental loyalty and commitment to the United States, and subscribe to a generally accepted set of values. For middlewestern Americans of the late nineteenth century these latter certainly included the value of work, success, individual opportunity, the political process, and the ideas of progress, sobriety, and deference to community definitions of social behavior. This constitutes cultural assimilation—acquiring an outlook and demeanor that essentially reflect the values of the host society. Structural assimilation occurs when the host society responds to evidence of cultural assimilation by unself-conscious acceptance of the immigrants or their descendants—usually the

[8] *Daily Commercial Times,* March 9, 1876; Milwaukee *Sentinel,* August 7, 1873.

latter—who have ceased to think of themselves as outsiders, or in any way different. There are obvious barriers to structural assimilation. Race is the most stubborn one. Religion was the most enduring one in the period under consideration, after the second and third generations had obscured differences of appearance, origin, and language. But other differences endured to set people apart, and there was no actual melting pot but rather a continuing consciousness of separate pasts.[9]

Was there a Wisconsin variation to our generalized picture of the assimilation process? While the American-born offspring of American-born parents—mostly of New England and Middle States antecedents—defined the society legally and maintained political control, they were decidedly in the minority. By 1880, the foreign-born and their children were 72 per cent of Wisconsin's population, somewhat concentrated in cities but quite generally distributed. First- and second-generation Germans and Scandinavians were more than 40 per cent of the total population, divided roughly four to one. Those with American-born parents—loosely termed the Yankees—were just 27.7 per cent of the total population and were outnumbered about three to two by these two largest continental European groups. First and second generations of British and Irish background, about five Irish to four British, were another 17 per cent. If we assume that those of British background were natural allies of the Yankees, fitting in easily with respect to language, religion, and political orientation, this leaves nearly five-eighths of the population quite

[9] Milton M. Gordon, *Assimilation in American Life: The Role of Race, Religion, and National Origins* (New York, 1964), chap. 3. See also: D. Aidan McQuillan, "Territory and Ethnic Identity: Some New Measures of an Old Theme in the Cultural Geography of the United States," in James R. Gibson, ed., *European Settlement and Development in North America: Essays on Geographical Change in Honour and Memory of Andrew Hill Clark* (Toronto, 1978), 136–169; Kathleen N. Conzen, "Immigrants, Immigrant Neighborhoods, and Ethnic Identity: Historical Issues," in the *Journal of American History*, 66 (December, 1979), 603–615; and Richard M. Bernard, *The Melting Pot and the Altar: Marital Assimilation in Early Twentieth-Century Wisconsin* (Minneapolis, 1980). Richard D. Cross in John A. Garraty's book *Interpreting American History: Conversations with Historians* (2 vols., New York, 1970), 2:21–42, concludes (p. 36): "If this country lasts a thousand years and we don't have any more massive immigration, probably it will become structurally assimilated too."

different in national or ethnic origin, in language, or in religion—and most of them in all three.[10]

Beyond the fact that each individual made, or failed to make,
adjustments to the host society, there were other variations. Most
adapted to an understanding of the national, regional, and local
society. If there was an established local social order to which
they were latecomers, they made some necessary adjustments.
Non-Germans who settled in Milwaukee and adjacent counties
north and west of the metropolis, where Germans were the
pioneers or early fillers-in, certainly acquired more than simply
a smattering of the German language. They took on some German social baggage, farming methods, and attitudes as well.[11]

Rural people found one another through their churches and
related social organizations which usually defined them ethnically, but also through simple neighborliness and a mutual
dependence that transcended ethnic and religious differences.
Common economic goals were more stable creators of a sense of
community than the Grange, which, though consciously created
for that purpose, failed to stay the course as a broad, popular
movement. The rural school, although regarded generally as a
disappointment by a succession of state superintendents, was
often the center for community affairs and social exchange.

Village people more readily found their like in church and
social organizations. Distinctions of economic gradation were
more sharply drawn than in the country, but some caring for the
resident disadvantaged was a common feature because people
knew one another's circumstances—with names and faces
attached. The village school system was a route to economic
mobility of quite a democratic character, since working for wages
was less of a possibility for adolescents. The village simply did

[10] Bernard, *Melting Pot and the Altar*, 5–9. Native-born of native-born parents were 27.7
per cent of the total population, British-born and their children 7.3 per cent, making 35
per cent. But by 1880 an unknown number of the former group had foreign-born
grandparents and doubtless still identified themselves with a particular ethnic and religious group other than what would be considered "Yankee."

[11] John Higham, "Another Look at Nativism," in Carl N. Degler, ed., *Pivotal Interpre-
tations of American History* (2 vols., New York, 1966), 2:150–151.

not represent so Darwinian a world as the rapidly growing industrial city.[12]

There were centrifugal forces at work in both rural and urban Wisconsin to overcome the persistence of enclaves. One such influence was the Northwest Ordinance of 1785, which set the pattern for the disposition of the federal public domain. The land was surveyed in a grid pattern of six-mile-square townships made up of thirty-six sections, each containing a square mile. This was an adaptation of the New England town system which had provided for orderly settlement by reserving space for a village, schools, common lands, public structures, ecclesiastical property, and so forth. While the New England system did not work exactly as intended, a strong sense of community among the colonial settlers made it a feasible one.[13]

The convenience of this orderly survey ensured accurate title descriptions without regard to the character of the land. Subsequent legislation by Congress dropped practically all reservations for community use, except for the familiar school section. This, however, was simply a reservation of a section for a school fund, not for the location of a school. The pressures for both exploitation and federal revenue resulted in a pattern of scattered settlement and rampant speculation in agricultural, timber, and mineral lands, waterpowers, and prospective townsites which was complicated further by land grants for canals, railroads, and other special purposes. But a six-mile square of scattered farms, uncultivated land, ridges, streams, and other natural barriers does not itself make a community. What did help to create a community was Wisconsin's system of town government, man-

[12] John A. Fleckner, "Poverty and Relief in Nineteenth-Century Janesville," in *WMH*, 61 (Summer, 1978), 279–299; Herbert G. Gutman, *Work, Culture and Society in Industrializing America: Essays in American Working-Class and Social History* (New York, 1976), 254–258, 307–312.

[13] Payson Jackson Treat, "Origin of the National Land System Under the Confederation," in Vernon Carstensen, ed., *The Public Lands: Studies in the History of the Public Domain* (Madison, 1963), 7–14. The presence of a formidable Indian society immediately adjacent to the colonial New England frontier also helped impose a relatively orderly frontier settlement.

dated by the state constitution. New York had borrowed the New England town and mixed it with the county form. Wisconsin is unique in the Midwest for its retention of the town—usually coterminous with the federal survey—as a basic unit of government.[14]

Because the Wisconsin town government was mandated, it was not a matter of waiting for a certain density of settlement or a felt need on the part of the residents. Where settlement was light, the town might be a huge jurisdiction which would later subdivide—normally by petition of the residents—usually along the lines of the federal township surveys or approximately so. In 1870, practically everyone in rural Wisconsin—or nearly three-fourths of the total population—was a resident of a town rather than of an incorporated village or city. Fortunately, we have a near-contemporary description of the formation of a Wisconsin town:[15]

> Monroe held her first town meeting April 3, 1849, at the court house. One hundred and forty-nine voters were present, but hardly any of them had ever attended a town meeting, and no one seemed to know how to proceed. After an awkward pause, some one tired of playing Mr. Micawber, exclaimed, "What do they do at town meetings?" Mr. Daniel S. Sutherland, who, when a boy, had attended town meetings in New York, replied,

[14] Robert C. Nesbit, *Wisconsin: A History* (Madison, 1973), chap. 10; John Brinckerhoff Jackson, *American Space: The Centennial Years, 1865–1876* (New York, 1972), 25–26; Wisconsin Constitution, Article IV, Section 23; David E. Spencer, "Local Government in Wisconsin," in *Wis. Hist. Colls.*, 11:502–511; George S. Wehrwein, "Town Government in Wisconsin," in *Wisconsin Blue Book, 1935*, pp. 95–107; James R. Donoghue, "The Local Government System of Wisconsin," in *Wisconsin Blue Book, 1968*, pp. 105–108.

[15] Wehrwein, "Town Government in Wisconsin," in *Wisconsin Blue Book, 1935*, pp. 96–99; Helen M. Bingham, *History of Green County, Wisconsin* (Milwaukee, 1877), 84. A common confusion is that the town (township) often shared its name with the hamlet or village that developed usually soon after the initial settlement period. Thus the incorporated (1858) Village of Monroe was the county seat of Green County; in 1880 it was chartered as the City of Monroe. Monroe (village and city) was "set off" from the Town (township) of Monroe and was governed by the Town of Monroe until incorporation. *Eleventh Census of the United States, 1890: Population, Volume I, Part 1*, p. 361; Snyder, Van Vechten & Company, comp., *Historical Atlas of Wisconsin, Embracing Complete State and County Maps, City and County Histories; also Special Articles on Geology, Education, Agriculture, and Other Important Interests of the State* (Milwaukee, 1878), 211–212.

"First they put someone in the chair, and then they go to work."
Mr. Sutherland was then called to the chair, and this is the work
they did: Taxes of $125 for contingent expenses, $25 for the
support of the poor, $200 for making and repairing roads and
bridges, and $300 for schools were voted; the running at large of
domestic animals, and, as the record says, other incidental questions were considered, and the usual town officers were elected.

What made town government unique was that voter participation was face to face. The electors of the town met as a legislative
body at least once a year, on the April town meeting day. This
meeting was not only to cast a ballot for town officers and the
town board of supervisors, but to review the administration of
town affairs and to legislate policies within the town's powers.
Town officers were truly administrative. Any actions that went
beyond the legislation of the town meeting could be embarrassing
to the supervisors. Town government also dealt with basic matters that could not fail to engage the interest of the newest
recruit. The town collected the property tax on real and personal
property for itself, the county, and the state. Property was
assessed for this purpose at the town level by an elected assessor,
and his work was subject to review by the town meeting. Everyone knew, or could find out, everyone else's property assessment. This included not only real estate but also animals,
machinery, vehicles, watches, household goods and furnishings,
and merchants' and manufacturers' stock.[16]

---

[16] Merle Curti, *The Making of an American Community: A Case Study of Democracy in a
Frontier County* (Stanford, 1959), 295–299; Wehrwein, "Town Government in Wisconsin," in *Wisconsin Blue Book, 1935,* pp. 105–107. Something over half of the general fund
income of the state came from the property tax assessed and collected at the town, village,
and city levels, according to the *Wisconsin Blue Book, 1881,* p. 313. In the early 1870's, the
*Blue Book* published an abstract from the assessment rolls, reported by counties, on
various types of property. Readers must have been bemused that the 2,009 swine of
Kewaunee County were worth only 48 cents each while the 3,807 in St. Croix County
had an average value of $3.78. And what of the single hog residing in Bayfield County
valued at $25? Another anomaly was that there were almost as many pocket watches in
Rock County as in Milwaukee County. The average value of a watch was $8.88 in
Marquette County and $39.35 in Milwaukee. From such discrepancies came boards of
equalization. The *Wisconsin Blue Book, 1873,* pp. 361–366, has the "Abstract from Assessment Rolls." It first appears in 1871. The "Abstract from Assessment Rolls" was

**COUNTY SEATS IN WISCONSIN, 1893**

If taxes and tax assessments were not enough to bring the town electors to meeting, the town government—as a body—could decide on the location of town roads, schoolhouses, and the districts for both roads and schools. Also the town cared for the

relegated to the secretary of state reports in *Wisconsin Public Documents* (also known as *Governors' Messages and Accompanying Documents*) for 1875, as an economy measure demanded by the legislature. See *Wisconsin Blue Book, 1875,* preface.

poor, set fines for stray animals, licensed the sale of liquor, and had many of the same powers as villages and cities. Many towns did not have town halls, but were building them by the eighties. This was a large item of expense and the location was determined by the town meeting. Of continuing interest, of course, was who got elected to what. This too was determined at town meeting.[17]

While it is commonly deplored that the federal survey township is simply a rectangular measure of land with no relation to patterns of occupancy or landforms, this feature had its virtues when the area was mandated as a unit of government. It meant that natural neighborhoods and ethnic enclaves fit the town lines most imperfectly. Except in a few towns with border-to-border Germans, the town usually represented a variety of ethnic and religious interests that found their initial contacts in town meeting. It was here that basic political alliances were made, based upon perceived common interests. True to the spirit of American politics, identification by party affiliation carried down to the town level. Nor was the town an isolated political unit. The chairman of the town board sat on the county board of supervisors, the legislative and executive body of the county. Immigrant groups largely formed their political loyalties on the basis of local experience and the issues of local and state contests. The tariff, the money question, or Reconstruction policies had less impact on them than such local questions as temperance legislation, Sabbatarianism, blue laws, school legislation, and how their ethnic and religious identities were recognized by contesting politicians and parties.[18]

It is difficult to find descriptions of the working of town government one hundred years ago beyond generalizations from the

[17] Wehrwein, "Town Government in Wisconsin," in *Wisconsin Blue Book, 1935*, pp. 96–97, 102–107. Also see Curti, *Making of an American Community*, 295–302; Delos O. Kinsman, *The Local Governments of Wisconsin* (Appleton, 1921), 23–35.

[18] Roger E. Wyman, "Voting Behavior in the Progressive Era: Wisconsin as a Case Study" (doctoral dissertation, University of Wisconsin, 1970), chap. 2; Richard J. Jensen, *The Winning of the Midwest: Social and Political Conflict, 1888–1896* (Chicago, 1971), preface; Paul Kleppner, *The Cross of Culture: A Social Analysis of Midwestern Politics, 1850–1900* (New York, 1970), chap 2.

laws. The familiar county histories usually are content with a brief account of the initial organizational meeting, followed by lists of all the elected officials over the years—which helped to sell books. The paucity of histories of town government and politics reflects the fleeting nature of local history, which was so much a part of everyday life and seemed infinitely less important historically than a county man who got to Congress. Reconstructing town government in detail takes time, personnel, money, and many pages. Such a study was undertaken in the 1950's for comparing voter lists with the manuscript censuses and a great variety of other records, along with a detailed examination of official town records. The published result, Merle Curti's *The Making of an American Community*, is a classic in American historical literature.

Curti's chapter, "Democracy at the Grass Roots: Town Government in Lincoln and Pigeon," looks at the town-organizing process, which in the 1870's was still in progress in the western uplands of Trempealeau County. The Town of Pigeon was split off from Lincoln in 1875, springing to life full-blown with its share of the budget and taxable wealth. Because of the rough topography, Trempealeau's towns were somewhat irregular in size and followed the ridge lines in a few instances. The reasons for creating the Town of Pigeon were that it had the requisite population and tax base, and that its settlement pattern ran off at a tangent up Pigeon Creek away from the main body of settlement in the Trempealeau River Valley. More importantly, Pigeon Creek had been settled later, and mainly by Norwegians.[19]

On the face of it, this appeared to be a mutually agreeable ethnic separation, which it was. But Lincoln, whose earlier settlers were mostly Yankees and British immigrants, after the separation still had about one-fourth Norwegians. More to the point, all of these elements had been politicized by 1875, when

---

[19] Curti, *Making of an American Community*, 295–319; Snyder, Van Vechten & Company, *Historical Atlas of Wisconsin*, 66 (map of the towns).

the split into two towns occurred. Leadership had emerged which was able to accommodate the ethnic variety present. But the Norwegians, being the newest, were voting as a bloc, while the English-speaking voters were contesting within the given rival political parties. This resulted in the minority Norwegians having two members on the three-member town board in the Town of Lincoln. The Norwegian leader, Peter Ekern, was therefore chairman, which meant that he sat on the county board of supervisors. This was more than reason enough for allowing the Pigeon Creek Norwegians to have their own town government.[20]

After the creation of the Town of Pigeon, which became the new and firmer base for Peter Ekern's political career, the remaining and diminished Norwegian minority in the Town of Lincoln continued to have representation on the town board and in other offices. Similarly, although the new Town of Pigeon had a clear Norwegian majority, the Yankee minority was greatly overrepresented among the elected officials in the early years of the town's independent history. The Norwegian electorate of Pigeon appreciated that the Yankee minority was a valuable resource, better able to handle such positions as town clerk and justice of the peace. In Lincoln, the minority Norwegians were regularly represented on both of the rival slates for town offices. These slates were common to town elections and closely paralleled Republican versus Democratic rivalry in county, state, and national elections. Parties cut across ethnic lines and an important strategy was the balanced slate which mirrored ethnic divisions and geographic interests. There was little evidence of overt prejudice against other ethnic groups, but rather a recognizable preference for your own being recognized on the slate of your party preference. The political parties recognized the necessity for making inroads on ethnic bloc voting. This made it difficult to treat anyone who belonged to a self-conscious ethnic group as an unwelcome stranger.[21]

As leaders emerged, the same names began to appear more

[20] Curti, *Making of an American Community*, 302–303.
[21] *Ibid.*, 316–319.

frequently in town offices, trading them around. This tendency can be readily seen in the many volumes of county histories. Slates for town elections were gotten up by partisans who had their tickets printed for distribution to voters at the polls, which were open all day on town meeting day, the first Tuesday in April. As for the degree of participation in town government, Curti's Trempealeau study included collating the eligible voters in the Town of Lincoln from the federal 1870 and 1880 manuscript censuses. Because of the high mobility rates, Curti compared them only with the elections for town chairman of those years. The results indicated a participation rate of 61.9 per cent of the eligible voters on town meeting day in 1870; for 1880 the rate was 72.7 per cent. Rural life was not particularly exciting in the seventies, but town meeting day qualified.[22]

The great equalizer in Wisconsin grass-roots democracy was, of course, language. Continental Europeans were at a disadvantage, but that too was relative. One student of economic and social mobility in pioneer Milwaukee remarked that the high rate of illiteracy among the Irish appeared to be a greater bar to advancement and acceptance than did the initial disadvantage of the language barrier for Germans and Scandinavians, who had a high rate of literacy in their own languages and the habit of schooling their children. It was not uncommon for town records to be written in other than English.[23]

Joseph Schafer noticed, as did others, that in the heavily German areas north of Milwaukee, English came more slowly. But he also noted that the very fact that Germans were the dominant

---

[22] *Ibid.*, 297, 300, 302–319. A century later, the mixing of suburban homes with adjacent farms in an urban shadow sometimes makes for strange antics when the suburbanites discover the pure democracy of town government affecting their lives. See James R. Donoghue, "Local Government in Wisconsin," in the *Wisconsin Blue Book, 1979–1980*, p. 138. For a description of town balloting, see George Brown, "Sovereignty and Democracy in Wisconsin Elections," in the *Wisconsin Blue Book, 1935*, pp. 81–84.

[23] Kathleen Conzen, *Immigrant Milwaukee, 1836–1860: Accommodation and Community in a Frontier City* (Cambridge, 1976), 59–60, 258n. Ray Stannard Baker, *Native American: The Book of My Youth* (New York, 1941), 20–24, tells of paying taxes in the eighties on his father's scattered holdings in Polk and Burnett counties to town treasurers "who in those days were pioneer farmers, usually Scandinavians who spoke little English."

group provided more opportunities for the German-born to have a political career at the county or state level. Those who aspired to a legislative career were generally well-educated, and they found it easier to get an adequate command of English than it would have been for the average Yankee to get beyond a little conversational German. Those German-born who enjoyed success in politics, business, or the professions were examples to others. "In fact," wrote Schafer, "unusual success in any field opened wide the door of social opportunity to the family of the successful immigrant. His children would be sure to attend the American high school or college; they could, if they chose to do so, intermarry with American families, and fraternize on equal terms with Americans of the older lineage in church, in lodge, and in the home."[24]

Nils P. Haugen (1849-1931), a Norwegian-born politician of the Progressive era, observed: "Time takes care of the question of language," even in solid ethnic enclaves. As for himself, he read Norwegian quite readily and had the alphabet by rote when he first went to a Wisconsin district school at age five. Nils started school in Rock County and finished it in Pierce County among "a good mixture of nationalities: mostly Norwegians, but some Americans, Irish, French and at least one German family. The melting pot was doing its work, and all the pupils lived together in the best of harmony and good will, which continued throughout their mature years." Haugen became a voter in 1870 and was elected a state assemblyman eight years later.[25]

The first requirement for intelligent participation in town meeting, beyond simply coming to the town hall to vote for your slate, was the ability to follow conversational English. As anyone who has been immersed in a foreign culture for any time knows,

[24] Joseph Schafer, *Four Wisconsin Counties: Prairie and Forest* (Madison, 1927), 185–186. Ernest Bruncken disagreed with Schafer. See Ernest Bruncken, "How Germans Became Americans," in *Proceedings of the State Historical Society of Wisconsin* (74 vols., Madison, 1875–1958), 1897, pp. 112–113, hereinafter cited as *SHSW Proceedings*.

[25] Nils P. Haugen, *Pioneer and Political Reminiscences* (Evansville, 1930), 17–19, 47; John Higham, *Strangers in the Land: Patterns of American Nativism, 1860–1925* (New Brunswick, 1963), chap. 3.

one generally gets the drift of things long before being able to reply in kind. There was surely a good deal of diffidence displayed by continental Europeans around Americans, which did not arise from a lack of understanding of what was being said so much as the difficulty of taking part. But most ethnic communities produced men who were anxious to take a leader's part in affairs and learned enough English to make themselves understood. For the others, it was difficult to confine dealings to their own kind. There were inevitable encounters with tax assessors, path masters, merchants, bankers, lawyers, grain buyers, machinery dealers, land agents, and so forth that spurred the comprehension, if not the flow, of the new language. The same encounters encouraged reciprocity. If a Yankee wanted their business or their votes, he soon acquired some conversational German or Norwegian.[26]

There were occasions when Norwegians in the Town of Lincoln were discriminated against, presumably because of language difficulties. Only 6 per cent of the jurors who served on local juries between 1873 and 1879 were Norwegians. This was far below their proportion of eligible jurors, while the American-born furnished 83 per cent. But there appears as well to have been selection favoring substantial property owners. The bilingual meeting was a standard feature of civic occasions in many places outside of Milwaukee. Courtrooms and public meetings commonly used interpreters. The generation of the seventies and eighties had a tolerance for oratory and discussion, even in bilingual form, which lies well beyond the ken of their present descendants.[27]

---

[26] Norwegians had an advantage over Germans in that there is a certain similarity with English in Norwegian vocabulary and word order, making it possible to mix English words readily into conversational Norwegian. See Richard J. Fapso, *Norwegians in Wisconsin* (Madison, 1977), 29. But colloquial German is also adaptable. To say "Die vinnt blase wie de dickens" would scarcely have baffled any Wisconsinite of the time.

[27] Curti, *Making of an American Community*, 315. Bill Hooker, *Glimpses of an Earlier Milwaukee* (Milwaukee, 1929), 41, describes Theodore Rudzinski, alderman from the South Side, who "spoke good English, Polish and German, the three languages then required for nearly every walk of life."

The bilingual meeting points to another contradictory feature of ethnic separation. It is easy to assume that relatively large clusters of an ethnic group, particularly continental Europeans, would be content to produce here a modified version of the society they knew. This is true, as many contemporary observers remarked. On the other hand, the very fact that they were a numerically important element in any larger community made it necessary that they be incorporated economically and politically into the whole, just as the Norwegians were accommodated in the Town of Lincoln. They had the confidence of numbers, and a stake which could not be ignored.[28]

The mere fact of numbers—less than one-third of Wisconsin's 1870 population was native-born of American-born parents—meant that locally the majority social group defining the norm was only occasionally made up of those of Yankee background. This was true in rural as well as urban Wisconsin. Where Oscar Hallam was raised, a few miles west of Dodgeville in the Town of Linden, of the 360 family heads in 1870, only seventy-four were American-born; 229 of them were English, eighteen Welsh, sixteen German, twelve Irish, and eight Scandinavian. The English were nearly all Cornish and, as the overwhelming majority, they afforded themselves the luxury of dividing into Methodists and Primitive Methodists. Hallam, of Cornish background, reflected upon how that majority sized up the neighborhood: "The Cornish and Manx of that community were honest, so were the few plain English and the few Norwegians and the Dutch and the Germans. . . . They were all of good credit and were good pay. They all owned their farms. They were industrious and thrifty. Getting over toward Diamond Grove, you had to look out more. There were some 'Murrikens'

---

[28] ". . . [T]he more an ethnic community approached the character of a true community in the fullest sense of the term, the more effectively it functioned to ease the transition from European to American life." Conzen, *Immigrant Milwaukee*, 3, has particular reference to Milwaukee's German community of the 1850's which was geographically separate, self-contained, and self-sufficient.

around there too who were not so thrifty or industrious. That country was wooded. Some of them would plow around the stumps instead of grubbing the stumps. There were some farmers there who worked on Sunday. They were not well regarded." The "Murrikens"—Americans—were the outsiders, yet the virtues which Hallam ascribed to the others could have come straight out of Emerson or McGuffey. Who then was acculturated?[29]

Town meeting day acquired its traditions in the latter nineteenth century. It was normally an all-day affair with heavy business in the early afternoon—listening to the reports of the town supervisors, clerk, assessor, treasurer—and generally reviewing town finances and the new budget. Later, they broke up into road district caucuses to choose road overseers. The last part of the meeting, which often went on into early evening, was concerned with the allocation of the various funds and voting on the tax rates to cover them. Town government was parsimonious. Citizens cherished a dollar and most worked out their road taxes. The total budget for 1885 for the fourteen towns and five villages in Trempealeau County came to $78,756.23, of which 26.7 per cent went for roads and bridges, 38.6 per cent for schools, 2.6 per cent for poor relief, 7.5 per cent for current expenses, and 24.6 per cent for other purposes.[30]

One tradition of the Wisconsin town meeting was that the wives came along, although they were not voters. As noted, it was an all-day affair and the inner man had to be sustained. The sale of liquor was illegal on annual town meeting day and fall election day, but that many men on a day off from chores needed watching. One way to hold the participants to their tasks was a grand feed. Meeting day was then an important occasion that included social exchange with people well beyond the usual rural

[29] Joseph Schafer, *The Wisconsin Lead Region* (Madison, 1932), 294; Oscar Hallam, "Bloomfield and Number Five: The American Way of Life in a Wisconsin Rural Community in the 70s, As Seen by a Small Boy," 159–162, in the Hallam Reminiscences.

[30] Curti, *Making of an American Community*, 298–310; *Wisconsin Blue Book, 1887*, p. 280; Hallam, "Bloomfield and Number Five," 70–71.

neighborhood. There were not many other events, including fairs, political meetings, or school and church affairs, that cast as wide a net or afforded so much contact with strangers.[31]

The fragmentary evidence on immigrant participation in town government is admittedly contradictory. A land agent for the Wisconsin Central Railroad, which had recruited large numbers of Germans and Bohemians to its land in Taylor County, commented: "The main difficulty with the adult immigrant from a monarchical government, is his imperfect comprehension of the great privileges and responsibilities of our system of popular franchise. . . . The effect of the grouping of the foreign element upon the older settlers . . . is to cause a desire to sell out and remove from the locality on account of distaste for their inefficient management of town and Co. government and their uncongenial society." Possibly the key phrase here is "their inefficient management," which implies that the older settlers—presumably English-speaking—were not free to run the town and county without consulting the interests of the newcomers, who doubtless were suspicious, difficult to communicate with, and clannish—but who showed up and voted![32]

Despite such testimony that Wisconsin town government did not always work as well as intended, there is considerable evidence that rural and village people identified readily with the Wisconsin town as a rural neighborhood or social unit, as well as a municipal corporation. Any number of memoirs assumed that a rural town name was as meaningful as that of a village. Bob La Follette, for instance, never felt that he had to explain his references to Primrose, although it was not a spot on a map. Joseph Schafer had no difficulty finding town historians for his *Town Studies* volume. And the Western Historical Company, which published the familiar 1879–1881 series of Wisconsin

[31] *Laws of Wisconsin*, 1859, p. 126, forbade liquor sales on town meeting day. It had subsequent refinements.

[32] S. C. Miles [Stetsonville] to John S. Roeseler, October 28, 1888, in the Roeseler Papers. Also see C. J. Galpin, *The Social Anatomy of an Agricultural Community*, University of Wisconsin Agricultural Experiment Station, Research Bulletin, no. 34 (1915), 22.

county histories, organized them by town, village, and city, with the town, by name, as the basic unit.

There is something to be said for the farm neighborhood as an environment for acculturating people of dissimilar backgrounds. This is based upon the well-established premise that most rural neighborhoods were ethnically mixed simply by the processes of geographic mobility, the natural effects of scattered initial settlement, and patterns of land ownership. Humans are social animals and will seek contact with whomever is available. Then, too, farming is one of man's few non-competitive enterprises, in the sense that one man's success is not going to drive his neighbor out of business. The neighbor wants to know how he does it, and the successful farmer delights in instructing him. Also, farm neighborhoods were more isolated than we can well imagine today. Winter, and mud in other seasons, limited travel for much of the year. Even in favorable weather, a trip to the village or hamlet took a large share of the day. If you went, you got the neighbor's mail and small purchases. Trading work was also a commonplace. Oscar Hallam says trading went well beyond that. When you butchered, you supplied the neighbors, who responded in kind.[33]

A wider neighborhood exchange resulted from the need for specialized services, which grew as farming became more commercialized. The average farmer's skills were not sufficient for raising a dairy barn or repairing equipment that required metalworking. Many of the foreign-born provided these skills, particularly German neighbors, as it was common for them to have a trade to which they had been apprenticed. They were millers, blacksmiths, builders, stonemasons, cabinetmakers, wheelwrights, and so forth, whose skills were not matched by Yankee handymen.[34]

Threshing was a fall activity that got the neighborhood together to trade field and kitchen work. Steam threshing was introduced

[33] Hallam, "Bloomfield and Number Five," 7–8.
[34] Schafer, *Wisconsin Lead Region*, 236.

in the seventies, but even the horsepowered threshers in common use, so lovingly described by Hamlin Garland, were expensive equipment that was served by a regular crew. Wisconsin grain fields were not all that extensive, which meant a lot of moving. Threshing went on into winter. Farmers put the grain, in the stalk, under cover, or stacked it until the threshers came around. Among other things, fall was election time—annually in Wisconsin until 1882. The harvest table was enlivened by political talk that gave young men of both foreign and domestic origins their baptism.[35]

As Wisconsin farmers made the transition to dairying, it involved those beyond the immediate neighborhood in a common endeavor. Cheese making was the widespread practice, except for very local urban milksheds. A rural cheese factory drew upon farmers within a two-to-three-mile radius. This required considerable organization on the part of those promoting the venture to get an adequate supply of milk. Ole Barton, a Norwegian farmer in Primrose Town, was a leader and organizer in 1878 of the co-operative Primrose Union Cheese Factory Association. He had earlier exercised his leadership in helping to organize the Primrose Mutual Fire Insurance Company and the Primrose Farmers' Club in 1873 which—like most granger groups—had a short life. Farmers' voluntary organizations that enjoyed more than a temporary existence were apt to have an economic rather than a primarily social or ethnic identity. As such, they recruited across ethnic lines and brought neighborhood leaders of diverse backgrounds together.[36]

Sickness, childbirth, and death more often brought rural neighbors than a physician. It was neighbors who nursed families stricken with common diseases that often laid all members low.

[35] Hamlin Garland, *A Son of the Middle Border* (New York, 1917), "The Last Threshing in the Coulee," 50–58; Hallam, "Bloomfield and Number Five," 90–98.

[36] Eric E. Lampard, *The Rise of the Dairy Industry in Wisconsin: A Study in Agricultural Change, 1820–1920* (Madison, 1963), chap. 4; Albert O. Barton, "Social History of Primrose," in Joseph Schafer, *Wisconsin Domesday Book: Town Studies* (Madison, 1924), 115–116.

The deceased were not sent to town for the amenities and burial. The neighbors took care of such details, and cemeteries were very local affairs—even family affairs.[37]

Children went to school together, all ages in the same room, and developed a society of their own. This was often a source of irritation for non-English-speaking parents. Nonetheless, the children were a bridge to English-speaking neighbors for such families. Young adults also shared in this process. Many young immigrants learned their English by hiring out to English-speaking families in the neighborhood. American farmers were often the tycoons of the neighborhood, for they had picked the best land early and enjoyed more resources and credit.[38]

Hamlin Garland was a sensitive interpreter of the Wisconsin of his youth. "Up the Coulee: A Story of Wisconsin" concerns the return of a man, who like himself had achieved success in the East, to the family farm in the western uplands. It is partly a political tract; Garland was an active Single Taxer interested in the western farmer as a debtor in an economic environment controlled by others. The story concerns Howard McLane, a successful actor-playwright, who returns rather tardily to visit his mother who lives with a younger son on a failing farm near the old homestead. Among Howard's first impressions that jar his nostalgia is the village: "How poor and dull and sleepy and squalid it seemed! The one main street ended at the hillside . . . between two rows of the usual village stores. . . . An unpaved street, with walled, drab-colored, miserable, rotting wooden buildings. . . ." The life of the village was symbolized by "the grouping of the old loafers on the salt-barrels and nail-kegs. He recognized most of them—a little dirtier, a little more bent, and

[37] Doane Robinson, "Beaver Creek Valley, Monroe County," in Schafer, *Town Studies*, 134–135, tells of his family being nursed through typhoid for weeks by the neighbors. It was a neighborhood of mixed ethnic strains. On another occasion, all joined to shivaree a German neighbor who married the daughter of a new settler.

[38] L[awrence] Kessinger to [Reuben G. Thwaites], September 14, 1888, in the Roeseler Papers; Laurence M. Larson, *The Log Book of a Young Immigrant* (Northfield, 1939), 20–21; Louis Larson, "Pioneering in Wisconsin and Minnesota," in La Crosse County Historical Society, *La Crosse Historical Sketches,* series 6 (La Crosse, 1942), 18–32.

a little grayer." (Clearly not much of community promise here!)

McLane hitches a ride with an acquaintance. The farm where he grew up, he is surprised to learn, is no longer where his family lives. When he inquires who does live there, the laconic reply is, "Dutchman." And the Dunlap place? " 'Nother Dutchman." He has a brief encounter with the German woman living on the home place that his brother, Grant, was forced by debt to relinquish. Howard can communicate with her in simple German, not because he had an average Wisconsin Yankee rural boyhood among German neighbors, but because of his cosmopolitan life since.

The old sense of Yankee community is briefly revived by a visit from neighbors whom McLane knew as a boy, but he is shortly overwhelmed by the narrowness and poverty of their lives. A young woman, a self-confessed old maid teacher of twenty-five, tells him that the hills are full of her kind as "most all the boys have gone west." When McLane demurs that she must have suitors, she replies: "Oh, a young Dutchman or Norwegian once in a while. Nobody that counts." Grant's wife, however, sees it differently, having given up independence as a teacher: "I was a fool for ever marrying."

Garland's story is a gloomy retrospective on the decline of a sense of community. The pioneer spirit of the neighborhood has fled with the young men gone West or to other careers, and with the whole families who moved on, as had the Garlands in fact. Those left behind are beaten or uncertain. They share with the village the sense of despair and decay. The foreign interlopers are more successful, but distant.[39]

"Among the Corn-Rows" is another Garland story from *Main-Travelled Roads*. It departs from the prevailing gloom of "Up the Coulee" and was therefore more congenial to the reading public of the nineties. It concerns Rob Rodemaker, a young German-

[39] Hamlin Garland, *Main-Travelled Roads* (New York, 1899; partially reprinted in paperback, New York, 1961), 59–110. Lewis Atherton, *Main Street on the Middle Border* (Bloomington, 1954), 14–22, has a brief account of Garland's career and is a book full of Wisconsin examples covering the years 1873–1893—a pleasant work of scholarly nostalgia. See also Jean Holloway, *Hamlin Garland: A Biography* (Austin, 1960).

American who is homesteading in Dakota, as Garland did briefly. Rob returns home to Waupaca County in search of a wife to share his claim. He persuades Julia, whose harsh Norwegian father has turned her into an unpaid field hand, to come away with him. It is not what she had in mind, but the reader accepts that she will do better than with the Yankee drug clerk who once looked at her with momentary interest.

Rob and Julia had gone to school with Yankee neighbor children. With the greater opportunity open to a young man, Rob had escaped the diminished prospects where "they wa'n't no chance there f'r a feller. We fellers workin' out back there got more 'n' more like *hands*, an' less like human beings." His Dakota pals, who give Rob a raucous sendoff on his errand, clearly accept him as a venturesome Yankee to be envied. Julia Peterson has found no such emancipation, and she daydreams of marriage to a Yankee as her means of escape. She discourages Norwegian suitors, but is losing contact with Yankee girl friends for shame over her uncouth life and imagined appearance. Such contacts are discouraged by her father, a "tireless, silent, and grim-visaged old Norse."

Rob Rodemaker turns out to be her Yankee suitor, but not by his initial design. He was simply going back home where "girls are thick as huckleberries." On his way from the station, he sees Julia "toiling back and forth between the corn-rows, holding the handles of the double-shovel corn-plough" while her little brother rides the horse. Rob stops to visit, incidentally getting an inventory of the neighborhood girls not yet married or engaged. "Do they keep up the ly-ceum and the sociables same as ever?" he asks. She says that they do, "but I don't . . . I don't get out often." A quick study, it dawns on Rob that he has found his huckleberry. He returns shortly to put his case: "[A] *rattlin'* good claim; a shanty on it fourteen by sixteen—no tarred paper about it, and a suller to keep butter in, and a hundred acres o' wheat just about ready to turn now. I need a wife." Julia agrees to run off to Squire Hatfield's to marry that night, "with a sudden realization of how far from her dreams of courtship this reality was.'' She offers to shake hands on it, but he manages a tentative hug and a kiss on the cheek.[40]

Given the high rate of geographic mobility of family units as well as the young, was the continuity of a sense of community and of community leadership possible? The answer lay in the continuing presence of a stable core of residents who generally enjoyed more economic success than did the peripatetic. It follows that those who achieved higher property values were apt to be more energetic in other fields. While residence in the hamlet or unincorporated village, where town government often centered, gave some advantage in filling the role of town clerk or treasurer, the Trempealeau County study cited earlier showed a preponderance of farmers in leadership roles before 1860 at both town and county levels, and the emergence of the foreign-born after 1860, especially at the town level. There was more chance to emerge as a leader at the county level in the pioneering period. This would accord with the idea that the period of greatest instability in a community occurred in the formative years, in a competitive environment where the rules and accepted social order were not yet clear. After this period of instability, the community established a sort of pecking order which could accommodate the comings and goings of individual members and families, with the newcomers fitting themselves into the existing order.[41]

Northern Wisconsin, as one moved beyond the advancing

[40] Garland, *Main-Travelled Roads* (1899 edition), 88–111. The intermarriage rate of those of German and Norwegian origin is of interest here. It is particularly difficult to establish in the 1880's for second-generation immigrants. But a fair sampling indicates that the children of Norwegian-born married within their ethnic group 85 per cent of the time. For those of German origin, the ratio was four out of five. But first they had to find one another, and the Norwegians were inclined to be more clannish in their settlement patterns as well. See Bernard, *Melting Pot and the Altar,* 117–118. See also Peter A. Munch, ''Social Adjustment Among Wisconsin Norwegians,'' in the *American Sociological Review,* 14 (December, 1949), 780–787.

[41] Curti, *Making of an American Community,* chap. 15; Richard S. Alcorn, ''Leadership and Stability in Mid-Nineteenth-Century America: A Case Study of an Illinois Town,'' in the *Journal of American History,* 61 (December, 1974), 685–687; Don H. Doyle, *The Social Order of a Frontier Community: Jacksonville, Illinois, 1825–70* (Urbana, 1978), 2–9; Allan G. Bogue, ''Social Theory and the Pioneer,'' in *Agricultural History,* 34 (January, 1960), 29–32.

farm frontier, presented a different type of rural population—the logging camp and isolated sawmill. Some of these counties were more urban than rural because mills congregated at a water-power and log boom site. Oneida County, about as large as Dane County in area, in 1890 had 2,658 of its total 5,010 population in the village of Rhinelander, and another 1,154 in the village of Eagle River. This left a rural population of only 1,198, mostly woodsmen and a few agricultural settlers, to divide up among the four large towns. Nearby Taylor County was similarly circumstanced, with more agricultural settlement by Central European immigrants who had been solicited and assisted by the Wisconsin Central Railroad. Both loggers and new immigrants had difficulties establishing community relations with other inhabitants.[42]

The logging camp or mill hamlet was something less than a community. The location was as temporary as the population. Even in an established mill village like Centralia (now part of Wisconsin Rapids in Wood County), two-fifths of the adult male population were unmarried in 1880, and two-thirds of those lived in dormitory-boardinghouses provided by the mills. Dormitories and logging camps were frequently towers of Babel, but the companies had to reckon with ethnic prejudices. William Holt recalled the camps run by his family in the 1880's: "In some camps the teamsters were a little hightoned and insisted on a camp of their own. Some of the lumberjacks called themselves 'white men' and would not bunk in the same room with Polacks, Finns, Russians, Montenegrins, and other foreigners. To tell the truth I never saw the men take any interest in a bath-house, except the Finns." These were not exactly the makings of Paul Bunyan's "jolly crew," despite literary efforts to the contrary, or of a community in any sense but that enforced by isolation and other hard conditions of life.[43]

[42] *Eleventh Census of the United States, 1890: Population, Volume I, Part 1,* pp. 363, 366; S. C. Miles to John S. Roeseler, October 28, 1888, in the Roeseler Papers.

[43] Peter Hruschka, "Centralia, Wisconsin, and Her Immigrants, 1860–1880," unpublished seminar paper in the author's files, January, 1969; William A. Holt, *A Wisconsin Lumberman Looks Backward* ([Oconto], 1948), 35.

The rural town and its government dealt not only with farms
and farmers. The rural hamlet, a small settlement in a primarily
agricultural area, offered services that usually included more
than a general store. But it lacked the village attributes of a grid
of streets and other near-urban amenities. The latter nineteenth
century was the heyday of the Wisconsin hamlet, before rural
free delivery and the automobile transformed or obliterated it.
Some did graduate to village status, but most were safe havens
from urban life. Before such transformations, they might occasionally have had a country doctor or other professional, and
usually a blacksmith, a tavern, and possibly a church or country
hotel. The farm community extended into the hamlet with a few
farmers who doubled as craftsmen or agents. Farm animals, well
beyond the limits an incorporated village would tolerate, lived
pastoral lives there. Hamlets were real competitors of the more
citified villages, and were an integral part of the rural scene.[44]

Beyond the legal definitions of what constitutes a rural town
government, a village, or a city, these are not hard and fast
descriptions of Wisconsin in the latter nineteenth century. Buffalo City was incorporated as a city in 1859, when it had 268
inhabitants, more than it had in 1890, but it was still a city
officially. (Remember that only thirty-eight villages had been
incorporated before 1885, and there were at least seventy-one
unincorporated villages of over 300 population according to the
1880 federal census.) Size was no guide. In 1880 McFarland, in
Dane County, was an incorporated village with 168 population;
Waukesha, Marinette, and Menomonie, with populations over
2,500, were unorganized parts of rural towns. Marinette and
Menomonie appear as cities in the 1890 census, but Waukesha
was only an incorporated village although it was larger than
Menomonie in both censuses. Incorporation was voluntary under

[44] Glenn T. Trewartha, "The Unincorporated Hamlet: One Element of the American
Settlement Fabric," in the *Annals of the Association of American Geographers,* 33 (March,
1943), 32–81, offers the definition of a hamlet as an unorganized settlement of no more
than eighteen houses and 150 inhabitants, most of them engaged in farming or farm
work.

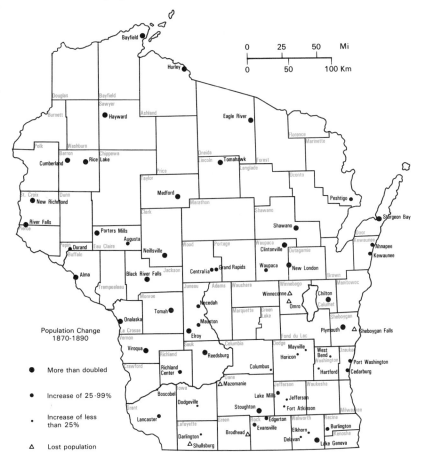

## WISCONSIN CITIES AND VILLAGES
## OF POPULATION 1,000–2,500 IN 1890

general rather than special laws for villages after 1872, but a city charter could still be obtained by a special legislative act until twenty years later.[45]

[45] *Laws of Wisconsin (Private and Local)*, 1859, pp. 350–385; *Tenth Census of the United States, 1880: Population, Volume I, Part 1*, pp. 336–375; *Eleventh Census of the United States, 1890: Population, Volume I, Part 1*, pp. 357–375; *Laws of Wisconsin*, 1872, pp. 275–304; George S. Wehrwein, "Village Government in Wisconsin," in *Wisconsin Blue Book, 1940*, pp. 161–170; Donoghue, "Local Government System of Wisconsin," in *Wisconsin Blue Book, 1968*, p. 109.

There were certain advantages to remaining unincorporated. The town had to provide police service from general revenues for unincorporated settlements, for instance. Presumably most such places were set aside as separate road and school districts using their own property tax base. Probably the full panoply of village or city officials appeared an unnecessary extravagance, and once elected they ran things. There was no direct democracy in village or city government such as was represented by town meeting day.[46]

Ernest Bruncken commented: "On the whole, the small town is most favorable to rapid Americanization, unless it is almost exclusively inhabited by foreigners, as does occasionally happen. In small cities or villages, the people are so universally and well acquainted with one another, both in business and social life, that the foreigners cannot easily form separate communities . . . ." The conclusion seems obvious. The village was necessarily more intimate than a rural town simply because of the density of the population and the visually observable limits of the village. Was not Bruncken right about the much greater social and economic contact on a day-to-day basis? Would not the rural residents also probably have more contacts with the villagers than with most of their fellow citizens of the diffuse rural town?[47]

Not necessarily so! As a British observer of midwestern culture remarked, social equality stopped at the village and city limits: "Levels and gradations of society formed in them, as they have done throughout history . . . . A right side and a wrong side to the new railroad tracks developed." Urbanites lived by different rules having to do with the individual's or group's place in a more complicated economic scheme of things. These were added

---

[46] *Revised Statutes of the State of Wisconsin*, 1878, pp. 234–254; Donoghue, "Local Government System of Wisconsin," in *Wisconsin Blue Book, 1968*, pp. 108–109. The 1890 federal census by minor civil divisions is a useful guide to the very active changes in county and town borders as well as the creation of incorporated villages and cities that went on during the eighties. These appear in the heavily footnoted schedule, *Eleventh Census of the United States, 1890: Population, Volume I, Part 1*, pp. 357–367.

[47] Bruncken, "How Germans Become Americans," in *SHSW Proceedings*, 1897, p. 107.

to the usual social signals emitted by one's ethnic and religious identity. The workmen who drew their wages from the village man of affairs did not ordinarily sit at his table. The villager of consequence was served by a "domestic," not by the neighbor's daughter come in to "help out." The distinction between the farmer's hired man, who usually appeared as part of the family, and the daily wage earner in the village or city, was a very real one. The perception was slow to die that the hired man was an apprentice farmer, even if the economic reality was that many would buy a horse and buggy rather than a neighboring farm or go to homestead in Dakota. Many newly arrived immigrants hired out to neighboring established farmers while making their own farms. Socially, they certainly were in a different category from the immigrant in an urban setting who had no marketable skill or property.[48]

And what of the farmer's view of the man in the village? There was a good deal of distrust involved, based upon other than ethnic or religious differences. Nor was this distrust confined to immigrants, who usually saw the villager as a Yankee or as one of their own studying to be a Yankee. Hamlin Garland reported that country boys were terrorized by the village boys. Garland's father briefly operated a Grange store in Osage, Iowa, a countryman among the urban sharpers. Hamlin saw himself as an uncomfortable "clod jumper" among more sophisticated youths at the village academy. William A. Titus resolved to go to the high school in Fond du Lac, a formidable institution with four teachers. "I, as a farmer boy, had no social standing," he said, and therefore he had no part in the students' social affairs. William Whyte said that farmers would drive several blocks out of their way to avoid passing the Watertown high school: "Should any farmer have the temerity to drive by the school with his empty sled, it would be taken possession of by the young ruffians . . . ." Maybe social affairs at the Fond du Lac high school were not that exhilarating, but Titus gives a notion of the social dis-

[48] David Graham Hutton, *Midwest at Noon* (Chicago, 1946), 127.

tance that lay between the rural residents and the villagers. And the inference is clear that the majority of high school students then were from the "right side of the tracks."[49]

An unrelieved picture of rural immigrant distrust of the villager is provided by Laurence Larson: "The Yankees were 'smart' and the immigrant had a lurking fear that he himself was not smart in the same way. . . . It is therefore not strange that he came to believe that he was being exploited . . . and often too the belief was well founded. . . . To the charges of idleness and dishonesty there was added that of coarse immorality . . . and their daughters, in growing numbers, were finding work as domestic helpers in town." Village lawyers were considered to be as hazardous to a farmer's financial well-being as a lightning rod salesman or a hop buyer. The Pigeon Creek Sentinels, a rural literary and debating society, once argued the question: "*Resolved*; that [commercial] agents have done more damage to farmers than grasshoppers." That was in America's centennial year.[50]

A common mistake that village merchants made, even as they ardently wooed their rural farm neighbors with pioneer day parades, civic barbecues, fairs, and other inducements, was their natural inclination to look upon themselves as urbanites and to identify more with the cities down the rails than with the farm community that sustained them. Any village with a railroad connection was certain of its destiny to become a manufacturing and distribution center. Destiny needed frequent harkings to greatness in the near future.[51]

The average Wisconsin village was not an accident of nature,

[49] Garland, *Son of the Middle Border*, 160–171; William A. Titus, "The Westward Trail," in *WMH*, 20 (December, 1936), 178; William F. Whyte, "Beginnings of the Watertown School System," in *WMH*, 7 (September, 1923), 89. The terms "hayseed" and "rube" apparently came into common parlance about the 1880's. See Mitford M. Mathews, ed., *A Dictionary of Americanisms on Historical Principles* (2 vols., Chicago, 1951).

[50] Larson, *Log Book of a Young Immigrant*, 68; Hallam, "Bloomfield and Number Five," 99–104, on lightning rod salesmen and hop buyers, and 330–334 on village lawyers; Curti, *Making of an American Community*, 413.

[51] Trewartha, "The Unincorporated Hamlet," *Annals of the Association of American Geographers*, 33:60.

nor was it a clustering of peasants in a life style familiar to Europeans. It was a promotion, usually the enterprise of speculative Yankees. The railroads added an extra dimension, but their most fertile field was in northern Wisconsin. Elsewhere, the landscape was pretty well covered, and the best that the railroads could do was to shake down the eager bidders along a flexible prospective route. In southern Wisconsin, Yankee village promoters had every expectation that they were planting future cities to be filled by industrious compatriots. Every thriving village promised wealth and a grateful posterity. Such thoughts must have been behind the enterprise of Luke Stoughton, native of Weathersfield, Vermont, and merchant-capitalist of Janesville, when in 1847 he bought from Daniel Webster the future site of the city that bears his name. Little did Stoughton foresee that by the time of his death in 1874 the leading enterprises there—the ones that put the village on the map, as it were—would be the large wagon and carriage manufacturing works of T. G. Mandt, Norwegian immigrant, and Messrs. Melaas, Steenerson & Co., importers and distributors for "the famous Lofoten Cod Liver Oil." Somehow, things had gone amiss. Today Stoughton bears its Norwegian identification proudly and with due celebration. But as pioneer Madison historian Horace A. Tenney generously conceded: "The wondrous career of the [Norwegian] race in material wealth and mental improvement under favorable and improving conditions, is, to the early American settlers, a marked phase in race development, conspicuous among all others witnessed in western life."[52]

Should this judgment of the visible environmental effects of association with true American society seem a bit condescending,

[52] In 1876, the bonded indebtedness of Wisconsin towns, villages, and cities for railroad subsidies amounted to $2,707,496.97; for schools, $242,601.45; for roads and bridges, $105,695.49. That amounted to $11 to aid a railroad for every $1 to build a school. See *Wisconsin Blue Book, 1877,* pp. 334–335. This gentle blackmail was curtailed in 1874 by constitutional amendment. See *Laws of Wisconsin,* 1874, pp. 43–45. See also *United States Biographical Dictionary and Portrait Gallery of Eminent and Self-Made Men. Wisconsin Volume* (Chicago, 1877), 178–179; and Horace A. Tenney, "Stoughton," in William J. Park and Co., *Madison, Dane County and Surrounding Towns. . .* (Madison, 1877), 338–349, 554.

listen to a Yankee whose haven had not yet been invaded: "Better is it for a place to start with a good moral influence, and to secure a good moral reputation, than to have a reputation for mere business and money-making. We can afford to spare the loose and low population, which might otherwise be crowded in here . . . . The population is mostly free from the foreign element found in almost every town elsewhere—the country is so much settled by native-born Americans, that doubtless this will always be its character. Society is of the Eastern tone, and we trust we have among us enough of the salt of the earth, to give controlling influence to it, and shape it to permanent morality. As to secular advantages, they are not lacking."[53]

The Yankees who staked out most of southern Wisconsin by the 1850's were not liberal-minded people bent upon building a new and freer society with whatever human material might come along to share their "secular advantages"—after paying a finder's fee. Most of them came from the backland villages and hill farms of New England. Theirs was a homogeneous society and continued largely so for the many who spent some time in western New York. It was the New Englanders who stayed home in the cities and growing mill villages who first learned to live with the French-Canadians, Irish, Poles, and Italians.[54]

The European immigrant was not generally any more worldly than his Yankee counterpart. With few exceptions, those who made their way to Wisconsin after 1850 were not dissatisfied with

---

[53] This paean to Yankeedom was written in 1852 by a pioneer Presbyterian minister to describe what became the somnolent village of Lodi in Columbia County. It was quoted, with approval and at considerably more length, in the *History of Columbia County, Wisconsin*, p. 779, published in 1880 by the Western Historical Company of Chicago. Whatever the "secular advantages," Lodi did not grow much after 1860 and the inhabitants thirty-five years later were safely 90 per cent American-born. Wisconsin Department of State, *Tabular Statements of the Census Enumeration and the Agricultural, Mineral, and Manufacturing Interests of the State of Wisconsin*, 1895, Volume 1, p. 66 (hereinafter cited as *Wisconsin State Census* by date).

[54] Whitney R. Cross, *The Burned-Over District: The Social and Intellectual History of Enthusiastic Religion in Western New York, 1800–1850* (Ithaca, 1950; Harper Torchbook edition, New York, 1965), 4–6; Page Smith, *As a City Upon a Hill: The Town in American History* (New York, 1966), 53.

their religion or their cultural baggage. They also were conservatives in that sense. What troubled them was their economic present or future in the Old World. And what attracted them was the promise of economic well-being and the incidental promise of cultural and religious freedom protected by democratic citizenship. They did not come to be Yankees, and they were equally parochial in outlook.[55]

What the village offered was a wider array of economic opportunities than did the countryside. The Germans and Scandinavians particularly were numerous enough and similarly motivated with the Yankees towards "secular advantages." The presence of Norwegian-born T. G. Mandt, who by 1880 was the largest employer and president of the village board of Stoughton, was in no way unusual. It should not be necessary to make a list of similarly successful immigrants. The county histories of the time are full of examples. Can it be doubted that Yankee perceptions of an immigrant group were colored by the conspicuous success in business of some of its members?[56]

There is not much evidence of ethnic groups forming enclaves in villages comparable to the recognizable enclaves of Milwaukee with its Irish third ward, the Germans on the Northwest Side, Yankee Hill, or the Polish and German South Side. About the only way to determine this is to follow the census taker down the village streets in the federal manuscript censuses. The most common pattern appears to be clusters or islands, rather than distinctive sections of the village identified with a single ethnic group. In other words, they could be found on both the right and wrong sides of the tracks, to use the common metaphor for the economic gradations already becoming apparent in housing, residential streets, and neighborhoods. Kinship and European provincial affinities evidently account for these small, scattered clusters. The size of the village made the immigrant church or other

---

[55] Marcus Lee Hansen, *The Immigrant in American History* (Cambridge, 1940; Harper Torchbook edition, New York, 1964), 75–83.

[56] Western Historical Company, *The History of Dane County, Wisconsin. . .* (Chicago, 1880), 1162. In fairness, Mandt arrived in Dane County at age two in 1848.

meeting places accessible to all. These, of course, tended to serve segregated communities, but not on the basis of geographical separation into enclaves.[57]

If the Yankee villager viewed his rural cousin with condescension, thus creating some tension, the latter was nonetheless ready enough to become a villager himself. The village offered broader social contacts, more economic opportunities, and a sense of being abreast of affairs. Looking at the county subscription histories of the time, one is surprised at the number of men who came initially as farmers and then opted for a commercial or professional place in the village. The transition was not so hard to make. The truth is, nearly everyone in the village of the 1880's came from a farm background. Their urban orientation was an acquired trait, and all the stronger for that reason. This, combined with the profit motive, helped to make village pride and the "boomer" spirit a secular religion of the time.[58]

Henry Van Hise, father of a future president of the University of Wisconsin, illustrated the process. Injured in an accident while farming, he determined to try his luck as a merchant in the nearby village of East Milton. He then moved to Evansville, also in northwestern Rock County, a larger village with a population in 1870 of about one thousand. Van Hise was a merchant there

[57] The author conducted a graduate seminar in 1968–1969 in which students analyzed Wisconsin villages using the federal manuscript censuses. The pattern described above was common to Palmyra in Jefferson County, Monroe and Brodhead in Green County, and Boscobel in Grant County. See the following unpublished seminar papers, all in the SHSW: Bernard Bazan, "The Immigrants of Palmyra, Wisconsin, 1850–1880"; William F. Birdsall, "The Immigrant in Monroe, Wisconsin, 1870–1900"; Richard G. Levis, "The Immigrant in Brodhead"; Bruce Oman, "The Foreign Immigrant in Boscobel, Wisconsin, 1860–1880."

[58] Evidences of village pride inevitably come from local newspapers. Nonetheless, it is difficult to believe that it was the sole possession of the editor of the village weekly: "Never speak anything to the disparagement of your own town. Do anything you can to aid your laborers, mechanics, doctors, ministers, and printers. Help build up your churches and schools. Help all enterprises of merit; encourage every movement that will bring a dollar to your town by honest means, and discourage everything that tends to drive away labor or capital. Stand by your own town at all times and under all circumstances. This is the way to make things lively and prosperous." Columbus *Democrat*, August 27, 1881.

in three different firms during the succeeding eight years. The village had been established since 1845 and was incorporated in 1867, so there had been time for more continuity. Henry Van Hise realized his ambition as a village merchant: to aquire a farm for each of his seven children.[59]

Expecting considerable stability of residence to achieve the shrill note of village pride so characteristic of the times, it comes as a surprise that many villagers were apparently more footloose than their rural neighbors. A store or an office had no more holding power than a piece of land. The Trempealeau County study found farm operators the most persistent part of the population. Business and professional people—villagers—had a persistence rate of only one-fourth of their members during the decade from 1870 to 1880. A similar study of five villages in southwestern Wisconsin, which were either stable or only modestly growing in numbers between 1880 and 1885, found that they were apparently mere way stations.[60]

There are two ways of looking at the matter of the population mobility of the time. One is the surprising number of comings and goings within seemingly static or modestly growing communities. Another is the reassuring note that a stable core of the

[59] Maurice M. Vance, *Charles Richard Van Hise: Scientist Progressive* (Madison, 1960), 9–10; Writers' Program, Wisconsin, *Wisconsin: A Guide to the Badger State,* compiled by Workers of the Writers' Program of the Works Projects Administration in the State of Wisconsin (New York, 1941), 506. Curti, *Making of an American Community,* 228, found that of thirty-five village businessmen identified for his study, fourteen evidently came from a farm background. Thirteen had some previous business experience. Only three had fathers who were in business.

[60] Curti, *Making of an American Community,* 70–71; Peter J. Coleman, "Restless Grant County: Americans on the Move," in *WMH,* 46 (Autumn, 1962), 19. Village population mobility is discussed at more length in Chapter 6. In a completely unscientific comparison of listings in the *Wisconsin State Gazetteer and Business Directory* for 1876 and 1884, the persistence rates were 45.6 per cent for Monroe, 34.0 per cent for Stoughton, and 37.2 per cent for Baraboo. The count was by identifiable names, as it was not unusual for someone to change his business or profession. Stoughton and Baraboo enjoyed strong growth between 1870 and 1890, while Monroe was quite static. The latter had a large German and Swiss component by 1870 which may account for its greater stability. *Ninth Census of the United States, 1870: Population, Volume I,* 289, 290, 293; *Eleventh Census of the United States, 1890: Population, Volume I, Part 1,* pp. 359, 361, 365.

community remained. The familiar county histories are equally reassuring. The people who subscribed—and therefore had their biographical sketches included—felt a sense of place and asserted their bona fides as community leaders. Even those passing through sometimes left a community legacy. Twelve citizens of Kilbourn City (modern Wisconsin Dells) were the charter members and officers of Dell Temple of the Temple of Honor at its May 16, 1876, installation. Three and a half years later, only three of the original twelve remained in the village, but a new set of members, each with an office to match, was meeting regularly every Thursday night. Given the indicated rates of mobility for villagers in the seventies and eighties, those who persisted for eight or ten years were a decided minority—but also a *decisive* minority. They gave a sense of permanence and stability to the community, set the tone of the society to which newcomers conformed, and decided on admission to the circle of those who made things happen.[61]

The village offered another type of mobility than simply the turnover of population coming and going. Those who chose the village required some expectation that they could stay above the fine line between independence and indigence. The evidence is that those at the lower end in skills and property were the most likely to have a brief residence. But almost everyone shared in the opportunity to succeed in some degree. The immigrant Irishman who appeared in one census as an apparently temporary member of a railroad construction gang might well reappear later as a maintenance foreman or stationmaster, and thus an established villager. The unskilled learned a trade or became useful employees with some security. The craftsman acquired a shop and a place on the property tax rolls. The clerk became a partner in a mercantile establishment. The teacher went to normal school and became the principal of the new high school or superintendent of schools. And so on. Population growth was not necessarily

[61] Western Historical Company, *History of Columbia County*, 810, 831; Alcorn, "Leadership and Stability in Mid-Nineteenth-Century America," *Journal of American History*, 61:685–687; Doyle, *Social Order of a Frontier Community*, 15.

an accompaniment to this rising tide that floated many boats, although growth broadened the movement. Rather, the rising tide was an accompaniment of economic changes in the way goods and services were delivered. The farm that formerly had produced most of what the family consumed was now devoted more to cash crops and milk for the cheese factory. The growth of the marketplace was good for the village.

And why was the village considered a superior environment for the more rapid assimilation of the immigrant into the American mainstream? For one thing, it was more difficult to function in the village without a working command of English than, say, in a rural neighborhood where one had a few countrymen as neighbors, or in the anonymity of a city with its large immigrant enclaves. And while there was a surprising turnover of those accepted as natural leaders, there also existed a set of values which was easily transferred from one person to another. These included standards of deportment and views deemed respectable, and the importance to everyone of the growth and improvement of the village as an expression of community pride. If the immigrant reflected these values, and proved useful, he could be accepted as an insider. The village concentrated the pressures demanding conformity simply because people lived closer together, watching others was a passion, and there was more economic interdependence. It was easier to be a curmudgeon, an eccentric, or a loner on your own piece of land, or in the city. If you owned a business in the village, you needed acceptance; and so did the artisan or casual laborer.[62]

Village life focused status rivalries of both individuals and groups. A common evidence of group rivalry, and also an expression of village pride, was in church architecture. Columbus, for example, called itself "a city of churches." The local historian recorded the cost of each. In 1877 the congregation of Zion Lutheran Church, principally Germans, having outgrown

[62] Edward M. Lang, Jr., "The Common Man, Janesville, Wisconsin, 1870 to 1900" (master's thesis, University of Wisconsin, 1968), 50-87, 107-109.

several churches, commissioned a design from Edward Townsend Mix, a prominent Milwaukee architect of Yankee extraction. There were plenty of German-trained architects available,
as Milwaukee's skyline proved, but Mix was considered the
city's best.[63]

Providing a community meeting place was yet another way of
expressing individual success or group identification. In 1880,
Columbus had an opera house made from the old Methodist
church, a frame structure which was moved to a new site. The
Turnverein Germania met there, while eight other fraternal
organizations met in rooms provided over three local stores. By
the nineties, Columbus had a Turner Hall, as did Monroe and
many other villages. In Boscobel, Hurd's Opera House, which
seated 800, was supplemented by Ruka's Opera House, with a
capacity of 600. This seemed adequate for a village of 1,500
population.[64]

It is evident that the foreign-born found their way into village
politics well before the eighties. This is confirmed by the lists and
biographies of local elected officers. A more concentrated source
may be found in the hundreds of legistator's biographies in the
Wisconsin Blue Book. Most legislators came up through the ranks
of local offices in town, village, county, and city. Offhand, it
would appear that the village politician had a better chance at a
legislative seat than did a farmer. In the Wisconsin assembly of
1889, thirty-two of the 100 members gave non-farm occupations
and village addresses. Twenty-nine of these listed local offices
they held or had occupied, usually more than one. Ten of the
thirty-two were foreign-born: three Germans, one Austrian, one
Swiss, one Dane, two Britons, and two Canadians.[65]

[63] Western Historical Company, History of Columbia County, 678–684; DWB; Milwaukee
Journal, June 21, 1981; Richard W. E. Perrin, The Architecture of Wisconsin (Madison,
1967), 95–97.

[64] Western Historical Company, History of Columbia County, 690 ff.; Western Historical
Company, The History of Grant County, Wisconsin. . . (Chicago, 1881), 773–798; Wisconsin
State Gazetteer and Business Directory, passim.

[65] Wisconsin Blue Book, 1889, pp. 475–477, 501–522. A total of thirty-seven in the
assembly were foreign-born; twenty of them were from continental Europe, and ten of
those were from Germany.

Normal expectations on both sides—leaving aside any sense of protecting vital self-interests—eased the process of working the foreign-born into local politics. They accepted the rules of the host society, particularly with respect to matters defined by law, which included government and politics, education, property rights, and so on. Disagreements over education were not over the state's right to require a minimum education for children, but over the language of instruction and parochial school independence and equivalency. Yankee interest in immigrant participation usually started with presidential races. It is no coincidence that the presidential year brought a surge in the total vote and in partisan enthusiasm. The problem faced by village political managers was to attract immigrant voters by aligning them into the two-party system which local politics commonly followed.[66]

How village politics functioned a century ago in Wisconsin remains somewhat of a mystery. The few official records that survive do not tell us very much. Village weeklies usually had their eyes on state and national politics. Party politics was a passion, but local conflicts were something that everyone who mattered knew about anyway, and a village editor could only lose friends, subscriptions, and printing business by pointing them out. In any event, consensus was the mortar of boosterism.[67]

Because village politics frequently concerned matters of village pride and aggrandizement, there was evidently a good deal of deference shown those with the larger property and commercial interests. If there was rivalry, it was generally kept within those bounds. The idea was widely accepted that the village fathers

[66] Curti, *Making of an American Community,* 103–104, 137–138, 303; Doyle, *Social Order of a Frontier Community,* 169–177. *Laws of Wisconsin,* 1897, pp. 691–702, recognized and regulated the party caucus "at all general, municipal, town and village elections . . . ," thus confirming custom.

[67] The bibliographical essay in Doyle, *Social Order of a Frontier Community,* 273–282, is an excellent recent guide to literature on the subject of attempting to reconstruct village politics. See also Arthur J. Vidich and Joseph Bensman, *Small Town in Mass Society: Class, Power and Religion in a Rural Community* (Princeton, 1958; Anchor paperback edition, New York, 1960), chap. 5.

should be mature men of substance who treated local office as a mildly burdensome duty to be borne by the public-spirited.[68]

Mazomanie, a village in northwestern Dane County, furnishes a glimpse of village politics of the time—some would say of our time as well. A minute book of the village board survives, covering the years 1885–1893, beginning with the incorporation of the village. The new village president and the village clerk were members of the town board before the incorporation. The village contained about two-thirds of the town (that is, the township) population, before incorporation.[69]

The initial village election in Mazomanie gave every evidence of being a party vote. The village presidency was uncontested. The other offices were contested on a straight party basis. Mazomanie had an identifiable German element and older Irish, British, and Yankee contingents. The Germans, a stable element in the community, did well economically and furnished candidates to both the Republican and Democratic parties. J. A. Schmitz became one of the six village trustees. Henry Schildt, on the Republican ticket, defeated Carl Butz for police justice.[70]

J. B. Stickney, the village president, John G. Knapp, trustee, and H. R. Learnard, village clerk, were constants on the board through the 1880's. The board usually met in Knapp Bros. Store, often following a token meeting in the village hall. (If no outsiders appeared, they went to the store.) There was never a record of a vote in the minutes, only the language "It was

[68] Doyle, *Social Order of a Frontier Community,* 225–226; Alcorn, "Leadership and Stability in Mid-Nineteenth-Century America," *Journal of American History,* 61:694–702.

[69] Village Board Minutes, 1885–1893, Village of Mazomanie, Dane Microfilm Series 7, WSA. A sketch of the unincorporated village as it existed in 1880 is in Western Historical Company, *History of Dane County, Wisconsin* . . . (Chicago, 1880), 935–943 and 1047–1056. The village population was 1,034 in 1890, and another 448 lived in the rural Town of Mazomanie. (Both town and village were named Mazomanie.) *Wisconsin Blue Book, 1897,* p. 379. See also William Kittle, *History of the Township and Village of Mazomanie* (Madison, 1900), 79.

[70] *Wisconsin State Census,* 1895, vol. 1, p. 68; Statement of Election Results, 1885, Village Board Minutes, Village of Mazomanie, Dane Microfilm Series 7, WSA.

decided,'' or sometimes "a ballot was taken,'' or "resolved that" if an ordinance was in order.[71]

The important business of the board concerned sidewalks, streets, the innovation of electric lights—ten of them supplied by the milling company that owned the dam—organizing a fire company, and the responsibilities of property owners for "trash and clutter" and for animals at large. The most important business was done annually in April, just before the May election of officers. This was the licensing of the saloons—seven of them in 1886—for $200 each. These fees supplied most of the village budget.[72]

Ironically, Mazomanie—the town—was supposedly founded in 1843 by the British Temperance Emigration Society; but the village itself was platted and sold by insiders associated with the Milwaukee and Prairie du Chien railroad, built in the fifties. A spur had been projected from Mazomanie to the La Crosse-Milwaukee line. The result was a settlement of Irish construction workers and more stable Irish who formed an early Catholic congregation. The Yankees and British evidently came with the townsite promotion, and the Germans soon after.[73]

Mazomanie was not too well integrated as a community, speaking of the ethnic elements which—even in this small village

[71] Kittle, *History of Mazomanie* 79, 119-122, 141-143; Village Board Minutes, *passim,* Village of Mazomanie, Dane Microfilm Series 7, WSA. J. B. Stickney is in the Mazomanie *Sickle,* April 9, 1909.

[72] The Mazomanie village board minutes, May 1, 1888, contain just one record approximating an annual budget for the village, a Statement of Financial Conditions for May, 1886, to May, 1887:

| | |
|---|---:|
| Receipts. Bal. on hand May 3, 1887 | $1,506.85 |
| Poll Tax | 149.00 |
| Ins. agent tax | 60.40 |
| Hall Tax | 2.00 |
| Police court fines | 5.00 |
| Liquor licenses | 1,200.00 |
| Impounded stock | 8.00 |
| | $2,931.25 |
| Disbursements | 1,703.24 |
| BALANCE | $1,228.01 |

[73] Henry Howarth and Henry Z. Moulton, "Mazomanie," in Park and Co., *Madison, Dane County and Surroundings,* 592-615; Kittle, *History of Mazomanie,* 48-58.

of 1,024 in 1885—were separated into recognizable enclaves. Even given such separation, the political parties accommodated them in a familiar way. The village fathers were the merchants up and down the main village street who represented the leadership of the dominant Republican party. The village board members, without embarrassment, put the street lights in front of their own or their supporters' stores and homes. The sidewalks— the subject of many meetings—seemed to run strategic courses. An embarrassed afterthought provided a sidewalk to the "German Church."[74]

The principal source of revenue for the village was the licensing of the saloons. Before the incorporation as a village, this money went to the Town of Mazomanie. After incorporation, this money went into the village general fund by an express village board ordinance. This accounts for the generous allocation of funds for sidewalks, street lights, and street improvements. It probably also accounts in part for the poor record of Wisconsin's militant dry forces after the passage in 1889 of the local option law which permitted municipalities—towns, villages, and cities—to vote prohibition. A villager had to be a determined prohibitionist to vote away that revenue.[75]

The temperance forces had more success with Republican legislators than with village elections. An 1885 law gave municipal bodies the right to decide whether to have no licenses, where the former choice had been only between high or low license fees. In village government, the village board decided on this option.

---

[74] Howarth and Moulton, "Mazomanie," in Park and Co., *Madison, Dane County and Surroundings,* 600–605; Kathryn S. Moore, "Immigrant and Yankee: A Case Study of Mazomanie, Wisconsin, 1850–1880," unpublished seminar paper in author's files, December, 1968; Village Board Minutes, *passim,* Village of Mazomanie, Dane Microfilm Series 7, WSA.

[75] Village Board Minutes, May 3, 1886, Village of Mazomanie, Dane Microfilm Series 7, WSA; *Laws of Wisconsin,* 1883, vol. 1, p. 119; *ibid.,* 1889, vol. 1, pp. 734–736; Peter R. Weisensel, "The Wisconsin Temperance Crusade to 1919" (master's thesis, University of Wisconsin, 1965), 117, 142, states that by 1909 Wisconsin was geographically half dry—but that half included only 9 per cent of the state's population.

The prohibitionist forces scored a legislative coup four years later with the option for local referenda on the issue of licenses or prohibition. The *Wisconsin Prohibitionist* pointed out that this would circumvent the possibility "of a board or council turning traitor on their constituents. . . ." The issue could be placed on the town, village, or city ballot by a petition of 10 per cent of the number of voters who voted in the last municipal election. This was no insurmountable barrier in most any community, although the outcome might be no surprise. As an officer of the Wisconsin Woman's Christian Temperance Union told the delegates to their 1892 state convention, the grand idea was to keep on "forcing license or no-license upon the voters at every spring election."[76]

Mazomanie's prohibition petition arrived on schedule. The village board minutes for February 27, 1890, acknowledge receipt of the petition, signed by sixty-eight citizens. The dull political races of the prior five village elections were signaled by J. B. Stickney's uncontested elections as village president. In 1885, he had received 191 of the 211 votes cast. The 1889 vote dropped to thirty-one, meaning that only four voters—10 per cent of the number voting in that election—could force a special election on the prohibition issue. It was a real weapon.

Two hundred and two voters turned out for the special election in 1890. The meaning of the village budget, financed almost entirely by saloon licenses, was not lost upon the villagers. The prohibition issue was defeated, 125 to 77. The village board then turned its attention to the congenial task of renewing saloon licenses. The election of the village board followed the special election on the prohibition issue in short order. The village fathers won a ringing endorsement. President Stickney, running unop-

[76] *Laws of Wisconsin*, 1885, vol. 1, pp. 432–433; *ibid.*, 1889, vol. 1, pp. 734–736; *Wisconsin Prohibitionist* (Madison), April 18, 1889; Woman's Christian Temperance Union, Wisconsin, *Reports*, 1892, pp. 88. As the historian of Wisconsin's dry forces remarked, they may have been inept in many ways, but they were formidably organized. See Weisensel, "Wisconsin Temperance Crusade," 17.

posed as usual, received 145 votes, as did most of the rest of the ticket.[77]

Feeling its oats a bit, the village board proposed a radical departure for financing its taste for sidewalks, street lights, street extensions, and fire protection. A conflagration on election night, two years before in 1888, had required the aid of Madison's fire department, presumably by rail. Subsequent efforts to develop a more satisfactory water supply for such emergencies had been unsatisfactory. Consequently, the board offered a proposal for a municipal bond issue of $3,000 to build a standpipe and hydrants for fire protection. In a special election in May, 1890, on the proposal, the bond issue was rejected by a vote of 106 to 67. The bond issue would have pledged a levy against property. The 1887 budget indicated that the villagers had not been taxed regularly for operations or improvements. The board responded in September, 1890 with a three-mill levy—the first mention of such a tax. Also for the first time, the board members signed the ordinance in the minute book. They had crossed their Rubicon.[78]

In 1891 Mr. Stickney announced his decision not to run for Mazomanie village president for a seventh term. J. A. Schmitz succeeded him, defeating Jonathan Jones by 101 to 76, and old board members were joined by some new ones. There was a return to two-party contests through the last of the surviving record to the end of 1893, but the old hands were not seriously challenged. The prohibition petition was not renewed through those years. The proponents, having rallied only nine votes more than the number signing the petition, evidently felt that positions were fixed and both sides would turn out to defend them.[79]

The incorporation of Mazomanie as a village in 1885 was not an isolated coincidence. Temperance forces, always strong in the Republican party, had put through the series of liquor license

[77] Village Board Minutes, April 1, May 6, 1890, Village of Mazomanie, Dane Microfilm Serices 7, WSA.

[78] Ibid., May 8, 1888, May 13, 29, September 17, 1890.

[79] Ibid., May 4, 5, 1891, May 3, 1893. The village population actually declined from 1,222 to 1,034 between 1880 and 1890, and to 902 in 1900. The number of saloons had declined from seven to six, but not the desire for village improvements.

Farmers' market, Juneau Street, Milwaukee, c. 1887.

North Chicago Rolling Mills, Bay View, c. 1887.

Unloading coal on the Milwaukee docks, c. 1887.

McDougall whaleback steamers in the American Steel Barge Company docks, Superior, 1893.

Casting room floor at Fairbanks, Morse and Company, Beloit, c. 1890.

Original Pawling & Harnischfeger machine and pattern shop, First and Florida streets, Milwaukee, c. 1884.

Tanneries along the Milwaukee River, c. 1888.

Pawling & Harnischfeger works, First and Oregon streets, Milwaukee, c. 1886.

Henry Harnischfeger, c. 1884.

Frederick Vogel.

The Mitchell Building (built 1876), Milwaukee, c. 1887.

Offices of the Chicago, Milwaukee & St. Paul Railway Company, Mitchell Building, Milwaukee, 1887.

Interior of the Allis Reliance Works, c. 1887.

Paul Grottkau.

Jeremiah M. Rusk.

Edward P. Allis.

Charles King, 1879.

Allis Reliance Works, Bay View, probably May 5, 1886. National Guardsmen visible in the middle distance, parallel to the tracks.

Guardsmen drawn up at the Reliance Works, May 5, 1886, the day of the fatal shootings.

Woodworking class at the state school for the deaf, Delavan (Walworth County), c. 1893.

Housecleaning day, Black River Falls (Jackson County), c. 1892

National Soldiers' Home, Milwaukee, c. 1887.

Jeremiah Rusk (white beard, center) and his staff at the funeral of
Ulysses S. Grant, 1885.

Joseph Schlitz brewery, Milwaukee, c. 1887.

Plankinton House dining room, Milwaukee, c. 1887.

John Pritzlaff.

Horace Rublee.

The home of shoe manufacturer Charles T. Bradley, Milwaukee, c. 1887.

John A. Johnson.

Cadwallader C. Washburn's residence, Madison, c. 1874.

Views of Madison (above, looking southeastward from the Vilas residence) and of West Washington Avenue (looking southwestward from the capitol), c. 1875.

View of the Milwaukee Exposition Building from the corner of
Eighth and Prairie streets, c. 1887.

changes noted above that had consequences other than those intended. The earlier prevailing rate for a license to sell could be set by the licensing town, village, or city, within a range of $10 to $40; a license to serve liquor from $25 to $150. The 1882 legislature changed these ranges to $25 to $50 for a license to sell, and $75 to $200 for a license to serve. Licenses to serve were the norm in villages and cities. In 1885 Mazomanie had seven saloon licenses to serve and one drug store licensed to sell only.[80]

Another temperance success in 1885 provided that a petition signed by twelve voters could require a special election on the level of saloon licenses. The voters had an option of voting license fees of $250, $350, $400, or $500, depending upon the current level set by the village board or city council. This option could be voted upon every three years, by petition, and the village board could not change the levels set by the voters.[81]

A great surge of village and city incorporations followed this general rise in saloon license fees and the suggested disposition of the funds for general purposes. The Milwaukee *Sentinel* remarked after the 1882 changes in the minimum and maximum license levels that this was a tempting windfall for municipalities. The boost in the minimum brought an additional $25,000 into Milwaukee's coffers. The 1890 federal census listed 154 incorporated villages, an increase of 116 over the 1885 total. In addition, thirty-five villages graduated to city status between 1882 and 1891, while fifty-eight cities incorporated directly, without ever achieving village status.[82]

Marinette, which made the transition during the 1880's from a lumber camp with a mostly transient population to a family

[80] *Ibid.*, May 10, 1886; *Laws of Wisconsin*, 1882, pp. 970–976.

[81] Village Board Minutes, May 3, 1886, Village of Mazomanie, Dane Microfilm Series 7, WSA; *Laws of Wisconsin*, 1885, vol. 1, pp. 268–273.

[82] Wehrwein, "Village Government in Wisconsin," in *Wisconsin Blue Book, 1940*, pp. 166–167; Milwaukee *Sentinel*, March 31, 1882; *Eleventh Census of the United States, 1890: Population, Volume I, Part 1*, pp. 357–367. It may be that some village incorporations were initiated to take advantage of the free high school subsidy law of 1875, discussed below. But the timing seems to favor the reasons noted above. Political scientists seem to have missed this connection between liquor regulation statutes and village incorporations.

community, was one of those cities that stepped (in 1887) directly from town to city government with no intervening period as an incorporated village. Its population increased from 2,750 in 1880 to 11,523 in the 1890 census. Typically, the decision to incorporate was made by Marinette's first citizen, Isaac Stephenson, without much reference to the rest of the population. Although some of the mill owners, merchants, and professional men were ardent drys, Marinette kept its saloons. The new city fathers set licenses at the top $500 figure. In 1893 Marinette had fifty-two licensed saloons and three of Wisconsin's sixty-odd known millionaires. The saloons carried their share of the city budget. Only sixteen Wisconsin villages had voted themselves dry by 1906, under the 1889 option law. It was a less stern decision for rural towns, 223 of them having voted themselves dry. They were particularly concentrated in northern Wisconsin, where mill owners could indulge their dislike for saloons without contending with a large urban population as in Marinette.[83]

Another predictable, but surely unintentional, result of the temperance and prohibition crusades was to bring many immigrant voters to the polls who might otherwise have been indifferent to local elections. Practically everyone had grown so in Mazomanie before the 1890 special election on prohibition.[84]

The temperance crusade brought out not just the immigrant voters who were affronted; it also developed the talents of their leadership. Local and state issues determined immigrant party affiliations more than did presidential elections. Village leaders

[83] Carl E. Krog, "Marinette: Biography of a Nineteenth Century Lumbering Town" (doctoral dissertation, University of Wisconsin, 1971), 247–252, 258; Wisconsin Bureau of Labor and Industrial Statistics, *Biennial Report,* 1905–1906, pp. 236–238. The Milwaukee *Sentinel,* May 23, 1892, has the story on Wisconsin's millionaires, taken from the New York *Tribune.*

[84] Holdings and county records inventories in the Wisconsin State Archives. The 1906 report of the Wisconsin Bureau of Labor and Industrial Statistics noted that there were 296 villages and cities that licensed saloons; roughly two-thirds at minimum license, the other third at maximum. The two-for-one constraint may have reflected determinedly wet constituencies or simply a desire not to kill the goose. No analysis is offered on this question. Wisconsin Bureau of Labor and Industrial Statistics, *Biennial Report,* 1905–1906, pp. 236–245.

got their state politics from city newspapers, which were carried daily on the growing railroad network. The folklore of the village loafers hanging around the railroad depot has a basis in fact: it was a scene of considerable activity along any main line and on important feeders. Milwaukee papers furnished the news for the man of affairs in the village; the *Sentinel, Seebote, Herold,* and *Germania* were general newspapers with political news as a staple.[85]

The running fights over temperance, prohibition, and Sunday observance give the impression of an unbridgeable gulf between the Germans and Irish on one side, and the Yankees and their immigrant allies on the other. The truth seems to be that these battles were not nearly so divisive as the newspapers, church, and temperance publications indicate. Many Catholic congregations, both Irish and German, supported temperance and abstinence societies—an indication of cultural assimilation. *The Catholic Citizen,* published in Milwaukee, was ardently temperance and for conforming to Yankee ideas of Sunday observance. Archbishop Frederick Katzer of Milwaukee found it necessary to warn his flocks against joining not just the Turnverein or other German secret orders, but the Masons, the Odd Fellows, and the Sons of Temperance as well. Inclusion of the latter organization is interesting, given the ethnic make-up of most Catholic congregations.[86]

American evangelical Protestantism, the main driving force behind the temperance and sabbatarian crusades, was changing towards accommodation, just as were the immigrant churches. The growth of denominationalism, nonsectarian organizations such as the Young Men's Christian Association, the American

---

[85] The German-language dailies and weeklies' combined circulation was about 92,000 in 1884, about twice that of the English-language dailies of Milwaukee, and obviously more than the city absorbed. See Bayrd Still, *Milwaukee: The History of a City* (Madison, 1948; reprinted, 1965), 264–265; and Fulmer Mood, "Frederick Jackson Turner and the Chicago *Inter-Ocean,* 1885," in *WMH,* 35 (Spring, 1952), 194.

[86] *Catholic Citizen,* June 24, August 19, 1882, March 24 and 31, 1883; Milwaukee *Sentinel,* May 1, 1892; Weisensel, "Wisconsin Temperance Crusade," 4–5.

Sunday School movement, and the nonsectarian religion of immensely popular evangelists like Dwight L. Moody, undermined the traditional differences between Baptists, Methodists, Congregationalists, Presbyterians, and others. While the churches were expanding their memberships, religion was becoming more a social activity and a matter of outward demeanor. Such changes were directed particularly at urban America, but they were also felt in Wisconsin villages. After all, part of villagers' sense of difference from their rural surroundings was their identification with urban culture. They became more tolerant of immigrant churches, including the Catholics. They were curious about one another and uneasy about being too different. Church membership was an outward sign of conformity. As one sign of this, village newspapers readily printed notices and items on church fairs, bazaars, suppers, and building plans of both immigrant and native churches.[87]

Some of the Yankee temperance organizations catered as much or more to the social needs of their members as to the assault on Demon Rum. A study of the Good Templars in Wisconsin notes that the order attracted mostly young people. Their participation was usually passive. Many lodges waxed and waned rapidly as this mercurial group passed on to other enthusiasms. A lot of effort was spent on social affairs, initiation ceremonies, and arguing about who was worthy to join. Visiting lecturers were a staple of the organization, and getting a respectable attendance was always a problem. The order had adopted a rule in 1866 against dancing at lodge functions—an interesting problem in itself. Funerals in regalia were possibly less attractive for some members. The county subscription histories devote a good deal of space to the various temperance organizations. Lodi's Perseverance Lodge, No. 272, I.O.G.T., was barely persevering. Begun

[87] Sydney E. Ahlstrom, *A Religious History of the American People* (2 vols., New Haven, 1972; Image Books paperback edition in two vols., New York, 1975), 2:191–249; Carter E. Boren, "Divided Protestantism: A Unifying Force in Nineteenth-Century American Culture," in Margaret F. Morris, ed., *Essays on the Gilded Age* (Austin, 1973), 19–50; Clifton E. Olmstead, *History of Religion in the United States* (Englewood Cliffs, 1960), 446–447.

in 1865, the lodge had 185 initiates, but had dwindled to fifteen by 1870, and 1871 was "a very dark [year] for the lodge . . . ." And so it went. People came and went while rival organizations nibbled away at the shifting membership. One gets little sense that they were savaging their German neighbors—or even their local saloonkeepers.[88]

When the Odd Fellows of Two Rivers broke ground for a new hall, the participants repaired to the Turnverein Hall where speeches were given by C. White in English and Henry Stoll in German. About the same time, 1873, the German and German-Swiss veterans of the American Civil War joined in building Monroe's Turner Hall. It was the village meeting place over the years. By the 1890's, however, the Turnverein and other German organizations were failing for want of new recruits. The German Lutheran pastor had to teach German so that the young people could learn their catechism for confirmation. There was little disposition to continue the old German societies like the Deutsche Gesellschaft or the Schuetzen Verein, "for want of interest as the American-born members appreciate American games and sports more and the German language has also been discontinued because members speak little German."[89]

Sectarian spirit thrived in the American churches despite the homogenizing influences of popular evangelism and other pressures for conformity. The immigrant churches also were split by doctrinal and other internal disputes. The many synods of the Lutherans are a familiar example. Even the Catholic church had difficulty adjusting to its international role in the United States. The clergy were often seized with more zeal than their parishioners, which sometimes loosened rather than strengthened bonds. As an example, Archbishop Michael Heiss ordered his clergy to deny the sacraments to parents who refused to support or send their children to parochial schools when ordered to do so.

---

[88] Joanne J. Brownsword, "Good Templars in Wisconsin, 1850–1880" (master's thesis, University of Wisconsin, 1960); Weisensel, "Wisconsin Temperance Crusade," *passim;* Western Historical Company, *History of Columbia County,* 786.

[89] Milwaukee *Herold,* March 12, 1874; Birdsall, "Immigrant in Monroe."

The opposite side of this, of course, was an inclination on the part of the laity towards assimilation into the general community. In Trempealeau County, a German Lutheran pastor refused permission to a lax member to have his wife buried with other members of the family in the church cemetery because the husband was a member of a secret fraternal order, the Odd Fellows. Such officiousness on the part of the immigrant clergy in the American environment could certainly loosen bonds—and promote the Odd Fellows as a more ecumenical outfit.[90]

Yankee society was indeed difficult to penetrate for the first-generation immigrant unless he made a determined effort to learn the language, conformed to standards, and enjoyed an economic position in the village commensurate with his ambitions. But this generalization is subject to qualification. Many foreign-born came to Wisconsin as children or young adults and were as ready as the second generation—born here—to desert the Turnverein for American social organizations. And the immigrant organizations, like their churches, trimmed to American models. They became less an assertion of their differences— just as Americans learned to hold meetings in Turner halls. The immigrants' political differences, frequently based upon ethnic and religious identifications as they were, nonetheless found expression through the mainstream parties of American politics. German Catholics may have been quite dependably Democrats, but not all Democrats were German Catholics. The major parties spread a wide net. As in village politics, they learned to accommodate those who delivered votes.

Just as the political parties reached out to the male immigrant of voting age, the public school was a vital agency of assimilation, although this function was not necessarily uppermost with those who supported a larger financial commitment to local schools. A historian of the village of Lodi records that in 1864 the state superintendent of public schools, in his annual report, had

---

[90] Minutes of a meeting of all Milwaukee Catholic priests, October 13, 1881, in File 31, Milwaukee Archdiocesan Archives, Salzmann Library, St. Francis Seminary; Milwaukee *Herold*, March 6, 1879.

placed the village in rather an unenviable light in comparison with Kilbourn City, Pardeeville, Wyocena, Cambria, Fall River, and Poynette, because Lodi had not elected to consolidate its schools and include a public high school. This "aroused the pride of the citizens of Lodi, and steps were at once taken to remedy the matter." This statement reflects the general superiority of the village over the rural town in the vital field of public education. The importance of the school as an agency of assimilation, together with a sense of community, cannot be overestimated. This function, quite aside from the necessity of preparing young people for a more rapidly changing world than their parents knew, required a changed attitude towards support of the schools. The truth is that the village, on the whole, responded much more satisfactorily than did the rural town (township). Maybe it was a simple matter of rivalry and pride, as expressed by the villagers of Lodi who consolidated their schools, graded them, took over a privately operated academy as a high school, and went to the legislature for special permission to issue school district bonds in the amount of $10,000—a not inconsiderable undertaking for the 725 inhabitants.[91]

Villagers often had a livelier appreciation of the advantages for their children of improved educational opportunity. It certainly was not because villagers were wealthier as a class. Quite the contrary in terms of property values, although merchants and others may have seen more cash during the year than the average farmer. A more likely conclusion seems to be that the pure democracy of the rural town, which pertained as well to the rural school district, did not work as well in educational matters as did the somewhat elitist democracy of the village with its accustomed deference to the "village fathers."[92]

Some of the enthusiasm for improving village schools may have come from the running argument over the role of parochial

---

[91] Western Historical Company, *History of Columbia County,* 784-785.

[92] Curti, *Making of an American Community,* 253-255. Lee Soltow, *Patterns of Wealthholding in Wisconsin Since 1850* (Madison, 1971), 127, does not have many data for the years 1870-1900, but concludes: "The greatest leveller of all is education."

schools. This is not subject to proof, and village energy was
applied to the problem before the eighties, when the strong drive
for Catholic parochial schools began. The competition of a graded
public school system (with a high school) required considerable
determination on the part of the Catholics or Lutherans in a
village to build a competing school. They obviously had such
determination. Mazomanie, a village of about 1,000 in 1887,
had a Catholic parochial school which was graded, taught by
three sisters, and claimed 100 pupils.[93]

Villages generally had a higher proportion than rural towns of
men with education beyond the common school, a surprising
number of whom had taught school while getting their education.
Even a larger number of village women experienced an interval
as country schoolteachers. Among the things that these people
had in common were intellectual and cultural interests, an appreciation of the appalling condition of the average country school,
an active distaste for farm life as experienced in their youth, an
appreciation of the advantages for all children of a vital school
program, and the desire to stir things up. This combination
worked particularly well in the confined environment of the village. One knew where to find allies, and which screws to turn—
though again this is not subject to proof in chapter and verse.[94]

Years after her first teaching exierence in 1872, in a rural
school district of enlightened Kenosha County, Mary Bradford
recalled her initial encounter with rural school conditions: "There
was not a farmer of any repute in that district . . . who, if obliged
by circumstances to find with a neighbor accommodations for
some of his young stock—valuable pigs, lambs, calves, or colts—

[93] *Hoffmann's Catholic Directory,* 1887, p. 74; "List of Free High Schools," in *Wisconsin Blue Book, 1887,* p. 461.

[94] Smith, *As a City Upon a Hill,* 222–234; Edgar G. Doudna, *The Making of Our Wisconsin Schools, 1848–1948,* reprinted by the state centennial committee (n.p., 1948) from the *Wisconsin Journal of Education* (January, 1948). Mary D. Bradford, *Memoirs of Mary D. Bradford: Autobiographical and Historical Reminiscences of Education in Wisconsin, Through Progressive Service from Rural School Teaching to City Superintendent* (Evansville, 1932), which also ran in part in the *WMH,* 14–16 (September, 1930–September, 1932), is the record of a country girl who taught school starting at age sixteen, and went on to an activist and professional role.

would have thought of placing them there until the prospective housing place for his property had been examined, and its suitability in every way determined; but the place where his children and those of his neighbor would spend six or seven hours a day for a period of three months received no thought from him. Hence, the filthy, unsanitary, unattractive old room which I entered on my first day as a country school teacher."[95]

The record shows that most rural school districts simply wanted the cheapest they could get, and many voters came to the annual school election meetings as recalcitrant taxpayers, not as concerned parents. What they often got, as many county and state superintendents regularly complained, was a sixteen-year-old girl from a country school, hired to teach by an uncle who was the elected school district clerk. The county superintendent certified teachers on the basis of their "moral character, learning, and ability to teach," but none of these qualities was required when a superintendent ran for his office. And since the educational qualifications for teaching were vaguely defined, certification was quite open-ended. There was even an escape clause, allowing the county superintendent to limit certification to one school whenever "he is satisfied that the applicant is not qualified to teach in every district of the town. . . ." Little wonder that a county superintendent complained of "many ministers of the Gospel, professors in our higher institutions of learning, physicians, rich merchants and persons of influence in all other positions in life— join in *urging* and often in begging or commanding the county superintendents to grant certificates to those who *cannot* pass."[96]

Seeking answers to the conditions of rural schools, the legislature, prodded by the growing body of those working to make teaching a profession, provided in 1869 for the consolidation of

---

[95] Bradford, "Memoirs of Mary D. Bradford," *WMH,* 14:370.

[96] Wisconsin Superintendent of Public Instruction, *Annual Report,* 1873, pp. 93, 136. The Waushara County superintendent noted that certificates were given to two persons fifteen years old; ten to sixteen-year-olds; and fifteen to seventeen-year-olds. See also Wisconsin Superintendent of Public Instruction, *Laws of Wisconsin Relating to Common Schools, Normal Schools and the State University* (Madison, 1873), 112–114; and Hallam, "Bloomfield and Number Five," 203–224.

rural town subdistricts into single town school districts. But the
plan was left optional, with no bait attached. The amount of state
support for schools, mostly derived from the income of the school
fund from school land sales, had fallen in the seventies to an
average forty cents per child per year. There was not much
leverage there, and the consolidated district plan found practically no interest on the part of rural towns. By 1881, only
nineteen rural towns, all of them in northern counties where they
had more geography than pupils, had adopted the consolidated
district. By contrast to the towns, the villages were quick to take
advantage of a similar option.[97]

The first order of business, when a village adopted the consolidated district plan, was to elect a school board. The board, in
turn, selected a principal or superintendent to administer the
schools. In the tradition of the "village elders," the board was
usually made up of business and professional men who rather
naturally deferred to the judgment of the professional administrator, if he or she commanded their confidence. Fortunately, the
relatively new normal schools and the revitalized University of
Wisconsin were supplying such people, as were the educational
institutions in older states.

The next advantage that fell to the village was the free high
school. The legislative decision in 1875 to subsidize high schools
was a happy circumstance of pressure from two strong state
superintendents, Samuel Fallows and Edward Searing, together
with the political upset of 1873 which split the normal Republican serendipity. This put the Liberal Republicans in position to
be courted by both Democrats and Republicans—a longer story
for a later chapter. A good many Germans followed Carl Schurz
into the national Liberal Republican movement in 1872, or the
Democratic-Reform coalition of 1873 in state politics. The results
put Prussian-born Frederick Horn of Cedarburg in the assembly

[97] J. W. Stearns, ed., *The Columbian History of Education in Wisconsin* (Milwaukee, 1893), 30-33, 55-57; Wisconsin Superintendent of Public Instruction, *Biennial Report,* 1884, pp. 215-217, 238-249; *ibid.,* 1888, appendix, pp. 127-155.

speakership in 1875. The high school bill was introduced by Herman Naber of Shawano, born in the Grand Duchy of Oldenburg. Both men had come to Wisconsin as adults and were familiar with Old World education. Much of the debate about needed change in the Wisconsin school system invoked the Prussian model—a conspicuous success in the seventies.[98]

Just after the passage of the free high school measure, State Superintendent Searing discussed his expectations under the title "Township High Schools." "A perusal of the law . . . will show that its leading purpose is to encourage the establishment of *township high schools,* and thus to afford to rural neighborhoods the benefit of the higher educational facilities usually found only in cities and some large villages." If, however, the rural town failed to take advantage of this opportunity, "then it may be for the interest of a village district therein to organize the same unaided. The law allows the single district to do so, and to the school established by it properly qualified pupils from other parts of the town may be admitted on payment of tuition." The county superintendents were queried. They responded with enthusiasm. "I believe it will dot the State thickly with *nuclei* of culture," commented one. Almost all mentioned prospective village sites. A few hit upon the causes that were to turn the high schools into village rather than rural town or joint ventures. "Those against it think it is taxing one location to benefit another," wrote the superintendent of Green County. "Opposition has usually come from persons living at a distance from the place of the contemplated school," said the superintendent of Dodge County. From

---

[98] Fallows, Searing, and Horn biographies in the *DWB;* Schafer, *Four Wisconsin Counties,* 236–239. Horn was Ozaukee County superintendent ten years earlier; he had previously served as speaker in 1851 and 1854. Searing wrote: "The superintendent takes pleasure in saying that not only in the legislature which enacted the law, but throughout the State, in the audiences he had previously addressed, the Germans were among the most appreciative and ardent supporters of the high-school plan. This appears but natural when we consider that Germany is universally acknowledged to be the world's educational center." Wisconsin Superintendent of Public Instruction, *Annual Report,* 1875, p. 48.

Kenosha County came the comment: "There is a general feeling, I think, that it would largely increase the amount of taxes,
while comparatively few would be benefited thereby."[99]

The high school became the vital link between the common
schools and institutions of higher learning. It also made it possible to recruit rural teachers from the ranks of high school students rather than those who came direct from ungraded country
or village schools. State Superintendent Robert Graham wrote in
his 1883 report that "these schools exert a useful and wide-
reaching influence . . . in the opportunity they afford young
people to prepare themselves in scholarship for the position of
teachers in the elementary schools."[100]

Apparently there was occasional criticism of the high schools,
some claiming that they served an elite. The 1892 report
answered these critics with a breakdown by family status, claiming that of 5,491 families with children in the high schools, 1,623
were farm families and 659 were those of day laborers. The
legislative bait, starting with an appropriation of $25,000 to
subsidize the program, had worked. By 1884, more than half the
amount of the state subsidy was being collected by high schools
to cover the tuition of nonresident pupils, doubtless most of it
from farm families sending children to village high schools.[101]

Dane County had ten high schools by 1891, located in Belleville, Black Earth, Cambridge, Madison, Marshall, Mazomanie, Middleton, Oregon, Stoughton, and Sun Prairie. The
village populations of four of these—Belleville, Black Earth,
Cambridge, and Marshall—were under five hundred. That was

---

[99] Wisconsin Superintendent of Public Instruction, *Annual Report,* 1875, pp. 33–54;
Stearns, ed., *Columbian History of Education in Wisconsin,* 56–57. The superintendent's
statistical reports of the time make scarcely any reference to village schools, lumping them
in town or county figures. But one may extrapolate from these. In 1883 there were 110
high schools in the free high school category, thirty-three of them in city systems with
superintendents independent of the county superintendents. The remaining seventy-
seven were located in villages. Wisconsin Superintendent of Public Instruction, *Biennial
Report,* 1884, pp. 215–217, 238–249.

[100] Wisconsin Superintendent of Public Instruction, *Biennial Report,* 1884, pp. 20–22.

[101] *Ibid.,* 1884, pp. 21, 238–249; *ibid.,* 1892, pp. 48–51; Stearns, ed., *Columbian History
of Education in Wisconsin,* 58–62.

fairly representative of the southern Wisconsin counties. It seems fair to conclude that the high school—which generally meant a substantial outlay, since village pride demanded a suitable structure not provided by the state subsidy—created an important focus for community life. For ambitious young people interested in a professional career, the common route now passed through this village institution.[102]

Cities are more difficult to define than are villages when discerning the development of a sense of community. There were many sorts of distancing factors within urban cultures that varied with their economic organizations, their ethnic and religious mix, community leadership, and so forth. Sawmill cities like Eau Claire, with their high proportion of unskilled and itinerant labor, were quite different from more settled and varied industrial cities like Appleton and Janesville, although all three were comparable in size in the 1880 census. One can only compare examples that have attracted some useful description and study for the period under discussion.

Among other social distancing factors which greater concentrations of population made possible were the opportunities for people of like origins, religions, economic circumstances, and fraternal interests to group together. Distance was no great limiting factor for finding one's own kind in a city of ten to fifteen thousand. In the twin cities of Neenah-Menasha, for instance, with a combined population in 1890 of 9,664, there were three Catholic churches serving Germans, Irish, and Poles respectively. The cities were not discernibly segregated—no distinct sections occupied by national groups. But ethnic and religious communities were present with sufficient numbers to maintain separate but overlapping parishes divided along ethnic lines and shared by the two cities. The Germans, Norwegians, and Danes

---

[102] *Wisconsin Blue Book, 1891,* pp. 546–547. Smith, *As a City Upon a Hill,* concludes (p. 255) from statistical studies made on the origins of Americans who were conspicuously successful: "The town . . . contributed disproportionately to the professions, but to business it contributed very little." He uses "town" in the sense of "small town" or village.

maintained separate Lutheran congregations. The German and Irish Catholics maintained separate parochial schools, as did the German Lutherans. Until late in the century, only a small percentage of the children of the immigrants attended public schools, even for the number of years required by law. Voluntary associations were equally exclusive. Immigrant organizations conducted affairs in their own languages. The immigrants, an overwhelming majority of them working-class, accepted prevailing values and were in turn looked upon tolerantly by the Yankee-dominated society. The fact that the growing papermaking industry in Neenah-Menasha was relatively stable in its employment contributed to this harmony.[103]

Nearby Appleton, with a similar population mix and industrial base, was described in a reminiscence of the son of an emigrant from England. Alfred Galpin described the Appleton his father knew in the latter 1800's:[104]

> With its economy so well distributed between agriculture and industry, Appleton had no slums or landless proletariat. . . . Our artisans and shopkeepers were predominantly "Dutch" (Deutsch) or "Holland Dutch." To clerk in a store required at least an elementary competence in German, which for decades was also the language of St. Joseph's Catholic Church and Franciscan friary, and of the services conducted for the Reformed Jewish congregation at temple Zion. Typical among Wisconsin's numerous ethnic enclaves, the neighboring village of Little Chute remained a homogeneous unit of Dutch Catholics. All these groups, including also Irish, Swiss, and Scandinavians, worked and lived together with little sacrifice of their religious or ancestral life-patterns. Rather than a melting pot, the Appleton area furnished a miniature model of a pluralistic society.

How typical of Wisconsin's secondary cities were Appleton

[103] Charles N. Glaab and Lawrence M. Larsen, *Factories in the Valley: Neenah-Menasha, 1870–1915* (Madison, 1969), 204–211; *Hoffmann's Catholic Directory*, 1887, p. 208; Stearns, ed., *Columbian History of Education in Wisconsin*, 643. Oshkosh (population 15,748 in 1880) presented a similar diversity. See Richard J. Harney, *History of Winnebago County, Wisconsin, and Early History of the Northwest* (Oshkosh, 1880), 186–189.

[104] Alfred Galpin, "Portrait of a Father," in *WMH*, 63 (Summer, 1980), 263–266. Edna Ferber, the novelist, and Harry Houdini, the magician, came from Appleton's small Jewish community.

and Neenah-Menasha? They were certainly similar to most others in southern Wisconsin. This was particularly true of those cities with a growing industrial base that attracted a generous share of the European immigrants who were increasingly slanting cityward because of their own economic circumstances, their inability to buy desirable cheap land or to make the capital investment required for farming. What they found in these cities was a ready-made society which fits the description of these Fox River Valley cities. The congregations, fraternal orders, benevolent societies, parochial schools, and other organizations that would put them in their separate spheres were already in existence, or simply needed more recruits to make them viable.[105]

One can find many variations of ethnic enclaves. The eighth ward in La Crosse, for instance, was over one-third foreign-born, 66 per cent of them German. The ninth ward was 36.4 per cent foreign-born, 90.3 per cent of them Scandinavian. These doubtless were actual enclaves, and there were others that were simply perceptions of contemporaries. Oscar Thompson, the son of Norwegian immigrants, recalling his 1870's boyhood in Beloit, thought of his own mixed neighborhood as normal, but the "wild Irish" boys from "across the river" were different from his own American, Norwegian, and Irish chums.[106]

It was not that the foreign-born were not there. If one subtracts Milwaukee's from Wisconsin's urban population (places 2,500 and larger), the remainder in 1870 had an average foreign-born component of 32.8 per cent, compared to 33.8 per cent for the combined village and rural population. By 1890, these figures were reversed: 31.9 per cent for the urban, 28.75 per cent for the villages and rural population. The secondary cities had

---

[105] John D. Buenker, "The Immigrant Heritage," in Nicholas C. Burckel, ed., *Racine: Growth and Change in a Wisconsin County* (Racine, 1977), 79–81.

[106] *Wisconsin State Census,* 1895, p. 82; Buenker, "Immigrant Heritage," in Burckel, ed., *Racine,* 85–91; Oscar T. Thompson, *Home Town: Some Chapters of Reminiscence* (Beloit, 1942), 6–7. A survey of the 1880 manuscript census of Omaha, as another instance, discovered nothing resembling solid clusters, except for the black ghetto, despite the vivid contemporary perceptions. See Howard P. Chudacoff, "A New Look at Ethnic Neighborhoods: Residential Dispersion and the Concept of Visibility in a Medium-Sized City," in the *Journal of American History,* 60 (June, 1973), 76–93.

absorbed more of the immigration from 1870 to 1890, but not so much as to set them off as terra incognita to a rural or village youth.[107]

General percentage figures give no indication of the distribution of the foreign-born. In general, the new cities in northern Wisconsin drew a higher proportion of new immigrants, that being the nature of sawmill communities. In southern Wisconsin the more vigorous industrial cities drew them. Like found like in familiar social organizations. The peaceable kingdoms that historians have found in Janesville and Madison were cities that had a near-average percentage and mix of foreign-born in 1870, and made comparatively modest population gains by 1890. But why were the others so generally peaceable as well?[108]

Deference was a real force in city life, as it was in the village. It simply was not in the order of things for newly dependent people to challenge the right and duty of men of affairs to run things. Such men had exhibited their competence by accumulating property and creating wealth and jobs; they clearly knew best. Running a city was assumed to be a thankless burden, unremunerated, that fell on those who could afford the sacrifice. That this also served their self-interest was easily accepted by the majority.[109]

Deference, however, was not a simple matter of economic circumstance. Deference to those who were propertied came quite naturally to people who had come to the city for the purpose of improving their condition. If we are often appalled by the circumstances that they accepted, our judgment does not generally

[107] *Ninth Census of the United States, 1870: Population, Volume I,* 287–295; *Eleventh Census of the United States, 1890: Population, Volume I, Part 1,* pp. 557–558.

[108] Lang, "Common Man in Janesville"; Peter N. Laugesen, "The Immigrants of Madison, Wisconsin, 1860–1890" (master's thesis, University of Wisconsin, 1966); J. Rogers Hollingsworth and Ellen J. Hollingsworth, *Dimensions in Urban History: Historical and Social Science Perspectives on Middle-Size American Cities* (Madison, 1979), 78–97.

[109] *Laws of Wisconsin,* 1889, chap. 326, created classes of cities and made explicit that mayors and aldermen were not salaried, except in Milwaukee. Presumably the special charters under which second- and third-class cities operated (Milwaukee was the only city of the first class) had not provided salaries for mayors or aldermen. Those special charters are an impenetrable jungle.

comprehend the living conditions they left behind. The immigrant was ready to identify with things as he found them. No better proof is needed of this than the ready adoption of a pecking order that reflected American attitudes. A rare article was a German who did not believe that he was several cuts above a Pole or an Italian, but who grudgingly deferred to the Yankee's superior command of the economic and political system.[110]

Another aspect of the politics of deference was the possibility of joining the charmed circle. Admission was primarily by conspicuous economic success, not by birth, breeding, or accent. As in state government, Yankees were overrepresented in city government, but at least the door was ajar. Green Bay, for instance, by 1880 had elected three mayors who were foreign-born—but they all fit the pattern of enterprise, wealth, and commitment to the received view of the civic interest. The foreign-born could more readily aspire to the office of city alderman, elected by wards.[111]

Even the almost ritualistic contests over liquor control and civic decorum in cities were usually carried on at a subdued level of ethnic antagonism. Republican politicians shied away from close identification with these issues, although recognizing that an important part of their natural constituency favored control of liquor. But German Protestants and anticlerics were a necessary element of the party's voters, and they found liquor control measures repugnant. Democrats exploited this Republican weakness, which was part of the ritualism. As in the villages, the revenues from liquor licenses were too important to be seriously tampered with. Also, we may well be in error if we assume that an overwhelming majority of Yankees found an occasional glass of beer or a Sunday band concert offensive. The relative anonymity of the city made these amenities more available to the

---

[110] Michael Parenti, "Immigration and Political Life," in Frederic C. Jaher, ed., *The Age of Industrialism in America: Essays in Social Structure and Cultural Values* (New York, 1968), 85–88; Buenker, "Immigrant Heritage," in Burckel, ed., *Racine,* 120–125.

[111] Donald A. DeBats, "The Political Sieve: A Study of Green Bay, Wisconsin, 1854–1880" (master's thesis, University of Wisconsin, 1967); Hollingsworth and Hollingsworth, *Dimensions in Urban History,* chap. 2.

general populace. It could also isolate the rougher establishments that were usually less ethnic in character than just plain rough.[112]

There is no final answer to the question of how much immigrant citizens shared in the enthusiasm for civic boosting, which was endemic at least until the 1893 panic. But, given the demographics of the Wisconsin voting population and the fact that Wisconsin cities had conspicuously high percentages of home ownership, the evidence is that the cities became seriously overextended in financing booster-related "improvements," which resulted in important political shifts in the nineties. In other words, one must assume that civic aggrandizement was joined in by the foreign-born voters because bond issues were subject to voter approval.[113]

Civic booming was, of course, the province of Main Street, not of the immigrant running the trimmer in the sawmill. But Prussian-born Anton Klaus, Green Bay's wealthiest citizen in 1870, was an enthusiastic booster. Klaus proved his bona fides by going spectacularly broke after the 1873 panic—overextended in real estate and allied development projects. Nonetheless, the more familiar image of the go-getter, even in Wisconsin, somehow suggests attributes that were quintessentially American. George Peck caught this on a visit in 1879 to recently rebuilt Oshkosh: "If I were asked to pick out a hundred men that would illustrate Western pluck and enterprise, I would go to Oshkosh, pick up the first man with a slouch hat on, and ask him to ring a fire bell and get the boys together, and the hundred men could be picked out in four minutes by the watch."

Presumably the hundred would include those who, after the devastating 1875 fire, had just rebuilt their business and manu-

---

[112] Laugesen, "Immigrants of Madison," 55–66; David P. Thelen, *The Early Life of Robert M. La Follette, 1855–1884* (Chicago, 1966), 88–100. Janesville, certainly a Yankee-dominated community, collected about $2.25 per capita in saloon license fees. See Hollingsworth and Hollingsworth, *Dimensions in Urban History*, 96, 103, 107, 114.

[113] Wisconsin, with 55.2 per cent home ownership in cities of 8,000 to 100,000 population, was highest in the country except for Nevada. *Eleventh Census of the United States, 1890: Volume XIII, Report on Farms and Homes: Proprietorship and Indebtedness in the United States*, 27–30; David P. Thelen, *The New Citizenship: Origins of Progressivism in Wisconsin, 1885–1900* (Columbia, 1972), 133–135.

facturing structures in brick and stone—persons and firms like:
R. Guenther—apothecary and later state treasurer and congressman; H. Kuehmsted; L. Mayer & G. W. Newman; Haben &
Buck; Voigt & Wendorff; J. Horning & J. Baumgartner; Heis-
inger Bros.; K. Dichmann & Son; Kaerwer & Henkle; F. Her-
mann; Metz & Schloerb; J. M. Weisbrod; H. Bammessel; C.
Ernst; A. Meisner; Wm. Klotsch; E. Luhm; A. Tietzen; C.
Kohlman & Bros.; and Wm. Suhl's Steam Bakery—in all, about
one-fourth of Peck's one hundred. Very likely many of these
owned a slouch hat.[114]

Boosterism reached other levels of the community with civic
celebrations arranged by the local advancement society, or by
whatever other name the businessmen's organization was known.
These were truly community affairs. July 4, 1877, in Madison
was typical. The central affair took place in Capitol Park. Burr
Jones was the orator of the day, the Männerchor sang "The
Star-Spangled Banner," the Turnverein gave an exhibition of
acrobatics, and the Capitol City Band gave a concert in Turner
Hall. Schützen Park was crowded as the Germans continued
their celebration. Traditionally they were ardent celebrants of
Washington's Birthday and the Fourth.[115]

Columbus Day, 1892, witnessed a parade of 10,000 in Milwaukee, viewed by 125,000 according to the *Sentinel.* The affair
was organized by the Catholic church societies. The various
Polish Catholic societies stole the show with the variety of their
colorful uniforms—some of their units were on horseback. In
Wausau that day, all of the stores, mills, and factories were
closed for "a holiday of all classes." A grand industrial parade
was included with speaking and music for an evening celebration. Obviously, the city fathers were ready for some sacrifice of

[114] Lee F. Pendergrass, "Businessmen and Politicians in the Urban Development of
Green Bay, Wisconsin, 1866-1882" (master's thesis, University of Wisconsin, 1968),
12, 86-87; Harney, *Winnebago County,* 157-161.

[115] *Wisconsin State Journal,* July 5, 1877. Anson Buttles noted in his diary that Washington's Birthday "was not very extensively noted today, [and] has not been for many years
back except by the foreigners mostly. The Germans take more interest in it than Americans. . . ." Diary of Anson Buttles, February 23, 1891, in the Buttles Papers.

business to mark what was identified primarily as a Catholic holiday.[116]

It might be expected that city schools were superior to village and country schools as instruments of integration in the community. This appears not to be so. The reasons for this were only partly owing to the much greater prevalence of competing parochial schools in the cities. A typical report of the state superintendent of public instruction, that for 1888, gives attendance figures of 45.8 per cent for cities, against 63.9 per cent for village and rural public schools. Even if one distributes the state's estimated parochial school enrollment as nearly two-thirds in the cities, it would not make up the disparities. City children had a longer school year, but a smaller percentage attended.[117]

The availability of factory employment in many cities for both boys and girls probably accounts for much of the poor school attendance in that setting. Both parents working outside the home, or indifference, were other causes. Street trades or the simple attractions of "hanging out" in the relative anonymity of the city kept boys out of school. Village youth fortunately fell somewhere between the rural youths' harvest and plowing seasons and the city children's factory jobs and anonymous streets. (What was then known as truancy is today's enlightened "open campus.")

Another failure of the city schools was that they did not serve foreign-born adults in their struggles to deal with a new language. The Milwaukee public schools began running evening classes in 1880, but these were for school-age children who were working and therefore not attending regular classes. The state

---

[116] Milwaukee *Sentinel,* October 16 and 22, 1892. Columbus Day fell on a Friday, for which the Pope had given a special dispensation to the American faithful to ignore dietary restrictions.

[117] Wisconsin Superintendent of Public Instruction, *Biennial Report,* 1888, pp. 5–6. The superintendent complained regularly about the failure of parochial schools to report any statistics. The basis for yielding the village schools a superior attendance record, even though the statistics are not separated from those of rural districts, was the universal and continuous lament of county superintendents over lax attendance and short terms in rural districts.

constitution specifically limited free education to children between the ages of four and twenty years, but that did not bar others who were willing or able to pay a nominal tuition.[118]

Milwaukee *Deutschtum* was forged early in the city's history. But there were Germans and there were Germans. The peak of German immigration in the 1880's brought more rural, landless peasants to the industrial centers of Europe and America who lacked previous experience of cities and industrial employment. These newcomers faced a gulf similar to that expressed in the current term "Anglo," which Milwaukee's most recent immigrant recruits—Latin Americans—use to designate those who make decisions concerning their daily lives: jobs, assistance, housing, schooling, and so forth.[119]

A century ago, if you were a Pole working in one of the big manufacturing plants on Milwaukee's South Side, the chances were that your "Anglo" was a German. And the communication gap was also less literal than cultural. If you were one of the Russian Jewish refugees who arrived in the city in the summer of 1882, the German Jews were your "Anglos." They were desperately promoting the shipment of the refugees westward; the presence of the newcomers was disturbing their comfortable position as accepted members of the German community—their "Anglos." It all had to do with status, determined by when your community took root in the city, its relative economic status, its consciously applied political power, and how exotic it appeared by contrast with the mainstream, which might be described as German-Yankee at the time.[120]

[118] Buenker, "Immigrant Heritage," in Burckel, ed., *Racine*, 104; Stearns, ed., *Columbian History of Education in Wisconsin*, 451-452; Wisconsin Constitution, Article X, Section 3.

[119] Conzen, *Immigrant Milwaukee*, 14, 189; Roger D. Simon, *The City-Building Process: Housing and Services in New Milwaukee Neighborhoods, 1880-1910* (Transactions of the American Philosophical Society, vol. 68, pt. 5, Philadelphia, 1978), 17-19; Hartmut Keil, "German Immigrant Workers and the American Labor Movement, 1878-1890," research proposal in possession of the author.

[120] Korman, *Industrialization, Immigrants and Americanizers*, 41-48; Milwaukee *Sentinel*, July 2, 7, September 1, 14, 1882; Louis J. Swichkow and Lloyd P. Gartner, *The History of the Jews of Milwaukee* (Philadelphia, 1963), 63-64, 70-87.

The familiar divisions within the Milwaukee German community, based primarily upon religious orientation as well as provincial and economic class distinctions, were present by mid-century. But in culture and language they appeared to be all of a piece to non-Germans. The Germans staked out their main enclave in the city's northwest sector, including that portion of what shortly became downtown—the commercial center. They soon developed a sense of community from which non-Germans felt excluded. The other ethnic groups also settled in enclaves, but they were not usually as complete in their representation of occupations and social classes. The Germans, because of sheer numbers, felt at home in other sections of the growing city, even as industrial employment opportunities were dispersed by Milwaukee's distinctive geographic setting.[121]

In the 1880's Milwaukee was growing explosively; but as a young city it did not provide a stock of central city houses and other buildings to be converted into cramped quarters for the newly arrived with their few resources. The closest approximation was the established Irish section in the third ward, immediately south of the East Side business district. The third ward was characterized by small individual homes rather than tenements. In 1892 a major fire swept much of the ward, after which it lost its identity as the Irish enclave. By the turn of the century, much of it had been taken over by the recent Italian immigrants, who were attracted by the Catholic churches already at hand and by employment in the adjacent warehouses and docks.[122]

Beginning in 1869, major improvements were made in the Menomonee Valley by dredging canals to provide dock space

[121] Still, *Milwaukee,* 111–130. In addition to Still's excellent general history of the city, there are four other detailed studies that deal with this period, three available in printed form: Conzen, *Immigrant Milwaukee;* Virginia Zarob, "The Family in an Expanding Industrial Economy: Economic, Occupational, Social, and Residential Mobility in Milwaukee, Wisconsin, 1860–1880" (doctoral dissertation, Marquette University, 1976); Simon, *City-Building Process;* and Clay McShane, *Technology and Reform: Street Railways and the Growth of Milwaukee, 1887–1900* (Madison, 1974).

[122] Simon, *City-Building Process,* 18–21; Leora M. Howard, "Changes in Home Life in Milwaukee from 1865 to 1900" (master's thesis, University of Wisconsin, 1923), 12–13.

and access. This created a greatly enlarged area available for industries, for coal, brick, and lumber yards, for railroad yards, shops, and sidings, and packinghouses. Since a cheap, effective transit system did not come into being until well after 1890, Milwaukee's rapidly expanding industrial army had to find housing within walking distance of these employers. A broad division of the newer South Side placed the Poles in their heaviest concentrations south of the Menomonee Valley, bounded on the east by the company village of Bay View, the extended harbor improvements and dredged channels in Kinnickinnic Creek (River), plus the Chicago and North Western railroad occupying the lakeshore north of Bay View. Intermixing, but generally concentrating to the west of this growing Polish community, were the more recent South Side German immigrants, though they obviously had more options where they could feel at home in the city.[123]

As Milwaukee's overwhelming ethnic group, the German community on the northwest side was extensive enough by the 1860's to offer an environment so pervasive that the German-born could remain within it and have few contacts outside or need for a command of English. This included opportunities for industrial employment as well as for more traditional urban occupations and services. On the other hand, the confidence of numbers and the readiness of many to move into the mainstream of politics, entrepreneurship, and employment meant (as a recent student of the Milwaukee scene put it) that "by the 1880's, Germans were usually thought of as being separate from other immigrant groups—almost as if they had gained the stature of native Americans."[124]

Frank A. Flower's *History of Milwaukee, Wisconsin,* published in 1881, graphically illustrates this process with the hundreds of

---

[123] Simon, *City-Building Process,* 11-15, 18-19, 37-39; John Gurda, *Bay View, Wis.* (Milwaukee, 1979), 12-15; McShane, *Technology and Reform,* 40-44; Still, *Milwaukee,* 396; Korman, *Industrialization, Immigrants and Americanizers,* 46-47.

[124] Conzen, *Immigrant Milwaukee,* 1-9, 148-191; Zarob, "The Family in an Expanding Industrial Economy," 218-219; Korman, *Industrialization, Immigrants and Americanizers,* 42-43. Published in 1967 from his 1960 doctoral dissertation, Korman's book did not catch the current nuances of the term "native Americans."

brief biographies of the city's professional, commercial, industrial, supervisory, and skilled people—logical customers for his book. Other early established immigrant groups of appreciable numbers, particularly those from Great Britain, moved into the community's mainstream with equal ease. The Irish, the largest among these English-speaking people, moved with somewhat less ease because most of them came without capital, education, or urban skills. But many of them were quick to adapt and took advantage of available educational opportunities and an affinity for American politics. The pioneer reporter Bill Hooker commented that many of the Irish who had clearly made the transition to American success nonetheless remained in the modest homes of the old third ward "for fear of being called aristocratic," until they were released by the 1892 fire.[125]

This divided city of ethnic neighborhoods did develop a general sense of community. First of all, not everyone stayed put in an enclave or occupation. Bill Hooker nicely illustrates this. When he was a boy in the late sixties, his family lived in a three-section brick "tenement" on Virginia Street on the near South Side. His father was a foundry shop foreman at the E. P. Allis Reliance Works and later a member of the legislature. Another occupant was John M. Stowell, New York-born, who had a varied business and political career (mayor of Milwaukee, 1882–1884) and was the Stowell of the sawmill machinery manufacturing firm of Filer and Stowell. The third occupant was John A. Hinsey, claims agent for the Milwaukee Road, who became the model Irish Democratic political boss in the city. C. T. Melms, pioneer Milwaukee brewer, was another near neighbor. These were all families on their way up who were not content to stay in rental property in an industrial neighborhood. Economic mobility was an important factor in creating a sense of the whole city

---

[125] [Frank A. Flower], *History of Milwaukee, Wisconsin . . .* (2 vols., Chicago, 1881). The title page claims "nearly four thousand biographical sketches of pioneers and citizens." See Conzen, *Immigrant Milwaukee,* 59–60, 91–92; and Hooker, *An Earlier Milwaukee,* 67–69.

as a community, even while its character seemed fixed by the many blue-collar ethnic neighborhoods that survived.[126]

A sense of being a part of a metropolis, all too close to the megalopolis of Chicago, and surrounded by envious lesser cities and rural bluenoses, aided a growing sense of civic loyalty. The Madison *Democrat,* in a tirade entitled "Milwaukee—The Cancer of Wisconsin," ended with advice to "business men of the state . . . to transact business in Chicago, and have as little to do with Milwaukee as possible and the less the better. . . ." The Milwaukee papers in several languages responded in kind, contributing to a consensus that the city was of a different order. Civic booming worked in Milwaukee too. It never grew too varied or sophisticated to fail to respond.[127]

In the upper reaches of both business and society in the city there were two communities: an English-speaking one, and another more comfortable in German. They meshed more easily in business, of course. Frederick Pabst and Valentine Blatz were asked to join the chamber of commerce in 1865, Guido Pfister of Pfister and Vogel was on the board of banks and insurance companies, and so on. Bankers, real estate men, manufacturers, and those carrying on the city's commercial life necessarily did business with one another, and were drawn into civic projects such as the building of the Industrial Exposition Hall or capturing the state fair. A rough count of the chamber of commerce membership lists for 1872, 1883, and 1892 indicates that the presumably German-speaking membership mounted from about 19 per cent in 1872 to 26 per cent in 1883, and in 1892 to 37 per cent.[128]

Immersing themselves in American business life was a simpler

---

[126] Hooker, *An Earlier Milwaukee,* 4–5; Stowell is in the *DWB*; [Flower], *History of Milwaukee,* 1285–1303, documents the international character of the city's big industrial shops by listing the names and ethnic origins of shop foremen and middle managers.

[127] Madison *Democrat,* March 10, 1877; Still, *Milwaukee,* 252–253.

[128] Wisconsin State Agricultural Society, *Transactions,* 1887, pp. 170–183; Milwaukee Chamber of Commerce, *Annual Reports,* 1872, 1883, and 1892. The count is based on names of obvious German origin.

process than entering the English-speaking social life. One will look usually in vain for the names of prominent German business figures in the doings of Milwaukee's "high society" in the seventies. Nonetheless, the German community placed its mark upon social occasions at all levels, from beer gardens to the best the city offered in the way of theater and musical events.[129]

Times changed. The St. Andrew's Society took over Schlitz Park in the summer of 1882 for its annual picnic. The crowd of 7,000 Scotsmen and their Anglo-American friends forced the Germans to go elsewhere that day for their Gemütlichkeit. Ten years later, a prominent guest among the celebrants of the St. Andrew's Society annual banquet was Captain Frederick Pabst, sporting a Scot's bonnet—maybe just selling beer, but mostly because he carried instant recognition as a sort of "Mr. Milwaukee."[130]

It was certainly true that assimilation and a sense of a wider community were more easily achieved at the upper reaches of the economic and social pyramid. The amalgam there is also much easier to trace. The enclaves where newcomers could be comfortable continued longer in Milwaukee than in most Wisconsin cities. This was not simply a result of a continued influx of foreigners. There were other important factors: the city's distinctive geography that split it into sections; the high incidence of home ownership in working-class districts; and the identification of families with particular churches and other social organizations within walking distance. The rapid development by the early 1890's of an adequate transit system, accompanied by the development of suburbs and the outward movement of industries, began to break the mold. The 1893 panic and subsequent depression dealt this dispersion process a hard blow. Nonetheless, cheap rapid transit, the necessity to solve urban problems at

[129] Milwaukee *Herold*, February 1, 1886; Theodore Mueller, "Milwaukee's German Heritage: 'Das Deutsch-Athen Am Michigan See,' " in *Historical Messenger of the Milwaukee County Historical Society*, 24 (September, 1968), 84–95.

[130] Milwaukee *Sentinel*, July 14, 1882, and December 1, 1892. The fact that the city's Scots took over the most prominent beer garden for their national celebration says something about the pervasiveness of German culture.

the city rather than the ward level, and the lure of "downtown" for shopping and entertainment—all served better than the continual drumbeat of civic boosterism to give most Milwaukeeans a sense of belonging to something larger than a neighborhood. Just as rural town and village politics gave ethnic neighbors an incentive to participate, the more highly organized politics of the metropolis—a source of suspicious concern to those "outstate"—aggressively Americanized the immigrant. It took determination to remain an outsider, except for that huge minority— the wives and daughters of immigrant workingmen. The fragile alliances of the mass working-class movements that culminated in the tragic Bay View confrontation of 1886 were evanescent. In its aftermath, there was more getting even than getting together.[131]

[131] Still, *Milwaukee,* 396–400. McShane, *Technology and Reform,* 42, notes that the development of the streetcar system had a limited effect on the mobility of Milwaukee's industrial workers. Simon, *City-Building Process,* 15, adds that in 1902 Milwaukee ranked twenty-first among twenty-three major metropolitan areas in per capita streetcar ridership.

# 8

---

# Labor

---

## THE FAILURE OF INDUSTRIAL UNIONISM

THE growing body of industrial workers in the 1880's came to a heightened consciousness of itself as a separate class. This consciousness had much to do with the sense of insecurity in dealing with employers, who hired toilers by scores and hundreds in factories and workshops where a minority of skilled workers directed the labors of those who provided mostly muscle or simply a pair of hands. Employers were equally insecure in a fiercely competitive economy subject to rapid technological changes and expansion of the marketing areas of the lowest-cost producers. It was a deflationary period which, in turn, hit the rural debtor particularly hard—moderating sympathy for the urban wage earner, who lived in a different world. Wisconsin industries were vulnerable to the frequent sinking spells experienced by the general economy, as well as more specific slow times that were often the lot of such major employers or customers as lumbering, railroad building, iron mining, milling, or grain farming.

The general society seemed more sympathetic to the insecurity of the entrepreneur-employer than to the worker who had only his daily labor to sell. Certainly the notion of the sanctity of private property and the right of the employer to control absolutely the terms of employment—as an extension of his private property—was widely accepted. This is scarcely surprising in a population that was mostly rural, property-owning, and subject to the vagaries of weather and markets.

Governor Jeremiah Rusk, probably the most effective politician to hold the office before Robert La Follette, understood the limits of respectable opinion in this regard. An immediate test came during his first weeks in office, when the failure of the latest recipient of the St. Croix land grant, the Air Line Railroad, left 1,700 construction workers stranded in the wilderness of northwestern Wisconsin. To pleas from the contractors for militia to control the desperate men, Rusk replied that these men needed bread, not bayonets. He dispatched relief and managed the eventual restitution of the state's costs and the men's wages from the solvent successor to the eternally troublesome grant. Rusk's biographer editorially concluded that his "timely action . . . was of more practical benefit . . . than all the demagoguery and buncombe of the professional agitators who live off the workingmen . . . ," thus putting in bold relief the prevailing opinion.[1]

But Governor Rusk was also the one who on May 5, 1886, directed the militia during the culmination of the Eight Hour Day agitation in Bay View—the day after the Haymarket bombing in Chicago. When the officer in command at the Bay View Iron Works reported that the "mob" was approaching, Rusk reportedly ordered him by telephone: "Very well, sir. Fire on them." This the militia did, with devastating effect.[2]

The history of Wisconsin's industrial workers' efforts to achieve collective action, whether by individual shop organizations, trade and industrial unions, broad federations of all such organizations, or united political action, paralleled the general fate of labor movements at the time. They sometimes enjoyed limited success in prosperous times, only to lose ground and generally disappear in the frequent depressions and recessions which characterized the period 1873–1893. The Knights of Labor, a national organization that flourished in the 1880's,

---

[1] Henry Casson, *"Uncle Jerry": Life of General Jeremiah M. Rusk, Stage Driver, Farmer, Soldier, Legislator, Governor, Cabinet Officer* (Madison, 1895), 167–173.

[2] *Ibid.*, 192; Jerry M. Cooper, "The Wisconsin National Guard in the Milwaukee Riots of 1886," in *WMH*, 55 (Autumn, 1971), 42–43.

enjoyed broad but shallow popular support. The vicissitudes of
the economy, judges who automatically equated unions with
conspiracy, and a public that found the words "strike," "boycott," and "riot" interchangeable, only begin the litany of
obstacles to collective action. Industrial workers were a part of
the general public and many shared these attitudes. However, at
the peak of its strength as a popular movement, the Knights of
Labor claimed a Wisconsin membership of 30,000. The enthusiasm generated during the months before that May Day "riot"
to challenge the status quo with strikes, boycotts, and mass demonstrations was certainly unique.[3]

There appears not to have been any appreciable shortage of
workers—even of those with particular skills—in Wisconsin
industry at this time. The cities continued to attract many immigrants, who were joined by a flow of young people from rural
areas. A common refrain in news stories about strikes—which
were usually spontaneous actions in individual shops—was that
the employer immediately filled their places with no difficulty.[4]

The ethnic pecking order which characterized most large plants
in Milwaukee and elsewhere made common action difficult. German, British, and Scandinavian skilled workers, who were more
union-conscious than Americans, assumed that Poles, Italians,
and other latecomers were incapable of sustained union activity,
and thus were readily available to employers as strikebreakers.
Women and children in industry bore much the same
reputation.[5]

[3] Gilson G. Glasier, ed., *Autobiography of Roujet D. Marshall, Justice of the Supreme Court of the State of Wisconsin, 1895–1918* (2 vols., Madison, 1923 and 1931), 1:62–63; Ruth M. Elson, *Guardians of Tradition: American Schoolbooks of the Nineteenth Century* (Lincoln, 1964), 251; Milton D. Small, "The Biography of Robert Schilling" (master's thesis, University of Wisconsin, 1953), 188–189; Wisconsin Bureau of Labor and Industrial Statistics, *Biennial Report*, 1885–1886, p. 317. Membership figures for the Knights of Labor are certainly suspect in the light of the rapid rise and fall of the order, but it was probably close to 30 per cent of the state's industrial labor force.

[4] Gerd Korman, *Industrialization, Immigrants and Americanizers: The View From Milwaukee, 1866–1921* (Madison, 1967), 21–36; Milwaukee *Sentinel,* January 13, June 3, September 12, 1882.

[5] Korman, *Industrialization, Immigrants and Americanizers,* 43–44, 51–53; Thomas W. Gavett, *Development of the Labor Movement in Milwaukee* (Madison, 1965), 25–26, 47.

As was illustrated in the Eau Claire "Sawdust War" of 1881, strike actions by other than established, disciplined unions of skilled workers were usually spontaneous in character, lacked competent leadership, had little chance of success without the cooperation of the skilled workers, readily attracted outsiders eager to fill the jobs, and commonly ended in ugly confrontations. Unless the employer capitulated immediately, the strikers usually faced a choice between either overt action (which would bring the police and courts and even the militia to the employer's aid) or a rapid melting away of their supporters (and the loss of their jobs to others). Picketing and boycotts were considered illegal activities. As Judge James A. Mallory put the case to striking cigar makers when their employer readily recruited replacements: " . . . [T]hey had an undoubted right to strike, if the conditions . . . did not suit them, but they had no right to hang around the shop they had left and intimidate those who wanted to work." Associations of employers to implement lockouts, import strikebreakers, or establish blacklists were looked upon with equanimity. The legal system did not offer much leverage to workers.[6]

The Sons of Vulcan, the skilled ironworkers' union at the Milwaukee Iron Works in Bay View, was one of the strongest unions in its ability to sustain discipline and win concessions. Iron reduction, unlike steelmaking, involved operations dependent upon highly skilled labor. The Sons of Vulcan were mostly of British origin and had little in common with the numerous unskilled workers who shared the unpleasant conditions of the seventy-two-hour week and the heat, noise, and hazards of the workplace for about one-fifth the wages. It was unskilled Poles who met the militia's gunfire on May 5, 1886, as they crossed over the boundary of Bay View Village from their enclave on Milwaukee's South Side. The Sons of Vulcan were inside the

---

[6] Milwaukee *Sentinel*, February 16, 1882. See also *ibid.*, January 18, 20, February 7, 1882; U.S. Senate Committee on Education and Labor, *Report Upon the Relations Between Labor and Capital, and Testimony Taken by the Committee* (4 vols., Washington, 1885), 1:279–280.

plant, taking no part in the Eight Hour Day agitation and unwilling to join the general work stoppage.[7]

Not the least of the troubles of Wisconsin's industrial workers was their lack of common agreement on means and goals. This was the proper function of leadership. Competence and a practical approach to the problems at hand did not necessarily accompany the attributes of bilingualism and commanding presence. By 1893, Victor Berger and Frank Weber, the architects of Milwaukee socialism and of the Wisconsin Federation of Labor (AF of L), provided the competence and practical sense in these roles. But earlier, leaders vied for center stage in the noisy struggles leading to the Eight Hour Day riots in Milwaukee, the climactic Bay View incident, and its aftermath.[8]

The career of Robert Schilling, who was the principal leader of the Wisconsin Knights of Labor through the eighties, may well stand as a metaphor for the trials of industrial labor in those tumultuous years. His was the most persuasive voice arguing for a community of purpose and action. He considered race, nationality, and religion irrelevant bars to participation in a common cause. His bluff honesty, general good nature, and readiness to seek sensible compromise gave him a central role wherever such a solution was possible. But he was essentially an orator and publicist, not much interested in organizational details, who readily mistook the word for the deed. Schilling started as a trade unionist, but soon found third-party politics more congenial; he always welcomed an opportunity to turn a labor union into a base for political action. No radical, he was a pragmatist whose talents were not disturbed by the tenets of any coherent philoso-

---

[7] John Gurda, *Bay View, Wis.* (Milwaukee, 1979), 13–14; David Brody, *Steelworkers in America: The Nonunion Era* (Cambridge, 1960), 7–10; Bernhard C. Korn, *The Story of Bay View* (Milwaukee, 1980), 54–56. Both the Sons of Vulcan and the Milwaukee Iron Works went through name changes in the 1870's and 1880's. The Sons of Vulcan was an English transplant which became part of the National Amalgamated Association of Iron and Steel Workers in 1875. The name "Sons of Vulcan" remained in common parlance, as did "Milwaukee Iron Works" or "Bay View Works," although the plant became a part of the North Chicago Rolling Mill Company in 1878 and part of the Illinois Steel Company at the end of the 1880's.

[8] *DWB*; Gavett, *Labor Movement in Milwaukee,* 90–95.

phy. Schilling achieved nationwide prominence as the national secretary of the People's (Populist) party at its 1892 convention in Omaha. The Milwaukee *Sentinel* wryly noted prior to the Omaha convention: "Robert Schilling has held his usual state convention and has decided to call his party the People's party this year. It continues to be the old Greenback and free coinage party, however, and smells just as sweet with one name as another."

Schilling is a neglected figure in Wisconsin history, usually given only passing mention as one of the leaders of the Eight Hour Day agitation in 1886 and for his role in Milwaukee third-party politics immediately before and after. While the Wisconsin Knights of Labor centered in the metropolis, where it had fully half of its membership at its peak, Schilling became a familiar figure in Wisconsin lumber centers and other industrial cities as the state organizer for the Knights, as a union negotiator, and as an accomplished stump speaker. In a day when political oratory ranked high as public entertainment—and could be piped into the home only on paper—Schilling provided it in both forms. He normally edited a minimum of two weeklies, in German and/or English, and was fluent in both. He often boasted of the distances he traveled and the number of speeches he had given in a day. Many Wisconsinites, in the 1880's and 1890's, readily recognized references to "Old Bob," and they did not mean La Follette but "Old Bob" Schilling.[9]

Robert Schilling came to this country from Saxony at age three and left school to go to work at thirteen after his father died. He apprenticed as a cooper in St. Louis in a shop serving the brewing industry. It was a trade shortly threatened by machine-made barrel staves. As skilled workers requiring a relatively lengthy apprenticeship, the coopers had a national union of some consequence. Schilling—fluent in German and English, an avid reader, and a competent public speaker—rose within the Coopers' International Union, which had had problems recruit-

[9] Small, "Robert Schilling," 64–65, 273, 337; *DWB*; Milwaukee *Sentinel*, May 30, 1886.

ing German-speaking members. Martin Foran, head of the Coopers' International, brought Schilling to Cleveland. The two men were compatible, since both looked beyond their trade to the general problems of workingmen in an industrial society increasingly dominated by large employers. Cleveland was the home of the Standard Oil Company, which could afford the expensive machinery for fabricating barrel staves to be assembled by coopers who had only modest skills. Ohio was also a hotbed of greenbackism, a monetary theory and hopeful basis for agrarian and urban labor political co-operation. Foran and Schilling were leaders in various efforts to organize industrial unions that would recruit across the lines of trades, skills, and occupations. A problem was that these efforts usually attracted theoretical reformers rather than rank-and-file members. Schilling was certainly inclined to think in terms of third-party platforms.[10]

The times were ripe for an organization to reach beyond the existing trade unions. The far from inevitable instrument for change was the Knights of Labor. What made the Knights different was that during its first seven years (1869–1876), the order, centered in Philadelphia, was controlled by pure and simple unionists who sought closer ties among the various craft unions but did not reach out to the unskilled as well. They professed no aims to rebuild American society and made no provisions to take in other than craftsmen and industrial workers. Given the problems of the times for unions, the order adopted the trappings of secrecy and ritual common to the popular fraternal organizations of the day. By 1878, however, the professional reformers had moved in on the Knights.[11]

[10] Small, "Robert Schilling," 5–14, 22–28, 32–34, 49–58; Milwaukee *Sentinel*, May 30, 1886; Albert S. Bolles, *Industrial History of the United States* . . . (Norwich, Connecticut, 1881), 510; John R. Commons et al., *History of Labour in the United States* (4 vols., New York, 1918–1935), 2:74–76; Norman J. Ware, *The Labor Movement in the United States, 1860–1895: A Study in Democracy* (New York, 1929; Vintage paperback edition, 1964), 11–18.

[11] Ware, *Labor Movement in the United States*, 26–42. The Knights of Labor "were the first to organize the unskilled workers of America . . . bringing these in large masses into the ranks of organized labor." Herman Schlüter, *The Brewing Industry and the Brewery Workers' Movement in America* (Cincinnati, 1910), 113–114.

Schilling's introduction to Wisconsin had come about through the agency of Edward P. Allis, whose conversion to monetary reform followed his brush with near bankruptcy. In 1877 Allis was running for governor on the Greenback ticket. He was shopping for an orator-editor who was strong in the faith and who could persuade the traditionally hard money Germans of the rightness of his cause. Schilling proved to be his man, making a great hit with Wisconsin audiences. Although he lost the election, Allis made his best showing in communities where Schilling had appeared. Schilling continued his forays into Wisconsin, where he was sponsored by businessmen and manufacturers who shared the views of Edward Allis—a sponsorship which pretty well defined Schilling's radicalism.[12]

In a broader context, Americans were newly aware of what would later be called "un-American activities." Doctrines such as socialism, communism, nihilism, and anarchism, which had their origins in Europe—many in Germany—now appeared in the American heartland. The violent activities of the Molly Maguires in the anthracite fields ended in late 1876, when ten Mollys were hanged. In the summer of 1877, widespread railroad strike-related riots erupted in Baltimore, Pittsburgh, Chicago, San Francisco, St. Louis, Reading, Altoona, Scranton, Buffalo, Toledo, and Louisville. In Pittsburgh, state militia units from Philadelphia were brought in to quell the disturbances and killed twenty-six people in dispersing a crowd. A day of looting and general destruction followed. There was a similar scene in Baltimore. President Rutherford B. Hayes sent federal troops to Baltimore to quell the riot there: the first occasion when they were used in what began as a labor dispute. The nation contemplated revolution coming from the city slums, and began to see Molly Maguires and unwanted foreign agitators in every minor labor dispute. The courts and newspapers began to talk of class war and conspiracy.[13]

---

[12] Small, "Robert Schilling," 100–104, 112–113, 119–121; Walter F. Peterson, *An Industrial Heritage: Allis-Chalmers Corporation* (Milwaukee, 1978), 72–75.

[13] Ware, *Labor Movement in the United States,* 45–49. Robert V. Bruce, *1877: Year of*

Wisconsin was not touched directly by the events of the 1877 summer, but there was certainly a growing consciousness that the metropolis was different. A socialist party flourished briefly in Milwaukee in the seventies, organized by men with such names as Brucker and Lyser. The Milwaukee *Commercial Times* warned: "Honest workingmen, Milwaukee's large class of little capitalists and savings bank depositors . . . will be very careful not to encourage the Brucker party. . . ." This was the socialist group which had the wit simply to suggest a slate of local candidates, some of whom were nominated by the Democrats, who could count votes.[14]

In the summer of 1880, Schilling moved to Oshkosh to join the editorial staff of the *Standard*, a greenback paper backed by Allis and other substantial greenbackers. The Oshkosh connection was a brief one. He shortly moved to Milwaukee to edit a German-language weekly, *Der Reformer,* for the local greenbackers. Milwaukee remained his home. He went to his first Wisconsin convention of the Greenback party about the time of his move to Milwaukee, where he took his accustomed place on the platform resolutions committee. The platform produced was pure Schilling, featuring quotations from Aristotle, Lincoln, Webster, Jefferson, President Grant, Edward P. Allis, and Republican and Democratic platforms that had wobbled on hard money.[15]

---

*Violence* (Indianapolis, 1959), reconstructs the events of the summer. Governor Harrison Ludington requested that the 300 residents of the Old Soldiers' Home at Milwaukee be mustered to save the city from "the laborer insurrection," which furnished a wan smile to President Hayes and his cabinet. *Ibid.*, 289.

[14] Ware, *Labor Movement in the United States,* 22–50; Milwaukee *Commercial Times,* April 1, 1876. The names of Joseph Brucker and Gustav Lyser were frequently invoked by the English-language press opposing "communism." It was assumed that they would "start something" during the 1877 railroad strikes. "Trusty citizens" and the militia were alerted. Many of these political activists, however, disappeared into the Greenback party in 1880, except for the dangerous Herr Brucker, who became a Republican. See Frederick I. Olson, "The Milwaukee Socialists, 1897–1941" (doctoral dissertation, Harvard University, 1952), 28–34; field notes for a biographical sketch of Joseph Brucker, in U.S., WPA, Wisconsin Biographies. Brucker shortly turned to real estate promotion in northern Wisconsin. See also Gavett, *Labor Movement in Milwaukee,* 27–34.

[15] Small, "Robert Schilling," 152–156, 161–165; Ellis B. Usher, *The Greenback Movement of 1875–1884 and Wisconsin's Part in It* (Milwaukee, 1911), 57–61.

The 1881 gubernatorial campaign was the last hurrah for the Greenback party in Wisconsin. Over his own objections, Allis was given the nomination and received about 4 per cent of the vote. Casting about for a constituency to support *Der Reformer,* Schilling's eye fell upon the union movement. He wrote his old friend, Terence Powderly, now national president of the Knights of Labor, who renewed his commission as an organizer for the order. Schilling wasted no time in reviving the Milwaukee Knights Assembly and attempting to steer it towards political action.[16]

Milwaukee labor history becomes intricate at this point. Interest in union activity was renewing rapidly, but the potential leadership was more interested in political activity than in practical unionism. The political action virus was endemic among those who specialized in editing union newspapers, composing union constitutions, and writing resolutions for reviving unions and trades assemblies.[17]

In 1885 everything began to break at once for Schilling. That summer, the Knights temporarily won recognition in a strike against the southwestern railroads controlled by Jay Gould. This short-lived triumph was largely responsible for the tremendous growth of the Knights in 1885 and 1886. At the same time, Schilling was making important gains outside Milwaukee. Michigan had passed a ten-hour workday law for industry. Across the river in Marinette, an eleven-hour day was standard, and the workers organized, preparing to strike. Schilling, who agreed with Powderly's rejection of the strike as a useful weapon, hurried to offer his services as arbitrator. It was a mark of his

---

[16] Usher, *Greenback Movement, passim*; Small, "Robert Schilling," 164–176. The resumption of paper-gold convertibility in 1879, combined with the Bland-Allison silver purchase act, gave the National Greenback party its deathblow. See Irwin Unger, *The Greenback Era: A Social and Political History of American Finance, 1865–1879* (Princeton, 1964), chap. 11. After the 1884 presidential campaign, in which Schilling was active as a popular speaker beyond Wisconsin's borders for the National Greenback Labor ticket, he closed down the *Reformer* and concentrated on the *Volksblatt,* which he had initially edited in the interest of the Milwaukee Trades Assembly.

[17] Gavett, *Labor Movement in Milwaukee,* 41–50.

conservatism, despite his oratory about heartless monopolists or the inequity of the national money system, that Schilling's services were so readily accepted by both sides. His mediation efforts resulted in a settlement of a ten-hour day for ten hours' pay and some wage concessions, but the mill owners were adamant against any real recognition of the workers' unions.[18]

Schilling's reputation was enhanced by the Marinette settlement, and calls came from around the state to organize new Knights assemblies. The Knights rapidly became the principal voice of labor in most Wisconsin cities and many lumber towns. Schilling's speeches had changed very little over the past ten years—sounding fiery when condemning monopoly and the "money power," but repeatedly counseling against violence and strikes. Unlike Powderly, he was prepared to use the boycott as a weapon, confident of his ability to sway public opinion. Conservatives feared him, but he was infinitely preferable to his immediate rivals.[19]

Schilling was also at odds with Powderly because of his enthusiastic acceptance of the growing eight-hour-day agitation. This was an old rallying cry that had excited occasional interest and support over the past quarter-century. In 1884 the Federation of Organized Trades and Labor Unions, from which emerged the American Federation of Labor two years later, had declared that the eight-hour day would become a fact by united action on May 1, 1886. The Knights inherited this impractical pledge as the ascendant labor organization at the time. Powderly wanted no trouble from this dubious promise, and suggested that local

[18] Ware, *Labor Movement in the United States,* 123–125, 139–145. The national membership of the Knights grew from 111,395 to 729,677 between July, 1885, and July, 1886. The decline was less rapid, but membership fell to 259,518 two years later. *Ibid.,* 66. "By May, 1886, there were forty-two local assemblies with over 12,000 members in Milwaukee and 25,000 members in the state," according to Gavett, *Labor Movement in Milwaukee,* 50. See also Small, "Robert Schilling," 191–195; Carl E. Krog, "Marinette: Biography of a Nineteenth Century Lumbering Town" (doctoral dissertation, University of Wisconsin, 1971), 222–226; Wisconsin Bureau of Labor and Industrial Statistics, *Biennial Report,* 1885–1886, pp. 238–246.

[19] Small, "Robert Schilling," 195, 197–200.

members write essays on the eight-hour day to be published on Washington's birthday. Somehow, this seemed to fall short of the popular expectation. So popular was the eight-hour-day idea with the rapidly growing rank and file of the Knights in Milwaukee that Schilling could not resist promoting it. Early in 1886, he formally organized the Eight Hour League in Milwaukee.[20]

A problem that continually plagued Schilling was that his left flank was exposed. A German expatriate socialist, Paul Grottkau, with roots in European anarchism (though he broke with the anarchists before Haymarket), moved to Milwaukee in March, 1886, where he edited the German socialist paper *Arbeiter-Zeitung*. Grottkau positioned himself to the left of the majority of German socialists but to the right of those willing to espouse violent action. He organized the Central Labor Union, which recruited actively among unskilled workers, although it also included some local craft unions. In numbers, the Central Labor Union had less than half as many members as Schilling's Milwaukee assembly of the Knights of Labor. Both organizations had substantial Polish contingents. This would be of some significance in the light of later events.[21]

Grottkau spoke for the majority of the German socialists, but the active members had undergone the usual schisms. Frank Hirth, a cigar maker who had edited socialist newspapers in Detroit and Chicago, had adopted the anarchistic doctrines which Grottkau had earlier rejected. Most of the public did not distinguish between socialism and anarchism. Hirth was prominent in a small faction that advocated violence against the ''bosses'' and the system. They were noisy participants at Eight Hour League

---

[20] *Ibid.*, 197, 200–201; Ware, *Labor Movement in the United States,* chap. 13.

[21] Gavett, *Labor Movement in Milwaukee,* 56–57; Small, ''Robert Schilling,'' 200–205; Morris Hillquit, *History of Socialism in the United States* (5th ed., New York, 1910), 209–220; Henry David, *The History of the Haymarket Affair: A Study in the American Social-Revolutionary and Labor Movements* (New York, 1936; revised paperback edition, 1963), chaps. 1–5; Howard H. Quint, *The Forging of American Socialism: Origins of the Modern Movement* (Columbia, South Carolina, 1953), 15–36; Milwaukee *Journal,* May 5, 6, 11, 15, 1886; Cooper, ''Wisconsin National Guard in the Milwaukee Riots of 1886,'' *WMH,* 55:36–37.

general meetings, particularly heckling Schilling for his lack of militancy.[22]

Schilling's part in the Eight Hour League was compromised by Master Workman Powderly's hostility towards the whole idea. Grottkau and Hirth successfully challenged Schilling's leadership, calling for a mass confrontation with employers on May 1, 1886. Schilling began looking for a way out. Late in February, the League held a hugely successful mass meeting at the West Side Turner Hall, with an estimated 3,000 in attendance. The purpose was to put pressure on the city common council to approve a resolution to adopt an eight-hour rule for all day laborers working for the city or on municipal projects. Schilling, who had become a friend of the Republican mayor, Emil Wallber, persuaded him to endorse the resolution. Shortly thereafter, the council adopted the resolution with only one dissenting vote, but it made no provision for enforcement.[23]

The action by the city council was advanced by Schilling as evidence that the triumph of the eight-hour day would be accomplished simply by the mobilization of public opinion and continued peaceful pressure. He predicted that this would come about by May first without the proposed general strike. This led to angry exchanges with the radicals, who scoffed at his timidity. Grottkau's new Central Labor Union had joined the Eight Hour League, and it now took over its direction as Schilling and the Knights' Milwaukee Central Committee, under pressure from Powderly, forced all but three of the thirty-seven local assemblies to abstain from participation in the proposed general strike action.[24]

---

[22] Small, "Robert Schilling," 190–191, 202; Milwaukee *Herold,* March 1, 1886. Gavett, *Labor Movement in Milwaukee,* 56–57, says that there were about 140 members of the German socialists who were followers of Grottkau and about forty members of the Hirth group.

[23] Wisconsin Bureau of Labor and Industrial Statistics, *Biennial Report,* 1885–1886, pp. 318–319; Cooper "Wisconsin National Guard in the Milwaukee Riots of 1886," *WMH,* 55:37; Milwaukee *Sentinel,* February 10, 11, 16, 27, March 19, 1886; Small, "Robert Schilling," 197.

[24] Small, "Robert Schilling," 199–205.

In Wisconsin, the strike threat in support of the eight-hour agitation was almost entirely confined to Milwaukee. Most of the city's industries depended upon a corps of skilled operatives who exhibited some organization and militancy, but who usually dealt with individual employers rather than engaging in general strike actions. The rapid growth of the Knights in 1886, plus the eight-hour-day agitation, added a new element—industrial union-ism—to labor relations in the city.[25]

Schilling was an opportunist driven swiftly by events, which he tried to influence. The Knights grew so rapidly in the spring of 1886—not alone in Milwaukee—that his days and nights were filled with engagements to speak and organize new chapters. He had little time to contemplate strategies or concentrate upon particular situations. It must have been largely fortuitous that he played a personal role in two Milwaukee strikes that were industry-wide in character, and involved industries particularly vulnerable to working-class pressure.

The Milwaukee cigar makers had engaged in a protracted strike in 1881–1882 that had broken the union and left bitter factionalism behind. The local of the International Cigar Makers was reviving at the same time that Schilling was recruiting a Knights assembly among cigar makers. The competing unions were about evenly matched in membership. The largest cigar-manufacturing firm struck a bargain with the international, abandoning a settlement being negotiated with the Knights. Schilling invoked a boycott, on which the conventional judicial view was that this constituted an illegal conspiracy, and some of the cigar makers went out on strike.[26]

The breweries presented a different type of target. Their employees worked unconscionably long hours for straight

<hr/>

[25] Wisconsin Bureau of Labor and Industrial Statistics, *Biennial Report,* 1885–1886, pp. 238–246, 249–251, 256–267, 282–296, 319–320, notes the shift from individual shop actions to industry-wide disputes.

[26] Small, "Robert Schilling," 203; Wisconsin Bureau of Labor and Industrial Statistics, *Biennial Report,* 1885–1886, pp. 256–267, 341–342, 372–382; Lawrence M. Friedman, *A History of American Law* (New York, 1973), 488–489; Gavett, *Labor Movement in Milwaukee,* 67; Milwaukee *Journal,* May 12, 1886.

wages—often as many as thirteen hours a day with some Sunday work expected. But much of this work, especially for those involved directly with the brewing process, was leisurely. There were also traditional privileges, such as free beer on the job. An old trade association existed among Milwaukee brewery workers—primarily a relief and benefit lodge, which was typical in the seventies. Schilling was especially effective in organizing brewery workers. Their standard language was German; coopers were involved both as employees and suppliers; and the nine Milwaukee breweries had a total payroll of "no less than 3,000 men."

Early in 1886 the brewery workers won substantial concessions from the brewers, who presented a united front. Working hours were reduced to ten and general raises totaling over 10 per cent were offered, to become effective on May first. Stunned by their easy victory—the brewers recognized a popular movement and knew who consumed their product—the brewery workers decided to hold out for their original demands and a closed shop. These concessions were not made. The men walked out on May 1, the Saturday when the eight-hour-day excitement began, adding to the crowds. The brewers conceded again on the wage demands but not on the closed shop. The men went back to work on May 6, the day after the shootings at Bay View.[27]

The Allis Reliance Works was organized as one of the largest (1,600 members) Knights of Labor assemblies. A senior molder was the spokesman, who doubtless felt that he and his men could strike a bargain on wages and hours without advice or assistance from others. In April, 1886, the negotiations with Edward P. Allis shortly came to an impasse. Allis agreed to an eight-hour day, but in a reasoned reply he also told his men that he could not compete on the basis of ten hours' pay for the eight-hour day. He agreed to some minor adjustments in pay for the common labor, but said he would simply shut down and await better

[27] Thomas C. Cochran, *The Pabst Brewing Company: The History of an American Business* (New York, 1948), 271–283; Milwaukee *Journal,* May 1, 1886.

times if the other workers insisted upon an eight-hour day at ten hours' wages.[28]

A committee of employees met with Allis and reported back that it was satisfied with his explanations. An initial meeting accepted these findings, but a subsequent meeting with a smaller attendance, which was evidently dominated by Grottkau's followers, repudiated the agreement. Bad blood developed between the two opposing factions. On May 1, there was a walkout of 150 men from the foundry, about 10 per cent of the work force. Allis said that he understood that these men were simply exhibiting solidarity with the eight-hour-day movement and would return on Monday. As May 1 was a Saturday, a general holiday atmosphere pervaded the city and many workers failed to report or left early.[29]

Schilling was concerned with the growing militancy of his abandoned creation, the Eight Hour League. There were crowds in the streets on Saturday, May first, and a grand parade and general meeting planned for the following day at the Milwaukee Garden, a large beer garden in the old German quarter west of the Milwaukee River. Schilling arranged a meeting for Monday night, May third, inviting businessmen and labor representatives to the West Side Turner Hall. His speech offered no practical alternatives and was simply a plea for calm. It received no particular notice in the press. Events had moved beyond his power to influence them. And Monday had offered more excitement than another speech from Schilling. Protesters invaded the Chicago, Milwaukee & St. Paul Railway car shops, attempting to shut them down, and part of the work force at the Bay View ironworks went out. Also, Governor Rusk arrived in town on Monday night in case he was needed.[30]

After the Sunday demonstration at the Milwaukee Garden,

---

[28] Wisconsin Bureau of Labor and Industrial Statistics, *Biennial Report*, 1885–1886, pp. 321–325.

[29] *Ibid.*, 323–326; Milwaukee *Journal*, May 1, 1886.

[30] Small, "Robert Schilling," 205–207; Milwaukee *Journal*, May 4, 5, 1886.

which was huge but orderly, the Milwaukee *Journal* acknowledged that the fears of many had not been realized, but deplored
the leadership that had come to the fore since the withdrawal of
the Knights from the Eight Hour League. The paper estimated
that there were 10,000 men on strike by May 1, but aside from
the brewery and cigar makers, most of the strikers were from less
concentrated industries: tailors, carpenters, coal yard hands,
German bakers, broommakers, brickyard employees, and
slaughterhouse hands.[31]

A mob of several hundred men had appeared at the CM&StP
car shops just before noon on Monday, the third. Late arrivals
kept coming until the number mounted from an estimated 300—
identified as mostly Poles by the Milwaukee *Journal*—to possibly
1,500, all milling about in the sprawling shops. They jostled
workmen at the machines, yelling and threatening. Some carried
sticks, and a few knives were in evidence. But the only violence
occurred when a group tried to reach the offices above the shop
floor and a shop foreman grabbed one of the interlopers and
threw him down the stairs. The group retreated.

The railroad shop men did not welcome their deliverers, whom
they clearly considered their social inferiors. Some wanted to
attack the interlopers, but cooler heads prevailed. The workmen
were directed to lay down their tools and go home to await a call.
The sides were about evenly matched, because the order to go
home had released another 1,800 to become spectators. Some
sheriff's deputies appeared but were helpless in the face of the
numbers involved and the extent of the shops. The company
brought in hired guards from outside, and their own employees
volunteered as "special police." Most employees were back at
work the following afternoon.[32]

[31] Milwaukee *Journal,* May 1, 3, 1886. May 1, 1886, was a national urban happening.
There were an estimated 80,000 workers out in Chicago, 45,000 in New York, 32,000 in
Cincinnati, and 9,000 in Baltimore. See Commons, et al., *History of Labour,* 2:385.
[32] Milwaukee *Journal,* May 3, 4, 5, 1886.

The incident at the car shops was not an isolated one. Euphoric with their assumed success there, some members of the crowd moved on to the Allis Reliance Works where they were repelled by fire hoses and strong words from the belligerent skilled workers. Another gang of about 200 Bohemian lumber shovers was also roaming the Menomonee Valley, closing down the lumberyards. Brewery workers from the West Side, estimated at about 650, passed over the Sixth Street bridge and marched down National Avenue to the Falk Brewery. The Falk workers had not gone out with the general brewery strike. This crowd was met by Sheriff George Paschen and deputies, plus Major George Traeumer and Adjutant Otto Falk of the Fourth Battalion. A committee was allowed to parley with the Falk workers, who refused to strike on this occasion.[33]

Governor Rusk was to emerge as the hero of the riots. He was a military man who had risen to the command of the Twenty-Fifth Wisconsin Infantry during the Civil War and been mustered out with the rank of brevet brigadier general. Rusk played the role of professional veteran to the hilt. He often traveled to Grand Army of the Republic affairs with a "staff" of "maimed heroes" which the press seldom failed to note. Rusk's adjutant general, Chandler P. Chapman of Madison, aided by Charles King of Milwaukee, had reorganized the national guard into a force of some 2,400 officers and men.[34]

Charles King, like his father Rufus who had made the *Sentinel* a power in Republican politics, was a West Point graduate, but

[33] *Ibid.*, May 3, 1886.

[34] Cooper, "Wisconsin National Guard in the Milwaukee Riots of 1886," *WMH*, 55:31–34, 39; Jerome A. Watrous, ed., *Memoirs of Milwaukee County: From the Earliest Historical Times Down to the Present, Including a Genealogical and Biographical Record of Representative Families in Milwaukee County* (Madison, 1909), 598–600; Casson, *Jeremiah M. Rusk*, 106–108, 223–225. Rusk's immediate predecessor, Governor William E. Smith, had been an enthusiastic advocate of a revived militia: "We cannot hope always to escape disorders and tumults similar to those which have arisen in other states and nations." *Wisconsin Public Documents,* 1880, Governor's Message, vol. 1, p. 22. In the summer of 1881, Smith had called out the militia to break the Eau Claire lumber strike, known popularly as the "Sawdust War." See Chapter 2 above.

had seen most of his service after the Civil War in Indian cam-
paigns in the Southwest. Invalided out in 1879, he joined the
Wisconsin National Guard as inspector and instructor. In this
capacity, King took no pains to hide his ultra-nativist views or
his opinion that Milwaukee harbored a population "from whose

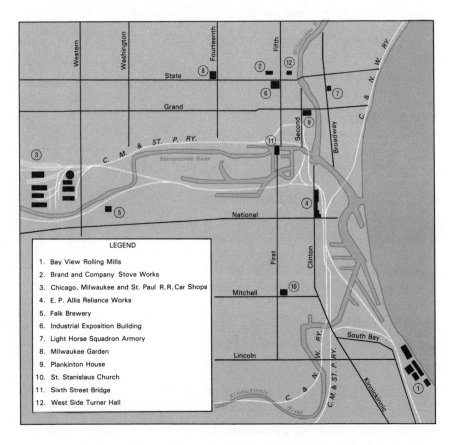

LEGEND

1. Bay View Rolling Mills
2. Brand and Company Stove Works
3. Chicago, Milwaukee and St. Paul R.R. Car Shops
4. E. P. Allis Reliance Works
5. Falk Brewery
6. Industrial Exposition Building
7. Light Horse Squadron Armory
8. Milwaukee Garden
9. Plankinton House
10. St. Stanislaus Church
11. Sixth Street Bridge
12. West Side Turner Hall

MILWAUKEE—BAY VIEW, 1886

dregs can be swept up . . . a mob [on] whom it might be a municipal blessing to fire. . . ." Strikes by laborers, he held, could only be the work of "designing demagogues" or "temporary insanity."[35]

Governor Rusk was watching the situation in Milwaukee. He distrusted Wallber and Paschen, the German mayor and county sheriff, on whose appeal he had to depend for any official call for aid. He was in touch with presumably more reliable witnesses, such as Colonel King and other prominent Milwaukeeans. King warned the governor that the pawn shops were being emptied of guns as the Reds prepared to take over the city. But a more practical man had set things in motion for the governor. When Alexander Mitchell, president of the CM&StP, found that his car shops had been closed by the strikers, he summoned Governor Rusk to the scene on a special train placed at his disposal. Rusk arrived that evening, Monday, May 3, and established his headquarters at the Plankinton House.[36]

Early on Tuesday morning, the fourth, the action shifted to the rolling mills at Bay View. A largely Polish crowd had assembled at St. Stanislaus Church, about a mile and a half away, to march on the mills and close them down. They were ready to set off by 8:00 A.M. Not long after, Mayor Wallber appeared at Schilling's door to persuade him to intervene. Sheriff Paschen had also sent a message to the same effect. Having persuaded all but three of the thirty-seven Milwaukee assemblies of the Knights to officially withdraw from the Eight Hour League, Schilling had become the voice of reason by contrast with Paul Grottkau and others now vying for leadership of the popular movement. Schill-

---

[35] *DWB*; Cooper, "Wisconsin National Guard in the Milwaukee Riots of 1886," in *WMH*, 55:34–35, quoting from the Wisconsin National Guard Association, *Proceedings*, 1884, pp. 2–3, 11; Charles King, "Memories of a Busy Life," in *WMH*, 5 (June, 1922), 371–373.

[36] King, "Memories of a Busy Life," *WMH*, 5:374–375; Cooper, "Wisconsin National Guard in the Milwaukee Riots of 1886," *WMH*, 55:38–39; Milwaukee *Journal*, May 4, 1886.

ing was memorialized by banners carried in the May Day parade: "Humbug, your name is Robert."[37]

Schilling arrived at Bay View to find a crowd surrounding the superintendent of the plant, who was not succeeding very well with his explanations of why the skilled laborers inside were not particularly interested in the eight-hour-day proposal. There were some hard words. The size of the crowd, estimated at over 1,000 men, caused understandable concern. The *Sentinel* described the superintendent, John C. Parkes, as standing in their midst with a big Pole at one side, a burly Pole on the other, a stout Pole behind, and a Samson Pole in front. Fortunately, the master workman of the Polonia Assembly was on hand, as he had been the day before, trying to calm things down. He seemed to be a minority of one.[38]

The crowd, recognizing Schilling, turned more good-natured, and agreed that he should head a delegation to go inside the plant and parley with the Sons of Vulcan. This delegation was just returning, with Schilling earnestly advising Parkes to close down, when the first contingent of the National Guard arrived by train near the front gate. Schilling, always confident of his ability to sway a crowd, was furious. In Schilling's absence, Sheriff Paschen had gauged the mood of the strikers and observed among them some who had been at the car shops the day before. Some were armed with clubs. He ordered them to disperse, and they asked him to repeat it in German. When he did so, the strikers answered, "Wir wollen nicht." The sheriff, fearing worse trouble, went to the phone and formally requested Governor Rusk to send the militia. When the troops first arrived, as the sheriff later stated, "The effect was magical . . . the turbulent mob was turned into quite an orderly assemblage." Then the Kosciusko Guard arrived, and came in last—a mistake, said the sheriff.[39]

[37] Small, "Robert Schilling," 206–208; Milwaukee *Sentinel,* May 5, 1886; Milwaukee *Journal,* April 28, May 4, 1886.

[38] Milwaukee *Sentinel,* May 5, 1886; Korn, *Story of Bay View,* 56.

[39] Milwaukee *Journal,* May 4, 1886; Small, "Robert Schilling," 208–209. Bay View was organized as a village, not part of Milwaukee, and therefore the county sheriff had

The scene that followed had much to do with the events of the next day. The guardsmen were forced to detrain and form ranks in the midst of the crowd. To make matters worse, the Kosciusko Guards were fellow Poles whose regular meeting place was in the parish school of St. Stanislaus. The strikers were more than threatening. Some grabbed for the soldiers' weapons, struck them from behind, and treated them to a shower of missiles. Captain Francis Borchardt was struck in the head by a stone. As the Kosciusko Guard reached the plant gate, five or six in the rear rank, without orders, turned and fired above the crowd. The strikers did not disperse, but the action brought some caution to the boldest, and they held their ground for some hours. The portentous Haymarket bomb exploded in Chicago that same evening.[40]

While the militia was moving in at the rolling mills, other events were unfolding in the city. Another mass meeting of strikers was taking place at the Milwaukee Garden on the German West Side. Paul Grottkau advised them that they had the power to close down the city. A large group formed and marched to the Brand and Company stove works, about three-quarters of a mile east near the Milwaukee River, and forced the plant to shut down. They were then within a few blocks of the Plankinton House where Governor Rusk had his headquarters. This, plus the news from Bay View, moved Rusk to call up units of the First Regiment, consisting of companies from Madison, Janesville, Beloit, Monroe, Darlington, Delavan, Whitewater, and Racine, since the only units he had in reserve were the Milwaukee Light Horse Squadron and the local artillery battery. The First Regiment units were all in the city by 5:30 that afternoon.[41]

---

full jurisdiction. Also see the Milwaukee *Evening Wisconsin,* May 3, 1886. Sheriff Paschen gave his version of the affair some months later; see the Milwaukee *Sentinel,* December 28, 1886; and David, *History of the Haymarket Affair,* 168-177.

[40] Cooper, "Wisconsin National Guard in the Milwaukee Riots of 1886," *WMH,* 55:40-41; Milwaukee *Journal,* May 4, 1886; Milwaukee *Sentinel,* May 5, December 28, 1886.

[41] Cooper, "Wisconsin National Guard in the Milwaukee Riots of 1886," *WMH,* 55:41-42; Milwaukee *Journal,* May 4, 5, 6, 1886; Milwaukee *Sentinel,* May 5, 1886; C. N. Caspar and H. H. Zahn, *Maps of the City of Milwaukee and of Bay View, Wis., 1886*

The men who had spent the previous day threatening the Bay View rolling mills reassembled the next morning (Wednesday, May fifth) at St. Stanislaus. They were better prepared, came in something resembling ranks, and had a standard bearer with a tricolor banner. On Monday, Schilling had held his poorly attended public meeting at Turner Hall and also met with the Milwaukee Knights of Labor executive committee, which called on all Knights to assist in maintaining order. The Knights Assembly at Bay View had met and offered its services as "special police" to protect the rolling mills, conditioned upon the removal of the militia. Instead, the four Milwaukee companies at Bay View were reinforced by two of the newly arrived companies from out of town. They spent an uncomfortable night, as it was cool and they had no blankets.[42]

As the strikers marching from St. Stanislaus came on, they presented an imposing array. Estimated at 1,500 men, they had a crowd of onlookers, including women and schoolchildren, tagging along. Major Traeumer had his command of six companies, numbering thirty-five to forty men each, drawn up in line just inside the plant fence.

Major Traeumer called the governor by phone when he was aware of the approach of the crowd. Rusk's orders were: "Should the rioters . . . attempt to seek an entrance, 'fight 'em.' " The approaching men were not visibly armed with anything other than sticks and stones. They apparently had no firearms and no shots were fired by them. Traeumer did not wait to learn their intent. He ordered them to halt when they were about a quarter

(Milwaukee, 1886). Wisconsin Adjutant General, *Biennial Report,* 1886, pp. 13–26, indicates that Company I of the Second Regiment from Watertown was also ordered to Milwaukee. Korn, *Story of Bay View,* 84–86, has a useful account from the perspective of the village.

[42] Schilling's Monday evening meeting was apparently lost in the Monday and Tuesday press accounts of more interesting events occurring in Chicago and Milwaukee. On Tuesday, May 4, he was in Madison for a scheduled appearance. See the Milwaukee *Journal,* May 4, 5, 1886; Milwaukee *Sentinel,* May 5, 6, 1886; Milwaukee *Evening Wisconsin,* May 4, 5, 1886; Small, "Robert Schilling," 206–208; and Cooper, "Wisconsin National Guard in the Milwaukee Riots of 1886," *WMH,* 55:40–41.

of a mile away, but obviously he was not heard and his hand signals were ignored. Receiving no response to his repeated commands to halt, he ordered his troops to fire. By Traeumer's own account, the distance was two hundred yards—somewhat more by the *Journal*'s account. Only the Sheridan Guard, posted where the fence dipped into a ravine, had a clear field of fire. Only two of the companies fired a full volley, despite prior orders that each man should pick his man and not fail to shoot. The *Journal* reported five killed and eight or ten wounded. The crowd fell flat, then withdrew with some of the wounded. Traeumer ordered a cease-fire when he saw the effect of his guardsmen's volley.[43]

The dramatic event at Bay View did not immediately end the agitation, but the shots fired and the presence of fresh troops made it clear that the momentum of the movement was gone. Colonel King took the Light Horse unit to deal with a crowd gathered for an early Wednesday morning meeting called at the Milwaukee Garden. Later action centered there throughout the day, with the cavalry and foot units exercising a restraining influence with horse, rifle butt, and occasional threats of sterner measures. King was sorely disappointed that Mayor Wallber not only refused him permission to clear the streets—the owner of the Garden having prudently locked up at the suggestion of Governor Rusk—but the Mayor also advised King to withdraw the military and leave affairs to the police. Wallber justified his action by mingling with the crowd, which was not hostile. He commented: "In the rear [of the crowd] on every street was a long line of buggies and wagons, containing men, women and children, who anticipated no danger, there simply 'to see the fun.' " With his usual temper, King reportedly gave his men orders "to shoot to kill, if the mayor is not obeyed." Wallber proved correct. The police earlier even made some arrests of men

[43] Cooper, "Wisconsin National Guard in the Milwaukee Riots of 1886," *WMH*, 55:42–43; Milwaukee *Journal*, May 5, 7, 1886; Wisconsin Adjutant General, *Biennial Report*, 1885–1886, pp. 18–19; Milwaukee *Evening Wisconsin*, May 5, 1886; Korn, *Story of Bay View*, 86–90. There is no way to reconcile the various newspaper accounts or official testimony about the distances involved or some other matters relating to the two occasions when the militia fired.

identified as known agitators, from among the crowd. Thursday was quiet.[44]

The majority of the state press was unreservedly favorable to Governor Rusk's prompt action, which was assumed to have saved Milwaukee from total anarchy. Few questioned the necessity for the shooting. The press reaction was colored by the nation's response to the Tuesday Haymarket bombing in Chicago. *Germania* contrasted Rusk's actions favorably with those of the vacillating governor of Illinois. Mayor Wallber was generally condemned for a want of resolution.[45]

The crisis passed quickly. The troops were discharged a few days later, despite anxious appeals from businessmen for Rusk to delay this action. The governor knew his business. The day after the shooting, he toured Bay View and the Polish section of the South Side by carriage, escorted by the Light Horse Squadron.[46]

The actions of Major Traeumer and his troops at Bay View were not seriously questioned. A coroner's jury pronounced the deaths and woundings justified. Major Traeumer was generally complimented for his humane action in ordering a cease-fire after a single volley. The *Journal* implied that the Sons of Vulcan could have handled the matter. They had irons heated and hoses hooked to the boilers with which to greet the crowd.[47]

The pride of the occasion may well have been dimmed by the list of the victims. Among the five killed outright was an elderly man feeding his chickens a half-mile away. Another was a schoolboy—he fell on his books—who was on the railroad embankment paralleling the road where the strikers were marching. The

[44] Cooper, "Wisconsin National Guard in the Milwaukee Riots of 1886," *WMH,* 55:43–44; Milwaukee *Journal,* May 5, 6, 1886. The firing at Bay View was confirmed by the *Journal* as occurring at 9:00 A.M. It therefore was known by the crowd at the Milwaukee Garden soon thereafter, and certainly by 3:15 P.M. when King asked permission to clear the streets. The Allis Works were opened that morning, with about 200 men reporting. They heard the firing at Bay View and made preparations. The militia was there with a Gatling gun to sweep the streets should a crowd appear.

[45] The Milwaukee *Journal,* May 8, 1886, carried comment from the press around the state. See also Milwaukee *Germania,* May 12, 1886.

[46] Milwaukee *Journal,* May 6, 8, 1886.

[47] *Ibid.,* May 7, 8, 1886.

directed fire struck the man carrying the banner at the head of the column; he was hit in several places and had his lower jaw carried away. (There was much editorial talk about the risks of carrying red banners, although this one was a tricolor.) Colonel King was still exulting over the affair thirty-six years later: "The mob was still nearly two hundred yards off, and flattened out at the crash of the rifles as though a hundred were hit, but only six were really punctured."[48]

Aside from the wisdom of Major Traeumer's ordering his men to fire at a range of two hundred yards, there was the troubling matter of the Kosciusko Guard firing towards the crowd without orders the day before. The fact is that these were "Sunday soldiers" and they were understandably confused and apprehensive in a situation for which they had neither been trained nor otherwise prepared. The drillmaster of the Wisconsin National Guard was Colonel King. The guards' brief training sessions used the Regular Army manual, which presumably prepared them to refight the Civil War. King treated the officer corps at summer camp to a lecture on "social disorder"—meaning strikes, which he found uniformly insane—and recommended Napoleonic instructions to fire two well-aimed volleys by battalion. King's other contribution to the mayhem, beyond this basic lack of instruction, was to secure 31,000 rounds of ball cartridge that could kill at a distance. "We had no riot guns and cartridges in those days, deadly at less than two hundred yards, but warranted not to harm innocent spectators a block or two away. Such as it was, however, the death-dealing ammunition came only just in time." (So much for the man feeding his chickens half a mile away.)[49]

The coroner's jury found that troops had followed orders and returned a verdict: "We hold the troops executing the orders, as well as the commander-in-chief, entirely blameless in the mat-

---

[48] Cooper, "Wisconsin National Guard in the Milwaukee Riots of 1886," *WMH*, 55:34–35; King, "Memories of a Busy Life," *WMH*, 5:376.

[49] Cooper, "Wisconsin National Guard in the Milwaukee Riots of 1886," *WMH*, 55:33–35, 42–43; King, "Memories of a Busy Life," *WMH*, 5:374–375.

ter." Those killed, including the boy, were "making an unlawful attempt to proceed to the rolling mills." Apparently Governor Rusk's order ("Should they attempt to enter . . .") had been liberally translated. The militiamen were showered with gifts, given public dinners, and inordinately praised. The *Journal* called for a halt to this: "The militia were in no danger; not a man of them that did not realize that the unorganized, unarmed mob of men and boys before them would scatter at the first shot. These facts are patent to everybody—to the greenest civilian as well as to the 'old veterans.' " This came perilously close to saying that the killings were unnecessary, but the *Journal* backed away from that. The inference seemed to be that the killings were justified by the results rather than by the immediate circumstances of Bay View.[50]

Twenty-five men were charged with "riot and unlawful assembly" as a result of the events of May 1–5, 1886. This was not necessarily an indication of their respective roles as leaders. Some were doubtless simply unlucky enough to be conspicuous at a given moment. The names of those charged are indicative: Bauer, Dampf, Hussfeldt, Gabrielski, Woicechowski, Hofer, Strehlow, Gastell, Runge, Luppnow, Heiber, Piepenberg, Gertz, Datara, Kroeger, Rozga, Dolnig, Andrsezewski, Ady, Skrezipenzinski, Protzmann, Lampel, Gondek, Datka, and Boncel. Those charged with "riot and conspiracy" were marked as the real ringleaders, wherever they were when events took place: Frank Hirth, Carl Simon, Anton Palm, Paul Grottkau, and Albert Moessinger.[51]

Nineteen men who had been arrested earlier were arraigned in Judge James Mallory's court on May eighth and charged with riotous behavior "with force of arms . . . for a space of five hours," involving assaults and beatings which terrified and

---

[50] Milwaukee *Journal,* May 8, 13, 1886. The paper suggested that the militia and businessmen making the gifts might well contribute to the widow of Mr. Kunkel, the man killed in his own yard.

[51] Wisconsin Bureau of Labor and Industrial Statistics, *Biennial Report,* 1885–1886, pp. 343–344.

alarmed peaceable citizens. Bail was set at $5,000 each for the nineteen, until the grand jury should sit.

A *Journal* reporter interviewed Grottkau and Hirth in their cells before their court appearances. Grottkau recalled his intentions in calling the second Milwaukee Garden meeting on the day of the Bay View shooting. He hoped "to keep them off the streets and away from the saloons." Under his lead, they were to create a central committee to ensure an end to the disorders. "The workingmen cannot be incited to riot by talk and they are not guilty of any violence, excepting that a few Polish laborers were noisy and demonstrative entirely against our wishes." He pointed out that his Central Labor Union was made up of independent unions over which he had no direct control. "The Knights of Labor are a centralized body, under dictatorship and may be used for good as well as for harm." Grottkau was at pains to charge the dictator, "R. Schilling," with having denounced him.[52]

Frank Hirth was at a loss to know why he was in jail. He was nowhere near the Milwaukee Garden, but was home, making cigars. "I do not know any of the Polish, and they do not know me. In fact, so far as I know they were under control of Schilling and are Knights of Labor. You will find that not a single socialist or member of the [Black] International society, that some people call anarchists, were in the troubles at Bay View or West Milwaukee [Milwaukee Garden] . . . . Schilling is the man who organized the Polish."[53]

Schilling had his own version. The events of Monday in the Menomonee Valley he blamed on "a number of ignorant Poles together with a few German anarchists and cranks . . . ." On the following day, before the first encounter between the strikers and the militia at Bay View, Schilling saw no evidence of

[52] Milwaukee *Journal*, May 7, 8, 1886. There were meetings called at the Milwaukee Garden on both Tuesday, May fourth, and the following day—the second one apparently by Grottkau, on a moment's notice, from concern that things were getting out of hand. See Wisconsin Bureau of Labor and Industrial Statistics, *Biennial Report*, 1885–1886, p. 333.

[53] Milwaukee *Journal*, May 7, 1886.

impending trouble. Sheriff Paschen, however, upon seeing so many people, "his heart had dropped into his pantaloons," and he had phoned for the militia instead of phoning Mrs. Schilling, as requested, to tell her that everything was under control.

Schilling said the militia was poorly led, which resulted in some of the Kosciusko Guard being roughed up. When the people, "mostly Poles," returned next day, "they were unarmed, and but about a dozen of them carried sticks, and, therefore, could not have intended an attack upon the heroes." The firing took place at such a distance that no one could have been warned. "To say it in plain German, 'It was cowardly, premeditated murder.' The most guilty man is the old know-nothing, Jerry Rusk . . . . The poor victims are dead and buried. They shall be revenged . . . . The intelligent citizens have a weapon mightier than the ball or the bayonet—the ballot."[54]

Whatever the Knights of Labor, the Eight Hour League, Grottkau's Central Labor Union, or other self-appointed leaders had briefly achieved towards a sense of community among the city's industrial work force was doomed by the spirit of these comments. Schilling was prophetic—and equally futile—in his return soon thereafter to his consuming interest, third-party politics. Unity at the ballot box did not require any real sense of community. In Milwaukee, in the fall of 1886, all that was required was a variety of reasons for getting even with somebody.

The drive for an eight-hour day died as a popular movement. Within two weeks the common council considered repeal of the eight-hour ordinance that had passed in March. Actual repeal came in July. Labor commissioner Frank A. Flower pronounced the epitaph of the movement in his biennial report: "Summing up all the facts, it may be safely stated that no benefits whatever have been derived from the agitation by any class of workingmen."[55]

[54] The Milwaukee *Journal*, May 20, 1886, printed this translation from Schilling's *Volksblatt*, and some comment by him on their translation on May 21, 1886, which did not alter the sense of the above.

[55] Milwaukee *Sentinel*, May 20, July 9, 1886; Wisconsin Bureau of Labor and Industrial Statistics, *Biennial Report*, 1885–1886, p. 345.

A grand jury met in Judge Mallory's court on May 19. After treating them to a homily about foreigners coming here for the honest purpose of accepting and sustaining our free institutions, he then stated that "men who by incendiary speeches and wild harangues cause breaches of the peace must be held to strict accountability. Our constitution does not protect any such freedom of speech. Our people have tolerated the reckless criminal conduct of anarchists and demagogues quite long enough." The jury later obligingly handed down fifty indictments against forty-nine men.[56]

Schilling, indicted twice for the earlier boycotting actions of his cigar makers, surrendered himself on June 7. He had been to a national assembly of the Knights in Cleveland when the indictments were handed down. He was put in an upper gallery of the jail with Frank Hirth and others who were starting their second month there, unable to make bail. Hirth greeted their new cell mate civilly, and observed that the Knights, socialists, trade unionists, and anarchists had chosen different ways for themselves "at the beginning of the labor movement . . . ." Pushing the lesson home, he said: "Now, after the utter failure of the movement and because we have quarreled with each other, we find ourselves here united. Do you not think that in spite of the different ways, we would have had success, had we not quarreled?" Schilling came unprepared for this discourse.[57]

Hirth and two of his companions got nine months at hard labor. Grottkau received a sentence of one year in the county jail, but served only six weeks before he was released on a technicality while awaiting trial on a different charge. Seven of the forty-nine indicted served prison terms; the other cases were variously disposed of after appeals and retrial. Schilling had a hung jury and the conspiracy charges against others for boycotting were not pressed. There was a noticeable disparity in the

---

[56] Milwaukee *Journal*, May 19, June 2, 3, 1886; Wisconsin Bureau of Labor and Industrial Statistics, *Biennial Report*, 1885–1886, pp. 343–344.

[57] Milwaukee *Journal*, June 7, 1886.

social status of those who served at hard labor and those who went free.[58]

Schilling returned to his accustomed place on the platform. "Our grand jury meets at the polls. Let this be the beginning of the war," he told a cheering audience come to inaugurate a new political party. As the manager of a new People's party, he was in his element. He thwarted the gubernatorial aspirations of Frank Powell, the mayor of La Crosse, and engineered the nomination of Master of the State Grange John Cochrane for governor. The platform committee's work was tossed aside in favor of a substitute offered by Schilling. He was back in the driver's seat of a vehicle which he understood.[59]

The People's party ticket for state offices was strictly for educational purposes. In Milwaukee, however, it was out for revenge. The first opportunity was in the 1886 fall elections, which included, aside from state offices, the county offices and the congressional district coterminous with Milwaukee County. Henry Smith, lately installed as master workman of the state assembly of the Knights of Labor, won the congressional seat with 43 per cent of the vote in a three-way race. The new party also swept most of the county offices, a state senate seat, and six of the twelve assembly seats for Milwaukee County. Newell Daniels, the founder of the Knights of St. Crispin—an early national union of shoemakers—and the organizer of the first assembly of Knights in Milwaukee, replaced Sheriff Paschen. It was a sweet victory.[60]

[58] Gavett, *Labor Movement in Milwaukee,* 67–68, 70, 75; Cooper, "Wisconsin National Guard in the Milwaukee Riots of 1886," *WMH,* 55:47–48; Wisconsin Bureau of Labor and Industrial Statistics, *Biennial Report,* 1885–1886, pp. 343–344.

[59] Small, "Robert Schilling," 217–223; Robert M. Rice, "The Populist Party in Milwaukee" (master's thesis, University of Wisconsin-Milwaukee, 1967), 18–20.

[60] Sarah C. Ettenheim, *How Milwaukee Voted, 1848–1968* (Milwaukee, 1970), 81; Small, "Robert Schilling," 222–223; Gavett, *Labor Movement in Milwaukee,* 68–70, 72; Rice, "Populist Party in Milwaukee," 20; Roger D. Simon, "The Bay View Incident and the People's Party in Milwaukee," research paper, 23–26, History of Wisconsin Project files; *DWB.* There were similar labor tickets in other major cities, but none enjoyed the sweeping success of the Milwaukee ticket.

The vote was largely a workingmen's revolt against incumbents and candidates favorable to the law-and-order stance represented by the Milwaukee *Sentinel* and the business community. But it was also, in part, an ethnic response to constant reminders that it was German radicals and demagogues who had led the credulous Poles astray. The German press was well aware of this. The *Germania*, admitting that most of the rioters were unfortunately German, took note of a cartoon in *Harper's Weekly* that showed Irish Alderman Pat Boodle talking to a shabby German anarchist, armed with a bomb and a red flag: "Keep at it, Hans Socialist . . . . I myself was once a rioter." Schilling had a surefire line for his working-class audiences: "When I mention the word *'Sentinel'* I always feel like wiping my mouth afterward."[61]

A study of Milwaukee voting patterns in the 1886 election found that the affluent second-generation Germans of the seventh ward remained stoutly Republican. But the more representative German thirteenth ward, part of the traditional German section on Milwaukee's West Side, with a high proportion of skilled workers, voted 65 per cent for Schilling's ticket. On the South Side, the Poles of the eleventh, twelfth, and fourteenth wards, as well as the newer German population of the eighth, gave the People's ticket majorities ranging from 62 to 80 per cent. The Poles voted for Henry Smith overwhelmingly, despite his well known freethinker sentiments and despite warnings from Father Hypolite Gurski of St. Stanislaus that Henry Smith had called Jesus Christ a tramp and was demanding that all church property be taxed.[62]

The momentum of the fall elections carried over to the April

[61] Milwaukee *Germania,* May 12, 19, October 27, 1886; Milwaukee *Freidenker,* May 9, 16, 23, 1886; Small, "Robert Schilling," 219. See also Milwaukee *Herold,* May 7, 1886, and January 2, 4, 1887.

[62] Simon, "Bay View Incident and the People's Party in Milwaukee," 24–26. Harry C. Heming, comp., *The Catholic Church in Wisconsin* (Milwaukee, 1895–1898), 339–340, 355–356, renders the name of the rector of St. Stanislaus as Hippolite Gonski, earlier as Gorski. The confusion is pardonable as he came to St. Stanislaus as assistant rector to Fr. Hyacinth Gulski, who founded St. Hyacinth and became rector there in 1884.

municipal elections, but with less success. Several factors were at work. Grottkau found it difficult to work for the ticket as his hatred of Schilling became obsessive. And the Republicans and Democrats had worked out a delicately balanced fusion, called the Citizens' Ticket, for fear that Schilling and Grottkau would take over the city government and the county courts in another three-way race. The principal contests citywide were for the circuit and superior court judgeships and the People's party candidates won these in the city, 12,656 to 11,248 for the circuit judgeship and a similar margin for the other. But these offices were county-wide, and outside Milwaukee the vote went 3,357 for the fusion candidate to 530 for the People's party candidate, reversing the results in the city. The People's party votes were concentrated in working-class wards with the result that its aldermanic candidates won in only three of the seventeen wards in the city, but the party already had two sitting council members. Of eleven constables—called "paper servers" by the *Journal*—the People's party won six, which heartened the party. The *Journal* remarked that the People's party vote was down only 218, comparing the circuit judgeship race with the congressional seat race of the previous November; but the citywide vote as a whole was off by 3,829, indicating that the fusion ticket was the heavy loser. Traditionally, the spring elections drew fewer votes.[63]

The Milwaukee Democrats persisted in their fusionist alliance with the Republicans, despite the efforts of party heads William F. Vilas, Ellis B. Usher, and others outside Milwaukee to dissuade them. Judge Mallory, who had been the Democratic candidate for governor in 1877, took charge of the fusion forces for

---

[63] Small, "Robert Schilling," 231–232; Simon, "Bay View Incident and the People's Party in Milwaukee," 28–31; Gavett, *Labor Movement in Milwaukee*, 72–73; Milwaukee *Journal*, April 6, 1887. The success of the labor party was not unique to Milwaukee, but the bitterness of the division doubtless was. Kenosha and Racine had similar contests with a Knights of Labor-led party opposed by the conservative Democrats and Republicans combined in a Citizen ticket. In Kenosha the Labor ticket won the mayoralty race, a majority of the other city offices, and four of five council seat races. A Labor ticket lost to the Citizen coalition in Racine in that spring of 1887. There were similar races in other Wisconsin industrial cities with less clear-cut results.

the April, 1888, municipal elections. He was aided by Grottkau's decision to enter a separate Socialist Labor ticket in the field after a final falling out with Schilling and the People's party. The Socialists drew fewer than 1,000 votes, but it was enough to defeat Schilling's ticket across the board by a margin less than Grottkau's Socialist total. It was the People's party's last hurrah.[64]

As the *Herold* had pointed out after the 1887 Milwaukee municipal election, no matter how well organized for political action the labor forces might become in Milwaukee and other cities, they would find efforts to win county, state, or national elections in vain. It observed that people outside the cities had no interest whatsoever in the labor movement. John Cochrane, the People's party candidate in the 1886 gubernatorial race, had received 60 per cent of his vote from the disciplined labor vote in Milwaukee. The county totals for Cochrane in 1886 show that another 27 per cent came from counties with an appreciable urban labor vote: Racine, Winnebago, Marinette, La Crosse, Sheboygan, Outagamie, and Fond du Lac. Cochrane's share of the state-wide vote was only 7.5 per cent. Workers united in their dislike of Jeremiah Rusk and their rejection of the Democratic candidate, Gilbert M. Woodward, a La Crosse attorney who insisted that Bay View was not an issue between Republicans and Democrats. The vote was scarcely an endorsement of Cochrane, and it certainly presaged no alliance of industrial labor and the farm vote.[65]

The rise of the American Federation of Labor led to a more fruitful political alliance between the AF of L in Milwaukee and Victor Berger's Socialists (Sozial-Democratischer Verein, or Social Democrats as they became known after 1896). Schilling was only intermittently concerned with the Knights of Labor, which was melting away rapidly. Powderly, with his enthusiasm

---

[64] Small, "Robert Schilling," 238–240; Gavett, *Labor Movement in Milwaukee,* 74–76; Simon, "Bay View and the People's Party in Milwaukee," 31–33; Horace S. Merrill, *William Freeman Vilas: Doctrinaire Democrat* (Madison, 1954), 153–154.

[65] Milwaukee *Herold,* April 6, 1887; *Wisconsin Blue Book, 1887,* pp. 250, 371–372.

for temperance, drove out the brewery workers. In 1886 the American Federation of Labor was beginning to gather in the fragmented trade unions.[66]

With the emergence of the AF of L as the dominant labor organization in Milwaukee, something was gained in the way of a trades-oriented labor organization that could assert itself— often effectively—in the hostile environment that followed the Bay View riot. The AF of L more was successful than Schilling's Knights of Labor with its loose coalition, ill-defined aims, and politically oriented leadership. The difference was well summed up by one old-time Milwaukee trade unionist: "After working for more than twelve years in the city, five years ago I hardly knew any craftsmen except those working with me in the same shop. To-day I am personally acquainted with four-fifths of all the men engaged at my trade, and everybody seems to know me. This fact I appreciate more than almost anything connected with my social position." A sense of genuine community was the source of strength of the trades union movement.[67]

Equally revealing were the observations about the Knights of Labor made seventy years later by Charles Jopke, who had come to Milwaukee from rural Germany in 1881 when he was thirteen. Jopke had gone to work in one of the Pfister and Vogel tanneries four days after his arrival. One Sunday in 1886, he recalled, a red-whiskered organizer from the Knights had talked to the tanners in a meeting hall on Second Street, urging them to put down a dollar each and declare themselves union men. There was a lot of pressure: "Well, we didn't know no better. Everybody came along and said 'Come on, you've got to join. You'd better join that.' Well, they fooled you, you didn't know. Then we went along with the bunch and went up the steps to the second floor and paid him a dollar, and we didn't get—he took

---

[66] Gavett, *Labor Movement in Milwaukee*, 74–79, 90–97, Bayrd Still, *Milwaukee: The History of a City* (Madison, 1948; reprinted, 1965), 294–296; Olson, "Milwaukee Socialists," chap. 1; Small, "Robert Schilling," 228–238; Cochran, *Pabst Brewing Company*, 282–283. See also Victor L. Berger and Frank J. Weber in *DWB*.

[67] Wisconsin Bureau of Labor Statistics, *Biennial Report*, 1883–1884, p. 122; Gavett, *Labor Movement in Milwaukee*, 41–42.

all the money and landed in jail.'' Jopke's experience with the
Knights of Labor organizer doubtless colored his view of unions
generally, reinforced by his loyalty to his longtime employers.[68]

In 1892 the Brotherhood of Tanners and Curriers in Milwaukee struck against an across-the-board wage reduction of 5 per
cent. Pfister and Vogel joined an association of the other large
tanneries in the city which was pledged to break the union. The
tanners began by firing all known union members. It turned into
a long and sometimes violent contest.[69]

Charles Jopke's memory of the 1892 strike was indicative of
the times and of the changes that a few years could make in the
outlook of a young immigrant worker.

> HOLBROOK: Do you remember the strike of 1892? Was that bad;
> was that a little tough?
> JOPKE: That didn't bother me. I had a foreman job then and I
> didn't mix in there. . . . But they never bothered me because I
> didn't interfere, I'd just go along and didn't say nothing.

Some craftsmen identified more readily with their employers
than with their fellow workmen. The rural Germans and Poles of
Milwaukee's South Side, who were part of the ''New Immigration'' of the eighties, had been the shock troops of the 1886 riots.
Six years later, some had left behind the sense of insecurity and
frustration of being part of the faceless crowd waiting at the plant
gate for a day's work. They had become the dependable, skilled
workers and the lower echelons of management, preferred over
immigrants who arrived later.[70]

The results of Bay View were disastrous for Milwaukee's
Polish community, which had provided the unskilled labor at the

[68] Transcript of Charles Jopke interview, February 25, 1952, in the Matson Holbrook
Interviews.

[69] *Ibid.*; Wisconsin Bureau of Labor, Census and Industrial Statistics, *Biennial Report,*
1891–1892, pp. 120–122; Milwaukee *Sentinel,* February 26, March 13, April 16, 27, May
22, August 11, 1892.

[70] Jopke Transcript; Hartmut Keil, ''German Immigrant Workers and the American
Labor Movement, 1878–1890,'' research proposal, 1975, in the author's possession;
Korman, *Industrialization, Immigrants and Americanizers,* 35–40; Albert C. Vogel to Matson
Holbrook, February 21, 1952, in the Holbrook Interviews.

rolling mills. Speaking for the business community of Milwaukee, the *Sentinel* commented: "The Poles of the city are under the greatest obligations to the members of the Kosciusko Guards who alone have prevented the entire race from falling under the public ban."[71]

The fact is, many Poles *did* fall under a ban. The majority of the Kosciusko Guard were small businessmen, a few professionals, and clerks. Their armory had been the parish school of St. Stanislaus, which evicted them. They were treated as pariahs by the rest of the Polish community, which boycotted their businesses. On the other side, a committee of Milwaukee manufacturers served notice that they would not hire any Pole who did not have a recommendation from an officer of the Kosciusko Guard. Other Polish workers were simply let go as suspect. Alderman Theodore Rudzinski, who was as outspoken as Schilling against Governor Rusk and the actions of the militia, was excoriated by all right-thinking citizens. Such antagonisms divided the Polish community for years—a burden Poles had to bear along with the actions and opinions of those who did most of the hiring and firing in Milwaukee.[72]

To Robert Schilling's discredit, he—like Grottkau and Hirth— was quick to disavow the Poles. To his credit, he continued to speak out against the shooting at Bay View as a cruel, bungled, and unnecessary act. In part, this was a defense of his own course and of his friend, Mayor Wallber, who became a symbol of German timidity and ineptitude in the face of a presumed revo-

[71] Milwaukee *Sentinel,* May 12, 1886. The Milwaukee *Journal* carried the following advertisement on May 7, 1886: "WANTED: Mechanics in all departments of carriage and sleigh building. Also a few laborers and boys to learn the trade. Will pay good wages. . . . Polanders and drunkards need not apply. NORTHWEST SLEIGH COMPANY. Apply at 20 Canal Street." Five days later, the *Journal* carried a lengthy and spirited editorial defense of Milwaukee's Polish citizens: "The simple fact is, they are no better nor worse than other nationalities, except possibly they may be hot-headed and more easily misled. . . ." Milwaukee *Journal,* May 12, 1886.

[72] Cooper, "Wisconsin National Guard in the Milwaukee Riots of 1886," *WMH,* 55:46–47; Milwaukee *Journal,* May 11, 12, 14, 1886; Milwaukee *Herold,* May 7, 11, 14, 1886. Rusk revoked Rudzinski's commission as a notary public, then came to Milwaukee to testify against the alderman before the grand jury. Milwaukee *Journal,* June 3, 4, 1886.

lution led by German radicals. Schilling's initial political successes in 1886 and 1887 were aided by the German community's rejection of blame for the affair.

The Poles lacked an English-language forum comparable to the newspapers commanded by the other elements in the affair. But young Michael Kruszka, editor of the weekly *Krytyka* and soon to become editor of the country's first Polish daily newspaper (and a national leader among Poles from his base in Milwaukee), did his best by writing to the *Journal.* He said there were "not more than 100 Polanders" in the Monday crowd, "while the largest part consisted of German laborers and socialists, the rest being laborers of other nationalities . . . ." He complained that the reporters of Milwaukee's English-language press seemed to lack "knowledge of nationalities, as they generally call every laborer, who does not speak English and does wrong, a 'Polack.' " The few members of the Polonia Assembly of the Knights who did march on the Bay View rolling mills, Kruszka continued, were not armed except for about two dozen men with sticks.[73]

Schilling's overriding fault was that he saw the Knights of Labor primarily as an instrument with which to pursue his career as a political reformer. He made no sustained effort to pick up the pieces after Bay View. He had no conception of the Knights as an experiment in industrial unionism. The success of the American Federation of Labor in the years following was made at the expense of a general working-class movement. For the future, it would be the skilled workers who would define themselves as "the working class."[74]

---

[73] Milwaukee *Journal,* May 8, 1886; *DWB.*

[74] Ware, *Labor Movement in the United States,* xii–xviii, advances the thesis that the AF of L was a regression to "sauve qui peut . . . a strategic retreat of a few craft unions disturbed for their own safety. . . ." See also Gavett, *Labor Movement in Milwaukee,* 78.

# 9

# Inequalities

"NO one certainly will rejoice more heartily than the present Commissioner when the Indians of this country cease to be in a position to dictate . . . to the Government; when, in fact, the last hostile tribe becomes reduced to the condition of suppliants for charity. This is, indeed, the only hope of salvation for the aborigines of the continent. . . . They must yield or perish; and there is something that savors of providential mercy in the rapidity with which their fate advances upon them. . . ." Commissioner of Indian Affairs Francis A. Walker, the author of these lines, was a distinguished Boston economist of enlightened views who had a notable public career.[1]

Commissioner Walker's comment referred to western hostiles, although the statement reflects complacency about the contemporary plight of those—like Wisconsin's Indians—who were powerless and presumably dying out. He did recognize the obligation "to make good to these original owners of the soil the loss by which we so greatly gain." His appeal was to practical rather than humanitarian considerations, because—as he said—he understood congressional appropriation committees. The answer was simple: "The Government should extend over [the Indians] a rigid reformatory discipline . . . requiring them to learn and

---

[1] Francis A. Walker, U.S. Commissioner of Indian Affairs, *Annual Report*, 1872, as excerpted in Wilcomb E. Washburn, comp., *The American Indian and the United States: A Documentary History* (4 vols., New York, 1973), 1:183–184. See the *DAB*.

practice the arts of industry at least until one generation has been fairly started on a course of self-improvement. . . ."²

Walker's "rigid reformatory discipline" was official policy over the years following 1871, when the practice of treating Indian tribes as sovereign nations ended. This placed them under the President's executive power, as implemented by the U.S. Commissioner of Indian Affairs in the Interior Department, thus ending the more or less dual control of the commissioner and the army. The House of Representatives embraced this solution because the "sovereign nation" fiction invoked the treaty powers of the Constitution and involved only the President and the Senate.³

The new policy was partly precipitated by the infamous massacre at Sand Creek, late in 1864, by Colorado troops who indiscriminately slaughtered and mutilated some 150 Cheyenne men, women, and children after they had surrendered their weapons and engaged in peace negotiations. Senator James Doolittle of Wisconsin was chairman of a joint congressional committee set up to inquire into the general conditions of American Indians and their relations with military and civil officers. Out of this came the creation in 1867 of the Peace Commission, made up of senior army officers and civilians with humanitarian interests. Their report, highly critical of past policies, became an important source for reformers. This was followed by the creation of the Board of Indian Commissioners, a citizens' board to function as an advisory and oversight body. Its creation is identified with President Ulysses S. Grant's policy of turning Indian education over to the churches.⁴

The object of American Indian policy was to force the individ-

² Washburn, comp., *American Indian and the United States*, 1:185–187.

³ Robert F. Berkhofer, Jr., *The White Man's Indian: Images of the American Indian from Columbus to the Present* (New York, 1978; Vintage paperback edition, 1979), 166–170; Henry E. Fritz, *The Movement for Indian Assimilation, 1860–1890* (Philadelphia, 1963), 83 ff.

⁴ Francis Paul Prucha, *American Indian Policy in Crisis: Christian Reformers and the Indians, 1865–1890* (Norman, 1976), 10–29; Fritz, *Movement for Indian Assimilation*, chaps. 3 and 4; Loring B. Priest, *Uncle Sam's Stepchildren: The Reformation of United States Indian Policy,*

ual Indian eventually into something resembling citizenship. This involved a number of strategies: undermining tribal government by close supervision; breaking up the reservations by individual land allotments; Christianizing the Indians; and separating the younger generation with a system of boarding schools and insistence upon the use of English. As these policies reflected back upon Wisconsin Indians, who had long since lost any military power, or—in the case of many—any possessory power over land in tribal or individual ownership, the enforcement of these general policies was anomalous.

The circumstances of Wisconsin Indians as tribes, subgroups, or individuals were simply too varied to permit any generalized description of what happened to them during the last quarter of the nineteenth century with respect to their status, general character, and even the numbers of the various Wisconsin Indians at any given time between the 1870's and the 1890's. The U.S. Commissioner of Indian Affairs included in his annual reports edited returns from the individual agencies. But agency heads came and went, since the jobs were considered patronage plums, and the headcounts were not always accurate. Between 1871 and 1882, the Wisconsin agencies at La Pointe and Green Bay, which oversaw all reservations in the state, had changes of agents five times. This was not an unusual turnover. One soon begins to note other important discrepancies. For example, it was quite usual for an agent to find conditions distressing in his first year, but much improved the next.[5]

1865-1887 (New Brunswick, 1942; reprinted, New York, 1969, and Lincoln, 1975); Berkhofer, White Man's Indian, 169–171; Robert H. Keller, Jr., "The Protestant Churches and Grant's Peace Policy: A Study in Church-State Relations, 1869–1882" (doctoral dissertation, University of Chicago, 1967), revised and published as American Protestantism and United States Indian Policy, 1869–1882 (Lincoln, 1983).

[5] Keller, "Protestant Churches and Grant's Peace Policy," 345–346. As to numbers, the federal census reported "civilized Indians" and the agencies reported those on reservations. There were many Indians in Wisconsin like the Winnebago who fitted neither category. See Reuben Gold Thwaites, ed., "The Wisconsin Winnebagoes," Wis. Hist. Colls., 12:416–418. Eleventh Census of the United States, 1890: Population, Volume I, Part 1, pp. 401, 450, 484–485, gives counts of Wisconsin's civilized Indians (not on reservations) for 1860: 1,017; 1870: 1,206; 1880: 3,161; 1890: 3,835; then by counties and by urban places for the same years. The county returns, p. 450, are more interesting than

In 1873, Wisconsin Indians furnished examples of the bankruptcy of past government policies and of the hazards of those advocated by Commissioner Walker and those who followed him, which culminated in the Dawes Severalty Act of 1887. The Winnebago were the last tribe east of the Mississippi to be subjected to forcible removal, which was done in 1873–1874 by the army. Removed earlier to reservations in Iowa and Minnesota, they repeatedly had drifted back.[6]

Most Wisconsin tribes were characteristically divided between those who held to traditional ways and those who were making some effort—at least outwardly—to adapt to white society. The distinction is often described as one between pagans and Christians, although it frequently had other connotations. Those Winnebago who had returned to Wisconsin are generally described as traditionalists who rejected white culture. They ranged over various stretches of western Wisconsin, generally along the rivers and streams between the Mississippi and Wisconsin rivers, following an age-old pattern of hunting and gathering over a countryside that still had much nonagricultural land. The country also had many isolated farms, and some Winnebago were aware that many whites feared them. A few Indians around a village selling moccasins or blueberries was quite a different matter from an unknown number of Indian males in an isolated rural setting.

The result of neighboring whites' agitation was that the army rounded up about 1,000 Winnebago a little before Christmas in 1873 and herded them—part way on foot—to a reservation in Nebraska. About 860 Indians actually arrived. The Winnebago Agency report for 1874 was quite optimistic about the progress being made by those who had not returned to Wisconsin; the recent Wisconsin catch, however, "appear to be of dissolute

---

the rapid increase overall. Jackson County, for instance, which was Winnebago country, counted none in 1870, seventy-eight in 1880, and one in 1890.

[6] The Dawes Severalty Act allotted a quarter-section (160 acres) to each Indian family head and granted citizenship to those who received the land. Reuben Gold Thwaites, ed., *Civil War Messages and Proclamations of Wisconsin War Governors* (Madison, 1912), 230–231; Richard N. Current, *The History of Wisconsin. Volume II: The Civil War Era, 1848–1873* (Madison, 1976), 319–323; Thwaites, ed., "Wisconsin Winnebagoes," *Wis. Hist. Colls.*, 12:407–410.

habits." Three-fourths of the latter were gone again by 1875 . . . which did not distress the agent.[7]

The Wisconsin Winnebago took advantage of an 1875 law which offered Indians not in their tribal relations the benefits of the 1862 homestead act without losing their rights to tribal annuities. Many took forty-acre homesteads, which were tax-free, simply to guarantee their rights as Wisconsin residents. Some located their homesteads in their familiar haunts; others never bothered to visit theirs. Needless to say, what land was left to enter by 1875 was not choice farmland.[8]

The implementation of "severalty"—the policy of persuading Indians to accept individual land holdings—had been earlier applied in 1839 to those New York Indians who had been removed to reservations south of Green Bay. The towns of Stockbridge and Brothertown, on the east shore of Lake Winnebago in Calumet County, are mementoes of this experiment. The Stockbridge were the remains of the Housatonic—a Mahican tribe—and the Munsee who, by contemporary accounts, were "civilized Indians," meaning that they were more or less indistinguishable from whites in their outward mode of pioneer life. But, as one of their leaders expressed it: "Our God hath made us a people distinct from you—we must remain so or perish. We can never participate in the wealth or the social privileges of the whites, however we might be made participants in their political privileges."[9]

---

[7] Nancy O. Lurie, "The Winnebago Indians: A Study in Cultural Change" (doctoral dissertation, Northwestern University, 1952), 167–169; Gilson G. Glasier, ed., *Autobiography of Roujet D. Marshall, Justice of the Supreme Court of the State of Wisconsin, 1895–1918* (2 vols., Madison, 1923 and 1931), 1:109–114; Thwaites, ed., "Wisconsin Winnebagoes," *Wis. Hist. Colls.*, 12:399–433.

[8] Thwaites, ed., "Wisconsin Winnebagoes," *Wis. Hist. Colls.*, 12:415–421; Lurie, "Winnebago Indians," 254–257.

[9] Joseph Schafer, *The Winnebago-Horicon Basin: A Type Study in Western History* (Madison, 1937), chaps. 3 and 4; Wilcomb E. Washburn, *The Indian in America* (New York, 1975), 235; T. J. Brasser, "Mahican," in *Handbook of North American Indians. Volume 15: Northeast* (Washington, 1978), 207–209; W. A. Titus, "Historic Spots in Wisconsin. Brothertown: A Wisconsin Story with a New England Background," in *WMH*, 21 (March, 1938), 293–300; W. A. Titus, "A Brief Account of the Stockbridges," in *WMH*, 30 (June, 1947), 423–432; *Eleventh Census of the United States, 1890: Volume X, Report on Indians Taxed and Indians Not Taxed in the United States (Except Alaska)*, 613, 618, 623.

Being the first agricultural pioneers in Calumet County, and outwardly adapted to the society that would shortly surround them, did not alter the usual course of events. White pioneers wanted their land. The Brothertown accepted severalty—individual land ownership—in 1839; a dozen years later—in 1851—ex-Governor James Doty hailed the results as proof that severalty was the true policy of the future, the Brothertown having become part of the general community, according to him.[10]

The example of the Brothertown Indians, however, was a poor one to generalize upon, as they were a collection of Algonquian tribal remnants who by invitation in the late eighteenth century formed a community on Oneida tribal lands in New York. By the time they reached Wisconsin, English was their common language and they had generous admixtures of European and African blood. Those few Brothertown who remained in the vicinity of Lake Winnebago were accepted, provided that their mixed ancestry was primarily white. Many of them sold out to German farmers within the next two or three decades after their special severalty act.[11]

The Stockbridge had a more complicated destiny. Unlike the Brothertown they had a strong tribal tradition, despite setting an early example as Christian Indians. The question of severalty split them into two parties. Those opposing severalty were characterized as the "ablest," who agreed that they must remain separate from the whites or perish. This was not entirely disinterested, because these men generally were also the leaders of the tribe, who with severalty would lose their dominant positions in the tribe's relations with the federal government. In any event,

---

[10] Schafer, *Winnebago-Horicon Basin*, 53–55.

[11] *Ibid.*, 47–59; Titus, "Brothertown," *WMH*, 21:293–300; Ives Goddard, "Delaware," in *Handbook of North American Indians. Volume 15: Northeast*, 222; Jack Campisi, "Oneida," in *ibid.*, 481. Lyle M. Stone and Donald Chaput, "History of the Upper Great Lakes Area," in *ibid.*, 609, conclude of these New York Indians: "This melange of Indians of different linguistic and cultural backgrounds accelerated the process of changing life-styles. There came to be in the Green Bay vicinity a new Indian way of life, far removed from the hunter-trapper-canoe traditions of the 1660s." See also *Eleventh Census of the United States, 1890: Volume X, Report on Indians Taxed and Indians Not Taxed in the United States (Except Alaska)*, 618–619.

the government prevailed in 1856 when land was alloted to the minority who chose that option—the "citizens"—and the remainder of the land was opened to general entry. The tribal party was moved to its third location since coming to Wisconsin: a reservation in Shawano County adjacent to the Menominee. Just a few of the citizens' party remained at Stockbridge in Calumet County when the trust provisions of the allotments—which prevented them from selling—ran out by the eighties.[12]

Those who moved to the new reservation found the land indifferent for their style of farming. The principal resource, as with the Menominee, was pine timber. But the Indians' attempts to exploit it resulted in a ruling that their right to the land was for occupancy only. The title to the timber remained with the government. This resulted in a rape of the timber by lumbermen, led by Congressman Philetus Sawyer of Oshkosh, who in the early seventies got a bill through Congress putting up part of the Menominee and much of the Stockbridge timber for sale.[13]

The course of the remaining Stockbridge was not yet run. In 1871, they were again offered severalty; and again they divided into "Indians" and "citizens" factions. The "citizens" each received about $700 cash with which to buy farms, as some did, but others ended up with little except the brief experience of having money. The "Indians" remained on the reduced reservation. A few farmed. Others turned to logging or other seasonal

[12] Schafer, *Winnebago-Horicon Basin*, 55–76; Titus, "Stockbridges," *WMH*, 30:423–432. About one-third of the tribe moved to Kansas during the argument over taking allotments.

[13] Richard N. Current, *Pine Logs and Politics: A Life of Philetus Sawyer, 1816–1900* (Madison, 1950), 72–74; Current, *Civil War Decade*, 557. Titus, "Stockbridges," *WMH*, 30:431, ironically suggests that "perhaps as a reward for their patriotic military service" in the Civil War, the government arranged to sell the timber without notifying the Stockbridge. See also Felix M. Keesing, *The Menomini Indians of Wisconsin: A Study of Three Centuries of Cultural Contact and Change* (Philadelphia, 1939; reprinted, New York, 1971), 183. Clarence J. Milfred et al., *Soil Resources and Forest Ecology of Menominee County, Wisconsin*, Wisconsin Geological and Natural History Survey, *Bulletin*, no. 85 (Madison, 1967), contradicts significantly the long-held belief that the lands in question were not suitable for farming.

Chippewa Red
Cliff Reservation

Chippewa Bad River
Reservation

0    25    50    Mi

0    50    100 Km

Chippewa Lac du
Flambeau Reservation

St. Croix
Band of
Chippewa

Chippewa Lac Court
Oreilles Reservation

Forest County
Potawatomi

Mole Lake Band
of Chippewa

Menominee
Reservation

Stockbridge-Munsee Reservation

Oneida
Reservation

Scattered
Winnebago

Brothertown
remnants

Maximum areas of reservation
shown; boundaries frequently altered.

INDIANS IN WISCONSIN, C. 1875

work for whites, or continued trapping and berrying while awaiting their $30 annuity payments.[14]

The Oneida Indians from western New York, who came to
their new home contemporaneously with the Stockbridge and

[14] Schafer, *Winnebago-Horicon Basin*, 75–76; Keller, "Protestant Churches and Grant's
Peace Policy," 205–206; Washburn, comp., *American Indian and the United States*, 1:536–
538; Priest, *Uncle Sam's Stepchildren*, 177–178; Titus, "Stockbridges," *WMH*, 30:431–
432.

Brothertown, occupied a reservation immediately southwest of the city of Green Bay. They experienced similar frustrations with the management of their forest resources, but their land was better adapted to farming than that of the Stockbridge and Menominee. The Oneida petitioned for severalty and citizenship in 1877, but then split into factions over the issue. It was 1890 before allotments were made to those who elected to have them, and the reservation acreage was consequently reduced. Those taking allotments were given title in fee simple in 1906, and most of them promptly sold out. Few became successful farmers.[15]

The Oneida maintained a strong sense of their identity, despite their divisions over allotments between those preferring traditional ways versus those wanting citizenship status, and their religious divisions into Episcopalians, Methodists, and Catholics. Mission schools were operated by all three churches, in addition to the Indian Bureau and public schools. There was relatively little intermarriage with the nearby Stockbridge and Menominee or with whites. They did mix with the wider society as workers in logging and even in city mills.[16]

Although the Wisconsin Oneida had long been Christian and brought little of their traditional Iroquois political structure with them, the 1890 federal census special report on Indians observed: "The Oneidas generally are at present not far enough advanced to become citizens. The provision of the Dawes bill admitting them indiscriminately to citizenship after the expiration of 25 years will not ameliorate their condition." The writer favored a selective process of immediate citizenship for those (he gave no estimate of numbers) who were willing and able to make competent citizens. This cavil was evidently based in part upon obser-

[15] Robert E. Ritzenthaler, "The Oneida Indians of Wisconsin," in the *Bulletin of the Public Museum of the City of Milwaukee*, 19 (November, 1950), 13; Milwaukee *Christian Statesman*, January 11, 1887; U.S. Commissioner of Indian Affairs, *Annual Report*, 1876, p. 146; *ibid.*, 1877, p. 202.

[16] *Eleventh Census of the United States, 1890: Volume X, Report on Indians Taxed and Indians Not Taxed in the United States (Except Alaska)*, 619–621; Ritzenthaler, "Oneida Indians of Wisconsin," *Bulletin of the Public Museum of the City of Milwaukee*, 19:14; Campisi, "Oneida," in *Handbook of North American Indians. Volume 15: Northeast*, 485–487.

vations of a serious educational gap. The "majority of the old people speak English, and many of them are able to read and write. . . . There are scarcely any on the reservation between the ages of 25 and 50 who are able to read and write English understandingly. Persons of this class can read and write who neither understand nor speak English." This was doubtless intended as a slap at the two mission schools—Episcopal and Methodist—which were "the most.patronized" although they competed with four public schools taught by Oneida graduates of the Carlisle Indian Industrial School in Pennsylvania. The problem seemed to be that few of the children used English at home, knew it only mechanically at school, and conversed with their peers only in Oneida.[17]

The Oneida belied the common belief that the American Indian was dying out. To be sure, counting Indians was less than an exact science under the circumstances that obtained in Wisconsin at the time—a fact that the federal census bureau acknowledged. Its figures indicated a decline of those counted as reservation Indians from 10,312 in the 1870 census to 7,637 in 1880 and 6,095 in 1890. But those outside the agencies' purview (counted either as Indians taxed or self-sustaining and not in any tribal relationship) steadily increased in the same census reports from 1,206 to 3,161 to 3,835, while the combined totals declined from 11,521 in 1870, to 10,798 in 1880, and to 9,930 in 1890. The great majority, who did not make a transition to living somewhat like their white neighbors, existed mostly in dire poverty. Some made a partial transition, living in small, ill-constructed houses, often without floors or similar amenities, and crowded with extended families. With a less than adequate diet, and plagued by alcoholism and chronic diseases, those who attempted this compromise were probably less healthy than those

[17] Campisi, "Oneida," in *Handbook of North American Indians. Volume 15: Northeast,* 486, 621; *Eleventh Census of the United States, 1890: Volume X, Report on Indians Taxed and Indians Not Taxed in the United States (Except Alaska),* 619–621. See Prucha, *American Indian Policy in Crisis,* 272–282, on Carlisle. "As a tribe, they [Oneida] are like boys sixteen or seventeen years old; they know too much to be Indians and too little to be white people." Or so states the U.S. Commissioner of Indian Affairs, *Annual Report,* 1874, p. 186.

who shunned white ways. An 1881 report on Wisconsin's reservation Indians noted 161 births and 183 deaths. Dr. Joseph Hobbins noted consumption as the principal hazard of the Chippewa, pneumonia as the common scourge among all tribes, and scrofula and consumption more particularly among the Winnebago. There simply were not reliable reports to draw upon, Hobbins complained, for comparisons with the health of the white population.[18]

One factor in the persistence of an Indian population in Wisconsin may well have been the widely deplored practices of polygamy and early marriage. Moses Paquette observed that the annuities were commonly paid by head: "The inducement to have a numerous progeny is powerful, and the Indians take advantage of the premium thus placed by the government on child-bearing." The Indian Bureau seer who wrote the "Historic Review of Indians in the United States" commented of the American Indian: "While an enigma he is of a magnificent race, physically. When we consider the ravages of disease, intermarriage, exposure, starvation, and the white man, and then consider the number of Indians now here . . . the Indian would seem to be a startling example of the survival of the fittest."[19]

The Menominee were, like the Winnebago and Chippewa, a pre-Columbian Wisconsin tribe. They had ceded their lands by

---

[18] *Eleventh Census of the United States, 1890: Volume X, Report on Indians Taxed and Indians Not Taxed in the United States (Except Alaska)*, 21–28; General James S. Brisbin, from a letter to the New York *Herald* reported in the *Wisconsin State Journal*, April 2, 1881. Joseph Hobbins, "Health in Wisconsin," appears in all the Wisconsin county histories published by the Western Historical Company, always on pp. 230–249. Scrofula is tuberculosis of the lymph glands.

[19] Thwaites, ed., "Wisconsin Winnebagoes," *Wis. Hist. Colls.*, 12:420; *Eleventh Census of the United States, 1890: Volume X, Report on Indians Taxed and Indians Not Taxed in the United States (Except Alaska)*, 56; Robert E. and Pat Ritzenthaler, *The Woodland Indians of the Western Great Lakes* (New York, 1970), 38–40. Ideas of Indian morality were, of course, usually measured against accepted American Protestant standards of the time. The biases of these judgmental descriptions are rather clear: Christianity and the use of English would improve the character of most Indians. And such opinions carried weight, as they were contained in an official document of the federal government: *Eleventh Census of the United States, 1890: Volume X, Report on Indians Taxed and Indians Not Taxed in the United States (Except Alaska)*, 619–625.

1848, and were scheduled for removal to a reservation in Minnesota. But the Menominee refused to accept removal. In 1854 the federal government granted them a reservation on the present site on the upper Wolf River. Many Menominee families were related to citizens of Green Bay, whose families went back to the period of the French and British fur trade. This helped them to prevail in their long struggle to preserve their present home. Like the neighboring Stockbridge, they had a difficult time maintaining their rights to the timber on their reservation. It was the timber that united them, particularly against the 1871 act of Congress to permit its sale to whites. Despite the usual deep division of the tribe between traditionals and Christians, or citizens, the Menominee always mustered a majority against allotments or the sale to outsiders of their timber. The Indian Bureau, responding to the lumber barons, allowed the Menominee to harvest and market their logs in the 1880's. Their agent attempted to limit logging privileges to those who would farm during the summer. This accorded with the purposes of the Dawes Severalty Act—individually owned farm acreage and eventual citizenship to replace tribal government. Lumbering was better suited than agriculture to a traditional life style based on hunting and gathering. Lumbering was seasonal and a communal activity, resembling the hunt in demanding skills and stamina. Apparently the better land on the reservation was covered by timber. The open land they were encouraged to farm was often as indifferent for their style of farming as their attitude towards that type of work.[20]

Like the Oneida, the Menominee were, according to the 1890

[20] Keesing, *Menomini Indians of Wisconsin*; Menominee Indian Centennial Committee, *Menominee Indian Centennial, 1854–1954* (n.p., 1954), 43-55; Patricia K. Ourada, *The Menominee Indians: A History* (Norman, 1979), 107-156; Stephen J. Herzberg, "The Menominee: From Treaty to Termination," in *WMH*, 60 (Summer, 1977), 269-284, 329; Willard H. Titus, "Observations on the Menominee Indians," in *WMH*, 14 (September–December, 1930), 93-105, 121-132; Mathilda E. Eggener, "History of the Menomini Indians" (bachelor's thesis, University of Wisconsin, 1911); Walter J. Hoffman, "The Menomini Indians," in U.S. Bureau of Ethnology, *Annual Report, 1892–1893* (Washington, 1896), pt. 1, pp. 3–328; Milfred et al., *Soil Resources of Menominee County*.

census, taking advantage of educational opportunities. There was a similar lack of command of English among those in their middle years, but unlike the Oneida, few old people spoke or read English. Agency schools and mission schools operated both as boarding schools as well as day schools and also served children from the Oneida, Stockbridge, and Chippewa reservations. The traditionalists among the Menominee were fewer than one-fourth of those on the reservation. The remainder were nominally Catholic. The Catholic church had not accepted the Protestant domination of Indian reservations confirmed by the Grant administration policies, and opened its own school on the Menominee reservation.[21]

The Chippewa Indians fell on difficult times as the fur trade declined in northern Wisconsin, to be succeeded by lumbering and settlement. A hunting, fishing, trapping, and gathering culture characterized by relatively loose tribal government described the Chippewa in the nineteenth century. Because of the nature of the land they inhabited and their adaptation to it, they spent much of the year in small roving bands or family units. The reduction of their land holdings to the relatively small reservations of the 1854 treaties put constraints upon their traditional way of life. Not that they confined themselves to these reserves; but they were in competition with lumbermen, settlers, private owners, and white trappers over much of what had been their range before 1854. Many Chippewa did adapt to lumbering, particularly winter work in the woods, but they had problems similar to the Menominee in protecting or profiting from their own limited timber holdings.

The Wisconsin Chippewa had refused to move westward to a reservation in Minnesota adjacent to their traditional Sioux enemies. By treaties in 1854 they were granted four reservations that exist today: Lac du Flambeau in the southern corner of

---

[21] *Eleventh Census of the United States, 1890: Volume X, Report on Indians Taxed and Indians Not Taxed in the United States (Except Alaska)*, 621–623; Thomas A. Downs, "Francis Xavier Krautbauer, Second Bishop of the Green Bay Diocese" (master's thesis, St. Paul Seminary, St. Paul, Minnesota, 1963), 42–44; Ritzenthaler and Ritzenthaler, *Woodland Indians*, 97.

adjoining Vilas and Iron counties; Lac Court Oreilles in Sawyer County; Bad River adjacent to the present city of Ashland; and Red Cliff hugging the northern tip of Bayfield County on Lake Superior. The landlocked Lac Court Oreilles and Lac du Flambeau reservations harbored 65 per cent of the Wisconsin Chippewa. They did only a little cultivating of their land and profited little from sales of reservation timber. The Lac Court Oreilles people appear to have been more militant about the protection of their timber. The 1890 census report on these people stated that they were about one-third Christians (mostly Catholic) who sent their children to the mission or government schools and spoke English. The Christians were characterized as comfortable by comparison with the more numerous "pagans." The Christians, presumably, were the ones trying to keep their keepers and the lumbermen honest. By contrast, the Lac du Flambeau people were overwhelmingly "pagan," roving, and "in a destitute condition."

The Bad River Chippewa were divided about half-and-half between Christians and pagans, only the former using English and sending their children to school. They, too, had continuing trouble over the exploitation by whites of their timber, and, being close to Ashland with a railroad running through the reservation, they had contacts with whites who were little concerned with violations of Indian property or other basic rights. Their streams were used for log drives through their lands without regard to their use by the Chippewa for fishing, trapping, or travel. The reservation agent, however, did not assign Indian complaints that whites "make their women bad and bring in much fire water" as the reasons for condemning the Bad River Indians as "the most immoral of the Chippewas." (The root of the Indians' problem was alleged to be a former addiction to polygamy and a present one to drunkenness.) Bad as the Bad River Indians were, the pagans were especially bad, while the Christians existed in some comfort by contrast.

At a greater remove from the influence of Ashland's randy population, the Red Cliff people were seen as "the most civilized of all the Chippewas." They cut wood, fished, made maple sugar, and farmed successfully. They were relatively well-housed, used English, and sent their children to the two Catholic schools maintained there.

Given the character of the land on which most of the members of this most numerous Wisconsin tribe were confined, their prospects were not bright. Individual land ownership could not make farmers of them even had the climate and most of the land been suitable. Their principal legacy appears to have been the prompt sale of the timber from their allotments in a marketplace even more rapacious than the fur trade had been. After all, a fur trader hoped to see his Indian trappers and hunters back with a catch the following year, and he often financed that enterprise. What good was a treeless Indian to a lumberman?[22]

With a confidence totally at variance with the evidence in hand, the special report of the 1890 census concluded:[23]

> In all future dealings with the reservation Indians let them understand that they must become self-sustaining; make them understand this by the law; show them the way; give them the means to become self-sustaining and they will succeed. Teach the Indian that it pays to be clean, to be industrious, to have but one wife, to have property, to have but one family of children, and teach him to follow the best habits of white people. Show him that it is to his interest to be like other men.
>
> Whatever is to be done with the reservation Indians do it at once. Ten years can close this question up. Do not dole this out through another 50 or 100 years. . . .

Impatient as it was with agency and mission schools on the reservation, the government's advice was:

---

[22] Robert E. Ritzenthaler, "Southwestern Chippewa," in *Handbook of North American Indians. Volume 15: Northeast*, 743–747, 753–754; Stephan Thernstrom, ed., *Harvard Encyclopedia of American Ethnic Groups* (Cambridge, 1980), 74–75; *Eleventh Census of the United States, 1890: Volume X, Report on Indians Taxed and Indians Not Taxed in the United States (Except Alaska)*, 617–618, 623–624; Ronald A. Janke, "The Development and Persistence of United States Indian Land Problems as Shown by a Detailed Study of the Chippewa Indians" (doctoral dissertation, University of Minnesota, 1975), 273–275, 296–297, 324–329; Edmund J. Danziger, Jr., *The Chippewas of Lake Superior* (Norman, 1978), 91–109.

[23] *Eleventh Census of the United States, 1890: Volume X, Report on Indians Taxed and Indians Not Taxed in the United States (Except Alaska)*, 72, 74.

University of Wisconsin class of 1876, with
Bascom Hall in the background.

Frederick Jackson Turner as a
student, 1884, and later as professor of history, 1892, at the University of Wisconsin.

Oscar Hallam, 1887.

Lucius Fairchild (center) and guests at the Fairchild residence, c. 1892.

William D. Hoard.

George W. Peck.

Nils P. Haugen.

William Freeman Vilas (right) in his Washington office, 1890.

John Coit Spooner.

Matthew Hale Carpenter.

Philetus Sawyer.

Elisha W. Keyes.

Campers at Lake Kegonsa near Stoughton (Dane County), c. 1880.

Winnebago Indians, probably Wood County, c. 1885.

Baseball, Jackson County, c. 1890.

Camping out, probably Marinette County, c. 1890.

Saloon, Grantsburg (Burnett County), 1886.

Bethesda Springs, a spa near Waukesha.

Women's outing, near Green Bay, c. 1882.

Men's outing, Green Bay area, c. 1890.

Bicyclists, Green Bay, c. 1890.

Suppertime at Sturgeon Bay (Door County), c. 1890.

Indian children on reservations should be placed as soon as possible in the public school systems of the states and territories in which they live and where English alone is taught. There is no serious objection to their going to these public schools, for there is not the prejudice existing against the Indian that there is against the negro. . . . Public schools are not denominational schools and creed is not taught in them, so this would be an advantage.

Wisconsin furnishes evidence to the contrary. Ray Stannard Baker grew up in St. Croix Falls where the family moved in 1875 when Ray was five years old. His parents were of New England background and his father, Major Joseph Baker, was proud of family links to the Underground Railroad and abolitionist activism. Ray Baker would later write the best-known progressive tract on American race relations, *Following the Color Line: American Negro Citizenship in the Progressive Era*. But his views on Indians were quite different.[24]

In the seventies and eighties, St. Croix Falls had a "Quailtown" inhabited by "fragments of the once powerful tribe of the Chippewa, degraded by liquor and the diseases of the white man, demoralized by the breakdown of the stern tribal usages which from time immemorial had constituted the morals and buttressed the religion of a courageous and hardy people. In all the settlements there were many half-breeds, 'half Indian and half river-driver,' as the saying went, and often a dominating white 'squaw-man,' who had all the vices of both races."[25]

Joseph Baker, on the other hand, found the Indians interesting. He regularly bought articles of food and moccasins from them. When the Dream Dance was introduced among the Chippewa, an Indian scare ensued which brought the isolated immigrant settlers swarming into St. Croix Falls with their worldly

[24] Ray Stannard Baker, *Native American: The Book of My Youth* (New York, 1941), 1-3, 11-15, 305; Ray Stannard Baker, *Following the Color Line: American Negro Citizenship in the Progressive Era* (New York, 1908; Harper Torchbook edition, New York, 1964). *Following the Color Line* appeared first as a series of articles in *The American Magazine*, a venture controlled by Baker, Lincoln Steffens, Ida Tarbell, and other prominent "progressive" journalists.

[25] Baker, *Native American*, 4.

goods. Major Baker was sure that the alarm was unfounded. Over his wife's strong objections, shared by their son, Joseph Baker set out to discover the source of the alarm. A few days later, he returned with word from some leaders of the Chippewa that the ceremonies planned were of a religious rather than a warlike nature, "to express the sorrow of the Indian over his lost estate."[26]

It is worth noting that the confident policies of the Bureau of Indian Affairs, confirmed in 1887 by the Dawes Act, were meant to integrate the Wisconsin Indians into Ray Stannard Baker's generation, not that of his more tolerant father. Ray Baker wrote: "In the after years of my boyhood I had no patience in reading of the 'noble red man' . . . for I remembered vividly the filthy camps of the Indians I knew and the drunkenness and worse." He went to school with Indian and half-breed children, whom he obviously kept at a distance. Baker's progressivism was as qualified as most other progressives' on the score of true equality.[27]

One evidence of an Indian sense of community that transcended the isolation of assigned reservations or past tribal rivalries was in religion. Not, however, from the assignment of Wisconsin Indians to the Congregational missionary societies or the Catholic response to that assignment, but rather through traditional religious practices and adaptations of Christian teachings. There was no hard and fast line between those who clung to a traditional religious observance and those who were nominal Christians.[28]

---

[26] *Ibid.*, 5–8.

[27] *Ibid.*, 4, 100–101; Baker, *Following the Color Line*, xiv; Ray Stannard Baker, *American Chronicle: The Autobiography of Ray Stannard Baker* (New York, 1945).

[28] Prucha, *American Indian Policy in Crisis*, 150–161; Keller, *Protestantism and Indian Policy*, 180–187. The 1874 policy of assigning each reservation to a specific religious denomination was set aside in 1881 by Secretary of Interior Carl Schurz. Intolerance towards American Indian religions did not officially end until 1934. For religious beliefs and practices of the Oneida, Winnebago, and Chippewa, see Campisi, "Oneida," in *Handbook of North American Indians. Volume 15: Northeast*, 488; Nancy O. Lurie, "Winnebago," in *ibid.*, 695–696; Ritzenthaler, "Southwestern Chippewa," in *ibid.*, 754–757; and index in *ibid.* for other references to medicine societies. See also Ritzenthaler and Ritzenthaler, *Woodland Indians*, 87–100; and Thwaites, ed., "Wisconsin Winnebagoes," *Wis. Hist. Colls.*, 12:423–425.

The Dream Dance, or Drum Dance, originated among the Sioux—possibly the Omaha—sometime in the seventies. A young woman hid from U.S. soldiers by swimming into a lake, where she remained in the shallows for some ten days. She experienced a vision wherein she was instructed to carry the ritual to her people, who accepted it as direct revelation. The Dream Dance cult spread from tribe to tribe, and with minor variations, it superseded older ceremonies of a similar kind.[29]

It is probable that the rumor of an uprising of the Chippewa referred to by Ray Stannard Baker was in fact the arrival among the Chippewa of the Dream Dance ceremony. The Santee Sioux had conveyed the ceremony to the Minnesota Chippewa, who had in turn conveyed it to the Wisconsin Chippewa. The ceremony thus spread, by the gift of a special drum and the ritual, among groups and tribes, to become common to almost all Wisconsin Indians.[30]

It would seem that learning English and the competing dogmas of Christianity did less to create a sense of community among Wisconsin's Indians than did their constant awareness of being outsiders. The value system being forced upon them had a limited application to their situation. This encouraged traditional enemies among the Indians to find common ground in shared ceremonies and a darkening destiny.

\* \* \*

Wisconsin had a very small and scattered Negro population in the latter decades of the nineteenth century. It comprised no

[29] S. A. Barrett, "The Dream Dance of the Chippewa and Menominee Indians of Northern Wisconsin," in the *Bulletin of the Public Museum of the City of Milwaukee*, 1 (November, 1911), 256-257; Ritzenthaler and Ritzenthaler, *Woodland Indians*, 83-95, 293-296. The common thread was a strong pan-Indian movement in the face of white pressure.

[30] Baker, *Native American*, 7-8. Barrett, "Dream Dance," *Bulletin of the Public Museum of the City of Milwaukee*, 1:297, places the arrival of the Dream Dance in Wisconsin sometime in the 1890's. Ritzenthaler and Ritzenthaler, *Woodland Indians*, 93, say sometime in the 1870's. The Dream Dance ceremony did not have the messianic overtones of the Messiah Craze, or Ghost Dance cult, which originated among the Nevada Paiute Indians in the early 1890's and did not reach Wisconsin until much later. See the annual report for 1891 of Commissioner of Indian Affairs T. J. Morgan on the "Messiah Craze," in Washburn, comp., *American Indian and the United States*, 1:560-564.

more than two-tenths of 1 per cent of the state's population, was highly mobile in most locations, and was subjected to the usual prejudices, employment restrictions, and indifference to basic rights. Lacking political power and faced with a waning interest in the problems of Negro citizens on the part of former champions—a situation not unique to Wisconsin—the usual lot of the Negro citizen was discontent, normally masked by a protective deference to the white majority. Some found an economic niche, their security depending upon complacent white patronage; but they certainly did not find acceptance as equals.[31]

Negroes had more opportunity than Indians to seek a place of their own within the confines of the surrounding white society—remembering always their "proper" place. To that extent, they benefited from official indifference. The Negro community also produced more leaders whose concerns could occasionally impinge upon white consciousness. Black activists scored a minor legal point now and again, but they were in a discouraging environment, generally one of massive indifference broken by occasions of hostility.

The nominal increase of Wisconsin's Negro population between 1870 and 1890 reflects a very high mobility rate among blacks. The census of 1870 reported 2,113 Negroes in Wisconsin; that of 1880 reported 2,702; and that of 1890, 2,444. In the census of 1900, Negroes had increased only to 2,486. Fifty-one per cent of Wisconsin-born Negroes lived elsewhere by 1900, compared with 22.8 per cent of Wisconsin-born whites.

Wisconsin's Negroes came from a variety of backgrounds. A few dated back to the fur-trade era. Most of those from the territorial period had arrived with the border state Southerners of the lead region. A few came with the army as officers' servants. By the 1870's there were two identifiable rural Negro communities: Pleasant Ridge near Lancaster in Grant County, and Cheyenne Valley in northeastern Vernon County. Both

---

[31] C. Vann Woodward, *The Strange Career of Jim Crow* (New York, 1955), 52–53. The term "Negro" was common to all sources of the time and is therefore used instead of the post-1960 term "black."

communities were created initially by freed and escaped slaves.[32]

Cheyenne Valley was the more stable community, doubtless because Negroes pioneered the settlement and were gradually infiltrated by Irish, Bohemian, and Norwegian immigrant families who arrived with fewer preconceptions about these American neighbors. Their integrated school and Methodist church were accepted as community institutions. Relations with white neighbors were generally harmonious with some intermarriage in the seventies and eighties, and this harmony continued until after the turn of the century. Also, the Negro community maintained a balance of the sexes.

The Pleasant Ridge community in Grant County was less advantageously placed to endure. It was only half the size of the more isolated Cheyenne Valley settlement. Its origins went back to 1848 with the arrival of the Horner family, a southern white family, and their former slaves. While the school district and a small United Brethren church were integrated, the Negroes were expected to "keep their place." In 1883, a white neighbor killed a black man he suspected of paying attention to his daughter. Samuel Gadlin, the murdered man, was an example of the problem. He was a latecomer who was attracted to Pleasant Ridge long after the Civil War had produced an influx of escaped or recently freed slaves. White neighbors were resentful of these latecomers. Like many Northerners, they adjusted complacently to the imposition of Jim Crow in the South during the 1870's, which was followed by a more conscious segregation in the North. Gadlin was a recently widowed Union veteran, but he "presumed."

Whatever the degree of acceptance of the earlier Negro residents, the Pleasant Ridge community went into decline by the 1880's. Partly this was a result of aspirations on the part of young people and the lack of opportunity locally. The community had

[32] *Eleventh Census of the United States, 1890: Population, Volume I, Part 1*, pp. 435–436; *Twelfth Census of the United States, 1900: Population, Volume I, Part 1*, pp. 690–693, 702–705; Zachary Cooper, *Black Settlers in Rural Wisconsin* (Madison, 1977), 5–19; James K. Phillips, "Negro-White Integration in a Midwestern Farm Community," in *Negro Heritage*, 7 (February–March, 1968), 55–58, 62–64.

also lost its character as a place where harmony reigned. An annual picnic which had featured an agreeable mixing of the neighbors thereafter continued as a mostly Negro affair. The white neighbors had rechristened Pleasant Ridge ''Nigger Ridge,'' and while the black children continued in the integrated school, they had little to do with their white schoolmates outside.[33]

Sympathy and a shortage of farm labor late in the Civil War brought about the importation of a large colony of Negroes to Fox Lake in rural Dodge County. They were recruited through a New York relief agency. Known locally as ''Squire Barron's carload of Negroes'' after Quartus H. Barron, the local justice of the peace who made the arrangements, there were seventy-one of them counted in the 1870 federal census. Only thirty-eight remained fifteen years later. They established their own church in the 1870's, but the worshippers were often harassed by local white youths. By 1900, just three charter members of the congregation remained.[34]

Even allowing for uncertainties about the accuracy of the censuses, the high mobility of the Negro population was characteristic in both urban and rural settings. Milwaukee was the only distinctly urban center where Negroes actually increased substantially, although not as rapidly as the general population. The most obvious reasons for this were a lack of employment opportunities, open hostility or indifference, and the failure to maintain a sense of community, which was ordinarily represented by a church congregation. Negroes were not particularly welcome anywhere. Where they did appear, they were often met with hostility as readily as with curiosity.[35]

Fond du Lac, which had a comparatively large and persistent Negro community from 1870 to 1900, had a patron saint in Joshua Goss, a white farmer who beggared himself in collecting

[33] Cooper, *Black Settlers in Rural Wisconsin*, 19–27; Laura Johnson, Lancaster, Wisconsin, to John O. Holzheuter, February 2, 1980, in research files, History of Wisconsin Project.

[34] Central Lakes Publishing Company, *Fox Lake, Wisconsin: 125 Years, 1838–1963 (A History)* (Fox Lake, 1963), 35–36.

[35] Current, *Civil War Era*, 559–562.

and finding employment for them. Beloit, Janesville, Racine, and Madison similarly had colonies that were reminders of early abolitionist sentiment. These colonies were characterized by a friendly interest on the part of a white elite which hired them as domestics. As one presumably white friend put it, Madison's early Negro residents were of a high character and "had no time to breed mischief, even if they had had the inclination." This statement quite well defined the relationship.[36]

Scattered through the general community in dependent circumstances, Negroes found it difficult to attain a community of their own. Madison's Negro population, for instance, declined from sixty-two to forty-one between 1870 and 1895, although the city's population increased by 74 per cent. They were distributed through three wards, the first and fifth on the city's west side and the second on the east side, but until 1902 they had no church.[37]

It was very difficult for Negroes to achieve an independent status as businessmen and they generally catered to the white community. Even the very few Negro professionals were dependent upon mostly white clienteles. Negroes themselves tended to have more confidence in whites to provide their needs for goods or services. Another part of this difficulty was that most Negroes simply did not have much money in hand to pay for these needs.[38]

Negroes were also often identified as strikebreakers. Since few unions would admit them, they had nothing to lose in this regard. They also were accustomed to being let go when a strike ended. They were considered cheap labor, fitted only for fringe jobs.

[36] Bill Hooker, "Fond du Lac, Its Sawmills and Freedmen—A Sketch," in *WMH*, 16 (June, 1933), 423-427; Velma F. Bell, "The Negro in Beloit and Madison" (master's thesis, University of Wisconsin, 1933), 6-10; Barbara R. Shade, "I Am the Darker Brother: The Story of Madison's Black Citizens, 1865-1900," manuscript in History of Wisconsin Project files, 17, published in part as an eight-part series in the Madison *Capital Times*, May 14-22, 1979.

[37] Bell, "Negro in Beloit and Madison," 54; *Wisconsin State Census*, 1895, p. 68; C. M. Foote and Co., *Plat Book of Dane County, Wisconsin . . .* (Minneapolis, 1890), 34-35, 38-39.

[38] Thomas R. Buchanan, "Black Milwaukee, 1890-1915" (master's thesis, University of Wisconsin-Milwaukee, 1973), 32-33.

Hostility from those they competed with or displaced was the rule.[39]

In 1895 Milwaukee had nearly one-fourth of Wisconsin's Negroes, compared to about one-twelfth in 1870, but they had decreased slightly as a percentage of the city's total population. Several cities—Fond du Lac (1 per cent), Beloit (.76 per cent), Superior (.69 per cent), and Racine (.40 per cent)—had higher concentrations of blacks than Milwaukee in 1895 (.22 per cent), but all of these others save Superior had experienced absolute reductions in numbers of Negroes since the 1870 census. As the percentages indicate, they were a tiny minority in all of these cities.

Milwaukee Negroes were concentrated immediately west of

---

[39] *Ibid.*, 18–21; Thomas W. Gavett, *Development of the Labor Movement in Milwaukee* (Madison, 1965), 25–26.

WISCONSIN'S NEGRO POPULATION, 1870–1895

| City | 1870 | 1880 | 1890 | 1895 |
|---|---|---|---|---|
| Milwaukee | 176 | 304 | 449 | 551 |
| Superior | – | – | 68 | 185 |
| Fond du Lac | 179 | 178 | 112 | 129 |
| Racine | 141 | 142 | 108 | 102 |
| Waukesha (village) | 31 | n.a. | 57 | 70 |
| Beloit | 66 | 96 | 67 | 59 |
| La Crosse | 101 | 55 | 61 | 56 |
| Oshkosh | 68 | 77 | 56 | 55 |
| Madison | 62 | 63 | 44 | 41 |
| Janesville | 62 | 71 | 42 | 28 |
| Kenosha | 9 | 17 | 17 | 25 |
| Eleven-City Totals | 895 | 1,003 | 1,081 | 1,301 |
| Wisconsin Totals | 2,113 | 2,702 | 2,444 | 2,450 |

SOURCES: *Ninth Census of the United States, 1870: Population, Volume I*, 287–295; *Tenth Census of the United States, 1880: Population, Volume I*, 425; *Eleventh Census of the United States, 1890: Population, Volume I, Part 1*, pp. 435–436; *Wisconsin State Census*, 1895, pp.60–111. Of the 1890 Negro population of 2,444 in Wisconsin, 1,432 were urban (2,500+ population) which was 58.6 per cent compared to 33.2 per cent for the general population.

the Milwaukee River in the fourth ward, where the Plankinton House was one of their principal employers. The Plankinton House hired Negro waiters when it opened in 1868, and they were among the elite of the black community, with as many as forty-five regularly employed. It continued this policy. The competing Newhall House hired a black dining room staff late in 1880, then abruptly dismissed them a year later in favor of white girls. (The Milwaukee *Sentinel* commented: "The experiment of using Negro men for waiters instead of white girls did not prove satisfactory to the management of the Newhall House. The 'coons' will be discharged to-day and the girls discharged about six months ago will be reinstated.") Three-fourths of Milwaukee's Negroes were in the fourth ward in 1870, and over half were there twenty years later. By 1895, four-fifths of them were concentrated in the fourth and the immediately adjacent wards. The remainder were very thinly distributed in the other parts of the city.

The Negro community's location in old housing mixed with marginal commercial structures along the Milwaukee River—itself not an attractive stream—created a section known as the "Bad Lands" along both sides of the river. As the name suggests, it was the gambling and red-light district, operated and patronized by all races. The black community was indelibly associated in the public mind with the "Bad Lands" because it lived (or was trapped) there.[40]

Milwaukee Negroes were more various in their employment and in their perceptions of their "place" in the general community than in most Wisconsin urban communities. The majority were limited to the usual Negro jobs as servants and unskilled industrial employees. But the city was large enough to offer entrepreneurial and some semiprofessional opportunities. Many of those who succeeded were light-skinned Negroes who had enjoyed some educational advantages. If there were any advan-

[40] Buchanan, "Black Milwaukee," 9–10.

tages to living in a northern city, they probably related to skin color and the fact that Negroes were not confined to segregated schools.[41]

Because of their identification with white culture and values, albeit ambivalently, Negroes occasionally produced leaders willing to test the limits of white tolerance. The evidence is that this tolerance diminished in the post-Civil War years. It was easier to sympathize with Lo, the Poor Indian, who wasn't met with in an urban setting running a blind pig or striving for middle-class respectability.

But even in Milwaukee, where black aspirations ran the full gamut, there were not many legal victories between the seventies and the nineties. An earlier victory in 1866 had been engineered by Radical Republicans who arranged for a lawsuit in the interest of Ezekiel Gillespie, "a person of mixed African blood," who was refused the right to vote. Three times—in 1849, 1857, and 1865—referenda on extending voting rights to Negro citizens had apparently failed. Taking the case to the state supreme court, Byron Paine won a reversal based upon the 1849 referendum, which had carried but had been ruled void because only a minority of those voting in the election expressed themselves on the issue. After the Gillespie appeal succeeded, Negroes voted, often under hostile conditions, until an 1882 amendment on voting rights, which struck from Article III of the Wisconsin Constitution the references to "white" citizens and "white" persons of foreign birth. William Green, a black activist attorney in Milwaukee claimed that most Negroes were effectively prevented from voting prior to this 1882 amendment, despite the 1866 court ruling in Gillespie's favor.[42]

[41] Ibid., 16–31. The Milwaukee Northwestern Recorder, January 14, 1893, listed businesses belonging to Negroes, and concluded: "In a short time our city will be largely inhabited by respectable colored citizens." The Recorder started in 1892, as the Wisconsin Afro-American. In 1890 Wisconsin's blacks were counted 1,007 as Negro, 782 as mulatto, 290 as quadroon, and 365 as octoroon. See Eleventh Census of the United States, 1890: Population, Volume I, Part 1, p. 397.

[42] Leslie H. Fishel, Jr., "Wisconsin and Negro Suffrage," in WMH, 46 (Spring, 1963), 180–196; John O. Holzhueter, "Ezekiel Gillespie, Lost and Found," in WMH, 60 (Spring, 1977), 179–184. Milwaukee County Historical Society, The Negro in Milwau-

A last gasp of Radical Republicanism was the congressional civil rights act of 1875, which forbade discrimination in places of public accommodation. This was struck down by the U.S. Supreme Court in 1883, which ruled it an unconstitutional infringement on private rights. The only cure offered was state legislation on the issue. Wisconsin did not hurry to fill the void, and few Negroes were inclined to press the issue. Overt discrimination was their daily experience, and the Negro community of Milwaukee turned inward and created its own social groups and hierarchy. Their gradual increase in numbers made this possible, as did the philosophy of Booker T. Washington (endorsed by many whites) that Negroes should prove their worth and not intrude where they were not wanted.

It was six years after the 1883 Supreme Court decision before a formal test came in Wisconsin. Then Owen Howell purchased a ticket by messenger to a play at Milwaukee's Bijou Opera House. When he arrived to take his seat on the main floor, he was told that he could be seated only in the gallery. Howell was testing the system. He filed suit against Jacob Litt, the owner, who had other theaters in Chicago, New York, St. Paul, and elsewhere. Litt was a chosen target, as subsequent newspaper stories made clear. Whites, he said, did object to sitting next to Negroes but he generously provided restricted seating for the latter. But it was whites, he stated, who made his theaters pay. Howell won his suit against the owner of the Bijou, with costs and an award of $100.[43]

A white activist attorney and former congressman, Gerry Whiting Hazelton, acted for Howell. There was fairly wide sup-

---

*kee: An Historical Survey* (Milwaukee, 1968), 5-11, contains a reprint of an article by William T. Green, "Negroes in Milwaukee," originally published in the Milwaukee *Sentinel*, October 16, 1895. See also *Laws of Wisconsin*, 1882, pp. 899-901. In Oshkosh, local Negroes hired carriages to go to the polls in November, 1876, and received a notice in the Milwaukee *Sentinel*, November 8, 9, 1876, for this bit of bravado.

[43] Leslie H. Fishel, Jr., "The Genesis of the First Wisconsin Civil Rights Act," in *WMH*, 49 (Summer, 1966), 328-329; Harry H. Anderson, "Landmark Civil Rights Decisions in Wisconsin," in Milwaukee County Historical Society, *The Negro in Milwaukee*, 22-29; Buchanan, "Black Milwaukee," 54-65. The suit asked $2,500 damages, according to the Milwaukee *Herald*, October 15, 1889.

port for Howell in the black community, and many Negroes attended the jury trial. William T. Green, who would be the first black graduate of the University of Wisconsin Law School, emerged as the leader of the movement while still a student. Green and others organized a meeting in Milwaukee in late November, 1889, which issued a call for a state civil rights league. This was not an isolated action. While Milwaukee did not yet have a Negro newspaper, the editor of the New York *Age* was promoting a national movement for a similar organization.[44]

Milwaukee newspapers generally took the new evidence of local black militancy calmly. The *Sentinel* pointed out that there was no legislative remedy for "senseless prejudice," but Negroes must simply prove their worth. The Milwaukee *Journal* wrote approvingly of the test case against the Bijou owner, but took no notice of the meetings of the new Civil Rights League after its formal creation. Liberal but Democratic in its politics, the *Journal* reflected a southern viewpoint about Negroes. The League was viewed by the *Journal* as a typical Republican ploy to organize the black vote: "Cultivated northern workmen cannot be kept down unless African inferiority is used to rule them."[45]

Green and his supporters found an advocate in the Republican assemblyman from their fourth ward, Orren T. Williams. Williams could count votes, and he obligingly introduced a public accommodations measure which was largely Green's draft. Everything was right except the timing. The bill came before the legislature elected in 1890, in which the Republicans were an unaccustomed minority. Democrats were normally hostile towards Negro aspirations, and some were voluble on the subject. "Where is the man on this floor who will say the colored man is the equal of the white man? God did not create them equal," declared a Democratic member of the assembly commit-

---

[44] Fishel, "First Wisconsin Civil Rights Act," *WMH*, 49:327. The Milwaukee *Herald*, October 15, 1889, said that seventy-five Milwaukee Negroes attended the initial meeting to censure the owner of the Bijou.

[45] Milwaukee *Sentinel*, November 29, 1889; Milwaukee *Journal*, September 30, October 9, and an editorial, "Negro Labor," October 8, 1889.

tee considering the bill. Passed in emasculated form in the assembly, the bill died in the senate.[46]

Not until the Republicans returned to control of the legislature and executive office after the 1894 election, did Wisconsin finally pass the 1895 comprehensive civil rights act, more or less in the form drawn by William Green. Meanwhile, in 1892, Green had been presumably the first Negro to sit as a delegate in a state Republican convention. The triumph of Wisconsin's civil rights statute was not an isolated event. Similar measures were adopted or strengthened from 1890 to 1900 in Washington, Iowa, Ohio, Colorado, Massachusetts, Nebraska, New York, Minnesota, and California.[47]

These apparent victories were a part of a growing Republican party interest in the urban Negro voter. While Milwaukee did not have a large Negro community by comparison with other cities of the Upper Midwest, its Negroes were concentrated in a single ward that constituted an assembly district, and they were politically active. The fact that William Green could get seventy-five, out of a total city black population of 449, to a meeting in the Bijou Theater case was evidence enough. The fourth ward was a potential swing district. A Democrat had won in the district in 1882, and again ten years later.

Aside from this political interest in Negroes, which had been kept alive by a few friends from the Radical Republican tradition such as Byron Paine and Gerry Whiting Hazelton, there was not much to cheer about in the later years of the century. The growing national indifference was reflected in Milwaukee. As a historian of the Milwaukee black community concludes: "By the turn of the century, Milwaukee Negroes were treated with indifference or hostility. The benevolent paternalism and street-nodding familiarity that had once seemed to characterize relations

[46] Fishel, "First Wisconsin Civil Rights Act," *WMH*, 49:329–330; Roger E. Wyman, "Wisconsin Ethnic Groups and the Election of 1890," in *WMH*, 51 (Summer, 1968), 269–293.

[47] Fishel, "First Wisconsin Civil Rights Act," *WMH*, 49:330–333.

between blacks and whites in the city had given way to a cold and formalized pattern of race relations."[48]

The Republican *Sentinel* caught the spirit of this attitude in a news story, "The Colored Four Hundred." It recorded, in what was considered the appropriate dialect, a "Big Cake Walk" contest held at the Exposition Building. Judges for the contest were local white sporting types; music was furnished by Christopher Bach's orchestra with "a programme of old colored melodies." Four thousand spectators came to watch twenty-two black couples compete. The *Sentinel* continued: "As one negro girl expressed it, 'all de white folks have come out to watch de darkies' fun.' " The crowd booed when their favorites, a mulatto/quadroon couple, took only second prize. Coins were showered on the performers. Negroes were amusing—in their place—was the message.[49]

\* \* \*

Did Wisconsin women achieve any greater sense of community in the post-Civil War decades, based upon the enlarged role which they played? Women had appeared in unaccustomed roles during the war, and they were finding new opportunities in education and the professions as well as in service and industrial employment. Women made up only 8.72 per cent of those reporting gainful occupations in 1870; by 1890 this percentage was 14.07. While most of this increase was in domestic and industrial employment, women also made notable gains in office work and in retailing, and they increased their majority position in teaching, which had been considerably upgraded as a professional occupation. A very few were appearing where they had not been before—as lawyers, doctors, and as teachers in co-educational institutions of higher learning.[50]

[48] Buchanan, "Black Milwaukee," 54–56.

[49] Milwaukee *Sentinel*, March 6, 7, 1892; Barbara R. Shade, "Reconstruction Offered Tantalizing Hint of Freedom," in the Madison *Capital Times*, May 18, 1979.

[50] See Chapter 5 above. See also *Ninth Census of the United States, 1870: Population, Volume I*, 698, 764; *Eleventh Census of the United States, 1890: Population, Volume I, Part 2*, pp. 302, 624; Current, *Civil War Era*, 369–371, 387–389; Ethel A. Hurn, *Wisconsin Women in the War Between the States* (Madison, 1911); and Victoria Brown, *Uncommon Lives of Common Women: The Missing Half of Wisconsin History* (Madison, 1975), 13–24.

The problem with treating women as a separate community—as Negroes and Indians assuredly were—imposed upon by
serious legal, economic, and societal disadvantages is that women
reflected all of the normal divisions of the wider society based
upon economic circumstances, ethnicity, religion, their neighbors, and their presumptions of social class. There is no better
illustration of this fact than a simple story that ran on the editorial page of the *Sentinel* in the middle of February, 1886, two and
a half months before the Bay View riots. Titled "Women Who
Work," it was a reflection upon the increasing number of women
found working not just in stores where they had become a familiar sight, but in other occupations. In the middle of this matter-
of-fact story appeared the following: "The collection of garbage
is largely left to Polish women, who look upon a barrel of decayed
potatoes and table scraps with as much delight as some of their
fair sisters contemplate a Charlotte-Russe."[51]

The implications of this gratuitous characterization are plain.
This was the editorial page of the state's largest English-language
newspaper. Certainly very few copies circulated in the Polish
community, but the *Sentinel* had more than one German-speaking
member on its editorial staff. It speaks volumes that this reference was intended as a humorous aside to the *Sentinel's* audience
that would offend no one. It was, of course, entirely consonant
with references to Poles that appeared after the Bay View shootings, but this was some weeks before that event. While the
*Sentinel* was a hotly partisan political organ, the advertisements,
social page, and serialized stories—a common feature—certainly
implied a large and faithful audience of women. What does the
remark in "Women Who Work" say about any supposed feeling
of identification of the "fair sisters" with these later arrivals?[52]

*Germania,* the conservative voice of the German Lutheran community, observed of the Eight Hour League Parade of May 2,

---

[51] Milwaukee *Sentinel,* February 18, 1886.

[52] The majority of Milwaukee's Poles, as elsewhere before 1890, came from German-
controlled provinces and spoke the language. Presumably the German-speaking editors
were as insensitive as anyone else to this characterization of Polish women in the
community.

1886, which it generally disapproved: "Were those fine, young ladies who watched from their pretty carriages (though there were certainly not many of them), sympathetic to demonstrating seamstresses and dressmakers, who otherwise are seen on the streets carrying heavy bundles of dress material?" *Germania* managed to look both ways on many issues, and this was one of them. The paper decided that the "fine young ladies" were there because: "Pleasant Spring weather, rather than a commitment to any particular ideology, brought the many spectators out into the streets."[53]

Frank A. Flower, who headed Governor Jeremiah Rusk's bureau of labor and industrial statistics, also noticed this complacency towards the interests of working women:[54]

> No class of wage-workers is more deserving yet receives less attention from reformers, philanthropists and law-makers than the girls and women of cities who are compelled to support themselves, and frequently dependent relatives also, by their daily labors.
> While the workingmen can exercise their power and influence at the ballot-box, hold meetings, and demand redress and the passage of laws, form labor unions, go on strikes and even have their own newspapers as well as representatives in legislatures and municipal councils, the working girls, patient, timid and weak, must bear their ills without many public champions and without much public sympathy. . . .
> Men belong to various lodges, associations, unions and benevolent organizations, so that when thrown out of employment or crippled by misfortunes, they are looked after and succored. Working women are not thus provided for. They have fewer influences behind them—fewer props than men. . . .

Why this evident lack of interest or concern? Because those who had a relatively secure and comfortable place in their society were adept at justifying their comfort, which is common enough. Who wished to question a system that provided a maid of all work in the home for $2 a week with room and board—no questions about hours? It was easy to applaud Messrs. Rich and

[53] Milwaukee *Germania*, May 5, 1886.
[54] Wisconsin Bureau of Labor Statistics, *Biennial Report*, 1883–1884, p. 109.

Silber, who proposed to employ some 300 hands in their new dry goods and merchandising establishment. "We have in Milwaukee a population including many young women not compelled to work for a living, and yet willing to engage in light employment that will afford what seems to them a fair remuneration. The possession of this class gives Milwaukee a great advantage as a center for the manufacture of garments for women's wear," commented Mr. Rich, one of the firm's "plucky managers." What a blessing that the sewing machine offered these fortunates "what seems to them a fair remuneration" for relieving their fair sisters of the time-consuming task of making clothing for a family. Why rock such a comfortable boat?[55]

Gentlewomen were probably more active in charitable concerns after the Civil War. Society was more attuned to the necessity for private charity because of the very inadequacies of local and state governments, particularly in times of emergency. The war offered such times, and made it more difficult to rationalize that dire poverty was generally a sign of defective character. The war also offered certified widows and orphans. Mrs. Cordelia Harvey, the governor's widow, was only one of those women who learned how to deal productively with bureaucracy to get things done that required doing. Women continued to apply this hard-won knowledge.[56]

But women activists were generally prisoners of their society in the sense that their concern for working women was based upon some common assumptions. One was that "working women" were necessarily widows, or women who had to provide for their families because a husband failed to do so. The Woman's Industrial Exchange, which opened in Milwaukee in 1882, is often cited as evidence of early practical concern for working women on the part of the economically secure. Its avowed purpose was to "teach and promote industries among women, and

[55] Milwaukee *Northwest Trade Bulletin*, February 5, 1883.

[56] Current, *Civil War Era*, 392–397, 512–516; Anna B. Butler, Emma C. Bascom, and Katherine F. Kerr, eds., *Centennial Records of the Women of Wisconsin* (Madison, 1876), 1–80; Robert C. Nesbit, *Wisconsin: A History* (Madison, 1973), 257–258.

to provide a place for the sale of woman's work." The breadth of concern was somewhat less than later commentary suggests. The secretary of the new organization reported to the state's bureau of labor statistics: "It has provided itself a great benefit to gentle-women who have, through misfortune, become reduced. . . ." This was not exactly addressed to a broad definition of the "working women" of Wisconsin.[57]

Beyond the limits of social class, ethnicity, and religion, there were others. An indication came in a shocked report in the Milwaukee *Commercial Times* of December 17, 1877, entitled "An Indecent Outrage." A new organization called the Sunday Lecture Society had engaged Susan B. Anthony, whose announced topic was "The Homes of Single Women." But Miss Anthony substituted a lecture on "Women and Social Purity" in which "she proceeded to shower upon her helpless audience the most revolting statistics concerning prostitution, abortion, infanticide and venereal diseases. Her hearers were thunder-struck. . . . The whole performance was . . . an outrage upon decency and a shameful insult to the people of Milwaukee. . . ." The reason for the outrage was that the large audience supposed "that they were about to listen to a lecture containing nothing which could justly offend the most modest young girls there. Fathers took their daughters, brothers their sisters and gentlemen their lady friends, under this mistaken impression . . . for which the degenerate Sunday lecture society is accountable."

The *Commercial Times* was not innocent about Miss Anthony's subject. Not too long before, it had reported a police crackdown on the "social evil factories" on River Street. "The result will be that the 'dives' will all be cleansed out—as they should be—while there are other places of more respectability that will not, as we are informed, be molested. Milwaukee is particularly fortunate in the fact that as compared with other cities of equal size, the social evil here is decent and respectable. Even the worst resorts here are far superior in conduct to what would be called

[57] Ruth De Young Kohler, *The Story of Wisconsin Women* (Madison, 1948), 46–47; Wisconsin Bureau of Labor Statistics, *Biennial Report*, 1883–1884, pp. 113–114.

high-toned houses in many other cities.'' There were subsequent stories about saloons using pretty girls—not above some friendly interest in the customers—as waitresses, and the introduction of the "concert saloon" from New York. Another story concerned Mother Anderson's saloon on Cedar Street, which catered to ''a very promiscuous crowd . . . of both white and colored distinction.'' Miss Anthony, who was evidently flat out against such institutions, simply was not up to handling the grading system accepted locally.[58]

This editorial ambivalence delineates society at the time of America's centennial. Society was not interested in hearing about its inconsistencies. Ladies generally thought of "working women" as gentlewomen in reduced circumstances. The other category was "working girls," popularly considered as a brief, temporary condition prior to marriage. This was understandable, as the majority of those visible in industrial occupations were young—often very young. And a lady's concern was most often touched by the working girl's vulnerability rather than by the meagerness of their wages and lives. When women who organized the Milwaukee Home for the Friendless looked beyond their concern for widows and their children, they added in 1873 the "Young Woman's Home" which offered a wholesome environment for working girls. This charitable operation provided room and board for $2.50 per week. It would have been difficult to find many working girls in Milwaukee earning more than a dollar a day, and seventy-five cents would have been closer to the average.[59]

This is not to say that there was no consciousness of the lot of working girls on the part of middle-class women of Yankee background, but rather that one must search for the evidence. The

[58] Milwaukee *Commercial Times*, May 14, 26, 1875; May 1, 1876; April 17, December 17, 1877.
[59] Butler, Bascom, and Kerr, eds., *Centennial Records of the Women of Wisconsin*, 3–6. Wisconsin Bureau of Labor and Industrial Statistics, *Biennial Report*, 1888–1889, pp. 152–155, gives representative wages. See, for instance, "Boxes—paper and cigar." This industry employed many children and young women, and 292 of the 391 reported earning less than 80 cents per day.

Woman's Christian Temperance Union (WCTU), for instance,
highly organized under Frances Willard's dictum to "do everything," largely overlooked this field. The annual reports of the
organization in Wisconsin contain no reference to working
women among the many departments into which its efforts were
directed. One of these departments was charged with influencing
the press and various deliberative bodies; others oversaw the
traffic in unfermented wines, work among foreigners, and so on.
The department on the relation of capital and labor apparently
was concerned only about alcohol consumption. By 1893, with
twenty-seven departments, the closest the WCTU came to working girls was a home for women. This agency cared for unwed
mothers and found Christian homes for the babies and domestic
positions for the graduates, of whom twenty-one of twenty-two
"are leading good, true, virtuous lives, deeply grateful. . . ."[60]

Oddly, a fire served to divert rather than to focus attention on
the employment conditions of working girls. On January 9, 1883,
the Newhall House, an unprofitable firetrap which had once
been Milwaukee's largest and most elegant hotel, was destroyed
by fire. The seventy-one confirmed deaths made it America's
worst hotel fire, a record which stood for sixty-three years. Forty
young women, mostly chambermaids, were housed on the top
floor, and many among them were lost. The tragedy led to a
more militant concern with fire safety measures in public accommodations and workplaces. Wisconsin's bureau of labor statistics
was created in 1883, and its principal powers initially were in the
field of fire safety. This was largely admonitory because until
1885 no funds were provided for an inspector. Enforcement powers concerning working women were strongest with respect to
underage children (twelve years, initially) and the hours they
worked.[61]

---

[60] Woman's Christian Temperance Union of Wisconsin, *Annual Report*, 1889, pp. 63–
106; *ibid.*, 1893, pp. 5, 95–132.

[61] Country Beautiful Corporation, *Great Fires of America* (Waukesha, 1973), 114–116;
Daniel R. Madden, "Factory Safety in Wisconsin, 1878–1911" (master's thesis, Univer-
sity of Wisconsin, 1968); Wisconsin Bureau of Labor and Industrial Statistics, *Biennial
Report*, 1898–1899, pp. 116–124; *ibid*, 1885–1886, pp. 487–522.

Were working women able to achieve any sort of unity in the face of the sixty-hour week for wages about half or less than those received by men? The short answer is no. Most working women in Wisconsin's industries fit the popular notion that young women worked during a brief hiatus in their lives between school and the serious business of life—meaning marriage and family. Work was considered a transition between domination by their fathers to domination by their husbands, and most young women were indifferent to other possibilities.

In the summer of 1884, the *Sentinel* surveyed the scene of "Working Women in Milwaukee." The emphasis was upon young women who were Americanized, and particularly upon store clerks. If they were through with their schooling, they worked to "occupy their time, to yield them a pin-money source of revenue or to escape the Bridget-work at home." Asked why they worked at these low-paying jobs rather than at something else open to women such as telegraphy or typesetting, one who claimed to know replied: "Because every girl, no matter how homely and unattractive, expects to get married. . . ." They needed no occupational skills. Lower-class women worked harder and were "elbowing their way into all the departments of trade which have been supposed to be occupied exclusively by men." The immediate example was the great number of Polish girls in Milwaukee's many cigar factories.[62]

In 1881, the Milwaukee cigar makers had joined in a long strike which ended disastrously for their union. Women were recruited to replace them. The typesetters faced a similar situation. Women were considered a threat both as cheap labor and as union busters. When Wisconsin workmen were asked: "What in your opinion, could be done either by legislation or employers, to improve the general condition of your trade?" it was the cigar makers, typesetters, and tailors who most wanted young women out of the work force, although among other male workers child

[62] Milwaukee *Sentinel*, June 30, 1884.

labor and immigrant competition were generally the most mentioned.[63]

The common conception that most working women in factories were "working girls" certainly was correct. In 1890, of the 129,295 persons aged ten and over engaged in Wisconsin's manufacturing and mechanical industries, 20,805 were females (16.1 per cent) and 13,239 of those were under twenty-five years of age (63.6 per cent). By comparison, only 29,947 of the 108,490 males so employed (27.6 per cent) were under age twenty-five. Might one not assume that young women who saw themselves as prospective wives and mothers would discover some sense of community beyond their immediate fellow workers? They certainly knew themselves to be exploited. Not infrequently, boys proved to be more united and militant than older fellow workers. Why not young working women?[64]

Women appear to have been little attracted to unionism or to militant action. The *Sentinel* conducted surveys of shops just before May Day, 1886, to see which were affected by the eight-hour agitation. The paper discovered no problem at the three large knitting mills which hired several hundred young women. The 300 employees at Kalamazoo Knitting, mostly girls, expressed themselves as "satisfied" with $2.50 to $4 for a sixty-hour week. The Cream City Knitting Mill managers had thoughtfully turned off the machinery and announced that any woman interested in the Eight Hour Movement could draw her pay and leave. No takers.[65]

When the Eight Hour League was enjoying some early successes, Robert Schilling recruited some working girls into the Knights of Labor. His initial effort in Milwaukee was a standoff.

[63] Wisconsin Bureau of Labor Statistics, *Biennial Report*, 1883–1884, pp. 83–84, 140–141; Wisconsin Bureau of Labor and Industrial Statistics, *Biennial Report*, 1887–1888, pp. 51–64.

[64] *Eleventh Census of the United States, 1890: Population, Volume I, Part 2*, pp. 339, 370–371; Wisconsin Bureau of Labor and Industrial Statistics, *Biennial Report*, 1885–1886, pp. 305–306.

[65] Milwaukee *Sentinel*, May 1, 1886; Wisconsin Bureau of Labor and Industrial Statistics, *Biennial Report*, 1885–1886, p. 471.

An estimated fifty young women came to the Odd Fellows hall on a March night. After the preliminaries, Schilling announced that they were welcome to join a regular assembly of their choice for half the regular fee, or have their own exclusive female assembly. After some further explanatory remarks, he asked those wishing to join to remain and he would sign them up. He needed their name, address, and age. The reference to age brought a decided chill and half of the audience left. Schilling evidently improved his technique, as forty "young ladies" signed up to organize a strictly female assembly a week later.[66]

It appears that young women in some trades were interested in organization. During the Civil War they had definitely won a place for themselves in printing and publishing. Initially used as strikebreakers in typesetting, the union finally had the wit to recruit them. Women in men's tailoring were caught in a strike in 1886 between the manufacturers and the contractors, who exploited women doing piecework. It was a difficult trade to define. Apparently many of the contractors themselves were women.

The strike situation gave the women who made the garments an opportunity to display some militancy. Their average returns on piecework had dropped some 30 per cent over the past ten years. The contractors, who naturally passed on these reductions from the manufacturers, were organized and on strike. Unfortunately, those pieceworkers who belatedly organized in late April were confronted with rival unions—the Knights of Labor or Paul Grottkau's Central Labor Union. They split about half and half.[67]

Paul Grottkau was all graciousness when half those women who initially joined the Knights seceded to form a local in his Central Labor Union. He sent musicians to play for them while

[66] Milwaukee *Sentinel*, March 7, 15, 1886; Norman J. Ware, *The Labor Movement in the United States, 1860-1895: A Study in Democracy* (New York, 1929; Vintage paperback edition, New York, 1964), 346-349.

[67] Gavett, *Labor Movement in Milwaukee*, 10-12, 41; Milwaukee *Sentinel*, May 1, 1886; Wisconsin Bureau of Labor and Industrial Statistics, *Biennial Report*, 1885-1886, pp. 267-268, 282-291.

they organized, then appeared to address their meeting. He featured these new acquisitions in the grand demonstration planned for Sunday, May second, of which Grottkau was chief marshal. He must have been disappointed. Carriages for the "ladies" were provided in the first division of the parade, but it required only six to accommodate the participating female tailors and bookbinders. (One wonders why young women who worked ten hours a day required carriages to take part in the parade.)[68]

Describing a brief strike in 1885 by forty sewing girls working at Bradley and Metcalf's shoe factory a few months before the general demonstrations of 1886, the state's commissioner of labor and industrial statistics said that the strike was directed at a forewoman: "The matter was treated lightly, the girls apparently being anxious for a few holidays and an excursion on Lake Michigan." Two girls were fired as ringleaders, and the rest returned shortly to the old conditions.[69]

Shoe manufacturers employed a good many young women at wages of $3.50 to $5.50 per week. "Officers of the Bureau visiting one of the factories employing over one hundred girls, noted that a number of them were singing, showing that the work is not unpleasant nor the conditions surrounding them unacceptable." A strike of shoemakers in February, 1886, against smaller firms to meet the piece rates of Bradley and Metcalf involved only men, who won an advance. The settlement excluded women employees. We do not know if they continued to sing at their work.[70]

Most of what we know about the organized activities of Wisconsin women in the latter nineteenth century implicitly con-

---

[68] Milwaukee *Sentinel*, May 1, 3, 1886; Milwaukee *Journal*, May 1, 3, 1886. Mari Jo Buhle, *Women and American Socialism, 1870–1920* (Urbana, 1981), 33, says that Paul Grottkau had urged the mobilization of women in the socialist movement when he was a new arrival from Germany.

[69] Milwaukee *Sentinel*, May 1, 1886; Wisconsin Bureau of Labor and Industrial Statistics, *Biennial Report*, 1885–1886, p. 296, for the 1885 strike.

[70] Wisconsin Bureau of Labor and Industrial Statistics, *Biennial Report*, 1885–1886, pp. 292–295, 311. The singers were probably at Bradley and Metcalf, judging by the number of women employed.

cerns the Anglo-American or Yankee community. That community was scarcely more than a quarter of the total population, but in many ways it determined the standards to be adopted, consciously resisted, or ignored by the remainder. For want of information or synthesizing studies, and because of the variety of women involved, there is little to draw upon to describe the three-fourths of the female population comprising the immigrants and their daughters. It is worth recalling in Hamlin Garland's story, "Among the Corn-Rows," that Rob and Julia fit a pattern of second-generation immigrants most likely to adapt to Yankee ways. They went to public school in a neighborhood of mixed ethnic background in rural Waupaca County. Rob was thoroughly Americanized and accepted as such. Julia desperately wanted to be, but found it infinitely more difficult for the reason that she was a woman. How much more difficult was this transition for the majority of women caught in enclaves dominated by the ethnic home, language, churches, social organizations, and often the parochial schools. An estimated half of these women were Catholic—a serious barrier stoutly maintained by both Yankees and Catholics.[71]

In a very real sense, Yankee women were the dominant force in their churches, although most of them were no more conscious of that fact than were the ministers who thought themselves in full charge. Most immigrant churches suffered no such confusion. But the immigrant churches also offered women a central role as guardians of religious instruction, practice, and traditions in the home, and as mainstays of the churches' social life. The Catholic church went a step beyond this. Its more highly developed parochial school system and eleemosynary institutions gave a wide scope to women parishioners as well as to those who took vows. The story of Sister Mary Emily Power, an immigrant Irish girl who in 1867 at age twenty-three became prioress of the

[71] Hamlin Garland, *Main-Travelled Roads* (New York, 1899), 88–111; David P. Thelen, *The New Citizenship: Origins of Progressivism in Wisconsin, 1885–1900* (Columbia, 1972), 11–22; Lawrence L. Graves, "The Wisconsin Woman's Suffrage Movement, 1846–1920" (doctoral dissertation, University of Wisconsin, 1954).

Dominican St. Clara Academy at Sinsinawa Mound in Grant County, tells of the opportunity for a distinguished career as well as the building of a vital community. It is doubtful that any of the ten or so women who in 1891 held the elective office of county superintendent of schools could have had more challenging careers or a wider influence than did Sister Mary Emily Power.[72]

Middle-class urban women were the principal beneficiaries of the escape from the domestic treadmill offered by cheap domestic help, and by plumbing, gas and electricity, manufactured clothing, and whatever kitchen and laundry improvements the times offered. The city gave such women the widest scope to join in whatever seemed to them meaningful activities. They found it a man's world and much of the concentrated discontent and determination to change things came from these women. They represent most of the contrast that one finds between their restricted role in the centennial celebration of 1876 and the clarion calls that rang from the Woman's Building of the 1893 World's Columbian Exposition in Chicago.[73]

The Woman's Christian Temperance Union became the principal vehicle for Wisconsin women in small towns and villages who wished for a larger sense of purpose and to belong to a wider community. Frances Willard, the long-time president of the WCTU (1879–1898), lived on a farm near Janesville from the age of six (1846) until she went away to school in the spring of 1857 to Milwaukee Female College, and then to Evanston, Illinois, to attend—at her father's insistence—Northwestern Female College. After a varied teaching career, she returned to Evanston

[72] Ann Douglas, *The Feminization of American Culture* (New York, 1977), 3–13. Butler, Bascom, and Kerr, eds., *Centennial Records of the Women of Wisconsin*, reviews many church-related women's organizations. See also Mary Synon, *Mother Emily of Sinsinawa* (Milwaukee, 1954); Mary Paschala O'Connor, *Five Decades: History of the Congregation of the Most Holy Rosary, Sinsinawa, Wisconsin, 1849–1899* (Sinsinawa, 1954); J. W. Stearns, ed., *The Columbian History of Education in Wisconsin* (Milwaukee, 1893), 685–690; and *Wisconsin Blue Book, 1891*, p. 545.

[73] Eleanor Flexner, *Century of Struggle: The Woman's Rights Movement in the United States* (Cambridge, 1959; revised edition, 1975), 182–189; Butler, Bascom, and Kerr, eds., *Centennial Records of the Women of Wisconsin*, 70–223; *Wisconsin Blue Book, 1877*, pp. 491–499; Mary K. O. Eagle, ed., *The Congress of Women, Held in the Woman's Building, World's Columbian Exposition, Chicago, U.S.A., 1893* (Chicago, 1894; reprinted, New York, 1974).

as a professor and then as dean of the Lady's College of Northwestern University. In 1874, she abruptly resigned the deanship to become corresponding secretary of the WCTU. A woman of great ability, her interest in the WCTU extended well beyond the temperance cause—witness her slogan, "Do everything." The fact of her Wisconsin background added to the attractions of the organization for Wisconsin women of similar background.[74]

There is no doubt of the small-town character of the Wisconsin WCTU. The temperance movement began in 1874 in a small Ohio town. It appeared shortly thereafter in Wisconsin in a similar form: ladies kneeling in prayer in front of saloons, then being serenaded in return with "sauerkraut songs" in Ripon, that font of militant Republicanism. Frances Willard brought to the crusade a broader program and more effective organization. It rapidly outgrew the small woman's suffrage movement, which split nationally in 1869 and 1870 into two rival groups.[75]

The great strength of the WCTU in villages and smaller cities was its appeal to women of an evangelical temper, who rejected association with the militant suffragists because the latter talked of women's rights rather than of the sacred nature of the Christian home. Willard, who was interested in the suffrage movement, saw the possibilities of the broader base offered by the WCTU to bring the evangelicals around to support of suffrage as a practical response to the problems of influencing legislators.[76]

[74] Mary Earhart, *Frances Willard: From Prayers to Politics* (Chicago, 1944), 24–145; Madison *Northwestern Mail*, February 24, 1898; *DAB*; Flexner, *Century of Struggle*, 185–189; Andrew Sinclair, *The Emancipation of the American Woman* (New York, 1966), 222–224.

[75] Flexner, *Century of Struggle*, 182–186; Sinclair, *Emancipation of the American Woman*, 222–224; Earhart, *Frances Willard*, 144; Milwaukee *Christian Statesman*, May 21, 1874; Carol Hymowitz and Michaele Weissman, *A History of Women in America* (New York, 1978), 159–160.

[76] Flexner, *Century of Struggle*, 182–186; Sinclair, *Emancipation of the American Woman*, 222–224. According to Sinclair (p. 223): Willard "appealed to that very ideal to which the anti-suffragists appealed. And because, among politically minded women, the respectable were many and the radical were few, the Woman's Christian Temperance Union prospered. The supreme cleverness of Willard was to use this conservative organization to advocate woman suffrage and child labour laws and other progressive legislation, always in the name of purity and home."

The pattern of organization and activities of the WCTU in Wisconsin revealed its strengths and weaknesses. Organized on the basis of congressional districts and the counties within them, it made scarcely a dent in the Fifth Congressional District, which ranged along the lakefront north of Milwaukee, and remained vestigial in other areas that were also heavily German. Because it was an active organization, it could prosper only where members could readily meet. As with similar organizations, there was a continual turnover of membership. But there was more social pressure in small communities to keep members active. Taking a treasurer's report at random, it is interesting to note that the 1890 dues, based upon local membership, show that Baraboo returned half again as much as Madison, Stoughton almost equal the amount from Milwaukee, and Black River Falls twice that of La Crosse. The WCTU was great on meetings at all levels of its complex organization. As for the number of women involved, the district reports reflect pride, coyness, evasion, and a simple lack of accurate information—everything but usable totals. Taking the total of paid-up dues and dividing by the twenty-five cents per member which the WCTU constitution required be paid to the state organization, it seems to have been a steadily growing body. Membership totaled approximately 1,014 in 1885; 2,265 in 1887; 3,940 in 1891; and 4,525 in 1893.

Considering the regular turnover of members, those whose dues were in arrears, and the fact that some local unions led intermittent lives while others flourished, it is probable that double and more of these numbers considered themselves part of the organization. The reason for the success of the WCTU was its organizational structure, which required a flow of information up and down from local, county, district, and state officers. This was duplicated in some measure by the various departments carrying on a great variety of activities: franchise; influencing the press; prison, jail, and almshouse work; legislation; state and county fairs; systematic giving; parlor meetings; work among foreigners; work among lumbermen; scientific temperance instruction; and so on. There was a wheel for every shoulder, and this was a formidable community reaching far outside the usual activities of women's social organizations.[77]

Farm women had much less opportunity to establish a sense of broad community. The most important statewide organization in the period was the Grange. It had a much rockier career than the WCTU, because it built to more than 18,000 members in 1875, then rapidly declined. Having forsworn its disastrous co-operative and other business ventures, the Grange returned to emphasis upon its social role to help overcome the isolation of farm life.[78]

The Grange was the first secret order to grant full membership to women. Significantly, there were special offices in the organization specifically designated for women, and not many served in general offices at the state level. In the second annual state meeting in 1874, the votes for general offices ranged from 190 to 250; for the four women's offices, only twenty to thirty-five votes were cast. Presumably these represented the women present. In 1883, seventy-seven delegates were present; sixteen of them were women who were most probably the wives of other delegates. A women was elected state treasurer, and women served on twelve of the fourteen standing committees. They did not have much to say from the floor, except as they were called upon for occasional committee reports. Ten years later, only thirteen delegates were in attendance, five of them women, four of whom were wives of other delegates. A resolution in favor of woman suffrage was adopted, having been approved by the locals.[79]

---

[77] Woman's Christian Temperance Union of Wisconsin, *Annual Report*, 1890, pp. 41–43; *ibid.*, 1892, p. 5.

[78] See Chapter 1 above. Women were a minority of the Grange's membership. Given the fact that the rural farm population outnumbered that in villages and small cities by about five to one by 1890, the proportion of women in the Grange was very small compared to those in villages and small urban centers (under 2,500 population) involved in the WCTU. Grange membership had declined to 8,592 by 1878. LaVerne H. Marquart, *Wisconsin's Agricultural Heritage: The Grange, 1871–1971* (Lake Mills, 1972), 8–21, 28.

[79] Sarah M. Stephenson, "The Social and Educational Aspects of the Grange, 1870–1934" (master's thesis, University of Wisconsin, 1935), 1–59; Patrons of Husbandry, Wisconsin State Grange, *Proceedings*, 1874, pp. 10–12; *ibid.*, 1883, pp. 6–7, 19–20, 40; *ibid.*, 1893, pp. 4, 7, 20–22.

All in all, farm women accepted a subordinate role in state organizations which included both men and women. A reading of the *Transactions* of the state agricultural society reveals that women were generally content to play their traditional role while men tended to the serious business. Women were invited to read papers they had given at local Grange meetings that some male officer found elevating and recommended for the agricultural society meeting. A fair sample was "The Proper Advancement of Women," given by Mrs. Fannie B. Dennett of the Du Lac Grange of Milton Junction. No militant, she was willing to wait for the ballot, but asked for the right of more leisure for the farm wife, whose "realm, and her chief delight should be to make home all that is bright and lovely." A realistic right was for "more time, time to improve and fit herself for the duties that are now devolving upon her; time to read, to study and think, to keep equal with the man in intelligence, to be his helper and adviser as well as his housekeeper."[80]

Women did make legal and professional advances. Many of these legal changes came from the determination of individuals to test the system. Miss Rhoda Lavinia Goodell of Janesville, whose father was a minister widely known for his abolition and temperance agitation, became the first woman admitted to the bar in Wisconsin. A year later, in 1875, she sought admission to practice law before the state supreme court. Chief Justice Edward G. Ryan was aghast at the idea. For a woman to practice law he characterized as a departure "from the order of nature; and when voluntary, treason against it." (Ryan was prolix when agitated, and that was his normal condition.) The other justices concurred. The Milwaukee *Sentinel*, critical of the decision, was a fair Republican bellwether. The 1877 legislature quickly passed a statute eliminating gender as a consideration for admission to practice before any state court.[81]

---

[80] Wisconsin State Agricultural Society, *Transactions*, 1874–1875, p. 464.

[81] Milwaukee *Sentinel*, June 19, 1874; February 16, 24, April 4, 1876, January 31, April 25, 1879; *Laws of Wisconsin*, 1877, p. 616; *DWB*; *Wisconsin Reports*, 39:232–246; Alfons J. Beitzinger, *Edward G. Ryan: Lion of the Law* Madison, 1960), 39–42; Snyder, Van Vechten and Co., comps., *Historical Atlas of Wisconsin . . .* (Milwaukee, 1878), 146.

Goodell persisted, and in April, 1879, she applied again. On June 18, with the chief justice absent from the bench, the court admitted Miss Goodell—its last decision in its January term. She died not long after, in March, 1880; Ryan followed her in October. Moses M. Strong, president of the state bar association, spoke for the late chief justice. Commenting on Miss Goodell's brief career, he found it a matter of satisfaction "that besides the pioneer female lawyer of the state whom death has removed to the immortal bar, only one other has thought fit to seek after the honors, the distinction or wealth which the pursuit of our profession may, by some, be supposed to furnish, and she has wisely selected so circumscribed a sphere as New London, in Waupaca County, for the exercise of her professional powers." Strong's satisfaction would be short-lived.[82]

The drive for woman's suffrage meanwhile inched forward. There was a good deal of male apathy on the subject, rather than the stubborn resistance that is often assumed. This was especially so on the part of those of Yankee background who made up the basic support of the usual majority party. Republican politicans knew that a fair minority of their constituents supported woman's suffrage and recognized the source as their wives, who were coming to share Frances Willard's view that the ballot was necessary to their purposes. The results—recorded in a useful barometer of this constituency, the Milwaukee *Sentinel*—make up a mixture of solid support, but often enlivened by light-hearted comment or downright burlesque. The source of this ambivalence was not only the apathy of the majority of men, but also the knowledge that this apathy was shared by many of their wives.[83]

[82] State Bar Association of Wisconsin, *Proceedings*, 1881 (reprinted, Madison, 1905), 58, 134; Vol. O, Supreme Court Journals, 1836–1960, Series 2030, WSA. Thirty years later, Justice Roujet Marshall objected to women as court employees, let alone as lawyers. See Glasier, ed., *Roujet D. Marshall*, 2:388–389.

[83] Milwaukee *Sentinel*, April 4, 1873, March 23, 1874, July 17, 1876, March 6, 1880, February 8, 11, 1881, September 10, October 2, 1882, March 27, 30, 1885; Graves, "Wisconsin Woman's Suffrage Movement," chaps 1 and 2. The Milwaukee *Sentinel*, February 8, 1881, commented: "The only successful opponents to woman suffrage are women themselves . . . nobody really cares about the issue." In the October 2, 1882, issue, United States Attorney Gerry Whiting Hazelton was quoted: "I may be old fogyish

The issue suffered as much from ardent advocacy as from the indifference of lukewarm friends. As the *Sentinel* remarked in 1882, there was a "general disinclination—among the Teutonic races at least—to be dictated to by those who have not the power to enforce their will," thus raising the usual specter that woman's suffrage meant prohibition. At a suffrage conference later in 1882 held in the senate chamber in Madison, featuring Susan B. Anthony and Olympia Brown, who was later president of the small Wisconsin Woman's Suffrage Association, the pair agreed that the time would come when a petition by 5,000 women would have as much weight "as one signed by the same number of negroes, Irishmen, Germans and Polacks." This was a frequent theme of the diplomatic Reverend Olympia Brown.[84]

One area of public policy where it seemed safe to allow women some voice was that relating to education. The state superintendent, Edward Searing, remarked in his report for 1874: "Women, as a class, are more immediately interested in schools than men are. The majority of our teachers are women. . . . Who are better fitted than they to know what should be the character of the schools. . . ?" This sentiment appealed to the liberal legislature of 1875, which passed an act to allow women to stand for election as director, treasurer, or clerk of school districts in towns and villages, for city school boards, and for county superintendent. That there were four identifiable women county superin-

in the matter, but my traditions and early education have been against it. I may be wrong in my views, but I do not care to change them." Hazelton was the same man who successfully represented Owen Howell, the Negro in the Bijou theater discrimination case.

[84] Milwaukee *Sentinel*, September 10, October 2, 1882, December 2, 1886; Wisconsin Woman's Suffrage Association, *Wisconsin Woman Suffrage Directory, Prepared by a Member of the Wisconsin Woman Suffrage Association for the Use of Its Officers, Members and Other Friends of the Cause* (Milwaukee, 1885). One of Olympia Brown's biographers suggests that a real paranoia developed in her speeches, as she found it "unbearable" that women were "the political inferiors of all the riffraff of Europe that is poured upon our shores." See Charles E. Neu, "Olympia Brown and the Woman's Suffrage Movement," in *WMH*, 43 (Summer, 1960), 281; *DWB*.

tendents five years later, and nine by 1885, indicates a general acceptance of the measure.[85]

In 1885, after several legislatures had narrowly defeated general suffrage measures, resort was had to what was described as a "sop"—a fallback position. A referendum was submitted to the voters. The ballots read: "For woman suffrage in school matters" or "Against woman suffrage in school matters." The referendum was equally vague. After defining such voters to include women, it stated that in "any election pertaining to school matters, [they] shall have a right to vote at such elections."[86]

The vote on the referendum was an anomaly. In Milwaukee and several other cities, the measure was considered irrelevant because the school commissioners were appointed by the city council. The 1886 election was held prior to the adoption of the Australian ballot, meaning that ballots were prepared by contesting parties. Separate ballot boxes for the referendum were supposed to be provided, but no widespread effort was made to provide these or the ballots. Only 877 votes were cast on the referendum in Milwaukee, where the vote for governor totaled 31,508. Statewide, only 28.8 per cent of those who voted in the gubernatorial race cast a ballot on the referendum. The measure

[85] Wisconsin Superintendent of Public Instruction, *Annual Report,* 1874, xcvii–xcviii; Conrad E. Patzer, *Public Education in Wisconsin* (Madison, 1924), 454–455; *Wisconsin Blue Book, 1881,* pp. 422–423; *ibid., 1885,* p. 407. The count of female superintendents is based on the common practice of identifying them as "Mrs." or by Christian name. But because nearly half of the persons on these lists are identified only by initials, it is not always possible to determine gender.

[86] Milwaukee *Sentinel,* February 11, 1881, March 27, 1885, November 10, 25, 1886; Patzer, *Public Education in Wisconsin,* 460. The acceptance of this watered-down woman's suffrage measure was largely the work of Miss Alura Collins of Mukwonago, who chaired the legislative committee of the Wisconsin Woman's Suffrage Association. She actively lobbied the 1885 session of the legislature which passed what became Chapter 211 of the 1885 session laws. The state constitution required that the measure be submitted to the electorate, as it was in the 1886 general election. Graves, "Wisconsin Woman's Suffrage Movement," 51–53.

narrowly carried by just 15.2 per cent of those who voted in the governor's contest.[87]

The election details are interesting. Janesville, which one would suppose was a center of Yankee activism on the issue, recorded only fifty-eight votes on the referendum, fifty-four favorable. In the gubernatorial election, 1,931 votes were cast. In neighboring Beloit, 1,072 gubernatorial votes were cast, 352 on the referendum. Obviously Beloit had something of a campaign on the issue, which drew 284 in favor and sixty-eight votes against. Also, it may be inferred that ballots were provided in Beloit and probably not in Janesville.

Adams County registered 1,322 votes in the race for governor and 755 on the referendum, which passed 474 to 281. The county had no incorporated cities or villages, meaning that women won the vote in all school districts. All towns voted on the issue, indicating that ballots were available. Dane County cast 12,504 votes for governor, but only 2,677 on the referendum, which carried by 1,679 to 998 votes. Eight rural towns in Dane County cast no ballots on the measure, others only a scattering. Only 15 per cent of those voting in Madison (the headquarters of the Wisconsin WCTU and the Woman's Suffrage Association) cast a ballot on the referendum. Oshkosh was more responsive than Madison. Voters there cast 3,712 votes for governor and 2,181 votes on the referendum, which lost by 1,557 to 624—a spirited contest compared to Janesville and Madison.[88]

Why was there such a mixed record on this vote? Partly, it may be that city voters, who were most likely to be politicized on the issue, were indifferent because—as in Milwaukee—the school

---

[87] Milwaukee County Board of Canvassers, election return statements, November 10, 1886, in Series 211, Records of the Secretary of State, WSA; Milwaukee *Sentinel*, November 10, 1886; *Wisconsin Blue Book, 1887*, p. 250; *ibid., 1979–1980*, p. 343. Negro voting rights had been confirmed in an 1866 court ruling on the basis of a similar favorable response of the minority who had voted on the issue in an 1849 election. Following that precedent, the school franchise referendum passed.

[88] Adams, Dane, and Winnebago county boards of canvassers, election return statements, 1886, in Series 211, Records of the Secretary of State, WSA; *Wisconsin Blue Book, 1887*, pp. 209–249.

commissioners were appointed rather than elected. But why not fight for the voting privilege for the majority of Wisconsin women who lived in rural towns and unincorporated villages? It would appear that this was an opportunity the proponents of woman's suffrage simply overlooked. Maybe the *Sentinel* was correct in its assessment that a similar measure adopted earlier in Massachusetts did not spur a wider interest in general woman's suffrage, and that few women used the privilege.[89]

The referendum received little official attention from the WCTU, which was by far the largest organization that logically should have been actively behind it. The twelfth annual state convention was held in October, 1885, seven months after the legislature determined to include the measure in the November, 1886, election. Yet not a word relating to the referendum appears in the forty-six pages of the session minutes, and there was no report from the superintendent of the department of franchise. It was a divisive issue in the Wisconsin WCTU.[90]

The language of the referendum—that women could now vote in "any election pertaining to school matters"—brought confusion. The attorney general decided that this meant only at school district meetings, but prominent attorneys argued that it probably meant that they could vote for city officials—mayors, councilmen, or aldermen—if these officers appointed the school commissioners. When the municipal election day came in April, 1887, the confusion was compounded. Most election officials stoutly guarded the ballot boxes in villages and cities where school officials held appointive office, but a few allowed women

[89] Milwaukee *Sentinel*, March 27, 30, 1885.

[90] Woman's Christian Temperance Union of Wisconsin, *Annual Report*, 1885; Theodora W. Youmans, "How Wisconsin Women Won the Ballot," in *WMH*, 5 (September, 1921), 14-15. The president of Wisconsin's WCTU, Miss Amy C. Kellogg of Fort Atkinson, commenting on the suffrage question, observed (p. 11): "Some of those who thoroughly believe in woman's suffrage, do not believe in trying to solve the two questions [liquor control and suffrage] together, but rather in settling each upon its own merits. Others, and some of our best workers too, have not yet come to the point that woman needs or should have the ballot." The Wisconsin Woman's Suffrage Association resolved in 1894: "That the indifference of women has been a greater obstacle to the success of the cause than the selfishness of men." *Wisconsin Citizen*, November, 1894.

to vote for municipal officials. In Ripon, which elected its school commissioners, 194 women cast ballots and Mrs. Lydia Brown was among those elected. A number of lawsuits were generated among those women refused the franchise elsewhere. The issue came to rest upon the suit entered by Olympia Brown, who with others was refused the right to vote for municipal officials in Racine.

Judge John B. Winslow of the first circuit court, a resident of Racine and later chief justice, ruled in favor of Olympia Brown. Appeal was taken to the supreme court, which in early 1888 reversed Judge Winslow. The law was declared to be restricted to school elections only, on a separate ballot in a separate ballot box. Olympia called down divine retribution upon the court. In effect, the court's decision rendered null the right of women to vote in city and village elections, unless separate ballot boxes and ballots were provided for women voters on school issues or the election of school officials. It was 1901 before the legislature required that separate ballot boxes be provided. This does not mean that the law was a dead letter. Rural and most village school districts held meetings, like town meetings, where women could vote. Incorporated villages and cities responded variously as their individual charters pertained to school matters and as local election officials complied with the supreme court's 1888 ruling.[91]

Woman's suffrage in Wisconsin saw few victories after the 1886 school election referendum was carried with a marked lack of enthusiasm. There are no statewide municipal election records, as with the initial constitutional referendum, to see how it was implemented at the local level. Olympia Brown and her followers continued to test the measure in municipal and county elections. The violence attending the Eight Hour League agitation in Milwaukee in May, 1886, brought a conservative reaction which stubbornly defended things as they were. Also, prohibition

---

[91] Youmans, "How Wisconsin Women Won the Ballot," *WMH*, 5:16–17; Milwaukee *Sentinel*, March 27, April 1, 5, 6, 7, 9, 10, 23, June 18, 1887, January 14, February 1, 6, April 12, 13, 14, 20, 1888; *Wisconsin Blue Book, 1887*, p. 418.

was a more lively issue than woman's suffrage, having come before the legislature in 1878, 1879, 1880, 1881, and 1882, as the Republicans sought to placate the prohibition forces. Most of Wisconsin's large foreign-born contingent saw little merit in woman's suffrage, even if limited to school matters. When aroused, the huge German vote could be formidable. In the Town of Berry in Dane County, 166 of the 173 men who cast ballots in the 1886 election voted ''no'' on the school franchise referendum; the other seven were silent. The Town of Berry was initially settled by members of the British Temperance Emigration Society, but by 1877 it was reported: ''The town now is almost entirely Germans, who, by-the-way, make our very best citizens.''[92]

The suffrage issue simply stalled in the face of Wisconsin's heavily German and Catholic culture, which saw the issue as a nativist attack in truculent terms. Both the militant suffragists and the temperance forces constantly harped on the inequity of foreigners of deplorable ignorance and customs having the ballot, when women (native-born of native-born parents, of course) did not. If that were not enough, there were constant legislative skirmishes over the liquor laws, fostered by the Republican majority to woo the prohibitionists. Finally, the Edgerton Bible fray and the Bennett Law fight at the end of the eighties added to the freshet of intemperate language on both sides.[93]

Women made some gains in legal status during the period, but usually it was on the basis of their special needs rather than from any general conception of equality between the sexes. What did occur was a legislative recognition that common-law notions of woman's innate inferiority and her subservient position in mar-

[92] Youmans, "How Wisconsin Women Won the Ballot," *WMH*, 5:16; Milwaukee *Sentinel* Index, 1880–1890, entries under "Woman's Suffrage," microfilm copy in SHSW; A. M. Thomson, *A Political History of Wisconsin* (Milwaukee, 1900), 225–228; Otto Kerl and Wm. S. Crowther, "Berry," in William J. Park and Co., *Madison, Dane County and Surrounding Towns . . .* (Madison, 1877), 267–268.

[93] Graves, "Wisconsin Woman's Suffrage Movement," chap. 7, summarizes many of these weaknesses in the movement. See also Neu, "Olympia Brown and the Woman's Suffrage Movement," *WMH*, 43:281.

riage did not fit an urban industrial society well. Since this concept was deeply embedded in Blackstone's *Commentaries*, it doubtless helps to explain the marked lack of enthusiasm among the older generation of lawyers and judges towards women in that profession. At the legislative level, changes came about in the definitions of married women's property rights, their ability to sue as individuals, and their control of children of previous marriages. In 1883, married women became liable to suits for damages and their husbands were not necessarily liable. Legislation to recognize their special status and to limit women's working hours and conditions and to set age limits for industrial labor all became frequent legislative concerns.[94]

The state medical society had to state in defense of itself that while "there might be some prejudice against them," women were not excluded from practice if they were graduates of recognized medical schools. Some women did find less conspicuous professional employment. Theodora Youmans, a suffrage leader, discovered thirty women, many doubtless unaware of the others, engaged as journalists, editors, and publishers. While many of their publications were directed at women, a fair number were general newspapers. Both the Green Bay *Advocate* and the *Gazette*, principal newspapers there at the time, were managed by women in the late 1880's. Since women provided the bulk of the popular novels of the time, it was probably less traumatic for men to see them in newspaper offices. But most of Mrs. Youmans' examples were widows of newspapermen who had gone to their reward.[95]

By far the largest numbers of professional women were in teaching. The new normal schools, the introduction of the free high schools, and particularly the growth of the educational

[94] Flexner, *Century of Struggle*, 235; Claude D. Stout, "The Legal Status of Women in Wisconsin," in the *Marquette Law Review*, 14 (February–June, 1930), 66–80, 121–129, 199–211, particularly 77–79 for a catalog of statutory changes; Donald J. Berthrong, "Social Legislation in Wisconsin, 1836–1900" (doctoral dissertation, University of Wisconsin, 1951), chaps. 2 and 3.

[95] Theodora W. Youmans, "Women as Journalists: Some Who Conduct Successful Papers in Wisconsin," in the Milwaukee *Sentinel*, March 15, 1891; Ada T. Griswold, comp., *Annotated Catalogue of Newspaper Files in the Library of the State Historical Society of Wisconsin* (second edition, Madison, 1911), 334–335.

enterprise in villages and cities presented a great opportunity for women. The number of certified women teaching in public schools increased 38.8 per cent between 1874 and 1890, while the number of male certified teachers declined 6.7 per cent. While there was a substantial increase of men in city systems, the percentage increase of women was greater there as well. Women also were firmly entrenched in the faculties of the expanding normal school system, and not just in pedagogy. In 1874, it required 8,709 teachers to fill 5,522 positions in the public schools because of split terms and the usual practice of hiring men for the winter term when the bigger boys attended. Teaching had become more professionalized and the school terms longer and less discontinuous in most locations twenty years later. The actual expenditures for the public school system more than doubled between 1870 and 1892, which was a period of deflation, making the actual increase even greater. The largest part of the school dollars went for teachers' salaries.[96]

The issue of co-education in Wisconsin was fairly well settled by the early seventies. The Civil War helped to hasten this change simply because of the small number of available men students. Co-education at the University of Wisconsin was delayed briefly by the presidency of Paul Chadbourne (1867–1870), who was adamantly opposed, but this policy was vigorously reversed by his successors, particularly John Bascom (1874–1887). Other institutions reacted variously, most having been co-educational from the start. Co-education, of course, did not necessarily imply equality of treatment, but rather reflected current views of women's special requirements and capacities.[97]

The problem for women in the field of education, at whatever level, was the expectations of the general society and of those

[96] Wisconsin Superintendent of Public Instruction, *Annual Report*, 1874, pp. 230-232, 255-256, 275; *ibid., Biennial Report*, 1888-1890, pp. 143-145, 178-179; Stearns, ed., *Columbian History of Education in Wisconsin*, 64-68, 287-293; Patzer, *Public Education in Wisconsin*, 453, 458, 465.

[97] Current, *Civil War Era*, 506; Merle Curti and Vernon Carstensen, *The University of Wisconsin: A History, 1848-1925* (2 vols., Madison, 1949), 1:219-225, 290-292; Helen R. Olin, *The Women of a State University: An Illustration of the Working of Coeducation in the Middle West* (New York, 1909); William F. Allen and David E. Spencer, *Higher Education in Wisconsin*, U.S. Bureau of Education, Circular of Information, no. 1 (Washington,

who exercised oversight. It was a field in which a woman could not readily act as a leader of change in social relations and basic attitudes, except by indirection. To that degree, the teaching profession was more suitable for the complacent, who probably provided more role models for girls than did the actively rebellious. One characteristic of the times, however, was the frequent reference to a teacher who had a profound impact upon a career—usually a boy's career, to be sure—and more often than not the teacher was a woman.[98]

Everyone should have a favorite candidate in the pantheon of Wisconsin women who advanced the cause. A likely nominee is Dr. Juliet Severance (1833–1919) of Milwaukee and Whitewater, a woman who seldom appears in the standard works. A graduate in 1858 of the Hygeo Therapeutic College of New York City, she appeared in Whitewater shortly thereafter as a medical practitioner, radical feminist, and leading spiritualist. She married Anson B. Severance in 1869, a member of a Milwaukee family of musicians, dancing masters, and spiritualists. Mrs. Severance became a well-known lecturer in the Midwest on politics, spiritualism, and feminism. She was a friend of Robert Schilling and of Congressman Henry Smith; the three belonged to a society of freethinkers in Milwaukee. She was a leading figure in the organization of Schilling's People's party in 1886 and of the Greenback party earlier. She appeared before and could hold large audiences. Despite her friendship with Schilling, she was a strong supporter of Paul Grottkau, sitting at the table with his counsel at his trial following the disturbances of May, 1886, in Milwaukee. The Grottkau trial produced the liveliest descriptions of Mrs. Severance: "Her tall and somewhat angular form and decisive manners, her quickly observant eyes, and the firm lines of her curveless mouth, show Mrs. Severance to be a woman of

1889), 37–41; John Rury, "Women and Minorities in Wisconsin Higher Education: A Historical Perspective," University of Wisconsin, Department of Educational Policy Studies, n.d., a paper in possession of the author.

[98] This observation is based on a fairly wide reading in memoirs and other sources. A boy or girl was less likely to go on to a professional career after 1870 without formal higher education. It was often a teacher in the grades or in high school who made an adolescent aware of the possibilities.

strong will. . . . Her eyes are blue and penetrating, and her smile is always an index to her mood, the lines of her face denoting real pleasure, sarcastic acquiescence, or strong antagonism, as the case may be.''[99]

Juliet Severance got around. Despite her busy schedule as medical practitioner, spiritualist lecturer, and third-party gadfly, she found time to go where any group required some needling. In the winter of 1885 she appeared at the annual meeting of the Wisconsin State Agricultural Society in Madison. This was a group pretty well adjusted to things as they were. After some give and take that galled her, she arose and delivered herself of the following:[100]

It always gives me a kind of sick feeling when I am attending a convention and a gentleman gets up and accidentally, or incidentally, or from a sense of courtesy, alludes to the women, he at once puts on a kind of a simpering tone, as though he was going to talk to a baby instead of a person that is his equal and should so be recognized everywhere in society. Where do you expect intelligence on your farms unless the mothers of the farmers have intelligence? Are you men that have reared cattle and stock of every kind so ignorant that you do not know that its pedigree determines its intelligence and its qualities in every way . . . ? When women are cultivated in all these departments the same as men are, when they have equal liberties everywhere that men have, when they are not relegated to home and home alone and flattered with the idea that they are queen in the realm of home, when they are never queen except when the king is gone. [*Laughter.*] It is nonsense; we want to be addressed as intelligent human beings the same as you are. No flattery, no particular attention, but merely, simply, equal justice everywhere in the world, and in agricultural education as well as anywhere else. Then your sons will go to agricultural schools when the girls are educated there as well as the boys [*laughter and applause*], and they should never go until they are so arranged.

[99] Whitewater *Register*, October 16, 1919; Mary F. Bednarowski, "Spiritualism in Wisconsin in the Nineteenth Century," in *WMH*, 59 (Autumn, 1975), 17–18; Milton M. Small, "The Biography of Robert Schilling" (master's thesis, University of Wisconsin, 1953), 162; [Frank A. Flower], *History of Milwaukee, Wisconsin . . .* (Chicago, 1881), 594, 597; Milwaukee *Sentinel*, December 6, 1886.

[100] Wisconsin State Agricultural Society, *Transactions*, 1885, pp. 254–255.

# 10

---

# Life and Times

---

B Y 1873, for most of Wisconsin's people, the pioneering phase of settlement was in the past and there was little to differentiate the life and surroundings of the rural, village, or city resident from those of his counterpart in, for example, western New York state. A minor difference probably was a more immediate sense of a pioneering past. Those born in Wisconsin since 1860 were often reminded of this by the older generation, whose members frequently remarked on the contrasts between their surroundings and a past less remote in years than in change. For as recently as 1850, the state's population was almost entirely confined to the southern one-third as defined by the Fox-Wisconsin waterway. The future metropolis of Milwaukee then had a population of only 20,061; its nearest rival, Racine, had 5,107; and only these two, plus Kenosha (1,451), had been incorporated as cities. There was not yet a mile of railroad in the state, and therefore people and goods moved at a slow pace over a minor network of execrable roads. Oddly, there was by 1849 a primitive telegraph system that connected Milwaukee with Chicago and the East; but it reached only a few interior points for want of sufficient use.[1]

---

[1]Robert C. Nesbit, *Wisconsin: A History* (Madison, 1973), 197–201; *Wisconsin Blue Book, 1880*, p. 449; *Seventh Census of the United States, 1850: Volume I, Part 2*, pp. 918–924. The preceding volume in this *History of Wisconsin*, Richard N. Current's *Volume II: The Civil War Era, 1848–1873* (Madison, 1976), 28, 596–597, concludes on this note of wonder at how things had changed by 1873 for those who had arrived twenty or more years earlier. By then, a sure-fire line at farmers' meetings was: "Now, gentlemen, I have lived here forty years. I thought when I carried wheat from here [Dane County] to Milwaukee. . . ." The remainder matters but little; that opening gambit set up the audience for a celebration of a pure-hearted and rugged past compared to the effete or corrupted present. See Wisconsin State Agricultural Society, *Transactions*, 1885, p. 314.

A train whistle was a familiar daily sound by 1873 for the majority of Wisconsinites. There were 2,379 miles of railroads built by that year (1,093 miles since 1870), 3,896 miles completed by the end of 1883, and 5,925 miles ten years later. It was not, however, simply a matter of increased mileage. Railroads underwent technological changes after 1870 that vastly increased their carrying capacity and speed. Fares and freight rates were substantially lower, accompanied by new standards of comfort, convenience, and reliability. In 1890, Janesville was served by thirty scheduled trains daily—not an unusual number for a southern Wisconsin city. The railroad was simply the only way to travel any distance or to ship goods overland economically. Even where water transportation was available, the railroads— with their much greater speed, better transfer facilities, and all-weather operation—competed successfully for all but the bulkiest commodities.[2]

The railroad made the local depot the nerve center of nearly every city and village. In doing so, it profoundly affected the economies, life styles, and employment opportunities of everyone who even remotely came within its orbit. It created an information explosion by making metropolitan newspapers and national magazines available in post offices along the line with a speed little improved upon today. The railroad brought the theatrical troupe, the drummer, new products, fashions, the itinerant lecturer, the statewide political candidate, the circus, the National Education Association convention (to Madison in 1884), tourists, Chautauqua, and seemingly the whole wide world.

Besides broadening travel opportunity, the railroads immediately tied the rural populace of most of southern Wisconsin more firmly to the commercial-industrial economy. They also brought a new standard of living that required a higher and more assured income to enable participation. This became the dilemma of farmers who were close enough to a substantial village or second-

---

[2]*Wisconsin Blue Book, 1897,* p. 611; Ruth B. Jeffris, "Influences on Family Life in the United States During the Eighties" (master's thesis, University of Wisconsin, 1928), 100–101; quoted from the Wisconsin Bureau of Labor, Census and Industrial Statistics, *Biennial Report,* 1895–1896, pp. 147–149.

ary city to be drawn into its orbit. A sizable farm within an urban shadow represented an investment which put the farmer, in terms of visible wealth, on a par with successful merchants and professional men. If his rural church had closed its doors to combine with the village congregation, and his children expected to attend the village high school, the farmer became a participant in village life and measured his success and life style against the village standard.[3]

Rural remoteness was certainly reduced, although not much before the mid-nineties. Between 1872 and 1891 the number of post offices in Wisconsin increased from about 1,135 to 1,690. One might assume that the largest share of the additions were in the northern counties, but a comparison of the lists will disprove this. For instance, Dane County post offices increased from fifty-four to sixty-two, although its rural population was nearly stable in numbers by 1870, with the population growth of the next twenty years accounted for almost entirely by its urban centers (2,500+) where the number of post offices did not increase. The extension of the railroad network probably had something to do with the proliferation of fourth-class post offices, but congressional pressures, patronage, and the advantages to a village or hamlet storekeeper of having a fourth-class post office in his store had more. These tradesmen naturally became strong supporters of the system.[4]

There is a point in noting the increase of rural post offices to

[3]Joseph Schafer, *A History of Agriculture in Wisconsin* (Madison, 1922), chap. 10, has a fine appreciation of the dilemma of the southern Wisconsin farmer in this respect. Also see Rowland Berthoff, *An Unsettled People: Social Order and Disorder in American History* (New York, 1971), 187.

[4]*Wisconsin Blue Book, 1873,* pp. 376–384; *ibid., 1891,* pp. 341–352; Wayne E. Fuller, *RFD: The Changing Face of Rural America* (Bloomington, 1964), 13–16, 84–87. The calculation of the number of post offices is based upon a count of a few pages and estimating the totals; the rough approximation of their locations geographically, by comparing the two alphabetical lists through the ABC's. (The numbers in Dane County were actually counted and subsequently corrected, with complaints, by my editor.) Morton Keller, in *Affairs of State: Public Life in Late Nineteenth Century America* (Cambridge, 1977), 310, writes: "In many rural areas there was one fourth class postmaster for every hundred voters . . . 'scattered everywhere, the walking representatives of the dominant party constantly within the gaze of the people.'"

serve a population that was stabilized in numbers or actually decreasing in some counties. It meant that more rural people were within easier reach of a hamlet or village post office, and they had developed the habit of going to town. It was not only the dairy cow and cheese factory that put farmers more frequently onto their unsatisfactory roads. The post office brought the catalogue from "The Original Grange Supply Store," which was the name borne by Montgomery Ward in 1872, and from its many imitators and competitors. The mails brought the mail-order merchandise as well. The village and nearby city merchants could also reach the farmer through the pages of a city or village newspaper which came by mail. In 1873 Wisconsin had approximately 175 newspapers, only sixteen of them dailies originating in nine cities. By 1891 the number of papers had increased to about 490, of which forty-nine were dailies originating in twenty-two cities. While many of the weeklies were speciality papers—religious, agricultural, fraternal, foreign-language—all found a wider audience created by the expansion of the railroads and the postal system. Advertising, mail-order houses, the newspapers and inexpensive magazines by mail, a regular income supplied by the dairy cow, factory-made spring buggies and wagons, merchants' associations, and the attractions of crossroads grown into hamlets, hamlets into villages, and villages into nascent cities drew the farmer and created the tradition of Saturday night in town, which became as sacrosanct for farmers as Monday washday was for their wives.

Newspapers participated in this transformation and were themselves transformed between 1873 and 1893. The Beaver Dam *Argus* of May, 1873, and May, 1893, illustrates the changes that took place in small-town newspapers to reach a wider rural audience. It was a four-page weekly through these twenty years. In 1873, there was little enough of Beaver Dam news and less about the surrounding rural population. The issues in 1893 reveal a front page that oddly resembles that of the 1982 format of *The Wall Street Journal*. The "boiler plate" and local general store ads were gone from the front page, which was devoted to international, national, and Wisconsin news. The second and third pages carried news on Beaver Dam and rural folks ranging from the mayor's inaugural address, the doings of the common council, the budget of the board of education, and county court jury list with names from every rural town, to a column, "Our Folks and Our Friends." The ads were not very different from those of twenty years earlier—just about half as many. The price: $2 a year—in advance—in 1873; $1.50 in 1893. Subscriptions evidently paid more than Lydia Pinkham et al.[5]

All in all, the information, conveniences, and merchandise available to the farmer were not much different from those available to the villager. Nonetheless, as noted before, there remained a sense of alienation based upon the villagers' adoption of urban values. America's true values were said to flow from its agrarian past. "Dangers to republican institutions come from cities and from aggregations of men in other vocations and the stability of our government is most intimately connected with its agricultural system." This was a truism accepted by many, including politicians who had left the farm for an urban professional career. They were all for keeping rural youth down on the farm where hearts were true, and faith and patriotism were unsullied.[6]

Why was there a continuance of this seeming gulf between farm people and villagers, when contacts and interdependence were increasing? The relative living standards were similar. The log cabin of the pioneer family with a profitable farm had given way to a house that compared favorably with those of the village merchant and tradesman. Like the farmer, the village resident got his water from a well, lacked indoor plumbing, read by lamplight, and had no utility service other than a volunteer fire department. If the villager kept chickens, a horse, and a cow, he

[5]Fuller, *RFD*, 249-251. Rural free delivery, which doomed many hamlet post offices, came a few years after 1893. See *Wisconsin Blue Book, 1873*, pp. 372-375; *ibid., 1891*, pp. 331-340; Lewis Atherton, *Main Street on the Middle Border* (Bloomington, 1954), chap. 2; Schafer, *Agriculture in Wisconsin*, 176-177.

[6]Glenn T. Trewartha, "The Unincorporated Hamlet: One Element of the American Settlement Fabric," in the *Annals of the Association of American Geographers*, 33 (March, 1943), 60; Wisconsin Bureau of Labor, Census and Industrial Statistics, *Biennial Report, 1895-1896*, p. 5, quoting a statement contained in the tenth federal census (1880).

was considerably more inconvenienced in confining, feeding, and cleaning up after them. Neighbors in 1885 did not complain if a farmer kept hogs and fed fat cattle.

What was there, then, to envy about the villager? Was it simply a feeling of being left out of a future promise, rather than a rejection of the unjustified pretensions of urbanity on the part of the villager? Could it have been the steadily eroding prices of farm products that characterized the period, accompanied by the assumption that the prices farmers paid for goods they purchased did not decline? Were Wisconsin farmers oppressed by debts, incurred in better times at higher interest rates and arranged by the village banker or loan agent? Were the railroads still oppressing him, despite the fright of the 1874 Potter Law? Was it that the farmer was capitalized at a figure which, despite good management and hard work, did not afford an adequate return? Or was farming simply such a speculative venture, fraught with uncontrollable variables—weather, prices, pests, oversupply— that it required a gambler's temperament, which not every farmer possessed?

It is fair to suggest reasons other than purely economic ones for rural discontent. One is simply that other opportunities were beckoning. The matter was well summed up in 1880 by Grant Showerman's father, talking to his ten-year-old son: "I hope you won't have to drudge the way I've had to. I've had to do a lot of hard work in my day, and sometimes I wasn't really equal to it. . . . I want you to be a lawyer. I might have been a lawyer if I'd only had an education. But I never got much schoolin', except what I give myself. . . ." Twenty years later, the son became a professor at the University of Wisconsin.[7]

Hiram Showerman was not alone in his dissatisfaction with farm life. Governor Cadwallader C. Washburn indiscreetly told the Wisconsin State Agricultural Society that he had little but painful recollections of his youth on a New England farm. What he remembered was long hours of work with the sickle and flail.

[7]Grant Showerman, *A Country Chronicle* (New York, 1916), 29, 148–149; *DWB*.

He refused to feel uplifted by it. Robert M. La Follette made a not unusual transition. His stepfather was a demanding but indifferent farmer. Robert did not rejoice in farm work. After the stepfather's death, the La Follette farm was rented to Robert's brother-in-law, while Robert took the chance of moving his mother and other sister to Madison while getting a university education. Later, La Follette bought a Maple Bluff farm and joined other successful Madisonians as a gentleman farmer. He cherished the notion that he joyfully plowed a straight furrow. Emanuel Philipp made much the same transition from a hard-scrabble farmer's son to millionaire owner of a model farm. William Dempster Hoard celebrated the rewards of farm life from his editorial offices in Fort Atkinson, and on any public platform.[8]

The trouble with farming, particularly after 1870, was not so much that it didn't pay those who were enterprising, but that the farming practiced after the wheat era simply tied the farmer and his family to an endless round of hard work. After all, wheat farming had a seasonal rhythm to it that allowed considerable leisure between spells of hard labor. Mixed farming—dairying, hogs, corn, hay and other feed crops, cattle fattening, potatoes, tobacco—was a daily round of chores. The short-sighted farmer, who saw the completion of these tasks as the business of life, was loath to allow schooling or social contacts for his children to interfere. A man like Grant Showerman's father tempered his immediate necessities by his hopes for his son.

There is little doubt that many men of the older generation were of another bent than farming or business; but where were the professional opportunities, outside of law, doctoring, or the pulpit? Contemporary memoirs are full of stories of men who

[8]The Wisconsin State Agricultural Society, *Transactions*, 1873–1874, p. 111, has Governor Washburn's confession. The society's president that year was William R. Taylor, who introduced the governor and defeated him the following November. See Belle Case La Follette and Fola La Follette, *Robert M. La Follette* (2 vols., New York, 1953), 1:13–27; David P. Thelen, *The Early Life of Robert M. La Follette, 1855–1884* (Chicago, 1966), 19–20; Robert S. Maxwell, *Emanuel L. Philipp: Wisconsin Stalwart* (Madison, 1959), 4–8; *DWB*; Milwaukee *Sentinel*, June 30, 1904.

were indifferent farmers because they were bemused by other things, but whatever was their potential will never be known. There existed a limited market for professors, professional musicians, artists, philosophers, scientists, and scholars.[9]

Hamlin Garland had a sense of this common problem, that the generation before his simply lacked opportunities for using talents it possessed. His Grandfather McClintock "was as weirdly unworldly as a farmer could be." His Uncle William's "small unpainted dwelling seemed a natural feature of the landscape, but as the years passed and other and more enterprising settlers built big barns, and shining white houses, the gray and leaning stables, sagging gates and roofs of my uncle's farm, become a reproach even in my eyes. . . ." Jabez Brown, a pioneer farmer in Sauk County, had nine children, but "when father was writing, he seemed oblivious to the confusion around him. He not only wrote articles for the papers but was always writing 'Temperance Lectures,' 'Peace Lectures,' and the like. It seemed rather a waste of energy to deliver these lectures in some of the small villages, for we had seldom heard of any intemperance in the surrounding country, and for the most part people lived fairly peaceably."[10]

That the idea of social class in post-bellum America was largely an urban phenomenon is generally accepted, whereupon what are called "middle-class values" became the standard. Wisconsin's rural peoples came to share these values, not only by increasing contact with urban society through what they saw, heard, and read, but also as a consequence of their mobility, their treatment of the land as a commodity, and their engaging in farming primarily as a business rather than a way of life. In truth, there were differences in viewpoint based upon ethnic background, but the pattern of mobility from farm to farm and from farm to village was not confined of those of Yankee back-

---

[9]*Wisconsin Blue Book, 1881,* pp. 338–347.

[10]Hamlin Garland, *A Son of the Middle Border,* ed. Henry M. Christman (Macmillan paperback edition, New York, 1962), 16–20; Melissa Brown, "The Jabez Brown Twins: A Family Portrait," in *WMH,* 30 (September, 1946), 40–42.

ground. It was in the villages and smaller cities that all people encountered American middle-class values in relatively uncomplicated, ready-made form.[11]

It was not all that difficult for a successful farmer to make the transition from farm to village. Often that success required not much more than having claimed or purchased superior land, advantageously located, to realize a substantial capital gain. Nothing is more stimulating to the human ego than unsweated wealth, or more encourages the notion that one is well equipped to compete with others. Any number of farmers acted upon this exciting knowledge. They sold or rented out and moved to town. A man with some capital behind him could easily fit into the village middle class as merchant, loan agent, implement dealer, insurance agent, liveryman, commission merchant, or hotelkeeper. The gazetteers give evidence that these services were expanding, even in villages that experienced little population growth.[12]

There are many available witnesses who experienced the times in Wisconsin. Probably the best known of these is Hamlin Garland, whose experience particularly found expression in his collected stories, published as *Main-Travelled Roads*. Garland was of two minds about the Wisconsin village of the latter eighties. A vision of decay and lost hopes appears in his story "Up the Coulee," and the village's redeeming qualities are discerned in "God's Ravens." The latter story reverses the role of the observer. Instead of a successful man of the world returning to his roots, we see the village through the eyes of a farm boy grown to manhood who has been whipped in spirit and in health by the metropolis—in this case, Chicago. He moves his family back to the Wisconsin village of his youth in search of renewal. But the proposed cure does not work at first: "He grew almost to hate the people as he saw them coming and going in the mud, or

[11]Berthoff, *An Unsettled People*, 196–210; Howard Mumford Jones, *The Age of Energy: Varieties of American Experience, 1865–1915* (New York, 1970), 44–45; Richard Lingeman, *Small Town America: A Narrative History, 1620—The Present* (Boston, 1980), 323–325.

[12]*Wisconsin State Gazetteer and Business Directory,* 1876–1877, 1886, 1895–1896. The county histories for Wisconsin, published by the Western Historical Company of Chicago, 1879–1891, have hundreds of biographies that confirm the above generalization.

heard their loud hearty voices sounding from the street. He hated their gossip, their dull jokes. The flat little town grew vulgar and low and desolate to him."

The change comes when he collapses on his daily walk to the post office. The concerned villagers make him their charge, and bring him through a crisis and extended convalescence. The brief story ends with the recovering invalid exclaiming to his wife: "We know our neighbors now, don't we? We can never hate or ridicule them again." She replies, "Yes, Robert. They will never be caricatures again—to me." She suspects the permanence of his mood. It could have been Zona Gale's "Friendship Village."[13]

Another genre is the view of some who did not share Garland's Yankee background. One remembers Laurence Larson's comment that, to the Norwegian immigrant, the village was the stronghold of Yankees who "were 'smart' and the immigrant had a lurking fear that he himself was not smart in the same way." Thorstein Veblen, born of Norwegian parents on a Wisconsin frontier farm, wrote: "The country town of the great American farming region is the perfect flower of self-help and cupidity standardized on the American plan. . . . The country town is one of the great American institutions; perhaps the greatest, in the sense that it has had and continues to have a greater part than any other in shaping public sentiment and giving character to American culture."[14]

The contrast between a village and a secondary city was not so

[13]"Up the Coulee" can be found in most editions of Hamlin Garland's *Main-Travelled Roads.* "God's Ravens" can be found in William A. Titus, comp., *Wisconsin Writers: Sketches and Studies* (Chicago, 1930). Larzar Ziff, *The American 1890s: Life and Times of a Lost Generation* (New York, 1966; Viking Compass edition, 1968), 93–119, is a useful treatment of Garland's experience in this early part of his long career. Atherton, *Main Street on the Middle Border,* 76, who certainly saw the midwestern village through a golden haze, found Zona Gale's Portage—"Friendship Village"—too heavy on "sweetness and light."

[14]Laurence M. Larson, *The Log Book of a Young Immigrant* (Northfield, 1939), 68–69; Max Lerner, ed., *The Portable Veblen* (New York, 1948), 407, quoting from Thorstein Veblen, *Absentee Ownership and Business Enterprise in Recent Times: The Case of America* (New York, 1923), 142. See Atherton, *Main Street on the Middle Border,* 49–57, for a critical view of this Veblen essay.

sharp a century ago. They all had hopes, and their styles of life, like their appearances, were not greatly different. Janesville and Beloit, with populations in 1870 of 8,789 and 4,396 respectively, still practiced the village custom of turning the family cow into the street to shift for herself as an urban marauder or to find her way to more open grazing on the edge of town. "No house was considered complete unless it had a barn or stable for the horse, cow, and pig."[15]

Beloit rated a brief description in the 1880 census special volume on the social statistics of cities. Not only did the city in 1880 have no water system, neither did it have any drainage system—a condition it shared with larger cities, including Madison and Oskosh. Removal of garbage, manure, household wastes, and human excrement in Beloit was left up to individual householders. There were no ordinances on the subject. A committee of the city council could order a householder to abate a nuisance, usually in response to a complaint. A street crew occasionally gathered up manure on the downtown streets and "spread [it] upon the higher and less fertile parts of the public grounds"— presumably including the centrally located, ten-acre, unimproved public park. Sidewalks, where they existed, were wooden, provided by the abutting property owner. Only downtown were sidewalks somewhat uniform, being generally raised on posts to keep them dry.[16]

In villages, a man's social world generally revolved around his

---

[15]Oscar T. Thompson, *Home Town: Some Chapters of Reminiscence* (Beloit, 1942), 14–15. John A. Fleckner, "Poverty and Relief in Nineteenth-Century Janesville," in *WMH*, 61 (Summer, 1978), 282–283, writes that the "cow question" occupied the city council during most of the decade of the seventies. David V. Mollenhoff, *Madison: A History of the Formative Years* (Dubuque, 1982), 153–154, notes that the urban cow was banished from the capital city finally in 1886, but the law had forbade it to graze at will thirteen years earlier.

[16]*Tenth Census of the United States, 1880: Report on the Social Statistics of Cities, Volume XIX, Part 2*, pp. 642–643, 656–659, 679–681; Thompson, *Home Town*, 14. Mollenhoff, *Madison*, 207–212, 219–227, details the building of a water system in the early eighties, but it was after 1900 before a satisfactory sewage disposal system was built. Albert H. Sanford and H. J. Hirshheimer, *A History of La Crosse, Wisconsin, 1841–1900* (La Crosse, 1951), 184–187, note that La Crosse began its city water system in 1877, mostly for fire protection.

business and business contacts, his home, fraternal organizations, and church. The forty-hour week was nowhere in vogue.
Village businesses kept unconscionable hours. By the 1870's
grocery stores had replaced the less specialized general stores in
Beloit. They continued the general-store tradition, remaining
open in the evenings, six days a week, and functioning as informal social clubs in this transplanted New England village.[17]

Businessmen were naturally the keepers of the village flame. If
some improvement was needed, it had to originate in the business community or find approval and backing there. The same
was true of village celebrations, such as July Fourth, a Pioneer
Day, or a fair, to instill local loyalty and attract farmers who had
alternative trade centers to patronize. Thorstein Veblen claimed
that co-operation among village merchants was made easier by
their deliberate avoidance of price competition—at least overtly—
by not advertising cut prices. (Ads ordinarily spoke of the availability of goods, not of a specific price.) One interest that village
merchants had in common was the problem of doing business on
credit, a rural and village custom of long standing. It was not
usual to send bills, which creditors viewed as a reflection upon
their characters. Nor was it common to charge interest on long-
due accounts, which was one justification for the higher price
structure. Cash stores, mail-order houses, and ads from department stores in neighboring cities were common problems for
village merchants, as were the later chain stores that located in
small towns and villages. The organization of a "credit union"
in 1874 among the village merchants of Darlington was remarkable enough to attract the notice of the Dodgeville *Chronicle*, some
twenty miles away. Not a credit union in the present sense, it
was an organization of village merchants who met weekly to

[17]Thompson, *Home Town*, 19, and Showerman, *Country Chronicle*, 26–31, 263–279, have
descriptions of the village and hamlet stores as informal gathering places for men. The
same characters were always there in the evening. Schafer, *Agriculture in Wisconsin*, 177,
observes: "The village merchant is not often credited with a social function, yet his store
was a genuine social center. Perhaps for the older people it was the most important single
social opportunity aside from the church, and its value for that purpose varied with the
character of the storekeeper."

compare lists of "dead beats" on their books. The Dodgeville
editor noted with delight that the dead beat list "is said to
embrace some of the most prominent citizens of the town."[18]

Fraternal organizations were found even in small villages. In
1880, West Salem in La Crosse County had a population of 432,
and four secret societies: Masons, Odd Fellows, Ancient Order
of the United Workmen, and the Sons of Temperance. (Despite
its name, the last was open to women.) The prestigious lodge
was the Masons (A.F. & A.M.), which had sixty members and a
two-story building that provided the village meeting place. The
Odd Fellows and United Workmen had twenty and twenty-seven
members respectively. The numbers involved would have
exhausted the complement of adult males in the village and
nearby, except that there was much overlapping of membership.
All of the lodges met weekly. Add to this a weekly prayer meeting, a fund-raising supper at one of the churches, a business or
board meeting for school or village, and it made for a full week
of fraternizing for some.[19]

In a larger village, Columbus, with 1,876 inhabitants in 1880,
not only were there more lodges, but also a greater variety of
meeting places over three of the local stores. Robert Griffiths,
whose furniture store provided one of the meeting places, was an
indefatigable lodge goer. He appeared as an original member or
officer of five organizations. While the rental of his hall may have
been an uncommon spur to his fraternal impulse, he also
belonged to the Rebeccas, who met over the Bassett and Davis
store. Like many furniture dealers of the day, Griffiths was also
an undertaker, and doubtless cultivated his future clientele.[20]

Not every village adult male fit the description of a business-

[18]Lingeman, *Small Town America*, 332–336; Atherton, *Main Street on the Middle Border*,
49–57; John E. Brush, "The Trade Centers of South-Western Wisconsin: An Analysis
of Function and Location" (doctoral dissertation, University of Wisconsin, 1952);
Dodgeville *Chronicle*, March 6, 1874.

[19]*Eleventh Census of the United States, 1890: Population, Volume I, Part 1*, p. 362; Western
Historical Company, *History of La Crosse County, Wisconsin* (Chicago, 1881), 701–702.

[20]Western Historical Company, *History of Columbia County, Wisconsin* . . . (Chicago,
1880), 690–692, 967.

man-joiner, of course. But there were few villages that harbored much in the way of industrial activities beyond the crafts that could withstand the competition of factory production. For example, Janesville, already a minor industrial city in 1870, had more women employed as domestics (379) than there were men (326) listed as general laborers. There probably were many clerks, bookkeepers, and others working in trade or offices who identified themselves with the village businessmen. They were among the joiners and were eligible for the less prestigious among the various fraternal orders.[21]

Women's lives centered upon the home, family, and church. Social club activities were little known in villages and small cities, except among the socially elite. Middle-class women found their available leisure occupied with the church, missionary society, temperance society, and various money-raising schemes such as church suppers or bake sales. Quilting parties or similar combinations of social and practical activities also brought them together. (Afternoon card parties lay in the future, as did study clubs.) The growing industry of readymade clothing was devoted mostly to the needs of men and boys. Women's fashions were elaborate and—for middle-class women—a consuming occupation, even though the local seamstress was called in for the finer productions.[22]

Given the average life span of the period, the hazards associated with much employment, and the common age gap between husband and wife, the times abounded with single-parent families—generally widows. They and their single daughters bore the brunt of poverty and hard work, usually in domestic service in a village for the smallest wages. Many families lived close to the bone, with periodic help from neighbors or occasional help from local poor relief. There is little to say about their lives and times, which must have been narrow and bleak.[23]

---

[21]Fleckner, "Poverty and Relief in Janesville," *WMH,* 61:284.

[22]Mary I. Wood, *The History of the General Federation of Women's Clubs For the First Twenty-Two Years of Its Organization* (New York, 1912), 3-40; Thompson, *Home Town,* 5, 55-56.

[23]Fleckner, "Poverty and Relief in Janesville," *WMH,* 61:283-284.

As it was a man's world, so it was a boy's world as well, and nowhere more so than in the village. It is no coincidence that we associate Tom Sawyer with village life. Village boys could find little in the way of regular employment, and household chores were not onerous, even if they included the care of some livestock, a garden, and supplying the household with fuel and water. Outside of these chores, a boy usually had time to be with his neighborhood gang. Other neighborhoods were hazardous because they were the domain of other gangs—not necessarily rivals, but simply a matter of the territorial imperative. These limits were flexible for the purposes of going to school, the village center, the fairgrounds, the waterpower or riverfront, industrial areas, or wherever the family cow wandered.[24]

Boys in gangs have always been a minor hazard to the community. The Dodgeville *Chronicle* complained about "boys, (some of them of tender age,) who nightly congregate on our street's and in bar-rooms, and stores, and indulge in cathawling each other, around swearing and useing indecent language. . . ." A Janesville woman, a public alcoholic, asked to enter the poorhouse after she injured herself while fleeing from a gang of taunting boys. Farmers avoided driving by the village high school, especially in winter when the boys felt confined and their snowballs could disconcert horses, with amusing results.[25]

Girls' lives were more home-centered than those of juvenile males. While a change of costumes—to long pants—was the traditional recognition of the end of childhood for boys, the change was more marked for girls, although little reference was made to the reasons for this. In the mid-eighties, Frances Willard contrasted her earlier rites of passage, when at seventeen her hair was "done up," and her feet became "entangled in the skirt of my new gown," with the more active roles that were opening to

[24]Thompson, *Home Town*, 4–11.

[25]Dodgeville *Chronicle*, January 16, 1874; Edward M. Lang, Jr., "The Common Man, Janesville, Wisconsin, 1870 to 1900" (master's thesis, University of Wisconsin, 1968), 14; Fleckner, "Poverty and Relief in Janesville," *WMH,* 61:291; Mollenhoff, *Madison*, 242–243.

girls to take part in literary society debates, or even to consider medicine as a career. ''I had an aspiration; you have opportunity. I breathed an atmosphere laden with old time conservatisms . . . you are exhilarated by the vital air of a new liberty.''[26]

Frances Willard was being more polemical than accurate. Most young women accepted the world as it was, and the goal was pure love and an ideal marriage to an up-and-coming young man, for whom she would create a sanctuary from life's battles. She did have much more freedom than traditional European societies allowed, and was not excluded from adult society. She consorted as an equal with her brother's friends on unchaperoned outings. ''The price paid by society for treating its young people in this fashion was that of keeping itself in a public state of total innocence so that nothing would offend or corrupt the young person.'' This was the genteel tradition, which made the saccharine, trite, moralistic novels of scribbling women the standard American fare.[27]

Girls, like boys, had rather special opportunities in a village or small city. Hired domestic labor was available and cheap for a family of modest circumstances. Everyone who belonged to the broad middle class knew everyone else, and the freedom allowed to young people could be more confidently indulged. Then there was the village high school, which flourished in the eighties. The village high school of West Salem graduated its first class in 1880: Carrie Walker and Belle Spaulding. The following June, there were six graduates. ''The commencement exercises were held in the Baptist Church, with the following programme: Music, Select Choir; Essay, 'Wasted Lives,' Jessie Viets; Essay, 'Light, More Light,' Julia Smead; Essay, 'Power in Music,' Mamie Clark; Music, Select Choir; Oration, 'Voices of the Dead,' John McConnell; Essay, 'For Pearls We Must Dive,'

---

[26]Mrs. Levi B. Pease, ''Girlhood Recollections,'' in La Crosse County Historical Society, *La Crosse County Historical Sketches,* series 5 (La Crosse, 1940), 33–40; Frances E. Willard, *How to Win: A Book for Girls* (Chicago, 1887), 16–18.

[27]Lingeman, *Small Town America,* 267–274; Ziff, *The American 1890s,* 41–44; James D. Hart, *The Popular Book: A History of America's Literary Taste* (New York, 1950; reprinted, Berkeley, 1961), 96–97, 306, 308.

Ella Edwards; Essay, 'Sunshine and Shadows' (with valedic-
tory), Bay Ladd.'' Here was a capsule account of the new higher
learning of the Wisconsin village. Four girls and two boys: girls
read essays while boys orated, and there was no difficulty about
picking a valedictorian.[28]

Village young people had to improvise much of their own
entertainment and social activities. Such were not greatly different from those of surrounding rural neighborhoods, and attending rural dances at Grange halls was a favorite diversion. Dancing
meant the four-couple quadrille. A fiddler, with or without other
accompaniment, usually supplied the melody and called the figures. Dances were commonly attended by all ages, and most
parents would have balked at dances strictly for teen-agers. Ball-
room dancing was for decadent city types, but even the annual
ball of Milwaukee's Light Horse Squadron, the social event of
the season, offered quadrilles, mixed with what were termed
''round dances'' such as the waltz or more vigorous polka or
schottische.[29]

Joseph Schafer celebrated the country dances of his youth:
''From the standpoint of social training, the country dance performed a service of obvious value'' for ''many an awkward youth
[whose] 'first dance' was his 'social baptism with fire'. . . .'' But
not everyone approved this pastime. Most evangelical churches
were adamantly opposed to dancing and cards, and this included
the stricter sects of the Lutherans. Even Schafer acknowledged
that perhaps ''no one thing did more to impair the social unity
of neighborhoods, and to paralyze plans for providing wholesome
recreation, than the eternal question of dancing or no dancing.''
It split the Yankees, much as the liquor question split both
Yankees and Germans.[30]

The eternal question, as Schafer put it, was a constant spur to
the churches to involve young people in more ''wholesome''

[28]Western Historical Company, *History of La Crosse County*, 696.

[29]Showerman, *Country Chronicle*, 35–58; Jeffris, ''Family Life in the United States,''
96–97; Schafer, *Agriculture in Wisconsin*, 175–176; Milwaukee *Daily Journal*, April 30, 1886.

[30]Schafer, *Agriculture in Wisconsin*, 175–176.

recreation. Unitarians, Universalists, Episcopalians, and Catholics solved the problem by combining dancing with other social occasions. But as the list indicates, Presbyterians, Methodists, Baptists, Congregationalists, many Lutherans, and other immigrant evangelical sects were dead set against dancing. They were the ones heard from in the running battle with Satan, at a time when church membership was steadily gaining but the influence of the churches on individual conduct was just as steadily declining. One response was the parish house or the enlargement of church structures to include rooms for Sunday schools, activities for young people, and for women to quilt, hold church fairs, and meet. By the nineties, young peoples' organizations such as the Epworth League were formalized on a denominational basis. Temperance organizations, particularly the Good Templars, attracted young people as social organizations as much as for their avowed purpose.[31]

The Young Men's Christian Association was the most important interdenominational organization to appeal to young males. Introduced from England to New England before the Civil War, it was conceived as an instrument to bring into the fold young men who were flocking to the cities, by providing needed services and an opportunity to serve others. The movement had already reached Wisconsin by 1870, when twelve associations were reported, most of them located in lesser cities.[32]

Village and small-town life was not all church- and lodge-centered for social occasions. Fairs, circuses, community observances of the Glorious Fourth, or any other excuse for parades, orations, and public feasting were supplemented by commercial entertainment and lectures, which could bring together a broad cross section of the village population. The Wisconsin gazetteer for 1886 listed about seventy cities and villages with opera houses,

[31]Atherton, *Main Street on the Middle Border,* 186–190; Robert D. Cross, "American Society: 1865–1914," in John A. Garraty, *Interpreting American History: Conversations With Historians* (2 vols., New York, 1970), 2:37; Joanne J. Brownsword, "Good Templars in Wisconsin" (master's thesis, University of Wisconsin, 1960).

[32]Winthrop S. Hudson, *American Protestantism* (Chicago, 1961), 112–115; Young Men's Christian Association, *Proceedings,* 1870, p. xxx.

theaters, or public halls. The number had grown by nearly another 100 ten years later. Boscobel, with a population of 1,479 in 1895, had two opera houses seating 800 and 600 respectively. Lodi, with a population of 975, had a 500-seat opera house.[33]

What sort of entertainment did opera houses, theaters, and halls offer? Itinerant road shows, variety acts, musicians and musical organizations, and lecturers were standards. Many originated in Wisconsin. Beloit had a local group called Clement Brothers and Forrester, professional singers and entertainers who traveled continuously, returning to Beloit's opera house once a year for a "Home Concert." In the eighties, Beloit also had a dance band that played a regular circuit in Wisconsin and Iowa. The Columbus *Democrat* voiced a not unusual complaint: "There is no better town of its size in this state for a first class entertainment to stop at than Columbus. But the place has been rode down with snide shows, concerts and slight of hand performers, who only come here to get the price of admission. . . . The *Democrat* will puff no poor affair, but will always say a good word for any company that deserves it. Snide shows and broken down variety troupes will do well to bear this in mind."[34]

The *Democrat* had earlier given evidence of its discriminating taste: "At the Opera House . . . Wednesday evening . . . Prof. L. B. Hudson, the eminent elocutionist, will give one of his popular entertainments, [rendering] in his unsurpassed voice and manner, some of the choicest gems in English literature. He personates twenty or more characters . . . commingling fun and pathos. Admission 25 cents and 15 cents for students. Give him a good hearing; his entertainment is worth more to you than twenty nigger shows." As well as elocutionists, there was a thriving market for lecturers in places that never expected to see Mark Twain or Henry Ward Beecher. George W. Peck, one of the few

[33] *Wisconsin State Gazetteer and Business Directory,* 1886, 1895–1896.
[34] Thompson, *Home Town,* 44; Columbus *Democrat,* August 20, 1881. Apparently the opera houses of Wisconsin were quite as much a wasteland as the glowing tubes in every home today. But it was communal, and if you paid to endure it you were entitled to an opinion.

intentional humorists among Wisconsin's governors, went on the lecture circuit with two set pieces. His smasher was "How Private George W. Peck Put Down the Rebellion, or the Funny Experiences of a Raw Recruit." Peck was in the Twain tradition and probably did not have to advertise that he was funny, although present-day readers may be a bit puzzled by what all the hilarity was about. He gained a national reputation with his stories about "Peck's Bad Boy," which became part of the language. Spawning village opera houses did not exhaust the talents of local builders and architects nearly so rapidly as it did the available talent to grace their stages.[35]

The favorable aspect of indifferent and intermittent commercial entertainment was that villagers could provide their own without worrying about comparisons with professional standards. This is why several hundred would appear at a high school graduation featuring six graduates from a student body of thirty or forty. They wanted to hear how Ella spoke her piece. The youth of the village was surrounded by encouraging friends of all ages who knew which youngster could be levied upon to play the piano, sing, give a humorous recitation successfully, orate as well as anything heard around the courthouse, or have an occasional poem in the weekly paper. Editors, lawyers, doctors, and teachers knew likely young people who might be drawn into their professions. Burr Jones, who served one term in Congress and sat on the state supreme court, had little to measure himself against in Evansville, but listened with interest when he was advised to think of going to college.[36]

The negative aspect of this supportive but sheltered existence

---

[35]Columbus *Democrat,* January 9, 1875. Peck is in the *DAB*; Marilyn Grant, "One More Civil War Memoir," in *WMH,* 65 (Winter, 1981-1982), 122-129. The lecture, "How Peck and Another Mule Crushed the Rebellion," is in George W. Peck, *Peck's Fun: Comprising All the Choice Gems of Wit, Humor, Sarcasm and Pathos from the Prolific Pen of George W. Peck* (Chicago, 1890), 204-226. William D. Hoard was another acknowledged humorist as governor, though not for pay. Hoard's humor seems much less contrived. He modeled his style on Lincoln's use of the apt illustration. See George W. Rankin, *William Dempster Hoard* (Fort Atkinson, 1925), 24-30; Wilbur H. Glover, "W. D. Hoard's Humor," in *WMH,* 35 (Spring, 1952), 185-187.

[36]Burr W. Jones, *Reminiscences of Nine Decades* (Evansville, 1937), 32; *DWB*.

was that young people readily accepted the conventional wisdom of the older generation. Differences of opinion were defined by the elders, not by the young, and did not extend much beyond conventional political or religious controversy. Elders went to high school graduations to hear the eternal verities affirmed in graceful imagery. Young people responded in kind.

When the national guardsmen from Janesville and Madison were ordered to Eau Claire to restore order in the so-called Sawdust War, the young men preferred to think of themselves as being engaged in something analogous to war duty. If they had any reservations about their role as strikebreakers, or sympathy for the men whom they were placing in their stockades or harassing in the streets, they left no record of such doubts. They were young romantics who identified themselves with the Civil War veterans who were part of every community.[37]

A sterner test came with the Milwaukee riot duty in May, 1886. The guardsmen who were dispatched to Bay View were poorly trained and led, poorly quartered, poorly fed, and badly frightened. The Madison *Democrat* was incensed by this and editorialized about the pusillanimous leadership that permitted the guardsmen to be pelted by the mob. Later, it charged that the men of the First Regiment were "mad all over" about the favoritism shown Milwaukee's Light Horse Squadron, the elite unit, while they were sent to Bay View. "Janesville boys swear that if they ever go to Milwaukee again they will kill more than six, and several other companies vow they will not do guard duty another week on lemons and raw eggs at $1 a day . . . the town that ever needs the present First regiment again will have the biggest funeral ever held in this state."[38]

In the absence of direct testimony from the young men involved, this editorial report indicates that the militiamen assumed that the shootings were more than justified. Their elders

---

[37]Jerry M. Cooper, "The Wisconsin Militia, 1832-1900" (master's thesis, University of Wisconsin, 1968), 252-255.

[38]Wisconsin Adjutant General, *Biennial Report*, 1885-1886, pp. 34-35; Madison *Democrat*, May 11, 29, 1886.

told them so from every side. Boys from "out state" cities and villages had confronted the immigrant mob from the city. What irritated them most was that Milwaukee's fancy horse guards spent most of the time at their downtown armory and did not share the discomfort and trauma of duty at Bay View. The victims apparently concerned these boys from out of town less than did their own inconvenience.[39]

This attitude of complacency was part of village and small-town life. These young men were accustomed to approval from their elders, and found little reason to question the conventional wisdom. The greatest hazard of which they could conceive—the Civil War—had been dealt with by their parents' generation, and the heroes were accorded due deference. The older generation played its part to the hilt. They were the ones who had endured the hardships of pioneering, of hauling wheat to Milwaukee by wagon, and fighting the war that ended all threats to America's boundless future. They were not remote. They walked the streets, and one could identify them readily by the style of hats they wore and the commonly inflated military or honorific titles by which their fellows addressed them. They also were filled with parental concern. In 1880, when General Grant visited the Wisconsin State Fair, on the grounds of Camp Randall, he congratulated the assemblage that the site had been transformed: "I hope that these grounds may never again be the scene of warlike preparations . . . and may the young men and boys before me, and these fine-appearing militia-men, never be called upon to witness the scenes of strife which these old veterans have gone through."[40]

Other bases for a friendly interest and deference between generations existed in the uncertainty of life itself. The birth rate was dropping dramatically in the years after the Civil War, but

[39]Cooper, "Wisconsin Militia," 266, 281–282, confirms the middle-class background of most of the guardsmen.

[40]Wisconsin State Agricultural Society, *Transactions,* 1880–1881, pp. 95, 189. Most of the "old veterans" on the scene in 1880 would have been between the ages of thirty-five and forty-five. The Civil War was a real gulf that service at Bay View, or the later brief adventure of the Spanish-American War, could not bridge.

not the hazards to life. On the average, about one in five infants who reached the age of one year would not survive through age five. And the teens were perilous times—consumption, scarlet fever, diphtheria, typhoid, and polio favored the young. A lively appreciation of the opportunities open to young people in a rapidly changing society alternated with apprehension over the moral and physical hazards. Parents and elders were indulgent, partly because the young accepted authority more readily and were offered rewards not available so readily to their parents.[41]

Wisconsin cities of the time were not simply villages writ large, although they exhibited village ways in many respects. This difference extended beyond family cows browsing in residential streets, unimproved roadways, and a lack of such rudimentary services as water, drainage, sewers, and trash collection. The British novelist Anthony Trollope observed the essential differ- ence in 1861 on a visit to Milwaukee—a typical new western city:[42]

> In the principal business streets of all these towns one sees vast buildings. They are usually called blocks, and are often so denom- inated in large letters on their front. . . . Men build on an enor- mous scale, three times, ten times as much as is wanted. The only measure of size is an increase on what men have built before. Monroe P. Jones, the speculator, is very probably ruined, and then begins the world again, nothing daunted. . . . He is greedy of dollars with a terrible covetousness; but he is greedy in order that he may speculate more widely. . . . As an individual I differ very much from Monroe P. Jones. The first block accomplished, with an adequate rent accruing to me as the builder, I fancy that I should never try a second. But Jones is undoubtedly the man for the West. It is that love of money to come, joined to a strong disregard for money made, which constitutes the vigorous frontier mind. . . .

[41]*Wisconsin's Changing Population* (Science Inquiry Publication, no. 9, Bulletin of the University of Wisconsin, serial no. 2642, general series no. 2426, Madison, 1942), 27; Joseph F. Kett, *Rites of Passage: Adolescence in America, 1790 to the Present* (New York, 1977), 189; J. C. Bartholf, "Our Boy Crop," in Wisconsin State Agricultural Society, *Transac- tions,* 1883–1884, pp. 247–256.

[42]Anthony Trollope, *North America,* eds., Donald Smalley and Bradford A. Booth (New York, 1951), 127–128.

Love of money to come, and a willingness to risk money in hand, marked the real city builders. As Trollope observed, they commonly guessed wrong, or if they guessed right they overextended their optimism and resources. But if they happened to be in the right place at the right time, things moved. It was this sense of being where great opportunities existed that set cities apart from villages. Few conspicuous fortunes were won in villages. City entrepreneurs could dare and win more. They were also more likely to translate their success into public benefactions: libraries, parks, even art collections. Villagers were conservators. It did not require as much to establish a standard of conspicuous consumption. It can well be argued that the triumph of the Wisconsin village was in the field of education, modestly subsidized by the state. Another advantage was that the village did not ordinarily levy on its youth for labor to create the conspicuous fortunes.

Villages had merchants' associations whose aim was to retain or enlarge their farm clientele. Cities had advancement associations, boards of trade, and similar organizations whose purpose was to attract manufacturers, enlarge the city's wholesale trade area, and attract capital to provide services and amenities. The very word "Oshkosh" became a symbol of manic energy devoted to this purpose. This hyperthyroid intensity had implications for the inhabitants.[43]

Oshkosh was all get up and go. Its downtown streets and stores were illuminated by electricity by the summer of 1882—quite early in terms of the available technology. "There is no city in the state where so many people may be seen promenading on the main thoroughfares in the evening as in Oshkosh. Bands of music, electric lights, fairs and festivals, entertainments, are the . . . attractions that keep the evenings in constant bustle of activity and life. The next project talked of is a public park or a grand

[43]Joseph Schafer, *The Winnebago-Horicon Basin: A Type Study in Western History* (Madison, 1937), 279–280, was of the opinion that "the success of Oshkosh must be ascribed to superior social cooperation in community enterprises, and to superior, at least bolder, leadership in the period of the 1870's." He was comparing the fortunes of Fond du Lac and Oshkosh.

boullvard [sic] along the lake shore. Waterworks are much discussed. . . ." A $30,000 opera house was going up, another railroad was building through the city. "To add to these projects, all going on at the same time," the state's pharmaceutical association met that summer in Oshkosh, as did the encampment of the Second Regiment. Businessmen of Wausau, 400 strong, were due as guests of Oshkosh for two days, and this was to be followed by the Northern Wisconsin State Fair, which Oshkosh had secured from rivals along with the normal school and the Northern State Insane Asylum. The municipal cup ran over.[44]

An interesting contrast to all of this bustle was the following critique of Oshkosh in the 1880 federal census: "There are no water-works." "There are no public parks and pleasure grounds." "The city has no system of sewage." "*Liquid household wastes.*— Chamber slops, laundry waste, and kitchen slops are all disposed of in the same way, but in what way is not reported, except that none of it goes into sewers, because there are none. The overflow from cesspools and privy-vaults is thought to contaminate water more or less."[45]

Oshkosh is singled out here, not because its sanitary arrangements were conspicuously less satisfactory than those of some other Wisconsin cities, but because it had more opportunity to do something about them. Known as the "Phoenix City," it had lost most of its business and industrial district in fires of 1874 and 1875, repeatedly rebuilt it in brick and stone, but gave little attention to its festering problems. Situated as it was, at an average elevation of only seven feet above the level of shallow Lake Winnebago, and growing pell-mell, it might better have given some thought to its water supply and sewers rather than its electric lights and opera house.[46]

---

[44]Milwaukee *Sentinel*, August 27, 1882; Forrest McDonald, *Let There Be Light: The Electric Utility Industry in Wisconsin, 1881–1955* (Madison, 1957), 69–72.

[45]*Tenth Census of the United States, 1880: Report on the Social Statistics of Cities, Volume XIX, Part 2*, pp. 680–681.

[46]Oshkosh, seemingly ill-starred, had burned in 1859, 1861, 1866, and twice in 1874 prior to what became known as the Great Fire of 1875. See Reuben Gold Thwaites, *The History of Winnebago County & The Fox River Valley, 1541–1877* ([Oshkosh? 1984?]), 95–96.

Children faced some special health problems, and even schools could be a hazard. An article in the 1881 annual report of the state superintendent goes far to explain why. The superintendent invited architects to submit plans for school buildings adapted to the needs of rural, village, and small city locations. A plan submitted by Edbrooke and Burnham of Chicago for a small city school especially struck the superintendent's fancy. The building was two stories plus a basement. Four classrooms furnished space for 140 to 200 scholars. The novel arrangement was that the privies were in the basement, adjoining the separate playrooms for the girls and boys for use in inclement weather. "The crowning feature of this school-house consists in the arrangement for the ventilation of all its parts," which required that the hot-air furnace draw the exhaust air from the school rooms through the privy vaults. "Only about one-sixth of these faeces by weight remains in the vaults after being subjected to this process; and this residuum is, easily and with no offensive odor, shoveled occasionally into baskets and carried out of the building. . . . It has been tested with complete success in private houses and institutions of learning; and the testimony is that no impure air, even in the summer season, rises from the vaults and penetrates the apartments of the houses."[47]

It is worthwhile to examine public attitudes towards standards of sanitation. If there is a central fact about youth in late-nine-teenth-century Wisconsin, it is the uncertainty of maintaining health among the hazards to which children were exposed unwittingly. There was also a great deal of public inertia. People asked

[47]Wisconsin Superintendent of Public Instruction, *Annual Report,* 1881, pp. 142–148. "The privy vault problem seems to be the question of the hour. For many years the kind hearted and generous people of the city have been preserving their excrement for the benefit of future generations. They have not suffered it to be washed away into the bosom of the lake and diluted to annihilation nor have they permitted the destroying agencies of the atmosphere to rob it of its precious virulence nor yet have they allowed it to be returned to mother earth and rendered harmless by the formation of new and kindly compounds, but have boxed it up and cherished it with watchful care in all its pristine deadliness. . . . Sanitary work is the crab of modern civilization. . . ." Quoted from the Oshkosh health officer's report in the Wisconsin State Board of Health, *Annual Report,* 1889–1890, pp. 131–132.

what seemed a perfectly logical question: How did we and our ancestors survive, if what we are told is true? The proof of Louis Pasteur's findings had been established for a score of years, but it certainly did not find general acceptance. Partly, this was a problem of the medical profession, which had no great claim on public confidence.[48]

Even professors of chemistry suffered a credibility gap. In 1885 Dr. Erastus G. Smith, chemistry professor at Beloit College, was invited to address the meeting of the state agricultural society on the topic "Sanitary Problems." He chose to discuss the sanitary conditions encountered on the farm and in the village, observing that "insiduous [sic] germs of disease sown broadcast and running riot through the crowded tenement districts of the city" were a familiar subject. He cited Pasteur's more recent work, followed by commonsense warnings about the positioning of the family well and privy.[49]

The following day, apropos of nothing in particular, an anti-germ enthusiast seized the floor. He said in part: "We have no time for splitting hairs ourselves, nor pay others for doing it, only but to a very limited extent. Splitting hairs is contrary to nature, and microscopical observations are contrary to nature, or else our eyes would be made into microscopes, and we must look out for these microscopical observations. If our eyes were microscopes, there is not probably anything on the face of the earth that we would eat. Because we would see bacteria and such things everywhere." The speaker seems not to have limited himself to scorning germs. As a member of the board of visitors of the Platteville Normal, he probably made the following comment (part of the board's report), which bears his touch: "It is a lamentable fact that many children who have no other advantages than such as the country district school affords have lost

[48]Wisconsin began to license pharmacists in 1882, but only debated licensing physicians. The Milwaukee *Sentinel*, on February 2, 1882, argued against the latter measure. Also see Guenter B. Risse, "From Horse and Buggy to Automobile and Telephone: Medical Practice in Wisconsin, 1848–1930," in Ronald L. Numbers and Judith W. Leavitt, eds., *Wisconsin Medicine: Historical Perspectives* (Madison, 1981), 25–45.

[49]Wisconsin State Agricultural Society, *Transactions,* 1885, pp. 189–202.

many precious hours of youth's most precious time, because their teacher had *too much education* to be able to impart to them in a practical, simple way the first rudiments of knowledge. He perhaps knew Botany well, had the 'ologies at his fingers' ends, but could not successfully teach the country child the three 'r's.'' A surfeit of education rather fits with the hazards of microscopical vision.[50]

Prospects for longevity may not have been improved by living in a Wisconsin city before the turn of the century, but it could be a more interesting life, particularly for those lucky enough to be a part of the expanding middle class. The sense of drive and destiny that possessed communities was not all cynicism. Anthony Trollope was close to the heart of it when he characterized this sense as more a competitive urge than a certain prospect of riches. It is difficult to explain the invitation from the Oshkosh business community to 400 of its counterparts from Wausau for a two-day visit in purely practical, acquisitive terms. Those businessmen had visions of Oshkosh as a future commercial and wholesale center for north-central Wisconsin, to be sure. But beyond that, they were enamored of the largeness of the gesture.

The business community of La Crosse indulged a similar fantasy when a hardy band of businessmen, sixty-one strong, foraged their way through the communities to the westward as far as the Missouri River. They were marking out a territory for what they confidently called "The Gateway City." Their dream faded with the rapid rise of Minneapolis and St. Paul. On a quieter note a decade later, the board of trade printed a winning essay on the subject, "La Crosse, a City of Homes," which closed: "It would be disloyal not to believe with all our hearts that the United States is the best country on this round earth, Wisconsin the best state, and this city of La Crosse, where our fortunate lot is cast, the very best city."[51]

Much of the cost of this urban competition was passed on to

---

[50]*Ibid.,* 319; Wisconsin Superintendent of Public Instruction, *Biennial Report,* 1886, p. 101. Emphasis in the original.

[51]La Crosse Board of Trade, *Annual Report,* 1881, pp. 3–23, and *ibid.,* 1890, p. 32.

the future. This was not done unjustly, it was thought, for the
rosy future seemed to justify the transfer. Available revenue and
borrowing capacity were severely strained to provide amenities
supposedly necessary to true urban status: surfaced streets, curbs,
sidewalks, storm drains, and downtown lighting. Some cities
even thought of sewers. Municipal ownership was not a popular
doctrine. It appeared perfectly reasonable to franchise water systems, public transit, and gas and electricity to private capital.
The indirect cost of this practice proved expensive in the long
run: inadequate service, the corruption of politics, and overge-
nerous concessions that the courts usually upheld. These problems soon became apparent, particularly with the 1893 depression
and the end of the boom.[52]

Frederick Jackson Turner, who became Wisconsin's most celebrated historian, was not an average man. But in many respects,
he was representative of his generation, shaped by the changes of
his times. He spent his boyhood in a Wisconsin village that was
becoming a minor city. His parents, Andrew Jackson Turner
and Mary Hanford, came from New England stock. Jack Turner
had little schooling and much hard work on a frontier farm. He
escaped this by seizing an opportunity to learn the printer's
trade, and in 1858 landed in Portage. Having married Miss
Hanford, a schoolteacher from Friendship in Adams County,
Jack Turner became the owner and editor of the principal weekly
in Portage in 1861, the year Frederick, the first of three children,
was born.

Portage was a village of 2,879 population in 1860, and had
grown to 4,346 twenty years later, by which time Fred Turner
was at the University in Madison. Portage was a pleasant place
in which to grow up. It was small enough for a boy to enjoy the
adjoining countryside, and to know everyone and be known by
them. The winters were long and hard, but there was sledding
and skating on the canal and rivers. Summer brought the big
Fourth of July celebration at the courthouse, usually with an out-

[52]The above is the theme of David P. Thelen, *The New Citizenship: Origins of Progressivism
in Wisconsin, 1885–1900* (Columbia, 1972), 130–141.

of-town orator, the two local bands, and appropriate songs by
the Liederkranz Society—Portage was more than one-third foreign-born in 1870, with its quota of Germans. Then the straw-
berry and ice cream festival season began, with the ladies of the
various churches and charitable groups vying for honors and
collections. The Columbia County Fair came in the fall, at least
one of Wisconsin's many small circuses visited the town annually,
and the opera house offered out-of-town fare with some
regularity.

When Fred Turner was thirteen, he joined with other young-
sters to organize a series of young peoples' dances to imitate their
parents who met fortnightly in a local hall with a hired band.
The older generation enjoyed the show. In 1876, when he was
fifteen and inspired by the national centennial, he and his friends
organized a military company to take part in the celebration.
The organization lived on, and its annual ball became an important social occasion, particularly after the elder Turner took over,
secured fancy uniforms and rifles, and entered the company in
state competitions. Fred was also attracted to oratory, and at age
fifteen he delivered a Memorial Day declamation to his fellow
citizens. He excelled in school and carried off the prize in the
1878 graduation exercises of the high school.[53]

When Fred Turner began at the University in Madison in the
fall of 1878, he was classed as a subfreshman because of the
inadequacy of the Portage high school, although he had taken a
special preparatory course in Greek to qualify for matriculation
in the ancient classical course. Madison and the University were
a wider world. But it was not yet entirely a modern world:[54]

> Theorists in those days held that mental faculties could not be
> trusted to mature without proper guidance; strict mental and
> moral discipline was needed to develop the mind. This, rather
> than the acquisition of knowledge, was the purpose of schooling.
> Students were not to question or even to reason; learning was by

[53]Ray Allen Billington, *Frederick Jackson Turner: Historian, Scholar, Teacher* (New York, 1973), 3–11.
[54]*Ibid.*, 18–20.

rote, and the classroom a means of testing their ability to recite the set body of material they had memorized. They were never to doubt the rigid prescriptions imposed by their elders.

Burr Jones, born near Evansville in 1846, was fifteen years older than Fred Turner and had had an education which was quite different. There being no high schools outside the cities, he attended a Methodist-supported seminary in Evansville. He characterized his attendance as "more or less desultory and not continuous. . . ." Coming from a typical rural district school, Jones found "no entrance examinations, and . . . like all others who could pay a little fee, was cheerfully admitted." Jones was a youth at a time when boys owed their labor to their fathers until age twenty-one, and he expressed his gratitude to his stepfather who never mentioned the matter. This common-law doctrine is seldom encountered in the memoirs of men born after 1860.[55]

After a couple of terms of teaching, Jones felt that he could attempt the University. Professor John Sterling, the acting head, invited him to come to a faculty meeting so that Jones and the faculty could look one another over. He was accepted without any reservations. During his first year, 1866, there was serious discussion of whether to close the institution, but the legislature adopted a more generous policy. Jones concluded of his time at the University in the late sixties: "It was a dumb fellow, or one thoroughly lazy, who could not pass in those halcyon days. It was necessary then to fill the ranks and keep them filled rather than to drop the undesireable."[56]

Fred Turner came to quite a different University a dozen years later. President Paul Chadbourne (1867–1870) had set the institution on a new course. After an interlude (1871–1874) with John H. Twombly, who looked the part but was deemed incompetent, John Bascom came to the presidency, which he occupied until 1887. During Bascom's tenure the University made significant strides towards more exacting requirements, broader programs,

[55]Jones, *Reminiscences*, 27–28.

[56]*Ibid.*, 37–49; Merle Curti and Vernon Carstensen, *The University of Wisconsin: A History, 1848–1925* (2 vols., Madison, 1949), 1:170–173.

and other methods of instruction, although much of the old authoritarianism remained. It was, all in all, a period of transition.[57]

The difference between the entrance requirements at the University of Burr Jones and of Fred Turner a dozen years later in 1878 defines one of the most important changes of the times. Not that there was a dramatic increase in the proportion of young people who went on to the University or to college—at least not until the latter eighties. The change was in the new emphasis upon the role of formal education in society, and a general overhaul of the school system.

The problems of rural schools were many. Aside from casual attendance by those enrolled at the two or three short terms— usually taught by different teachers—and a paucity of teaching materials, most teachers were sadly prepared. Many of them had no more schooling than what they were giving to their pupils, and sixteen-year-old teachers were not unusual. The legal age for attendance—there being no compulsory attendance law until 1879—was from four to twenty. Mothers were not averse to sending four-year-olds. One can imagine the instruction received in one-room schoolhouses with fifty—or even fifteen—scholars of that age range reciting from whatever texts the family could provide. Recitation was the basic technique, and was necessarily brief for the individual child. The bright child was the one who committed much material to memory. Whatever their many virtues, most texts, like the famous McGuffey readers, bore little relation to children's experiences. We hear only of those young people who were avid to read and excel. They were the ones who wrote memoirs and reminiscences.[58]

[57]Curti and Carstensen, *University of Wisconsin,* 1:218–498. Also see Frederic A. Pike, *A Student at Wisconsin Fifty Years Ago: Reminiscences and Records of the Eighties* (Madison, 1935).

[58]Ruth M. Elson, *Guardians of Tradition: American Schoolbooks of the Nineteenth Century* (Lincoln, 1964), is an excellent survey of the contents and uses of textbooks. Belle C. Bohn, "Early Wisconsin School Teachers," in *WMH,* 23 (September, 1939), 58–61, and Mary D. Bradford, *Memoirs of Mary D. Bradford . . .* (Evansville, 1932), which also appeared in *WMH,* 14–16 (September, 1930–September, 1932), describe the rural district schools of the early seventies.

This scheme of the blind leading the blind began to change in the seventies. Aside from a growing argument over compulsory education resulting from the 1870 federal census figures on illiteracy and from the state superintendent's statistics on attendance, the real problem was to create a more rational school system out of what was at hand. This effort moved by fits and starts, with much argument and viewing with alarm. The most significant act of the seventies was the creation of the modestly subsidized free high school system. As elsewhere described, it was the villages and small cities that took advantage of the legislation. The rural towns ignored the opportunity.[59]

The graded school was not a leap from a one-room school to six or eight separate classes in separate rooms. For most villages or small cities, a graded school meant simply a two- or three-room schoolhouse where the children could be divided into primary and elementary divisions. Cities settled for two or three-room graded schools, located by wards or subdistricts, rather than consolidating them on the principle of more age and grade leveling. This seemed eminently reasonable at a time when most high schools at the top of the system often had only two to four teachers.[60]

A simultaneous problem was the improvement of teacher qualifications. An earlier effort to subsidize normal departments in academies and private colleges proved fruitless. It was this experience that led to the creation of the normal school system and a normal department in the University. This department, and

---

[59]J. W. Stearns, ed., *The Columbian History of Education in Wisconsin* (Milwaukee, 1893), 54–62. Until 1861, when the office of county superintendent of schools was created, town superintendents (no educational qualifications required) had decided on the qualifications of teachers. A friend of Mary Bradford's was asked by a local board of supervisors to draw a map of Ireland and identify its counties as a test of her qualifications. Bradford, "Memoirs of Mary D. Bradford," *WMH*, 14:162.

[60]In 1880, Dane County had 246 schools, only ten of them with two or more departments (rooms). This did not include the single city system, Madison, which had six schools with three or more departments, plus a high school with twelve teachers and 254 students. Wisconsin Superintendent of Public Instruction, *Annual Report,* 1881, pp. 296, 354–357, 362–363.

normal schools at Platteville, Whitewater, Oshkosh, River Falls, Milwaukee, and Stevens Point, came into being within a thirty-year period between 1863 and 1894. The normal schools had the problem of taking many of their students from ungraded district schools. Given the state of their previous education, it is not surprising that the emphasis was upon a liberal arts program, minus the usual emphasis upon ancient and modern languages. The idea that a college education consisted of the memorization of textbook material, to be recited on demand, died hard. But students, parents, and the faculties of the normal schools were pleased to think of the institutions as local, state-supported, liberal arts colleges.[61]

The shift from untrained teachers straight from the ungraded one-room schools to normal school graduates was not quickly accomplished. The high school was conceived to fulfill a dual role. One was to provide teachers for the ungraded rural schools; the other to provide students with some uniformity of background for the University and colleges. This would allow the University to relinquish the embarrassing task of operating a preparatory department. By defining the high school curriculum necessary for tuition-free entrance to the University, the University effectively gained control over the standard high school program. The University also filled the role of inspector of high schools, and eventually (in 1880) discontinued its preparatory department. There was much tinkering with the normal school programs to fit them for the role of preparing teachers for the various levels of public ungraded, graded, and high schools. As

[61]Conrad E. Patzer, *Public Education in Wisconsin* (Madison, 1924), 134–146; William T. Anderson, "The Development of the Common Schools," in *Wisconsin Blue Book, 1923*, pp. 116–117; Richard P. Bailey, "The Wisconsin State Colleges, 1875–1955, With Respect to the Function of Preparing Secondary School Teachers" (doctoral dissertation, University of Wisconsin, 1959); William H. Herrmann, "The Rise of the Public Normal School System in Wisconsin" (doctoral dissertation, University of Wisconsin, 1953); Jurgen Herbst, "Nineteenth-Century Normal Schools in the United States: A Fresh Look," in the *History of Education*, 9 (September, 1980), 224–227; Walker D. Wyman, ed., *History of the Wisconsin State Universities* (River Falls, 1968), 1–13.

normal school requirements increased, they invariably placed emphasis upon academic subjects rather than upon the art of teaching.[62]

A limitation upon the professionalization of teaching was the system of certification, which was based upon examinations given by county and city superintendents and also by a state board. Superintendents could issue certificates of three grades, carrying various limitations as to teaching level, duration, and jurisdiction. The coveted state certificate covered all levels, and was either limited or unlimited as to subjects. Candidates were examined in the following areas, nine required by statute, the others taken by choice: United States history, arithmetic, geography, United States Constitution, Wisconsin constitution, physiology, algebra, reading, grammar and analysis, penmanship, geometry, natural philosophy, orthography, orthoepy, English literature, mental philosophy, general history, geology, political economy, botany, zoology, and theory of teaching. The examination was exclusively subject-oriented, with only the faintest nod towards pedagogy. The questions would easily defeat the average Ph.D. today. For example:[63]

- Tabulate the chief doings of the "Army of the Potomac" under each of its commanders.
- When it is noon, January 1, at Washington (77° west), what time is it at Pekin (116° 27" east)?
- What writs may the higher courts of Wisconsin issue to the lower, and what does each mean?
- Trace the circulation of the blood, from the right auricle through the liver, back to the right auricle again.
- A dam of 15 feet head has a hole 6 feet from its foot. At what distance from the foot will the leakage strike?

---

[62]Curti and Carstensen, *University of Wisconsin,* 1:482–498; Herrmann, "Rise of the Normal School System," 236–238; Herbst, "Nineteenth-Century Normal Schools," *History of Education,* 9:225–227.

[63]Patzer, *Public Education in Wisconsin,* 126–128; Herrmann, "Rise of the Normal School System," 260–261. The examination for a state certificate, August 9–12, 1881, is reproduced in the Wisconsin Superintendent of Public Instruction, *Annual Report,* 1881, pp. 277–290. In 1881, one unlimited certificate was won by Thomas J. Walsh of Two Rivers. He became the senator from Montana and chairman of the committee that uncovered the Teapot Dome scandal of the Harding administration. *Ibid.,* 1881, xxxiv; *ibid.,* 1882, p. 36; *DAB.*

County and city examinations offered a way to continue to qualify for those who had pursued teaching for years. Not until later did a normal school diploma confer a certificate to teach. For years, more teachers qualified by local examinations than by attending normal schools, colleges, or the University of Wisconsin. The principal mode for conveying pedagogical instruction and professionalism to teachers was through teachers' institutes and professional associations. It is a moot question whether these flourished because of a strongly felt need on the part of teachers, or because teachers practiced outward conformity and were subject to pressure to take part.[64]

One comes away from the state superintendents' annual reports, which contain generous excerpts from county superintendents' comments, with an impression that here was a profession that was indeed building esprit. One straw in the wind was that the number of persons who reported themselves as "teachers and professors" grew from 4,164 in the 1870 census to 11,707 twenty years later. The total population of the state had grown some 60 per cent in that interval. It was not that the actual number of teachers had nearly tripled, but that in 1890 they readily identified themselves as teachers. Being a teacher was no longer an occasional trade that placed a man somewhere below the salt, or identified a woman as condemned to spinsterhood.[65]

The enormous changes that took place in Wisconsin's public school system did not grow entirely out of Yankee middle-class concern about children's preparation for a changing future, or from competitive civic pride, although both were important. Another powerful impetus came from the strong flow of immigration that came in, particularly after the depression of the

[64]Patzer, *Public Education in Wisconsin*, 156–157; Ellis B. Usher, *Wisconsin: Its Story and Biography, 1848-1913* (8 vols., Chicago, 1914), 2:382–384.

[65]Wisconsin Superintendent of Public Instruction, *Annual Report*, 1881, p. 227; *Ninth Census of the United States, 1870: Population, Volume I*, 764; *Eleventh Census of the United States, 1890: Population, Volume I, Part 2*, p. 624. Lloyd P. Jorgenson, *The Founding of Public Education in Wisconsin* (Madison, 1956), 156–157, notes that in 1870 only 231 persons in Dodge County reported to the census taker that they were teachers, but the state superintendent reported 354 there.

seventies, accompanied by the growing strength of the immigrant churches, and especially the Catholic church with its expanding parochial school system. While the antagonism between public and parochial schools is usually ascribed to the prejudice of the Yankees, they had allies among the foreign-born and their children. Most of the rapid growth of the Catholic church in Wisconsin after 1870 was owed to German, Polish, and Bohemian immigration, mostly from German and Austrian sovereignties. The earlier German immigrants, most of whom were Protestant or anticlerical freethinkers, were equally hostile to the growth of Catholicism.[66]

The sheer size of the Catholic church in relation to other religious groups, plus the tendency of this later immigration to cluster in urban-industrial settings, made Catholics more noticeable to others as well as more assertive themselves. The hierarchy and most of the laity of Wisconsin Catholicism were German, well acquainted with their Lutheran and anticlerical critics, and much aware of Bismarck's Kulturkampf of the seventies.[67]

Milwaukee's German press, because it represented religious and political views in all their diversity, was in a continual family row, monitored gleefully by the *Sentinel's* German-speaking editors. One thing that the Lutheran *Germania* and the liberal *Herold* did agree upon was the evidence of Catholic clerical dictation to the laity in political matters. This was supplemented by continual suspicion of Catholic purposes: to get part of the public school and eleemosynary institutions' tax revenues; or, alternately, to gain control of the public schools. *Germania*, for instance, once counted all the Catholics who held posts as school board members, superintendents, or principals. This, according to *Germania*, could only be for the purpose of subverting the public schools. Of course, a favorite route for the Irish to middle-class circum-

[66]Koppel S. Pinson, *Modern Germany: Its History and Civilization* (New York, 1966 ed.), 175.

[67]Colman J. Barry, *The Catholic Church and German Americans* (Milwaukee, 1953), vii. The Kulturkampf refers to Chancellor Bismarck's efforts to impose some state control over Catholic schools and the appointment of bishops. The dogma of papal infallibility, proclaimed in 1870, was the ostensible reason. Pinson, *Modern Germany,* 186–189.

stances was through teaching in the public schools. One could not count German Catholics by looking at lists of names. But Irish names were readily recognized, and universally assumed to be Catholic and up to no good.[68]

The American middle class had long since overcome its prejudice that the public schools were meant for the lower orders of society. Indeed, it was frequently charged that the high schools were elitist institutions designed to replace, at public expense, the private academies formerly patronized by the middle and upper classes. One indication that the middle class now felt that the public schools were meant for everyone was a growing interest in the statistics of school attendance. Superintendent Robert Graham brought this into sharp relief in his 1882 report. He observed that while city schools on the average held longer terms and had much better attendance records for those enrolled, they enrolled only an average 47 per cent of those of legal school age—between four and twenty—while the village and country schools had 64 per cent enrolled. He regretted that he lacked figures on private school (parochial) enrollments, since they obviously had a greater impact on city statistics. Nor was he able to get the desired data on those of "*real* school age, ages seven through fifteen." He nonetheless noted that "we have pretty definite data for determining that already causes are at work in our larger cities which, unchecked, must soon result in a large illiterate class."[69]

The legislative session of 1885 was a particularly productive one for public education. Superintendent Graham's 1882 report

---

[68]Milwaukee *Germania,* October 29, 1879. On April 6, 1874, the Milwaukee *Seebote,* semi-official organ of the Catholic hierarchy, complained that the Milwaukee *Herold* talked only about the religion of Democratic candidates, not where they stood on the issues. See also Carl H. Knoche, *The German Immigrant Press in Milwaukee* (New York, 1980), 237–264; the Milwaukee *Christian Statesman,* February 6, 1873, January 27, 1876, and January 8, 1880; and the *Salesianum,* 2 (May, 1874), p. 4, and 4 (February, 1877), p. 4, which discuss the pros and cons of church property taxation.

[69]Usher, *Wisconsin,* 2:386–387; Edgar G. Doudna, *The Making of Our Wisconsin Schools, 1848–1948* (reprinted by The State Centennial Committee, 1948, from the *Wisconsin Journal of Education,* January, 1948), 21–22; Wisconsin Superintendent of Public Instruction, *Annual Report,* 1882, pp. 13–14, 177–179, 218–219.

had directed attention to the problems of growing illiteracy in the cities, despite the enlarged role of the parochial schools there. Successive superintendents and governors had pointed out the penurious role of the state government in supporting the public schools, which according to the constitution were the ultimate responsibility of the state. Governor Jeremiah Rusk, in his messages to the sessions of 1883 and 1885, noted the favorable circumstance that the state's general fund was running a substantial and growing surplus.[70]

As if to bring everything into conjunction, Science Hall, opened in 1876 as the most commodious building on the University campus, was destroyed by fire in December, 1884. While it may seem strange to celebrate such an event, it forced the 1885 legislature to face the problem of the inadequate nature of the state's support of the University, the common schools, and other state institutions. To add to the felicity of the occasion, Colonel William F. Vilas, a regent of the University and an acknowledged leader in the Democratic party, was elected to the assembly. He took charge of the crisis presented by the destruction of Science Hall to get the legislature committed to rebuilding and to continued support of the University, before leaving to join President Cleveland's cabinet.[71]

Yet another conjunction occurred just before the burning of Science Hall. In November, 1884, Milwaukee's Archbishop Michael Heiss returned from a plenary council of the American bishops with word that parochial schools were to be practically

[70]The school fund, entirely separate from general fund tax monies, was based upon the sale of lands allotted at the time of statehood, plus some escheats. Not only was there an established notion that the school lands and funds had been grossly mismanaged a generation earlier, but funds had been borrowed from it during the Civil War without subsequent full restitution. The contribution of these funds to the support of the common schools had fallen by the seventies to about 40 cents per child per year. Doudna, *Making of Our Wisconsin Schools,* 4–5; Patzer, *Public Education in Wisconsin,* 454–455, 460–462.

[71]Pike, *A Student at Wisconsin,* 21–27; Horace S. Merrill, *William Freeman Vilas: Doctrinaire Democrat* (Madison, 1954), 68–75.

mandatory for the faithful. The nature of this decision was no secret. The anti-Catholic press was eager to spread the news.[72]

The legislature, given the circumstances—namely, its past failure to support the public schools financially; the prosperous condition of the general fund; its recent generosity to the University; the threat of an urban subclass of illiterates; and a determination on the part of the Catholic hierarchy to press for the broadest possible parochial school system, which usually meant instruction in the language of the majority of the parish—saw the light. Legislation was passed to fix a one-mill levy on the state's property tax to be dedicated to the school fund. It was no tremendous boon, since it initially only trebled the pittance of state support for the school fund. Nonetheless, it marked the legislature's path towards a sterner compulsory attendance law than the ineffective 1879 statute, and focused attention on the problem of "urban illiteracy," which came to be interpreted as the inability to read and write in English. It must be observed that Bay View and Haymarket were but a year away.[73]

Suffice to say, the gloomy 1873 report of Superintendent Samuel Fallows on growing illiteracy, massive nonattendance, the casual short terms of rural schools, and the lack of preparation of the nonprofessional teaching force was quite in contrast with the optimistic review offered twenty years later by his successor in the office, Oliver E. Wells. Wells remarked that the 1890 federal census indicated that nonattendance had fallen from Fallows' figure of one-third to about 6.4 per cent: "The fact is that very few children grow up to the age of 20 without gaining a rudimentary education in school." Although the receipts from taxes fell as the 1893 depression took hold, teachers' wages had not suf-

[72]Barry, *Catholic Church and German Americans*, 186. See also Richard J. Orsi, "Humphrey Joseph Desmond: A Case Study in American Catholic Liberalism" (master's thesis, University of Wisconsin, 1965). Desmond supported public schools.

[73]Patzer, *Public Education in Wisconsin*, 76–77, 461. Archbishop Heiss had earlier given confidential instructions that confessors must force parents to support parochial schools. See the minutes of the Milwaukee Archdiocese, October 13, 1881, in file 31 of the Archdiocesan Archives at the Salzmann Library, St. Francis Seminary.

fered. "This, in connection with the longer tenure of teachers, shows that the people begin to value good teachers as of first importance to the school. . . . There is notable improvement in the qualification of teachers. Naturally, the cities absorb most of the product of the normal schools. A few years ago, none of the normal graduates, and but few under-graduates could be found in the country schools. Now they constitute one-tenth of the country teaching force. . . ." He noted that the training of teachers who enrolled at institutes had changed dramatically. Just 1,629 of them had attended common school only, while 1,396 had attended colleges or normals, and 3,337 came from the high schools.[74]

Attendance and teacher preparation may have improved, but learning remained much by rote and students were not to question the rigid prescriptions imposed. When President John Bascom met with Fred Turner's sophomore class to inaugurate their first real year as University students rather than preparatory initiates, there was no discussion of intellectual values or of a wider world being opened to them. Bascom instructed them in the dangers of eating between meals, urged them to have their food well cooked, to eat slowly, to exercise, and—above all—to shun alcohol in any form.[75]

The older generation that was improvising this new educational system was looking beyond its own children. It left to the pulpit and to the religious press the impolite attacks upon the Catholic church, its many foreign-language parochial schools, and its militant clergy. This generation was aware that many Germans of the earlier immigration considered themselves liberals, which included most of those who were attracted to politics

[74]Wisconsin Superintendent of Public Instruction, *Annual Report,* 1873, pp. 3–32; *ibid., Biennial Report,* 1894, pp. 29–33. These attendance figures are based on the more realistic school ages, seven to fifteen. In 1873, of 7,619 teachers' certificates issued, 6,986 were of the lowest grade, indicating a common school education only.

[75]Billington, *Turner,* 20. Charles Van Hise found Bascom's officiousness in the regulation of the boys in the dormitories silly and childish. The incident described fits this conclusion. Maurice M. Vance, *Charles Richard Van Hise: Scientist Progressive* (Madison, 1960), 15–16.

and political office, and who were readers of the *Herold* or possibly of *Germania*, rather than of the Democratic and Catholic *Seebote*. They were allies and political partners, in other words. If the higher reaches of the new educational system reached only a privileged few, there remained the problem of bringing those outside the public school system to a proper understanding of the organized institutions of society.

The steady lengthening of the school term, until it approached nearly the present-day school year for children between ages seven and fifteen, was a logical outcome of the professionalization of public school teaching. It answered the employment needs of the profession as well as those of middle-class children. It also—presumably—provided an escalator for the children of those lower on the socio-economic scale. As observed earlier, this doubtless worked best in the village, where there were fewer demands for a child's labor than on a farm, or in the city where child labor in factories was centered. Another need to be answered by the public schools was the inculcation of the language, social values, and citizenship requirements of society into the school-age children of the immigrants.

The first compulsory school law in 1879 required only twelve weeks of attendance annually, and that not continuous. It was also loaded with exemptions: living more than two miles from school by the nearest traveled road; the child's labor needed by the family; or reasons of health on the part of the child or someone else in the family. The 1879 law's weaknesses reflected the state superintendents' uncertainty over the solution to a recognized problem, but the easy exemptions and lax enforcement by the local school boards rendered it largely unheeded. The long step forward was to be the 1889 compulsory education statute known as the Bennett Law, which defined not only attendance but also what constituted a legal school. The latter provision put the fat in the fire, but this story properly belongs with the discussion of politics.[76]

[76]Wisconsin Superintendent of Public Instruction, *Annual Report,* 1873, "Special Report on Compulsory Education," 33–72; *ibid.,* 1874, liii–lxviii; Patzer, *Public Education in*

Concern for young people and the acquisition by immigrants of an appreciation for American values and culture reached beyond the schools. The free library movement in Wisconsin owes something to this concern. Prior to the seventies, Wisconsin's libraries were generally maintained by organizations such as a lyceum society or young men's association. These had discontinuous histories, for by their nature libraries require broad general support. They need space, professional oversight, someone in attendance, and a budget for continuous new purchases. The impetus towards public tax support was generally a Yankee concern. A Janesville assemblyman initiated an 1872 law authorizing public support, with a one-mill levy if accepted by the voters in a village or city.

Libraries were objects of philanthropy before Andrew Carnegie turned this into a wholesale operation. Among such was Cadwallader C. Washburn's gift in 1882 of $50,000 for a public library in La Crosse. Similar gifts resulted in libraries in Ashland, Merrill, Menomonie, Beaver Dam, Oshkosh, and other cities within the next dozen years. They usually memorialized the donor or a relative. Donors expected public commitment for the continuance of the institutions. Public support had become widespread by the nineties. A state library association was formed in 1891, followed a few years later by the Wisconsin Free Library Commission.

One may read all sorts of motives into the library movement: provision of a wholesome environment and center of interest for youth; an alternative to the saloon for workingmen; an Americanization center for immigrants; and even public toilets for farmers in town for the day. In general, libraries found their best customers among school children, young women who were the principal audience of the popular novelists of the time, and wom-

---

*Wisconsin,* 75–77, 458–465; Wisconsin Bureau of Labor and Industrial Statistics, *Biennial Report,* 1897–1898, pp. 490–554. Evidently rural objections to a compulsory statute declined as rural schools became more accessible and attention centered on urban problems. The Bennett Law retained the modest twelve weeks' requirement, which was certainly a concession to rural school attendance patterns.

en's study clubs. It was a difficult task to improve the minds of those who did not come around.[77]

Private philanthropy became an important force in fields other than libraries as personal fortunes mounted, although much giving was by those of less spectacular means. Certainly most philanthropy of the time went to churches. But Wisconsin's private colleges also depended heavily upon gifts, particularly for buildings. Lawrence and Ripon, for instance, were recipients of generous gifts from lumbermen Philetus Sawyer and Orrin Ingram. Beloit College had an important financial angel in a Chicago real estate operator, as well as local supporters. As a rule, businessmen tended to add some strings, often requiring commitments from others. The Washburn observatory on the University of Wisconsin campus was given contingent upon legislative support. Beloit College also received the gift of an observatory— considered essential for an institution with scholarly pretensions.[78]

"The Methodist people began their camp meeting the 3rd at this place. They have had but three pleasant days: Saturday, Sunday, and Monday. We went Saturday afternoon and all day Sunday. They have a very nice tent furnished with camp chairs which are very comfortable. Heard some good speaking and met

[77]John C. Colson, " 'Public Spirit' at Work: Philanthropy and Public Libraries in Nineteenth-Century Wisconsin," in *WMH,* 59 (Spring, 1976), 192-209; David I. Macleod, "Carnegie Libraries in Wisconsin" (master's thesis, University of Wisconsin, 1967), published with the same title (Madison, 1968); Kathryn Saucerman, "A Study of the Wisconsin Library Movement, 1850-1900" (master's thesis, University of Wisconsin, 1944); Frank A. Hutchins, "Free City Libraries," in Stearns, ed., *Columbian History of Education in Wisconsin,* 413-421; Theresa West, "Milwaukee Public Library," in *ibid.,* 422-427; Clarence B. Lester, "The Library Movement in Wisconsin," in Milo M. Quaife, *Wisconsin: Its History and Its People, 1634-1924* (4 vols., Chicago, 1924), 2:411- 432. See also Alice E. Smith, "Business and Culture in Nineteenth-Century Wisconsin," in *Transactions of the Wisconsin Academy of Sciences, Arts and Letters,* 54, Part A (1965), 82; and Lilly M. E. Borresen, "Young Men's Library Association and Other Antecedents of La Crosse Public Library,' " in La Crosse County Historical Society, *La Crosse County Historical Sketches,* series 2 (La Crosse, 1935), 37-50.

[78]Smith, "Business and Culture," *Transactions of the Wisconsin Academy of Sciences, Arts and Letters,* 54, Part A, 77-82; Richard N. Current, *Pine Logs and Politics: A Life of Philetus Sawyer, 1816-1900* (Madison, 1950), 294-297; Edward D. Eaton, *Historical Sketches of Beloit College* (New York, 1928), 82-83; Curti and Carstensen, *University of Wisconsin,* 1:356; Stearns, ed., *Columbian History of Education in Wisconsin,* 87-293.

a good many acquaintances." So wrote Mrs. Maria Merrill of Sechlerville in rural Jackson County on a June day in 1890. It is worth quoting for what is left out, for that is all she wrote about the event, although her journal contained many references of a conventional religious nature. It is difficult to imagine such a person experiencing a Methodist camp meeting forty or fifty years earlier, then coming away with no more than a comment on the fixtures, meeting friends, and hearing some good speaking. The fire had been going out for some time, but the victory of the sentimental evangelists was complete by the time of Mrs. Merrill's pleasant visit. Henry Ward Beecher, Dwight L. Moody, and others had intervened. They had changed the nature of the revival experience. It was conducted with more decorum. "What the fear of hell-fire had been in an earlier day, bathos and nostalgia were to Moody's."[79]

Early in the nineteenth century, New England youths were expected to undergo a period of religious anxiety beginning at about the age of eight to twelve, which was to culminate in a conversion experience in their latter teens. Like the fear of hell-fire, this Calvinist orthodoxy had undergone serious revision for Wisconsin's young people of New England ancestry. For one thing, the Calvinist notion of election was muted, and the Congregational and Presbyterian denominations identified with it had not transplanted to Wisconsin nearly so successfully as the free-will Methodists and Baptists.[80]

[79]Entry for June 10, 1890, in the Maria (Morton) Merrill Journal (typewritten copy); Bernard A. Weisberger, *They Gathered at the River: The Story of the Great Revivalists and Their Impact Upon Religion in America* (Boston, 1958), 217.

[80]Joseph F. Kett, "Growing Up in Rural New England, 1800–1840," in Tamara K. Hareven, ed., *Anonymous Americans: Explorations in Nineteenth-Century Social History* (Englewood Cliffs, 1971), 4–5; Current, *Civil War Era*, 547–548. Successful preachers were as sought after as successful coaches today, and commanded spectacular salaries from fashionable city congregations. The Reverend Doctor John L. Dudley was called to Plymouth Congregational Church in Milwaukee in 1868 from Middleton, Connecticut. His liberal theology so attracted local Unitarians that their own church closed, it was claimed. Wealthy Milwaukeeans purchased a suitable home for him, and his sermons appeared verbatim in a local paper. Frederick I. Olson, "My Search for Mrs. Dudley," in the *Historical Messenger of the Milwaukee County Historical Society,* 13 (December, 1957), 12.

A sort of benign denominationalism had overtaken American Protestantism. As America's mobile population moved from state to state, farm to village, and village to city, church membership soared and sects proliferated, but most of them acquired a comfortable interchangeability, although retaining a strong competitive urge. An attempt at an "Evangelical Alliance for the State of Wisconsin" (1874–1877), composed of the largest Yankee denominations—Methodists, Congregationalists, Baptists, and Presbyterians—foundered at its second meeting. The purpose of the alliance was to serve small communities with interdenominational churches. No thought was given to co-operation with immigrant evangelical churches.[81]

The status of the American churches is suggested by the minutes of the annual meetings of the Congregational Church in Wisconsin. In 1882, the membership of 12,905 showed a decrease of 382 for the year, despite 923 new members. Wisconsin was contributing more members elsewhere than it gained by immigration: "This was not so in the earlier years of our history. Then our growth was from immigration as well as by conversion; not so now." The decline in the Sunday school program was even more disturbing. Over the preceding ten years, the average number reported in classes had fallen from 18,756 to 14,011— not exactly a prospering enterprise.[82]

One might have expected that the subjects of the Bay View riots and the relations of capital and labor would have been central topics of the annual meeting held in September, 1886, just four months after the tragic events in Milwaukee. Not a word. Milwaukee did draw attention: "We have also seen that our commercial metropolis has been made the scene, and the Lord's day the occasion of a drunken carousal and the celebra-

[81]Evangelical Alliance for the State of Wisconsin, Papers; Carter E. Boren, "Divided Protestantism: A Unifying Force in Nineteenth-Century American Culture," in Margaret F. Morris, ed., *Essays on the Gilded Age* (Austin, 1973), 19–50; Sydney E. Ahlstrom, *A Religious History of the American People* (New Haven, 1972; Image Books paperback edition in two vols., New York, 1975), 2:324.

[82]Congregational and Presbyterian Convention of Wisconsin, *Annual Meeting Minutes*, 1882, p. 15. The joint convention with the Presbyterians was dissolved in 1883.

tion of inebriety. . . . We understand that the Lord's day was singled out from all the days devoted to the late Sangerfest, as the day on which to launch the greatest number of excursion trains . . . from all over the state to Milwaukee.'' But Milwaukee was not uppermost in the Congregationalists' minds. They were supporting missionaries in India and Turkey, and—closer to home—trying to save some of ''the lowest class of Germans'' who had been attracted to Utah by the Mormons.[83]

Young people were not particularly attracted to doctrinal differences among the American evangelical denominations. The ways to attract and hold them became more and more through meeting their social needs, not just in their home setting but also when they left home. The YMCA and YWCA, which grew rapidly in Wisconsin after 1870, were typically nondenominational, but recognizably American evangelical. The Sunday School Union, revived in 1872 by a Chicago businessman allied with evangelist Dwight L. Moody, supplied the uniform lesson plans used by many of these churches, and led to interdenominational institutes for Sunday school teachers. Sunday school had been traditionally an adult activity in village and rural churches. It succumbed to grading and an emphasis upon children and young people. The Social Gospel movement, presumably designed to bring American churches closer to immediate social problems, was also interdenominational in character, as was the new style of revivalism.[84]

The American evangelical churches of Wisconsin met on interdenominational grounds by means of a series of axioms that set them apart from the foreign-born and their children. These axioms were: That the public schools were properly nonsectarian, meaning that they were based upon a nondenominational creed acceptable to American evangelicals; that everyone should

[83]Congregational Convention of Wisconsin, Annual Meeting Minutes, 1886, pp. 21, 98, 108–109.

[84]Ahlstrom, *Religious History of the American People,* 2:197–201, 260–273; Young Men's Christian Association, *Proceedings,* 1870, xxx; *ibid.,* 1879, lxxxiii; *ibid., Year Book,* 1890, pp. 95, 138–139, 151; Hudson, *American Protestantism,* 118–121; Hugh H. Knapp, ''The Social Gospel in Wisconsin, 1890-1912'' (master's thesis, University of Wisconsin, 1968).

support the public schools financially and ensure their children an American education, taught in English, and covering the subjects defined by legislation as necessary to educated citizenship; that the American Sabbath, as received from New England Puritanism, was enjoined by the Bible and properly enforced by statute and local ordinances; that the regulation or prohibition of alcohol was desirable and properly a subject for general law rather than local custom or individual preference; that Catholics, being subjects of a foreign authority concerning whatever that authority chose to define as matters of faith and morals, could not be expected to exercise properly the duties and obligations of American citizenship as intended by the founding fathers.

Everyone who professed membership in or attachment to the American evangelical community did not necessarily subscribe with equal vehemence to all of the above axioms. But they were pretty sure to affirm the description of the public schools and to view Catholics with some suspicion. That took in a lot of territory, even if one granted laxness on Sunday observance and the regulation of liquor. The problem for the moderates on these latter scores was that the terms of the debate were usually defined by the clergy, who had a vested interest in pressing for action.

In Wisconsin, a Catholic disadvantage in the debate was their clerical leadership, given the strictly authoritarian nature of the church's organization and the conservative German hierarchy in Wisconsin. Pope Pius IX (1846–1878) had witnessed the revolutions of 1848, the loss of the papal temporal power in Rome, the overthrow of Napoleon III in France, the Paris Commune, and Bismarck's Kulturkampf in Germany. In reaction, he gave two important hostages to American evangelical prejudice. The 1864 encyclical, *Syllabus errorum*, was taken as a condemnation of democracy. The doctrine of papal infallibility in matters of faith and morals, pronounced in 1870, gave new fuel to anti-Catholicism, which had been somewhat subdued since the Civil War. The German-American hierarchy was sympathetic to Pius IX's views. His successor, Leo XIII (1878–1903), a diplomat of rare skill, had to deal with the strong nationalist movements within the church in the United States resulting from the increasing numbers of large ethnic groups congregating in the cities. It was one thing to accommodate within the Catholic church national differences between countries, and quite another to accommodate them within an American city or parish. In Wisconsin, Irish and German Catholics had long been at odds. By the eighties the growth of the Polish community, and of other Catholics in lesser numbers, complicated problems.[85]

The evidences of cultural and religious conflict between American Protestants and immigrant Catholics tend to obscure the role of other important groups. Useful numbers are difficult to come by. Census forms never inquired directly about church affiliation, and the definition of affiliation differed among churches. An informed guess is that by 1890 the proportions of church membership in Wisconsin were approximately one-half Catholic and one-third Lutheran, the remainder belonging to other Protestant churches. This applied not to the whole population, but to the one-third that was claimed as active communicants or members.[86]

Yankees could not remain unaware that the Lutherans were somehow allied with them, and that they were no monolithic communion as Yankees perceived the Catholics. One did not have to be particularly observant to know that German and Scandinavian Lutherans organized separately and were as addicted to schismatic proliferation as were the American churches. (At one time there were sixty-six independent Lutheran church synods in the United States.) Germans represented much

[85]Ahlstrom, *Religious History of the American People*, 2:298–353; Clifton E. Olmstead, *History of Religion in the United States* (Englewood Cliffs, 1960), 426–434. Barry, *Catholic Church and German Americans*, deals mostly with the conflicts within the American hierarchy between the Irish and Germans.

[86]Current, *Civil War Era*, 543, estimates that Catholics comprised not more than 25 per cent of church members in 1860, and had grown slightly larger than Methodist membership by 1870. According to the 1890 census, Catholics outnumbered Methodists, 249,829 to 43,696, and all of the various Lutheran synods numbered 160,919. Together, the Catholics and Lutherans equalled 73.8 per cent of Wisconsin's 556,355 church members. *Ninth Census of the United States, 1890: Statistics on Churches in the United States, Volume IX, Part 1*, pp. 38–44. There was, of course, no uniformity in the ways the various churches counted their communicants, which generally gave the Catholics a considerable edge.

the largest Lutheran population in Wisconsin, despite the fact that most Scandinavians were Lutherans. Ernest Bruncken succinctly stated the central fact about German Lutherans in Wisconsin: "There are no 'liberal' German churches in this country. . . . If a German-American becomes a 'Liberal' (Freisinnig), he at once severs all connection with churches of any kind, unless he has become so Americanized as to prefer attendance at a native-American church."[87]

In general, the tendency of German and Scandinavian Lutherans was to reject the formalism which characterized the church in their homeland, where it was a state church associated with upper-class privilege. The men who assumed leadership here were opposed to everything that this represented, but were not in agreement on their American alternatives, hence the extreme fragmentation. To vastly oversimplify, the largest synods in Wisconsin became the confessional Missouri and Wisconsin synods. While the several German Lutheran synods became designated by states—Missouri, Wisconsin, Ohio, Michigan, Iowa, Minnesota—this referred to their origins and not to their geographical distribution. What they were generally agreed upon was a strict conservatism, the importance of the German language to maintenance of the faith, and separation of church and state. Missouri and Wisconsin synod Lutherans resembled the Catholics in their emphasis upon a parochial school system, and they actively discouraged their young people from social intercourse with others, even of different Lutheran synods.[88]

While it is hazardous to generalize about such a diverse group, the Scandinavian Lutherans generally split along national lines,

[87]Ahlstrom, *Religious History of the American People,* 2:215–223; Roy A. Suelflow, *A Plan for Survival* (New York, 1965); Ernest Bruncken, "How Germans Become Americans," in *SHSW Proceedings,* 1897, p. 109.

[88]A prominent fault line in German-American Lutheranism was the insistence upon theological consensus of the Missouri and Wisconsin synods. Carl F. W. Walther (1811–1887), founder of Concordia Seminary of the Missouri synod, was accused of being "a crypto-Calvinistic predestinarian." This type of controversy split many German and Norwegian congregations in the later nineteenth century. Ahlstrom, *Religious History of the American People,* 2:217–219. The Milwaukee *Sentinel,* August 6, 1882, and Milwaukee *Germania,* October 20, 1880, have stories on such battles within congregations.

as when the Norwegians split from the Scandinavian Augustana synod because of the preponderance of Swedes in the synod. Further schisms involved doctrinal conflicts loosely described as between low church and high church elements—pietists and liturgists. To the outside observer, the readiest difference between German Lutherans and Scandinavian Lutherans was the willingness of the latter to send their children to the public schools, and to give them religious instruction elsewhere. At the same time, it should be noted, few ethnic groups have so successfully maintained their identity and language as have the Norwegians.[89]

The central assumption of the Yankee churches was that strangers should know enough to conform to Yankee standards. A notable example of this attitude was an article, "The German Sunday," by William E. Armitage, Wisconsin bishop of the Protestant Episcopal Church. Armitage wrote a gently chiding sermon which appeared in the initial issue of the *Transactions* of the new Wisconsin Academy of Sciences, Arts and Letters. The Continental Sunday was, as he pointed out to his compatriots, an issue on which Catholics, Lutherans, and anticlerics from Germany would unite to defend. His Yankee audience could have learned something right there. What it came down to was that the Germans should be persuaded "in return for American opportunities and rights . . . to give up the custom, or be held responsible for the flood of evil to which it opens the gates."[90]

American Protestant suspicions of the Catholic church were historic as well as grounded in contemporary perceptions. There were many points of friction, including the "exotic" public spectacles of the church in the metropolis. Mounted Polish Knights were something relatively new in Milwaukee's experience. When Michael Heiss returned to Milwaukee as an archbishop in April, 1882, the *Sentinel*, which always turned an unfriendly eye on the Catholics at election time, devoted ten columns to the event. Nine years later, James Cardinal Gibbons was the celebrity at

[89]Suelflow, *A Plan for Survival*, 141–151; Ahlstrom, *Religious History of the American People*, 2:215–216, 220–222.
[90]*Transactions of the Wisconsin Academy of Sciences, Arts and Letters*, 1 (1870), 62–71.

the investiture of Heiss's successor, Archbishop Frederick Katzer.[91]

What outsiders failed to understand about the German Catholic hierarchy of Wisconsin, which appeared to be in firm control, was that hierarchy's perception of its own precarious hold. Because of their experience with the Prussian state and Yankee hostility, immigrant German Catholics were suspicious of the state here, and they were devoted to the preservation of German Catholicism as a separate entity on the American scene. This goal was largely achieved in Wisconsin, at the cost of considerable friction with smaller national groups. But the real problems mounted with the growth of the Polish population in Wisconsin, and with the national recognition of the Irish hierarchy as the leaders of the movement to Americanize the Catholic church. In other words, Wisconsin Catholicism was not a monolith at all, and what often seemed single-minded offensive tactics sprang from a fearful defensive psychology.

Nationally, the Irish won the day. Archbishop John Ireland of St. Paul, Minnesota, led in making concessions on the issue of parochial versus public schools. While the German-American bishops were quite ready to seek European aid in maintaining their stance on separate parishes for representative nationalities, and even proposed a similar formula for the American hierarchy, Gibbons and other Americanists deftly undercut them in Rome. The final act came in 1891, when Cardinal Gibbons officiated at Archbishop Katzer's investiture. He told the assembled Germans in Milwaukee that there could be only an American Catholic church here. Reminiscing years later, Cardinal Gibbons recalled: ''It was one of the most audacious things I ever did, but it had to be done. When I finished they were aghast. . . .''[92]

It is all too easy to assume, from the ubiquity of references to

[91]Milwaukee *Sentinel*, April 24, 1882; Milwaukee *Germania*, April 2, 1884. *Germania*, the Lutheran German paper, thought the Catholics particularly adept at creating public spectacles and demonstrations, especially as election time neared. Barry, *Catholic Church and German Americans*, 161–163.

[92]Barry, *Catholic Church and German Americans*, 163. Barry's book is the extended account of this struggle to define the Catholic church in the United States.

the ongoing controversies that centered on religious and cultural differences, that this was a dangerous minefield for politicians. But there is ample evidence that despite the sound and the fury, there were wide areas of tolerance. Robert M. La Follette enjoyed a successful political career as a three-term congressman in the eighties, while representing a district dominated by Yankee types, without being a churchgoer. As he cheerfully admitted: "I got fed up on that sort of thing as a boy. My step-father insisted on entertaining the Baptist minister every Sunday." His own father had been an agnostic. Burr Jones, who held the same congressional seat just before La Follette, greatly admired his (Jones's) step-father, who was an agnostic in a community that was more familiar with the word "unbeliever."[93]

Religion bore rather lightly on many successful politicians of the day. One finds little reference to their own religious identity or its influence on them in the biographies of such successful political figures as William F. Vilas, Philetus Sawyer, and Matthew Carpenter, or in Isaac Stephenson's autobiography. One may hazard that the religious diversity of Wisconsin's electorate discouraged more than the most general references to religious faith on the part of these successful political practitioners. Of course, United States senators—and all four of the above were that—were elected by the legislature in their time, not by the general public. When a Methodist minister took advantage of the invitation to offer the opening prayer for the Wisconsin assembly to condemn dancing and the exhibition of too much gaiety and fun on the part of the assembly members, "the prayer caused a good deal of merriment, and was looked upon in the light of a good joke."[94]

When the minister of a Milwaukee Methodist congregation led a drive to prevent the managers of the Industrial Exposition Building from offering door prizes to boost attendance, he was told to mind his own business by one of the directors, who pointedly remarked that his colleagues were leading businessmen

---

[93]Thelen, *Early Life of Robert La Follette*, 13–14; Jones, *Reminiscences*, 12, 20–21.
[94]Milwaukee *Sentinel*, March 20, 1873.

who "also support the churches." The *Sentinel* editorialized: "A man with a dull sense of the ordinary courtesies of civilized life, a man intolerant and hungry for notoriety, can hardly do better than to go into the pulpit if he can find a congregation that will endure him." These were strong words from the state's leading spokesman for Republican orthodoxy.[95]

If one were asked to name a sport, recreational activity, or amusement that was in any way unique to Wisconsin, or peculiarly identified with it, it is likely that the circus would be on any short list. But in fact the circus was in no way really unique to Wisconsin; rather, Wisconsin simply became the base for some early companies that happened to move to Delavan from the crowded field of western New York, following the Mabie Brothers Circus which arrived there in 1840. The Circus World Museum, established in 1959 at Baraboo, where the Ringling Brothers started their circus in the eighties, has done much to fix Wisconsin's reputation in the circus hierarchy. Delavan was the home for twenty-six circuses over the years—they folded and reorganized regularly—and between 1873 and 1893 at least nine towns and small cities in Wisconsin were home bases for one or more circuses.[96]

One might well argue that a more characteristic Wisconsin development than the circus, particularly in the years 1873–1893, was the mineral spring spa. Most Wisconsin history buffs have heard of Waukesha's past as the "Saratoga of the West." A wealthy New Yorker, Colonel Richard Dunbar, a sufferer from diabetes, decided that a Waukesha mineral spring had restored him to health. He organized the Bethesda Mineral Spring Company in 1869 to exploit his discovery. Dunbar was

[95]*Ibid.*, October 18, November 9, 1892.

[96]Richard E. Conover, *The Circus: Wisconsin's Unique Heritage* (Baraboo, 1967). Ayres Davies, "Wisconsin, Incubator of the American Circus," in *WMH*, 25 (March, 1942), 283–296, covers much the same ground, as does *Wisconsin Circus Lore,* compiled by the Federal Writers' Project of the Works Progress Administration (Madison, 1937). The best modern study of Wisconsin's role in circus history is Dean Jensen, *The Biggest, The Smallest, The Longest, The Shortest: A Chronicle of the American Circus from Its Heartland* (Madison, 1975).

aware of the rising popularity of the spa on the American scene. The idea of a summer vacation was reaching downward into an enlarging middle class, which was transforming such places from exclusive playgrounds for the conspicuously wealthy.

The literature on Waukesha emphasizes the brilliance of its season, and its clientele of wealthy Southerners and ailing national figures. This tends to miss the point, which entrepreneurs quickly grasped. The place was a gold mine. A pair of Chicago promoters with more imagination than Dunbar built an elaborate summer hotel, the Fountain Spring House, of dazzling size and magnificence. When it burned down four years after its opening, its 1878 replacement was one of the largest hotel structures west of the Alleghenies. It had a 300-foot frontage, featured deep verandas on three main floors, 300 rooms and suites, and impressive public rooms and dining facilities which made it the center for those who had come to be seen. By the nineties, Waukesha had thirty hotels and many boardinghouses, although the village had a modest permanent population. The Milwaukee Road claimed that it brought 8,000 to 10,000 passengers to Waukesha annually. The village was also served by the Chicago and North Western. The crowds vanished by late September. There were at least ten widely advertised springs in and around Waukesha by then, all with appropriate names: Bethesda, Glenn, Hygeia, Silurian, Arcadian, White Rock, Fountain, Clysmic, Lethean, and Vesta.

This hydrological bonanza was in trouble by the nineties. The depression was not the only factor. There were competing attractions of similar character. Every spring in southern Wisconsin, where the underlying strata of limestone produced water of similar properties, became a potential spa. Madison's Tonyawatha Springs Hotel, on the southeast shore of Lake Monona, became a competitor. There were similar promotions in Beaver Dam, Sparta, Palmyra, Beloit, Appleton, and other centers of life-prolonging waters. Probably the most certain income from this growing seasonal business was that of Professor Gustave Bode of

Milwaukee', an analytical chemist who provided the analyses, if not the proof, of curative powers.[97]

The railroads were quick to exploit and encourage the growing American penchant for active outdoor recreation. Strolling or riding about a spa in Waukesha did not satisfy the generation of men who had discovered the New York version of baseball in the Union army. Touring, hiking, fishing, sailing, and hunting offered more activity, variety, and a better respite from the summer's heat than did Waukesha and its like. Also, the mileage from Chicago to Ashland, or to St. Paul and beyond, was more profitable to Wisconsin railroads, which all terminated in Chicago. The Wisconsin Central, which went more directly northward than its rivals, built the rambling Chequamegon Hotel in Ashland that took several trainloads of vacationers and sportsmen to fill.[98]

One can readily perceive the changes of a few years. A brochure of 1879 advertising the new reach of western railroads, *The Golden Northwest*, included the Dakotas—then Dakota Territory—as well as northern Wisconsin and Minnesota. One illustration shows two fishermen, in business suits and bowlers—precursors of Calvin Coolidge—in a sylvan setting at the base of an impressive Minnesota waterfall. Just eight years later, a Chicago, Milwaukee & St. Paul Railway booklet, *Gems of the Northwest*, included a cut labeled "Camping Out." Again a sylvan setting,

---

[97]Lillian Krueger, "Waukesha: 'The Saratoga of the West,' " in *WMH*, 24 (June, 1941), 394–424; James Maitland, *The Golden Northwest* (Chicago, 1879), 19–45; Chicago, Milwaukee & St. Paul Railway, *Gems of the Northwest: A Brief Description of Prominent Places of Interest Along the Lines of the Chicago, Milwaukee and St. Paul Railway and Connecting Roads* (Milwaukee, 1885), 19–43; William J. Park and Co., *Madison, Dane County and Surrounding Towns* . . . (Madison, 1877), 214; Wisconsin Central Railroad, *Along the Line* ([Chicago?, 1893?]), 30. An interesting hustler was Dr. George E. Swan of Beaver Dam, who developed a spring in his pasture whose fanciful pavilion—all that remains of the busy spa—is now on the National Register of Historic Places. A homeopathic physician who had a highly successful patent medicine for "female weakness," Swan trumpeted: "I name this water Vita—or life—life to the whole urinary economy. . . ." See Larry A. Reed, "Dr. Swan's Restorative Waters," in *WMH*, 64 (Winter, 1980–1981), 124–126.

[98]Wisconsin Central Railroad, *Along the Line*, 1–2, 28.

From Maitland, *The Golden Northwest* (1879), 66.

it shows four sportsmen in nondescript costumes suitable for such activity, cooking a mess of fish beside their commodious tent. Their world illustrates many of the comforts and implements that American enterprise had quickly provided for the outdoorsman. The two men in the 1879 illustration appear to have transported direct from a street corner in Chicago's financial district to their wild setting, and provided only with pole, string, hook, and worms for the business at hand.[99]

[99]Maitland, *The Golden Northwest,* 46–66; Chicago, Milwaukee & St. Paul Railway, *Gems of the Northwest,* 69. The latter booklet is literature: it records the travels of a Boston millionaire's son who meets an acquaintance, a learned and widely traveled doctor from New Orleans, accompanied by his anxious daughter. Full of chance meetings that strain coincidence, it is recommended for those who would like some respite from thirty-second shrinking hemorrhoid commercials in favor of an earlier advertising style.

From CM&StP Railway,
*Gems of the Northwest* (1887), 50.

Joseph Schafer noted an important change in rural custom
that occurred during his youth:[100]

> About the year 1880 or 1881 (at least in southwestern Wisconsin)
> farm boys began to organize baseball clubs modeled after those
> already familiar in the towns. Having no Saturday afternoon
> holiday, the practice meets and games were played on Sunday
> afternoon. They attracted all the young folks, and a good many
> of the elders, and of course the farm hands. The result was
> wholesome in several ways. Though the games cost the players
> doubly sore muscles for a day or two during each week, and
> occasionally a broken finger, these gatherings put the cumulative

---

[100]Schafer, *Agriculture in Wisconsin,* 175; John R. Betts, *America's Sporting Heritage: 1850–
1950* (Reading, Massachusetts, 1974), 92–97; Barbara Greenwood, "Majors Return to
Milwaukee," in *Wisconsin Then and Now,* 16 (July, 1970), 1–3, 8; Robert Obojski, *Bush
League: A History of Minor League Baseball* (New York, 1975), 64–67; Dodgeville *Chronicle,*
May 12, 19, 1876, home of the Monitors, "of our glorious National Game."

force of social coöperation behind the unuttered demand of children for the recognition of the right to play. Incidentally, they went far to abolish Sunday work on farms and, by a natural reaction on the part of the church people, led in many places to the custom of a Saturday half-holiday.

Baseball was by all odds the great American game by the seventies. Milwaukee's earliest participation in a league dates from 1865, when the Northwestern Association was started in Chicago. Milwaukee had professional teams off and on from that date, but not for more than a year or two at a time until it joined the Western Association in 1888, from which eventually evolved the present American League. By the 1880's, semiprofessional teams were a regular feature of other cities, and even small towns. Almost every village and hamlet boasted an amateur team with avid fans.

If there was one aspect of organized recreation that was somewhat distinctive to Wisconsin, it was the Turnerbund and the many local Turner halls that featured gymnasia. Most YMCA's followed this model where they were able to be built. In 1880, George Brosius, director of the normal department of the German-American Turnerbund, led a team from Milwaukee to an international Turnfest at Frankfurt am Main, where the Milwaukee gymnasts took several prizes. A feature of Chicago's great fair of 1893 was a mass demonstration of turning exercises by 4,000 members of the Turnerbund.[101]

The University of Wisconsin was no leader in the introduction of sports. Although the normal schools at Platteville and Whitewater fielded baseball teams as early as 1867 and 1868 to play neighboring town teams, the University did not have a baseball team until 1882. These teams were organized and managed by students, but without a student association to give them continu-

[101]Henry C. A. Metzner, *A Brief History of the North American Gymnastic Union*, trans. Theo. Stempfel, Jr. (Indianapolis, 1911), 50–51; John A. Krout, *Annals of American Sport* (*The Pageant of America* series, vol. 15, New Haven, 1929), 209; Lizzie R. Johnstone, "Camp Brosius," in *WMH*, 10 (December, 1926), 170–174; Emil Dapprich, "National German-American Teachers' Seminary," in Stearns, ed., *Columbian History of Education in Wisconsin*, 317–319.

ity there were periods when no teams were fielded. Nor did the University teams worry much about gate receipts beyond providing travel expenses, even as sports and sporting news assumed a central place in the American male consciousness. The Milwaukee *Herold* boasted in 1886 that it was the first German-American newspaper in the nation to have a news wire service and the first to have a regular baseball column. But when the University belatedly took up football in 1887, by which time Ivy League teams had created an audience for the game, it created no great stir. In 1892, the University eleven played Northwestern University in Milwaukee before a Thanksgiving Day crowd of 500. On the same day, a crowd of 4,500 turned out to watch six hours of bicycle races at Milwaukee's Industrial Exposition Building. The *Sentinel* chided its readers for their lack of enthusiasm for football, which was a Thanksgiving Day staple in the Northeast.[102]

One problem with college athletics was the lack of homogeneity of the student bodies. At the normal schools until well into the nineties, most of the students were schoolteachers of all ages trying to catch up with new requirements for upgraded teaching certificates. As late as 1889–1890, Oshkosh Normal had only twenty-eight high school graduates in a student body of nearly 500. Also, there was the simple matter of emphasis. The traditional literary and debating societies remained a central interest of student life. A biographer of Robert M. La Follette compared his triumph in a six-state oratorical contest in 1879 as the nearest thing to a Rose Bowl victory a century later.[103]

There was much that was faddish in athletic activities. Sports came to receive more and more attention because, as even the German-language Milwaukee *Herold* recognized, baseball, football, horse racing, sculling, yachting, bicycle racing, and other sports news sold papers. Most of these sports could be enjoyed

[102]Ronald A. Smith, "Athletics in the Wisconsin State University System: 1867–1913," in *WMH*, 55 (Autumn, 1971), 3–6; Pike, *A Student at Wisconsin*, 136–155; Milwaukee *Herold*, October 9, 1886, April 1, 1890; Milwaukee *Sentinel*, November 25, 1892.

[103]Smith, "Athletics in the Wisconsin State University System," *WMH*, 55:8; Thelen, *Early Life of Robert La Follette*, 44.

vicariously by amateurs. News stories created sports personalities and contests which became subjects for animated conversations in shops and offices. Some professional and amateur sports caught the public fancy only momentarily. Pedestrianism was such a fad in the seventies. People paid to watch walkers circle an indoor track in endurance and distance contests, or followed the exploits of long-distance walkers in the press. Archery had a vogue, as did croquet, probably because women could take part despite their restrictive costumes. There was a great boom in roller rinks in the eighties. There was very little pavement even in cities, so skating was not an activity that people learned in childhood. But rinks were expensive to build and to maintain, and "proper people" frowned upon the mixing of classes and forbade their children to go. As with many contrived and commercialized diversions, the interest quickly faded.[104]

A consuming interest was horses. The railroads made it possible for people to see well-known trotters in local meets, handicapped against local favorites. J. I. Case owned a world-class harness horse, Jay-Eye-See, and it was a thrill to see Val Blatz's $5,000 matched pair pulling a sleigh along Grand Avenue (now Wisconsin Avenue) when a fresh snowfall made conditions right. Every community had comparable horses, and with more variety than even automobiles offer today.[105]

The horseless carriage—as a competing form of transporta-

[104]George S. Hage, "Games People Played: Sports in Minnesota Daily Newspapers, 1860–1890," in *Minnesota History*, 47 (Winter, 1981), 321–328, summarizes much that can be found as well in Wisconsin's press of the time, only no one has done it. See also Ted Vincent, *Mudville's Revenge: The Rise and Fall of American Sports* (New York, 1981), 36 ff; and Foster Rhea Dulles, *America Learns to Play: A History of Popular Recreation, 1607–1940* (New York, 1940), 182–185, 191–196.

[105]Frances Stover, "Trotting Races at Cold Spring Park," in the *Historical Messenger of the Milwaukee County Historical Society*, 10 (June, 1954), 14–16; John L. Mitchell, "Fine Horses and Horse-Breeding Facilities," in W. J. Anderson and Julius Bleyer, eds., *Milwaukee's Great Industries: A Compilation of Facts Concerning Milwaukee's Commercial and Manufacturing Enterprises, Its Trade and Commerce, and the Advantages It Offers to Manufacturers Seeking Desirable Locations for New or Established Industries* (Milwaukee, 1892), 117–122; Milwaukee *Sentinel*, January 13, 1892; Bill Hooker, *Glimpses of an Earlier Milwaukee* (Milwaukee, 1929), 47–49.

tion—lay well in the future. In 1872–1873, an epizooty—an outbreak of equine distemper—incapacitated most urban horses for a number of weeks, and probably enhanced interest in Dr. John W. Carhart's steam buggy, which appeared on the streets of Racine briefly. But Carhart's vehicle was ahead of its time. The horse epidemic also brought a legislative challenge of $10,000 to anyone who could offer a mechanized substitute, "cheap and practical," that could win a race of 200 miles over the public roads between Green Bay and Madison. The offer brought two entries for the trial of July, 1878. One ungainly monster, the Oshkosh entry, actually finished the course, but it scarcely fit the conditions of the challenge, since it looked more like a primitive locomotive than a roadster.[106]

The "safety" bicycle—with wheels of the same size—was introduced in the eighties and quickly found an avid following. It probably had as much influence on the good roads movement of the 1890's as did farmers' organizations or the appearance of the first real automobiles. Milwaukee had two widely recognized competitors in cycling, W. C. Wegner and Walter C. Sanger, in a day when cycling was looked upon as a serious sport and recreation rather than as a way to get from here to there.[107]

Milwaukee was somewhat different among major American cities in how its people relaxed and enjoyed themselves. The city was well over half German in background, and Germans dominated important sectors of business, industry, and finance as well as furnishing the upper echelons of craftsmen, foremen, and managers. It is little wonder that Milwaukee was looked upon as a sort of transposed Rhineland city in physical appearance, cuisine, recreational facilities, and general ambience. Few of its rivals in size with large populations of German origin offered as much

[106]Howard Mead, Jill Dean, and Susan Smith, *Portrait of the Past: A Photographic Journey Through Wisconsin* (Madison, 1971), has pictures of the early mechanized age of transportation. The 1878 winner is on p. 96. See also Wisconsin State Highway Commission and United States Public Roads Administration, *A History of Wisconsin Highway Development, 1835–1945* (Madison, 1947), 19–20.

[107]Ballard Campbell, "The Good Roads Movement in Wisconsin, 1890–1911," in *WMH*, 49 (Summer, 1966), 276–278; Milwaukee *Sentinel*, October 20, 1892.

German theater and music as regular fare. The Continental
Sunday so deplored by Bishop Armitage held full sway. Milwaukee became a favorite convention city because of its beer gardens
and parks, its varied amusements, its competitive and generous
brewers, and its relaxed attitude towards types of entertainment
that scandalized Yankee sensibilities.[108]

Milwaukee's panorama painters gave the artistic community
an extra dimension. These were German artists who exploited a
European art form—a huge circular canvas displayed in special
buildings where the spectator stood on a platform surrounded by
the painting. Actual artifacts were placed in the foreground to
force perspective and fool the eye. The panoramas were usually
battle scenes, and certainly not art of the highest order. But the
artists were well-trained and it required quite a number to produce the works, which were a cut above the older style of panorama paintings that were rolled from one spool to another while
a pianist attempted to drown out the noise. Like the other professional men who made up the closely knit German intellectual
community, the panorama artists helped to fix Milwaukee in the
American and European consciousness as a distinctive American
city.[109]

A characteristic manifestation of western metropolitan status
was narcissism. Most any civic occasion provided an excuse for
another promotional pamphlet or a substantial commemorative
book fearlessly plagiarized from predecessors. Milwaukee was
not behindhand in this. Typical of the genre, and on an ambitious scale, was *Milwaukee's Great Industries: A Compilation of Facts
Concerning Milwaukee's Commercial and Manufacturing Enterprises, Its
Trade and Commerce, and the Advantages It Offers to Manufacturers*

[108]Bayrd Still, *Milwaukee: The History of a City* (Madison, 1948; reprinted, 1965), 257–
267; Theodore Mueller, "Milwaukee's German Heritage: 'Das Deutsch-Athen Am
Michigan See,' " in the *Historical Messenger of the Milwaukee County Historical Society,* 24
(September, 1968), 84–95; Hooker, *An Earlier Milwaukee,* 45–46, 67–70.

[109]Mueller, " 'Das Deutsch-Athen Am Michigan See,' " *Historical Messenger of the
Milwaukee County Historical Society,* 24:84–95; Frances Stover, "The Panorama Painters'
Days of Glory," *ibid.,* 12 (June, 1956), 2–7; Norman J. Kaiser, "A History of the
German Theater of Milwaukee from 1850 to 1890" (master's thesis, University of
Wisconsin, 1954); Porter Butts, *Art in Wisconsin: The Art Experience of the Middle West
Frontier* (Madison, 1936), 136.

*Seeking Desirable Locations for New or Established Industries*, published in 1892 by the Association for the Advancement of Milwaukee. No modest undertaking, it contained 365 pages, about 110 of them advertising. It began with two pages of one-liners about the city's wonders: "Milwaukee in a Nutshell." This was crowded with facts and figures about industries, transit facilities, gallons pumped by the water system, postal receipts, available bank capital, the absence of crime, poverty, and health problems, and so on. Buried among the exhilarating truths: "Milwaukee has one of the finest art galleries in the land [a gift of the pork packer Frederick Layton], and several of the best private art collections in the country." "Milwaukee has the best public school system of any city in the United States." "Milwaukee is recognized the world over as one of the great musical centers of the United States."[110]

No doubt Milwaukee's art world had improved since the report of the superintendent of the fine arts department of the state fair, held in Milwaukee in 1873: "Some sore head, each year the fair has been held in Milwaukee, has growled because no better exhibition was made in this department. This year, as recommended in my last report, this department was left entirely to the enterprise of Milwaukeeans, and they freely and generously contributed, *one oil painting* and *three chromos*, proving that the citizens of the metropolis of the state either had nothing to exhibit, or that they were wanting in pride and enterprise sufficient to make an exhibition."[111]

---

[110]Anderson and Bleyer, eds., *Milwaukee's Great Industries,* ix–x. Similar volumes, which might seem superfluous considering the dates: Milwaukee *Evening Wisconsin, City of Milwaukee, Souvenir Edition, 1892,* being a reprint of J. C. Miller, pub., *Milwaukee, Wisconsin, The Cream City: Its Unexampled Growth and Brilliant Prospects, A Glance at Its History, A Review of Its Commerce and A Description of Some of Its Business Enterprises . . .* (Milwaukee, 1891); Caspar & Zahn, *The City of Milwaukee: A Guide to the "Cream City" for Visitors and Citizens, Giving a History of the Settlement, Development and Present Importance of the City, With a Chronology of Interesting Events* (Milwaukee, 1886); Phoenix Publishing Co., *Milwaukee of Today: The Cream City of the Lakes, Its Growth, Resources, Commerce, Manufactures, Financial Interests, Public Institutions and Prospects* (Milwaukee, 1893). Similar effusions reached backward and forward through the years.

[111]J. O. Eaton, "Fine Arts," in Wisconsin State Agricultural Society, *Transactions,* 1873–1874, pp. 130–131.

To use the state fair exhibit as a measure of local taste is probably unfair. At its opening in 1881, the Milwaukee Industrial Exposition Building contained extensive art galleries. Local art patrons, particularly Mrs. Alexander Mitchell, generously loaned from their private collections. Mrs. Mitchell boldly collected the works of contemporary European and American painters, including works by James McNeill Whistler. The galleries were crammed: 242 oils, 118 watercolors, and several hundred etchings and copies of European art, most of it for sale. These industrial expositions had become commonplace in western cities, and eastern galleries took advantage of them to display their wares in the provinces.[112]

When John Fiske, a popular lecturer identified with advocacy of the theories of Charles Darwin and Herbert Spencer, came to Milwaukee in 1872 to lecture, he met his Harvard classmate, the linguist Jeremiah Curtin. Fiske found a warm welcome from some in the community: "I have Germans at my lectures, and I am smiled at at the big beer garden where a glass is ordered for 'Herr Professor'. . . ." He also dined with "Mr. and Mrs. E. P. Allis which have got 13 children and swear by Spencer." In the music department, Fiske attended a concert where "the music was good and would have been magnificent if performed by the Harvard orchestra and the Handel and Haydn. As it was, the singers were a little crude, and in the orchestra there was a predominance of brass. Three trombones against two double basses—Oh Lord! in an orchestra of 30 performers. Duly to appreciate this, you should remember that in the Harvard orchestra of 70 performers there are usually two trombones against seven double basses, which is the true proportion. This rasped my ear horribly; and the hautboy playing was fearfully

[112]Milwaukee Industrial Exposition Association, *Catalogue of the Art Department,* 1881 and 1892; Butts, *Art in Wisconsin*; Charlotte R. Partridge, "Wisconsin in the Field of Art," in the *Wisconsin Blue Book, 1929,* pp. 103–110; Walter F. Peterson, "Ladies' Art and Science Class: An Experiment in Adult Education," in the *Historical Messenger of the Milwaukee County Historical Society,* 19 (September, 1963), 2–6.

provincial." Milwaukee has always had problems measuring up to the "true proportions" of Boston and Cambridge.[113]

It would not do to leave the impression that the finer things were exclusively the province of the German-Americans. William Metcalf, of the successful shoe-manufacturing firm of Bradley and Metcalf, was from New York, the son of a portrait painter, Eliah Metcalf. A man of broad and scientific interests, William felt keenly that he had missed an education while amassing a fortune. He was an avid Sunday painter. Another of his enthusiasms was Wisconsin's famous photographer, H. H. Bennett of Wisconsin Dells, whom Metcalf subsidized, as well as becoming a valuable advisor on the artistic values of Bennett's craft.[114]

Ella Wheeler, the precocious poet of rural Dane County, quite astonished her audience, who remembered her verses in the temperance cause, when her volume *Poems of Passion* was published in 1883. She was summoned to Milwaukee to the salon of the reigning "Madame de Staël," Marion Churchill Dudley, the wife of the elderly Reverend Doctor John L. Dudley. Dudley was the city's leading preacher in the seventies. Mrs. Dudley, who briefly published her own and others' verses in *Spectroscope,* advised Ella that her "little love wails" were "calculated to spoil all chance of a desirable marriage."[115]

Vinnie Ream Hoxie (1847–1914), another talented female artist, was born in Madison, but her active career as a sculptress

---

[113][John Fiske], "Milwaukee, 1872," in the *Historical Messenger of the Milwaukee County Historical Society,* 8 (December, 1952), 7–10, four letters from John Fiske to his wife. Fiske did add: "On the other hand, flute was excellent, 'cello fair, and leading violin perfectly exquisite." See also Frederick I. Olson, "The Story of Jeremiah Curtin," *ibid.,* 9 (March, 1953), 3–7; and Joseph Schafer, ed., *Memoirs of Jeremiah Curtin* (Madison, 1940), 61.

[114]Sara Rath, *Pioneer Photographer: Wisconsin's H. H. Bennett* (Madison, 1979), 37–58. On Metcalf, see *The National Cyclopedia of American Biography* (53 vols., New York, 1893–1971), 3:249.

[115]*DWB*; Jenny Ballou, *Period Piece: Ella Wheeler Wilcox and Her Times* (Boston, 1940), 72–126; Olson, "My Search for Mrs. Dudley," *Historical Messenger of the Milwaukee County Historical Society,* 13:11–15. Ella Wheeler Wilcox has much of a page in Bartlett's *Familiar Quotations,* plus four notes. Mrs. Dudley is a Milwaukee footnote.

was pursued elsewhere.* The same was true of Helen Farn-
sworth Mears (1876–1916), after she found an audience with her
"Genius of Wisconsin," a sculpture that she did for the Wisconsin exhibit at the Chicago World's Columbian Exposition and
which now stands in the state capitol. Both women were extraor-
dinarily precocious, and both eventually made it into the *Dictionary of American Biography.*

Like the artists, Wisconsin's professional musicians of stature
who wished to pursue a career as soloists generally betook themselves elsewhere for training and opportunities. Milwaukee
aspired to a symphony orchestra in the nineties, but patronage
remained a barrier. There were professional artists, actors, and
musicians, mostly of German background, who could make a
living in Milwaukee if they supplemented their income by teaching. But there is not much to be said that sets these people apart
from their counterparts in other midwestern cities.

In the field of architecture, Edward Townsend Mix (1831–
1890) could accommodate himself to almost any desired style.
He designed the Industrial Exposition Building in Milwaukee, a
wondrous contraption, as well as the Mitchell Building and the
Alexander Mitchell residence. He was the state architect from
1874 to 1887, having held the post earlier in the sixties. He also
designed a number of churches in Milwaukee and elsewhere, and
the main building of the National Soldiers' Home in
Milwaukee.[116]

When Matson Holbrook conducted his interviews with Milwaukee workmen whose careers went back to the 1870's and
1880's, he usually asked them what they did for entertainment,

*Evidence from the 1850 and 1860 manuscript census schedules strongly suggests that
Vinnie Ream was born, not in 1847, but in 1842 or possibly 1841.

[116]Winifred V. Miller, "Wisconsin's Place in the Field of Music," in the *Wisconsin Blue
Book, 1929,* pp. 97–102; Smith, "Business and Culture," *Transactions of the Wisconsin
Academy of Sciences, Arts and Letters,* 54, Part A, 83; Wisconsin Federation of Music Clubs,
*Wisconsin Composers* (n.p., 1948); Herbert W. Rice, "Architect of Milwaukee," in the
*Historical Messenger of the Milwaukee County Historical Society,* 11 (June, 1955), 10–11; Mary
E. Pagel, "Edward Townsend Mix," *ibid.,* 21 (December, 1965), 110–116; Richard W.
E. Perrin, *The Architecture of Wisconsin* (Madison, 1967), 79–97; Randy Garber, ed., *Built
in Milwaukee: An Architectural View of the City,* Milwaukee Department of City Development
(Milwaukee, [1981?]), 37, 80, 98, 101–102, 107, 138, 140, 185.

assuming they had an acquaintance with the Schlitz Palm Garden, the Stadt or Pabst theaters, or other local wonders of the time. They often took some prodding. E. T. Stamm responded with some puzzlement: "In the evenings? No, why, when we got home we were so darned tired nobody'd want to go anywhere." Leo Wieland, an office worker at Pritzlaff Hardware, mentioned two factors that mitigated against an active social life. His hours were 7:30 A.M. to 6:00 P.M. six days a week, and "we didn't have much money to spend." His response to the query "What was your idea of a good evening's entertainment?" was succinct: "Staying home." Worse yet: "I never liked beer very much." Frank Fiedler remembered: "Practically the only recreation was the purchase of a so-called pint of beer for five cents. It was a two-quart pail, the inside rubbed with butter to keep down the foam. This was the evening's feast for the worker, his family, and possible guests." Fiedler implied that those workers who frequented the saloons were not going to get ahead in the world and own a little property. Besides, their nickel pint was a pint. Of course, Mr. Fiedler, who took his two-quart "pint" home in a bucket, was not hitting the free lunch. (This may help to clear up the mystery of the "free lunch.")[117]

In 1892, the *Sentinel* estimated that fully one-half of every man's earnings in Milwaukee was spent on eating and drinking. The average daily earnings were $2.25, but of the 90,000 family heads, 30,000 averaged $2.00. Twenty thousand earned only $1.50, and 15,000 earned $1.00 per day. A lucky 15,000 earned $3.00, and the numbers dwindled rapidly above that figure. The five-cent pail of beer at home was more characteristic than a night of revelry. It was the thirsty visitors from Chicago, up for the day on the whaleback excursion steamer *Christopher Columbus,* who sought the sybaritic pleasures of Das Deutsch-Athen.[118]

[117]Transcripts of interviews with E. T. Stamm, January 22, 1952, Leo Wieland, January 16, 1952, Frank H. Fiedler, February 19, 1952, and Charles Jopke, February 15, 1952, in the Matson Holbrook Interviews. Jopke, who took *his* pint standing at the bar, had fond memories of the competing free lunches.

[118]Milwaukee *Sentinel,* December 4, 1892; Theodore Mueller, "Sails and Steam on the Milwaukee," in the *Historical Messenger of the Milwaukee County Historical Society,* 10 (Decem-

At another level, the hundreds of comments by workmen recorded in the reports of the commissioner of labor statistics give a firm impression that Charles Jopke, who on his own volition went down to the tannery every Sunday morning to check the vats, was more typical than those who were swayed by the socialist rhetoric of Paul Grottkau. As Jopke remarked: "The Vogels had done something for me and I could do something for them." When asked whether he and his fellows talked about tanning on social occasions, Jopke replied: "Tanning? That's all we talked." He may have been more of a company man than the average, but it was from such attitudes that there arose the bread-and-butter unionism of the Wisconsin Federation of Labor and Victor Berger's peculiarly conservative socialism.[119]

One special group in Wisconsin society which came to have a profound effect upon the times was made up of Civil War veterans. The usual assumption is that the Grand Army of the Republic (GAR), organized in 1866, was a power in community and political life from that date. But its lasting influence dates from 1880, when a national encampment held in Milwaukee attracted 40,000 veterans and 100,000 other visitors to see the affair. Prior to this meeting, the GAR nationally had seemed to be withering on the vine.[120]

Wars that turn out to be more than adventures tend to alienate the participants. At its peak, the Grand Army of the Republic recruited no more than a fifth of the available veterans. Most veterans simply went home to no particular public welcome or

---

ber, 1954), 3–6, 16; Hooker, *An Earlier Milwaukee*, 45–47, 101–102. The *Sentinel* was complaining in 1882 about the rural Germanic custom of local businessmen who closed up shop and went home for the main meal of the day—not fitting for an enterprising city. Ten years later, it noted that the new electric street cars were at their busiest from noon to 2:00 P.M. because the custom persisted. Milwaukee *Sentinel,* December 3, 1882, December 4, 1892.

[119]Jopke Transcript.

[120]Walter Monfried, "Milwaukee Remembers the GAR Reunions," in the *Historical Messenger of the Milwaukee County Historical Society,* 12 (September, 1956), 8–11. The standard history of the GAR is Mary R. Dearing, *Veterans in Politics: The Story of the G.A.R.* (Baton Rouge, 1952). See also Jackson R. Horton, "The Demobilization of Wisconsin Troops After the Civil War" (master's thesis, University of Wisconsin, 1952).

concern and took up their lives; others were made restless by the wartime experience. One must remember that most of them were men in their twenties at war's end.

Being a professional veteran was a well-established career before the eighties—for officers—but rank-and-file enthusiasm did not last long after the 1868 and 1872 presidential races. The original GAR had developed within Illinois Radical Republican politics, and had a difficult time surviving the sea change to something other than a political pressure group. Despite its Illinois origins, however, the Wisconsin GAR had more staying power. In 1879, Berlin, Wisconsin, had the oldest continuous post in the nation. But only three Wisconsin posts were represented at the national encampment that year. The Wisconsin militia had fallen on equally lean days.[121]

Those interested in the continuance of the GAR determined to put the organization back in business with the 1880 grand national encampment in Milwaukee. The city was learning how to mobilize the engines of publicity—and remember those generous brewers—which turned war reminiscences into a national industry. A compelling line, used over and over by those promoting the affair, went: "Comrades, attend to this at once, or we shall not know whether you are dead, proud or gone to Texas." Generals Ulysses S. Grant and Philip Sheridan graced the occasion, which was a huge success.[122]

The impact of the Grand Army of the Republic may be seen in the politics of the eighties. The 1877 *Wisconsin Blue Book* reveals that not one of the six state elective officers, governor through

---

[121]Dearing, *Veterans in Politics,* chaps. 6 and 7; Horton, "Demobilization of Wisconsin Troops," 10–46, 81–84; Cooper, "Wisconsin Militia," chap. 4; Martin K. Gordon, "The Milwaukee Infantry Militia, 1865–1892," in the *Historical Messenger of the Milwaukee County Historical Society,* 24 (March, 1968), 2–15.

[122]Monfried, "Milwaukee GAR Reunions," *Historical Messenger of the Milwaukee County Historical Society,* 12:10. The Milwaukee *Sunday Telegraph* was regularly carrying a page devoted to war reminiscences, which became a staple of Sunday papers of the time. See issues during April and May, 1886, for example. The national encampment of 1889 was also held in Milwaukee in recognition of the role that the city had played in reviving the GAR. This was the peak year in terms of membership. Irascible General William T. Sherman was the main attraction in 1889.

schools superintendent, was a veteran. Ten years later, only the lieutenant-governor was a non-veteran. The secretary of state and the state treasurer had lost arms at Chickamauga and Laurel Hill respectively.[123]

As the war years receded, veterans came to occupy a special place in the society of their times. Part of this was simply organization and the place they claimed for themselves by that success. Part of it was the political coming-of-age of the former "Boys in Blue." Part of it was sheer sentimentality, so much a part of the way people of the times expressed themselves and what they looked for in literature, the news, on the stage, the pulpit, and platform. And, most of all, the veterans carried the aura of men who had settled, by long and bloody service, the only apparent threat to American destiny. As the saying now has it, theirs was a hard act to follow. That the phoenix of the GAR officially arose from the ashes in the congenial atmosphere of Milwaukee is worth remembering.

[123] *Wisconsin Blue Book, 1877,* pp. 445–446; *ibid., 1887,* pp. 482–484. There were two more offices in 1887, railroad commissioner and insurance commissioner. The railroad commissioner was Norwegian-born in 1847. The insurance commissioner, English-born in 1841, enlisted in April, 1861, participated in five major battles, and was discharged for wounds received at Antietam. By 1877, it appears that veterans included military service in their legislative biographies.

# PART III

# Politics and
# Government

"We may sneer at the politician, but he has his uses, and
he has been found to be an essential factor in modern
affairs, and under any form of government, democratic
or aristocratic."

ALEXANDER M. THOMSON
Speaker of the Assembly, 1868 and 1869
In *A Political History of Wisconsin* (1900)

# 11

# Old-Time Politics

Wisconsin has a wealth of published and unpublished political history and biography for the years between 1873 and 1893. Much of the early writing followed the nineteenth-century notion that history was simply past politics, organized by presidential administrations nationally and by the procession of governors at the state level. Glance through the state and county histories and observe this progression of gubernatorial figures who supposedly placed their stamps upon the historic years of their administrations. It may have been this promise of immortality that brought many of them to the office, for it was a modest post and a certain modesty was expected of the occupant. Robert M. La Follette broke a tradition of about twenty years by delivering his 1901 message to the legislature in person and by directing his legislative allies in the same manner.[1]

The wealth of later treatments of Wisconsin's political history for this period is owing to a variety of circumstances, one of

---

[1]John W. Tebbel, *A History of Book Publishing in the United States* (4 vols., New York, 1972–1981), 2:533. Consul W. Butterfield's "History of Wisconsin" as it appears in Western Historical Company, *History of La Crosse County, Wisconsin* (Chicago, 1881), 19–109, is a standard part of the county histories published by this company. Clark S. Matteson, *The History of Wisconsin from Prehistoric to Present Periods* (Milwaukee, 1893), 279 ff, presents chapters by governors' administrations "interspersed with realistic and romantic events," as noted on the title page. Snyder, Van Vechten and Co., comps, *Historical Atlas of Wisconsin* . . . (Milwaukee, 1878), 129 ff, follows the same scheme. *Wisconsin Blue Book, 1881*, p. 471, lists the employees of the governor's office. Aside from the lieutenant-governor, these were a private secretary, an executive clerk, and a janitor. The secretary of state had ten employees. A review of senate and assembly records indicates that Governor Jeremiah Rusk altered previous practice by sending his 1882 address to be read by a clerk. See Robert M. La Follette, *La Follette's Autobiography: A Personal Narrative of Political Experiences* (Madison, 1911; reprinted, 1960), 105.

which was the need to set the record straight. Alexander M. Thomson, a pioneer newspaperman and politician, was assembly speaker in the 1869 session and editor of the Milwaukee *Sentinel* from 1870 to 1874. In 1872, he consorted with the Liberal Republican anti-President Grant movement and contracted a nervous coalition with the Democrats. U.S. Senator Matthew Hale Carpenter of Wisconsin was the most effective apologist for the ripening scandals of the Grant administration. Nervous about his chances for re-election in 1875, Carpenter and his stalwart friends bought the *Sentinel* from under Thomson and sent him packing. Thomson was then described as the one who "headed the successful opposition to his [Carpenter's] re-election in 1875." Mellowed by intervening years, Thomson wrote *A Political History of Wisconsin* during his last months of life.[2]

Robert M. La Follette carries a heavy responsibility for the commonly accepted view of the political character of Wisconsin in the last quarter of the nineteenth century. He took his cue from Edward G. Ryan's often-quoted address of 1873 to the University of Wisconsin law school: "The question will arise, and arise in your day . . . , which shall rule—wealth or man; which shall lead—money or intellect; who shall fill public stations—educated and patriotic free men, or the feudal serfs of corporate capital." La Follette made this the central theme of his extended quest for the governorship and control of the Republican party in Wisconsin. La Follette's success, his subsequent career, and his political autobiography, which was accepted by his admirers as gospel, fixed the common view of what had gone before.[3]

[2]Alexander M. Thomson, *A Political History of Wisconsin* (Milwaukee, 1900), iv, 189–207, 214, 308–309; E. Bruce Thompson, *Matthew Hale Carpenter: Webster of the West* (Madison, 1954), 104, 109–118, 205–207, 223–230; Milwaukee *Herold,* March 21, 1872; Milwaukee *Sentinel,* June 10, 1898 (Thomson's obituary); Matteson, *History of Wisconsin,* 490–494; *Memorial Addresses on the Life and Character of Matthew H. Carpenter (A Senator from Wisconsin) Delivered in the Senate and House of Representatives, January 26, 1882* (published by 47 Cong., 1 sess., Washington, but not in the congressional serial set). See also entries under Carpenter, Matthew Hale, in the SHSW Library subject catalog.

[3]Alfons J. Beitzinger, *Edward G. Ryan: Lion of the Law* (Madison, 1960), 104–106; La Follette, *Autobiography,* 11–12, 83–86. For some exceptions to La Follette's version, see Isaac Stephenson, *Recollections of a Long Life, 1829–1915* (Chicago, 1915), 212–223; and Nils P. Haugen, *Pioneer and Political Reminiscences* (Evansville, [1930?]), 111–115. La

Frederick Jackson Turner set the agenda for generations of undergraduate and graduate students at the University with his 1893 paper, "The Significance of the Frontier in American History." Turner's prestige in this new profession helped to create one of the country's largest graduate programs in American history, based in large part upon the growing collections of the state historical society. A flood of books, theses, and dissertations concentrated on the westward movement, the origins of Wisconsin progressivism, and the political milieu from which progressivism evolved.[4]

Party identification, then as now, was the strongest factor in voting behavior for those who could trace their political roots back two or three generations. A man generally inherited his politics—speaking now of those who could look back that far, meaning principally those of Yankee background in Wisconsin. This is a broad term which included people like William A. Titus, of Pennsylvania Dutch antecedents, who, like most of his neighbors in Eden and Empire townships, Fond du Lac County, never doubted his American identity. A man might move far from his parents' circumstances, taking his politics with him. It was something not easily changed, but more readily rationalized whenever one's faith was tested by new circumstances.[5]

If a Yankee emerged from the 1850's, the Civil War years, and Reconstruction still a dedicated Democrat, he was likely to remain one—at least until William Jennings Bryan and 1896. In Wisconsin, the majority of Yankees had undergone the various sea changes from Jacksonian Democrats or Whigs to Republicans in the 1850's or from Unionist Democrats to Republicans

---

Follette was not unique in his view; one will find confirmation, on a national scale. See Leonard D. White, *The Republican Era: A Study in Administrative History, 1869-1901* (New York, 1958), 1. See also David P. Thelen, *The New Citizenship: Origins of Progressivism in Wisconsin, 1885-1900* (Columbia, 1972).

[4]Ray Allen Billington, *Frederick Jackson Turner: Historian, Scholar, Teacher* (New York, 1973), 565-569; Emanuel L. Philipp, *Political Reform in Wisconsin*, eds. Stanley P. Caine and Roger E. Wyman (Madison, 1973), vii–xii.

[5]William A. Titus, "The Westward Trail," in *WMH*, 20 (March, 1937), 310–316; Roger E. Wyman, "Voting Behavior in the Progressive Era: Wisconsin as a Case Study" (doctoral dissertation, University of Wisconsin, 1970), 6–12.

during the war or Reconstruction. It was the Civil War that had molded the two major parties to the pattern of the 1870's, 1880's, and early 1890's.

The first introduction the majority of immigrant voters had to politics was to the basic units of the system: the rural town, village, and city ward. Early settlement was often made up of ethnic enclaves, and many of them maintained a strong sense of their origins even after the astonishing mobility of the times had obscured this original identity in the census reports. But the immigrant voter early caught on to the significance of local government units that determined tax assessments, the allocation of revenues, the location of roads and schools, tavern licensing, and ordinances that attempted to regulate other ordinary affairs of life.[6]

While many immigrant voters were indifferent to essentially national issues such as Reconstruction policy or the tariff, they *were* aware that state government affected them directly on matters of more immediate interest. It was the Wisconsin legislature that argued the taxation of church property in the seventies, passed the Graham liquor control law in 1872, adopted the compulsory school attendance law in 1879, and occasionally debated the role of parochial schools in hostile terms. The rulings on prayers in school and Bible reading came from Madison, as did decisions on state support of eleemosynary institutions run by church-affiliated groups and on who could earn a fee by providing ministerial services in state-run institutions. If this range of issues seems tightly drawn around religious differences, so it was—a justification for giving religion a primary position in considering ethno-cultural factors in nineteenth-century voting behavior.[7]

---

[6]David L. Brye, *Wisconsin Voting Patterns in the Twentieth Century, 1900 to 1950* (New York, 1979), 38–43; Merle Curti, *The Making of an American Community: A Case Study of Democracy in a Frontier County* (Stanford, 1959), 296–297; Joseph Schafer, *The Winnebago-Horicon Basin: A Type Study in Western History* (Madison, 1937), 162–163.

[7]Frederick W. von Cotzhausen, *Historic Reminiscences and Reflections* (5 pts., Milwaukee, 1906–1918), pt. 2, pp. 14–19, pt. 4, pp. 48–49; Herman J. Deutsch, "Yankee-Teuton Rivalry in Wisconsin Politics of the Seventies," in *WMH*, 14 (March–June, 1931), 262–

While Wisconsin voters represented a rich mixture of ethnic groups and religious affiliations, the Germans, Norwegians, Irish, and Poles received the most attention. The Germans made up nearly half (46 per cent) of the foreign-born and their children, or about one-third of the total population by the end of the seventies. The Irish were a large but diminishing contingent, more sophisticated politically and most visible in Milwaukee Democratic politics, which guaranteed their being noticed by Yankee Republicans. The Norwegians were the second-largest immigrant group by the latter seventies—and growing. Outnumbered more than four to one by the Germans in 1890, they were generally Republican and mostly rural. The Poles were noticeable because they were concentrated in Milwaukee, Portage, and Marathon counties, were Catholic, and voted Democratic as a bloc—except for some special occasions to be remarked.[8]

The Milwaukee *Sentinel* is the most accessible observer of Wisconsin's ethnic voters. Speaking for the Yankee element that seldom had any serious challenge to control of the Republican party, the *Sentinel* had no difficulty defining Yankee interests. The Irish were equally easy. They were Democrats and saw everything through the prism of Anglo-Irish differences. The English and Scots were Republicans because they were eminently reasonable—and because the Irish were Democrats. The Poles were Catholic, ignorant of American politics, and were allegedly voted like cattle by their priests and the Irish politicians. The Norwegians were dutifully Republican, worth mollifying with a nomination for secretary of state, state treasurer, or other minor

---

282, 403–418; Conrad E. Patzer, *Public Education in Wisconsin* (Madison, 1924), 74–77. See Milwaukee *Sentinel*, February 8, March 1, 1882, for argument on the Bate Bill to eliminate the exemption of taxation on church property. See also the Milwaukee *Germania*, February 15, 23, 1882, for the German Lutheran view; and Thomas C. Hunt, "Catholic Education Policy and the Decline of Protestant Influence in Wisconsin's Schools During the Late Nineteenth Century" (doctoral dissertation, University of Wisconsin, 1971).

[8]Richard M. Bernard, *The Melting Pot and the Altar: Marital Assimilation in Early Twentieth Century Wisconsin* (Minneapolis, 1980), 5–7; M. Justille McDonald, *History of the Irish in Wisconsin in the Nineteenth Century* (Washington, 1954; reprinted, New York, 1976), 150–193.

offices, but otherwise they should be left alone to pursue their real passion, religious controversy.

The everlasting puzzle was the Germans. Not only did they come in the largest numbers, but they also presented no united front politically, except on the question of "personal freedom," which the Yankees chose to translate as a devotion to beer, saloons, and the Continental Sunday. The Germans replied that they simply meant to pursue a life style free of meddlesome interference. Politically, the Germans had found the Democrats most congenial on this point. But the Protestant Germans moved slowly away from an identification politically with the Catholics—German, Irish, or Polish. The anticlerical Germans had moved into the Republican ranks in the 1850's, and clung to the hope that the party would continue as the liberal—or even radical—party in American politics. How could the *Sentinel* deal with such a quixotic notion?[9]

The Germans were not only the most numerous and most varied of the ethnic groups to be considered by political managers; they were also excessively inward-looking, considering their well-established position in Wisconsin's economic, social, and political life. The *Sentinel* had long maintained German-speaking newsmen on its editorial staff and frequently addressed itself to the German community. By the 1880's many people of German origin were equally at home in German or English. While the German papers gave an inordinate amount of space to observing, correcting, and ridiculing one another, they were deeply interested in American politics, a common source of disagreement among them. The three principal German-language papers were the Milwaukee *Seebote*, *Herold*, and *Germania*, representing respectively the Catholic, liberal, and German Lutheran points of view, and usually the Democratic, Liberal Republican, and unalloyed Republican party positions—until something came up to offend Germandom. Dependably, something did.[10]

[9]Milwaukee *Sentinel*, November 4, 1882. The *Sentinel* discovered and embraced the more conservative Lutherans and other German Protestants as natural allies.

[10]Carl W. Wittke, *The German-Language Press in America* (Lexington, 1957), 155–208; Carl H. Knoche, *The German Immigrant Press in Milwaukee* (New York, 1980), 237–264;

One characteristic that irritated the *Sentinel* was the ability of the German press and community to smother their political differences in the face of perceived threats to common German interests. Unfortunately for the Germans, such common ground was not religious freedom, an end to ethnic or racial slurs, or some equally noble cause. In the eyes of many Yankees, it all somehow boiled down to a defense of drinking beer on Sunday with a band playing. Worse, from the standpoint of the *Sentinel's* Republican orthodoxy, *Der Herold* and *Germania* rationalized an occasional Democratic victory outside Milwaukee, provided some deserving German was elected to something. (There were few undeserving Germans.)[11]

There was a variety of reasons, beyond the German psyche, for the tensions between the German community and the major political parties—and their representative newspapers. Religious tensions have been mentioned, which irritated both Catholic and Lutheran Germans who were accustomed to church-related schools, hospitals, and charitable institutions receiving state support. One must also remember the long depression that began in the fall of 1873. Industrialization and urbanization attracted growing streams of immigrants to the cities, which led to increasing pressure to control immigration and to examine the processes and prospects of assimilation. The Woman's Christian Temperance Union brought a new dimension to the immigration question. Olympia Brown and other suffragists were inveighing against foreign men having the ballot while American women had no voting rights. This, and identification with the leadership of labor radicalism and the Bay View riots, put Germans on the

---

Milwaukee *Sentinel,* August 6, 1882. See the Milwaukee *Herold,* February 8, 1872, for a typical editorial on the insensitivity of the English-language press in its ignorance of German identity, customs, and language.

[11]See the Milwaukee *Herold,* October 30, 1873, October 24, 1878, October 21, 1880, Milwaukee *Germania,* March 30, November 2, 1881, March 27, 1884, Milwaukee *Seebote,* January 13, 1873, October 31, 1878, April 3, 1884, and April 8, 1886, for typical cheering for a German candidate. The Milwaukee *Sentinel,* August 14, 1882, found something suspicious about the Milwaukee German community celebrating—with a grand banquet—the election of Peter Deuster, Democrat of Milwaukee, and Richard Guenther, Republican of Oshkosh, to the United States House of Representatives.

defensive. Even German liberals began talking about revising Wisconsin's generous franchise for immigrants and requiring five years' residence. It was not just beer, the Continental Sunday, school prayers, and the 1889 Bennett Law that set them apart.[12]

As was normal in Wisconsin, Republicans won eight of the eleven gubernatorial races held between November, 1871, and November, 1892, and allowed Democratic coalitions to control the assembly only in 1874, 1878, and 1883 prior to the 1890 Democratic sweep. However, their hold was not so secure that they could be cavalier—as they often were—with the immigrant vote. The best allies of the Republicans in maintaining their favorable balance were their counterparts, the Yankee Bourbon Democrats, who controlled their party at the state level. Irish "Boss" John A. Hinsey may have exercised considerable control of local Democratic affairs in Milwaukee during his long reign from 1874 to 1894, but he had little influence outside the metropolis. The German press did not miss the significance of the parochial role of Germans in both parties. Beyond the usual token candidate in one of the lesser state elective offices, Germans claimed that they seldom received appointive offices or were appointed chairmen of important committees in the legislature.[13]

It was the narrowness of the usual margin between the main contesting parties—generally within the range of 51 to 55 per cent for the Republicans in gubernatorial races—that set Republicans to studying the sometimes fickle German vote. For those whose feet were set in the cement of party loyalty, it also accounts for the intense dislike of their Yankee counterparts of more pliant

[12]See the Milwaukee *Herold*, May 11, 1886, and Milwaukee *Seebote*, November 4, 1886, on revising the franchise for the foreign-born.

[13]James R. Donoghue, *How Wisconsin Voted, 1848–1972* (Madison, 1974), 11, 97–102; Kathleen M. Carlin, " 'Boss' John A. Hinsey," in the *Historical Messenger of the Milwaukee County Historical Society*, 18 (June, 1962), 2–6. See the Milwaukee *Herold*, October 14, 1875, June 15, 1876; and the Milwaukee *Germania*, January 27, 1881, for typical complaints about the dearth of Germans in important party positions or in state appointive offices.

natures. General E. E. Bryant of Madison characterized one of these recreant Republicans as "a man with just enough of talent and culture to render his asininity conspicuous. . . ." Alexander Thomson called the same worthy, Dr. O. W. Wight, who helped organize the Reform movement in Milwaukee that coalesced with the Democrats in 1873, "an able, learned man but deficient in common sense. . . ." The idea of staunch party loyalty was widely accepted as the desirable norm by Yankees despite the many third parties of the times.[14]

As already suggested, it took a bit more steadfastness of character for a Yankee to emerge from the political traumas of the 1850's and 1860's as an unyielding Democrat. The opposite implication of this is that the Republican party harbored the more flexible types. And this is true, in the sense that the Republicans are identified as the activists of the times who prized solutions and change. This left to the Democrats the role of the conservatives who deplored an expanded role for government. It followed that the enthusiasts who seized upon single issues usually came from the Republican ranks: prohibitionists, inflation enthusiasts, Sabbatarians, civil service advocates, voting franchise reformers, antimonopolists, railroad regulators, and the advocates of other measures generally associated with the platforms of the Greenback and Populist parties. Republicans had to consider accommodation to these enthusiasms or risk the rise of splinter parties that might imperil their thin majorities. There was always the risk that these splinter parties would work out alliances with the minority Democrats, who had the advantage of both a statewide and a national organization in place. The Democrats had money, political talent, and allies in Congress where the party occasionally controlled one or both houses, and they polled more popular votes for the presidency nationally in 1876, 1884, 1888, and 1892. Wisconsin's Democrats may have harbored a limited vision of the role of government, but not of the rewards of controlling it.

---

[14]Donoghue, *How Wisconsin Voted, 1848-1972*, pp. 97-102; E. E. Bryant to Lucius Fairchild, June 14, 1874, in the Fairchild Papers; A. M. Thomson to Elisha Keyes, June 12, 1873, in the Keyes Papers.

Did the immigrants vote in other than local elections in proportion to their numbers? The potential numbers, of course, were awesome. The Milwaukee *Seebote* reminded its readers of the arithmetic, saying that neither the Republican nor Democratic managers seemed to know who the voters were. The *Seebote* claimed that of the 146,219 votes cast in the 1871 gubernatorial election, 54,350 were Germans, compared to only 48,105 American-born voters. However the editor arrived at this comparison, the 1870 census showed 156,517 males of twenty-one and over who were foreign-born, to 98,642 American-born. If one includes the voting-age sons of foreign-born parents as ethnic voters, the disparity continues with a vengeance, despite the lessening percentages of foreign-born.[15]

The large size of the immigrant vote is affirmed not only by the numbers. Voter registration, particularly for Milwaukee, became a Republican enthusiasm in the 1870's because of the top-heavy Democratic majorities there. Nearly one in eight of the Democratic gubernatorial votes in 1873 came from Milwaukee County, where four out of five people lived in the metropolis. As often happens with such enthusiasms, the legislature put a registration law in place—for Milwaukee only—in 1879, at which time the imaginative manager of Republican party affairs in Milwaukee, Henry Clay Payne, reversed the city's Democratic tide.[16]

[15]The Milwaukee *Seebote*, November 3, 1873, was extrapolating from the figures given in the *Ninth Census of the United States, 1870: Compendium*, 442. See also *Ninth Census of the United States, 1870: Population, Volume I*, 619; *Eleventh Census of the United States, 1890: Population, Volume I, Part 1*, pp. 788–789. Translating the percentages of males of voting age, without regard to how many were actually eligible, it appears that voter participation ran approximately 56 per cent in the gubernatorial election of 1879, 50 per cent in 1881, 77 per cent in 1888, and 67 per cent in 1890. (Of course, 1888 was a presidential election year; and the elections of 1879 and 1881 did not include congressional races.) Donoghue, *How Wisconsin Voted, 1848–1972*, pp. 2–5, indicates that the turnout of voters by these rough estimates compares favorably with those of 1940–1972, and was considerably higher than those of 1920 and 1930.

[16]The Milwaukee *Herold*, April 4, 1878, and April 4, 1879, worried about Irish "repeaters" and railroad workers imported to inflate the Democratic vote in the Irish third ward. It was 1893 before a statewide voter registration law was passed. See *Laws of Wisconsin*, 1879, pp. 328–333; *ibid.*, 1893, pp. 391–454, esp. 396. See also William W. Wight, *Henry Clay Payne: A Life* (Milwaukee, 1907), 40–47; and Thomson, *Political History of Wisconsin*, 448–450, for a biographical sketch of Payne.

Charles Jopke recalled that he was "just waiting for that day" when he reached twenty-one and could take out his citizenship papers. This became a mass exercise, organized by those interested. Jopke was gathered up by his alderman, along with other young fellows, in "a big wagon with a fence around [it], and he took us right down there to the courthouse. He took us there and we all had to march in. Then he got all the papers and by golly, was I glad to get my papers!"[17]

In summary, Wisconsin elections could revolve around the perceptions held by the large number of immigrant voters about issues that mattered to them. These were not generally the issues on which the parties differed at the national level. The immigrants responded more certainly to state and local issues that dealt with their ethno-cultural identities. Politics was a passion with many, and was not limited to those of American background. This was a generation that savored political oratory; the generation, too, that packed circuit courtrooms in small towns to relish battles of wits. In part this was so for want of other diversions. Politics had all of the elements of professional sports today: glamorous stars who received continuous publicity; journeymen players deserving support, instruction, or total rejection; bets to be won or lost; a season culminating in a gripping playoff; victory or defeat; deep analysis of the results; and the promise of another trial of strength in the near future.[18]

For the participant, whether as candidate or officeholder, politics could be an avocation. Even a congressman spent extended

[17]Transcript of Charles Jopke interview, February 15, 1952, in the Matson Holbrook Interviews. The Milwaukee Seebote, October 30, 1876, complained that it was difficult for rural Germans to comply with the requirements for initiating citizenship, which was done in a state court of record.

[18]Roger E. Wyman, "Wisconsin Ethnic Groups and the Election of 1890," in WMH, 51 (Summer, 1968), 269–270; Paul Kleppner, The Cross of Culture: A Social Analysis of Midwestern Politics, 1850–1900 (New York, 1970), 35–91; Richard J. Jensen, The Winning of the Midwest: Social and Political Conflict, 1888–1896 (Chicago, 1971), 58–88. The burden of the message is that economic and class distinctions had less to do with immigrant voting than did religious and other determinants. "During 'court week' the wagons of farmers were tied up about the court house square and an appreciative audience watched the fine points of a trial-game as an urban audience might watch the fine points of a professional baseball game." See Roscoe Pound, Criminal Justice in America (New York, 1930), 163.

periods at home between the standard long and short sessions of the time. A state legislator could anticipate an average sixty-six calendar days in Madison, extending from mid-January to the latter part of March or even mid-April. With the adoption of biennial sessions and with longer terms beginning in 1885, the average session (to 1893) was ninety-six calendar days. This may account, in part, for the decreasing number of farmers in the legislature and the increasing number of lawyers. Many local and county offices were not demanding, daily tasks.[19]

There were no primary elections, of course. A man with political ambitions or an interested participant in the process started at the district, ward, or precinct level by attending caucus meetings where delegates were chosen to attend the county, assembly, senate, congressional, and state conventions at which candidates were nominated. Robert M. La Follette rang the changes on the functions of this caucus and convention system, which he replaced with his cherished primary. The caucus and the convention, La Follette said, "answer no purpose further than to give respectable form to political robbery." Since attendance at caucuses and conventions took time and money, participation was usually limited and the results fairly easy to manage. It is not surprising that men of considerable wealth were among the most successful operatives at the top levels: Alexander Mitchell, Philetus Sawyer, Isaac Stephenson, and William F. Vilas were representative. There is little evidence that these men paid much time or attention to winning the hearts and minds of the voters, particularly the immigrant voter. Only for those on the lower rungs of the political ladder, such as John A. Hinsey of Milwaukee, was the individual voter sometimes a daily concern.[20]

---

[19]*Biographical Directory of the American Congress, 1774-1949* (Washington, 1950), 327–439; *Wisconsin Blue Book, 1979-1980*, p. 364. Nils Haugen, a former court reporter, remembered "service in the assembly was pleasant and agreeable, and not nearly so strenuous as reporting." Haugen, *Reminiscences*, 48.

[20]La Follette, *Autobiography*, 85–86. Isaac Stephenson's *Recollections* deal only with those who mattered. See also Carlin, " 'Boss' Hinsey," *Historical Messenger of the Milwaukee County Historical Society*, 18:2–6; Richard W. Hantke, "Elisha W. Keyes, the Bismarck of Western Politics," in *WMH*, 31 (September, 1947), 29–41; Horace S. Merrill, *William Freeman Vilas: Doctrinaire Democrat* (Madison, 1954), *passim*; and McDonald, *History of the Irish in Wisconsin*, chap. 5.

In the game of politics, a professional could savor the fine points best with a worthy opponent. A Democratic railroad attorney wrote to his friend, Republican ex-governor Lucius Fairchild, after the stunning Democratic upset victory in 1873: "But we did beat you fellows awfully. *We* did it, but who is We? that is the question: Why we Democrats, Grangers, Reformers, Liberal Republicans, aided a little by other influences which it is not necessary now to mention."

The 1873 election, discussed above in connection with railroad regulation, was indeed a conjunction of a variety of political forces. Anti-railroad sentiment reached a pitch that year, accompanied by the suspicion that Republican echoes of such sentiment were hollow. Added to that was the Liberal Republican bolt, led by former Wisconsin political figure Carl Schurz among others, from the renomination of President Ulysses Grant in 1872. In Wisconsin, Liberal Republicans were mostly Germans incensed by Republican slurs against Schurz and the feeling that their support was unappreciated by the regular Republican party. These were the Milwaukee *Sentinel's* "enlightened Teutons," in revolt for these reasons as well as their opposition to the Graham liquor control law, which they saw as Yankee meddling through the medium of the Republican party. As if that were not enough, Alexander Mitchell had a bone to pick with the incumbent Republican governor, Cadwallader C. Washburn, over the veto of a railroad bridge bill to allow a crossing of the Mississippi north of La Crosse, Washburn's home town. The financial panic began in the fall of 1873, and the Wisconsin Grange caught fire. These were the "other influences" not necessary to mention by Fairchild's exultant Democratic friend.[21]

[21]George B. Smith to Lucius Fairchild, May 1, 1874, in the Fairchild Papers. See Chapter 3 above; Richard N. Current, *The History of Wisconsin. Volume II: The Civil War Era, 1848-1873* (Madison, 1976), 584–594; Robert C. Nesbit, *Wisconsin: A History* (Madison, 1973), 382–385; Deutsch, "Yankee-Teuton Rivalry in Wisconsin Politics," *WMH,* 14:262–282; Herman J. Deutsch, "Disintegrating Forces in Wisconsin Politics of the Early Seventies," in *WMH,* 15 (December, 1931–June, 1932), 168–181, 282–296; Graham A. Cosmas, "The Democracy in Search of Issues: The Wisconsin Reform Party, 1873–1877," in *WMH,* 46 (Winter, 1962–1963), 93–108; *DAB.*

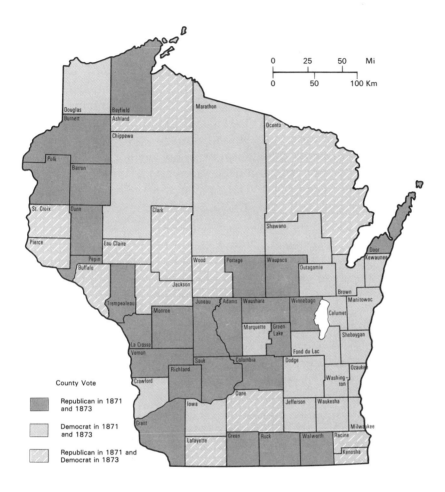

GUBERNATORIAL ELECTIONS, 1871 AND 1873

The Germans bore the brunt of Republican ire for their surprising defeat. The gubernatorial vote for Republican Washburn
was down 12,077 from 1871, and the Democratic-Reform candidate's total was 12,689 higher than the Democratic total of 1871.
Thirty-eight per cent of that increase came from Milwaukee
County, and 24 per cent from ten additional counties in south-

eastern Wisconsin (Ozaukee, Sheboygan, Manitowoc, Calumet, Winnebago, Fond du Lac, Dodge, Washington, Jefferson, and Racine) which in 1870 had the highest concentrations of German-born in the state. Republican managers assumed that it was primarily the anti-Graham Law campaign, bankrolled by the brewers and distillers, that had energized the Germans. It had been simple enough for Alexander Mitchell, who was paymaster for the Democratic party in Milwaukee—and elsewhere in the state when convenient—to engineer an alliance of the Liberal Republicans and some independent reform groups with the Democratic party. This was an operation that has fascinated historians because of the disparate elements involved in the coalition. What brought them together has been suggested earlier. The Democrats had a permanent party organization in place; they had consistently opposed temperance and other sumptuary legislation; and they had polled 47 per cent of the 1871 gubernatorial vote. Even reformers like to win, and the Democrats were hungry indeed.[22]

Horace Rublee, a Madison newspaperman who was very much a Republican activist, had been state chairman of the party from 1859 to 1869, when he was rewarded with the post of minister to Switzerland. The view from Bern enhanced his mordant wit in consoling the defeated Governor Washburn: "You have been the victim of a situation created by the follies or worse than follies of the party. Moreover, with a Granger who had the support of the railways, & a Good Templar who had the confidence of the whiskey & beer ring. . . . The unholy alliance, however, of Democrats & soreheaded Republicans, Grangers & Railroad

[22]Donoghue, *How Wisconsin Voted, 1848–1972,* p. 97; Current, *Civil War Era,* map on p. 419; Deutsch, "Yankee-Teuton Rivalry in Wisconsin Politics," *WMH,* 14:262–282; Cosmas, "Democracy in Search of Issues," *WMH,* 46:93–101; David B. Leonard, "A Biography of Alexander Mitchell, 1817–1887" (master's thesis, University of Wisconsin, 1951), 116–134. Mitchell had followed Senator James Doolittle out of the Republican party, as a supporter of President Andrew Johnson's policies. He may have been attracted to the Democrats because they consistently won in Milwaukee local elections, although a Republican seemed a fixture as congressman from there until Mitchell won the office (1871–1875). It probably is somewhat generous to attribute Mitchell's change of parties to his concern for Reconstruction policy.

men, Good Templars & saloon keepers will dissolve pretty rapidly. . . .''

"The most important circumstance as it seems to me," Rublee continued, ''. . . is that we have driven the whole German vote into the embrace of the Democracy, & I don't exactly see how we are going to recapture them. What with the pig-headedness & infatuation of the temperance men, & the sensitiveness of the Germans to whatever threatens to interfere with their supply of beer, the business is a difficult one to manage. . . . The Germans comprise I suppose nearly one-third of our people, & some regard ought to be paid to their sentiments, even if we had the power, which we have not, to maintain & enforce temperance laws.''[23]

In a more familiar vein, Rublee wrote to Elisha W. Keyes that he trusted that the Madison Regency would be well drilled: "No lobby influences allowed about the legislature. . . . Corruption withered at its sources. The railroad barons shorn of their power. . . . Virtue everywhere triumphant or about to triumph! How do you, my unregenerate friend, find the world and existence therein in the presence of these great innovations?''[24]

Horace Rublee proved an accurate prophet when he predicted that the "unholy alliance" concocted by the Democrats with the forces of "reform" would dissolve "pretty rapidly." By a series of fumbles, the railroad regulation measure—the Potter Law—

[23]Rublee to Washburn, December 4, 1873, in the C. C. Washburn Papers. The letter is quoted in Joseph Schafer, "Editorial Comment: Washburniana," in *WMH*, 14 (March, 1931), 318–319.

[24]Horace Rublee to Elisha Keyes, March 29, 1874, in the Keyes Papers. Henry C. Campbell, ed., *Wisconsin in Three Centuries, 1634–1905* (4 vols., New York, 1906), 4:274–276, shows a readier understanding of the forces that defeated Washburn. He gives more credit to Sam Rindskopf, Milwaukee distiller and organizer of German indignation over the Graham Law. Campbell makes the point that the Graham Law, as it is almost always called in political accounts, was otherwise named the Civil Damage Law. It required saloonkeepers to post a $2,000 bond and be liable for damages for serving a drunkard. That could dry things up at the source. Deutsch, "Yankee-Teuton Rivalry in Wisconsin Politics," *WMH*, 14:277, affirms that, although the railroad regulation issue was featured by both party platforms, and the liquor regulation issue muted, "the liquor contest was probably the determining one . . . disaffection from the Republican party was greatest in the cities, especially those with a large German population. . . .''

was written by Republicans intent upon redeeming their agricultural following. Alexander Mitchell, president of the CM&StP, was displeased with Governor William R. Taylor's acceptance of the Potter Law and his subsequent appointment of Edward G. Ryan as chief justice to enforce it. He had really achieved very little by financing the 1873 upset election. He had, of course, helped to defeat Governor Washburn, whom he disliked intensely. Oddly, Mitchell feared former Governor Washburn's anti-railroad stance more than he did Taylor's, but he had not counted on the Republican legislators finessing a strong railroad law of their own creation. Also, the Reform coalition had strengthened the hands of Democratic leaders outside Milwaukee, who were much less conservative than Mitchell, some even inclining towards greenback inflation. Disillusioned with his brief flirtation with reform, Mitchell did not open his capacious moneybags to the coalition again.[25]

The 1874 general election brought out a larger vote, a normal pattern for even-year elections involving congressional races, than had the gubernatorial upset the preceding November. The total vote was up 26 per cent, and the Republicans claimed over two-thirds of the increase this time. With a remarkably close congressional vote of 93,029 Republican to 93,504 Democratic, Republicans nevertheless won five of the eight congressional seats. The Democratic-Reform coalition lost twenty-three seats in the state assembly, losing control to the Republicans, who also retained their one-vote margin in the senate.[26]

It was not only Mitchell's financial support that was missing

[25]Mitchell's major-domo in 1873 was George H. Paul, a reform-minded Democrat who put the coalition together for Mitchell, then went to Madison as a Reform wing manager and speech writer for Governor Taylor. Taylor was a difficult article to manage, being both naive and stubborn. Paul solved his dilemma by resigning as party chairman and was appointed to the new railroad commission. See Cosmas, "Democracy in Search of Issues," *WMH,* 46:95–107; Edward L. Gambill, "A Biography of Edward S. Bragg" (master's thesis, University of Wisconsin, 1960), 96–100; Deutsch, "Disintegrating Forces in Wisconsin Politics," *WMH,* 15: 282–296, 391–397; and Richard W. Hantke, "The Life of Elisha William Keyes" (doctoral dissertation, University of Wisconsin, 1942), 263 ff.

[26]*Wisconsin Blue Book, 1873,* pp. 428–429; *ibid., 1875,* pp. 232–235, 306–307; Donoghue, *How Wisconsin Voted, 1848–1972,* p. 97; Milwaukee *Herold,* April 4, 1879. The

from the Reform-Democratic coalition's state election campaign of 1874; the brewers, distillers, and saloon owners had also lost interest after the 1874 legislature satisfactorily modified the Graham Law. This was no cause for regret for many Germans who were active in politics. They grew tired of the Republican charge that their only political interest was in the free flow of beer. These centrifugal forces brought disarray to the improvised Reform-Democratic coalition. In 1874, legislative candidates who were not ready to return to the major parties contested under a variety of labels: Reform, Liberal Reform, Independent Republican, Liberal Republican, Independent Reform, Independent Democrat, Liberal Democrat, People's Reform, and just plain Independent. These odd labels generally described disillusioned members of the 1873 coalition, and the mix-up worked to the advantage of the Republicans. In Milwaukee, two Republicans won election to the assembly with a minority of the vote in three-way races, giving the Milwaukee County delegation the unusually high number of five Republicans plus one Liberal Republican among its eleven assembly members. In Dodge County, "Reform" candidate Harman Grube beat "regular Reform nominee" Thomas O'Meara, which sounds more like an international incident than an assembly race.[27]

---

Republican-dominated legislature elected in 1872, meeting in the first months of 1873, gerrymandered a reapportionment of the state. It is evident that this was a delicate operation that won them five of the eight seats in 1874. The Democrats won their three seats by margins of 5,895 votes, 2,501 votes, and two votes—the last an obvious Republican miscalculation. The Republicans won their five seats by margins of 3,441 votes, 3,036 votes, 1,135 votes, 217 votes, and ninety-two votes. The Democrats were inured to this species of Republican arithmetic and contented themselves with calling the kettle black. See H. Rupert Theobald, "Equal Representation," in *Wisconsin Blue Book, 1970,* pp. 96–104; Matteson, *History of Wisconsin,* 542–552; and Thomson, *Political History of Wisconsin,* 243–257. Thomson summed up the problem nicely (pp. 244–245): ". . . [T]he Democratic votes being bunched, as it were, on the lake shore section of the State, while the Republican vote was so distributed over the western and northern sections as to enable the Republicans to carry a majority of the counties and legislative districts."

[27]Cosmas, "Democracy in Search of Issues," *WMH,* 46:105; Milwaukee *Herold,* June 5, October 23, 1873; *Wisconsin Blue Book, 1872,* pp. 436–460; *ibid., 1875,* pp. 310–338; *ibid., 1876,* pp. 451–486. The *Blue Books* give brief biographies of legislators and the election results. The designation of party affiliation in the biographies does not always agree with that in the statistical lists of members that follow.

As the triumphant Republicans came to Madison in January, 1875, their paramount task was to fill the United States Senate seat held by Matt Carpenter. Battle lines were soon drawn between two powerful candidates: the incumbent, and Cadwallader Washburn, former governor. As a party, the Republicans had a clear majority. But the important part was to agree upon their nominee. The drill was for the legislators from both houses to hold party caucuses—with plenty of lobbyists around—and try to arrive at a consensus. The main contestants were there also. Carpenter addressed a joint session of the legislature. After this initial maneuvering, each house voted separately. If there was not a clear winner by a simple majority of the total members, they balloted formally, each day thereafter, until they arrived at a majority.

Senator Carpenter had become a popular figure in Wisconsin politics because he was a compelling personality and a peerless orator in an age when oratory was appreciated. As the leading defender of the Grant administration, Carpenter was regularly on the front pages of New York and other metropolitan newspapers. By 1875, however, the Grant administration was becoming increasingly unpopular, and as a nationally known lawyer of formidable reputation, Carpenter had defended a long list of unsavory characters and causes associated with the administration.[28]

Carpenter and his principal ally, Elisha W. Keyes, the state Republican party chairman who helped control the patronage that was the senator's due, worked manfully in the election of 1874 which produced the comfortable Republican majority in the assembly. Carpenter's re-election seemed assured, but when the first test came, eighteen members of the party refused to attend the party caucus to choose a nominee. This left Carpenter short of an absolute majority when the eighteen proved adamant

---

[28]Thompson, *Carpenter, passim*; Frank A. Flower, *Life of Matthew Hale Carpenter* (Madison, 1883), 402; Bill Hooker, *Glimpses of an Earlier Milwaukee* (Milwaukee, 1929), 57–58. Carpenter's technique owed much to well-prepared rashness. His greatest problems seem to have been a bubbling wit, a lack of discretion, and some brushes with conventional morality.

through successive ballots, scattering their votes among several other candidates. There was much complicated maneuvering, but the gist of it was the determination of Washburn and his supporters to deny the election to Carpenter. On the Democratic side, there was a like determination on the part of Alexander Mitchell and former Senator James Doolittle to prevent any defections to Carpenter. Finally, a deal was made between the Republican bolters and the Democrats to hold a single test vote on someone acceptable to the minority Democrats. They agreed upon Angus Cameron, a Republican railroad lawyer from La Crosse, who was considered innocuous enough by the Democrats not to become a formidable political power. Cameron was elected, and he did not contradict the Democrats' assessment—although he did not reward his benefactors either.[29]

One may readily gain the impression that legislators of the time found themselves pawns in more political games than they had bargained for. They were subject not only to the unrestrained blandishments and threats of the usual lobbies, but the richest man in the state, who controlled half its railroad mileage, also appeared in the guise of a party boss to place his orders. The senatorial contests involved everyone on the federal payroll in the state down to the hamlet postmaster, the jobs of all of whom depended on the outcome. "Boss" Keyes, Madison postmaster and Republican state chairman, dispensed much of the postal patronage as well as that for internal revenue collection and other federal agencies, and levied on federal jobholders heavily for party contests. Keyes appeared at all Republican caucus doors to crack the whip. As for the legislators, there was little continuity of membership or leadership to prepare the members for this onslaught.[30]

---

[29]Thompson, *Carpenter*, 218–230; Campbell, ed., *Wisconsin in Three Centuries*, 4:269; Milwaukee *Sentinel*, March 8, 1875; Herman J. Deutsch, "Carpenter and the Senatorial Election of 1875 in Wisconsin," in *WMH*, 16 (September, 1932), 26–46.

[30]Ballard C. Campbell, *Representative Democracy: Public Policy and Midwestern Legislatures in the Late Nineteenth Century* (Cambridge, 1980), 31–32, states that, on the average, only one in four legislators returned in the succeeding legislature, and fewer than 4 per cent served three consecutive terms.

Becoming the leading apologist for the Grant administration was liability enough for Carpenter. But given his role with the Grant forces, he inevitably took on Senator Carl Schurz of Missouri as well. This displeased those liberal Germans who had followed Schurz into the Liberal Republican movement of 1872. It also displeased some Protestant Germans who were distancing themselves increasingly from their Catholic countrymen by voting Republican. There was a growing recognition among knowledgeable Republicans that a significant shift of the German vote could have seismic consequences in Wisconsin elections. It simply made no sense to conclude: "What is the use of catering to the d–n Dutch. They don't vote the ticket any way." No, they voted German; and the non-Catholic German vote was huge and volatile.

Carpenter forces courted the Germans in the 1875 legislature. Republican Zebulon P. Burdick of Janesville nominated Frederick W. Horn of Cedarburg for assembly speaker. This was obviously a party move, as it was the only Republican nomination. Horn had been a staunch Democrat in eleven legislative sessions between 1848 and 1872, and he was to return as a Democrat in 1882. But he came to the 1875 assembly as an Independent Republican—a time of shaken loyalties. Horn's support of Carpenter seems to have been a bit quixotic. He wrote to Keyes a couple of years later: "I know all those little weaknesses of Mr. C. [Carpenter] as well as anyone, yet he really is a great man and you certainly would rather see him there than any of these small potatoe fellows with fish blood, *if any,* in their veins."[31]

As the 1875 state elections approached, the Republicans knew that they had a hard nut to crack. "Farmer" Taylor, as the governor was familiarly known, had mollified his German allies with a recommendation that the Graham Law be modified to dispense with "obnoxious provisions, without in any degree

---

[31]Deutsch, "Yankee-Teuton Rivalry in Wisconsin Politics," *WMH,* 14:414, quotes the Madison *Democrat,* August 21, 1873, on the "d—n Dutch." Milwaukee *Sentinel,* January 14, 1875; *DWB.* Horn and Burdick biographies are in *Wisconsin Blue Book, 1875,* pp. 331, 333. See also F. W. Horn to Elisha Keyes, December 19, 1878, in the Keyes Papers.

impairing the appropriate power of the state to regulate and restrain the traffic in intoxicating liquors. . . .'' This was about as far as a Good Templar could go. The coalition worked quite smoothly on this matter, finding a compromise that removed the features most obnoxious to the Personal Liberty League and other German organizations, yet not selling out temperance as a principle. The Republican senators knew where their German vote had gone, and agreed to the changes. Taylor had also recouped the error of allowing the Republicans to write the railroad regulation law, when he got his back up over the intransigence of the railroad tycoons who refused to abide by it.[32]

The Republicans finessed Taylor in 1875 with the pioneer businessman and popular three-term mayor of Milwaukee, Harrison Ludington. Ludington had sagaciously referred the problem of the Graham Law to the city attorney, Emil Wallber. Wallber's answer was that the law was unconstitutional under the licensing power granted to the city. This convenient opinion was appealed by temperance forces and overturned by the state supreme court. But no legal action followed, although the chief justice declared that the Milwaukee licenses issued were null and void. Milwaukee continued to ignore the law, which Governor Taylor and the legislature changed the following year. The Germans appreciated this legerdemain, and gave more credit to Ludington than to Good Templar Taylor. The two gubernatorial candidates were well matched. Neither could give a speech, but Ludington avoided the possibility by appearing at county fairs— popular events in the fall—where he steadfastly refused to make speeches and instead chatted amiably with all comers. Unfortunately the governor had to prove his incapacity for speechmaking. Taylor was narrowly defeated, but the rest of the Democratic-Reform state officers survived the test.[33]

Ludington's narrow victory was revealing for the Republicans.

---

[32] *Wisconsin Public Documents,* 1873, Governor's Message, vol. 1, pp. 15–16; Deutsch, "Yankee-Teuton Rivalry in Wisconsin Politics," *WMH,* 14:277–280; Cosmas, "Democracy in Search of Issues," *WMH,* 46:102–105.

[33] Deutsch, "Yankee-Teuton Rivalry in Wisconsin Politics," *WMH,* 14:271–272; Cosmas, "Democracy in Search of Issues," *WMH,* 46:108; Nesbit, *Wisconsin,* 370.

In 1873, Taylor had carried Milwaukee County with 10,435 votes to Republican Washburn's 2,837. The 1875 vote for governor in Milwaukee County was 7,415 for Taylor, 6,042 for Ludington. The total vote cast in the county was practically the same in 1873 and 1875 (13,272 and 13,457), but Taylor's vote was down 3,020 while the Republican vote was up 3,205. Ludington won the state by the razor-thin margin of 841 votes. Republican organizer Henry Payne levied on Democrat Alexander Mitchell for the Republican campaign. Mitchell was rewarded by the more acceptable Vance Law, which replaced the stringent railroad regulation of the Potter Law. Other heavily German counties—Manitowoc, Ozaukee, Sheboygan, Washington, Jefferson, and Winnebago—made lesser but significant shifts in favor of Ludington. Alexander Mitchell's support of Taylor in 1873 had strained the faith of many grangers that the Reform-Democratic ticket would really achieve a true regulatory law. By the 1875 election the Republicans could claim the Potter Law as their creation because of Reform ineptitude.

No clear mandate emerged from the 1875 elections. The Reform-Democrat incumbents of the lesser state offices were as narrowly returned as was Ludington. Dissatisfaction with the 1874 legislative session, in which Republicans were an unaccustomed assembly minority of forty-one, had led to their triumphant return with a majority of sixty-four the following year. This majority was badly eroded in the 1875 election, despite Ludington's victory, indicating that the election was more a repudiation of Governor Taylor. But in the state senate, with larger constituencies than the assembly, and with only half the members' seats at risk, Republicans substantially increased their narrow one-vote majority in the 1874 and 1875 sessions to a margin of nine after the 1875 election.[34]

[34]Donoghue, *How Wisconsin Voted, 1848-1972*, pp. 97–98; Frank N. Elliott, "The Causes and the Growth of Railroad Regulation in Wisconsin, 1848–1876" (doctoral dissertation, University of Wisconsin, 1956), 306–317; Deutsch, "Disintegrating Forces in Wisconsin Politics," *WMH*, 15:391–411; Cosmas, "Democracy in Search of Issues," *WMH*, 46:102–108; *Wisconsin Blue Book* for 1874, 1875, and 1876.

**GUBERNATORIAL ELECTIONS, 1871, 1873 AND 1875**

| COUNTY | 1871 Doolittle (Dem.) vs. Washburn (Rep.) | | 1873 Taylor (Ref.-Dem.) vs. Washburn (Rep.) | | | 1875 Taylor (Dem.) vs. Ludington (Rep.) | | |
|---|---|---|---|---|---|---|---|---|
| | TOTAL VOTE | % REP. | TOTAL VOTE | % CHANGE IN TOTAL, 1871–1873 | % REP. | TOTAL VOTE | % CHANGE IN TOTAL, 1873–1875 | % REP. |
| Brown | 3,074 | 43% | 3,326 | + 8.2 | 39% | 4,101 | +23.3 | 42% |
| Dane | 8,036 | 52 | 8,055 | .24 | 47 | 9,280 | 15.2 | 48 |
| Dodge | 7,113 | 36 | 6,390 | −10.2 | 29 | 7,188 | 12.5 | 35 |
| Grant | 5,125 | 62 | 4,509 | −12.0 | 53 | 5,500 | 22.0 | 58 |
| Green | 2,691 | 65 | 2,768 | 2.9 | 51 | 3,555 | 28.4 | 55 |
| Iowa | 3,089 | 47 | 2,883 | − 6.7 | 46 | 3,258 | 13.0 | 49 |
| Jefferson | 5,092 | 44 | 4,580 | −10.1 | 36 | 5,238 | 14.4 | 44 |
| La Crosse | 3,172 | 57 | 3,605 | 13.7 | 60 | 3,611 | .2 | 52 |
| Lafayette | 3,228 | 50 | 2,724 | −15.6 | 48 | 3,315 | 21.7 | 50 |
| Manitowoc | 3,285 | 44 | 3,546 | 7.9 | 23 | 4,026 | 13.5 | 35 |
| Milwaukee | 9,321 | 40 | 13,272 | 42.4 | 21 | 13,457 | 1.4 | 45 |
| Outagamie | 2,965 | 41 | 3,123 | − 5.3 | 33 | 3,715 | 19.0 | 32 |
| Ozaukee | 1,869 | 16 | 2,074 | 11.0 | 11 | 2,112 | 1.8 | 22 |
| Pierce | 1,762 | 70 | 1,428 | −19.0 | 48 | 1,856 | 30.0 | 57 |
| Richland | 2,410 | 58 | 2,214 | − 8.1 | 52 | 2,654 | 19.9 | 57 |
| Rock | 5,165 | 71 | 4,626 | −10.4 | 72 | 5,452 | 17.9 | 68 |
| Sheboygan | 3,870 | 49 | 3,929 | − 1.5 | 37 | 3,938 | .23 | 44 |
| Trempealeau | 1,282 | 77 | 1,262 | − 1.6 | 73 | 1,597 | 26.5 | 67 |
| Washington | 3,037 | 22 | 2,797 | − 7.9 | 17 | 3,028 | 8.3 | 24 |
| Waukesha | 4,942 | 49 | 4,727 | − 4.4 | 44 | 4,994 | 5.6 | 51 |
| Winnebago | 5,024 | 60 | 5,449 | 8.5 | 52 | 6,225 | 14.2 | 58 |
| WISCONSIN | 147,211 | 53% | 147,823 | + .42 | 45% | 169,469 | +14.6 | 50.2% |

SOURCES: James R. Donoghue, *How Wisconsin Voted, 1848–1872* (Madison, 1974), 97–98; Joseph Schafer, *A History of Agriculture in Wisconsin* (Madison, 1922), 137–139.

Harrison Ludington's political coattails in November, 1875, were nonexistent. The legislature that he met in January, 1876, had only forty-nine Republicans in the assembly, who faced forty-eight Democrats and three Independents: Peter Fagg and Henry Fink of Milwaukee, and William Carbys of Ozaukee. Fagg was born in Holland, Fink and Carbys in Germany. *Der Herold*, which was still sulking over the Republicans' treatment of the Liberal Republicans and of Carl Schurz, commented that the Republicans took Fagg, Fink, and Carbys into camp, and with their votes organized the assembly. *Der Herold* hoped that these apostates could explain themselves to their constituents.[35]

The Republicans actually learned something from the confused political contests of the mid-seventies: there was a German Republican vote out there that had to be nurtured. Henry C. Payne taught Republicans a good deal about this, having started his Young Men's Republican Club in Milwaukee in 1872, where he naturally turned to a study of the immigrant vote. Payne was energetic, intelligent, and played to win. The resounding 1875 Republican victory in Milwaukee County put Payne in line for the state chairmanship.[36]

The rise of Henry C. Payne as a new manager of Republican strategy, sensitive to the party's need for a broader constituency, was matched by the decline of Elisha W. Keyes. Keyes had worked his way up in Whig and Republican politics, beginning with the 1851 election of Governor Leonard Farwell. Since 1869, Keyes had been state chairman of the Republican party, and he

---

[35] *Wisconsin Blue Book, 1875*, p. 328; *ibid., 1876*, pp. 471–472, 474; Milwaukee *Herold*, January 13, 1876. Apparently only Fink and Carbys were gathered into the Republican fold. The *Blue Book* for 1876 counted fifty-one Republican members to forty-nine Opposition (as they were labeled). The "Statistical List of Members of the Assembly" has Peter Fagg as a Democrat, Fink as an Independent, and Carbys also as an Independent. Carbys' biography lists him as an Independent Republican. See *Wisconsin Blue Book, 1876*, pp. 474, 481, 484–485.

[36] Nesbit, *Wisconsin*, 375–376; Wight, *Payne*, 40–47; *DWB*; Campbell, ed., *Wisconsin in Three Centuries*, 4:278; Deutsch, "Yankee-Teuton Rivalry in Wisconsin Politics," *WMH*, 14:411. Payne was on the Republican national committee from 1880 until his death in 1904. He was offered the national chairmanship in 1892 but declined. He ended his political career as Theodore Roosevelt's postmaster general, dying in office.

was Madison postmaster for twenty-one years. He levied heavily on federal officeholders over a wide area. He was also identified with the interests of the Chicago and North Western and allied railroads. Keyes carried a burden in dealing with Germans and Irish, for he had been vice-president of Madison's Know Nothing lodge early in his political career. The term ''Boss'' came to symbolize Keyes. Not a man of wealth, he simply loved power, which he wielded without much tact.[37]

The beginning of Keyes's fall began in early 1875 with his stubborn fight to carry the re-election of Senator Carpenter. He was generally blamed for the stalemate which brought about the election of Angus Cameron. Keyes held off his detractors, and, calling on all of his political capital, he was triumphantly reaffirmed as state chairman. It was a naked illustration of the power of patronage, and of the fact that it was minor officeholders who had the time, tenacity, and self-interest to attend party caucuses and conventions. But more trouble was in the offing. Keyes was for James G. Blaine in 1876, but Rutherford B. Hayes won the Republican nomination and the presidency in the famous disputed election of America's centennial year. Hayes was a moderate reformer who ordered federal officeholders to choose between their federal jobs and important party positions. Keyes opted to keep his Madison postmastership, resigning the party chairmanship. In 1877, he was succeeded in the state party chairmanship by Horace Rublee, who was back from Switzerland.[38]

Keyes continued to harbor political ambitions well beyond his power to gratify. In 1879, he determined to take the United States Senate seat graced by Timothy Howe for eighteen years. Howe had no thought of retiring. But while Howe and Keyes

---

[37]Hantke, "Elisha Keyes, Bismarck of Western Politics," *WMH*, 31:29–41, is a summary of his doctoral dissertation, "The Life of Elisha William Keyes" (University of Wisconsin, 1942), of which pp. 76–83 cover his association with the Know Nothings. See also David P. Thelen, "The Boss and the Upstart: Keyes and La Follette, 1880–1884," in *WMH*, 47 (Winter, 1963–1964), 103–105; Deutsch, "Disintegrating Forces in Wisconsin Politics," *WMH*, 15:285.

[38]Hantke, "Elisha Keyes, Bismarck of Western Politics," *WMH*, 31:36–38.

were maneuvering, Matt Carpenter's desire for vindication was kindled. Many Republicans felt that for all his public and private faults, Matt was a great man in whose veins ran something more than "fish blood, if any." The rehabilitation of discredited politicians is a common American phenomenon. After a long, three-way battle, Carpenter won.[39]

Philetus Sawyer of Oshkosh, the millionaire lumberman and friend and ally of Senator Howe and former Governor Washburn, had been a congressman from 1865 to 1875, where his understanding of the processes of legislation was formidable. As a public figure he was looked upon as unlettered and unprepossessing. But he went a long way on shrewdness, generous geniality, a willingness to spend money, and a practical approach to getting what he wanted. Keyes, still a power in the party despite his twice-clipped wings, continued to harbor senatorial ambitions. He waited expectantly for the end of Angus Cameron's term in 1881. But Sawyer, who had been attending to his business affairs since leaving Congress six years before, had his eye on the senatorial toga. As he commented elegantly to Washburn: "I have kissed a-s enough for the privlage of doing peoples Chores and I have got *through.*" Keyes, like a sinking ship firing on its rescuers, had managed to alienate Henry C. Payne, the other Wisconsin postmaster with real power, and Payne was added to Sawyer's widening circle of allies. It was no contest. Senator Sawyer replaced Cameron.

Then, abruptly, Carpenter died in February, 1881, and the same legislature which had elected Sawyer moved swiftly. This time Keyes's friends did not bother to nominate him. The Republican majority quickly endorsed Senator Sawyer's choice, Angus Cameron, the surprised recipient of a second term in the august Senate of the United States. Sawyer's alliances had made him the acknowledged boss of Wisconsin Republican politics. Lesser satraps—even Payne—acted accordingly. Sawyer's amiability, capacious pocketbook, and offhand suggestions of where

[39]*Ibid.*, 31:38–39; William H. Russell, "Timothy O. Howe, Stalwart Republican," in *WMH*, 35 (Winter, 1951), 98; Thompson, *Carpenter*, 259–263.

duty lay were easier to bear than had been Keyes's peremptory demands.[40]

As the Republicans were adjusting to changes in leadership and their newly recognized constituency, the Democrats continued their schizoid existence, seeking an identity beyond that of complacent Bourbons, Alexander Mitchell's influence, or the Irish, Polish, and German Catholic shock troops of Milwaukee and lesser urban centers. Fortune smiled on them occasionally. The Whiskey Scandal nationally was largely a Republican affair, the impact of which was reflected best in the state assembly. There were sixty-two Republicans—plus two independents who voted with them—in the 1875 assembly elected in the fall of 1874. The scandal broke locally with seizures of records of Milwaukee distilleries in May, 1875, and trials were going on as the fall elections approached. The result, when the new assembly met in January, 1876, was that there were only forty-nine Republicans, who (as noted above) had to recruit among the three Milwaukee and Ozaukee Germans who had run as Independents to organize the assembly.[41]

Though the Democratic-Reform coalition faded rapidly after its astonishing 1873 success, a new threat to Republican serendipity now loomed. As the agricultural depression deepened in the 1870's, farmers discovered another villain: the money supply. It was a complicated controversy, but what it boiled down to was that the Civil War had largely been financed by the printing press. The state banks had been forced out of bank note issuance, which was replaced by a national currency—greenbacks—with no specie backing. Greenbacks had always been discounted for gold, but they were legal tender. The result was inflation. This

---

[40]Richard N. Current, *Pine Logs and Politics: A Life of Philetus Sawyer, 1816–1900* (Madison, 1950), 146–184. Nils Haugen, who served in Congress from 1887 to 1895, recalled Sawyer as "congenial and pleasant in his personal relations" although he "lacked entirely that dignity generally ascribed to the members of the United States Senate." Haugen, *Reminiscences,* 49–51, 102–103.

[41]Milwaukee *Herold,* October 14, 21, 28, November 11, 1875; Milwaukee *Sentinel,* September 25, 1877; *Wisconsin Blue Book, 1875,* pp. 338, 341–343; *ibid., 1876,* pp. 484–486; White, *Republican Era,* 372–374.

had eased with the Union victory, but prices remained inflated. The national debt was a hodgepodge of notes and certificates (bonds), some silent on the medium of redemption, some pledging gold. Republican Congresses had determined to retire the greenbacks and eventually return to a specie base. The result was a steady deflation, increasing the relative value of the dollar and lowering prices. Those who had contracted long-term debts, such as farm mortgages, were in a squeeze with lower prices in trying to meet fixed interest and debt with more expensive dollars. In these circumstances, it was natural to blame the current depression on this Republican monetary policy.

The idea of a national currency, based on the faith and credit of the federal government rather than on the relatively fixed supply of gold (or gold and silver), was not new. It bobbed up as regularly as the cycle of panics and depressions, which by nature were deflationary. In 1876, advocates from labor, agriculture, and business came together and entered a ticket in the presidential race as the Greenback party. Its presidential candidate polled only 1,509 votes in Wisconsin, and Wisconsin Republicans heaved a sigh of relief.

The virus, however, had not run its course. The Greenback party flowered in the state elections the following year, led by Edward P. Allis as its gubernatorial candidate. (Remember that he had been forced to the wall financially in 1876, but had been aided locally—with considerable embarrassment—to satisfy his creditors and retain his business. The Milwaukee business and financial community had recognized that Allis could not be allowed to go under. It was difficult to argue that he had not been caught by deflationary pressures as well as by the business slump.) Greenbackers like Allis, President George McK. Steele of Lawrence College, and George Esterly, the Whitewater farm implement manufacturer, could not be dismissed by such characteristic jocular comment as the *Wisconsin State Journal's* description of a Greenback meeting in Stoughton: three ruralites, a boy, and a bulldog.[42]

[42]Nesbit, *Wisconsin*, 387; Irwin Unger, *The Greenback Era: A Social and Political History of American Finance, 1865-1879* (Princeton, 1964); *Wisconsin Blue Book, 1877*, pp. 406-408;

Hard times bring out third parties. The 1877 gubernatorial race had five parties represented, but only three were taken seriously: Republicans, Democrats, and Greenbackers. Greenbacker Edward P. Allis drew 26,216 votes, almost 15 per cent of the total. This was, of course, frightening to the Republicans, because they recognized that most of the Greenback votes came from their Yankee constituency.[43]

A Socialist on the state ballot in 1877 represented the appearance of the fabled "cloud no larger than a man's hand." It was an exotic party, imported by German radicals, with a small following of German workingmen and English radicals. Briefly evident in the mid-seventies, it arose again to take a prominent part in the events in Milwaukee of May, 1886, and early in the 1890's finally found skilled leadership in the person of Victor Berger. In 1877 the Socialists nominated a Scot, Colin Campbell, to show the flag. While he drew only a scattering outside Milwaukee—being on the ballot only where a significant number of German radicals were present—Campbell received a nominal 2,176 votes. But 1,407 of these came from Milwaukee, eclipsing the 1,228 Greenback votes there for Edward P. Allis.[44]

Horace Rublee had returned from abroad in 1877 and again

---

Ellis B. Usher, *The Greenback Movement of 1875-1884 and Wisconsin's Part in It* (Milwaukee, 1911); Walter F. Peterson, *An Industrial Heritage: Allis-Chalmers Corporation* (Milwaukee, 1978), 15-16; Milwaukee *Commercial Times,* January 21, 1876; *Wisconsin State Journal,* October 29, 1877.

[43]One must remember that whatever the vote total, the true support for a third party on a statewide basis was pure speculation. This was because the state did not provide uniform, single ballots until 1893, leaving it to the party organizers to supply party ballots in hundreds of voting districts. Where they did not provide ballots, third-party enthusiasts could only hope that their supporters would "scratch" the designated candidate on a Republican or Democratic ballot and write in their third-party choice. This is why the Democrats, normally in the minority, were tempted to absorb third-party movements by the most unlikely compromises. They had the ballots everywhere, and their organization was always in place. See Florence E. Baker, "A Brief History of the Elective Franchise in Wisconsin," *SHSW Proceedings,* 1893, pp. 113-130; *Laws of Wisconsin,* 1893, pp. 407-413; *Wisconsin Blue Book, 1878,* pp. 404-405.

[44]Bayrd Still, "The Development of Milwaukee in the Early Metropolitan Period," in *WMH,* 25 (March, 1942), 303-304; Cotzhausen, *Reminiscences,* pt. 4, pp. 57-58; Milwaukee *Sentinel,* April 20, 1876; Frederick I. Olson, "The Milwaukee Socialists, 1897-1941" (doctoral dissertation, Harvard University, 1952), chap. 1; *Wisconsin Blue Book, 1878,* pp. 404-405; Campbell, ed., *Wisconsin in Three Centuries,* 4:282.

assumed the party chairmanship which he had held earlier. One of his first problems was the party platform which had, in Alexander Thomson's phrase, "prevaricated and dodged" on the currency question. The greenback heresy was a virus that infected both major parties. Both Rublee and 1877 gubernatorial candidate William E. Smith were hard money men. With the support of Smith, Rublee boldly organized a rump convention which rewrote the offending platform plank to endorse a hard money position. Rublee had identified this change as essential to hold the Republican party's German constituency.[45]

Harrison Ludington was persuaded to step aside after his single term. He had his thin margin of victory in 1875—one-half of 1 per cent—to think about, as well as other liabilities. Although he had no recommendations in the field of liquor control, his past was remembered as soft by temperance Republicans. And his strongest recommendation in his inaugural message had been to rescind the Potter Law, which Republicans claimed as their own. This was not calculated to please Republican grangers and others who felt victimized by the railroads.[46]

William E. Smith of Milwaukee, the successful Republican nominee of 1877, was Scottish-born but had come to the Midwest as a child. He had been a businessman in Fox Lake until 1872, when he moved to Milwaukee as the chief partner in a wholesale grocery firm with J. A. Roundy. Smith had served in the legislature off and on, as was common, since 1851, was state treasurer for two terms in the latter sixties, and in 1871 was

[45]Ellis B. Usher, *Wisconsin: Its Story and Biography, 1848-1913* (8 vols., Chicago, 1914), 3:548-550; Campbell, ed., *Wisconsin in Three Centuries*, 4:280-283; Thomson, *Political History of Wisconsin*, 209-211. The Milwaukee *Seebote*, the principal German Catholic paper, confirms (November 8, 1877) the German prejudice against paper money. The Milwaukee *Herold*, October 21, 1875, a liberal Republican German paper, had identified William E. Smith as leader of the liberal wing of the state Republicans who had been shut out by state chairman Keyes and his patronage troops—the Madison Regency—in the 1875 state convention that nominated Harrison Ludington. See Current, *Pine Logs and Politics*, 33-34, 166; Dorothy Ganfield Fowler, *John Coit Spooner: Defender of Presidents* (New York, 1961), 55-56; Thomson, *Political History of Wisconsin*, 294.

[46]Campbell, ed., *Wisconsin in Three Centuries*, 4:277-278; *Wisconsin Public Documents*, 1874-1875, Governor's Message, vol. 1, pp. 9-12.

elected assembly speaker. He had also served as a regent of the normal school system and on the prison board. He had other prominent business and education directorships—in short, the profile of a politically active Republican businessman. Smith considerably improved upon Ludington's margin of victory, although he won only by a plurality because of the Greenback candidate, Edward P. Allis. In his second race (1879), Smith won by a clear majority as the Greenback tide receded. He gained almost 22,000 votes over his 1877 total, while the Democratic gain was only 4,544, indicating that most of the 1877 Greenback voters were Republican deserters. The Democrats were in real disarray in 1879. They nominated Alexander Mitchell for governor, who curtly declined, which was not a rousing start for James G. Jenkins, a Milwaukee lawyer, who accepted.[47]

Voters could wander afield more readily in the legislative races. Governor Smith's first legislature (1878) had only forty-five Republicans in the assembly, faced by forty-one Democrats, thirteen Greenbackers, and one Socialist. The Greenbackers held the balance and one of them was elected speaker: Augustus R. Barrows, a lumberman from Chippewa Falls, serving his first term in the legislature. The Republican *Wisconsin State Journal* remarked that the assembly worked fairly well, despite a lack of organization along party lines. The usual Republican majority was restored the following year, and held until 1882, which was a Democratic year nationally and in Wisconsin.[48]

[47]*DWB*; Thomson, *Political History of Wisconsin,* 208–214, 327–329; *Wisconsin Blue Book, 1878,* pp. 404–405; *ibid., 1881,* pp. 302–303; *ibid., 1960,* pp. 120–126; Milwaukee *Herold,* October 21, 1875, January 10, 1878.

[48]*Wisconsin State Journal,* March 21, 1878; *Wisconsin Blue Book, 1878,* pp. 465–466, 486, 489–491. Smith's two terms as governor receive little mention in standard accounts. He was overshadowed by Senator Carpenter's second election in 1879, the two senatorial elections of 1881, the presidential campaign of 1880, and President James Garfield's assassination the following summer. "Governor Smith's first term, though offering little for the historian to seize upon, was marked by painstaking work, a freedom from acrimonious political discussion and a quiet dignity. . . ." Campbell, ed., *Wisconsin in Three Centuries,* 4:284; Thomson, *Political History of Wisconsin,* 219, 311–312; *Wisconsin Blue Book, 1960,* pp. 125–126. If Smith is remembered, it is for calling out the militia to settle the Eau Claire "Sawdust War" in July, 1881.

Genial political boss Philetus Sawyer was always on the look-out for new talent to add to his stable. He was a good judge of men and handled them with a light rein, expecting them to create their own initiatives and alliances, which might at times be at odds with his own. Unlike Boss Keyes, whose main stock in trade was his readiness to control the jobs of others, Sawyer was worth listening to for the simple reason that he possessed that evidence of superior success, a conspicuous fortune. But he did not bulldoze people as did his Democratic counterpart, Alexander Mitchell. Two Sawyer allies who went on to wider fields and comfortable fortunes with his blessing were Postmaster General Henry C. Payne and U.S. Senator John C. Spooner.

Payne, who became the arbiter of Republican affairs in Milwaukee, we have looked at before. Sawyer acquired Spooner along with his interest in the "Omaha Line," the railroad made up of various land-grant roads in northwestern Wisconsin. Spooner was the principal attorney for the West Wisconsin Railroad, which had a tenuous hold on the St. Croix land grant. Spooner's contribution was to save the grant and engineer its transfer to the Omaha in 1882. The grant had been the subject of scandal and manipulation for almost thirty years, and Sawyer would extend this record.[49]

Spooner was useful in other ways. As a young man, he had served as Governor Lucius Fairchild's private secretary. He was a Madison resident, attended the University, and married Annie Main, sister of the Dane County sheriff, who was accounted a member of the "Madison Regency," as was John Spooner's older brother Philip. Following the family trade, John became a lawyer and moved to Hudson, where he became the West Wisconsin's attorney. The West Wisconsin also retained William F. Vilas, who lived at the seat of power in Madison. Vilas would emerge as Wisconsin's leading Democrat, holding two cabinet posts in the Cleveland administrations. Their early collaboration was handy to both men despite their different party affiliations.[50]

[49]Fowler, *John Coit Spooner*, 26–64; Current, *Pine Logs and Politics*, 132–143.
[50]Fowler, *John Coit Spooner*, 16–56; Merrill, *William Freeman Vilas*, 35–36; *DWB*. Vilas and Spooner were close in age, born in 1840 and 1843 respectively. The difference was

Spooner also had political talents and ambitions. He spent the summer of 1880 stumping for legislative candidates who would be partial to Sawyer's candidacy for the U.S. Senate seat to be decided by the 1881 legislature. This was in the days when courtrooms furnished entertainment, and Spooner was a show. He wrote to a political ally that his strategy was to accept cases for trial only in scattered locations, in neighboring counties, where he could politick without being too obvious about it. Sawyer credited his 1881 election to the U.S. Senate much to the yeoman work of Payne and Spooner, who helped legislative candidates favorable to his cause. Sawyer thought so well of Spooner that, four years later, it became Senators Sawyer and Spooner. By that time Spooner was growing beyond a dependence on Sawyer's favor. Like Matthew Hale Carpenter, he became nationally known, one of an inner circle of Republican senators who determined the party's agenda.[51]

Jeremiah Rusk's huge form and patriarchal beard dominated the state political landscape of the 1880's. While he was a successful Vernon County farmer, tavern keeper, and stage owner near Viroqua, his real vocation was politics. He had served as county sheriff before the war, went to the assembly in 1862, resigned to accept a commission, and rose to command of the Twenty-Fifth Wisconsin, leaving the army as a brevet brigadier general. He returned to farming and politics, serving as bank comptroller in the Fairchild administration until 1870, when the office was abolished. Looking about for his next office, he naturally turned to the political powers in western Wisconsin. Cadwallader C. Washburn represented western Wisconsin in Congress from 1867 to 1871, and as early as 1868 he had his eye on the senatorship. But in 1869 Matt Carpenter stampeded the proceedings and ran off with the prize. Washburn, who did not want a third term in the House, put his blessing for successor on

---

that Colonel Vilas had a distinguished military career and Captain Spooner did not. Spooner became a United States Senator in 1885, and Vilas succeeded him in the seat in 1891. Spooner reclaimed the seat in 1897 and held it until 1907.

[51]Fowler, *John Coit Spooner,* 52–56, 201–202, 213–216, 262–268; Current, *Pine Logs and Politics,* 178–184; Nesbit, *Wisconsin,* 374–375; *DAB.*

a supporter, Jerry Rusk, who served three terms (1871–1877), when he fell into hot water.[52]

In the 1875 Carpenter-Washburn fight for Carpenter's senatorial seat, which finally fell to the considerably surprised Angus Cameron, a big issue was a letter that Washburn had written in 1871 when he received the party nomination for governor— apparently as the gift of Senators Carpenter and Howe. The letter supposedly disavowed any intention of ever contesting the senate seats of either Howe or Carpenter. Was the letter a confirmation of a deal, disposing of offices of sacred trust, or simply momentary picque expressed by an ambitious politician who had compromised his chances to become a senator? At any rate, the letter had been written to Jerry Rusk, who made the contents known four years later. Washburn was upset, and he responded in print before Rusk actually provided copies. A rift with Washburn was inevitable, and the indication of it was that Rusk lost his congressional seat. Washburn still had power in his western district even though he was a waning power in state politics. Rusk immediately began shopping for another sponsor to keep himself in public office. He turned to Elisha Keyes to help him get appointed as railroad commissioner, but Keyes was no longer the "Boss" he had been.[53]

Rusk's transfer to a more seaworthy political craft than Keyes's was made through ex-Senator Howe, who remembered him favorably as a congressman who ran errands and cheerfully traded favors. Sawyer had also been in Congress during Rusk's first two terms, and Sawyer and Howe were close. Rusk aligned himself with Sawyer and Payne. When it came time for Sawyer and his friends to find a more favorably disposed gubernatorial candidate with popular appeal, Rusk came to their minds. As the still-hostile *Sentinel* put it: "The big ponderous form of Jerre

---

[52]George H. Wood, Jr., "A Diamond in the Rough—A Study of the Administration of Governor Jeremiah McLain Rusk, 1882–1889" (master's thesis, University of Wisconsin, 1970), 1–23; Henry Casson, *"Uncle Jerry": Life of General Jeremiah M. Rusk, Stage Driver, Farmer, Soldier, Legislator, Governor, Cabinet Officer* (Madison, 1895), 111–157.

[53]Wood, "Administration of Governor Rusk," 21–29.

Rusk stalks majestically through the corridors . . . conscious of the power of the machine to make a governor out of him.''[54]

Rusk had made a party splash the year before, which added to his availability. He was a delegate to the 1880 Republican national convention which featured a long deadlock among supporters of a third term for General Grant, those for James G. Blaine, also a frequent contestant, and men favoring John Sherman, the party's financial wizard from the crucial state of Ohio. Rusk, who was born and raised in Ohio, had a long acquaintance with James A. Garfield, then a recently elected senator from Ohio and manager of Sherman's campaign. With many others, Rusk was convinced of the availability of Garfield, who—under the circumstances—had to plead the opposite. Rusk led a movement within the Wisconsin delegation to break the deadlock by switching to Garfield, the dark horse of the convention. Wisconsin was strategically located at the end of the roll call of the states, a good position from which to lead the break. On the thirty-fourth ballot, sixteen of Wisconsin's twenty votes were switched to Garfield, who was not formally among the contenders. The deed was done. The grateful Garfield offered Jerry Rusk any appointment he desired, but all that came out of the patronage maneuvering was the post of chargé d'affaires to Paraguay and Uruguay. Rusk declined the dubious honor, and friends felt that he deserved balm. It came in the form of the longest run to date as Wisconsin's governor (1882–1889). Rusk practically owned the job but declined a fourth term, going soon after into the cabinet of President Benjamin Harrison as secretary of agriculture.[55]

Jerry Rusk provided the popular figure that the Republicans

[54]*Ibid.*, 23–30; Current, *Pine Logs and Politics,* 184–187; Milwaukee *Sentinel,* September 21, 1881. The *Sentinel* was still in the hands of Matt Carpenter's friends.

[55]Wood, "Administration of Governor Rusk," 28–34; Allan Peskin, "The 'Put-Up Job': Wisconsin and the Republican National Convention of 1880," in *WMH,* 55 (Summer, 1972), 263–274. Rusk went to Washington in June, 1881, and Garfield assured him that he would do better by him, but an assassin's bullet felled Garfield before the matter was settled.

needed, although he bore the initial burden of being the candidate believed to be dictated by Sawyer. The Rusk boom among Sawyer's lieutenants began with a rumor that Elisha Keyes might recoup by backing Hans B. Warner, a Norwegian-born wounded veteran who had survived a Confederate prison. Warner was just completing two terms as secretary of state. He was from Pierce County in northwestern Wisconsin. The counter-candidate whom Sawyer's forces needed was a nonpareil from western Wisconsin, someone with a distinguished war record and evidence that he had acquitted himself in some statewide office. Jerry Rusk filled the bill on all counts.[56]

Jerry Rusk was no shoo-in for the nomination, or in the general election. A good deal of earnest horse trading went on to fill the other statewide offices with regional and ethnic allies. Ernst G. Timme, German-born, who had lost an arm at Chickamauga, replaced Warner, the Norwegian, as secretary of state. The Norwegian vote was placated by the nomination of Nils Haugen, from the same county as Warner, to fill the newly created post of state railroad commissioner. Philip Spooner, the Madison ally of Keyes, was nominated for another elective post as insurance commissioner.[57]

Rusk won the governorship by a plurality rather than a majority, primarily because the prohibitionists formed a new party and fielded a full slate of candidates for the statewide offices. This was because the new Republican management failed to satisfy the prohibition forces in the platform. The prohibitionists took nearly 8 per cent of the total vote, mostly from the Republicans. This fact registered with the Republican legislative candidates, many of whom were always ready to entertain temperance legislation whatever the official party line. In 1881, the legislature rejected prohibition proposals and petitions but passed an anti-treat law, providing a fine for anyone buying a drink for another person, causing some hilarity in distant newspapers. (Apparently

---

[56]Wood, "Administration of Governor Rusk," 29–32. The *Wisconsin Blue Book, 1881,* pp. 491–492, contains a brief biography of Warner.

[57]Wood, "Administration of Governor Rusk," 31–34.

the "Dutch treat" was not understood by the Yankees.) It was repealed in the 1882 session, but liquor-control legislation could count on earnest maneuvering in any session. In 1885, the high license law was passed. Rusk took the defensive position that sobriety could not be legislated, which cheered German voters.[58]

Governor Rusk and the Republicans appeared to have a slippery hold on the Wisconsin electorate as he took over the governor's office in January, 1882. While Rusk had a comfortable majority of almost 11,000 votes out of 151,551 cast for the major party candidates, there were 20,227 votes for third-party candidates: 13,225 for the Prohibition candidate and 7,002 for Greenbacker Edward P. Allis, who was a reluctant candidate. There was little evidence that the soft money or temperance enthusiasms were going to abate, and the majority of these enthusiasts came from the ranks of the Republican voters. The seriousness with which Rusk and his sponsors treated the temperance issue was an indication of their intention to counterbalance their losses to the new Prohibition party by increasing their hold upon the Protestant Germans. This was successful, if the German press and Milwaukee voting are taken as indicators.[59]

There were other hazards to Governor Rusk's long-term political future. The Milwaukee *Sentinel* had come into the temporary control of owners and editors who were hostile to the so-called "Madison Regency" and to Senator Sawyer and his political allies. The paper had been controlled by Senator Carpenter and friends, but Carpenter's unexpected death in February, 1881, left the *Sentinel* somewhat adrift. The tone of its news and edito-

[58]Thomson, *Political History of Wisconsin,* 225-228; Milwaukee *Seebote,* March 31, November 3, 1881; Milwaukee *Herold,* March 31, November 3, 1881; Milwaukee *Germania,* February 2, 1881. The high license law was a Republican sop to temperance forces, baited with revenue for municipal corporations. Campbell, ed., *Wisconsin in Three Centuries,* 4:297-299.

[59]The Milwaukee *Herold* was actively pro-Rusk in 1881. It had earlier distanced itself from the Republicans as a result of the Liberal Republican bolt of 1872. Rusk narrowly carried Milwaukee County in 1881, the second Republican gubernatorial candidate to do so. Governor Smith had carried it in 1879, but he was a Milwaukeean running for a second term while Rusk was (to Milwaukeeans) a relatively new face from the wilds of Vernon County. See Milwaukee *Herold,* March 31, October 20, 1881.

rial pages was patronizing towards the new governor—whom it saw as Sawyer's creation—describing Rusk's inaugural as follows:

> The face of nature was unclouded and beamed benevolently, and so did the small legion of friends of the new Governor from the home of that gentleman, in anticipation of the loaves and fishes that were his to distribute. . . . The martial spectacle has not had a parallel in the history of this city [Madison] since the bellum days when the boys in blue quartered at Fort Randall panted for the privilege of pouring hot shot and shell into the ranks of the Johnnies. . . .

This complacency shortly turned to tones of alarm as the editors discovered a plot, fronted by Horace Rublee and other more shadowy figures, to destroy or take over the *Sentinel*. This "ring" was the result of the legislature's lamentable course in electing Sawyer to the Senate. The failure to heed the *Sentinel's* warnings about what would happen to the party if it elected Sawyer, and thus let wealth gain control of the party, had brought to power a ring which was allegedly destroying the normal Republican majorities. Rublee won control of the *Sentinel* in May, 1882, announced the change of management, and the next day the paper appeared as the *Republican-Sentinel*, a change that was not long continued. Willard G. Bleyer, the first director of the University's journalism school, described Rublee, who edited the *Sentinel* until his death in 1896, as the man who made the state's most important morning paper more than a party organ—rather Wisconsin's leading paper. His editorials were widely quoted by the state press as well as nationally. Rublee was a stout supporter of Governor Rusk as Rusk's political career blossomed well beyond what had been expected by those who supposedly raised him to the office.[60]

Other hazards to Rusk's future political career were within the

---

[60]Milwaukee *Sentinel,* January 3, 14, 24, 30, February 1, March 13, May 19, 22, 23, 1882; Milwaukee *Evening Wisconsin,* May 19, 20, 22, 1882. Willard Bleyer's assessment of Horace Rublee is in the *DAB*; Bleyer and Rublee are in the *DWB*. The *Sentinel* came strongly to Governor Rusk's support, particularly after the riots of May, 1886, in Milwaukee. The Milwaukee *Sentinel* Index, 1880–1890, reflects the change in Rusk's coverage after Rublee became editor.

Republican party nationally. Most readers will be aware of the disputed election of 1876, which ultimately brought Rutherford B. Hayes to the presidency. Probably a majority of Americans believed that this election had been won by Samuel J. Tilden of New York, the Democratic nominee. Moreover, Hayes was mildly a reformer at war with the Stalwart faction within the party. As we have seen, Rusk played a prominent role four years later in thwarting the Stalwarts in the 1880 national convention which gave the nomination to James A. Garfield. But Garfield's assassination removed him from the scene less than six months after his inauguration. His successor, Vice-President Chester A. Arthur, a Stalwart, never overcame the circumstances of his becoming President. Arthur was shunted aside by the 1884 national convention in favor of a perennial candidate, James G. Blaine, who lost to Grover Cleveland.

As one would expect from this record, the state Republicans had some nervous moments. In 1884, Wisconsin gave its electoral college vote to Blaine by a narrow majority of 50.4 per cent of the popular vote, and Rusk won re-election by the only slightly larger margin of 51 per cent. Two minor parties, the Greenback and Prohibition, ran candidates at both the national and state levels in that election—the first Wisconsin gubernatorial election to be held in a presidential election year. Presumably both of these minor parties, particularly the latter, cost the Republicans more than they did the Democrats. The election was too close for comfort, as had been three of the four Republican gubernatorial victories since Ludington's narrow win in 1875. Rusk was elected by a minority of the state's voters in the first and last of his three gubernatorial elections. Yet he emerged from this as a presumptive nominee for the presidency in 1888. His was truly an interesting political career.[61]

[61]Milwaukee *Sentinel,* April 5, 10, 1882; George H. Mayer, *The Republican Party, 1854–1966* (New York, 1967), 189–213; Donoghue, *How Wisconsin Voted, 1848–1972,* pp. 77, 98–100; *Wisconsin Blue Book, 1960,* pp. 129–130. The Milwaukee *Sentinel,* March 28, 1888, carried a lead editorial entitled "The Old Wisconsin Ironsides," which was a quote from the New York *Sun* reporting that Rusk, who was visiting in Washington, D.C., had been mentioned as presidential timber.

Rusk had little of Harrison Ludington's diffidence about presenting his message and recommendations to the legislature
within a few days of his first inauguration. The message gives
every evidence that Rusk had done his homework and of his
continuing interests: agriculture, education, the militia, and
improvements in institutional care. His subsequent messages
show a sure hand in this regard. An activist spirit also marked
his role as a political leader. He asserted himself, though as a
rule genially. He was not without a touchy sense of amour-
propre, but he soon developed the authority to back it up. He
had always taken a vital interest in the advancement of his own
political career, but, much like Senator Sawyer, he was not
distressed by the give-and-take normal to politics or by occasional evidence of independence on the part of allies or even
appointees. He soon felt secure in his own political base and
became an ameliorating influence between the inevitable factions
within the party. Rusk worked equably with Republicans who
found Sawyer's role as party boss difficult to abide. With these
qualities, he brought his party through some rough political
waters. One need only note that he faced a heavy Democratic
majority in his second legislature, and in 1885 the Democrat
Grover Cleveland succeeded to the White House, a most unaccustomed event for Republicans.[62]

Rusk was immediately handed a golden opportunity to refute
the charge that he was the creature of Senator Sawyer and his
money. During the first month of his governorship, a railroad
company building in northwestern Wisconsin went bankrupt,
stranding some 1,700 workmen in northern Burnett and Douglas
counties. January was no time of the year to be there in any case,
and to be abandoned with no prospect of payment, food, or
lodging created a desperate situation. The men took the understandable course of seizing anything of value, threatening to

---

[62]Wood, "Administration of Governor Rusk," is the best source on Rusk as politician
and governor. Casson, *Jeremiah M. Rusk,* is a panegyric, but a useful source. See also
Fulmer Mood, "Frederick Jackson Turner and the Chicago *Inter-Ocean,* 1885," in *WMH,*
35 (Spring, 1952), 193.

burn the bridges they had built, and otherwise visit their displeasure on the company. Some lumbermen who were supplying the railroad felt that they were unfairly at hazard and appealed to the new governor for troops to restore order and protect their property. Rusk replied with humanity and a useful phrase: "These men need bread, not bullets," or (equally alliterative), "bread, not bayonets."[63]

Rusk sent food and transportation, and through intermediaries persuaded the workmen to leave their wage claims to a committee and to his care. There was a way out. The defunct company, the Chicago, Portage and Superior, commonly known as the "Air Line," had a claim on a part of the St. Croix land grant which, although it came from the federal government, was in the gift of the state legislature. Because the Air Line was well behind its mandated completion date as well as clearly failing financially, Senator Sawyer and his allies of the "Omaha Line" were busy negotiating for the transfer of line and grant. Rusk was well aware of this, and proposed that the Omaha company assume the outstanding debts for work and materials of the former. This gesture obviously made the transfer of the land grant politically more palatable. A deal was quickly sealed, sweetened with the promise of part of the land grant and trackage rights for Alexander Mitchell's CM&StP to forestall yet another unseemly battle among the titans. The legislature responded with alacrity, and the deal, largely the work of Sawyer's attorney, John C. Spooner, safely delivered the various elements. Sawyer got the timber and the workmen eventually got their pay.[64]

Rusk similarly declined to respond to calls for the militia in strike situations in Superior in the spring of 1883 and two years later in Eau Claire. The contrast between Rusk and his predecessor, Governor Smith, who responded with regimental force in the Eau Claire "Sawdust War" of July, 1881, was plain to see.

[63]Casson, *Jeremiah M. Rusk,* 167–169.

[64]*Ibid.,* 169–173. Casson (p. 170) saw all of this as: "A happy thought struck the Governor." Current, *Pine Logs and Politics,* 140–143, and Wood, "Administration of Governor Rusk," 39–44, look beyond the "happy thought."

Strikes in isolated lumber towns were by the nature of things likely to lead to some sharp, brief confrontations. Rusk looked upon such events with equanimity. He had his eyes elsewhere. Following two days of rioting in 1884 in Cincinnati that received national attention, he told the militia companies in Milwaukee that they should form a battalion, and he had them hold joint exercises in August of that year.[65]

The 1882 fall election was a Democratic triumph nationally, a reaction to the accumulation of liabilities described above of a national party too long in power. Despite the Republican reapportionment of Wisconsin's congressional districts as a result of the 1880 federal census, the voters made a shambles of the Republican arithmetic. The Democrats regained control of the House of Representatives in Washington, having lost it temporarily in the 1880 election. Wisconsin took a share in this reverse. Normally a safely Republican state, in 1880 it had returned six Republicans and two Democrats to the lower house of Congress. The 1880 census brought an additional seat to Wisconsin which the Republican legislature incorporated in the 1882 redistricting. But the election that fall brought a humiliating defeat. The Republicans carried only three seats to the Democrats' six. Republican legislative district lines held no better. Where the party had had comfortable majorities of twenty-three Republicans in the senate and sixty-four in the assembly in the 1882 session, in the November election of that year they barely clung to control of the state senate and became a minority of forty-three in the one-hundred-member assembly.[66]

[65]Wood, "Administration of Governor Rusk," 50–51; Wisconsin Adjutant General, *Biennial Report,* September 30, 1884, pp. 15–16. Rusk's military instincts were never far below the surface. His last legislative message, January 13, 1887, in *Wisconsin Public Documents,* 1887, Governor's Message, vol. 1, p. 22, comments that the practical test "made in May last has demonstrated that the state troops can be assembled in any emergency . . . , and that, when assembled, they are loyal, subordinate, and under admirable instruction and discipline."

[66]*Wisconsin Blue Book, 1882,* pp. 314–317; *ibid., 1883,* pp. 312–315, 509–513. It should be noted that the Democrats, whatever their normal expectations in Wisconsin, controlled the House of Representatives during seven of the ten congresses between 1873 and 1893—fourteen of the twenty-one years—but held the White House for not quite five of

Governor Rusk could bear his party's 1882 defeat with some equanimity. For one reason, Wisconsin's voters had just approved in that election a constitutional amendment adopting the biennial system. The change meant that the legislature would meet biennially rather than annually, and the terms of assemblymen went from one year to two, senators from two years to four. As part of the change, the state officers elected for two-year terms in November, 1881, were not subject to election again until November, 1884. This gave Rusk and his fellow Republican state officials an added year to recover from the jolt of the 1882 election. Another mitigating factor was that the 1883 legislature did not present an opportunity to elect a United States Senator, but Senator Cameron's seat would be up in the 1885 session. Sure enough, serendipity reigned. When the legislature met in 1885, the Democratic threat had receded. There were only thirteen Democrats in the senate and thirty-nine in the assembly. While the Democrats could look forward to the inauguration of a Democratic President—the first one elected in twenty-eight years—before the end of their session, the returned Republican majority in Wisconsin would fill Senator Cameron's senatorial chair.[67]

Governor Rusk was a politician always alert to ensure his continuance in office. Fortunately, his interests were in accord with those of a large part of the electorate. As a successful farmer, he naturally undertook an active interest in the development of practical aid to agriculture. He allied with those who were agitating for an independent college of agriculture. While this purpose was thwarted, it did galvanize the regents and administration of the University of Wisconsin to adopt a program of farmers' institutes and short courses to reach a broad farm clientele. Rusk was a strong ally of William Henry, who came to the University

those twenty-one years (President Cleveland, 1885–1889 and 1893–1897). Wisconsin Democrats were so accustomed to Republican gerrymanders, and so astonished by the favorable 1882 election results, that they forgot to complain. The Republicans would not be so forgiving after the next (1890) census, when the Democrats were in control of the legislature.

[67] *Wisconsin Blue Book, 1885*, p. 33; *ibid., 1979–1980*, pp. 338–342, 362.

as professor of agriculture in 1880 and was the first dean (1891) after the creation of the separate college of agriculture in the University. The governor successfully promoted the office of state veterinarian, another step which established his popularity with farmers.[68]

Rusk's interest in agriculture did not grow out of his political ambitions, but he was not a man to neglect an opportunity. His Democratic opponent in the elections of 1881 and 1884 was a Racine farmer-banker, Nicholas D. Fratt, who was president of the Wisconsin State Agricultural Society. Rusk was aware of the average farmer's opinion of the society, which was run by life members who had paid a $200 membership fee. Fratt fit the mold. (It was reasonable to assume that a Racine banker would seldom be out plowing.) The society, a quasi-public agency which received a subsidy from the state, was principally in the business of directing the annual state fair and contributing to regional fairs. These fairs involved the eternal questions of whether they should be sponsoring harness races and authorizing beer tents as their principal attractions and sources of revenue. Therefore Governor Rusk was not above picking an occasional public row with the society's managers, then appearing jovially in a rear seat at their annual meeting in Madison to lobby the general membership.[69]

Every legislature since 1879 had entertained measures to make punishment for "vagabondage" even harsher. Rusk allowed such a measure to pass without his signature in 1883 when the Demo-

[68]See Chapter 1 above; also *Wisconsin Public Documents,* 1883, Governor's Message, vol. 1, pp. 7–8, and *ibid.,* Governor's Message, 1885, vol. 1, pp. 18–19, which suggest Rusk's approach. In the governor's 1883 message, two-thirds of his comment on the University concern Professor Henry and his work in agriculture. In 1885, he endorsed a separate agricultural school, divorced from the University, and "devoted purely to training men to be better farmers, [which] would operate to check the dangerous rush of farmer boys to the cities and into the professions. . . ." See also Wilbur H. Glover, *Farm and College: The College of Agriculture of the University of Wisconsin, A History* (Madison, 1952), 89–111; Merle Curti and Vernon Carstensen, *The University of Wisconsin: A History, 1848–1925* (2 vols., Madison, 1949), 1:467–468, 544.

[69]Wood, "Administration of Governor Rusk," chap. 5, esp. 70–75; Wisconsin State Agricultural Society, *Transactions,* 1885, pp. 376–380; Nicholas D. Fratt obituary in Milwaukee *Free Press,* November 13, 1910.

crats controlled the assembly and a Racine Democrat had introduced the bill. The law provided prison terms of up to a year for convicted vagrants sentenced in counties that did not maintain workhouses. (A vagrant was a male of sixteen or over, not resident where charged, and with no visible means of support.) The more usual sentence was not less than fifteen days on bread and water. Both the Milwaukee *Sentinel* and Madison *Wisconsin State Journal* commented on the law's severity. Governor Rusk soon had an opportunity to redeem his apparent oversight of allowing the bill to become law without comment or approval. In the next legislature, Republican Pliny Norcross, a Janesville lawyer, introduced yet another amendment to the vagrancy statute. The bill, which passed both houses, provided that convicted vagrants could be limited to a diet of bread and water for all or part of their sentences, which could run to ninety days in county detention. In a ringing veto message, the governor pointed out that nothing prevented this Draconian sentence from including hard labor as well as the extended diet of bread and water only. He observed that a diet of bread and water for felons in Waupun was limited to twenty days, the maximum term for solitary confinement. The application of punishment far in excess of these limits for vagrancy he characterized as sheer terrorism, calculated to deter others rather than simply to punish the individual.[70]

The governor had a sure sense of the popular pulse. His veto message made good copy. It was difficult to make the case that he was simply the tool of moneyed men or an ignorant Know Nothing, as Robert Schilling angrily characterized him after the

---

[70]Lawrence M. Friedman, *A History of American Law* (New York, 1973), 503–505, notes the passing of common law into specific statute law, as in these vagrancy laws which regularly came before the legislature. Citing a study of Chippewa County courts in criminal cases, he states that only 0.5 per cent of these were appealed. He was writing of the latter nineteenth century. See *Laws of Wisconsin*, 1879, pp. 273–276; *ibid.*, 1883, pp. 300–302; *Assembly Bills*, 1883, Bill 170; *Wisconsin Assembly Journal*, 1883, p. 798; *Milwaukee Sentinel* and *Wisconsin State Journal*, April 3, 1883. The *Wisconsin Assembly Journal*, 1885, pp. 997–998, has Rusk's veto message. See also Wisconsin Board of Charities and Reform, *Annual Report*, 1878, pp. 53–56 ("The Rights of Labor" and "Tramps"), and *ibid.*, *Annual Report*, 1880, pp. 95–96. The *Laws of Wisconsin*, 1887, pp. 524–528, rewrote the entire code on the subject of vagrancy. The definition remained essentially the same.

Bay View shootings the following year. The Milwaukee journalist Bill Hooker aptly described Rusk as not scholarly, "and sometimes he did get tangled up in his grammar, but he was far from being an ignoramus." Hooker added: "No man, in my time as a reporter, who occupied the exalted post of governor of the Badger State was more popular with the masses than Jeremiah Rusk, former stage driver."

The governor transcended the circumstances of his first nomination for the office and soon established his own political base from which he could deal as an equal. Rusk readily assumed the role of peacemaker within the party. His whole political career had been based upon making regional, factional, and ethnic alliances, which were a necessity for an aspiring politician from an outlying rural county. It is surprising how rapidly Rusk overcame the charge that he was the genial, bumbling tool of Philetus Sawyer and his henchmen.[71]

Rusk was an activist in more ways than simply recommending the expansion of state services in the vital fields of agriculture, education, institutional care, and health. He was also an effective lobbyist who worked the legislative corridors, made it his business to know legislators, employees, and lobbyists, and was available to and talkative with newsmen. His legislative messages give the impression of the man in charge. "For the rebuilding of the west steps and portico, which I found to be in a dangerous condition," the necessary repair was ordered. "I have also caused to be placed in the boiler room, at a cost of $2,200, two new boilers. . . ." While the new wings were being added to the capitol in November, 1883, a disastrous accident occurred. An exterior wall of the south wing collapsed, carrying forty workmen

[71]Casson, *Jeremiah M. Rusk,* 174–178; Hooker, *An Earlier Milwaukee,* 56–57. White, *Republican Era,* 235–237, says that the U.S. Department of Agriculture was extremely fortunate in its first three secretaries, the first being Jeremiah Rusk: "The vision of this man of the people was remarkable. He was equally concerned with pure and applied research, with the education of farmers in improved methods, with aid to marketing at home and abroad, and with the inspection of food products on a large scale. He it was, educated in the common schools alone, who sent experts abroad to establish contacts with agricultural institutions in other countries. . . ." See also Wood, "Administration of Governor Rusk," chap. 6.

with it. Six men died and seventeen were injured. Rusk ordered that the expenses of the injured be paid. "Perhaps, in strictness, this expenditure was beyond the law. . . . In the circumstances, I felt if I did less the people of Wisconsin would not justify me."[72]

The governor's resolution of Milwaukee's May Day riots in 1886 simply confirmed his growing popularity. Even though the Prohibition party vote peaked in 1886, with 6 per cent of the gubernatorial ballots, and Robert Schilling's People's party drew another 7.5 per cent, Rusk's percentage of the major party vote increased. The Democrats were uncommonly helpful to Rusk. They obliquely endorsed the governor's actions in the Bay View affair, preferring to denounce the Republicans for making political hay from an issue upon which both parties agreed. The conservative Bourbon element remained in firm control of the Democratic party, with Alexander Mitchell still active until his death in 1887, and a new star much in the ascendant in the person of William F. Vilas of Madison, who became President Cleveland's political right arm in 1885 as Postmaster General of the United States.[73]

The accession of Vilas to the chief patronage post in the nation marked another change in Rusk's status in his party. In March, 1885, the nation's post offices began to change hands. These, of course, were the principal sources of patronage, comprising three-fourths of the non-military federal employees. It was a great advantage to have every village and hamlet postmaster ready to distribute party material and aware of who fit where politically. Senators Sawyer and Spooner endured a four-year drought while Vilas tended the patronage spigot. This could only have had the effect of magnifying the minor patronage in the hands of the

---

[72]Wood, "Administration of Governor Rusk," chaps. 4 and 5; Hooker, *An Earlier Milwaukee,* 56–57; *Wisconsin Public Documents,* 1885, Governor's Message, vol. 1, pp. 4, 19–20.

[73]*Wisconsin Blue Book, 1887,* pp. 209–250. Sixty per cent of granger John Cochrane's vote was in Milwaukee County. Fifteen lumbering and industrial cities accounted for another 28.9 per cent. See also Robert M. Rice, "The Populist Party in Milwaukee" (master's thesis, University of Wisconsin-Milwaukee, 1967), 18–20; *Wisconsin Blue Book, 1887,* pp. 370–372; Merrill, *William Freeman Vilas,* 114–121, 185–187.

governor. As Democratic Governor George Peck complained a few years later, "two hundred and sixty-five more persons drew pay from the State Treasury for personal services in 1889 than in 1878."[74]

An important reason for the growing state payroll, aside from the rapid growth of population and an increase in the areas of service and regulation entered by the state, was the cheering existence of a surplus from year to year in the state's general fund. In 1880, special taxes on railroads and insurance companies provided $459,493.91 of the $1,049,406.73 taken in for the general fund. For 1888, these sources, enlarged to include telephone, telegraph, and sleeping-car companies, amounted to $1,155,715.77. The general fund began running a surplus, which led Governor Rusk in his 1885 message to declare a moratorium on property tax levies for state government. For some years thereafter, collections against real and personal property by the state were only those millages mandated for the public schools and the University. This accounts in large measure for the aggressive role that Governor Rusk was able to play in expanding the areas of direct state concern and intervention—as well as expanding the state payroll. The 1880's, of course, were more expansive after the long depression years of the seventies. Rusk took full advantage of this.[75]

Governor Rusk naturally played upon his war record and expressed his concern for the veterans, who constituted an effective lobby and a political force nationally. Rusk's biography contains a wonderful group portrait of the patriarchal governor, surrounded by seventeen members of his Grand Army Staff, known popularly as the "Maimed Heroes." The limits of veterans' politics had been tested earlier by another maimed hero, the one-armed Lucius Fairchild, whose biographer entitled his work *The Empty Sleeve.* Fittingly, Fairchild's manager, when he tempted

[74]Merrill, *William Freeman Vilas,* 98–108; *Wisconsin Public Documents,* 1891, Governor's Message, vol. 1, pp. 3–4.

[75]*Wisconsin Public Documents,* 1881, Governor's Message, vol. 1, p. 4; *ibid.,* 1885, vol. 1, p. 6; *ibid.,* 1887, vol. 1, pp. 6–7; *ibid.,* 1889, vol. 1, pp. 2–3.

fate in 1869 by running for (and winning) an unprecedented third term for governor, was Jeremiah Rusk, who later took advantage of the precedent. Then, after a decade abroad in a variety of diplomatic posts, Fairchild returned early in 1882 to a hero's welcome in his home town, Madison. The honors were done by his old friend and political ally, Jerry Rusk, newly installed as governor.[76]

Fairchild was somewhat surprised by the fervency of his welcome and the general belief that he would, in the natural course of things, return to politics. As he put the matter facetiously to Mrs. Fairchild, he had been mentioned as an active candidate for "President—Vice President—Senator—Congressman, Minister to England—& perhaps Alderman of Madison." He remained wary, as well he might, for the political booming seemed to come from Republicans who disliked Senator Sawyer's domination of the party, and looked upon Fairchild's assumed political potency as the magic that would relieve them of this embarrassment. Unfortunately, Fairchild finally was persuaded of his political puissance and offered himself for the senatorial nomination before the 1885 legislature. Sawyer had already designated the seat for his political ally from Hudson, John C. Spooner. (One of the ironies of this was that, as a young man, Spooner had been Governor Fairchild's secretary.) Fairchild stood forth and was smothered, with the utmost courtesy and deference, by Sawyer's allies. Governor Rusk was doubtless pleased by the outcome. It removed a potential rival with similar qualifications and a claim on the veterans. The humiliating defeat turned Fairchild's political energies to the Grand Army of the Republic. He won the office of national commander at the 1886 encampment held in San Francisco. Wishing to appear in style

---

[76]Casson, *Jeremiah M. Rusk*, 223–227; Sam Ross, *The Empty Sleeve: A Biography of Lucius Fairchild* (Madison, 1964), 117–119, 160–182. The potency of the veterans as a lobby and political force was such that Senator Sawyer—not a veteran—ingratiated himself with veterans by constituting himself as the court of last appeal for those who needed a special bill put through Congress for their specific pension cases. Sawyer set up a "Pension bureau" in his Washington home and shepherded countless special bills through the Congress. Current, *Pine Logs and Politics,* 219–228.

at the veterans' encampment of the following year, he indicated his desire to borrow the "Maimed Heroes," but Rusk—a national hero as a result of Bay View—had need of his entourage for the affair.[77]

Both men had by this time been stung by the presidential bee. But Fairchild, as national commander of the GAR and indefatigable worker of the veterans' circuit, had been turned livid by President Cleveland, who in Fairchild's view was much too conciliatory with the rebels of twenty years before, as well as too hard on special pension bills for Union veterans. It was a vendetta that professional veterans cherished. In 1887, at a GAR function in New York, it was announced that President Cleveland had just ordered the return of all captured Confederate battle flags to the respective southern states. National Commander Fairchild, honored guest at the affair, suited his impassioned words to the occasion: "May God palsy the hand that wrote that order! May God palsy the brain that conceived it! And may God palsy the tongue that dictated it!" (He was afterward known as "Fairchild of the three palsies.") When the Wisconsin Republicans went to their national convention at Chicago in 1888 with their wealth of riches in potential national leadership, it was Jeremiah Rusk who carried the ringing endorsement for the presidency from the Wisconsin state Republican convention; and it was John C. Spooner who, late in the proceedings, placed Rusk's name before the national convention. This did not lead to the nomination, but it did lead (after some uncertainty) to Rusk's appointment by President Benjamin Harrison as the nation's first secretary of agriculture with cabinet rank. Harrison rewarded General Fairchild with an appointment to the Cherokee commission.[78]

Political alliances are seldom based on bedrock, and Rusk's were subject to occasional shifts. The 1888 Republican national convention where he was offered as a presidential nominee was

[77]Ross, *Empty Sleeve*, 182–202; Wood, "Administration of Governor Rusk," 93–96; Mood, "Turner and the Chicago *Inter-Ocean*," *WMH*, 35:188–194, 210–214.

[78]Ross, *Empty Sleeve*, 202–211; Casson, *Jeremiah M. Rusk*, 213–227, 235–237.

held in June. As the summer progressed, Rusk was being urged to accept nomination for a fourth term as governor. Benjamin Harrison's election, or his gratitude to the Wisconsin delegation for quickly deserting favorite son Rusk's candidacy for his, was no secure anchor to windward for Rusk. But the governor doubtless felt that it ill became recent presidential timber to cling tenaciously to the bird in hand. There were a number of eager aspirants signaling their availability to succeed Rusk. A leading contender among them was Horace A. Taylor, popularly known as "Hod" Taylor, a fellow townsman of Senator Spooner and editor-owner of the Hudson *Star and Times*. Active in Republican affairs as well as successful in land, timber, mining, and banking enterprises, Taylor had been state chairman of the party (1883–1887) and was considered a "skilled manipulator" and "one of Spooner and Sawyer's pin-setters." Spooner was among Taylor's backers, but Rusk and Sawyer were not persuaded. Rusk and Sawyer, as noted earlier, were both tolerant of differences with political friends and allies. But Rusk's sensibilities in this particular matter are easy enough to understand. Taylor was a power in state politics in western Wisconsin, which was Rusk's base. Spooner, also from western Wisconsin, properly felt obligated to Taylor, because Taylor had skillfully managed his senatorial race in the 1885 legislature. Spooner himself intensely disliked this part of politics, and particularly disliked being in the middle. Taylor was insistent, and could be shrill.[79]

At this point, Rusk confirmed his role as a conciliator within the party, and demonstrated the independence he had achieved. He sent a general letter to the press asserting firmly that he could not be drafted for a fourth term: "The position of Governor, while a high and honorable one, is not one to be coveted for an indefinite length of time." Then, trusting to the short memories of the general electorate, as opposed to those relative few who could appreciate the irony, he went on: "There will be presented for the consideration of the Republican State Convention, the

---

[79]Current, *Pine Logs and Politics*, 189–190, 247–251; Fowler, *John Coit Spooner*, 119–120; *DWB*.

names of several gentlemen, who are all worthy and competent. . . . I have faith that the convention will choose wisely, and that their action will be indorsed [*sic*] by the people. Believing that it would be unwise and contrary to Republican principles, for men who are holding high positions at the hands of the Republican party, to attempt to control or dictate its nominations, I shall refrain from taking a part in the interest of any of the candidates, knowing that the convention will be composed of intelligent gentlemen, having the best interests of the party at heart.''[80]

The Milwaukee *Sentinel*, now under Horace Rublee's editorship and control, had become a reasonably objective Republican newspaper. Rublee must have had his problems with Hod Taylor and Henry Payne, equally peremptory types who managed state party affairs in the 1880's through offices located in Milwaukee. The *Sentinel* started a boom for a political outsider with a prominent article published on May 26, 1888, many weeks before the state convention, suggesting the availability of William D. Hoard, the widely known "cow editor" of Fort Atkinson. Hoard had a wide acquaintanceship across the state as the most prominent champion for a dairy economy as the salvation of Wisconsin farming. He was also a popular performer as an orator, with a fund of pointed, humorous stories. There were frequent references to his Lincolnesque appearance and style. Hoard's interest in politics had not included a time-consuming office—he was a busy man as editor and agricultural expert—which is probably why—when it came—his political career was meteoric: bright and brief.[81]

The *Sentinel* suggestion immediately caught fire. Hoard followed the advice of one of the many who seconded this bolt from the blue: "Keep still. Say nothing. Let the molasses run." Hoard did, the boom built, and he declared himself available. Rusk's statement warning that the usual deal among the kingmakers

[80]Casson, *Jeremiah M. Rusk*, 211–212; Rusk, "To the Editor," August 6, 1888, in the Rusk Papers.

[81]Current, *Pine Logs and Politics*, 247–248, 260; Wight, *Payne*, 47; George W. Rankin, *William Dempster Hoard* (Fort Atkinson, 1925), 81–83; Wilbur H. Glover, "W. D. Hoard's Humor," in *WMH*, 35 (Spring, 1952), 185–187; *DWB*.

would be unwelcome put them on notice. Sawyer and Rusk were content with Hod Taylor's frustration, while Spooner contented himself with a statement that he favored Taylor over the field. The untrammeled Republican convention went to Hoard, who handily won the general election.[82]

William Dempster Hoard was a man of enthusiasms and supreme self-assurance. He was known as the "Jersey Cow" candidate for one of his best-known enthusiasms: the single-purpose dairy cow. This was expressed with equal parts of humor and exasperation. Hoard knew what he knew and was not to be deflected. It went with his background. Both sides of his family were of New England stock. Hoard was born in upstate New York in a rural Madison County community about ten miles south of Oneida. His father was a Methodist circuit rider. Their neighbors were nearly all of the same background. The homogeneity of the people where he grew up, their strong religious convictions, and the certitude of their views were a strong influence on Hoard. He moved to Wisconsin in 1857 when he was twenty, served in the Civil War, and became a newspaper owner in 1870, first in Lake Mills, then in 1873 moving to Fort Atkinson. In 1872 he was one of the organizers of the Wisconsin Dairymen's Association, and in 1885 he launched *Hoard's Dairyman,* which soon became one of the nation's leading agricultural journals.[83]

Jefferson County was heavily German. In 1880, out of a population of 33,530, there were 8,202 German-born. Germans, together with their children and grandchildren, thus constituted a major element of the population. Hoard assumed that he knew these people well. A gregarious man, he doubtless did have a wide acquaintance among them. But they were not his people.

[82]Rankin, *Hoard,* 84–90; Fowler, *John Coit Spooner,* 120.

[83]Rankin, *Hoard,* 1–14; *Wisconsin Blue Book, 1960,* pp. 132–134; *DAB*; Eric E. Lampard, *The Rise of the Dairy Industry in Wisconsin: A Study in Agricultural Change, 1820–1920* (Madison, 1963), 145, 171–172, 250, 333, 340–341. Whitney R. Cross, *The Burned-Over District: The Social and Intellectual History of Enthusiastic Religion in Western New York, 1800–1850* (Ithaca, 1950; Harper Torchbook edition, 1965), 356, explains the transplanted Yankees.

Hoard recalled his mother, of Vermont background, as "the best-read woman I have ever known, in spite of the fact that she never had an opportunity for schooling except such as the district school afforded." It was not a long reach from this to the governor who insisted that everyone (which would include German supporters of parochial schools) deserved, and must have, the blessings of the district school.[84]

One senses an immediate difference between Rusk's gubernatorial messages to his legislatures and Hoard's with relation to a subject that had explosive potential in Wisconsin. Rusk had been complacent about the progress of Wisconsin's public school system, an attitude certainly justified by the reports of State Superintendent Robert Graham (1882–1887). Graham's last biennial report showed a steady increase of the school population seven to fifteen years of age enrolled in school, from 83.2 per cent in 1884 to 86 per cent two years later. While most of the children outside the cities attended public schools, fewer did so in the cities. This was not surprising, he wrote, because in the cities the expanding parochial schools could more readily reach their parishioners. This fact "corroborates the opinion that but comparatively few of our minor population are likely to become illiterate adults." Governor Rusk, in his last message, contented himself with congratulations on the liberal support given Wisconsin's schools, remarking: "The proportion of persons who cannot read or write is very small, and they reside mostly in the large cities. The common schools are eagerly sought, and the percentage of attendance is equal to that of any state in the Union."[85]

Graham's successor as state superintendent, Jesse B. Thayer, did not disagree with Graham's figures. He simply remarked

[84]Rankin, *Hoard*, 4; *Eleventh Census of the United States, 1890: Population, Volume I, Part 1*, pp. 667–668.

[85]Wisconsin Superintendent of Public Instruction, *Biennial Report*, 1884–1886, pp. 7–9, 18–20; *Wisconsin Public Documents*, 1885, Governor's Message, vol. 1, p. 15. Superintendent Graham had experienced a change of opinion since his 1882 report, where he remarked that "we have pretty definite data for determining that already causes are at work in our larger cities which, unchecked, must soon result in a large illiterate class." He had, evidently, reassured himself on the score of attendance in the urban parochial schools. Wisconsin Superintendent of Public Instruction, *Annual Report*, 1882, pp. 13–14.

that the methods of reporting had been improved to eliminate duplications, and the results showed a decline in attendance among children seven to fifteen years old from the 1886 figure of 86 per cent to 82.4 per cent for 1887 and 79.3 per cent for 1888. Even allowing for such special conditions as the severe winter of 1886–1887, a rise in epidemics of what were known as "the usual childhood diseases," the expansion of new, thinly populated country districts occasioned by the extension of railroad lines in the north, and the growth of the parochial schools which simply did not report attendance, he found attendance and the average days attended declining. The more accurate statistics, Thayer stated, "do not show that the public school has kept pace with the growth in population." He deplored the lack of statistical information on the growing parochial school population and concluded: "If it means that the public school is losing in any degree the confidence of the community, that should lead to inquiry as to causes. If it means that private schools are becoming successful rivals by offering a better course of study, better teachers, and better training in the essentials of a common school education, that also should lead to careful investigation, and application of remedies at the proper points."[86]

Governor Rusk and Superintendent Graham had not raised the question of the equivalency of public school and parochial school education. To them, literacy was literacy, whether in English, German, or any other language. They were sensitive enough to the Wisconsin electorate to know that a huge minority of eligible voters were more at home in German than in English, that German was the language of their churches, and that they were accustomed to parochial schools as the norm. By 1888, probably most parochial school teachers understood and spoke English, but German usually was the language they read, wrote, and expressed themselves in most fluently. As one county superintendent reported, the carry-over from English taught to German-speaking children in a German settlement was slight. They

[86]Wisconsin Superintendent of Public Instruction, *Biennial Report*, 1886–1888, pp. 4–19.

could be taught to speak, read, and write in English, but it was strictly a school exercise—rote learning. Among themselves, they spoke German as they did at home. If they read outside of school, it was in German, because that was what was available at home.[87]

Governor Hoard charged full tilt into this thicket. He knew what he knew. Part of this mental stance must have been the product of an uncommonly successful newspaper career. A small-town editor was expected to have valuable insights and opinions on a great variety of subjects. Just as *Hoard's Dairyman* reached well beyond Fort Atkinson, Hoard's opinions reached well beyond his readership, and he was a popular speaker around the state for any occasion. But he had not cultivated the arts associated with political prominence, which sometimes called for blurring or evading divisive issues. Reading examples of his platform wit and wisdom, one gets the sense of a man whose inner audience remained his fellow Yankees of Munnsville, New York.

Superintendent Thayer had challenged the legislature to look more closely at the expanding parochial school systems, but he did not directly connect this with language instruction. Governor Hoard, whose function it was to draw attention to problems needing legislative action, did not react like a seasoned Republican politician dealing with a sensitive issue. The solution was clear enough to him. No admirer of higher education, Hoard disposed of the state's university and normal schools in a single sentence, then leaped aboard his hobby: "The child that is, the citizen that is to be, has a right to demand of the State that it be provided, as against all contingencies, with a reasonable amount of instruction in common English branches. . . . In this connection I would recommend such legislation as would make it the duty of county and city superintendents to inspect all schools for

[87]Addie Neff to J. S. Roeseler, November 23, 1888, in the John S. Roeseler Papers. Neff (who was Clark County's superintendent of schools) was reporting on a German Lutheran congregation that supported an English-language school for six months of the year. It was not a success, for the reasons she noted.

the purpose, and with the authority only, to require that reading and writing in English be daily taught therein.''[88]

The resulting legislation, known popularly as the Bennett Law, made a one-term governor of William D. Hoard, helped to sweep all but one of the seven Republican congressmen from office, and gave the Democrats control of state government for four years. There were, of course, other elements to this political reversal, such as the McKinley tariff, agricultural discontent, and the generally indifferent record of the Harrison administration. There were also some skeletons in the closets of previous Republican state administrations for the Democrats to rattle. But the Bennett Law was the central issue for that huge and quite various segment of voters not firmly attached to either party: Wisconsin's Germans.[89]

In a sense, Governor Hoard was on his own with his call for instruction in English in *all* schools. No mention of this appears in the respective 1886 and 1888 reports of state superintendents Graham and Thayer. Both men remarked the lack of statistics on parochial school attendance. Their statistics derived from an annual census of school-age children gathered by district school clerks. By an 1887 statute, this was the responsibility of the town clerks. In 1887, according to the state superintendent's report, there were 5,977 school districts and subdistricts, aside from city schools, to filter their reports through town clerks. These clerks were simply citizens fulfilling a necessary obligation in their spare time. The usefulness of the statistical record may be imagined, even without taking into account the lack of parochial school attendance records. Superintendent Graham pronounced

---

[88]*Wisconsin Public Documents,* 1889, Governor's Message, vol. 1, pp. 16–18. Rankin, *Hoard,* 69–71, says that Hoard observed of a college education that it was like small doses of laudanum (an opiate) that had to wear off before the victim could adjust to the ordinary duties and responsibilities of life. He also resented the influence that administrators in higher education assumed in defining the curriculum of the common school.

[89]Wyman, ''Wisconsin Ethnic Groups and the Election of 1890,'' *WMH,* 51:269–293. Most embarrassing of the ''skeletons'' would be the so-called ''Treasury Cases,'' which are discussed below. See Thomson, *Political History of Wisconsin,* 241–243.

the 1879 compulsory attendance law a dead letter which should be repealed or rewritten. It was used by busybodies to harass neighbors of whom they did not approve, he said, and the onus fell on the local school board to act on such complaints. They were supposed to investigate and bring suit—an unpleasant proceeding.[90]

Governor Hoard put the worst possible face upon the supposed failure of the 1879 compulsory attendance law by simply citing the wrong figures from Superintendent Thayer's statistics. As Thayer and previous superintendents pointed out, the statistics Hoard used for the legal school age, four to twenty, were much less meaningful than for the seven-to-fifteen-years age group defined in the 1879 compulsory attendance statute. With these seven-to-fifteen-year-old figures, one gets a discrepancy of 62,359 supposedly not attending, rather than Hoard's 302,225. Super-intendents Graham and Thayer also had been at pains to make clear that they were not at all sure of the number of pupils in private and parochial schools. Superintendent Graham's opti-mistic appraisal ("but comparatively few of our minor popula-tion are likely to become illiterate adults") obviously assumed that the private and parochial schools were making up much of the 62,359 gap—those in the seven-to-fifteen age group reported as "not attending."[91]

The statistics cited by Governor Hoard, though wildly inaccu-rate, had the virtue of coming from an official report—and they did not end in three zeroes, as did the other educated guesses. In any event, figures per se did not particularly interest the gover-nor. His attention was on his recommendation that *all* schools—

---

[90]Wisconsin Superintendent of Public Instruction, *Biennial Report*, 1886–1888, pp. 1–2, 7, 17; *ibid.*, 1884–1886, p. 42; *Laws of Wisconsin*, 1879, pp. 155–156. Also see Patzer, *Public Education in Wisconsin*, 63–64.

[91]*Wisconsin Public Documents*, 1887–1888, Governor's Message, vol. 1, p. 17; Wisconsin Superintendent of Public Instruction, *Biennial Report*, 1887–1888, pp. 4–5; *ibid.*, 1885–1886, p. 20; *ibid.*, 1891–1982, pp. 17–18. The 1891–1892 report came up with a figure of 55,000 pupils in Catholic and Lutheran parochial schools, fully 11,000 of whom were not included in the statistical reports. See also William W. Updegrove, "Bibles and Brick-bats: Religious Conflict in Wisconsin's Public School System During the Nineteenth Century" (master's thesis, University of Wisconsin, 1970), 77–78.

public and private and parochial—meet a requirement "that reading and writing in English be daily taught therein."

The proposed bill to respond to Governor Hoard's recommendations was introduced by Senator Levi E. Pond of Westfield in Marquette County. Pond's biography reads much like Hoard's: born in western New York; came to Wisconsin as a young man in 1857; a war veteran. He was in his first term as a senator as part of the large Republican majorities of both houses—one of nine New York-born senators who made up over one-fourth of the membership of the 1889 session.[92]

There were later charges that the Pond bill was simply a Trojan horse masking the Bennett bill, which passed through both houses without significant debate. Senator Pond's bill met swift and massive resistance by petition and press, dying in his hands. It was really an ingenious effort simply to extend the provisions of the 1879 compulsory attendance law. It provided that private and parochial schools, or diocesan directors, should report attendance statistics to the state superintendent through the county or city superintendents—a not unreasonable demand, given uncertainty about their attendance. The 1879 law required "a fair knowledge of the branches of learning ordinarily taught in the common schools of this state." Pond's bill, as amended, extended this to instruction in English, defined as "having received suitable elementary instruction in that language to the extent that they are able to speak and to write the same with reasonable ease and correctness. . . ."[93]

The Bennett bill, introduced in the assembly at almost the same time, received no complaint from members of the legislature who were sensitive to the issue, nor from outsiders anxiously looking for similar measures on the legislature's agenda. Since both the Pond and Bennett bills defined a common school edu-

[92]Janet C. Wegner, "The Bennett Law Controversy in Wisconsin, 1889–1891: A Study of the Problem of 'Americanization' in the Immigrant Church and Its Relation to the History of Church and State in the United States" (master's thesis, Brown University, 1966), 6; *Wisconsin Blue Book, 1889,* pp. 474, 499.

[93]Wegner, "Bennett Law Controversy in Wisconsin," 6–9; *Laws of Wisconsin,* 1879, p. 155; *Wisconsin Senate Bills,* 1889, Bill 147, as amended.

cation as one providing instruction which would ensure the ability to speak, read, and write English, this appears not to have been the bone of contention at this point. Rather, it was the issue of requiring reports from parochial schools, which was fraught with future conflicts in the forbidden area of state and church relations. This was a point familiar to both Catholic and Lutheran Germans, and a current concern in Bismarck's Germany.[94]

The Bennett Law avoided the issue of parochial schools reporting anything to the state superintendent or local school officials, whether directly or through diocesan or other church officials. It simply repeated the formula of compulsory attendance for children between the ages of seven and fourteen (changed from fifteen) for a minimum of twelve weeks a year. They were to attend a public, private, or parochial school, in "the city, town or district" where the child resided, and "no school shall be regarded as a school . . . unless there shall be taught therein, as part of the elementary education of children, reading, writing, arithmetic and United States history, in the English language." Enforcement was left to the local school board, which alone could initiate complaints. Fines could be assessed by a local court. It was much less lenient than the 1879 law in the definition of exceptions. There were two pages of stern admonitions and possible fines for truancy and unauthorized employment, although any child over ten could be granted a work permit by a county judge on a showing that the child could read and write the English language and the family needed the income.[95]

Assemblyman Michael John Bennett, a Catholic of Irish descent, was a native of rural Iowa County serving his second consecutive term as a Republican legislator. He had a high school education and had both farmed and taught country school. He

[94]William F. Whyte, "The Bennett Law Campaign in Wisconsin," in *WMH*, 10 (June, 1927), 371-372; Wyman, "Voting Behavior in the Progressive Era," 70-71; Robert J. Ulrich, "The Bennett Law of 1889: Education and Politics in Wisconsin" (doctoral dissertation, University of Wisconsin, 1965), 176-178; Koppel S. Pinson, *Modern Germany: Its History and Civilization* (second edition, New York, 1966), 180.

[95]*Laws of Wisconsin*, 1879, pp. 155-156; *ibid.*, 1889, pp. 729-733.

had not actually conceived and written the bill that made his name famous. Months after its nearly unanimous passage, when a furor over its terms and origins arose, it was revealed that the Bennett Law had originated with the North Side Turnverein in Milwaukee, "to knock child-labor in the head and make it compulsory for all children under 14 years of age to attend school." An assistant city attorney, Robert Luscombe, had drafted the bill, drawing upon similar bills in Ohio and Illinois, which in turn were patterned after laws in Massachusetts and New York. Recognizing the tactical advantage of a sponsor from outside Milwaukee, they had asked Assemblyman Bennett, chairman of the education committee, to introduce it. But Bennett was not merely a passive agent in this transaction; he discussed the bill with other members of the legislature and mailed 300 copies to Wisconsin educators to solicit their opinions. One recipient was the legal editor of Milwaukee's weekly *Germania,* a newspaper addressed to a wide German Lutheran audience. Bennett asserted that he had received almost no negative response to his mailings, and the bill became law.[96]

The tocsin was first sounded by the German Lutherans, some months after the Bennett Law was on the books. While the root of their objections came down to the requirement that English must be the basic language of instruction, it was generally recognized that this appeal was largely limited to Germans who were supporting parochial schools.[97]

Governor Hoard was adamant. The English-language provi-

[96] *Wisconsin Blue Book, 1889,* p. 509; Wegner, "Bennett Law Controversy in Wisconsin," 8–13, citing the Milwaukee *Journal,* March 25, 1890; Milwaukee *Sentinel,* October 28, 1889, March 11, 13, 1890. Governor Hoard, thirty years later, claimed authorship of section 5 of the Bennett Law, which defined a legal school as one that taught reading, writing, arithmetic, and United States history, in English. See Louise Phelps Kellogg, "Notes of an interview with Ex-Governor William Dempster Hoard, at his home at Fort Atkinson, August 12 and 13, 1918," in the Louise Phelps Kellogg Papers. Hoard's assertion should be taken with a grain of salt, considering the date during World War I. For the popular mood at that time, see Ellis B. Usher to Hoard, August 27, 1917, and Hoard's reply, August 29, 1917, in the William D. Hoard Papers.

[97] Wegner, "Bennett Law Controversy in Wisconsin," 14–18; Wyman, "Voting Behavior in the Progressive Era," 71–73.

sion was the very heart of the law. He stood as the protector of the German child forcibly confined in an alien culture by dark-minded clerics and obstinate parents. He had lived among Jefferson County's heavily German Lutheran population for twenty years, secure in the knowledge that they all voted Democratic and knew about cows, but did not read his paper or expect to find an informed reference to themselves or their affairs therein.[98]

The political battles that followed, in which the Bennett Law figured most prominently, must be dealt with in broad strokes. The early skirmishes involved Milwaukee's *Germania* for the Lutheran Germans, trading volleys with Horace Rublee's Milwaukee *Sentinel,* which had inspired the draft for Hoard in 1888. The *Herold,* Milwaukee's liberal German voice which was back again generally as a Republican paper, took to printing its anti-Bennett Law editorials on the front page, in both German and English, doubtless distrusting the *Sentinel's* translations—the usual way for Yankees to get their views of what the German press was saying on political issues.[99]

Democratic politicians scented unaccustomed victory in the wind. Payne, Rusk, Sawyer, Spooner, and other practical Republican politicians foresaw the loss of their usual small but comfortable lead, which had secured the governorship since 1875 and had elected all of the United States senators since before the Civil War. Should the Democrats win a majority in the legislature in the 1890 election, Senator Spooner's seat would be lost, and Senator Sawyer's seat would be up in the 1893 legislature—too close in time for Republican comfort. This made the 1890 race more crucial than the prospect of merely losing the governorship and other executive offices.

In early 1890, Edward C. Wall became state chairman of the Democratic party. He was a man of modest means, the manager

---

[98]Rankin, *Hoard,* 131–134; Hoard to Ellis B. Usher, August 29, 1917, in the Hoard Papers.

[99]Wegner, "Bennett Law Controversy in Wisconsin," 14. The Milwaukee *Herold,* March 9, 1890, also printed statements critical of the Bennett Law by ex-governor Rusk, Senator Sawyer, and Henry Payne. Whyte, "Bennett Law Campaign in Wisconsin," *WMH,* 10:337.

of Badger Electric, a small Milwaukee utility. He had an office in the same building with Henry C. Payne, also a utility executive but of much broader means. The two were friendly rivals politically—professionals. Wall was deferential to Colonel Vilas, the acknowledged leader of the party since Alexander Mitchell's passing. Vilas was back in Madison as Wisconsin's leading Democrat after President Cleveland lost the 1888 election.

Vilas, Wall, and the Democrats generally were all set to base their 1890 campaign on the tariff—a tried and true issue that had Yankee farmers thumping their agricultural journals. The latest Republican-sponsored measure, known as the McKinley tariff, was a good issue, and one which was generally conceded to have cost the Republicans dear in the past. The argument was that higher tariff schedules on manufactured goods would hurt grain, hog, and cattle farmers, both in higher machinery prices and European retaliation against American grain and meat. There was in fact a downward trend in the late 1880's in the prices of those farm commodities. However, emphasis upon the tariff did not so much cause Yankee and Scandinavian farmers in central and western Wisconsin to shift from their traditional Republican loyalty. Rather, they simply stayed home on election day.[100]

What diverted the Democrats from yet another campaign fight on the much-used tariff issue was the rising German Lutheran campaign against the Bennett Law. The German Lutherans realized that they would have the support of Wisconsin's German Catholic hierarchy as well. Indeed, this led to the strange spectacle of German Lutheran and Catholic clergymen meeting

[100]Merrill, *William Freeman Vilas,* 159–163; *The Statistical History of the United States from Colonial Times to the Present* (Stamford, 1965 edition), 290, 297; Walter H. Ebling et al., *A Century of Wisconsin Agriculture, 1848–1948,* Wisconsin Department of Agriculture, Wisconsin Crop and Livestock Reporting Service, *Bulletin, No. 290* (1948), 75; John D. Bowman and Richard H. Keehn, "Agricultural Terms of Trade in Four Midwestern States, 1870–1900," in the *Journal of Economic History,* 34 (September, 1974), 603; Donoghue, *How Wisconsin Voted, 1848–1972,* p. 101. Elisha Keyes summed up the 1890 fall election results: "If the school question had been out of the canvass, the heavy weight of the McKinley Bill would have beaten the state ticket, but we should probably have saved the legislature. The school bill was the cause that lost us the legislature. . . ." Keyes to Jeremiah Rusk, July 6, 1892, in the Jeremiah M. Rusk Papers.

together. Democratic chairman Wall, who had a superb under-standing of the nuances of Wisconsin's huge ethnic and religious vote, immediately grasped his role. It was to persuade the Ger-man Catholic hierarchy to assume what is now called "a low profile." It was time to fish seriously for the German Lutheran vote, and Wall knew that many Lutherans would balk at voting for something enthusiastically supported by Catholic bishops. Let the Catholics work their own flocks while the German Lutherans sought some issues in the Bennett Law that might appeal to persons other than those committed to the preservation of the German language in school, church, and home. They found this in the provision that an approved parochial school must be in the same district as the public school where the child lived—an obvious error in the law that even Hoard was willing to forego. Also objectionable was the provision that the elected local school board had the power to bring complaints and to certify whether or not a parochial school in the district met the requirements of instruction in English. This, the Lutherans claimed, was mixing church and state affairs with a vengeance.[101]

The arithmetic of the Wisconsin electorate was readily appar-ent. The state's population was over 30 per cent foreign-born, and their children were another 43 per cent. Over half these people were of German background. An educated guess would be that this huge German group was about half Catholic and one-third Lutheran. The great majority of Catholics were Dem-ocratic in politics, as was the growing Polish minority. The German Lutherans were the swing vote, and they were probably divided about half and half between the two major parties. Edward Wall and Henry Payne knew this. Governor Hoard thought he knew better. He was convinced that few Germans could be counted as Republican voters.[102]

[101]Wegner, "Bennett Law Controversy in Wisconsin," chap. 4; Wyman, "Voting Behavior in the Progressive Era," chap. 3; Jensen, *Winning of the Midwest,* 122–148; Merrill, *William Freeman Vilas,* 162–169; Current, *Pine Logs and Politics,* 252–255.

[102]*Eleventh Census of the United States, 1890: Abstract,* 39, 46, 49; Wyman, "Voting Behavior in the Progressive Era," 84–100; Kleppner, *Cross of Culture,* 158–171.

Events moved against the Republicans. In the 1890 spring election in Milwaukee, the Bennett Law was the only issue of consequence. Henry Payne, who had painstakingly wooed a substantial number of German Lutherans over to the Republicans since the mid-seventies, watched them melt away while the Republican *Sentinel* derided their objections to the school law. Both parties presented non-German candidates for mayor. Thomas H. Brown was the incumbent Republican, and the Democrats chose George W. Peck, a popular newspaperman whose *Peck's Bad Boy* series had made him a humorist of national reputation. Archbishop Michael Heiss died and his funeral fell on election day, with his stern orders for all Catholics to rally against the Bennett Law ringing in the ears of the faithful. Peck maintained a light touch: "Let the public schools in our state be the best in the Union, and let the schools that are maintained by private societies bring up children in religion without being molested."[103]

Another blow to the Republicans had fallen just before the April local elections. A legal battle, carried to the state supreme court by Humphrey J. Desmond, a lawyer and editor of the *Catholic Citizen* of Milwaukee, scored a victory for Catholic parents of children in the public schools of Edgerton in Rock County. Their suit was based on the claim that prayers and readings from the King James version of the Bible constituted sectarian instruction in violation of Wisconsin's constitution. The Edgerton parents lost their suit in the circuit court, but on March 17, 1890, the state supreme court unanimously reversed that decision. (Wisconsin thus became the first of seven states to take such a position.) Three separate concurring opinions were written. That of Justice Harlow S. Orton provoked howls of rage from the Yankee churches that had jealously guarded the interpretation that "nonsectarian," in constitutional terms, simply meant non-denominational exercises acceptable to them. Orton said: "There is no such source and cause of strife, quarrel, fights, malignant

---

[103]Bayrd Still, *Milwaukee: The History of a City* (Madison, 1948; reprinted, 1965), 260–261, 296–297; Wyman, "Voting Behavior in the Progressive Era," 73–75.

opposition, persecution and war and all evil in the state, as religion."[104]

The Edgerton decision was one in a long series of skirmishes between the Catholic and the Yankee churches. Reversing a long series of Yankee victories—or simple assumptions of victory— the decision was bound to cause a new exchange of recriminations. *Our Church Work,* a monthly publication of the Wisconsin Congregational churches, may serve as an example: "The three contending forces today are American Christianity, Secularism, and Roman Catholicism." A month later *Our Church Work* approvingly published a resolution of the La Crosse presbytery: "We are amazed at the decision and declare it unconstitutional and rendered at the bidding of a foreign church and lawless elements in society, whose interests are antagonistic to the growth, order and permanency of the republic." The Janesville Baptist Association found the decision "an expression of a form of sectarianism in the interest of Roman Catholicism and infidelity, which have proven themselves . . . to be the worst foes of religious and civil liberty." German Catholics were equally sure that the Bennett Law was a plot against them, and replied in kind.[105]

George Peck won the April, 1890, Milwaukee mayoralty race in a landslide. The thirty-six-member board of aldermen acquired

---

[104]Richard J. Orsi, "Humphrey Joseph Desmond: A Case Study in American Catholic Liberalism" (master's thesis, University of Wisconsin, 1965), 83–94; *DWB*; Thomas C. Hunt, "The Edgerton Bible Decision: The End of an Era," in the *Catholic Historical Review,* 67 (October, 1981), 589–619; Thomas C. Hunt, "The Reformed Tradition, Bible Reading and Education in Wisconsin," in the *Journal of Presbyterian History,* 59 (Spring, 1981), 73–88. See also James I. Clark, *Education in Wisconsin* (Madison, 1958), 24–27; Joseph Schafer, "Editorial Comment: The Courts and History," in *WMH,* 9 (March, 1926), 347–357; Updegrove, "Bibles and Brickbats," 88–102.

[105]Deutsch, "Yankee-Teuton Rivalry in Wisconsin Politics," *WMH,* 14:403–418; *Our Church Work,* April 17, May 15, 1890; *Twenty-Ninth Anniversary of the Janesville Baptist Association, Held with the Baptist Church of Clinton, Wisconsin,* September 2–4, 1890, p. 12; Wegner, "Bennett Law Controversy in Wisconsin," 54–59, 71–72. Allegations that the Bennett Law was a plot of the Masonic order or the American Protective Association were common. The APA, however, was not active in Wisconsin until later. See Donald L. Kinzer, "The Political Uses of Anti-Catholicism: Michigan and Wisconsin, 1890–1894," in *Michigan History,* 39 (September, 1955), 315.

a clear majority of nineteen Germans, and Edward Wall had found his issue for the November state elections. Governor Hoard, who knew that the Republican kingmakers had been forced to accept him in 1888 because of Rusk's call for an unmanaged convention and the *Sentinel's* orchestrated draft, knew also that the party leaders would face disaster if they tried to dump him after one term. He was adamant that the 1890 campaign should be based squarely upon the "Little Red School House" and stern defense of the Bennett Law. He expressed a willingness to see some concessions on minor details, but not on the requirement of a minimum curriculum taught in English.[106]

The results in Milwaukee pointed clearly towards the coming November election. George Peck had scarcely warmed his chair as mayor of Milwaukee before he was catapulted into the gubernatorial race as the Democratic candidate to face the intractable Governor Hoard. The governor was sure that the Yankee rank and file of the party, as well as the Scandinavians, were in basic agreement with him on the central issue of the Bennett Law. The German Protestant minority in the party had naturally dwindled, but Hoard dismissed this with the argument that non-German Catholics would come over to the Republicans on that issue. In any event, he did not believe that his party had really ever had a significant German Protestant vote. Several meetings were held by Senator Spooner and Henry Payne with Hoard and Horace Rublee of the *Sentinel*—who was just as fixed on the Bennett Law issue—seeking a formula of concessions on the measure. These came to naught on the essentials. Hoard had his way. Defense of the law occupied about the first two-fifths of the party's state platform. By contrast, all that the Democrats needed to say was that they were for repeal of this manifestation of the "settled Republican policy of paternalism" and of "needless interference with parental rights and liberty of conscience," add-

---

[106]Still, *Milwaukee,* 296–297; Wyman, "Wisconsin Ethnic Groups and the Election of 1890," *WMH,* 51:269–293. The 1890 spring municipal election helped the Democrats in Milwaukee by bringing back to the fold their Polish and German Catholic voters who had been voting the various tickets devised by Robert Schilling following the Bay View riots. The Bennett Law now claimed center stage.

ing piously that the spread of the English language would take care of itself.[107]

Chairman Wall's strategy worked for the Democrats, thanks to all the help that Governor Hoard supplied. Nils Haugen's was the only one of seven Republican congressional seats to survive the debacle. Haugen actively supported the Bennett Law in the campaign, feeling that the McKinley tariff was probably more crucial in the Upper Midwest and among his constituents in western Wisconsin. (In fact, his assessment is borne out by recent scholarship.) The balance in the legislature between the sessions of 1889 and 1891 shifted from only six Democrats to nineteen—a majority—in the senate, and from twenty-nine to sixty-six in the assembly. The rout was complete. Traditional Republican areas suffered from the tendency of voters to stay home when displeased with their party's stand on economic issues—the tariff, in this case. Catholic voters were formidably aroused—at least those of continental European origins—and the disaffection of the estimated half of the German Protestant voters who had earlier drifted into the Republican party completed the party's disaster. Senator John Coit Spooner, who had reason to be bitter—his term expired in March, 1891—said of the losses: "The school law did it—a silly, sentimental and damned useless abstraction, foisted upon us by a self-righteous demagogue."[108]

Senator Spooner was replaced by William F. Vilas, the acknowledged head of the Democratic party in Wisconsin. The Bennett Law was repealed in 1891 and replaced with what was essentially a restatement of the 1879 compulsory school attendance law. The principal addition was a provision for the appointment of truant officers, "acting discreetly, to apprehend upon view, all children between seven and thirteen years of age, who

[107]Fowler, *John Coit Spooner*, 146–149; *Wisconsin Blue Book, 1891*, pp. 390–391, 393–394; Wyman, "Wisconsin Ethnic Groups and the Election of 1890," *WMH*, 51:269–293; McDonald, *Irish in Wisconsin*, 168–180.

[108]Haugen, *Reminiscences*, 94–96; Wyman, "Wisconsin Ethnic Groups and the Election of 1890," *WMH*, 51:281–293; *Wisconsin Blue Book, 1979–1980*, p. 362; Fowler, *John Coit Spooner*, 153, citing Spooner to H. M. Kutchin, November 18, 1890, and to Henry C. Payne, November 19, 1890, in the Spooner Papers in the Library of Congress.

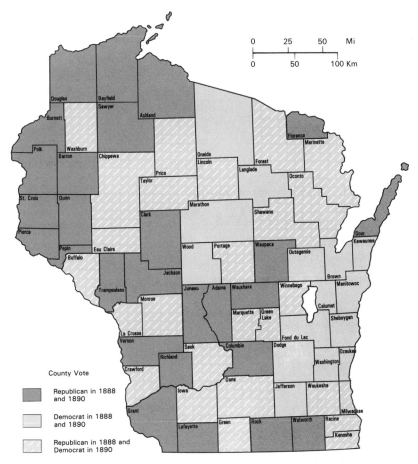

Douglas
Bayfield
Sawyer
Burnett
Ashland
Florence
Marinette
Polk
Washburn
Barron
Chippewa
Oneida
Lincoln
Forest
Langlade
Oconto
Price
Taylor
St. Croix
Dunn
Marathon
Shawano
Clark
Pepin
Eau Claire
Door
Kewaunee
Buffalo
Wood
Portage
Waupaca
Pierce
Outagamie
Jackson
Brown
Trempealeau
Juneau
Adams
Waushara
Winnebago
Manitowoc
Monroe
Calumet
Marquette
Green
Lake
Sheboygan
La Crosse
Vernon
Sauk
Columbia
Fond du Lac
Richland
Ozaukee
Crawford
Washington
Dane
County Vote
Jefferson
Waukesha
Iowa
Grant
Milwaukee
Green
Rock
Walworth
Racine
Lafayette
Kenosha

Republican in 1888
and 1890

Democrat in 1888
and 1890

Republican in 1888 and
Democrat in 1890

GUBERNATORIAL ELECTIONS, 1888 AND 1890

habitually frequent or loiter about public places, and have no lawful occupation. . . ." This disposed of the troublesome problem of making school board members the active agents in pursuing truants.[109]

Chairman Wall found that the Bennett Law was still his prime issue in 1892, even though it had been set aside by the Demo-

[109]*Laws of Wisconsin,* 1891, pp. 3, 217–219.

cratic legislature the year before. He was aided in this, of course, by the continuing fulminations of William D. Hoard and his supporters. This was often at the level of simply exchanging epithets. The Democrats had only to make reference to their "repeal of the Republican assault upon individual rights" to provoke Hoard, who kept the issue alive because he had become the center of the opposition within the party to the control exercised by Sawyer, Spooner, and Payne. Hoard's biographer was at pains to deny that Hoard's subsequent role in the Republican party—he made an early alliance with Robert M. La Follette—was simply an outcome of his embitterment over the active or covert opposition to the Bennett Law and to his gubernatorial nominations by the three, and particularly by Henry Payne, who became anathema to Hoard. Not surprisingly, much of Hoard's most vocal support came from those who approved the Bennett Law.[110]

The Bennett Law would not die as an issue. It touched the deepest chords of ethnic differences and religious animosities. Payne, Sawyer, Rusk, Spooner, and others in the Republican high command devoutly wanted the issue behind them, but Hoard and his rank-and-file followers were not mollified. As Payne remarked to Rusk: "The worst feature of the situation is the almost hopeless task of getting back our German Republicans without whose help it is impossible to carry Wisconsin."[111]

The Democrats had other arrows in their quiver, now that for the first time in thirty-five years they controlled all of the executive offices and both houses of the legislature. After Vilas claimed

[110] *Wisconsin Blue Book, 1893,* p. 419; Fowler, *John Coit Spooner,* 176–177; Rankin, *Hoard,* 92–109; Belle Case and Fola La Follette, *Robert M. La Follette* (2 vols., New York, 1953), 1:86–87, 102–104, 114. When Hoard returned to his home after his defeat in the 1890 election, he was presented with a gold watch inscribed: "He signed the Bennett Law." Rankin, *Hoard,* 97.

[111] Payne to Rusk, December 2, 1890, in the Rusk Papers; Merrill, *William Freeman Vilas,* 170–197. Rankin, *Hoard,* 92, reflects the contrary belief of Hoard and many of his supporters that it was "the 'stay-at-home' Republican vote [that] was the cause of Hoard's defeat," rather than a dramatic desertion of their German voters to the Democrats.

Senator Spooner's seat, they turned to the congenial task of reapportioning the state on the basis of the 1890 federal census. As Payne ruefully commented to a Democratic acquaintance on this prospect: "Grab all you can get. We fellows always did while we had the power." The Milwaukee *Journal*, published by Lucius Nieman, who was careful to consult on the paper's political positions with Vilas and Wall, relayed this hotel lobby conversation, remarking that Payne was not in sympathy with crybaby politicians.[112]

As it turned out, Payne's manly stoicism did not rule the Republican party's response. Assuming that they had an equal right to draw electoral district lines in conformance with the rules of gerrymander (as the Republicans "always" had, according to Payne's bluff comment), the Democrats were astounded when the Republicans took them to court. This was a new tactic. As another old Republican warhorse, Alexander Thomson, commented: "It must, in fairness, be admitted that these [Republican] apportionments were not always models to be introduced into equity practice; the Republicans, however, were never forced to the hard necessity that the Democrats were in their endeavor to retain control of the Legislature, the Democratic votes being bunched, as it were, on the lake shore section of the State. . . ."[13]

The first Democratic reapportionment was set aside by the state supreme court. In the summer of 1892, the resilient Democrats returned in special session, hoping to mend their plan in time for the November elections. Again the Republicans took

---

[112]Merrill, *William Freeman Vilas*, 181, citing the Milwaukee *Journal*, October 31, 1891.

[113]*Ibid.*, 180–185; Thomson, *Political History of Wisconsin*, 243–257. The Wisconsin Constitution, Article IV, Sections 2, 3, 4, and 5, as it appears in the *Wisconsin Blue Book, 1889*, pp. 15–16, required districting of state assembly and senatorial districts "by county, precinct, town or ward lines, to consist of contiguous territory, and be in as compact form as possible," with senatorial districts made up of unbroken assembly districts. This redistricting came every five years based upon the federal and state censuses. For congressmen, the requirement was less specific as to districts. (See the Constitution of the United States, Article I, Section 2.) The state constitution made no mention of equality of population numbers among districts.

them to court successfully, and a second special session had to adopt a reapportionment plan that met the court's objections.[114]

Still the Democrats retained their advantage. Republican charges that the unwieldy Democratic majority in the legislature was inept and lacked leadership, while fairly made, did not shift allegiances. Governor Peck had become the apostle of economy and the opponent of "centralization and paternalism and all mischievous meddling with rights of conscience and religion, especially in the care and education of children." Democratic attempts to gerrymander the state were not calculated to shock the ordinary voter, however much they excited Republican politicians and prospective office seekers.[115]

The fall election of 1892 occurred in a presidential election year with the Republicans defending the presidency. Benjamin Harrison had not been a popular President. The best indicator of this, so far as Wisconsin was concerned, was that the state's Republican delegation went to the national convention uninstructed. But by far the most damaging blow to Wisconsin Republicans in 1892 came from the so-called "Treasury Cases." For years, Wisconsin's state treasurers had been farming out public money to "pet" banks. The justifications for this were various: the state constitution and statutes were no clear guides to what to do with the funds; it was impractical to keep thousands of dollars in the inadequate vault in the state treasurer's office; the state lacked a system for drawing on bank accounts by check; and so on. Half-hearted legislative efforts to turn off this spigot were never quite adequate. It was a political time bomb, simply because it was general knowledge that the banks paid interest on the state deposits and the interest did not appear as credited to the state.

Subsequent testimony showed that over many years several

---

[114]Thomson, *Political History of Wisconsin*, 243–257; *Wisconsin Blue Book, 1979–1980*, p. 362; H. Rupert Theobald, "Equal Representation," in *Wisconsin Blue Books, 1970*, pp. 96–104, 245–246; Donoghue, *How Wisconsin Voted, 1848–1972*, pp. 78, 102.

[115]*Wisconsin Blue Book, 1893*, p. 419. See the *Wisconsin State Journal*, April 23, 1891, and Milwaukee *Sentinel*, April 23, 1891, and November 3, 1892, on Democratic ineptitude.

hundred thousand dollars in interest had simply gone into some unidentified pockets. The state treasurers' pockets were the most obvious. The trial testimony also revealed that this interest was mostly collected indirectly by politicans' henchmen, who used it—presumably—for party purposes. But enough of the payments had reached the various elected state treasurers to make the office attractive. A state treasurer clearly had to be a party insider. Wisconsin's Republicans did their best to cover the trail, but Nieman's Milwaukee *Journal* kept the issue alive. When brought into court to testify, former treasurers displayed wondrous lapses of memory and incredible naiveté.

The Democrats had not shared in this largess since the 1870's, and therefore their indignation was real. The complaint fit well with their stance of strict economy and an end to Republican mismanagement. With a Democrat as attorney general, the fat was soon in the fire. Since the most recent state treasurers had had Senator Sawyer as their bondsman, the trail led directly to an Oshkosh bank in which Sawyer was a principal stockholder. An officer of the bank had been acting as the conduit through whom the treasurer placed the state funds in favored banks. The Oshkosh bank official collected the interest. The inference was that Senator Sawyer, and possibly others, drew on it for political expenditures. In one instance, a bank sent the interest direct to the state treasurer. That worthy testified: "I didn't know they were paying anything, but I knew there was $470 they sent in there and I took it."[116]

The litigation turned out to be both lengthy and dull, as well as not an unalloyed joy for the Democrats because of the involve-

[116]Fowler, *John Coit Spooner*, 165–168; Current, *Pine Logs and Politics*, 255–258, 272–275; Payne to Rusk, May 2, 1892, in the Rusk Papers; Arlan Helgeson, "The Wisconsin Treasury Cases," in *WMH*, 35 (Winter, 1951), 129–136. See Mayer, *Republican Party*, 232–234, on the 1892 convention. Thomson, *Political History of Wisconsin*, 241–243, has an abbreviated and sanitized account of the "Treasury Cases." He mentions the total amount of the judgments against five former state treasurers: $725,000. Four of them were Republicans, one a Democrat. Jeremiah Rusk was also embarrassed by the disclosure that he was president of a Viroqua bank while governor and clearly a party to obtaining state funds for deposit.

ment of former Democratic state treasurer Ferdinand Kuehn, who had served two terms in the middle 1870's. Substantial judgments were returned against all five indicted, but a sympathetic legislature set aside the debts of two, including Kuehn, and reduced others.[117]

The real fireworks from the litigation had taken place earlier. Senator Sawyer was bondsman for two of the Republican ex-treasurers, Richard Guenther and Henry B. Harshaw, both of Oshkosh. The connection was obvious from the role played by Charles Schreiber, cashier of the National Bank of Oshkosh in which Sawyer was a principal stockholder. Schreiber was the one who directed the deposits of the state funds to favored banks and distributed the interest. Sawyer stood to lose as much as $200,000 as bondsman, as well as suffer the political damage involved. He compounded his troubles by approaching Robert M. La Follette, lately retired from Congress by the 1890 Bennett Law election, who had returned to his law practice in Madison. As La Follette later told the story, Sawyer asked La Follette to meet him at the Plankinton House in Milwaukee, without disclosing the purpose of the meeting. Assuming it was political business, La Follette was thunderstruck when—according to La Follette—the old man opened the conversation: "I wanted to talk with you about Siebecker and the treasury matter. These cases are awfully important to us. . . . I don't want to hire you as an attorney in the cases, La Follette, and don't want you to go into court. But here is fifty dollars, I will give you five hundred more or a thousand . . . when Siebecker decides the cases right." (Robert G. Siebecker was the Dane County judge who would hear the cases, and was also La Follette's brother-in-law!)[118]

La Follette left while Sawyer was attempting to rephrase the offer. "Nothing else ever came into my life that exerted such a powerful influence upon me as that affair," remarked the man who would finally depose the Republican Old Guard. "Sooner

[117]Helgeson, "Wisconsin Treasury Cases," *WMH*, 15:135–136.
[118]Current, *Pine Logs and Politics*, 255–260; La Follette, *Autobiography*, 63–64.

or later I probably would have done what I did in Wisconsin. But it would have been later."[119]

Silence fell for a few weeks. La Follette was counseling with a few intimates about what he should do. Finally, he agreed to ask the advice of a respected federal judge in Madison, Romanzo Bunn. It was unequivocal. La Follette must tell Judge Siebecker, which he did. Siebecker then disqualified himself, refusing to discuss his reasons. Newspaper speculation naturally followed, with the Chicago *Times* coming close to La Follette's version although he, too, had refused to comment on the speculation. This brought Senator Sawyer out with his version of the meeting, in the Milwaukee *Sentinel*. La Follette replied with a long letter to the *Sentinel* setting forth his story. This exchange occurred in late October of 1891—a year away from the next state and federal elections. But it was plain that more damage had been done to Senator Sawyer's reputation in the exchange. Nils Haugen, who like many other allies of La Follette eventually came to a parting of the ways, thought La Follette might have jumped to a hasty conclusion, and subsequently found political advantage in it. But when Haugen expressed his doubts to Speaker Thomas Reed of the House of Representatives that Sawyer could have been that crude, Reed remarked: "You can never tell about these old commercial fellows."[120]

The Democrats proceeded to sweep seven more of the fourteen remaining Republicans out of the state senate, retained a reduced but comfortable majority of fifty-five to forty-four in the assembly, held on to six of the ten congressional seats, and re-elected Governor Peck and the other Democratic state officials. Adding to the insult, for the first time since 1852, Wisconsin gave its

---

[119]La Follette, *Autobiography*, 64–65.

[120]*Ibid.*, 65–70. Current, *Pine Logs and Politics*, 260–269, observes that the differences between the La Follette and Sawyer versions were never tested in a court. He cites Horace Rublee's comment that Sawyer really had no reason to engage La Follette professionally at that stage of the proceedings against the treasurers. See also Nils P. Haugen, "Pioneer and Political Reminiscences," in *WMH*, 11–13 (December, 1927–December, 1929), 11:430–431.

electoral votes to a Democratic presidential candidate, helping to elect Grover Cleveland to a second term.

President Cleveland was confronted with the sharpest depression that the country had yet experienced. It began with a panic early in 1893, which closed even the Mitchell bank in Milwaukee and some elsewhere temporarily. (Twenty-seven others in the state closed permanently.) Wisconsin banks had escaped any such fate in the 1873 panic, but hard times followed both panics, worse for many in 1893 because Wisconsin was more urban and industrial. The Democrats, moreover, had their winning days behind them after the 1892 elections. Edward Wall, like Senator Vilas and President Cleveland, was then a hard money Democrat. Wall recognized that this was a stance which appealed to German voters, but Cleveland's management of the financial crisis and general distress that followed won him no plaudits. The remaining arrow in Wall's quiver was the old Bennett Law bugaboo, but this was wearing thin with the German Lutherans. The American Protective Association (APA) had replaced the Bennett Law as the symbol of anti-immigrant prejudice, but the APA was primarily anti-Catholic, which suited the Lutherans fine. The Republicans felt no need to defend the APA, although the organization naturally disapproved of the Democrats with their heavily Catholic constituency. Wisconsin Democrats contributed to their own problems by replacing the deposed Senator Sawyer with the son of Alexander Mitchell. John Mitchell's silver spoon was considerably tarnished because of the temporary closing of the family bank, and the *Sentinel* led in making him a heavy burden for his party.[121]

The Republican party returned massively to power in Wisconsin in the election of 1894, sweeping the state offices, regaining the senate comfortably, and reversing the assembly from a five-to-four margin for the Democrats to a four-to-one majority favor-

---

[121]Theodore A. Andersen, *A Century of Banking in Wisconsin* (Madison, 1954), 72–84; Merrill, *William Freeman Vilas*, 170–203, 219–221; Kinzer, "Political Uses of Anti-Catholicism," *Michigan History*, 39:318–319, 321–326. See also the Milwaukee *Sentinel*, November 4, 1892, for a typical treatment of John Mitchell, who was re-elected to a congressional seat that fall.

ing the Republicans. Despite the arithmetic of this election—the Republicans won the governorship with a record 58 per cent of the major party vote—it was less a resurgence of triumphant Republicanism than it was the rapid decline of Democratic appeal. The main villain was the panic and ensuing depression, which began almost at the moment that President Cleveland took office. True to his Bourbon stance, the President was not an imaginative executive. His instinct was to hunker down, and his attention was riveted on the gold reserves in the Treasury, to the exclusion of the human problems created by an increasingly urban, industrial society. Governor Peck had a similar mind set. While affable, he brought little more to the pressing questions of this darker time than increased economy in government. A political amateur like his predecessor Hoard, Peck was not stirred to any creative impulse by the office. In a lackluster convention, the Democrats renominated the unenthusiastic Peck to head the ticket for a third term. As Burr Jones wrote to Vilas: "At least 9 out of 10 democrats in farming districts would tell you if asked that they are in favor of a new deal. They give reason that they do not believe in 3rd terms." Chairman Wall clung to the hope that specialized appeals to ethnic blocs—particularly the German Lutherans—would work the old magic. But this was a worn-out device.[122]

The politics and politicians of the times may strike us as contrasting with those of our own day, but not unrecognizably so. The old saw held true: if one would be a leader he had better know where his followers are headed. The political fustian, campaign irrelevancies, and seeming blindness to the more compelling issues of an emerging urban-industrial society that characterized the major parties masked a growing dissatisfaction. The most obvious change to come was the determined rise of a competent dissident who did not divert his energies into third-party movements. But as a political society we have not lost our appetite for bombast.

[122]Donoghue, *How Wisconsin Voted, 1848–1972*, p. 102; *Wisconsin Blue Book, 1979–1980*, p. 362; Merrill, *William Freeman Vilas*, 220–223.

# 12

# Government

$R$OBERT M. LA FOLLETTE laid a heavy burden on those who governed the state from the time of his apparent awakening to the dark side of Wisconsin politics to his later turn to insurgency. His awakening, according to La Follette's own testimony, came in June, 1873, when he was in the audience for Chief Justice Edward G. Ryan's address to the graduating class of the University of Wisconsin. His turn to insurgency came in 1891, when La Follette alleged that Senator Philetus Sawyer attempted to bribe him in the Treasury Cases. The development of La Follette's indictment will be found at length in his *Autobiography,* and in an earlier version which he filtered through the uncritical ear of Lincoln Steffens, one of that band of journalists who joyfully adopted Theodore Roosevelt's intended epithet: "muckrakers." Recollecting in something less than a state of tranquility, La Follette remembered himself during that eighteen-year interval as considerably more of a political crusader than the facts appear to warrant. Nonetheless La Follette remained the touchstone for most subsequent descriptions of Wisconsin politics and government during the last thirty years of the century.[1]

[1] See above, Chapter 11, for accounts of Ryan's message and the Plankinton House incident between Sawyer and La Follette. See also Robert M. La Follette, *La Follette's Autobiography: A Personal Narrative of Political Experiences* (Madison, 1911; reprinted, 1960), 11–12, 60–70; Lincoln Steffens, "Wisconsin: Representative Government Restored: The Story of La Follette's War on the Railroads That Ruled His State," in *The Struggle for Self-Government: Being an Attempt to Trace American Political Corruption to Its Sources in Six States of the United States, with a Dedication to the Czar* (New York, 1906), 79–119; David P.

This is not to say that La Follette's view was unique to his perceptions and ambitions. In 1889 appeared a magisterial work, *The American Commonwealth,* by the Scottish scholar-statesman James Bryce, which quickly became an American standard, running to many editions and abridgements. General in tone, Bryce's assessment of western state government—which certainly included Wisconsin at the time he wrote—was: "The moral standard of Western America is not quite the same as that of England, just as the standard of England differs from that of Germany or France. . . . The newspapers accuse everybody; the ordinary citizen can seldom tell who is innocent and who is guilty. He makes a sort of compromise in his own mind by thinking nobody quite black, but everybody gray. And he goes on to think that what everybody does cannot be very sinful."[2]

If the powers and honors of the governor's office were paltry, at least its limited prestige exceeded that of the putative seat of the people's power to effect desired change: the legislature. During the 1870 session the Madison *Democrat* carried a spritely item about a police raid on a house of ill repute. Five "nymphs" were carried off to the station, but the customers were allowed to depart "for fear one or both houses of the legislature would be without a quorum, if they were held!" This about sets the tone for the following years. A perennial feature of the obligatory summary of the legislative sessions carried by Madison and Milwaukee newspapers was mention of the legislative "plunder boxes" made for the members by the state carpenter for $1.00 each, with lock and key. In these, "they have carried away a good many thousand dollars' worth of public property. . . ." In March of 1877 the *Sentinel* welcomed the end of another session:

---

Thelen, *The Early Life of Robert M. La Follette, 1855-1884* (Chicago, 1966); David P. Thelen, "The Boss and the Upstart: Keyes and La Follette, 1880-1884," in *WMH,* 47 (Winter, 1963-1964), 103–115; David P. Thelen, "Robert M. La Follette, Public Prosecutor," in *WMH,* 47 (Spring, 1964), 214–223. Emanuel L. Philipp, *Political Reform in Wisconsin,* eds. Stanley P. Caine and Roger E. Wyman (Madison, 1973), vii–xxviii, is an excellent brief guide to scholarly and popular assessments of La Follette's career.

[2] James Bryce, *The American Commonwealth* (2 vols.; second edition, revised, London, 1891), 1:524.

". . . [B]y to-morrow night Madison will have resumed its normal, graveyard appearance, and its many bartenders will take a rest. Yesterday the plunder boxes were lugged from the basement by the state carpenter, and now there is nothing loose about either chamber except the morals of the members. . . . Some of these fellows take everything home but a good reputation."[3]

The tone used in reporting the annual end of the session was not strictly partisan. The hotly Republican *Sentinel,* in March, 1877, was giving a heartfelt farewell to a legislature controlled in both houses by Republicans. The German-language Milwaukee *Herold* caught the same virus, characterizing the 1878 session as a yearly lawmaking swindle and carnival in Madison. The Milwaukee *Germania* heartily endorsed a proposal for biennial sessions, and wanted those sessions limited to six weeks or two months. The Madison *Democrat* awarded the 1881 legislature an accolade of sorts: "For stupid blunders the legislature that has just closed its labors, has no respectable rival in the history of the state." It is little wonder that governors, although not always as baldly as Governor Peck did in 1891, felt compelled to admonish the legislature to pass as few laws as possible, repeal a few bad ones as a better use of the legislature's time, stick to business, and go home as soon as possible. In 1893, Democratic Speaker Edward Keogh added that the legislature could easily cut four weeks from the length of the session if it would simply outlaw the railroads' practice of granting free passes to members. Free passes effectively shut down the legislature from Friday noon to Mon-

[3] Madison *Democrat,* February 9, 1870; Milwaukee *Sentinel,* March 13, 1874, March 8, 1877. The generally low opinion of the legislature was reflected in a renewal of the proposal for biennial sessions, which had been overwhelmingly rejected by the voters when it appeared on the ballot as a constitutional amendment in November, 1854. The proposal died in the assembly in the 1873 session. The amendment passed the sessions of 1880 and 1881 and was approved by a near four-to-one of those voters who voted on the measure in November, 1881. See the *Wisconsin Blue Book, 1979-1980,* p. 338; *Wisconsin Senate Journal,* 1874, p. 587; *Wisconsin State Journal,* March 13, 14, 1874; Milwaukee *Sentinel,* March 13, 14, 16, 17, 19, 1874; Madison *Democrat,* March 13, 14, 15, 18, 1874; *Wisconsin Public Documents,* 1875, Governor's Message, vol. 1, p. 6; *Wisconsin Assembly Journal,* 1875, p. 441, Joint Resolution 5A; *Wisconsin Senate Journal,* 1875, pp. 273, 291, Joint Resolution 3S; and *Wisconsin Blue Book, 1875,* p. 339.

day night every week as members hurried home—or somewhere.[4]

The wonder would seem to be that Wisconsin's state government was able to function in the people's interest at all. The governorship was constitutionally designed as a sort of chief clerkship among a gaggle of other elected officials, who could be members of opposing parties. In 1880, the governor had a private secretary, one clerk-messenger, and a janitor as his staff. At the end of the decade, the office had one additional clerk. The governor's appointive powers, to boards with mostly investigative and reporting functions, had increased; but the prevailing theory was that the power to make or enforce rules rested with the legislature, which could not delegate that power. This reservation of power was aggressively guarded by the courts, which had lately discovered the real possibilities of judge-made law. The legislature was therefore considered supreme—and was generally regarded as the biggest joke of all.[5]

Governor Harrison Ludington was a contrast with his successors, William E. Smith, Jeremiah Rusk, and William D. Hoard. Ludington was not an activist. He expressed "unaffected diffidence" in communicating his recommendations to the legislature, insisting that the legislative power resided there, "and the

---

[4] Madison *Democrat*, April 3, 1881; Milwaukee *Herold*, March 28, 1878; Milwaukee *Germania*, February 18, 1880; *Wisconsin Public Documents*, 1891, vol. 1, Governor's Message, p. 3; Madison *Democrat*, April 26, 1893, quoting the Milwaukee *News*. One can only conjecture as to the degree of obligation felt by legislators because they received railroad passes, particularly since they knew that weightier politicians received unlimited mileage while they had to apply for individual trips.

[5] *Wisconsin Blue Book, 1880*, p. 469; *ibid., 1889*, p. 446. Albert O. Barton, *La Follette's Winning of Wisconsin (1894-1904)* (Madison, 1922), 168, remarks: "The governor's office is in the main a clerical position, by courtesy made ornamental." See James D. Barnett, "The History of the Office of Governor in Wisconsin," in the *Iowa Journal of History and Politics*, 3 (April, 1905), 226-255; Frank M. Rice, "The Judicial Interpretation of the Executive Power in Wisconsin" (master's thesis, University of Wisconsin, 1954); Ballard C. Campbell, *Representative Democracy: Public Policy and Midwestern Legislatures in the Late Nineteenth Century* (Cambridge, 1980), 1-3; and Arnold M. Paul, *Conservative Crisis and the Rule of Law: Attitudes of Bench and Bar, 1887-1895* (Ithaca, 1960; Harper Torchbook edition, New York, 1969), xiv-xv.

THE HISTORY OF WISCONSIN

few recommendations which I shall make should be weighed by you in the light of this fact.''[6]

A problem that bothered the governor probably less than it did the secretary of state or the state treasurer was the highly diffuse nature of Wisconsin's government. While the county was the creature of the state for enforcement of most matters, nearly everything had to filter up to the county level from the town, village, or city level. The real bottleneck was town government, where property taxes were assessed and collected and where many reporting functions had to be initiated. Town government was carried out by people who gave it only a small part of their time and attention, before passing on a sheaf of often curious records—if any—to their successors. Assuming that village and city records were somewhat less of a problem, both because of their fewer numbers and more demanding duties, imagine the problems of Dane County officials in correlating the reports of thirty-five towns. Elsewhere, in newer counties, town governments were still proliferating by settlement and amoebic divisions. The state superintendent of public instruction had an even more difficult problem dealing with the district schools, which jealously guarded their independence from any suggested town system. The number of cracks into which assessment records, tax monies, and especially reports of all kinds could fall staggers the imagination. The state treasurer seemed to have the only real carrot and stick available. An 1858 law—modified in 1872—made it legal to withhold state monies due the county if a county were delinquent with the state's share of property taxes. The advantages of the county as the state's administrative arm at the local level are obvious. But, beyond the carrot of state funds, it was difficult to compel timely reporting or ensure its accuracy.[7]

[6] *Wisconsin Public Documents*, 1875, Governor's Message, vol. 1, pp. 1–2.

[7] James A. Wilgus, *The Government of the People of the State of Wisconsin* (Philadelphia, 1897), 10, 31–57, estimates that there were 1,050 town governments in the state by the mid-nineties. See also James D. Barnett, *Indirect Central Administration of Wisconsin* (University of Wisconsin, Bulletin no. 193, *Economics and Political Science Series*, vol. 4, no. 3, Madison, 1908), 400–402; and Raymond V. Phelan, *The Financial History of Wisconsin* (University of Wisconsin, Bulletin no. 193, *Economics and Political Science Series*, vol. 2, no. 2, Madison, 1908), 307–367.

The fact is that state government did function—and quite vigorously at times—apparently to the satisfaction of a majority of citizens whose expectations, fortunately, were less demanding than those of their heirs. One may make the case that Wisconsin, looking for its logical models among the northeastern states and its immediate neighbors, was not far behind those in the vanguard in accepting obligations for public health, public education, care for the dependent, and regulating as well as fostering economic interests clothed with a public interest. What may seem to later generations to be conspicuous blind spots generally accorded with majority opinion of the time. One need mention only the harshness of the law towards vagrancy, questions of law and order with respect to the relations of labor and capital, or the notion that prisoners should pay for their keep with enforced labor. It was a largely agrarian society that reflected these attitudes towards the problems of industrialization and urbanization. Given the rapidity of economic and social change, and the flood of European immigration posing the possibility of a Catholic majority, it is remarkable that the Yankee-dominated political and governmental machinery responded so well.

Acceptance of change is implicit in our political system. Wisconsin's franchise was generous to new citizens, and even included foreign-born males intending citizenship. Those few who ever considered changing this had to be satisfied with voter registration and the Australian ballot, first applied in Milwaukee. Newcomers could take care of themselves simply by adapting to the system, which essentially meant acquiring some political power as a group within one or the other of the major parties. As soon as an immigrant group was recognized as having some political cohesion and was making use of its common identity, it was worth courting. The process itself developed political leaders within the new bloc. Government proceeded from the premise that the party in power had best keep the allegiance of those who delivered the votes—maybe occasionally sullen, but less than mutinous. One may argue that much that was positive in the state's response to the needs of public education and the development of institutions for the dependent grew out of appre-

hensions about the aggressive growth of the various (and especially Catholic) parochial school systems, and the continental
Catholic tradition of serving the homeless, friendless, helpless,
and wayward. Not many politicians were baldly willing to express
this apprehension, but it satisfied a political need.[8]

The motivations for more state intervention in the lives of the
dependent sprang from concern for the social order, from appre-
hensions about the growing strength of what many considered to
be an alien religion, from the greater economy and control
afforded by institutionalizing rather than giving outdoor or casual aid, from a growing faith in experts on care and reformation,
from the necessity to isolate and possibly change the misfits who
were assumed to be a consequence of unrestricted immigration—or simply from disinterested humanity distressed by prevailing conditions. The question remains: How effectively did
state government respond? The record suggests that the political
system, allowing for its inherent weaknesses and popular attitudes towards it, responded with salutary changes, a considerable
expansion of services and resources, and actual leadership. This
record of change required governors and other officers who were
more than political hacks, and legislators who were alert to more
than orders from political bosses and interested in else besides
filling their "plunder boxes." The idea of giving some service to
the state did not originate with La Follette's embattled
progressives.

[8] Linda Erich, " 'For Heaven and Home and State': The Milwaukee Orphans' Asylum and Developments in Child Welfare, 1850-1930" (master's thesis, University of
Wisconsin-Milwaukee, 1976), 11-17. Erich notes (p. 32) that a real motivation of the
Milwaukee socially secure women who supported the orphan asylum was their concern
that only Catholic organizations had served this function. However, the ladies did have
standards: they did not accept illegitimate children. See also Peter Doyle, *Catholic Charities
of Wisconsin: Address of Peter Doyle of Milwaukee Before the State Conference of Charities and
Corrections, at Madison, Wis., March 2, 1886* (Milwaukee, 1886), 15. Mrs. William Pitt
Lynde of the state's board of charities and reform complained: "I learned from five
Roman Catholic convicts that their priest, (chaplain) although allowed access to the
wards, at proper and prescribed times, he never conversed with them in his capacity of
religious teacher and director, to show them the virtue of penitence or to help them attain
it, or attempted any efforts at reform or encouragement to a better life." Wisconsin
Board of Charities and Reform, *Annual Report*, 1875, p. 183.

Did wealth and privilege commonly suborn legislators and state officials to their purposes? Occasionally, no doubt, but not as a regular practice. Nils Haugen, a witness of good character, remembered his service in the state assemblies of 1879 and 1880 as pleasant and agreeable: "There was a mutual good-fellowship regardless of partisanship. . . . The legislative houses were open to outsiders, and anyone could enter at any time. The members did not fear their own corruption and seek protection for their own honesty behind closed doors." He continued: "Lobbyists were always on hand at the legislative sessions, but the danger of corruption was not even suggested. During my nearly thirty years of public service I cannot point to a single instance where I thought a public official was corruptly influenced. He may have been unduly influenced and swayed, but I have never thought 'bought,' as is often charged."[9]

The pre-eminent scholar of the legal history of Wisconsin's lumber industry concludes that "privilege" was a relative term. When the legislature conferred special privileges on corporations, it was seldom done in haste and there was little evidence of guile or overreaching on the part of those promoting the privileges. The privilege of damming a stream for a lumber consortium organizing a common boom company was typical. There is ample evidence of legislative caution and amendments which limited rights or increased obligations. The legislature seldom discovered a general principle to guide such deliberations, but responded rather to adversary proceedings, and was therefore usually careful to advertise such prospective legislation and seek those with possible conflicting interests.[10]

Governor Lucius Fairchild deserves credit for closing off the

[9] Nils P. Haugen, *Pioneer and Political Reminiscences* (Evansville, [1930?], 48, 54, 121–124. Haugen was, not so slyly, comparing the old political days with the paranoia of La Follette and his circle in these examples. Campbell, *Representative Democracy,* 201, substantially agrees with Haugen's assessment of the degree of corruption in Wisconsin state government of the time.

[10] J. Willard Hurst, *Law and Economic Growth: The Legal History of the Lumber Industry in Wisconsin, 1836-1919* (Cambridge, 1964), xii-xiii, 261-266; George J. Kuehnl, *The Wisconsin Business Corporation* (Madison, 1959), 190-191.

post-Civil War flow of petty changes in municipal corporation charters and special charters for business corporations. He lectured the legislature regularly on the waste of excessive legislation for private and local purposes, which took so much of the legislature's time. Upset that no result came from these warnings, he presented a model for a constitutional amendment which passed the required successive legislatures and won voter approval in the 1871 election. Fairchild's amendment also closed off the flow of special charters for towns and villages. City charters were not included in the prohibition until an 1892 amendment which had been urged repeatedly by Governor Rusk. A governor had an effective weapon in this campaign, which Rusk used on occasion: the veto. Fairchild and Rusk were the only three-term governors in the nineteenth century, and they accomplished these fundamental changes by persistence.[11]

Governor Fairchild set some precedents for activism, although he was a cautious man politically. As with the corporate charter amendment, he had a talent for seeking salutary changes that were of little concern to the general voting public but attracted significant support from influential and interested groups. Certainly the revival of the moribund state geological survey, pushed by Fairchild, was in that category. He also was the prime mover behind the establishment of the state board of charities and reform (1871) and appointed its first members, among whom Andrew E. Elmore, Hiram H. Giles, and Mary E. B. Lynde became rather well known in the field.[12]

[11] Kuehnl, *Wisconsin Business Corporation,* 163–168; *Wisconsin Public Documents,* 1866–1867, Governor's Message, p. vi; *ibid.,* 1881–1882, Governor's Message, vol. 1, pp. 20–21; *Wisconsin Blue Book, 1979–1980,* p. 338. The evidence of gubernatorial leadership in these changes can be seen in the voting record on the amendments noted as it appears in the *Blue Book* cited above. The vast majority of voters were indifferent. Only slightly more than one out of three voters in the 1872 election who voted on the governorship also voted on the amendment, but it carried overwhelmingly, 54,087 to 3,675. In the vote on Rusk's pet amendment, under 7 per cent of those voting for governor cast a vote on the amendment, and just 4 per cent voted approval and carried it. Sam Ross, *The Empty Sleeve: A Biography of Lucius Fairchild* (Madison, 1964), vii, emphasizes that Fairchild constantly played the role of the leader who did not lead.

[12] *Wisconsin Public Documents,* 1867–1868, Governor's Message, vol. 1, p. 15; *ibid.,* 1868–1869, Governor's Message, pp. 19–20; *ibid.,* 1869–1870, Governor's Message, vol. 1, p. 11; E. F. Bean, "State Geological Surveys of Wisconsin," in the *Transactions of the*

There is not space here to mark all the trends and changes in Wisconsin's government between 1873 and 1893. Many of them are suggested in previous chapters. The most conspicuous change surely was the slow retreat from legislative supremacy in all things great and small and from an extreme localism which permitted the widest latitude to town and county governments. This retreat logically stemmed from a society that was growing increasingly complex, creating new needs to provide services, regulations, oversight, and revenues with a degree of uniformity and equity that intermittent legislative oversight and extreme localism could not achieve. Obviously the change did not come about in a traceable straight line. There are some conspicuous signs along the way: the abandonment by an 1881 constitutional amendment of annual legislatures and legislative elections; the creation in 1871 of the state board of charities and reform with subsequent mutations, legislation, reforms, and efforts to achieve uniformity that flowed from the board's work; and the inevitable acquisition of powers to cite, make rules, or bring to court acquired by appointive officers and boards in areas of health, factory inspection, licensing, and oversight of businesses such as transportation, banking, and insurance.[13]

Wisconsin's commitment to an enlarged educational establishment has been discussed before. The rapid spread of free high schools logically called for a broader education for those who taught in them. In his 1880 message Governor Smith credited the improvement of the common schools to the professionalization of administrators and teachers: "It is, therefore, a serious misapprehension to assume, as I fear many do, that the only justification and reason for expending the large sums of money

---

*Wisconsin Academy of Sciences, Arts and Letters,* 30 (1937), 210–216; Dale W. Robison, *Wisconsin and the Mentally Ill: A History of the "Wisconsin Plan" of State and County Care, 1860–1915* (New York, 1980), 80–110; Eleanor J. Flynn, "The Development of Wisconsin's Administration of Charities and Correction and Present Trends in the United States" (master's thesis, University of Wisconsin, 1926), 141–146; Morton Keller, *Affairs of State: Public Life in Late Nineteenth Century America* (Cambridge, 1977), 124; Miriam Z. Langsam, "The Nineteenth Century Wisconsin Criminal: Ideologies and Institutions" (doctoral dissertation, University of Wisconsin, 1967), 118–130, 245–248.

[13] *Wisconsin Blue Book, 1873,* pp. 275–314; *ibid., 1895,* pp. 495–535.

necessary to equip and maintain our Normal Schools and University, are to be found in the direct and primary results of their labors in furnishing the opportunity and means of education to the pupils in attendance. These results, though in and of themselves by no means unimportant, are among the least of the benefits conferred by these institutions. Their full fruition is not seen without including the public schools, proper, and the good therein accomplished.'' Happily, Governor Smith was able to announce in the same message that the state's general fund had finally worked its way to a surplus, after accumulating juggled deficits during the long depression just ending. This fortunate condition (largely owed to the increasing flow of revenue levied on the gross receipts of railroads, license fees from insurance companies, and later additions to the corporate list) was what enabled the legislature in 1885 to suspend the collection of general property taxes for state operations and to substitute set millages for the public schools and the University to supplement their land-grant revenues. This created another stick and carrot for the state to press the counties into new fields of public service.[14]

Wisconsin state government was able to broaden and improve considerably the general level of institutional care for its citizens by a variety of circumstances and strategies. Governor Fairchild had pressed successfully for a second state hospital for the insane which opened at Oshkosh in 1873, and the original state hospital at Mendota was enlarged. As Fairchild pointed out in his 1869 message to the legislature: "Not less than four hundred insane persons in the state still remain without proper care and treatment. They are in our jails, poor houses, and private dwellings."

---

[14] *Wisconsin Public Documents,* 1878–1879, Governor's Message, vol. 1, pp. 9–10. Wisconsin's financial history during the period is given here in capsule form. It explains the equanimity with which most taxpayers were able to accept the increasing outlays for education and eleemosynary institutions. The state's share of direct taxes on the real and personal property of individuals rose only 7 per cent between 1873 and 1892; corporation taxes rose 382 per cent. The state's millage charged against real and personal property valuations was 1.96 in 1872; 1.558 in 1892. See Phelan, *Financial History of Wisconsin,* 461–464; *Wisconsin Blue Book, 1873,* pp. 357–361; *ibid., 1893,* pp. 330, 394–395.

He also expressed concern for orphaned children similarly confined, some of whom were sent to the state reform school simply
for want of better facilities. Fairchild also recommended the creation of a state board of charities and reform with powers limited
to investigation and advice which, he observed, had been useful
in other states. The governor wanted to simplify the system of
state institutional management that had developed, but not radically. The system—or rather lack of it—was that each institution
had an appointed board of trustees, with fixed overlapping terms,
charged with management. Given travel conditions and distances
a generation earlier, it was the custom to appoint local people in
the area where each institution was sited. A politically attuned
board with local business ties thus decided appointments and
contracts as well as general policies and general oversight. Fairchild merely recommended that these boards be limited to five
persons—no revolution.[15]

While needs may have seemed compelling enough, there were
several other important reasons for the considerable expansion of
institutional programs in the years following Governor Fairchild's advocacy. One was that this was an area where the chief
executive could have an impact. It was also an area that could
prove a source of embarrassment to an administration when
obvious needs were ignored or management scandals arose.
Another reason was the astonishingly small impact that the
expansion of institutions and programs had on the general fund
of the state to which institutional costs were charged. Allied to
this was the shift in the sources of general fund income to special
taxes upon corporations, the greater share of these from the
railroads which were, of course, growing rapidly. Another reason
that the expenses of state institutional programs failed to burgeon

---

[15] The Mendota state hospital, for instance, had a board of fifteen; the deaf and dumb
institute at Delavan had a nine-member board. *Wisconsin Public Documents,* 1867–1868,
Governor's Message, vol. 1, pp. 11–12; *ibid.,* 1868–1869, Governor's Message, vol. 1,
pp. 14–16; *ibid.,* 1870–1871, Governor's Message, vol. 1, pp. 11–16; *Wisconsin Blue Book,
1870,* pp. 342–343; Ross, *Empty Sleeve,* iv–vii; Richard N. Current, *The History of Wisconsin. Volume II: The Civil War Era, 1848–1873* (Madison, 1976), 452–455; Robison, *Wisconsin and the Mentally Ill,* 81–99.

was the large degree of self-sufficiency built into the system. The state prison, for instance, from 1875 into the latter nineties, contracted convict labor to a Chicago boot and shoe manufacturer despite complaints from competitors. (There was not yet an equivalent of the automobile license to occupy idle hands.) The reformatory institutions also supplied manufactured articles for the state institutions, and most of them had extensive farm programs using inmate or patient labor.[16]

There were gross inefficiencies in the system of patronage whereby the separate local boards managed the affairs of each institution. A scandal involving the board of trustees of the state hospital for the insane at Mendota came to a head in 1880, leading the following year to the creation of the state board of control, charged with financial and managerial responsibilities for the state institutions. It was a paid, full-time board of five, with a secretary. There were jurisdictional wrangles with the older board of charities and reform, but the latter board was not full-time. However, as we shall see, its impact was certainly greater, aside from the area of financial responsibility.[17]

One may hazard that the ardent localism of the times moved rural and village legislators to accept an expansion of county facilities rather than further expand state facilities when presumably Milwaukee and other industrial cities would provide more than their fair share of inmates. They also accepted charges for county patients in the state hospitals. But the truly most effective weapon of the state in developing institutional programs turned out to be the relatively toothless—bureaucratically speak-

[16] Phelan, *Financial History of Wisconsin*, 307–343, 363–367. General fund disbursements for the state institutions varied a great deal over the years, but the following series is indicative: (1872) $458,707.89; (1880) $419,014.52; (1890) $389,118.16. See the *Wisconsin Blue Book, 1873*, p. 358; *ibid., 1881*, p. 314; *ibid.*, 1891, p. 315. See also Oliver D. Weeks, "Development of County Government in Wisconsin" (doctoral dissertation, University of Wisconsin, 1924), 118–127, on the county role in tax collection.

[17] Milwaukee *Sentinel*, March 16, 17, 18, 1880; Madison *Democrat*, March 18, 1880; Donald J. Berthrong, "Social Legislation in Wisconsin, 1836–1900" (doctoral dissertation, University of Wisconsin, 1951), 1–2, 77–81, 382–400; Robison, *Wisconsin and the Mentally Ill*, 99–102. See also Bernett O. Odegard and George M. Keith, *A History of the State Board of Control and the State Institutions, 1849–1939* (Madison, [1939?]), 53–57.

ing—board of charities and reform. While its powers were mostly those of persuasion and publicity, these proved to be formidable. As the unsavory character of most county and local jails, poorhouses, and asylums came to light, the board was given the power to transfer county hospital inmates to those of neighboring counties and to level reimbursement. Since the state hospitals operated on the rule that only the curable would be accepted, it was up to the counties to make adequate provisions for those not accommodated by the state hospitals. The result was a great expansion of the county hospitals (asylums). Out of this grew what was described as the "Wisconsin Plan" of state and county care.[18]

Governor Smith's admonition to the legislature in 1880, on announcing the welcome change in the revenue picture, served as his own guide and that of his successor, Rusk. "It does not need, I think," remarked Governor Smith, "that I should amplify the views heretofore expressed upon the subject of appropriations and public expenditures. It is neither prudent nor popular to withhold what is necessary. The people of Wisconsin are not stingy, nor do they expect their representatives to be niggardly in the management of public business. They realize that penuriousness does not constitute economy, and therefore will approve wise expenditures and account them profitable investments." This was a note that continued until Governor Peck's first message which, largely for political reasons and reflecting his peculiarly narrow view of the state's areas of responsibility, called for retrenchment well beyond the necessities of the current financial situation.[19]

Given the improved state finances, Governor Smith was ready to implement one of his philanthropic interests—the relief of orphaned or homeless children who, for want of a proper state

[18] Weeks, "Development of County Government in Wisconsin," 182–188; Berthrong, "Social Legislation in Wisconsin," 384–389; Robison, *Wisconsin and the Mentally Ill,* 80–146; Odegard and Keith, *History of the State Board of Control and the State Institutions,* 154–163; Wisconsin State Board of Control, *Biennial Report,* 1893–1894, p. 2.

[19] *Wisconsin Public Documents,* 1878–1879, Governor's Message, vol. 1, p. 8; *ibid.,* 1891, Governor's Message, vol. 1, pp. 3–6.

facility, were often committed to correctional institutions or poor farms. Responding to the published reports of the board of charities and reform, the legislature had recently prohibited local authorities from placing these children in poorhouses. Out of Smith's initiative after some maneuvering, came the state public school for orphans at Sparta. By 1894, the school reported that it housed an average of 233 children; a total of 1,228 had been admitted since it opened in 1886. The disposition of their cases tells us something about the contemporary society: "At the last named date 743 children had been placed in homes, of whom 617 were indentured and the remaining 126 are on trial."[20]

The powers of the board of charities and reform were to inspect, report, and recommend. This included not only the state institutions, but also the county jails and poorhouses, which were the snake pits of the time. The impact of these reports, even at this distance, is overwhelming. This, for instance, is a description of the Jefferson County poorhouse as the board of visitors found it in 1873:

> The number of insane in this house is very large. Eleven of them have to be confined in their cells all the time. Some of them are very difficult to take care of, and the task is as disagreeable and revolting as can well be conceived of. Three of them have to be kept on straw, as they will not use beds. Several of them have been at the Hospital for the Insane, and have been sent back because their places were wanted for more hopeful cases. At the time this poor-house was visited it contained nine children. A German child two months old, illegitimate, the mother between 17 and 18 years of age, was also in the house.
>
> Another German woman was there with three children, two boys, one ten years old, and the other eight, and a girl four. The woman has a husband, but he will not live with her.
>
> There is still another German woman with four children, all

---

[20] *Ibid.*, 1878–1879, Governor's Message, vol. 1, p. 12; *Wisconsin Blue Book, 1895,* pp. 529–530. Oscar Hallam recalled that his kind-hearted parents had once taken "on trial" an orphan boy from the nearby county poor farm, which housed derelicts, orphans, the insane, and senile. They returned him the next day because of his foul language. Oscar Hallam, "Bloomfield and Number Five: The American Way of Life in a Wisconsin Rural Community in the 70s, As Seen by a Small Boy," 257–263, in the Hallam Reminiscences.

boys, 3, 6, 9, and 11 years of age. They are all unhealthy, with rheumatism and all disease inherited from the parents. The father is dead.

There is also a blind boy, the son of one of the women confined as insane. The boy is said to be idiotic, and yet it is said that at times he gives considerable evidence of intellect. He talks, commits verses and sings. Should he not have a chance at the Blind Institute?

This was not selected as an extreme example, though it is graphic enough. There are pages and pages of equally dismal descriptions in the board's reports. Dane County's poorhouse listed the reasons for commitment of its pauper population: "Intemperance direct twenty-nine; intemperance indirect twelve; insanity twenty-one; idiocy eighteen; blindness two; deaf mutes one; sickness three; lameness one; orphanage two; bastardy seven; and old age four." The county jails were infinitely worse, though this was a difficult standard to attain.[21]

Several hundred pages of such testimony, published annually by the state, are evidence that the board was discharging its function: inspecting and reporting. Did this have an impact? The accumulated index to the Milwaukee *Sentinel* shows a steady flow of news items on the work of the board. From the early seventies through 1879, the index cites an average of six to eight items annually on its work outside Milwaukee County, and considerably more than that on board visits and reports involving Milwaukee institutions. The items also show that private citizens, mostly representing women's organizations, followed and abetted the board's work.[22]

There had always existed a lively competition among communities to have a state institution with its payroll and supply expenditures. The go-getters of Oshkosh, for example, were envied for carrying off the prizes represented by a state hospital for the insane and a normal school. Envy brought constant scru-

[21] Wisconsin Board of Charities and Reform, *Annual Report,* 1873, pp. 140, 143–144.

[22] Milwaukee *Sentinel* Index. Robison, *Wisconsin and the Mentally Ill,* 91–92, calls the power of publicity that resided with the board of charities and reform "a potent lever for change."

tiny. If there was any advantage to this willy-nilly system of
siting, management, and control, it was that the state generally
gained a subsidy from the lucky community, usually in the form
of the site. Also, it made legislative approval of yet another
institution easier, which possibly had little broad popular political appeal, because of the hope of getting the institution on the
part of several competing counties or communities. The public
school for orphans, for instance, was located by the state's board
of supervision after consideration of proposals from Stevens
Point, Waupaca, Green Bay, Oshkosh, Fond du Lac, Ripon,
New Lisbon, Sparta, and La Crosse. (Sparta won with the gift of
a 165-acre site.)[23]

For the governor, the problem was that all of the individual
boards for each state institution went their merry individual
ways. This put the political party in power at hazard whenever
one of them too flagrantly mismanaged, in any of a variety of
ways. A disappointed contractor—or an overly greedy one—a
disgruntled vendor, or a displaced placeman (every job was filled
by someone's political preference, subject to replacement by
someone else's) was sure to sound an alarm. As Governor Smith
discovered, because the board of charities and reform had only
powers to investigate and recommend, it offered nothing in the
way of a lightning rod to relieve his office of these embarrass-
ments. As chief executive, the governor was assumed to be
responsible. Having endured one such surprise after the other,
in 1881 Smith gratefully acknowledged a recommendation by a
committee of legislators, whom he had appointed for the duty, to
abolish the separate boards for each institution and to create a
single board of supervision to oversee them all.[24]

The state board of supervision was created in 1881. It was a
five-member salaried board, with powers of both purse and
appointment. It could even declare a person insane, for routing

[23] *Wisconsin Blue Book, 1889,* p. 411.

[24] *Wisconsin Public Documents,* 1879–1880, Governor's Message, vol. 1, pp. 17–18;
Robison, *Wisconsin and the Mentally Ill,* 99–109, 231–238, 258; Kenneth C. Acrea, "Wisconsin Progressivism: Legislative Response to Social Change, 1891 to 1909" (doctoral
dissertation, University of Wisconsin, 1968), 170–171.

to a state hospital or county asylum. In other words, it decided who was curable. This board of supervisors naturally conflicted with the older board of charities and reform, which still had a good deal to say about the operations of the state institutions. As often happens in government, nothing was done about this conflict of wills and assignments. The problem was not resolved until the Democrats came to power in 1891 and abolished both boards, replacing them with a single board of control—starting fresh with Democratic appointees, of course. Like the previous board of supervision, it was more interested in controlling budgets and management than in the reforming spirit that had animated the old board of charities and reform.

In 1879 the board of charities and reform had reported that progress had been made, although there remained much to be done. The number of children under fifteen confined in poorhouses had dropped from 229 in 1871 to sixty-one during the preceding eight years. Of the sixty-one, forty-five were under fifteen years of age and "sound in body and mind." During those eight years, the number of county poorhouses had increased from twenty-four to thirty-six, but the inmate population had fallen from 1,240 to 1,119. This drop owed something to the growth of county asylums, subsidized by the state with a per capita payment of $1.50 per week for each inmate. This change somewhat rationalized the type of clientele left in the poorhouses, and relieved the state hospitals of those deemed incurable. The board of charities and reform, having its responsibilities curtailed by the creation of the board of supervision, increased its interest in county and city jails, which made newspaper copy. Somehow, the inmates of jails were more interesting than the anonymous inmates of the poorhouses.[25]

The state board of health was created in 1876, without much evidence of gubernatorial pressure. (This was the legislature that Governor Ludington addressed with "extreme deference," for he was reluctant to instruct the members.) The health board had

[25] Wisconsin Board of Charities and Reform, *Annual Report,* 1879, pp. 24–25, 55; Robison, *Wisconsin and the Mentally Ill,* 84–93, 111-144.

something less than the full confidence of the public. But the great advantage that health administrators had was fear of epidemic diseases. It was generally assumed that outbreaks of cholera, smallpox, diphtheria, scarlet fever, and other diseases usually began among the immigrant poor; but epidemics were no respecters of neighborhood barriers. With the growing cities on Lake Michigan dumping their sewage and taking their water supplies from the lake, they were bound to get a seasonal scare. The power to quarantine, vaccinate, order cleanups, and take other measures was inevitably going to be invested in health officers, whether or not the public believed in the germ theory of disease. This, in turn, undermined the prevailing theory that the legislature could not delegate any rule-making powers.[26]

Like the board of charities and reform, the board of health looked for sounding boards to spread its message. An important one was the state agricultural society, which printed some seventy pages of extracts from the health board's first annual report in its transactions. The returns on this were sometimes equivocal. Although Louis Pasteur's findings had been in the public domain for almost twenty years, not everyone was willing to subscribe to the possible existence of microorganisms in his well water. As an Oshkosh health officer lamented, "Sanitary work is the crab of modern civilization. . . ."[27]

Other state offices were created to answer the needs of particular clienteles. The state's commissioner of labor statistics, dating from 1883, moved from reporting on fire and safety conditions to grants of specific powers to correct them as well as

[26] Judith W. Leavitt, *The Healthiest City: Milwaukee and the Politics of Health Reform* (Princeton, 1982); Judith W. Leavitt, "Health in Urban Wisconsin: From Bad to Better," in Ronald L. Numbers and Judith W. Leavitt, eds., *Wisconsin Medicine: Historical Perspectives* (Madison, 1981), 155–175; Cornelius A. Harper, "The Work of the State Board of Health, 1876–1924," in Milo M. Quaife, *Wisconsin: Its History and Its People* (4 vols., Chicago, 1924), 2:323–330; Lyndon E. Abbott, "The Wisconsin State Board of Health and Its Relation to Federal and Local Health Administration" (master's thesis, University of Wisconsin, 1932); Louis F. Frank, *The Medical History of Milwaukee, 1834–1914* (Milwaukee, 1915); Robert L. Stefanik, "Public Health in Milwaukee: From Sanitation to Bacteriology" (master's thesis, University of Wisconsin-Milwaukee, 1967).
[27] Wisconsin State Board of Health, *Annual Report*, 1889–1890, p. 132.

deal with child labor and women in the work force. The office of the state veterinarian was created at Governor Rusk's request, and he went back to the next legislature for a definition of the veterinarian's powers, "to accomplish the objects for which it [the enabling law] is intended." Still other boards appeared as the professions began to assume that some formal, required training was necessary. The usual problem was to accommodate established practitioners who lacked this training, while weeding out those who had diplomas from schools that provided little else. The impetus, of course, came from those who were formally trained. It sheds some light on the medical profession in 1882 that the Milwaukee *Sentinel* favored the examination and licensing of pharmacists, but not of physicians: "Almost all treatment of disease is in the nature of experiment. This being the case it is obviously unfair to give to one class of experimenters the exclusive privilege of making the experiments." By 1893, there were boards of examiners for admission to the Wisconsin bar and to the pharmaceutical profession. There was also a board of dental examiners. But as yet there was no board to license the medical profession.[28]

The central agency in the creation of this expanded government was, of course, the legislature. How did it perform as other than a long-running newspaper joke? (One must remember the

[28] Wisconsin Bureau of Labor and Industrial Statistics, *Biennial Report,* 1898–1899, pp. 116–129; *Wisconsin Public Documents,* 1885–1886, Governor's Message, vol. 1, p. 17. Nils Haugen told how admission to the Wisconsin bar was handled in the late 1870's: "Wheeler being one of the older practitioners was usually one of the committee [appointed by the local court to examine applicants]. He had two standard questions which he never failed to put to the candidate: 'How would you endorse a verbal order?' 'Do you think a man can be convicted of highway robbery, if the highway is not legally laid out?' " Haugen, *Reminiscences,* 194. See Milwaukee *Sentinel,* July 23, 1892, on the board of dental examiners. The pharmacy board, created three years earlier, rejected 261 of 702 examined from 1882 to 1888. *Wisconsin Blue Book, 1889,* p. 452; *ibid.,* 1897, p. 548. The law governing the practice of dentistry excluded those in active practice at the time of passage from the examination procedure, as did the pharmacy law. *Laws of Wisconsin,* 1885, pp. 105–107; *ibid.,* 1882, pp. 493–499. See also Milwaukee *Sentinel,* February 2, 1882; *Wisconsin Blue Book,* 1893, pp. 566–572; Charles R. Bulger, "Wisconsin Administrative Government, 1870–1891: Years of Legislative Control and Local Enforcement" (master's thesis, University of Wisconsin, 1984); and Chapter 9 above for the basis of the public attitude towards the medical profession.

admonition of James Bryce: "The newspapers accuse everybody.") Outwardly, the Wisconsin legislature of the time
appeared both chaotic and managed: chaotic, because there was
little continuity of membership from session to session; managed,
because the majority party's political managers, although generally not members of the legislature, appeared to take a prominent
role in organizing and overseeing its work.[29]

There was no legislative staff except during sessions. The legislative quarters were simply empty most of the time: no officers,
no staff, no interim committee meetings. Continuity of membership was very low. The 1887 *Wisconsin Blue Book* contains a list of
about 2,500 men who served as assemblymen in the first thirty-
eight legislatures, 1848 through 1887. An average one in four of
them served in more than one session, but just under one in ten
(9.6) served in consecutive sessions. About one in thirteen served
in the senate at some time. The number to bear in mind is that
three-fourths of the assembly members, on the average, were
serving a single term. For these thirty-eight sessions, there were
thirty-two different speakers. Only three of the five men who
were speaker more than once were elected to that office in consecutive sessions. Only one of the five served three times, Frederick W. Horn of Cedarburg, who was speaker in 1851, 1854,
and 1875.[30]

Despite this lack of formal continuity, there was a tradition
which brought order out of the seeming disorder of a large
majority of new members appearing in Madison for the first
time, seeing the sights, looking for quarters, and wondering how

[29] Richard N. Current, *Pine Logs and Politics: A Life of Philetus Sawyer, 1816-1900*
(Madison, 1950), 82–84, comments that party chairman Elisha Keyes "coordinated the
efforts of Republicans in the legislature," and in 1872 put through a reapportionment
measure satisfactory to Congressman Philetus Sawyer, who drew his own district. Horace
S. Merrill, *William Freeman Vilas: Doctrinaire Democrat* (Madison, 1954), 182–183, 220–
221, illustrates how Democratic chairmen managed the Democratic legislative majorities
of 1891 and 1893. The *Wisconsin State Journal*, April 23, 1891, was outraged by the
Democratic bosses openly sitting in the chambers and cracking the whip. See also Campbell, *Representative Democracy*, 191–193, on Democratic chairman Edward C. Wall directing
legislative affairs "from his 'look-out' post on the Assembly floor."
[30] *Wisconsin Blue Book, 1887*, pp. 131–175.

things worked. While this was going on, the smaller body of incumbents, returning from the last session, met with party managers to prepare for an organizational caucus. In addition, the offices of chief clerk for the two houses provided a good deal of continuity. While only one of the fifteen speakers who served during the sixteen legislative sessions, 1873–1893, served two consecutive terms, two others had served previously in that capacity. They were assisted by nine different chief clerks, only four of whom were in that position for just one session. Charles E. Bross was chief clerk of the senate during nine consecutive sessions from 1878 to 1889. The senate, of course, had fewer organizational problems because senators' terms covered two sessions and were staggered. Republicans had more experienced legislators throughout these years, and ordinarily they managed the organization of senate and assembly much more readily than did the Democrats, who won both houses only in the sessions of 1891 and 1893.[31]

Beyond questions of patronage and chairmanships, which the Yankee legislators naturally assumed were mostly theirs—for they usually provided the leadership in both parties—there lay the terrain of party voting and discipline. It depends on how one defines issues—or roll calls, the only available record—as party issues. In general, partisanship was not nearly so high as in the contemporary United States Congress. Urban legislators usually exhibited more coherence on party matters than rural members, but oddly there was little evidence of urban-rural strife. The most identifiable party issues concerned social issues: liquor control, school laws, and anything touching ethnic or religious sensibilities. It was generally assumed that Milwaukee legislators knew best what was needed in the way of specific authority to handle the myriad problems peculiar to the state's only metropolis—the nineteenth-century version of "home rule." As early as 1885,

---

[31] *Ibid., 1895*, pp. 184–185. Campbell, *Representative Democracy*, 40–45, furnishes the best description of the usual organizational order from chaos. As the legislators' biographies in the *Wisconsin Blue Book* indicate, most legislators had previous experience in local political offices and were active in community affairs. But most of them were coming to Madison as legislators for the first—and often the only—time.

Milwaukee County was considered to be in a separate class because of its dominant urban center.

The least definable party lines occurred in dealing with such matters as franchises, charters, and economic issues. Faulty or hasty legislation was always a hazard, not usually a matter of corruption or crafty maneuvers but more a product of the universally accepted notion that politically the shortest session was the best one. Also, it must be remembered that two out of three biennial sessions had to deal with the election of a United States senator. These were usually lengthy contests occupying the center of attention of the controlling party. This activity did not seem to lessen the number of bills dropped in the hopper to demand hasty action or more likely to die in committee towards the end of each session.[32]

One may surely conclude that in the years 1873–1893, Wisconsin's governors, other executive officers, and legislators did a better job than newspaper opinion at the time or later progressive critics were willing to concede. Contemporary cynicism became a weapon in the hands of later critics. Wisconsin governors did govern, though probably more as auxiliaries to the legislature than as the executive heads of an expanding bureaucracy that controlled budgeting, personnel, licensing, police, land use, and the myriad other powers and expectations that have accumulated since. The other elected state executives, who generally had larger staffs and clearly defined areas of authority, were nonetheless inferior in power, prestige, and opportunities to influence events. As usual, Edward G. Ryan was dealing in hyperbole when he called the governorship a "paltry office."[33]

Until he called out the militia in May, 1886, to deal with the mob in Milwaukee, Governor Rusk was primarily the chief legislative officer of the state. The governor, if he asserted himself

[32] Campbell, *Representative Democracy,* 31, 45–49, 85–86, 97, 122–123, 205–217. See also Ballard C. Campbell, "Ethnicity and the 1893 Wisconsin Assembly," in the *Journal of American History,* 62 (June, 1975), 74–94; and the Milwaukee *Journal,* November 7, 1982, "Centennial Pages," on Milwaukee County government.

[33] Keller, *Affairs of State,* 351. Ryan so described the governorship in 1879, consoling a colleague who had been defeated in a gubernatorial election.

at all, was the one who defined the legislative agenda. What stands out about governors Rusk and Smith in particular is the attention they paid to some special segment of society that needed help, and their willingness to address things left undone. Additionally, the power of the veto helped to keep the legislators on the governor's business. Somehow, Wisconsin's people emerged from these years with a better chance at an education for their young, were slightly healthier, worked shorter hours generally, and were conscious that those who required custodial care were mostly better off than twenty years before. Workplaces were generally safer, standards were applied to professional people and businesses with a fiduciary trust, and public accommodations were meeting standards enforced by law and overseen by state agencies. Indeed, people had grown accustomed to the notion that the government—and Madison was infinitely more immediate than Washington—should do something about other problems. Of course, Wisconsin was not yet the Eden that those who followed have created.

# APPENDIX

## THE GOVERNORS OF WISCONSIN, 1873–1893

| Name | Birthplace | Party | Term in Office | Birth/ Death |
|---|---|---|---|---|
| CADWALLADER C. WASHBURN | Maine | Rep. | Jan. 1, 1872–Jan. 5, 1874 | 1818–1882 |
| WILLIAM R. TAYLOR | Connecticut | Dem. | Jan. 5, 1874–Jan. 3, 1876 | 1820–1909 |
| HARRISON LUDINGTON | New York | Rep. | Jan. 3, 1876–Jan. 7, 1878 | 1812–1891 |
| WILLIAM E. SMITH | Scotland | Rep. | Jan. 7, 1878–Jan. 2, 1882 | 1824–1883 |
| JEREMIAH M. RUSK | Ohio | Rep. | Jan. 2, 1882–Jan. 7, 1889 | 1830–1893 |
| WILLIAM D. HOARD | New York | Rep. | Jan. 7, 1889–Jan. 5, 1891 | 1836–1918 |
| GEORGE W. PECK | New York | Dem. | Jan. 5, 1891–Jan. 7, 1895 | 1840–1916 |

# ESSAY ON SOURCES

BIBLIOGRAPHIC AIDS AND SERIALS

THIS ESSAY does not presume to be complete or necessarily authoritative. The effort was to make it representative. On some topics there is all too much to choose from, on others both sources and scholarly treatments are all too scarce. The footnotes to the text contain numerous works not mentioned here.

Richard N. Current noted in his introduction to the Essay on Sources in *The History of Wisconsin. Volume II: The Civil War Era, 1848–1873* (Madison, 1976): "Directly or indirectly the manuscript collections of the State Historical Society of Wisconsin have served as the main sources for this volume . . . and, still more, for the monographs upon which it is largely based." With the exception of four pages devoted specifically to the Civil War, certainly four out of five items noted in the remaining twenty-nine pages of Current's essay on sources fit this present volume as well. This is certainly true of his discussion of "Local Histories," and there is a similar overlapping coverage in other categories. Faced with the need to select from among several thousand titles worthy of mention, it seems reasonable to concentrate upon sources that supplement those presented in Volume II, and particularly those that have appeared in intervening years, even though much repetition is inevitable.

An interest in the sources presumes an interest in the Society and its history. Clifford L. Lord and Carl Ubbelohde, *Clio's Servant: The State Historical Society of Wisconsin, 1846–1954* (Madison, 1967), is a useful guide, supplemented by Alice E. Smith, "Wisconsin's History: Written and Unwritten," in the *Wisconsin Magazine of History,* 44 (Winter, 1960–1961), 95–101. This journal, published quarterly since 1917, has a manageable number of cumulative index volumes as well as annual indexes. Also rich in materials are the twenty volumes of the *Collections of the State Historical Society of Wisconsin* (Madison, 1855–1915), indexed in Volume 21, and the *Proceedings of the State Historical Society of Wisconsin* (74 vols., Madison, 1875–1958). The 1893 *Proceedings,* for instance, carried the first published version of Frederick Jackson Turner's seminal essay, "The Significance of the Frontier in American History," making that volume a rare item. Another series, the "Wisconsin Necrology," a collection of newspaper obituaries covering the years 1846–1968, is in fifty-two volumes in the Society Library, indexed in the subject card catalog.

The Manuscripts Room of the State Historical Society of Wisconsin and its finding aids give access to both the manuscripts collections of the Society and the archives of the state and local governments. Published guides, available in many libraries, include Alice E. Smith, ed., *Guide to the Manuscripts of the Wisconsin Historical Society* (Madison, 1944); Josephine L. Harper and Sharon C. Smith, eds., *Guide to the Manuscripts of the State Historical Society of Wisconsin: Supplement Number One* (Madison, 1957); Josephine L. Harper, ed., *Guide to the Manuscripts of the State Historical Society of Wisconsin: Supplement Number Two* (Madison, 1966); and David J. Delgado, ed. and comp., *Guide to the Wisconsin State Archives* (Madison, 1966). Also on the fourth floor of the Society building are located the iconographic collections of the Visual and Sound Archives.

There are relatively few cumulative archival records from state officers and boards for the years 1873–1893. Available in published form are the official reports in the series, *Wisconsin Public Documents*. These contain the reports of the governors and other executive officers and of some boards and administrative agencies. Some of these reports also appear in separate individual series. Northern Micrographics, "Index to Wisconsin Public Documents, 1852–1912/14 and Supplement" (La Crosse, 1975), is a guide to their microfiche copies of these records. Marcia R. Nettesheim, ed., "Guide to Wisconsin State Agencies and Their Call Numbers" (2nd ed., Madison, 1984), will help locate these sources in the Public Documents wing of the Society Library, which is also an official depository for published federal document series. The best guide to these federal records are the documents librarians. For this volume, the most used federal documents were the relevant published census volumes. Carmen R. Delle Donne, *Federal Census Schedules, 1850–1880: Primary Sources for Historical Research* (Reference Information Paper No. 67, National Archives and Records Service, G.S.A., Washington, 1973), answers questions on how the information was gathered, supplementing the older Carroll D. Wright and William C. Hunt, *The History and Growth of the United States Census* (Washington, 1900). The manuscript censuses for Wisconsin for 1860 and 1870 are in the SHSW Library in bound volumes. Those for 1880 and 1900 are on film. The 1890 series was destroyed in a fire in Washington. The Constitution of Wisconsin required an interim state census. There is no published version of the 1875 state census, but the population enumeration schedules are on microfiche. There are published versions for 1885, 1895, and 1905, after which the requirement was dropped. See Wisconsin Department of State, *Tabular Statements of the Census Enumeration and the Agricultural, Mineral, and Manufacturing Interests of the State of Wisconsin, 1895,* with similar titles for the state censuses of 1885 and 1905.

The *Wisconsin Blue Book* expanded steadily after 1870, when it was still essentially a legislators' handbook. By the 1920's it was regularly incorporating special articles having historical dimensions, in addition to offering a much expanded coverage of state agencies and institutions. The 1954, 1964, and recent *Blue Books* contain cumulative lists of these special articles from 1919 to the present. Legislative Reference Library, "A Guide to the Wisconsin Blue Book, 1853-1962," *Research Bulletin*, no. 141 (1963), is supplemented by Northern Micrographics, "Wisconsin Blue Books and Indexes, 1953-1973" (La Crosse, 1975).

Keeping up with doctoral dissertations and masters' theses on Wisconsin subjects is a difficult task. There is an author and subject card catalog in the Memorial Library of the University of Wisconsin-Madison covering those produced on that campus. Robert C. Nesbit and William Fletcher Thompson, eds., *A Guide to Theses on Wisconsin Subjects*, compiled by Roger E. Wyman (Madison, 1964), and its 1966 *Supplement* compiled by Jeanne Hunnicutt Chiswick, await updating from the files accumulated for *The History of Wisconsin* series. Byron Anderson, *A Bibliography of Master's Theses and Doctoral Dissertations on Milwaukee Topics, 1911-1977* (Madison, 1981) — the years 1911-1977 being the dates of the monographs rather than the subjects — and University of Wisconsin-Platteville, Karrmann Library, "Masters Theses and Seminar Papers: U.W. Cluster, 1935-1976" (Platteville, 1979), are limited extensions of the *Theses Guides*. Another guide which should be updated and somewhat changed in format is Leroy Schlinkert, comp., *Subject Bibliography of Wisconsin History* (Madison, 1947), a flawed work that nevertheless serves as a guide to a variety of printed sources.

General biographies abound. The *Dictionary of Wisconsin Biography* (Madison, 1960), is particularly useful for the period 1873-1893. Each biography in the *DWB* closes with a list of sources for the sketch. Many of the state, county, and area histories include biographical sketches. Evelyn O. Koepke, "The Self-Styled Greeley of Wisconsin: Frank Abial Flower" (master's thesis, University of Wisconsin–Milwaukee, 1967), offers a useful sketch of Flower's career as editor of local histories of this genre, popularly known as "mugbooks." Darlene E. Waterstreet, comp., *Biography Index to the Wisconsin Blue Books, 1870-1973* (Milwaukee, 1974), is a guide for genealogists to the thousands of short biographies in the series. Alexander M. Thomson, *A Political History of Wisconsin* (Milwaukee, 1900), has biographies of the prominent political figures of the period. *The Columbian Biographical Dictionary and Portrait Gallery of the Representative Men of the United States: Wisconsin Volume* (Chicago, 1895), catches many prominent figures.

There are many general histories of the state, particularly multi-volume sets that usually include strictly biographical volumes. Most recent of single-volume, scholarly works are Richard N. Current, *Wisconsin: A*

*Bicentennial History* (New York, 1977), and Robert C. Nesbit, *Wisconsin: A History* (Madison, 1973). Two older texts are William F. Raney, *Wisconsin: A Story of Progress* (New York, 1940; reprinted, Appleton, 1963, 1970), and Milo M. Quaife, *Wisconsin: Its History and Its People* (4 vols., Chicago, 1924).

Since the publication of Volume II of this series in 1976, there has been an important change in the availability of the index to the Milwaukee *Sentinel.* Until recently, the index ran through the year 1879 and could be consulted only at the Milwaukee Public Library. Professor Herbert W. Rice, who directed the original Works Progress Administration project, brought to completion the monumental task of organizing the uncollated slips for the years 1880–1890, and the entire index is now available on film, thanks to a grant from the National Endowment for the Humanities. The broad use of the *Sentinel* and the other newspapers in this volume is indicated in the footnotes. Ada T. Griswold, comp., *Annotated Catalogue of Newspaper Files in the Library of the State Historical Society of Wisconsin* (Madison, 1911 edition), and Donald E. Oehlerts, comp., *Guide to Wisconsin Newspapers, 1833–1957* (Madison, 1958), remain useful although they preceded the massive microfilming project that brought many scattered files together in the SHSW. Carl H. Knoche, *The German Immigrant Press in Milwaukee* (New York, 1980), supplements Carl F. Wittke, *The German-Language Press in America* (Lexington, Kentucky, 1957). Histories of individual newspapers tend to be fugitive pieces in the newspapers themselves. Will C. Conrad, Kathleen F. Wilson, and Dale Wilson, *The Milwaukee Journal: The First Eighty Years* (Madison, 1964), is more substantial. Roland L. Strand, "History of the *Madison Democrat*" (master's thesis, University of Wisconsin, 1948), is one of the few studies in this form. Most of those who wrote local and state histories in the late nineteenth and early twentieth centuries were newspapermen who naturally included informed discussions of the press. Alexander M. Thomson, William G. Bruce, Henry C. Campbell, and Ellis B. Usher come to mind. Among continuing serials that one should know are *The Historical Messenger of the Milwaukee County Historical Society* (title changed to *Milwaukee History* in 1977); *Transactions of the Wisconsin Academy of Sciences, Arts and Letters;* and *Inland Seas,* the quarterly bulletin of the Great Lakes Historical Society.

## LAND AND THE ECONOMY

Arthur H. Robinson and Jerry B. Culver, eds., *The Atlas of Wisconsin* (Madison, 1974), is primarily a detailed locator but also contains sectional maps with physical details. Lawrence Martin, *The Physical Geography of Wisconsin* (Madison, 1916; 3rd ed., 1965); John T. Curtis, *The*

*Vegetation of Wisconsin: An Ordination of Plant Communities* (Madison, 1959); and Francis D. Hole, Marvin T. Beatty, and Gerhard B. Lee, *Soils of Wisconsin* (Madison, 1976), are the standard works on the natural environment. Snyder, Van Vechten and Co., comps., *Historical Atlas of Wisconsin, Embracing Complete State and County Maps, City & Village Plats, Together with Separate State and County Histories* (Milwaukee, 1893), tells it all and is particularly valuable for the years 1873–1893. Loyal Durand, "The Geographic Regions of Wisconsin" (doctoral dissertation, University of Wisconsin, 1930), is summarized or published in part in U.S. Department of Agriculture and Wisconsin Department of Agriculture and Markets, Wisconsin Crop and Livestock Reporting Service, *Bulletin No. 120* (1931), pp. 29–32, and in Loyal Durand and Leavelva M. Bradbury, *Home Regions of Wisconsin: A Geography of the State* (New York, 1933), a grade school text but the most easily accessible. Ernest F. Bean, "State Geological Surveys of Wisconsin," in *Transactions of the Wisconsin Academy of Sciences, Arts and Letters*, 30 (1937), 203–220, introduces Thomas C. Chamberlin, ed., *Geology of Wisconsin, Survey of 1873–1879* (4 vols., Madison, 1877–1883). James L. Greenleaf, "Report on the Water-power of the Northwest," in the *Tenth Census of the United States, 1880: Reports on the Water-power of the United States, Volume XVII, Part 2*, and Leonard S. Smith, *The Water Powers of Wisconsin*, Wisconsin Geological and Natural History Survey, *Bulletin* No. 20 (Madison, 1908), provide a perspective on a resource of diminishing expectations in southern Wisconsin. James A. Lake, *Law and Mineral Wealth: The Legal Profile of the Wisconsin Mining Industry* (Madison, 1962), has useful discussion of the geological surveys and the brief iron boom on the Gogebic Range in the 1880's.

Paul W. Gates, *History of Public Land Law Development* (Washington, 1968), U.S. Department of the Interior, Bureau of Land Management, *Public Lands Bibliography* (Washington, 1962), and Vernon Carstensen, ed., *The Public Lands: Studies in the History of the Public Domain* (Madison, 1963), are useful introductions to a vast subject. Any discussion of Wisconsin agricultural settlement, lumbering, and railroads begins here.

Joseph Schafer, *A History of Agriculture in Wisconsin* (Madison, 1922), is an introduction to his projected Domesday series and particularly to his *Wisconsin Domesday Book: Town Studies* (Madison, 1924), both with much on the land and pioneering. Frederick Merk, *Economic History of Wisconsin During the Civil War Decade* (Madison, 1916; reprinted, 1971), places the 1870's in context. Harvey S. Perloff et al., *Regions, Resources, and Economic Growth* (Lincoln, 1960), provides regional and national contexts for Wisconsin's development. David A. Wells, *Recent Economic Changes and Their Effect on the Production and Distribution of Wealth and the Well-Being of Society* (New York, 1890), offers a contemporary view, as does the series *Wisconsin State Gazetteer and Business Directory* beginning with the 1876–1877 volume compiled by Murphy and Co. (Milwaukee, 1876), and taken over subsequently by R.L. Polk and Co. of Chicago with the 1884–1885 volume. Ray H. Whitbeck, *The Geography of the Fox–Winnebago Valley,* Wisconsin Geological and Natural History Survey, *Bulletin* 42 (Madison, 1915), and Whitbeck, *The Geography and Economic Development of Southeastern Wisconsin,* Wisconsin Geological and Natural History Survey, *Bulletin* No. 58 (Madison, 1921), together with the later John W. Alexander, *Geography of Manufacturing in the Rock River Valley,* University of Wisconsin, School of Commerce, Bureau of Busines Research and Service, vol. 1, no. 2 (Madison, 1949), have self-explanatory titles. The Milwaukee Grain Exchange Papers are a mine of information on the commerce of the principal port as well as business opinion, supplemented by the Milwaukee *Daily Commercial Times* (1875–1878) and the *Northwestern Trade Bulletin* (1879–1884), also published in Milwaukee.

Eric E. Lampard, *The Rise of the Dairy Industry in Wisconsin: A Study in Agricultural Change, 1820–1920* (Madison, 1963), is the standard source, replacing older works such as Joseph Schafer's *A History of Agriculture in Wisconsin* (Madison, 1922). A pamphlet by the SHSW, *Joseph Schafer: Student of Agriculture,* foreword by Edward P. Alexander (Madison, 1942), lists all of his published work as a prodigiously busy author and editor, much of it on Wisconsin agriculture. His *Wisconsin Domesday Book* series (5 vols., Madison, 1922–1937), abounds with agricultural and social history, and includes, in addition to the volume above and the *Town Studies* previously mentioned: *The Wisconsin Lead Region* (Madison, 1932); *The Winnebago-Horicon Basin: A Type Study in Western History* (Madison, 1937); and *Four Wisconsin Counties: Prairie and Forest* (Madison, 1927).

Walter H. Ebling et al., *A Century of Wisconsin Agriculture, 1848–1948,* Wisconsin Department of Agriculture, Wisconsin Crop and Livestock Reporting Service, *Bulletin No. 290* (1948), is a reliable source for agricultural statistics, often presented in map form, with an analysis thereof. Ebling, *Wisconsin Agriculture in Mid-Century,* Wisconsin Department of Agriculture, Wisconsin Crop and Livestock Reporting Service, *Bulletin No. 325* (1954), supplements the earlier bulletin. Ebling, "The Development of Agriculture in Wisconsin," in the *Wisconsin Blue Book, 1929,* pp. 51–74, and Ebling, "A Century of Agriculture in Wisconsin," in *ibid., 1940,* pp. 185–196, are briefer treatments. Fred A. Shannon, *The Farmer's Last Frontier: Agriculture, 1860–1897* (New York, 1945; reprinted, 1968), treats agriculture in the Upper Midwest at length. Allan G. Bogue, *From Prairie to Corn Belt: Farming on the Illinois and Iowa Prairies in the Nineteenth Century* (Chicago, 1963), has much that is applicable to southern Wisconsin farming, as does Earl Hayter, *The Troubled Farmer, 1850-1900: Rural Readjustment to Industrialism* (DeKalb, 1968). John D. Bowman and Richard H. Keehn, "Agriculture Terms of Trade in Four Midwestern States, 1870-1900," in the *Journal of Economic History,* 34 (September, 1974), 592-605, suggests that market pressures on agricultural trade were not as negative as was widely assumed at the time. John G. Thompson, *The Rise and Decline of the Wheat Growing Industry in Wisconsin* (Madison, 1909), and Henrietta M. Larson, *The Wheat Market and the Farmer in Minnesota, 1858-1900* (New York, 1926), treat the general movement of wheat growing in southern Wisconsin towards the northwest.

Wilbur H. Glover, *Farm and College: The College of Agriculture of the University of Wisconsin, a History* (Madison, 1952), includes an excellent general history of the state's agricultural enterprise. Farming in northern Wisconsin is covered in Vernon Carstensen, *Farms or Forests: Evolution of a State Land Policy for Northern Wisconsin, 1850-1932* (Madison, 1958; reprinted, New York, 1979), and Lucile Kane, "Settling the Wisconsin Cutovers," in *WMH,* 40 (Winter, 1956-1957), 91-98. Arlan Helgeson, *Farms in the Cutover: Agricultural Settlement in Northern Wisconsin* (Madison, 1962), offers sobering reflections on the results of an enthusiasm summarized in William Henry, *Northern Wisconsin: A Handbook for the Homeseeker* (Madison, 1896). An example of several specialized studies is Alfred W. Booth, "The Geography of the Southeastern Dairy Region of Wisconsin" (doctoral dissertation, University of Wisconsin, 1936). Among useful serials on the subject, *Hoard's Dairyman* began as a weekly supplement to the Fort Atkinson *Jefferson County Union* in January, 1885, and continued as the nation's leading dairy journal. Two weeklies with the same name, *The Western Farmer,* were published in Madison from 1849 to 1874 and from 1882 to 1884. Accessible because the state printed and distributed many copies over the years are the *Transactions* of the Northern Wisconsin Agricultural Society and the *Transactions* of the Northern Wisconsin Agricultural and Mechanical Association. Not as formidable as they sound, they contain a wealth of social history.

The background of the Wisconsin lumber industry must begin with J. Willard Hurst, *Law and Economic Growth: The Legal History of the Lumber Industry in Wisconsin, 1836-1915* (Cambridge, 1964), a monumental study. The standard general work is Robert F. Fries, *Empire in Pine: The Story of Lumbering in Wisconsin, 1830-1900* (Madison, 1951), supplemented by Agnes M. Larson, *History of the White Pine Industry in Minnesota* (Minneapolis, 1949). Bernhardt J. Kleven, "Wisconsin Lumber Industry" (doctoral dissertation, University of Minnesota, 1941), offers useful material on technological changes. George W. Hotchkiss, *History of the*

*Lumber and Forest Industry of the Northwest* (Chicago, 1898), writes as a contemporary. Paul W. Gates, *The Wisconsin Pine Lands of Cornell University: A Study in Land Policy and Absentee Ownership* (Ithaca, 1943; reprinted, Madison, 1965), is a standard work, as is William G. Rector, *Log Transportation in the Lake States Lumber Industry, 1840-1918* (Glendale, California, 1953). Filibert Roth, *U.S. Forestry Conditions and Interests of Wisconsin,* U.S. Department of Agriculture, Division of Forestry, *Bulletin No. 16* (1898), is by an early professional in the field. There are a number of very readable memoirs by contemporaries engaged in the lumber business: Isaac Stephenson, *Recollections of a Long Life, 1829-1915* (Chicago, 1915), is both a business and a political memoir; John Emmett Nelligan, as told to Charles M. Sheridan, *The Life of a Lumberman* (n.p., 1929), remembers it as a rugged life; William A. Holt, *A Wisconsin Lumberman Looks Backward* (Oconto?, Wisconsin, 1948), was a second-generation lumberman from Chicago who in 1888 moved to Oconto in his early twenties to run the family firms.

The best scholarly history of several dealing with individual companies is Charles E. Twining, *Downriver: Orrin H. Ingram and the Empire Lumber Company* (Madison, 1975). Other representative studies are: A. R. Reynolds, *The Daniel Shaw Lumber Company: A Case Study of the Wisconsin Lumbering Frontier* (New York, 1957); Fred W. Kohlmeyer, *Timber Roots: The Laird, Norton Story, 1855-1905* (Winona, Minnesota, 1972); and Duane D. Fischer, "The John S. Owen Enterprises" (doctoral dissertation, University of Wisconsin, 1964). Ralph W. Hidy, Frank Ernest Hill, and Allan Nevins, *Timber and Men: The Weyerhaeuser Story* (New York, 1963), is bland enough not to offend.

TRANSPORTATION

James P. Kaysen, comp., *The Railroads of Wisconsin, 1827-1937* (Boston, 1937), is an essential guide to the construction and complicated ownership histories of individual companies. William F. Raney's Chapter X, "The Building of Wisconsin Railroads," in *Wisconsin: A Story of Progress* (New York, 1940; reprinted, Appleton, 1963, 1970), is the standard short account, and also appears in *WMH,* 19 (June, 1936), 387-403. There are several company histories. The most interesting is Roy L. Martin, *History of the Wisconsin Central* (Railway and Locomotive Historical Society, *Bulletin,* no. 54, Boston, 1941). Especially useful are studies that put Wisconsin railroads in a larger context. Albro Martin, *James J. Hill and the Opening of the Northwest* (New York, 1976); Julius Grodinsky, *Transcontinental Railway Strategy, 1869-1893: A Study of Businessmen* (Philadelphia, 1962); Alfred D. Chandler, Jr., comp. and ed., *The Railroads: The Nation's First Big Business* (New York, 1965); and Thomas C. Cochran, *Railroad Leaders, 1845-1890: The Business Mind in*

*Action* (Cambridge, 1953), are representative. Studies of efforts to control the railroads include: George H. Miller, *Railroads and the Granger Laws* (Madison, 1971); Robert S. Hunt, *Law and Locomotives: The Impact of the Railroad on Wisconsin Law in the Nineteenth Century* (Madison, 1958); Dale E. Treleven, "Railroads, Elevators, and Grain Dealers: The Genesis of Antimonopolism in Milwaukee," in *WMH,* 52 (Spring, 1969), 205–222; Robert T. Daland, "Enactment of the Potter Law," in *WMH,* 33 (September, 1949), 45–54; William L. Burton, "Wisconsin's First Railroad Commission: A Case Study in Apostasy," in *WMH,* 45 (Spring, 1962), 190–198; and the overwhelming body of material published in the Wisconsin Railroad Commissioner's annual and biennial reports, beginning in 1874. Dissertations and theses are represented by Richard L. Canuteson, "The Railway Development of Northern Wisconsin" (master's thesis, University of Wisconsin, 1930); Herbert W. Rice, "Early History of the Chicago, Milwaukee and St. Paul Railway Company" (doctoral dissertation, State University of Iowa, 1938); and Frank N. Elliott, "The Causes and the Growth of Railroad Regulation in Wisconsin, 1848–1876" (doctoral dissertation, University of Wisconsin, 1956). David B. Leonard, "A Biography of Alexander Mitchell, 1817–1887" (master's thesis, University of Wisconsin, 1951), found slim pickings in the way of personal and business records.

On roads and highways, William O. Hotchkiss, *Rural Highways of Wisconsin,* Wisconsin Geological and Natural History Survey, *Bulletin* No. 18 (Madison, 1906), was almost as close to the problem as J. C. Ford, "Our Country Roads," in the Wisconsin State Agricultural Society, *Transactions,* 23 (1885), 206–217, or John M. Olin, "Better Roads— A Plan for Improving County Highways in Wisconsin," in *ibid.,* 31 (1893), 283–319. Wayne E. Fuller, *RFD: The Changing Face of Rural America* (Bloomington, 1964), and Ballard Campbell, "The Good Roads Movement in Wisconsin, 1890–1911," in *WMH,* 49 (Summer, 1966), 273–293, sum it up.

A principal source for information on water transportation during the period 1873–1893 is federal documents, which are best consulted in the appropriate footnotes. Ralph G. Plumb, a Manitowoc historian, wrote a *History of the Navigation of the Great Lakes* (Washington, 1911), *Lake Michigan* (Manitowoc, 1941), and other works on harbors and shipping. The Mississippi was of minor importance for Wisconsin except for the log and lumber trade. H. J. Hirshheimer, "La Crosse River History and the Davidsons," in *WMH,* 28 (March, 1945), 263–276, and Mildred L. Hartsough, *From Canoe to Steel Barge on the Upper Mississippi* (Minneapolis, 1934), are supplemented by Louis C. Hunter, *Steamboats on the Western Rivers: An Economic and Technological History* (Cambridge, 1949), a fascinating social as well as technological study. George G. Tunell, "The Diversion of the Flour and Grain Traffic from

the Great Lakes to the Railroads," in the *Journal of Political Economy,* 5
(June, 1897), 340–375, 413–420, is by an expert who wrote some
government reports. The best history of the misconceived Fox–Wisconsin
waterway is Robert W. McCluggage, "The Fox-Wisconsin Waterway, 1836–1872: Land Speculation and Regional Rivalries, Politics
and Private Enterprise" (doctoral dissertation, University of Wisconsin, 1954). Samuel Mermin, *The Fox–Wisconsin Improvement: An Historical Study in Legal Institutions and Political Economy* (Madison, 1968), takes
the story farther.

INDUSTRY

There is no satisfactory large-scale general study of Wisconsin industry for the years covered by this volume. J. H. H. Alexander, "A Short
Industrial History of Wisconsin," in the *Wisconsin Blue Book, 1929,* pp.
31–49, is supplemented by Francis F. Bowman, *Why Wisconsin* (Madison, 1948), which is limited, and Wisconsin Regional Planning Committee, *A Study of Wisconsin: Its Resources, Its Physical, Social and Economic
Background* (Madison, 1934), a New Deal production with a historical
dimension. Otherwise, the many relevant federal census volumes are
most useful, with Harvey S. Perloff et al., *Regions, Resources, and Economic Growth* (Lincoln, 1960), as a guide to federal census series. Victor
S. Clark, *History of Manufactures in the United States, 1860–1914* (Washington, 1928), is a massive work with a good index. Of more recent
general treatments, Edward C. Kirkland, *Industry Comes of Age: Business,
Labor, and Public Policy, 1860–1897* (New York, 1961), remains a standard for background.

Most sources on industry deal with specific industries or companies.
Margaret Walsh has expanded on her published doctoral dissertation,
*The Manufacturing Frontier: Pioneer Industry in Antebellum Wisconsin, 1830–
1860* (Madison, 1972), with a series of articles: "Industrial Opportunity on the Urban Frontier: 'Rags to Riches' and Milwaukee Clothing
Manufacturers, 1840–1880," in *WMH,* 57 (Spring, 1974), 175–194;
"Business Success and Capital Availability in the New West: Milwau-
kee Ironmasters in the Middle Nineteenth Century," in *The Old North-
west,* 1 (June, 1975), 159–179; and "Pork Packing as a Leading Edge
of Midwestern Industry, 1835–1875," in *Agricultural History,* 51 (October, 1977), 702–717. Also important are Thomas C. Cochran, *The Pabst
Brewing Company: The History of an American Business* (New York, 1948);
Edgar M. Hoover, Jr., *Location Theory and the Shoe and Leather Industries*
(Cambridge, 1937; reprinted, New York, 1968); William O. Baldwin,
"Historical Geography of the Brewing Industry: Focus on Wisconsin"
(doctoral dissertation, University of Illinois, 1966); Robert T. Hilton,
"Men of Metal: A History of the Foundry Industry in Wisconsin"

(master's thesis, University of Wisconsin, 1952); the brief but interesting *Autobiography* of Henry Harnischfeger (Milwaukee, 1929); and Walter F. Peterson, *An Industrial Heritage: Allis-Chalmers Corporation* (Milwaukee, 1978).

The important agricultural machinery industry brings to mind Stewart H. Holbrook, *Machines of Plenty: Pioneering in American Agriculture* (New York, 1955), based much upon the career of James I. Case as distilled from personal and company papers. Harvey Schwartz, "The Changes in the Location of the American Agricultural Implement Industry, 1850 to 1900" (doctoral dissertation, University of Illinois, 1966), is basically a statistical study, while Agnes M. Larson, *John A. Johnson: An Uncommon American* (Northfield, 1969), celebrates a Norwegian-American who became Madison's most important industrialist. The "Autobiography" of George W. Esterly, a typescript in the George W. Esterly Papers, deals with the father and son who manufactured the Esterly harvester in Whitewater. Bernhard C. Korn, *The Story of Bay View* (Milwaukee, 1980), is derived from his 1936 master's thesis done at Marquette University. Maurice L. Branch, "The Paper Industry in the Lake States Region, 1834–1947" (doctoral dissertation, University of Wisconsin, 1954), discusses all aspects of a widely dispersed industry important to Wisconsin. Charles E. Schefft, "The Tanning Industry in Wisconsin: A History of Its Frontier Origins and Its Development" (master's thesis, University of Wisconsin, 1938), provides background for the several transcripts of interviews (SHSW) done by Matson Holbrook in early 1952 with elderly men who worked in the Milwaukee leather trade before 1900.

Much Wisconsin industrial history is centered on a locale rather than on a specific industry. Much cited here is W. J. Anderson and Julius Bleyer, eds., *Milwaukee's Great Industries: A Compilation of Facts Concerning Milwaukee's Commercial and Manufacturing Enterprises, Its Trade and Commerce, and the Advantages It Offers to Manufacturers Seeking Desirable Locations for New or Established Industries* (Milwaukee, 1892), because the local men who wrote about specific industries for the volume were presumably knowledgeable and reflect their times. The length of the title tells why many similar works must be indicated as a genre to be sought in the footnotes. Later scholarly works that concentrate on places include Charles N. Glaab and Lawrence H. Larsen, *Factories in the Valley: Neenah-Menasha, 1870–1915* (Madison, 1969), a social and industrial study of a smaller community. Others that reflect a similar approach are: Nicholas C. Burckel, ed., *Racine: Growth and Change in a Wisconsin County* (Racine, 1977); Michael P. Conzen, "Metropolitan Dominance in the American Midwest During the Later Nineteenth Century" (doctoral dissertation, University of Wisconsin, 1972); Beloit *Daily News, The Book of Beloit, 1836–1936* (Beloit, 1936); James B. Smith, "The

Movements for Diversified Industry in Eau Claire, Wisconsin, 1879–
1907: Boosterism and Urban Development Strategy in a Declining
Lumber Town" (master's thesis, University of Wisconsin, 1967); and
Carl E. Krog, "Marinette: Biography of a Nineteenth Century Lum-
bering Town" (doctoral dissertation, University of Wisconsin, 1971).
Forrest McDonald, *Let There Be Light: The Electric Utility Industry in
Wisconsin, 1881–1955* (Madison, 1957), begins, of course, in the cities.

How industry was financed for the period 1873–1893 is an elusive
topic. Two standard works are Theodore A. Andersen, *A Century of
Banking in Wisconsin* (Madison, 1954), and Leonard B. Krueger, *History
of Commercial Banking in Wisconsin* (University of Wisconsin, Studies in
the Social Sciences and History, no. 18, Madison, 1933), but they have
little to say about credit to industry. Michael P. Conzen, "Capital
Flows and the Developing Urban Hierarchy: State Bank Capital in
Wisconsin, 1854–1895," in *Economic Geography*, 51 (October, 1975),
321–338, is difficult for the layman. George J. Kuehnl, *The Wisconsin
Business Corporation* (Madison, 1959), is primarily a legal study but
drops an occasional nugget.

The biennial reports of the Wisconsin Bureau of Labor Statistics,
begun in 1883–1884, are basic documents for a view of people at work.
Gerd Korman, *Industrialization, Immigrants and Americanizers: The View
from Milwaukee, 1866–1921* (Madison, 1967), may be compared with
the contemporary writer Emile Levasseur, *The American Workman*, translated by Thomas S. Adams and edited by Theodore Marburg (Baltimore, 1900), who made extensive American observations in 1876 and
1893. Herbert G. Gutman, *Work, Culture, and Society in Industrializing
America: Essays in American Working-Class and Social History* (New York,
1976), is one of several concerned with the changing demands of an
urban-industrial society. Frank A. Flower's *History of Milwaukee, Wisconsin. . .* (2 vols., Chicago, 1881), is interesting for its literally hundreds
of brief biographies of skilled workers and small businessmen. George
B. Engberg, "Lumber and Labor in the Lake States," in *Minnesota
History*, 36 (March, 1959), 153–165, is one of several on this topic.
Daniel R. Madden, "Factory Safety in Wisconsin, 1878–1911" (master's thesis, University of Wisconsin, 1968), goes beyond the laws and
inspections. Again, the Matson Holbrook interviews give a picture of
work and workers' lives in the tanning industry.

## THE SOCIETY

The state and federal censuses are the basic sources for discussions of
Wisconsin's population. Walter H. Ebling, "Wisconsin Territorial and
State Censuses," in *Transactions of the Wisconsin Academy of Sciences, Arts
and Letters*, 55 (1966), 47–57, is helpful, and *Wisconsin's Changing Popu-*

*lation* (Science Inquiry Publication, no. 9, and Bulletin of the University of Wisconsin, serial no. 2642, general series no. 2426, Madison, 1942), contain summary information on the years 1870–1900. Guy-Harold Smith, "The Settlement and Present Distribution of Population in Wisconsin: A Geographical Interpretation" (doctoral dissertation, University of Wisconsin, 1927), is an impressive pre-computer study, summarized in Smith's "The Populating of Wisconsin," in the *Geographical Review,* 18 (July, 1928), 402–421, and "The Settlement and the Distribution of the Population in Wisconsin," in the *Transactions of the Wisconsin Academy of Sciences, Arts and Letters,* 24 (1929), 53–107.

Merle Curti, *The Making of an American Community: A Case Study of Democracy in a Frontier County* (Stanford, 1959), is the pioneering computer-assisted study of its type. Richard M. Bernard, *The Melting Pot and the Altar: Marital Assimilation in Early Twentieth Century Wisconsin* (Minneapolis, 1980), projects from nineteenth-century bases. Peter J. Coleman, "Restless Grant County: Americans on the Move," in *WMH,* 46 (Autumn, 1962), 16–31, follows Curti's lead. John E. Brush, "The Trade Centers of South-Western Wisconsin: An Analysis of Function and Location" (doctoral dissertation, University of Wisconsin, 1952), is a companion to Glenn T. Trewartha, "The Unincorporated Hamlet: One Element of the American Settlement Fabric," in *Annals of the Association of American Geographers,* 33 (March, 1943), 32–81, and C. J. Galpin, *The Social Anatomy of an Agricultural Community,* University of Wisconsin, Agricultural Experiment Station, *Research Bulletin* No. 34, (May, 1915), who is credited with originating rural sociology as a separate discipline. Robert R. Polk, "A Geographical Analysis of Population Change in the Hill Land of Western Wisconsin, 1870–1950" (doctoral dissertation, University of Wisconsin, 1964), is a later interpretive study. George W. Peck, ed., *Wisconsin: Comprising Sketches of Counties, Towns, Events, Institutions, and Persons, Arranged in Cyclopedic Form* (Madison, 1906), is a near-contemporary freeze frame, while Lewis Atherton, *Main Street on the Middle Border* (Bloomington, 1954), drew heavily upon the SHSW in this popular treatment.

Autobiographies and biographies tell us much about Wisconsin society. Oscar Hallam, "Bloomfield and Number Five: The American Way of Life in a Wisconsin Rural Community in the 70s, As Seen by a Small Boy," in the Hallam Reminiscences, is a gold mine, as is Gilson G. Glasier, ed., *Autobiography of Roujet D. Marshall, Justice of the Supreme Court of the State of Wisconsin, 1895–1918* (2 vols., Madison, 1923 and 1931). Ray Stannard Baker, *Native American: The Book of My Youth* (New York, 1941), recounts a boyhood in northwestern Wisconsin, and much of Hamlin Garland's best-known works reflect his boyhood in rural La Crosse County, especially *A Son of the Middle Border,* ed. Henry M. Christman (Macmillan paperback edition, New York, 1961). Burr W.

Jones, *Reminiscences of Nine Decades* (Evansville, Wisconsin, 1937), and Nils P. Haugen, *Pioneer and Political Reminiscences* (Evansville, Wisconsin, 1930?), earlier published in *WMH*, 11–13 (December, 1927–December, 1929), were men in their mid-twenties in 1873; Garland and particularly Baker were considerably younger. Grant Showerman, *A Country Chronicle* (New York, 1916), is unfortunately a rare volume, as is Oscar T. Thompson, *Home Town: Some Chapters of Reminiscence* (Beloit, 1942). Ray Allen Billington, *Frederick Jackson Turner: Historian, Scholar, Teacher* (New York, 1973), is a landmark because of Turner's importance in American historical scholarship and the book's recreation of his youth in Portage and at the University. Bill Hooker, *Glimpses of an Earlier Milwaukee* (Milwaukee, 1929), is an elderly newspaper reporter's collection of short reminiscences on any and every subject.

Don H. Doyle, *The Social Order of a Frontier Community: Jacksonville, Illinois, 1825–70* (Urbana, 1978), and Allan G. Bogue, "Social Theory and the Pioneer," in *Agricultural History*, 34 (January, 1960), 21–34, are helpful in describing the urbanizing society of 1873–1893. *The Tenth Census of the United States, 1880: Report on the Social Statistics of Cities, Volume XIX, Part 2*, pp. 641–686, reports on Beloit, Fond du Lac, La Crosse, Madison, Milwaukee, Oshkosh, and Racine. Bayrd Still, *Milwaukee: The History of a City* (Madison, 1948; reprinted, 1965), is a notable pioneer among scholarly urban studies, and he has watched over it in "Problems of an Urban Biographer," in the *Historical Messenger of the Milwaukee County Historical Society*, 23 (June, 1967), 34–43, and "Milwaukee Revisited: A Review Essay," in *WMH*, 60 (Summer, 1977), 330–333. Important recent studies of Milwaukee include Roger D. Simon, *The City-Building Process: Housing and Services in New Milwaukee Neighborhoods, 1880–1910 (Transactions of the American Philosophical Society*, vol. 68, pt. 5, Philadelphia, 1978); Kathleen N. Conzen, *Immigrant Milwaukee, 1836–1860: Accommodation and Community in a Frontier City* (Cambridge, 1976); and Clay McShane, *Technology and Reform: Street Railways and the Growth of Milwaukee, 1887–1900* (Madison, 1974). J. Rogers Hollingsworth and Ellen J. Hollingsworth, *Dimensions in Urban History: Historical and Social Science Perspectives on Middle-Size American Cities* (Madison, 1979), uses Wisconsin models. John A. Fleckner, "Poverty and Relief in Nineteenth-Century Janesville," in *WMH*, 61 (Summer, 1978), 279–299, and Edward M. Lang, Jr., "The Common Man, Janesville, Wisconsin, 1870 to 1900" (master's thesis, University of Wisconsin, 1968), complete a portrait of that city. Albert H. Sanford and H. J. Hirschheimer, *A History of La Crosse, Wisconsin, 1841–1900* (La Crosse, 1951), recently reissued, is an excellent city biography, as is the more recent book by David V. Mollenhoff, *Madison: A History of the Formative Years* (Dubuque, 1982).

Virginia M. Zarob, "The Family in an Expanding Industrial Economy: Economic, Occupational, Social, and Residential Mobility in Milwaukee, Wisconsin, 1860–1880" (doctoral dissertation, Marquette University, 1976), makes good use of local sources. Joanne J. Brownsword, "Good Templars in Wisconsin" (master's thesis, University of Wisconsin, 1960), examines a particular enthusiasm of the society of the time, as do Hosea W. Rood, "The Grand Army of the Republic and the Wisconsin Department," in *WMH*, 6 (March–June, 1923), 280–294, 403–413; Walter Monfried, "Milwaukee Remembers the GAR Reunions," in the *Historical Messenger of the Milwaukee County Historical Society*, 12 (September, 1956), 8–11; and Mary R. Dearing, *Veterans in Politics: The Story of the G.A.R.* (Baton Rouge, 1952), which has much on Wisconsin veterans. Michael P. Conzen, *Frontier Farming in an Urban Shadow: The Influence of Madison's Proximity on the Agricultural Development of Blooming Grove, Wisconsin* (Madison, 1971), fits with Gerald L. Prescott, "Gentlemen Farmers in the Gilded Age," in *WMH*, 55 (Spring, 1972), 197–212, taken from his 1968 doctoral dissertation. For a quick trip with a camera, see Howard Mead, Jill Dean, and Susan Smith, *Portrait of the Past: A Photographic Journey Through Wisconsin* (Madison, 1971). George Talbot, *At Home: Domestic Life in the Post-Centennial Era, 1876–1920* (Madison, 1976), illustrates the iconographic resources of the SHSW and of its curator of Visual and Sound Archives, who succeeded Paul Vanderbilt. Leora M. Howard, "Changes in Home Life in Milwaukee from 1865 to 1900" (master's thesis, University of Wisconsin, 1923), is impressionistic but the commentator is closer to the times. Joseph F. Kett, *Rites of Passage: Adolescence in America, 1790 to the Present* (New York, 1977), and Richard Lingeman, *Small Town America: A Narrative History, 1620–The Present* (Boston, 1980), are examples of more accessible works.

Sources not already noted covering labor strife include Milton M. Small, "The Biography of Robert Schilling" (master's thesis, University of Wisconsin, 1953), a competent and complete biography of the head of the Knights of Labor in Wisconsin. Jerry M. Cooper, "The Wisconsin National Guard in the Milwaukee Riots of 1886," in *WMH*, 55 (Autumn, 1971), 31–48, is the best summary account of the Bay View affair. Roger D. Simon, "The Bay View Incident and the Peoples' Party in Milwaukee" (unpublished research paper, January, 1967, copy in History of Wisconsin project files), is on the political aftermath. Thomas W. Gavett, *Development of the Labor Movement in Milwaukee* (Madison, 1965), is less pointed, while Robert V. Bruce, *1877: Year of Violence* (Indianapolis, 1959), discusses the earlier railroad strikes that were not directly felt in Wisconsin, although their spirit was. "Correspondence Concerning Strikes and Riots, 1858–1909," Records on Social Unrest,

Disasters and Relief, and Investigations, Series 88, Executive Department, WSA, pertains, as does particularly the Wisconsin Bureau of
Labor and Industrial Statistics, *Biennial Report,* 1885–1886.

IMMIGRATION

Early immigration history was largely engrossed with particular
immigrant groups, written by cheering members. By the 1920's it had
fallen to a low estate, given World War I and immigration restriction as
a settled policy. It is heartening to know that before Alex Haley and
*Roots* there was Marcus Lee Hansen, born in Neenah, Wisconsin, in
1892 of a Danish father and a Norwegian mother. With this dubiously
ecumenical beginning, he pioneered a less nationalistic history of immigration and made the field a respectable scholarly discipline. See Allan
H. Spear, "Marcus Lee Hansen and the Historiography of Immigration," in *WMH,* 44 (Summer, 1961), 258–268. Hansen's *The Atlantic
Migration, 1607–1860* (Cambridge, 1941), and *The Immigrant in American
History* (Cambridge, 1940; Harper Torchbook edition, New York, 1964),
were published posthumously, he having died at age forty-five in 1938.
For samples of what Hansen wrought, see particularly Stephan Thernstrom, ed., *Harvard Encyclopedia of American Ethnic Groups* (Cambridge,
1980), covering 126 distinct groups and with twenty-nine thematic
essays in 1,076 pages. Thomas J. Archdeacon, *Becoming American: An
Ethnic History* (New York, 1983), is a more manageable treatment
through a single lens, and is strong on Wisconsin sources. Kathleen N.
Conzen, author of "Immigrants, Immigrant Neighborhoods, and Ethnic Identity: Historical Issues," in the *Journal of American History,* 66
(December, 1979), 603–615, is a contributor to the *Harvard Encyclopedia*
who did her graduate study on Milwaukee. James R. Gibson, ed.,
*European Settlement and Development in North America: Essays on Geographical
Change in Honour and Memory of Andrew Hill Clark* (Toronto, 1978), com-
memorates a distinguished career in the University's geography department. David Ward, *Cities and Immigrants: A Geography of Change in
Nineteenth-Century America* (New York, 1971), is another member of that
department. Ingrid Semmingsen, *Norway to America: A History of the
Migration,* translated by Einar Haugen (Minneapolis, 1978), is a newer
name to add to that of Theodore Blegen of Minnesota, who pioneered
with others in making Norwegian-American history a forerunner in the
escape from immigrant history as hagiography. On the Finns, see John
I. Kolehmainen and George W. Hill, *Haven in the Woods: The Story of the
Finns in Wisconsin* (Madison, 1951; reprinted, 1965). Carl F. Wittke, *We
Who Built America: The Saga of the Immigrant* (New York, 1939), and *The
Irish in America* (Baton Rouge, 1956), deserve honorable mention. For
a worthy full-length Wisconsin study, see M. Justille McDonald, *His-*

*tory of the Irish in Wisconsin in the Nineteenth Century* (Washington, 1954; reprinted, New York, 1976). John D. Buenker, "The Immigrant Heritage," in Nicholas C. Burckel, ed., *Racine: Growth and Change in a Wisconsin County* (Racine, 1977), 69–136, should be noted.

## MINORITIES

The two minority groups dealt with at some length here are Negroes—the common term of the time—and Indians. There is a paucity of material on Negroes and the opposite with respect to Wisconsin Indians. Zachary Cooper, *Black Settlers in Rural Wisconsin* (Madison, 1977), is one of several brief pamphlets published by the SHSW on immigrant groups, women, and similar subjects of heightened recent interest. Thomas R. Buchanan, "Black Milwaukee, 1890–1915" (master's thesis, University of Wisconsin-Milwaukee, 1973), is comprehensive, readable, and valuable. William J. Vollmar, "The Negro in a Midwest Frontier City, Milwaukee: 1835–1870" (master's thesis, Marquette University, 1968), is less satisfactory. Thomas P. Imse, "The Negro Community in Milwaukee" (master's thesis, Marquette University, 1942), and Velma F. Bell, "The Negro in Beloit and Madison" (master's thesis, University of Wisconsin, 1933), are considerably earlier works. Leslie H. Fishel, jr., has written about early civil rights in "Wisconsin and Negro Suffrage," in *WMH*, 46 (Spring, 1963), 180–196, and "The Genesis of the First Wisconsin Civil Rights Act," in *WMH*, 49 (Summer, 1966), 324–333. Finally there is William T. Green, "Negroes in Milwaukee," in the Milwaukee County Historical Society, *The Negro in Milwaukee: An Historical Survey* (Milwaukee, 1968), 5–11.

A bibliographical guide to Wisconsin Indians by William H. Hodge is part of the "Feature Article" in the *Wisconsin Blue Book, 1975*, pp. 95–192, available in most libraries, not to be confused with Frederick W. Hodge, ed., *Handbook of American Indians North of Mexico* (in two parts, Washington, 1907, 1910). This latter, in turn, is succeeded by William C. Sturtevant, general editor, *Handbook of North American Indians, Volume 15: Northeast*, Bruce G. Trigger, volume editor (Washington, 1978), which has articles on all the tribes present in Wisconsin at the time, save the Sioux. Reliable and authoritative—a characterization that cannot be applied to many other recent studies of specific tribes—are Wilcomb E. Washburn, comp., *The American Indian and the United States: A Documentary History* (4 vols., New York, 1973), and Wilcomb E. Washburn, *The Indian in America* (New York, 1975). Nancy Oestreich Lurie, *Wisconsin Indians* (Madison, 1980), of the Milwaukee Public Museum, is a name to look for in your library card catalog, as is Francis Paul Prucha, *American Indian Policy in Crisis: Christian Reformers and the Indians, 1865–1890* (Norman, 1976). Fr. Prucha is a professor at

Marquette University who has published numerous works on Indian and U.S. Army history. A most valuable source is the *Eleventh Census of the United States, 1890: Volume X, Report on Indians Taxed and Indians Not Taxed in the United States (Except Alaska)*, which contains "Historic Review of Indians in the United States (Alaska Excepted)," 49–57; "Policy and Administration of Indian Affairs (From 1776 to 1890)," 61–78; and "Wisconsin," 617–626.

A longer bibliographical section on Wisconsin women will be justified when publications reach beyond the self-conscious recent past to matters other than brief biographies, suffrage compaigns, and feminist campaigners. Eleanor Flexner, *Century of Struggle: The Woman's Rights Movement in the United States* (Cambridge, 1959; revised edition, 1975), and Mary Earhart, *Frances Willard: From Prayers to Politics* (Chicago, 1944), are older standards to know. Andrew Sinclair, *The Better Half: The Emancipation of the American Woman* (New York, 1965), is a broad social history of feminism. More specific to Wisconsin is Mary D. Bradford, *Memoirs of Mary D. Bradford: Autobiographical and Historical Reminiscences of Education in Wisconsin, Through Progressive Service from Rural School Teaching to City Superintendent* (Evansville, Wisconsin, 1932), which may also be found in *WMH*, 14–16 (September, 1930–September, 1932).

### EDUCATION

The Wisconsin Superintendent of Public Instruction, *Annual Reports,* 1873 to 1882, and *Biennial Reports* thereafter are basic sources on the subject of Wisconsin public education. Fortunately there are two early works that complement one another nicely: J. W. Stearns, ed., *The Columbian History of Education in Wisconsin* (Milwaukee, 1893), which has chapters on parochial systems and higher education, while Conrad E. Patzer, *Public Education in Wisconsin* (Madison, 1924), is substantial with a strong historical dimension. Edgar G. Doudna, *The Making of Our Wisconsin Schools, 1848–1948,* reprinted by the State Centennial Committee (n.p., 1948), from the *Wisconsin Journal of Education,* 80 (January, 1948), 219–250, is a useful brief work. Thomas C. Hunt, "Catholic Educational Policy and the Decline of Protestant Influence in Wisconsin's Schools During the Late Nineteenth Century" (doctoral dissertation, University of Wisconsin, 1971), is stronger on the religious than the political conflicts. Wayne E. Schmidt, "Wisconsin Synod Lutheran Parochial Schools: An Overview of the Years 1850–1890" (doctoral dissertation, University of Wisconsin, 1968), is the only such study available. Joseph Schafer, "Genesis of Wisconsin's Free High School

System," in *WMH,* 10 (December, 1926), 123-149, provides a national context. William H. Herrmann, "The Rise of the Public Normal School System in Wisconsin" (doctoral dissertation, University of Wisconsin, 1953), and Walker D. Wyman, ed., *History of the Wisconsin State Universities* (River Falls, 1968), need a corrective which is offered either by Jurgen Herbst, "Nineteenth-Century Normal Schools in the United States: A Fresh Look," in *History of Education,* 9 (September, 1980), 224-227, or by Jeff Wasserman, "Wisconsin Normal Schools and the Educational Hierarchy, 1860-1890," in the *Journal of the Midwest History of Education Society,* 7 (1979), 1-9. Merle Curti and Vernon Carstensen, *The University of Wisconsin: A History, 1848-1925* (2 vols., Madison, 1949), is supplemented by Allan G. Bogue and Robert Taylor, eds., *The University of Wisconsin: One Hundred and Twenty-Five Years* (Madison, 1975). E. L. Luther, "Farmers' Institutes in Wisconsin, 1885-1933," in *WMH,* 30 (September, 1946), 59-68, has been expanded upon in Wilbur H. Glover, *Farm and College: The College of Agriculture of the University of Wisconsin, a History* (Madison, 1952). John C. Colson, " 'Public Spirit' at Work: Philanthropy and Public Libraries in Nineteenth-Century Wisconsin," in *WMH,* 59 (Spring, 1976), 192-209, and Kathryn Saucerman, "A Study of the Wisconsin Library Movement, 1850-1900" (master's thesis, University of Wisconsin, 1944), cover that public institution.

RELIGION

Among several large-scale surveys of American religious history, Sydney E. Ahlstrom, *A Religious History of the American People* (New Haven, 1972; Image Books paperback edition in two vols., New York, 1975), is good. Whitney R. Cross *The Burned-Over District: The Social and Intellectual History of Enthusiastic Religion in Western New York, 1800-1850* (Ithaca, 1950), explains the Wisconsin Yankee. Stephen J. Tordella, *Religion in Wisconsin: Preferences, Practices, and Ethnic Composition,* University of Wisconsin, Department of Rural Sociology, Applied Population Laboratory, *Population Series,* 70-13 (Madison, 1979), deals with the past and with bibliography. Denominational histories include E. Clifford Nelson and Eugene L. Fevold, *The Lutheran Church Among Norwegian-Americans: A History of the Evangelical Lutheran Church* (Minneapolis, 1960); John P. Koehler, *The History of the Wisconsin Synod,* ed. by Leigh D. Jordahl (St. Cloud, Minnesota, 1970); and two titles by Roy A. Suelflow which trace the history of Missouri Synod Lutherans, *A Plan for Survival* (New York, 1965), and *Walking with Wise Men: A History of the South Wisconsin District of the Lutheran Church—Missouri Synod* (Milwaukee, 1967). Barry J. Colman's *The Catholic Church and German Americans* (Milwaukee, 1953), is of fundamental importance. But when one gets beyond histories of the Catholic church in Wisconsin, which claimed about half the professing population, the fractions multiply too rapidly to hazard an incomplete list. John O. Holzhueter of the SHSW ought one day to execute a longer work than Tordella's, concentrating on Wisconsin society in the nineteenth century. Then, too, much religious history appears under the rubric of political controversy—for example the Bennett Law and the temperance crusade.

### Arts, Entertainment, and Sports

Again, the subject is so diverse as to defy containment in a paragraph or two, nor is there any general work to which to point. Those scholars who successively held the equivalent of the post as Director of Research of the SHSW were intrigued. See, for example, Louise Phelps Kellogg, "Wisconsin at the Centennial," in *WMH,* 10 (September, 1926), 3–16; Lillian Krueger, "Waukesha: 'The Saratoga of the West,' " in *WMH,* 24 (June, 1941), 394–424; and Alice E. Smith, "Business and Culture in Nineteenth-Century Wisconsin," in the *Transactions of the Wisconsin Academy of Sciences, Arts and Letters,* 54, Part A (1965), 77–85. Ayres Davies, "Wisconsin, Incubator of the American Circus," in *WMH,* 25 (March, 1942), 283–296, makes a claim typical of the subject. Sara Rath, *Pioneer Photographer: Wisconsin's H. H. Bennett* (Madison, 1979), substantiates a claim worth our notice. John R. Betts, *America's Sporting Heritage, 1850–1950* (Reading, Massachusetts, 1974), puts Ronald A. Smith, "Athletics in the Wisconsin State University System, 1867–1913," in *WMH,* 55 (Autumn, 1971), 3–23, in context. Richard W. E. Perrin, *The Architecture of Wisconsin* (Madison, 1967), has recently been joined by Randy Garber, ed., *Built in Milwaukee: An Architectural View of the City* (Milwaukee, 1981).

### Politics and Government

Every general history of Wisconsin covers politics and government. Alexander M. Thomson, *A Political History of Wisconsin* (Milwaukee, 1900), is probably the most authoritative of those written by a contemporary, though he had some conspicuous blind spots. Informative national histories to place Wisconsin in context are Morton Keller, *Affairs of State: Public Life in Late Nineteenth Century America* (Cambridge, 1977), and Leonard D. White, *The Republican Era: A Study in Administrative History, 1869–1901* (New York, 1958). James R. Donoghue, *How Wisconsin Voted, 1848–1972* (Madison, 1974), and Sarah C. Ettenheim, *How Milwaukee Voted, 1848–1968* (Milwaukee, 1970), furnish useful shortcuts to election figures. Herman J. Deutsch, "Political Forces in Wisconsin, 1871–1881" (doctoral dissertation, University of Wisconsin, 1926), is still the best guide to politics in the 1870's. Much of it is available in a series of articles: "Yankee-Teuton Rivalry in Wisconsin Politics of the Seventies," in *WMH,* 14 (March-June, 1931), 262-282, 403-418; "Disintegrating Forces in Wisconsin Politics of the Early Seventies," in *WMH,* 15 (December, 1931-June, 1932), 168-181, 282-296, 391-411; and "Carpenter and the Senatorial Election of 1875 in Wisconsin," in *WMH,* 16 (September, 1932), 26-46. Ellis B. Usher, *The Greenback Movement of 1875-1884 and Wisconsin's Part in It* (Milwaukee, 1911), was an active contemporary Democratic party leader and author of a multi-volume history of Wisconsin. Solon J. Buck, *The Granger Movement: A Study of Agricultural Organization and Its Political, Economic and Social Manifestations, 1870-1880* (Cambridge, 1913), is an old standard, supplemented by Graham A. Cosmas, "The Democracy in Search of Issues: The Wisconsin Reform Party, 1873-1877," in *WMH,* 46 (Winter, 1962-1963), 93-108, and D. Sven Nordin, *Rich Harvest: A History of the Grange, 1867-1900* (Jackson, Mississippi, 1974).

Recent analyses of politics in the 1880's and 1890's have drawn upon computer technology. For these see: David L. Brye, *Wisconsin Voting Patterns in the Twentieth Century, 1900 to 1950* (New York, 1979), which has revealing introductory remarks on earlier studies projected from the 1880's; Paul Kleppner, *The Cross of Culture: A Social Analysis of Midwestern Politics, 1850-1900* (New York, 1970), who is often more assertive than accurate; and Richard J. Jensen, *The Winning of the Midwest: Social and Political Conflict, 1888-1896* (Chicago, 1971), who also posts a warning about the technique in "History From a Deck of IBM Cards," in *Reviews in American History,* 6 (June, 1978), 229-234. Roger E. Wyman, "Voting Behavior in the Progressive Era: Wisconsin as a Case Study" (doctoral dissertation, University of Wisconsin, 1970), is a massive work unlike those above in that it is restricted to Wisconsin. Wyman has also published "Wisconsin Ethnic Groups and the Election of 1890," in *WMH,* 51 (Summer, 1968), 269-293, and "Agrarianism or Working-Class Radicalism? The Electoral Basis of Populism in Wisconsin," in the *Political Science Quarterly,* 89 (Winter, 1974-1975), 825-847. The origins and repercussions of Governor Hoard's fatal blunder are the subject of Robert J. Ulrich, "The Bennett Law of 1889: Education and Politics in Wisconsin" (doctoral dissertation, University of Wisconsin, 1965).

Lawrence L. Graves, "The Wisconsin Woman's Suffrage Movement, 1846-1920" (doctoral dissertation, University of Wisconsin, 1954), is the best available on that subject. Peter R. Weisensel, "The Wisconsin Temperance Crusade to 1919" (master's thesis, University of Wisconsin, 1965), is the best general history. On the Bennett Law, crucial in the 1890 election, the best is Janet C. Wegner, "The Bennett Law Controversy in Wisconsin, 1889-1891: A Study of the Problem of

'Americanization' in the Immigrant Church and Its Relation to the History of Church and State in the United States" (master's thesis, Brown University, 1966). William W. Updegrove, "Bibles and Brickbats: Religious Conflict in Wisconsin's Public School System During the Nineteenth Century" (master's thesis, University of Wisconsin, 1970), records a controversy that paralleled the better-known Bennett Law controversy. Two articles by Thomas C. Hunt, "The Edgerton Bible Decision: The End of an Era," in the *Catholic Historical Review,* 67 (October, 1981), 589–619, and "The Reformed Tradition, Bible Reading and Education in Wisconsin," in the *Journal of Presbyterian History,* 59 (Spring, 1981), 73–88, and Donald L. Kinzer, "The Political Uses of Anti-Catholicism: Michigan and Wisconsin, 1890–1894," in *Michigan History,* 39 (September, 1955), 312–326, add light to the political heat. Arlan Helgeson, "The Wisconsin Treasury Cases," in *WMH,* 35 (Winter, 1951), 129–136, and Robert M. La Follette, *La Follette's Autobiography: A Personal Narrative of Political Experience* (Madison, 1911; reprinted, 1960), help to round out Republican party embarrassment.

David P. Thelen, *The New Citizenship: Origins of Progressivism in Wisconsin, 1885–1900* (Columbia, Missouri, 1972), is a mature work on the thrust of political dissent. Thelen earlier wrote a prize-winning master's thesis, published as *The Early Life of Robert M. La Follette, 1855–1884* (Chicago, 1966). Thelen's articles on the young La Follette and his relations with the Republican Old Guard are instructive. See "The Boss and the Upstart: Keyes and La Follette, 1880–1884," in *WMH,* 47 (Winter, 1963–1964), 103–115, and "Robert M. La Follette, Public Prosecutor," in *WMH,* 47 (Spring, 1964), 214–223.

Other useful political biographies in the period include Richard W. Hantke, "The Life of Elisha Williams Keyes" (doctoral dissertation, University of Wisconsin, 1942), from which he extracted "Elisha W. Keyes, the Bismarck of Western Politics," in *WMH,* 31 (September, 1947), 29–47, and "Elisha W. Keyes and the Radical Republicans," in *WMH,* 35 (Spring, 1952), 203–208. Sam Ross, *The Empty Sleeve: A Biography of Lucius Fairchild* (Madison, 1964); Dorothy Ganfield Fowler, *John Coit Spooner: Defender of Presidents* (New York, 1961); and Richard N. Current, *Pine Logs and Politics: A Life of Philetus Sawyer, 1816–1900* (Madison, 1950), most competently span the political years 1873–1893. E. Bruce Thompson, *Matthew Hale Carpenter: Webster of the West* (Madison, 1954), and Horace S. Merrill, *William Freeman Vilas: Doctrinaire Democrat* (Madison, 1954), treat two national class orators of their day. George H. Wood, Jr., "A Diamond in the Rough—A Study of the Administration of Governor Jeremiah Rusk, 1882–1889" (master's thesis, University of Wisconsin, 1970), solidly supports Rusk's claim to competence. Uncritical but charming is Henry Casson, *"Uncle Jerry":*

*Life of General Jeremiah M. Rusk, Stage Driver, Farmer, Soldier, Legislator, Governor, Cabinet Officer* (Madison, 1895). Alfons J. Beitzinger, *Edward G. Ryan: Lion of the Law* (Madison, 1960), is a study of one of the era's most colorful jurists.

James A. Wilgus, *The Government of the People of the State of Wisconsin* (Philadelphia, 1897), is interesting as a first handbook on the subject. Charles R. Bulger, "Wisconsin Administrative Government, 1870–1891: Years of Legislative Control and Local Enforcement" (master's thesis, University of Wisconsin, 1984), is the latest word. James D. Barnett, *Indirect Central Administration of Wisconsin* (University of Wisconsin, Bulletin no. 269, *Economics and Political Science Series,* vol. 4, no. 3, Madison, 1908), covers the evolution of administrative offices. Raymond V. Phelan, *The Financial History of Wisconsin* (University of Wisconsin, Bulletin no. 193, *Economics and Political Science Series,* vol. 2, no. 2, Madison, 1908), is a companion work. Oliver D. Weeks, "The Development of County Government in Wisconsin" (doctoral dissertation, University of Wisconsin, 1924), clear but ponderous, is succeeded by James R. Donoghue, "The Local Government System of Wisconsin," in the *Wisconsin Blue Book, 1968,* pp. 73–281. George S. Wehrwein has contributed two useful articles to the *Wisconsin Blue Book:* "Town Government in Wisconsin," 1935, pp. 95–107, and "Village Government in Wisconsin," 1940, pp. 161–170. See also Daniel R. Madden, "City-State Relations in Wisconsin, 1835–1901: The Origins of the Milwaukee Home Rule Movement" (doctoral dissertation, University of Wisconsin, 1972). Marvin B. Rosenberry, "Wisconsin Courts: Their Origin, Organization and Work," in *Wisconsin Blue Book, 1925,* pp. 591–608, may be supplemented by descriptions of court work and individuals of the supreme court by John B. Winslow, *The Story of a Great Court: Being a Sketch History of the Supreme Court of Wisconsin, Its Judges and Their Times from the Admission of the State to the Death of Chief Justice Ryan* (Chicago, 1912), and two articles by John B. Sanborn, "The Supreme Court of Wisconsin in the Eighties," in *WMH,* 15 (September, 1931), 3–21, and "The Impeachment of Levi Hubbell," in *SHSW Proceedings,* 1905, pp. 194–213.

Miriam Z. Langsam, "The Nineteenth Century Wisconsin Criminal: Ideologies and Institutions" (doctoral dissertation, University of Wisconsin, 1967), is both descriptive and analytical. Eleanor J. Flynn, "The Development of Wisconsin's Administration of Charities and Corrections and Present Trends in the United States" (master's thesis, University of Wisconsin, 1926), is descriptive only, but useful. Dale W. Robison, *Wisconsin and the Mentally Ill: A History of the "Wisconsin Plan" of State and County Care, 1860–1915* (New York, 1980), is on the evolution of the system. Cornelius A. Harper, "The Work of the State Board of

Health, 1876–1924," in Milo M. Quaife, *Wisconsin: Its History and Its People* (4 vols., Chicago, 1924), 2:323–365, draws our attention to a resurgence in this field. More recent works are Ronald L. Numbers and Judith W. Leavitt, eds., *Wisconsin Medicine: Historical Perspectives* (Madison, 1981), a collection of essays on nineteenth-century health care, and Judith W. Leavitt, *The Healthiest City: Milwaukee and the Politics of Health Reform* (Princeton, 1982).

Ballard C. Campbell, *Representative Democracy: Public Policy and Midwestern Legislatures in the Late Nineteenth Century* (Cambridge, 1980), tells how Wisconsin's deliberative body dealt with problems of continuity and partisanship before there were professional legislators. Campbell's book was preceded by a useful article, "Ethnicity and the 1893 Wisconsin Assembly," in the *Journal of American History,* 62 (June, 1975), 74–94. Kenneth C. Acrea, "Wisconsin Progressivism: Legislative Response to Social Change, 1891 to 1909" (doctoral dissertation, University of Wisconsin, 1968); Gordon M. Haferbecker, *Wisconsin Labor Laws* (Madison, 1958); Gertrude Schmidt, "History of Labor Legislation in Wisconsin" (doctoral dissertation, University of Wisconsin, 1933); Daniel R. Madden, "Factory Safety in Wisconsin, 1878–1911" (master's thesis, University of Wisconsin, 1968); and Donald J. Berthrong, "Social Legislation in Wisconsin, 1836–1900" (doctoral dissertation, University of Wisconsin, 1951), all deal with social legislation, the last most broadly with great coverage of sources. James T. Burns, "A History of State Liquor Control in Wisconsin" (master's thesis, Marquette University, 1935), apparently did not have the last word.

# INDEX

Abbot, Edwin H., 121

Accidents, 225-226

Agriculture: 1-45; farm statistics (1870-1890), 1n; farmers' views, 43-45; effects of transportation revolution, 147; as industry, 150; loss of population to cities, 230; disappearance of undeveloped land, 267-268, 273; acreage statistics, 269; at University of Wisconsin, 589. *See also* Farmers and farming

Air Line Railroad, 381. *See also* Chicago, Portage and Superior Railroad Company

Alexander, John W., 182

Allis, Edward P.: 148, 174, 179, 202, 209, 538; as industrial entrepreneur, 167-171; as employer, 220; relations with labor, 241-242, 394-395; Greenback candidate for governor, 387, 389, 574-575, 577, 583; and Robert Schilling, 387. *See also* E. P. Allis and Company

Allis, Margaret Watson, 167

Allis Reliance Works, 148, 167-168, 169, 394-395, 397

Allis-Chalmers Corporation, 160

Alma, 276

Aluminum, 185

American Constitutional Union, 99

American Federation of Labor, 413-414

American Protective Association, 612n, 622

American Steel Barge Company, 135

American Sunday School Movement, 355-356

Anarchism, 387, 391

Ancient Order of the United Workmen, 486

Anthony, Susan B., 450, 451, 464

Appleby, John F., 181

Appleton: 187, 188, 239, 366-367; Irish in, 299

Apprenticeship, 231, 232-233, 253

*Arbeiter-Zeitung* (Milwaukee), 391

Architecture: 203, 540; as source of village pride, 345

*Argus* (Beaver Dam), 477-478

Armitage, William E., 524, 536

Armour, Philip D., 157

Art, 536, 537-538

Arthur, Chester A., 585

Ashland: 118-119, 190, 193-194, 275; Irish in, 299

Ashland County: lacks coal deposits, 151-152; Canadians in, 300

Assimilation: of immigrants, 309-311, 345, 358, 378; of Indians, 434

Association for the Advancement of Milwaukee, 211

*Attorney General v. the Railroad Companies* (1874), 105

Automobiles, 535

B. Stern and Son, 158

Babcock, Stephen M., 28

Bach, Christopher, 446

"Bad Lands" (Milwaukee), 441

Bad River Indian Reservation, 431

Badger Electric, 609

Baker, Joseph Stannard, 273-274, 433-434

Baker, Ray Stannard, 273-274, 433-435

Bammessel, H., 371

Banks and banking: 154, 160, 197n, 213; and lumber interests, 57; linked to political corruption, 618-621

Baraboo: 343n; wages in, 242

675

Wilcox, Ella Wheeler, 539
Wilde, F. A., 174
Willard, Frances, 452, 458–459, 463, 488–489
Williams, Orren T., 444
Winnebago County: Danes in, 298
Winnebago tribe: 304, 421; removal to Nebraska, 421–422
Winslow, John B., 468
Wisconsin: employees of, 593–594; governor, 625, 627–628; legislature, 625–627, 643–646
Wisconsin Academy of Sciences, Arts and Letters, 524
*Wisconsin Afro-American* (Milwaukee), 442n
Wisconsin and Minnesota Railroad, 120
*Wisconsin Blue Book,* 307, 346, 543, 644
Wisconsin Bureau of Labor and Industrial Statistics, 221, 251
Wisconsin Central Railroad Company, 33, 71, 109, 111, 115–121, 122, 124, 151, 191, 194, 326, 529
Wisconsin Dairymen's Association, 17–22, 25, 27, 28, 31–32
Wisconsin Dells, 344
*Wisconsin Farmer and Northwest Cultivator,* 9
Wisconsin Federation of Labor, 384, 542
Wisconsin Free Library Commission, 516
Wisconsin government: 624–647; record-keeping, 628; integrity of, 631; and schools, 633–634; and public institutions, 634–641; and public health, 641–642; and safety, 642–643; and licensing of professionals, 643
Wisconsin Immigration Commission, 123
"Wisconsin Lumber Line," 70, 82–83
Wisconsin Marine and Fire Insurance Company, 95
Wisconsin National Bank (Milwaukee), 160
"Wisconsin Plan," 637
*Wisconsin Prohibitionist,* 351
Wisconsin Railroad Commission, 102, 106, 127
Wisconsin River, 137–138, 152
Wisconsin State Agricultural Society, 22–23, 24, 144
Wisconsin State Fair, 495

*Wisconsin State Gazetteer,* 276
Wisconsin State Horticultural Society, 22–23
Wisconsin Terminal Moraine, 273
Wisconsin Valley Railroad Company, 109, 114
Wisconsin Woman's Suffrage Association, 464, 465n
Wm. Suhl's Steam Bakery, 371
Wolf River, 187
Woman's Christian Temperance Union, 351, 452, 458–461, 467, 552
Woman's Industrial Exchange, 449
Women: 446–473; in business, 167; in labor force, 244–249, 451–457; at town meetings, 325–326; occupations of, 446; as threat to working men, 453–454; attitudes towards, 447–449; and philanthropy, 449; and religion, 457–458; suffrage, 459, 463–464, 465–469; as professionals, 462–463, 470; as educators, 464–465, 470–472; legal rights of, 469–470; social activities, 487; girls, life of, 488–490
Woodman, Cyrus, 51
Woodward, Gilbert M., 413
World's Columbian Exposition, 458, 540
Worsley, Agnes, 250
Wyoming Territory, 10

Yankees: 312; pioneers of successive frontiers, 272; mobility of, 283–284; as arbiters of cultural values, 306–309; and mob violence, 307–308; dislike of by foreigners, 324–325, 337; condescension towards foreigners, 339–340, 342; and temperance movement, 355, 356; and religion, 522, 524; and political parties, 548–549, 550
Youmans, Theodora, 470
Young Men's Christian Association, 355, 491, 520, 532
Young Woman's Home, 451
Young Women's Christian Association, 520

Zion Lutheran Church (Columbus), 345–346

# ABOUT THE AUTHOR

ROBERT C. NESBIT came to the American history faculty of the University of Wisconsin–Madison in 1962 from Olympia, Washington, where he had been state archivist and supervisor of state purchasing. His grandfather, James W. Nesbit, was a high school principal in Wisconsin until 1906, when he moved to Ellensberg, Washington, as superintendent of schools. Robert Nesbit attended Central Washington College of Education in Ellensberg from 1935 to 1939, where a major influence on his career choice was Vernon Carstensen, later co-author with Merle Curti of *The University of Wisconsin: A History, 1848–1925* (1948). After serving in the Pacific during World War II, he earned his doctorate in history from the University of Washington in 1957, "an extended project made possible by the G.I. Bill." At Madison, he was active in reviving Wisconsin history as a regular course offering by the history department, and he is the author of the standard one-volume *Wisconsin: A History* (1973). He and his wife Marie, both natives of Washington, returned to Olympia following retirement in 1983.

# ABOUT THE BOOK

THE text was composed in Baskerville by TypeTronics of Madison on a Compugraphic 8600 digital typesetter. The book was printed by offset lithography on Warren's Olde Style, a long-lived sheet manufactured by the S. D. Warren Company. It was bound in Joanna Western Arrestox.